# A Natural History
# of Associations

*A Study in the Meaning of Community*

VOLUME TWO

Richard Maitland Bradfield

INTERNATIONAL UNIVERSITIES PRESS, INC.
New York

Published in 1973 by
International Universities Press, Inc.
239 Park Avenue South
New York, N.Y. 10003

Library of Congress Catalog Card Number: 73–5578
Volume I  ISBN: 0–8236–3495–7
Volume II ISBN: 0–8236–3496–5

Printed in Great Britain

# Contents of volume two

PART FOUR

# Environment and Adaptation

## Appendix to Part Four 495

*On the regulation of numbers in kin-based societies, with special reference to North American Indians*

# List of maps and text figures

## Volume two

PART THREE

# THE SOUTHWEST

# 10

# *Villages of Black Mesa*

The Hopi are the most westerly of the Pueblo Indians of New Mexico and Arizona. Traditionally they lived in seven villages perched on the southwesterly-projecting spurs of Black Mesa, in northeastern Arizona; this number was increased to nine by the founding of Hotevilla and Bakabi, following the split of Oraibi in 1906, and subsequently to eleven by the growth of new settlements at the foot of 1st, and 3rd Mesa, respectively. To-day the population of the eleven villages is about 4,500.

Black Mesa itself is a diamond-shaped plateau, some 60 miles in width and 6,000 to 7,000 feet above sea level, standing up between the basins of the Little Colorado and the San Juan rivers. Its surface tilts gently down to the southwest, and it is drained by four great washes (Moenkopi, Dinnebitto, Oraibi, and Polacca) extending almost the entire breadth of the plateau and carrying in their channels the precipitation that falls over three-quarters of its surface southwest towards the Little Colorado. The old Hopi villages stand on the spurs overlooking the valleys of the three southern washes, at the point where the valleys widen out on emerging from the plateau: the villages of 3rd Mesa (Hotevilla, Bakabi and Oraibi) on the spur between the Dinnebitto and Oraibi valleys, those of 2nd Mesa (Shungo'povi, Sipau'lovi and Mishong'novi) on the spur between the Oraibi valley and the Wepo (a tributary of Polacca wash), and those of 1st Mesa (Walpi, Sicho'movi and Hano) on the spur between the Wepo and Polacca valleys.

The fields of each village lie mainly in the valley overlooked by that village, the sites of the villages having been chosen no doubt, in the first place, with the double object of giving surveillance over the fields and defence against marauders.[1] During the last sixty years, defence needs being no longer operative, there has been a partial migration from the villages on the mesa top to new settlements which have grown up around the trading posts established at the foot of the mesa: notably to Polacca, at the foot of 1st Mesa, and to New Oraibi, at the foot of 3rd Mesa.[2] At the same time, and as a consequence of these demographic changes, the villages of Walpi on 1st Mesa and of Oraibi on 3rd Mesa have lost the dominant position they once held at the two poles of Hopi society.

[1] This is certainly so for the villages of 1st Mesa, and for Sipau'lovi and Mishong'novi on 2nd Mesa: cf. Mindeleff (1891), p. 223. Shungo'povi and Oraibi, however, are both sited on broad 'noses' of the mesa which would afford fairly easy approach to attackers, at least from one direction.

[2] The trading post at Toreva, at the foot of 2nd Mesa, has not attracted a settlement.

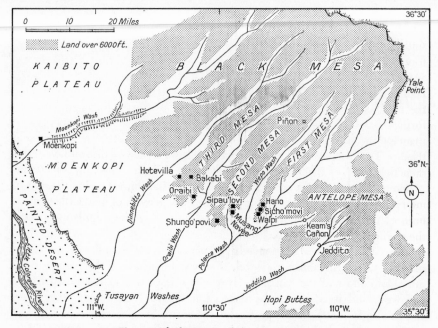

Fig. 27. Black Mesa and the Hopi villages.

*Ethno-geography of the Hopi.* Traditionally, the Hopi regarded the whole area covered by the map—and certain areas outside it—as their land (*tzü'rka*), and they travelled to different parts of it to hunt game and to collect plant, or mineral, products. They went to the canyon heads of Black Mesa to hunt mountain sheep, and to get oak for farming tools and spruce for katçina dances; to Grand Canyon for salt, yellow ochre, and the copper ore used for making blue-green pigment; to the San Francisco Mountains, to hunt deer and wild turkeys, and for spruce; to the Little Colorado river, for turtle shells, and for cottonwood roots for carving ceremonial objects; to the flats between the villages and the Little Colorado river, to hunt antelope, for white kaolin, and for the yucca roots needed for ceremonial washing of the hair; and in the spring to the Hopi Buttes, to take young eagles from the nest. Cotton was grown along Moenkopi Wash, and wild tobacco and other herbs gathered on the mesa slopes.

### PHYSICAL ENVIRONMENT OF THE VILLAGES

The houses are built of stone and adobe (clay), the stone being quarried from suitable places on the slopes of the mesa and the clay from deposits at the mesa foot. The rock that forms the mesa top is a relatively porous sandstone, known as the Toreva formation; beneath the sandstone, some 300 to 400 feet down, lie beds of shale. The great washes of Black Mesa have cut their way down through the beds of sandstone and deep into the Mancos shale; subsequently, due to further erosion of the sandstone, the valley floors have received an alluvial mantle some 60 to 120 feet deep, and it is on this mantle, of the main valleys and their principal tributaries, that the Hopi make by far the greater number of their fields.

Between each village on the mesa top, and its fields in the valley below, intervene some 300 to 400 feet of cliff face and talus slope. From the village a number of trails lead out, descending first the precipitous side of the mesa to the springs at the cliff foot from which, and from rock-cut cisterns on the mesa top, the villagers draw most of their water for domestic use, then on to the fields lying on the valley floor, and on past these and up the opposite mesa side to distant shrines and neighbouring villages. Each village thus stands at the centre of a web of trails, linking it to its water supply, to its fields, to its shrines and to its neighbours.

The principal crops grown by the Hopi are corn (maize), beans, melons, squash, gourds and sweet corn. Of these, the staple are corn and beans; and most of what I have now to say regarding Hopi agriculture[1] applies to the growing of the first of these two staples, corn, for it was on the corn harvest that the Hopi were ultimately dependent, in the old days, for their livelihood.

The Hopi farmer, who sets out to raise a corn crop in one of the valleys below the villages, operates within two sets of limits imposed by the environment, limits of time and limits of place: *when* to plant, and *where* to plant. I consider, first, the limits of *time* imposed by the environment.

The crucial factors that determine the dates of planting are snowfall, and frost. The winter in Hopiland sets in late in November and lasts until early March. During these months the weather is bitterly cold, with heavy falls of snow. In March the weather turns warmer, though the nights are still cold, and by mid April the ground is usually warm enough in sheltered places for planting early corn; the main corn crop, however, is not planted until the latter two weeks of May and early June. The fourteen weeks, from mid March to the end of June, are the driest in the year, and the total rainfall in this period may be no more than 1 inch. Early in July the weather changes, as the first rains of the summer rainy season set in, and some 3 to 4 inches of rain fall, on average, during July and August. Characteristically, at this time of year, the rain falls in a series of thunderstorms, often of great violence, usually lasting less than an

---

[1] On Hopi agriculture, see in particular Forde (1931), E. Beaglehole (1937), and Page (1940); also an article of my own (1971), 'The changing pattern of Hopi agriculture', upon which I draw in the account that follows.

hour and almost invariably accompanied by lightning. A further characteristic of these storms is their waywardness; great thunderclouds pile up in the south-west during the morning, and move slowly over the region during the after-noon; rain falls from these clouds as they move across the countryside, drenching everything in their path while it falls—but the area covered by any one shower may be no more than a few square miles, leaving the land on either side as dry as it was before. Early in September these storms gradually die out, giving way to the dry, sunny days of autumn, during which the main corn crop is harvested.

The total annual rainfall in the region of the Hopi villages varies from $8\frac{1}{2}$ to $10\frac{1}{2}$ inches, of which about a third falls in the course of July and August. Given the very high rate of surface evaporation that occurs during the summer months, this amount is generally insufficient *on its own* to bring crops to matu-rity. Consequently the Hopi have recourse to a method of farming widely practised in the Southwest, known as 'flood-water farming'. The simplicity of this method, as Kirk Bryan pointed out[1] many years ago, conceals its impor-tance in the economy of arid lands. Its essential feature is the selection, for planting, of a place overflowed by run-off from higher ground; in this way, the rain that falls over a large area is utilised on a small one.

Fields of this kind, known in the Southwest as *ak-chin* ('at the arroyo-mouth') fields, are commonly made at the point where a watercourse, carrying run-off from higher ground, fans out on reaching more nearly level ground. Such fields, at least in the region of the Hopi villages, have a distinctive soil profile: an upper layer 4 to 6 inches deep of fine sand, with a sand-and-clay loam beneath. The snowfalls of late winter saturate the ground as they melt; during April and May dry winds blow from the southwest, drying out the layer of fine sand that covers the field; but the sand layer, though itself dried out, acts as a mulch to prevent futher evaporation from the underlying loam. The loamy subsoil thus retains the moisture received from the snow melt at least until the end of May, and probably right through until the summer rains begin early in July.

A typical corn field is planted in rows, with some three paces between rows, and three to four paces between the 'hills' in a row: the seed itself being put well down in the moist subsoil, some 10 to 12 inches below the surface. The seed thus planted is dependent for germination on two factors: on the moisture retained in the subsoil from the snow melt,[2] and on the general warmth of the ground. Ordinarily it takes from ten to fourteen days, depending on the warmth of the ground, for the first leaves to appear. And it is here that frost plays its part in determining when the corn shall be planted; for if there is a frost after the leaves have opened, the young seedling will either be severely set back in its growth, or killed, depending on the severity of the frost.

---

[1] On flood-water farming in the south-west, see in particular Bryan (1929): also, the survey by Stewart (1940), especially—on Hopi farming—pp. 329-35.

[2] Hopi themselves are aware that good falls of snow the previous winter are a necessary pre-requisite to the harvest: cf. Stephen (1936), p. 239.

Hopi corn requires a growing period of 120 to 130 days,[1] depending on the season and on the location of the field where it is planted. The last killing frost of the spring usually occurs about mid May, and the first frost of the fall, towards the end of September; but both dates are widely variable. Moreover, some fields are more susceptible to frost than others; small fields made in gullies at the mesa foot are fairly well protected, since the nocturnal radiation of heat from the gully walls protects the young plants, while the large fields on the main valley floor, over which the damp air hangs at night, are more exposed. These variables the Hopi farmer has to weigh, in deciding when to plant a particular field. If he sows his field too early, he runs the risk of losing the whole crop to a late spring frost (and so have to re-plant the field, dangerously late in the season); if he plays safe and plants late, he may find his yield seriously curtailed by an early frost in the fall.

The remaining factor which exercises a critical influence on Hopi corn-growing is the rainfall of July and August. While the residual moisture held in the subsoil from the snow melt of early spring is probably sufficient on its own to tide the young plants over until the end of June, from then on they are dependent for their main growth on further falls of rain. But this rainfall, like the dates of the frosts in spring and fall, is widely variable in its incidence, both from year to year (ranging from less than 2 inches in a bad year, to over 4 inches in a good one), and locally from place to place; of two fields not more than a few hundred yards apart, one may receive enough moisture—in the form of direct rainfall plus surface run-off—to yield a crop in a given season, the other not enough. And it is this fact that makes the choice of field sites of such vital import to the Hopi.

The soils in the vicinity of the Hopi villages[2] fall into three main classes: *sands, sandy loams,* and *clays.*[3] *Sandy loams* occur on the mesa top, wherever the slope of the ground and the configuration of the rock permit the accumulation of more than a few inches of soil. Descending to the foot of the mesa, they form the soils of the 'side valley slope', the gentle declination which stretches from the edge of the talus nearly to the banks of the main wash, and of the fans of the tributary watercourses which traverse that slope. *Sandy loams* thus cover by far the greater part both of the mesa top and of the valley floor. *Sand* soils occur wherever sand has been deposited by the prevailing southwest wind: that is to say, in scattered dunes on the mesa top and on the valley floor, and on sand slopes on the lee side of the mesa. *Clay* soils, also, occur in two locations only: on talus

[1] '120 days or more': Carter (1945), p. 102.

[2] This account of soils is based on my own work in the Oraibi valley, summarised in an article (1969) on 'Soils of the Oraibi valley, in relation to plant cover'. The Oraibi valley carries relatively restricted areas of wind-blown sand, but is otherwise typical of the main valleys in the vicinity of the villages.

[3] Soils are conveniently classified according to their clay content. Taking a given soil sample as divisible into twelve parts, one with less than one part clay and more than ten parts sand is defined as a *sand*: one with between one and four parts clay, and the residue predominantly sand, as a *sandy loam* or a *sandy clay loam*: and one with more than four parts clay, as a *clay*.

slopes, where the soil represents the direct break-down product of the underlying rock strata, and on the floor of the main valley, in a belt some two to
three hundred yards wide, where the soil constitutes the old flood plain of the
main wash.

Each of the main soil areas carries its own distinctive plant association:[1]
the heavy *clay* soils of the main valley floor, where the ground has not been
cleared for cultivation, a cover of greasewood (*de've*): the *sandy loams* on the
side valley slope, a cover of snakeweed (*ma'övi*) and coarse grass, and on the fans
of tributary watercourses, a cover of rabbit-brush (*siva'pi*): the *silty clay* of
talus slopes, a cover of sagebrush (*davot'ka*), eriogonum (*powa'wi*) and Mormon
tea (*ös'vee*): the *sands* of sand slopes, an association either of bush-mint (*moñ-
dosh'habe*), or of black sage (*tçamukna*), with other shrubs: and the *sandy loams*
on the mesa top, an association of sagebrush with other shrubs (juniper, cliff-
rose, lemon bush or sumac), in varying proportions dependent on the depth of
the soil and the amount of sand that it contains.[2]

On each of the three main soil-types represented in the vicinity of the
villages the Hopi make, or have in the past made, fields. The majority of these
are indeed located now on the *sandy loams* of the fans of tributary watercourses,
at the point where the run-off from higher ground fans out on reaching the
valley floor; such are the typical *ak-chin* fields, and where the fans have not
been cleared for cultivation, they can be picked out from a distance by the
growth of rabbit-brush which they carry. But the Hopi have also made use in
places of sand slopes, chiefly for planting orchards of peach and apricot, and
also of the heavy clay soil of the old flood-plain of the main wash, for growing
corn; the latter was traditionally the best corn-land in the valley, and it is
only since the dissection of the main wash (i.e. below Oraibi) in the early years
of this century that the fields made there have been abandoned.

A survey of land cleared for cultivation—including land subsequently abandoned—in the Oraibi valley (see Figure 28), yields two conclusions: first, that
only a restricted area of the valley will respond to Hopi farming techniques, the
area which will so respond being clearly defined on the ground by its plant
cover;[3] and second, that within a radius of 4 to 6 miles of the parent village such
land has been pretty fully exploited *at one time or another* in the past. From these
two conclusions, a third follows: that, so long as the Hopi remained dependent

[1] On the plant cover of the Oraibi valley, see an article of my own (1968), 'Hopi names
for certain common shrubs, and their ecology'.

[2] Farther from the villages where the trees have not been cut for firewood, and stretching
for many miles to the northeast, the mesa top carries a cover of pinyon-juniper woodland;
at the north-eastern side of Black Mesa, and in the canyon heads, this gives way to Douglas
fir and ponderosa pine.

[3] Briefly, any soil with a sagebrush cover will not respond to cultivation; nor will a soil
with a cover of snakeweed, unless the snakeweed is mixed with rabbit-brush as on the fans
of tributary watercourses, or with bush-mint as on sand slopes. A soil with a greasewood
cover is likely to respond, provided it still receives run-off; where such soil has been cleared,
abandoned, and re-colonised by salt-bush (*sy'ovi*), it is unlikely to, as the salt-bush indicates
a fall in the level of the ground water.

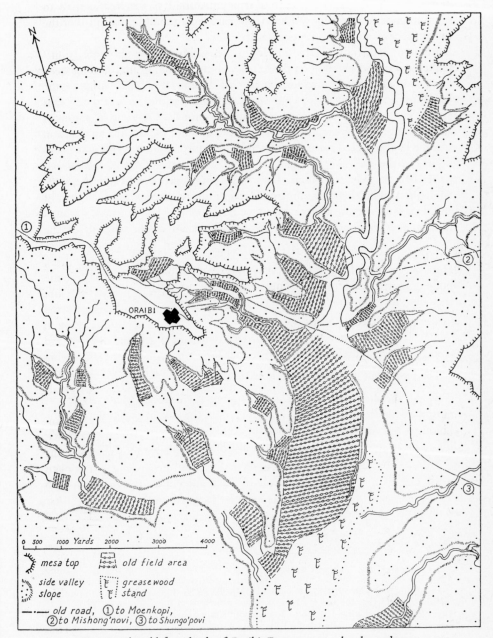

Fig. 28. The old farm lands of Oraibi. From a survey by the author.

on agriculture for their subsistence, the acreage of farmable land within reach of the several villages set a limit to their populations. It is, therefore, a matter of some interest to know how much land each household needed, in the traditional Hopi economy, to support itself.

An acre field, fully planted in Hopi style, yields on average some 10 to 12 bushels of corn, depending on the soil and on the season. From figures given by Stephen in his *Journal*,[1] it appears likely that the annual requirement per person for all purposes—that is, for consumption, for barter, for seed, and as a hedge against crop failure—lay between 20 and 24 bushels. To get that amount of corn, required an acreage of 2 acres per person; and in addition to this, there was the land required for vegetables, perhaps a further $\frac{1}{2}$ acre. This gives a total figure, in the traditional Hopi economy, of $2\frac{1}{2}$ acres of cultivated land per person: or between 15 and 20 acres for a household of six to eight persons. And at this point, before going any further into the relation between the Hopi and their land, we must break off to see how the land-holding unit, the matrilineage, and the consuming unit, the household, are structured.

### SOCIAL STRUCTURE OF THE HOPI VILLAGE[2]

Hopi society is made up of some thirty to forty matrilineal clans: the clan being a body of matrilineal kinsfolk, comprising one or more matrilineages. The clan is the only kin-group for which the Hopi have a term:[3]

pl. *nya'mü*,   people, clan:

        e.g. *hona'ni nya'mü*, badger clan:

sing. *wüñwa*, individual member of a clan.

The Hopi clan has three intrinsic attributes:

(*a*) All the members of the clan are supposedly *descended from a single ancestress*, the foundress of the clan. The clan is thus the widest group within which kinship is traced, and within which the child born into the clan learns to apply the terms of kinship (and the patterns of behaviour associated with the terms):

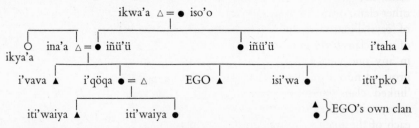

---

[1] Stephen (1936), pp. 954–5: cf. Curtis (1922), pp. 27–8.

[2] The account that follows is based on Titiev's analysis of the social structure of Oraibi. Titiev carried out his field work in 1932–4, and some of what he says refers to an earlier period still, i.e. to the period before the split of 1906; while, therefore, I use the present tense in this account, much of what I describe no longer holds to-day.

[3] Titiev (1944), p. 58. But there is some evidence that, just as the Banks Islanders use the term *veve* both for the clan and for segments of the clan, so the Hopi use the term *nya'mü*: Parsons (1936), p. 1067, n. 2.

In other words, for a boy, all the women in his clan of the generation above his own stand to him as *iñü'ü*, 'my mother', and all the men as *i'taha*, 'my uncle'; all the girls of the same generation as himself stand to him as *i'qöqa* or *isi'wa*, 'my elder (or younger) sister', and all the boys as *i'vava* or *itü'pko*, 'my elder (or younger) brother'; while all the children, male or female, of the generation below his own stand to him as *iti'waiya*, 'my sister's child'.

(*b*) Traditionally, the principal kinds of property, i.e. farm land, house sites, rights to ceremonial office, ownership of eagle-nesting cliffs, were held *in the name of the clan*. Of these assets, land was the most important; and myths recount how, as the ancestors of each clan arrived in the village, they were granted field sites in return for undertaking a ceremony in the annual liturgy.

(*c*) Each clan *has its own name*, its own sacred objects (*wuya*), and its own clan house in which the sacred objects are stored. Nearly all the names of Hopi clans are those of plants, of animals, of natural objects, or of deities or spirits.[1] These eponyms the Hopi also call *wuya*, or 'ancients'. Some of them are represented by masks, figurines or physical objects of various kinds, others have no tangible representation; but, in either case, 'there is a strong feeling of empathy and kinship between each group and its *wuya*. Those *wuya* which are in the form of physical objects are stored in the clan houses [i.e. of the clans that own them], and are so sacred that they are regarded as the "heart" of the clan.'[2]

Altogether, then, there are some thirty to forty clans, to one of which every Hopi belongs; and each clan is divided into a number of matrilineages. Owing to the general rule of matrilocal residence, the majority of the members of any given matrilineage will be found living in one village. The other matrilineages of the clan may be resident either in the same village, or in one (or more) of the other villages; no clan, so far as I know, has matrilineages resident in *all* the villages, nor is any clan confined to a single village.

Turning now to the village: each village has a nucleus of six or eight leading clans, in whose hands its principal ceremonies rest, and around this nucleus other clans, or matrilineages of other clans, have crystallised. Part of this process of 'crystallisation' has no doubt been due, as Hopi myth records, to the arrival of new clans from outside the village, and part to splitting of existing clans; for in any one village, e.g. Oraibi, the clans resident in it will be found to be grouped into a smaller number of phratries, i.e. groups of two, three or four 'linked' clans standing in a special relation to one another and practising exogamy within the group. Certainly at Oraibi, and perhaps at the other villages, each of the main kivas (underground ceremonial chambers) is associated with one of the phratries, and the principal ceremony done in that kiva rests in the

---

[1] For a comprehensive list of the clan names on the three mesas, see below pp. 200-9.

[2] Titiev (1944), p. 55. Titiev also gives the word *na'töla*, as alternative to *wuya*; *na'töla*, however, appears to refer not to the plant, animal or natural object from which the social group takes its name, but to the social group of which that object is the sign, whether it be phratry grouping, clan or lineage: see Stephen (1929), p. 60, and (1936), p. 836, and p. 1066, n. 3.

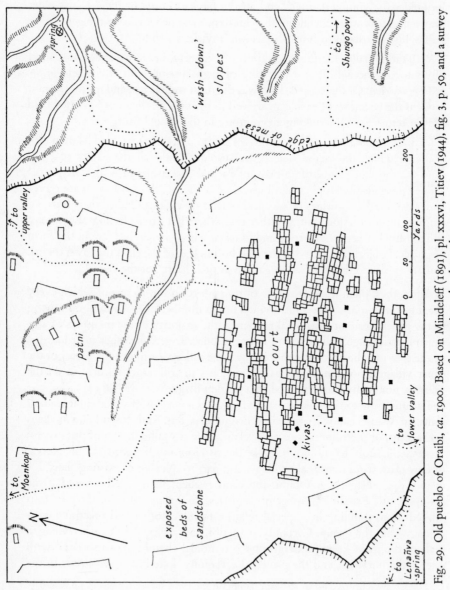

Fig. 29. Old pueblo of Oraibi, *ca.* 1900. Based on Mindeleff (1891), pl. xxxvi, Titiev (1944), fig. 3, p. 50, and a survey of the environs by the author.

hands of the leading clan of the phratry associated with it.[1] As each clan, apart from its primary name, 'owns' a number of secondary names for indicating its constituent matrilineages,[2] and as, further, each clan appears to have, apart from its primary *wuya* (in the sense of sacred object), several secondary *wuya*[3], the way lies open—when the clan reaches a certain size—for it to split into two, one half retaining the primary name, the primary *wuya* and 'ownership' of the ceremony associated with it, the other half taking one of the secondary names and one (or more) of the secondary *wuya*, and playing a subordinate rôle in the performance of the ceremony.

From a practical point of view, a Hopi village is thus made up of a number of matrilineal clans (or fragments of such clans), each comprising one or more closely related matrilineages, the clans themselves being linked loosely together into larger groupings termed phratries. Each clan is to a large extent autonomous, owning its own land and house-sites, choosing its own leaders, and transacting its own affairs with a good deal of independence. Such a social system, as Titiev points out,[4] rests on unstable foundations, for the more firmly people adhere to the clan, the weaker must be their village ties. The pueblo, indeed, is like one of those seed pods with a thin outer shell holding together a number of discrete segments: crack the shell, and the segments fall apart.

Theoretically, then, the Hopi villages are in constant danger of dividing into their component parts; in practice, however, there are two factors which counteract the tendency to disintegration. In the first place, marriage alliance creates new bonds which cut across clan ties; and in the second, the proper performance of ceremonies—upon which the welfare of the whole village depends—requires cooperation between the members of the different clans resident in it. To the part played by marriage alliance in linking clans together, both within the village and between neighbouring villages, I shall return later. Here I propose to consider how far the conditions of Hopi life, and in particular the singling out of individuals to take the lead in ceremonial, conduce to the emergence of leaders within the village: and what kind of authority such leaders dispose of.

---

[1] At Oraibi, the twenty-four principal clans represented in the village prior to the split of 1906 were grouped into nine phratries (Titiev, 1944, Table 3, p. 53):

| | | | | | |
|---|---|---|---|---|---|
| I | rabbit<br>katçina<br>parrot | IV | sun<br>eagle | VII | badger<br>gray badger<br>butterfly |
| II | bear<br>spider | V | greasewood<br>bow<br>reed | VIII | *pikyas* (young corn)<br>*patki* (water house) |
| III | sand<br>snake<br>lizard | VI | Masau'u<br>coyote<br>water coyote<br>*kokop* (firewood) | IX | sparrow hawk<br>squash |

For the links between the phratries and the main kivas in the pueblo, see below pp. 58–60.

[2] Parsons (1936), pp. 1067–8.

[3] Titiev (1944), p. 56, and n. 64.

[4] In the masterly chapter entitled 'The amorphous Hopi state', in *Old Oraibi* (1944), pp. 59–68.

On the ground each Hopi village,[1] though not especially tidy in its lay-out, is extremely compact; thus Oraibi, with a population (before the split of 1906) of 880 divided between 147 households, covered an area of less than 10 acres. Irregular blocks of houses, built wall to wall and often back to back, alternate with narrow thoroughfares, and these in turn converge on open courts, beside which the kivas are mostly to be found. A 'house', in Hopi, is *ki'hü*, a word which, as we shall see later, has wide extensions of meaning; and a 'cluster of houses' is *ki'qlö*, the suffix *-qölö* being one form for the plural. But there is no separate word for a 'village'. The term that is used is *ki-co'ki*, derived from *ki'hü*, 'house', and *co'ki*, 'any erect plant, as a bush or tree'; in other words, the village is conceived as the houses (*ki'hü*) standing up erect like a bush (*co'ki*), as indeed they do stand up when seen on the skyline from the valley below.

The word in Hopi, for a leader of any kind, is *moñ'wi* (pl. *moñ'mowitû*). Thus, the stem *ma'k-* means 'to hunt': hence *ma'k moñ'wi*, 'hunt leader', referring to the man who organises and directs a communal (rabbit) hunt. Yet the matter is not quite as simple as that, for the man who directs a communal hunt is responsible for carrying out the ritual on which the success of the hunt depends. And this brings us, at a step, to one of the key facts of Hopi life, namely: no leadership among the Hopi is without its ritual responsibilities, and conversely, all authority has a religious tap-root. As Titiev puts it:[2] 'the sacred and the civil are inextricably commingled in the political structure . . .'

At Oraibi and, from the scanty evidence available, the same seems to have been the case in the other villages,[3] the guidance of pueblo affairs rested in the hands of the six principal officers of the Soyal (the winter solstice ceremony), namely: the Soyal chief, generally the head of Bear clan: the head of Pikyas clan: Tobacco chief, generally the head of Rabbit clan: the head of Parrot clan: Crier chief (*tça'ak moñ'wi*), head of Greasewood clan: and War chief (*kale'taka moñ'wi*), drawn either from Reed or from Coyote clan. These six officers were responsible for carrying out the Soyal, and such political authority as they had stemmed in part from the headship of their own clans, and in part from their ritual office: this office being in turn backed, 'verified' in Titiev's words, by mythological sanctions.

Several myths link the Emergence from the Underworld, founding of the village, distribution of land and establishment of the ceremonial cycle, to the authority of the chiefs (*moñ'mowitû*). A composite summary of these myths runs as follows:[4]

[1] For plans of the seven old Hopi villages, see Mindeleff (1891), pp. 61–79.
[2] Titiev (1944), p. 59.
[3] Cf. Parsons (1933), pp. 53–7. The *structure* appears to have been the same in the several villages, but the offices were held by the heads of different clans: e.g. on 1st Mesa, the Village chief was head of Millet clan and leader of the Flute society (whereas, at Oraibi, he was head of Bear clan and leader of the Soyal).
[4] Based on the summary given by Titiev (1944), p. 61: itself based on the several myths recounted by Voth (1905c), pp. 1–30. On the significance of Masau'u as Skeleton, see further, below p. 288.

For some time prior to the Emergence from the Underworld, people had been hearing footsteps above them, but when they reached the surface of the earth it was cold and dark, and nothing could be seen. In due course they noticed a distant light and sent a messenger, who returned with the welcome news that he had discovered 'a field in which corn, water-melons, beans, etc., were planted. All around this field a fire was burning . . ., by which the ground was kept warm so that the plants could grow.'

Nearby the messenger found a man whose handsome appearance contrasted strangely with the grotesque death's head mask by his side. At once the messenger realised that it was Skeleton (*Masau'u*), 'whom they had heard walking about from the other world'. The deity proved kindly disposed, fed the messenger and sent him to fetch his companions. Here they built a large fire, warmed themselves, and 'Skeleton gave them roasting ears, and melons, squashes, etc., and they ate and refreshed themselves'.

In time the people left Masau'u and set out on the wanderings that were ultimately to bring them to their present settlements. For a while the Bear people settled at Shungo'povi, but they 'heard that Masau'u was living where Oraibi now is, and so they all travelled on towards Oraibi'. The Bear clan leader, Matçito, asked Masau'u to give him some land and to be the chief of his people, but Masau'u replied: 'No, I shall not be chief, you shall be chief here. I shall give you a piece of land, and then you live here.' And he stepped off a large tract of land, which he allotted to Matçito. Soon other clans began to arrive, each seeking to dwell at Oraibi and each offering in exchange to perform a beneficial ceremony for Matçito. If the trial performance proved pleasing to the chief, he would say: 'Very well, you take part in our cult and help us with the ceremonies', and then he would give them their fields according to the way they came. And that way their fields were all distributed.

Thus, as Titiev says, the myths 'explain'[1] the present state of things; for at Oraibi the leader of Bear clan is 'chief of the houses' (*ki'k moñ'wi*) or village head, Soyal leader, and theoretical owner of all the village lands, and the other clans in the village hold their land on condition of taking their share in the annual liturgy.

For his own clan, Bear clan leader chose a large tract of land to the southwest of Oraibi, on the old flood plain of the main wash. The western limit of this holding was marked by a boundary stone, on which a bear's claw was carved; beyond the stone, another large tract was allotted to Pikyas clan,[2] in return for the part played by Pikyas chief in the Soyal and Powamu ceremonies. Smaller plots were allotted to War chief and Tobacco chief, and to Parrot, Greasewood and Rabbit clans, for the part played by their leaders in the Soyal: and also to Spider clan, for their help in the Soyal and for their ownership of the Blue Flute ceremony. As a 'charter' for these grants, the Village chief at Oraibi has in his keeping a sacred stone, believed to have been brought from the Underworld

---

[1] For the myth relating how land was distributed at 2nd Mesa, see E. Beaglehole (1937), pp. 14–15.

[2] At some point later, the Pikyas succession failed and the land passed temporarily to Patki clan, of the same phratry; this is the origin of the Pikyas–Patki conflict. See Titiev (1944), pp. 201–2.

by Matçito and to show by the markings on its surface his intentions regarding control of the village lands. These are represented by a double rectangle, around which are grouped six figures, depicting the Soyal officers; each figure stands with the left hand across the chest and the right extended down to cover the genitals, a posture which is 'said to indicate that the chiefs are claiming the land enclosed within the central rectangles'.[1] Along the edge of the stone representing the east, there is a line of scratches, interspersed with occasional circles and crosses, depicting the 'path' which the chiefs are supposed to travel.

On the morning of the last day of the Soyal, the stone is brought out, the Soyal officers examine it closely, and then re-affirm their rights to hold office and their claims to the land. Then takes place the assembage known as *moñ lavai'yi*, 'chiefs' talk', at which first the Village chief, and then each of the other Soyal officers in turn, speaks, telling the people what has been done during the rites that have just concluded and ending with a prayer for good crops and long lives.

These 'chiefs' talks', of which the one that takes place at the conclusion of the Soyal is the most important, are the nearest that the Hopi come to any form of overt political control within the village. Even at these, however, the chiefs (*moñ'mowitû*) in no sense act as a law-making body; they only bring their authority to bear, to assert the traditional Hopi 'path'. What that 'path' is, we shall see later; here I am concerned with the roots of their authority.

This authority is both 'secular', and religious. To begin with, each Soyal officer is either the head or a leading member of his own clan; in other words, the *moñ'mowitû* are already big men in the village apart from their Soyal office. But where their position in their own clan is primarily 'secular', the holding of Soyal office invests their authority with a religious dye—expressed in a number of outward symbols.

Every major ceremony (*wi'mi*) in the annual cycle has its own *ti'poni*, or sacred object, made usually of a piece of cottonwood root—sometimes with a quartz crystal or a stone celt let into it—wrapped around with special feathers;[2] when not in use, the *ti'poni* is kept in the clan house of the clan that 'owns' the ceremony, in the care of the senior woman of the matrilineage from which the leader is chosen. Leadership in a ceremony ordinarily passes from the holder, as he ages, either to one of his younger brothers or to his sister's son; and ownership of the *ti'poni* belonging to the ceremony is the tangible sign that a man has become its leader. As a ruling Village chief (*ki'k moñ'wi*) grows old, he selects a successor from among his younger kinsmen and begins to teach him his future duties; when in course of time he dies, this man inherits from the late chief the *ti'poni* of the ceremony of which he was the head. At Oraibi, the Village chief was traditionally the leader of Bear clan, and it was the ownership of the Soyal

---

[1] Titiev (1944), p. 61: the stone itself is depicted there (Fig. 4, p. 60).
[2] The root of the word appears to be related to: *tih'ta*, to give birth, *po'no*, belly, *po'shi*, seed, *ti'poshi*, infant. According to Parsons (1936, p. 1305), 'it [the *ti'poni*] bears in its womb all seeds, hence is mother of all'.

*ti'poni* that marked his office; on 1st Mesa, it was the ownership of the Flute society's *ti'poni* that identified the Village chief.

At some time subsequent to receiving the *ti'poni* that marks his office,[1] the new Village chief is formally inducted into his office by the head of the Kwan (Agave) fraternity. Unfortunately, there is no first-hand account of such an induction; but the fact that Titiev refers to it as a 'baptism' suggests that it follows the common Hopi pattern of a washing of the head in yucca suds and the giving of a new name. What is significant, as throwing a flood of light on how the Hopi themselves envisage chiefship, is their own interpretation of the event. According to Tawaqwaptiwa,[2] the last traditional chief of Oraibi, the object of the 'baptism' is to fit the new leader for his position in the other world, thus putting him into close touch with the Cloud People (spirits of the dead) who control rain. 'Now I make you a chief', says the Kwan head, at the close of the ceremony, 'and now I give you a good path to lead us to the Sun. Now you are our father. Look forward for the good and not for the bad, and see that things go rightly so that we have good crops and long life.'

The Kwan leader also 'baptises' the other Soyal leaders when they succeed to office, with the exception of the War chief who is 'baptised' by the head of Kokop clan.

It is evident, from the words used by the Kwan head at his induction, that Hopi regard the Village chief primarily as intermediary between themselves and the Cloud People. He is responsible, at Oraibi, for carrying through the Soyal on which the welfare of the pueblo depends. Grouped with him in this enterprise are the other Soyal officers, known (like him) as *moñ'mowitû*, 'chiefs', and bearing (as he does) the outward signs of 'chiefship', namely the chief's stick (*moñ'kohü*) and the special clay markings on face, shoulders and leg which —only adopted on special ritual occasions—distinguish them from ordinary people.[3] As the leader of this group, the Village chief has special responsibility for maintaining harmony within the village; and it is in this context, as 'chief of the houses', that he wields a measure of political authority. Primarily, this authority is expressed in the settlement of land disputes, either in adjudicating between two claimants to a given piece of land, or in awarding damages for destruction of crops by livestock. Beyond this, his opinion may be sought on any issue affecting the village as a whole; but no compulsion is brought to bear to force people to take their disputes to the Village chief, and even in the old days, such decisions as he gave he lacked the power to enforce.

From this brief account of the 'political' structure of the Hopi village, certain points emerge. Each Village chief's jurisdiction is strictly limited to his own

[1] In practice, at the time of the first *wüwütçim* initiation following the new chief's entry into office: which may be three or four years later.

[2] Titiev (1944), pp. 63–4.

[3] These insignia pertain to all the Soyal officers, except the War chief: and also to the leaders of the Al (Horn), Kwan (Agave) and Tao (Singers) fraternities, who are likewise known as 'chiefs'.

pueblo. Within the pueblo, he is regarded as the 'father' of his people,[1] the people expect him to lead them on the 'path' of a good life, and to his prayers on their behalf they ascribe the success or failure of their crops. But he is looked upon, in Titiev's words,[2] 'rather as a guide and an adviser than an executive; and as an interpreter of Hopi tradition rather than as a legislator'; and he lacks, as we have seen, any real power to enforce his will.

So far as there was ever any cöercive power in the Hopi pueblo, this rested in the old days in the hands of the War chief and of certain disciplinary katçinas (men impersonating spirits). The War chief was traditionally responsible for preserving order within the village, while the katçinas had the more positive task of organising village working parties: e.g. for sowing the Village chief's corn crop, or for cleaning out the springs. But neither War chief nor disciplinary katçinas really fill the gap which we, with our notions of executive and judicial functions, feel to be there. In reality there can be no such gap, since Hopi society—until it began to disintegrate under western contact—'worked'; and the fact that we feel there to be one, is perhaps due to our employment of categories that are not appropriate to the task in hand. For the Hopi village presents the case of a social order in which the external forms of government—ἡ ἀρχή— have been reduced to a minimum; in its traditional form, it was as nearly *an-archic* as a tightly-knit, agricultural community can well be. This is to say, not that the village lacked social controls, but that the controls it had did not take the external forms[3] to which we are used (and to which our categories apply). These controls were two-fold: on the one hand, a general agreement regarding the ends of social life, defined as following the Hopi 'path'; and on the other, a peculiar sensitivity to public opinion, allied to fear of witchcraft.

The notion of social life as a 'path' (*pü'hü*) to be followed is one that we shall meet again and again in this account of Hopi society; it is indeed, as I hope to show in the sequel, one of the key concepts in Hopi thinking. The point I wish to stress here is that this concept has direct consequences in behaviour. For the 'path', to be travelled by each individual, is a specifically Hopi path; to travel it rightly requires certain modes of conduct, and these modes of conduct are equated, quite simply, with the Hopi way of life:[4]

> *ho'pi*: adj. (is) good, well-behaved, peaceable (Whorf):
>      good in every respect (Voegelin);

*Hopi'tû*: the wise people, *hopi* meaning tranquil, peaceable, wise (Parsons); and the worst that can be said of a person's behaviour is that he (or it) is *qa-ho'pi*, 'un-Hopi' (or, as we might say, 'un-English'), i.e. bad, mischievous, bold (Voegelin).

---

[1] On 2nd Mesa, for example, the communal sowing of the Village chief's cornfield is referred to as 'planting for the father': E. Beaglehole (1937), p. 38.

[2] Titiev (1944), p. 65.

[3] In Kardiner's terms, they are more *internalised* than the controls to which we are accustomed.

[4] See Parsons (1936), p. 1221: Whorf (1936), p. 1221: Voegelin (1957), p. 43, C3.

The primary sanction against such bad behaviour is fear of non-conformity: 'so marked is the dread of running afoul of public opinion among the Hopi,' writes Titiev,[1] ... that only a man of exceptional character dares to depart from conventional modes of behaviour in any important respects.' And this fear of public opinion, within the closely-knit village community, is backed by the fear of witchcraft.[2] For Hopi believe that witchcraft, or sorcery, is widespread, and that no one can tell which of his kinsmen or neighbours is likely to be a *po'aka*. Consequently they live in constant dread of sorcery, and early in life learn to avoid all appearance of having outstanding ability—for fear of arousing the envy of the 'two-hearted'.[3]

### THE HOUSEHOLD, AND THE ECONOMIC CYCLE[4]

While land and ceremonies are in theory 'owned' by the clan, in practice the rights to particular blocks of land, to ceremonial office, to house sites and to water cisterns (*patni*), are handed down within the separate matrilineages that make up the clan. The essential attributes of the matrilineage, as distinct from the clan, are that it has a time-depth of only three to four generations, and that all its members are *demonstrably* descended from a single ancestress. Any given clan in the village may be represented by one or more matrilineages; thus at Oraibi, with a population (before the split of 1906) of about 880, there were some thirty-nine matrilineages, one half of the twenty-four clans resident in the village being represented by one matrilineage only, and the remainder by two, three or four each.

Each matrilineage, in turn, comprises one or more segments; and it is the presence of the husband from another clan that converts the segment of the matrilineage, a kinship group, into the *household*, the consuming group. The household numbers, on average, some six to seven persons; and at Oraibi the thirty-nine matrilineages, referred to above, were made up of 147 separate households—an average of three to four households to each matrilineage. The several households that make up the matrilineage commonly occupy contiguous houses in one quarter of the village; but whether they do or not, there is constant coming and going between them. Boys and girls drop in for meals at the houses of their mother's sisters; and the children of the several

---

[1] Titiev (1944), p. 65. Cf. E. Beaglehole (1937), p. 12: 'The sanction for honest conduct ... is found in the power of public opinion.'

[2] See, especially, Titiev (1942). Witches, *po'akam*, may be of either sex; their special power, known as *duhi'sa*, is derived from an animal familiar with which each *po'aka* is intimately linked—hence they are referred to as 'two-hearted'; and they use this power to injure those whom they dislike, usually their own relatives. The principal prophylactic against witchcraft is ashes, particularly of cedar wood, smeared on the person.

[3] What is written here about witchcraft, applies to a period some years ago. While Hopi still today tend to avoid the appearance of having outstanding ability and are reluctant to take the lead in communal affairs, this is no longer motivated by fear of witchcraft; rather, it has become a basic feature of character formation in Hopi culture, and is likely to persist as long as the main lines of that culture persist.

[4] For this whole section, see E. Beaglehole (1937), especially pp. 22–45.

households of a matrilineage comprise the primary play-groups in the pueblo. It is, indeed, within his own household and the other households of his matrilineage that the child learns the norms of behaviour that constitute the Hopi 'path', perhaps first of all in relation to food and the eating of food; and it is to this aspect of pueblo life that I now turn—first to the getting and preparing of food, then to its consumption.

Conceptually, the Hopi divide the year into two halves, 'winter' and 'summer', made up of five or six moons (*mü'iya*) each. The year[1] begins in November, with *ke'le mü'iya*, 'sparrow-hawk or novice, moon'; 'with this moon,' Hopi say, 'everything is changed'. The first six moons, from *ke'le* (November) through to *kwiya' mü'iya* (late March—early April), are called *tü'müü*, 'winter'. They take their names either from the ceremonial event with which the moon co-incides, or from events in the agricultural cycle; thus, *ke'le* (November) refers to the initiation of novices in the Wü'wütçim ceremony and *powa' mü'iya* (February) to the Powamu ceremony, while *ö'sö mü'iya* (early March) takes its name from the sprouting of the new grass for grazing and *kwiya' mü'iya* from the erection of wind-breaks in the fields. The two latter moons, together with *haki'ton mü'iya*, 'waiting moon' (because people are waiting to plant their bean and corn crop), are known collectively as *ta'wa nyüña*, 'sun comes closer', i.e. spring.

The five (or six) moons, running from late May to the end of October, are called *ta'laa*, 'summer'. Each of these moons is known by at least two different names, one referring to what is happening in the fields, the other being that of the winter moon to which the summer moon is held to correspond: thus, *ü'yi mü'iya* (planting moon) is also known as *ke'le*; *wi'kya mü'iya* (hoeing moon), as *kya'*; *nasa'ñ mü'iya* (feasting moon), as *powa'*; and *tüho'os mü'iya* (the moon during which the harvest is carried in), as *ö'sö*. Further, three of the summer moons are sometimes named after the ceremonies with which they co-incide: *wi'kya* being referred to as the moon of the Nima'n ceremony (the home-going dance), *nasa'ñ* as the moon of the Marau' (one of the two harvest festivals), and *tüho'os* as the moon of the Lako'n (the other of the two harvest festivals). The Hopi year is thus divided as shown opposite.

The agricultural season opens early in March, as soon as the winter snows have melted. The first task is the clearing and preparation of the fields for planting. Traditionally, the implements used[2] were the digging stick (*so'ya*), used to lever up tufts of grass and bushes, the hoe (*wi'kya*), used for breaking the surface of the ground and—later in the season—for hoeing weeds, and the planting stick (*de've*), made of greasewood and used for digging the holes for the seed. Each household prepares its own fields, the bushes and weeds being collected together into piles, left to dry for a few days and then burned. The corn stumps of

---

[1] On the Hopi calendar, see Fewkes (1892a), pp. 151–3, and (1897a), pp. 255–8: Parsons (1933), pp. 58–61, and (1936), pp. 1037–9: Titiev (1938), pp. 39–42, and (1944), pp. 173–5.

[2] For the traditional agricultural implements used by the Hopi, see Hough (1918), pp. 236–7, and pl. xix.

the previous year's harvest are left in the ground to serve as a guide for planting (and also to help retain the soil), the new corn being set in rows between the rows of last season's crop.

Towards the middle of April, or later if the season is delayed, the planting of sweet corn, melons, squash and beans begins, followed a month later by the sowing of the main corn crop. The planting season extends over eight to ten weeks, up to about the third week in June. Within this period, the dates for planting the various crops are known by observing the sun rise behind a succession of points on the eastern skyline; each village has its own 'horizon calendar',[1] and a Sun Watcher, whose duty it is to watch the sun rise each morning and to let the people know as it reaches the successive points on the horizon.

Some ten days to a fortnight after planting, the first shoots of corn appear above the ground, and the main work of cultivation now begins. The soil around the seedlings has to be kept loose and free of weeds, in exposed places brushwood fences are put up to protect the young plants, and low banks of earth are sometimes raised round them to retain the moisture from rain or run-off. By the time the plants are knee high and the cobs beginning to form, towards the end of July, work in the fields slackens off; from then on, it is a matter of waiting for the cobs to fill out and ripen—a process that is dependent on the rainfall of the August moon (*pa' mii'iya*, 'moisture moon').

| *our month* | Hopi moon | Hopi season | Hopi moon | *our month* |
|---|---|---|---|---|
| November: | *ke'le* | | *ii'yi,* | late May –early June |
| December: | *kya'* | | *wi'kya,* | late June –early July |
| January: | *pa'* | *ta'laa,* summer: | *pa' mii'iya,* | late July –early August |
| February: | *powa'* | *tü'müü,* winter: | *nasa'ñ,* | late August –early Sept. |
| early March: | *ö'sö* | | *hiiu'ki mii'iya*[2]*, tüho'os,* | late September October |
| late March –early April: | *kwiya'* | *ta'wa nyüña,* spring: | | |
| late April –early May: | *haki'ton* | | | |

[1] For the 'horizon calendar' at Oraibi, see Titiev (1938), p. 40. My own observations (1966), regarding that 'calendar', are that the sun rises behind the point marked *kwiptuwi* about 20 April, and behind *moñya'ovi* about 4 May.

[2] 'Corn-husking moon', the name given this moon by Fewkes. Both Fewkes (1897a, pp. 255-8), and Titiev (1938, p. 40), insert a moon between *nasa'ñ* (= *powa'*) and *tüho'os* (= *ö'sö*); Parsons (1936, p. 1038, n. 1) remarks that this moon is *de trop*, on the ground that it falls between Marau' and Lako'n, which are celebrated in successive moons. Probably, however, this thirteenth moon is inserted whenever the lunar cycle gets out of phase with solar observation, the date of the Wü'wütçim ceremony being dependent on observation of the sun's rising point early in November.

The first crop to ripen is sweet corn; this is picked and roasted, in deep ovens close to the field, during August. Early in September, beans, squash and melons are ready for harvesting; squash and melons are carried up to the village as they are, but beans are left in the field until they are thoroughly sun-dried, then threshed out—by putting on a large blanket and beating with sticks. By late September, the main corn crop should be ripe. According to the size of the field, harvesting is done by the men of the household, or by small working parties of kinsfolk, and the crops transported to the village by burro or waggon; formerly, before animal power became available, the corn cobs were carried up to the pueblos on people's backs either in wicker carrying-baskets (*hoa'pu*) or in woven blankets.[1] As the corn is brought to the house, the women strip off the husks and spread the cobs on the flat roof tops to dry in the late October sunshine. The cobs are then stored in orderly rows according to colour, in the storehouse, one season's harvest being kept carefully apart from the previous year's[2] and a part of each being set on one side for seed. By early November when the first snows of the winter are due, the harvest should be collected and stored, and work in the fields comes to an end—until the following spring, when the agricultural cycle starts afresh.

### FOOD IN PUEBLO LIFE

Aristotle defined the household (*oikos*) as 'those who share a common meal tub'. Substitute corn store for meal tub, and the definition fits the Hopi household nicely.

In the old days, two cooked meals were served each day, one in the morning and one in the evening;[3] at mid-day, a light 'lunch' of waferbread and water was taken, either in the village or in the fields depending on the season. For almost every meal, corn provides the basic staple; and the preparation of meal from the corn, and its subsequent cooking, form the principal daily occupation of the women of the household. In the morning, therefore, the woman of the house goes to her corn store and fetches a basketful of cobs. After removing the kernels and collecting them into a flat yucca-fibre tray, she gets down to the serious business of grinding meal to the appropriate fineness. To grind is *ñü' manda*: a grinding stone is *ma'da*. Every house has at least two stones set in a

[1] How great that labour must have been is indicated by the belief that a widower, who courts a girl who has not already been married, is punished after death by having to carry a laden *hoa'pu* on the journey from the grave to the home of the dead.

[2] In the old days, and as late as the 1930s, each household endeavoured to keep a year's supply of corn in reserve, as a guard against crop failure.

[3] The following account of Hopi meals and cooking is based on P. Beaglehole (1937), pp. 60–71: checked, in places, by my own observations. So far as I know, the paper referred to by J. G. Owens (1892, p. 167, n. 2), 'Food resources and foods of the Hopi Indians', was never published. Perhaps the manuscript exists somewhere? (Owens' 'Notes on a collection of plants from the Hopi Indian region' was found and published by P. A. Vestal, in 1940.) Owens himself died of tropical fever in February, 1893, leading the second Peabody Museum Expedition to Central America, and was buried at Copan in western Honduras.

corner of the living room, one for the coarse first grinding, the other for the final fine grinding; some have a third *ma'da*, for grinding medium-fine meal.[1] Two kinds of corn—white, and blue—are chiefly used, together with sweet corn: the partially-ground meal being put in trays, and the chaff shaken out.

A Hopi meal ordinarily consists of one of the common preparations of corn-meal, served with a 'relish'—either a meat gravy, one of the cultivated vegetables (beans, squash, chili, onions), or wild greens. The corn-meal may be either boiled, baked in an oven in one of several different ways, or sand roasted. Out of these alternatives, the following ten common dishes are prepared:

(i) *pi'ki*, waferbread:

> *ingredients:* fine blue meal: burned *sy'ovi* ashes.

> *preparation:* a thin batter of blue corn-meal, mixed with water and burned *sy'ovi* (saltbush) ash, is prepared: the special *pi'ki* stone is heated and well greased. The woman sits on the floor before the stone, with all necessary paraphernalia within reach.

> A thin layer of batter, smeared over the surface of the hot stone, bakes instantly to a crisp. The sheet is at once peeled off, laid on a yucca-fibre tray, and left there until the next sheet is baked. It is then put back on the stone, on top of the sheet being baked, and the two sheets are folded together into a package about 2 inches wide, and 8 to 10 inches long. The packages are piled on a second tray, until the whole batch is done.

> *uses: pi'ki* was formerly the only food eaten at noon. Nowadays it is regarded as a delicacy, and is made especially in preparation for e.g. katçina dances, and weddings.

(ii) *somi'viki*, 'maiden's cake':

> *ingredients:* fine blue meal: burned *sy'ovi* ashes: sweet sauce prepared from sprouted wheat seeds, or sugar.

> *preparation:* a stiff dough is made by mixing fine blue meal with hot water and *sy'ovi* ash: the sweet sauce, or sugar, is then stirred into the dough. Corn husks, softened by soaking, are filled with the dough: the two ends being folded over, and the whole tied tightly with yucca fibre (or string) in two places, so that when unwrapped the package consists of three equal sections. The packages are then boiled for half an hour.

> *uses: somi'viki* is regarded as a special treat.

> Girls give it to their boy-friends, in the course of the Powamu ceremony and on the occasion of mixed hunting parties and picnics; it is served on the day of the head-washing of bride and groom, and subsequently during the weaving of the wedding garments; and women serve it to men on their return from e.g. salt-gathering expeditions.

---

[1] Nowadays, in many houses, the grinding stones have fallen out of use, and grinding is done in mechanical mills, either hand operated or electrically operated. The three grinding stones, set in a row, form a characteristic feature of archaeological sites throughout the region.

(iii) *tçükü' viki*, 'bride's cake'.

    *ingredients:* as for *somi' viki*.

    *preparation: tçükü' viki* is made of the same sweetened batter as *somi' viki*. Instead of being wrapped in corn husks, the dough is shaped into crescents some 5 to 6 inches long, wrapped in corn leaves, and boiled.

    *uses: tçükü' viki* is served at weddings, and again, alternately with *somi' viki*, during the weaving of the wedding garments.

(iv) *mömö' k-viki:*

    *ingredients:* coarse-ground blue meal.

    *preparation:* a batter of coarse blue meal and hot water is kneaded into a thick dough. The dough is moulded into dumplings, and boiled until the water thickens.

    *uses:* served with fried chili, this was formerly the common breakfast dish.

(v) *dañü' viki:*

    *ingredients:* coarse-ground blue meal: sweet sauce, or sugar.

    *preparation:* a sweet batter is made as for *somi' viki*, but with a coarse meal. The dough is put in one end of a corn husk, the sides and ends of which are folded over and tied. The packets are then baked in a special pit oven, prepared by placing a lining of hot stones at the bottom of the pit; the oven is filled with alternate layers of food packets and hot stones, the top covered over with a mat, and the whole lot left to cook for several hours.

    *uses: dañü' viki* is served, usually with meat, gravy or beans, at the evening meal.

(vi) *pi' kami:*

    *ingredients:* fine-ground white corn-meal: sweet sauce.

    *preparation:* the dried kernels are soaked in water, until the shells fall off and the kernels become soft. The corn is then ground very fine, boiling water added, and the whole stirred until a smooth thin batter results. Sweet sauce is then stirred in.

      The batter is poured into a pottery cooking vessel and covered over with corn husks. This is placed in a hot pit-oven, in mid-afternoon; flat stones are laid over the top, and the cracks filled with sand. Over the top of the oven, a fire of sheep dung is made and left to smoulder all night; early the next morning, the pudding is taken out and served.

    *uses: pi' kami* is a very special dish.

      It is served on such occasions as the naming feast for a newborn child, breakfast on the day of a katçina dance, and on the day the loom is set up for weaving the bride's wedding garments.

(vii) *hödzö' sögi:*

    *ingredients:* coarse-ground white corn-meal.

    *preparation:* coarsely ground white corn meal is added to boiling water, and boiled until thick. The pudding is then removed from the cooking pot, and served on a yucca-fibre tray.

    *uses:* in the old days, *hödzö' sögi* was commonly served with a meat gravy (*wi' pala*), either for breakfast or as a special dish for communal working parties. The pudding is pinched-off in small pieces and dipped in the gravy.

(*viii*) *kwö'mi*:

    *ingredients*: sweet corn, dried and finely ground.

    *preparation*: the sweet corn is baked over-night in hot embers, then ground very fine, and mixed with water into a stiff dough. The dough is shaped into rolls, then baked.

    *uses*: *kwö'mi* is made on special occasions: especially by a girl to give to her boy-friend, as an engagement gift.

(*ix*) *wida'ka*:

    *ingredients*: fine blue meal: sweet sauce, or sugar: sweet-corn, dried and coarsely ground.

    *preparation*: fine blue meal is added to boiling water, and boiled until thick. It is then transferred to a bowl, and sweetened. In the meantime, dried sweet-corn has been coarsely ground. The sweetened blue-meal batter is poured over the ground sweet-corn, and the two are boiled together until the sweet-corn is soft.

    *uses*: in the old days, *wida'ka* was commonly served with a number of different wild foods, e.g. sumac berries, wild spinach (*dö'mi*), wild mint (*moñdosh'habe*). Alternately, *wida'ka* may be served with cultivated vegetables: either with squash (*patña*) cut into pieces, or with beans, boiled with fat and salt.

(*x*) *nyö'kwivi*, hominy or mutton stew.

    *ingredients*: mutton, corn kernels, salt.

    *preparation*: dried corn kernels are boiled, with ashes of sheep dung, until the shells are ready to drop off the kernels. The kernels are then strained, washed, and added to a salted mutton stew, the whole being cooked until tender.

    *uses*: hominy is the occasional dish *par excellence*.

    No feast is complete without *nyö'kwivi* as the main course.

'In the total cultural complex,' writes Mrs. Beaglehole,[1] 'the importance of food, especially corn, and of eating cannot be over-estimated. No Hopi gives an account of an expedition or visit without specifying when, where, and exactly what he ate.' I propose now to consider this aspect of Hopi culture in its bearing on the upbringing of children; for perhaps the first explicit lesson the Hopi child receives is in relation to food and its use.[2]

'Food' in Hopi, in the sense of dishes served and ready for eating, is *no'va*; and the invitation to guests arriving at meal-time is: *katü'ü, ita'm no'nova-ni*, 'sit down, we are going to eat'. The typical meal consists, as we have seen, of one of the common preparations of corn-meal,[3] served with a 'relish'—either a meat gravy, one of the cultivated vegetables usually cooked with salt and fat, or wild greens. This division is recognised, both in nomenclature and in manners. In nomenclature a special term, *ö'ñgala*, refers to most of the items which we should describe as 'relishes' or 'condiments'. Traditionally, *ö'ñgala* foods included meat and fat, salt and sugar, all *ne'pni* or edible wild plants, together with chili, onions and most other vegetables grown in irrigated gardens. In other words,

---

[1] P. Beaglehole (1937), p. 60.

[2] Cf. the upbringing of Don Talai'yesva: Simmons (1942), pp. 52–6.

[3] Owens reckoned (1892, p. 163) that, in the old days, at least 90 per cent of the vegetable food eaten by the Hopi was made from corn.

*ö'ñgala* foods are those which are, or have in the past been, scarce; and they tend to be more tasteful than the rather monotonous staples of the Hopi dietary, with which they are implicitly contrasted.[1]

A Hopi meal was customarily served, on a cloth or blanket, on the floor just inside the entrance to the house, so that passers-by could be invited in to eat.[2] When all were 'seated' at table (in practice, adults commonly knelt to eat), the hot dishes were brought in, the bowls of gravy (*wi'pala*), boiled beans (*ö'ñgava*) or greens (*ne'pni*) being set down in the middle of the 'table'. Each person breaks off a piece of whatever kind of bread or pudding is being served and, holding it in the first three fingers of his right hand, leans forward, dips it into one of the bowls and conveys the morsel to his mouth. To dip as far as the distal joint of the fingers was considered proper; to dip as far as the proximal joint, was held to be greedy. As each in turn finishes, he rises, wipes his hands on his thighs and, if he is a guest, thanks the women of the household for his meal. The patterns of etiquette and manners are thus directed to ensuring the adequacy of a limited food supply, and in this respect reflect the division between staple foods and *ö'ñgala*. Asked about the latter, Hopi are likely to say that *ö'ñgala* foods are those which, as children, they were taught to eat sparingly of: 'that is *ö'ñgala*', they were told, meaning that it should be used lightly and only as a flavouring for corn and beans. For in the old days, even when there chanced to be plenty of it at the time, it was considered bad manners to eat heartily of an *ö'ñgala* food; such behaviour represented misuse of the food, according to the Hopi notion of its purpose.

This completes the main sequence of food production, and its consumption. Apart from house-building and weaving, agriculture constituted—in the traditional Hopi economy—the principal activity of men, and food preparation, with basketry and pot-making, the principal activity of women. Nearly all the food produced was grown by the household on its own land, and by far the greater part of the food consumed was eaten, again by the household, within its own four walls. To this generalisation there are two exceptions, namely: in production, the working parties of kinsmen and neighbours, chiefly at planting and harvest time, which cut across the boundaries of household and even of matrilineage; and in consumption, the elaborate series of gift exchanges that accompany such social events as childbirth, initiation and marriage. With these two exceptions, the complete sequence takes place within the household or, at the widest, within the several households that comprise the matrilineage; and it is within this group, and to a large extent in relation to economic

---

[1] On *ö'ñgala* foods, see Watson (1943), pp. 49–52. The 'tastefulness', or piquancy, of *ö'ñgala* foods is brought out in the etymology of the word, which is evidently related to the stem *ö'ñga*, salt. The same stem may also be present in the word for boiled beans, *ö'ñgava*; Stephen observes (1936, p. 354) that, in the days before the Hopi had sheep and goats, boiled beans were considered the same as meat.

[2] Such a meal, spread on the floor ready for the guests to eat, was known as *tünüshvoñya*: from *tü'moita*, to convey food to the mouth with the fingers, *nüsha*, to eat, *poñya*, in a circle; Stephen (1929), p. 24, n. 1.

activities, that the Hopi child learns the further patterns of behaviour that are expected of him, or of her.

## UPBRINGING OF THE HOPI CHILD

Much of the education of the child is unformalised, in terms of play—'most things a boy just teaches himself', Hopi say. But such self-teaching is aided by personal advice and, as the child grows older, by more formal instruction. From the time of a boy's katçina initiation, that is from about the age of 6 or 7,[1] a boy begins to accompany his father to the fields and learns from him how to judge soils and prepare them for crops, how to plant and tend fruit trees, how to care for livestock, and how to perform the ritual on which the fertility of both field and livestock depends. From his hunting 'father', he learns the skills of the experienced hunter, and in the winter months, after he has mastered these every-day activities, he starts frequenting his father's kiva; there he is taught how to spin and weave wool, how to dye cotton and to make moccasins, and how to dance.

In much the same way, through constant attendance on the women of her own household and matrilineage, a girl learns all that she needs to know about domestic duties and the care of children; how to prepare foods, the qualities of different coloured corns, the uses of herbs and wild plants. Above all, she must become proficient at grinding[2] and baking, for in the old days no girl was considered ready to marry until she was skilled in these arts, especially in the making of *pi'ki*; indeed, the four days' grinding that precedes the head-washing ceremony in marriage serves as a test, both practical and symbolic, of the bride's fitness to undertake her new responsibilities.[3]

[1] See Titiev (1944), p. 109, n. 5. One of the principal reasons why the Hopi objected to compulsory schooling for their children was that it prevented them from taking part in the economic activities of the household: E. Beaglehole (1937), pp. 19–20.

[2] Owens reckoned (1892, p. 164) that, in the old days, a Hopi woman spent *on average* three hours a day grinding corn.

[3] Reading this chapter in proof (1972) has made me sharply aware of the gap between the 'ethnographic present', in which it is written, and the actual present. Many of the details of food production and consumption described here no longer apply, or only apply now in an attenuated form.

# II

# *The Hopi 'road'*

In this chapter I give a full ethnographic description of the stages through which the Hopi pass, on the 'path' from birth to death and beyond death, to the land of the dead; and in the three chapters that follow, an equally full description of the principal segments of the annual ceremonial cycle. I make no apology for describing these events in detail; for, in their detail, we may hope to find the recurrent patterns of conceiving things, or categories of thinking, which it will be our eventual object to isolate.

## BIRTH, AND NAMING[1]

Hopi are well aware that conception is the result of sexual intercourse, and are able to list the signs which show the woman that she has conceived: first, her periods cease, then in the second month she feels sleepy and lazy, is without appetite, and suffers from morning sickness; later on, the state of the pregnancy is measured by judging the size of her belly. They believe, however, that conception may be influenced by prayers to the appropriate spirits. Thus, a woman who desires a child should pray to the sun early every morning, and to help her have an easy labour, she should again rise early and repeat her prayers to the sun. At the same time, 'she should grind corn and not sit around all day':[2] so closely are the practical and the religious linked in Hopi life.

Usually the only woman called to the house when a girl goes into labour is her own mother—or, if she is no longer living, one of her mother's sisters. This woman prepares a 'bed' of sand, a small brush made of fine stiff grass, and a sprig of juniper. The actual delivery[3] takes place alone, the girl taking up a squatting position over the 'bed' of sand. Apart from its practical use, the 'bed' of sand has a religious significance, as this account relates:[4]

> The first woman on earth . . . had her baby in the open air on the sand. This first infant was born on the sand and was rubbed with sand to remove the blood. Sand

---

[1] The account that follows is based on that given by E. and P. Beaglehole (1935), pp. 30–8, with notes from Owens (1892, pp. 161–75), Voth (1905a, pp. 47–61), and Parsons (1921, pp. 98–104). Beaglehole's account applies to 2nd Mesa, Voth's to 3rd Mesa, Owens' and Parsons' to 1st Mesa.

[2] E. and P. Beaglehole (1935), p. 28.

[3] To hasten labour, a weasel (*pi'wani*) skin is passed up and down over the stomach—to cause the child to slip out easily, the weasel being an animal that goes in and out (of holes and crevices) quickly: Parsons (1921), p. 99, cf. Owens (1892), p. 165.

[4] Told to Dr. Beaglehole (1935, p. 30) by 'a very old man'. Cf. on the use of sand at child-birth, Voth (1905a), pp. 47–9.

is therefore the Mother of babies. We make prayers to the sand for the fertility of the women.

Once the child is born, the attendant woman enters the room again, gives the mother a little of the juniper to chew, and usually some warm corn-meal gruel. The after-birth is expressed by kneading the abdomen; if that fails, she takes the little grass brush and strokes the patient's hips and back, at the same time pulling gently on the cord. The cord is tied about a finger's length away from the navel, with a piece of woollen twine, and then cut, a further finger's length beyond the knot, on an arrow-shaft in the case of a boy and on a stirring-stick for a girl: 'because the boy will later become a hunter and have to carry the firewood, and the girl stir the food in the pan and grind corn'.[1] Finally, the attendant scrapes the sand and blood off the floor on to a tray, puts the placenta on top, sprinkles it with corn-meal ('because it would be dangerous if the after-birth had not come out'), runs to the mesa edge and throws the tray with its contents over the edge.

The delivery completed, the twenty-day period of confinement begins. This period is known as *navwö'la*, the word used for any period of ritual abstinence. During this period the mother may not taste salt or meat, abstains from sexual intercourse, and may drink only warm water or a tea made by boiling the twigs of juniper:[2] the first two restrictions, those on diet and sex, being common to all periods of ceremonial fasting.

The father now calls in either his own mother, or his elder sister, to take charge of the mother and child; this relative the child will in due course call his *(i)so'o*,[3] and the relationship involves lasting duties and obligations on both sides. The *so'o* comes to the house, bringing with her a bowl of water, a piece of yucca root, some corn meal, and a single large ear of corn, which will serve as the infant's 'mother corn': these she brings, 'because the baby will be hers after she washes it'.[4]

Until the fifth day, neither mother nor child may see the sun; the first duty of the *so'o*, on her arrival, is therefore to hang blankets over the windows and doors to keep out the sun. Various explanations for this are offered,[5] the common element being that it is necessary to exclude the sun in situations of danger. The *so'o* then takes a bowl of warm water, prepares suds from the yucca roots she has brought, and washes the child all over with the suds. After drying it, she rubs the baby with soft ashes obtained from burned juniper, wraps it in a

[1] Voth (1905*a*), pp. 47–9: cf. Parsons (1921, p. 101), who adds that fine ashes are put on the navel. When, later, the cord falls off, it is tied to the arrow or stirring-stick, which is then hung in the rafters of the house, as a wish or prayer that the boy may become a good hunter, the girl a good housewife: Voth (1912*c*), items no. 290, 296.

[2] E. and P. Beaglehole (1935), pp. 31–4: cf. Owens (1892), pp. 166–7. Voth (1905*a*, p. 50) says that *all* her food must be prepared with juniper.

[3] The term *(i)so'o* is applied to both paternal and maternal grandmothers, and usually, also, to the father's eldest sister: the term *(i)kya'a* is used for the father's sister, other than the eldest, and for the father's sister's daughter: E. Beaglehole (1937), p. 6.

[4] E. and P. Beaglehole (1935, p. 32), quoting a Hopi informant.

[5] E. and P. Beaglehole (1935), pp. 32–3: Voth (1905*a*), p. 48.

blanket, and puts it in a cradle woven out of sumac (*sö've*) twigs, with the
'mother corn' placed by its side to watch over it. Next, the *so'o* takes some of
the corn meal in her hand and, using the palm of her hand, makes on each of the
four walls of the room four parallel lines, about 2 inches wide and 14 inches long:
first on the north wall, then on the west, south, and east walls, then on the
ceiling and the floor. The name given to these lines is *ki'hü*, 'house';[1] and they
are said to represent 'a house for the baby'.

The day after the birth, the *so'o* boils some sweet corn and juniper sprigs
together; this is the first solid food served the mother. On that day, and on every
day until the end of the *navwö'la* period, the infant is bathed each morning by
the *so'o*; after its bath, the child is rubbed with ashes to prevent sores. On the
fifth morning, and again on the morning of the tenth and fifteenth days, the
*so'o* washes the hair of both mother and child in yucca suds, using the child's
'mother corn' which she dips four times for each into the pounded yucca suds.
After this, the lowest of the four lines on the four walls are scraped off by the
mother,[2] or by *her* mother if she is not well enough; she scrapes the meal into her
hand, goes to the edge of the mesa, holds the meal to her lips, utters a short
prayer, and casts it towards the rising sun. On the tenth day, the second of
the meal lines is scraped off; and on the fifteenth day, the third. After the
washing of her head on the fifth morning, the mother puts on her moccasins,
resumes charge of the household affairs, and is now free to go out of the
house.

On the twentieth day after birth, the principal ceremony takes place. This
consists of three distinct parts: the purification of the mother, the naming of the
baby, and the presentation of the baby to the sun, followed by the naming
breakfast. For the ceremony, and especially for the breakfast that follows it,
considerable preparations are needed, and these begin on the afternoon of the
nineteenth day. First, the female relatives of the child's father assemble at the
mother's house, each bringing woven trays filled with corn meal, as presents.
Two particular dishes, *nyö'kwivi* or hominy stew, and *pi'kami*, are required for the
feast;[3] and during the afternoon the ingredients for these are prepared, and the
fires lighted for cooking them. About sunset, the *so'o* arrives; as soon as she
comes, she takes charge of things generally, and late that evening it is her duty
to wipe the last of the four corn-meal lines off the walls of the house.

Early next morning, before sunrise, the *so'o* and other female relatives of the
child's father return to the house to carry out the *asnaya* rite, that is, the washing
of the baby's head and the bestowing of a name. First, however, the mother has

[1] The fullest description of drawing the 'house' is given by Owens (1892, pp. 168–9);
Owens, however, says that it is done early on the morning of the twentieth day. The other
accounts—Voth (1905*a*, p. 49), Parsons (1921, p. 102), Beaglehole (1935, p. 33)—agree that
it is done on the first day, but Beaglehole says that the lines are made with ashes, not with
corn meal.

[2] Voth (1905*a*), pp. 53–4.

[3] Owens (1892), p. 167: Parsons (1921, p. 100) says that the women also bake *pi'ki*,
waferbread.

to be purified.[1] A bowl of yucca suds is placed on the floor, and before this the mother kneels, her hair falling into the soapy water. The *so'o* takes an ear of corn, dips it four times into the suds, and each time touches the head of the kneeling girl with the tip. All the females relatives of the father who are present do the same. The ear of corn is then laid aside, the *so'o* lathers the girl's head vigorously, rinses the suds out of her hair, and bathes her arms and legs with a decoction made by boiling juniper twigs in water. Finally, the mother is 'fumigated': a bowl with some hot stones in it is put on the floor, she stands over it wrapped in a blanket, and at intervals the *so'o* pours a little of the juniper water on the heated stones, producing a steam which envelopes her body.

Next come the bathing and naming of the baby. A second, smaller bowl of yucca suds is used, the infant's head being washed in the same manner as that of the mother, first by the *so'o*, then by each of the other female relatives of the father in turn. The *so'o* then bathes the baby, dries it, rubs it all over with fine white corn-meal and hands it to the mother to hold. Kneeling before the mother, she takes some fine corn-meal and rubs it first on the arms, neck and face of the mother, then on the face of the child. Then, taking the infant's 'mother corn' in her left hand and a pinch of corn-meal in her right, she first prays over the baby, circling the ear of corn four times over its head in a counter-clockwise direction, and then names it:[2]

> May you live to be old, may you have good corn,
> may you keep well, and now I name you. . . .

She lays the 'mother corn' on the floor, and each of the paternal aunts follows her in turn, each one giving the baby a different name.

The *so'o* now takes a handful of coarse meal, and with it makes a line of meal about 2 inches wide from the far wall, across the floor, to the door and out; this line is called *püh'tabi*, 'road'. In the meantime the mother, if this is her first child,[3] puts on the larger of her two white bridal robes and her bridal moccasins. Then just as the sun is about to rise, the *so'o* and mother, each with some corn-meal in one hand and a prayer-feather in the other, the *so'o* leading the way and carrying the baby wrapped in a blanket, the mother following, walk out through the door, along the corn-meal 'path', to the mesa edge. They stand facing the rising sun, each plants her prayer-feather in the ground, and as the sun appears above the horizon, the *so'o* pulls back the blanket from the baby's face, holds the meal to her lips, breathes a short prayer over it, then sprinkles it towards the rising sun. She hands the baby to the mother, who does the same; then both return to the house, the *so'o* still leading the way, but the mother now carrying the baby.

---

[1] Only Owens (1892, pp. 169–70) describes this in full; Beaglehole (1935), pp. 35–6 omits the 'fumigation' of the mother in juniper steam.

[2] This prayer is given in Owens' account (1892, pp. 170–2): Voth (1905a, p. 54) gives a slightly different version. Beaglehole (1935, p. 36) says that the *so'o* takes the 'mother corn' in her left hand: Owens, that she takes it in her right hand.

[3] Voth (1905a), pp. 55–6.

On their return, the naming breakfast is eaten. It is on this occasion that the salt and meat restriction on the mother is lifted, indicating that she is through the *navwö'la* and back in village life again.

Out of this account of the rites attendant on child-birth, two points may engage our attention. The first concerns the purification of the mother. It is evident, from the care taken to seclude the mother during the first five days after delivery and from the purificatory rites on the twentieth day, that the *navwö'la* is considered a period of potential danger.[1] Wherein, precisely, this danger resides, we are not yet in a position to say. But we may here introduce a concept, which we shall meet with again later, namely:

> *kya'*-, stem of *kya'la* v. is powerful, potent, full of mysterious power, sacred, causing dread to touch, perilous to approach: (Whorf, 1936, p. 1242).
> *kya mü'iya*, dangerous, sacred moon: i.e. December moon.
> *kya'kyauna*: adj. sacred. (Parsons, 1936, p. 1242).

The left hand is regarded as sacred (*kya'kyauna*) and used in placing or removing mask; and in the left hand are placed prayer-sticks and feathers and meal offering. The right hand is called *tünüsh' ma'htü*, food hand. It is the hand used for carrying food to the mouth, and is to that extent regarded as ceremonially defiled (*ka-kya'kyauna*).

> (Stephen, 1936, p. 371, n. 2).

The second point concerns the naming of the child. Each Hopi clan, as we have seen, carries the name of an animal, a plant or an object in the environment, and every clan has a stock of names at its disposal, referring to the animal, plant or object after which the clan takes its name; thus, the name *Loma'hongioma*, 'standing up gracefully', if bestowed by a member of Reed clan would refer to the straight, erect-growing reed plant, and if by a member of Butterfly clan, to the upright wings of the butterfly. When, on the twentieth day, the infant is given a number of names by its paternal aunts,[2] one of these 'sticks' and becomes, in course of time, the name by which he or she will be known throughout childhood. The naming ceremony, therefore, may best be regarded, in Beagle-hole's words,[3] 'as a rite of adoption, or initiation of the child into its father's clan; the child is henceforward known as "member" of his mother's clan, but "child" of his father's clan group'. And the significance of this way of regarding the ceremony is that, at every subsequent initiation in his life,[4] a person *receives a new name*, conferred by his sponsor in association with a ritual washing of the

---

[1] E. and P. Beaglehole (1935), pp. 37–8.

[2] That it is the *paternal* aunts who bestow names on the infant, is established by Owens (1892, pp. 170–2), Parsons (1921, pp. 100–2), E. and P. Beaglehole (1935, p. 36). Voth's statement (1905*b*, p. 67) that the 'child-names' are given to the infant by the *maternal* grandmother and aunts, is clearly an error, as his own earlier account (1905*a*, pp. 57–61) makes clear.

[3] E. Beaglehole (1937), p. 7.

[4] That is, at katçina initiation: at hunting initiation (for boys), and at the puberty rite (for girls): at Wü'wütçim initiation: on joining any one of the ceremonial societies, e.g. the Flute society: on returning from a salt expedition: and, following death, at the washing of the corpse before burial, and again on the arrival of the 'breath' at the land of the dead.

head. In other words, the giving of a new name marks one's joining, and incorporation into, a new group: the only group one does not receive a name on joining is the one into which he or she is *born*.

This aspect of naming is brought out in the next two rites I propose to consider: hunting initiation for boys, and the dressing of a girl's hair in butterfly whorls.

## HUNTING INITIATION FOR BOYS[1]

This takes place, or used to take place, in connection with rabbit hunting; but it is looked upon as a general hunting initiation, that is, to antelope and wild-sheep hunting as well. 'In this sense,' writes Beaglehole,[2] 'it is merely a continuation of the same interest in hunting that dictates the custom of cutting the umbilical cord of a boy on an arrow shaft and the wrapping of the dried cord round the shaft before thrusting it into the roof beams of the house; all this, that the boy may develop into a good hunter in after years.'

Hunting initiation is performed on the occasion of a lad's killing his first jack-rabbit, *so'wi*, as distinct from cotton-tail (*ta'vo*). When this happens, the hunt stops temporarily: the boy's father chooses the best hunter on the field to act as *ma'k na'adta*, 'his hunt father': all the men form a circle, the lad is stripped to the waist and bends forward, while his 'hunt father' draws the dead rabbit across his back in each of the four cardinal directions, leaving a trail of blood across his back each time. The hunt is then resumed.

On returning home, the boy enters on a four-day period during which he abstains from salt and meat. Each morning, before sunrise, his 'hunt father' takes him to a spring below the mesa; there he immerses the boy four times in the water, then gives him four prayer-sticks, which the boy deposits on the four sides of the spring, praying at the same time for strength and skill as a hunter. On the afternoon of the fourth day (counting the day on which he killed the jack-rabbit as the first, or 'going-in', day), the boy's paternal aunts make *pi'kami*, and his mother prepares a *nyö'kwivi* stew; in the evening, a hunt is announced for the following day. Early the next morning, the hunt breakfast is held at the mother's house, at which the boy eats salt and meat again. He then[3] goes to the house of his 'hunt father's' sister; his hair is washed and he is given new names by his 'hunt father's' female relatives, who also present him with gifts of *pi'ki* and *kwö'mi*.

His 'hunt father' now presents the boy with two curved throwing-sticks, and dresses him in white ceremonial shirt, sash and moccasins, which he has made

---

[1] See, in particular, Beaglehole (1936), pp. 14–17: (1937), pp. 73–5. The age at which hunting initiation takes place depends on the boy himself, but in the early 1930s, boys from about the age of 12 upwards were in the habit of going out regularly with the hunters: Beaglehole (1936), pp. 16–17.

[2] Beaglehole (1936), pp. 14–15.

[3] This is the order in which Beaglehole relates the events. It seems likely, however, by analogy with other similar ceremonies, that the head-washing and naming take place *first*, followed by breakfast at the boy's home.

for him. His body is painted with a broad yellow line across the chest from shoulder to shoulder, with short parallel bands above and below each elbow and each knee; each cheek is painted with two vertical lines of red ochre, and the rest of his face is rubbed over with white corn-meal. The boy's 'hunt father', who is to act as *ma'k moñwi*[1] of the hunt, also dresses in ceremonial shirt and moccasins, with a feather in his hair, yellow paint on his body and limbs, and red ochre on his face. On arrival at the place of the hunt, he carries out the usual ritual.[2] He makes a small hole in the sand, sprinkles corn meal towards it from the four cardinal directions, places a prayer-stick on each line of meal, lays some dry grass and rabbit droppings in the hole, and sets fire to the grass; each of the hunters, in turn, passes his throwing-stick through the smoke. The boy's new name is then announced to all present, and the hunt begins.

From this account, again, two points may engage our attention. The first concerns the relationship between the boy and his 'hunt father'. The 'hunt father', as we have seen, acts as the boy's sponsor; he makes the prayer-sticks which the boy deposits at the spring, and prepares the shirt, sash and moccasins which the boy dons on the morning of the hunt, and it is his sisters who wash the boy's hair and give him his new name. In return, the boy presents his 'hunt father' with the first few rabbits which he kills in the hunt, and his mother makes a return gift of corn-meal and *pi'ki* to the latter's sisters for their part in her son's initiation. This pattern of reciprocity characterises the relationship of sponsor and novice in all Hopi ceremonies. Thus, before a young man is initiated at Wü'wütçim, he is expected to work for his ceremonial 'father', and after, whenever the latter requires help, e.g. in agricultural work, sheep herding, or salt expeditions; in return, the ceremonial 'father' prepares the kilt and moccasins which his 'child' needs, and at the close of the ceremony his sisters wash the young man's hair and may present him with a blanket.

The second point concerns the significance of the throwing-stick, and of the markings on the boy's face and body. The throwing-stick is made out of a flat piece of wood, about 15 inches long and 2 to 3 inches wide, with a dog-leg bend in its length, a handle at one end and a cutting edge at the other. It is traditionally associated with the Hawk deity, Kih'sha, being modelled on the shape of a hawk's wing and referred to as *masha'adta*, 'his wing'.[3] Kih'sha, in Hopi myth, is the great hunter, especially of rabbits; and Whorf, in the Hopi glossary (1936, p. 1229), gives the following:

> *ke'le kömay'ta*, is painted with bars like a sparrow-hawk.

This suggests that the markings on the boy's body are intended to represent the bars on the body of the sparrow-hawk: the sparrow-hawk being the

[1] See above, p. 12.
[2] Cf. Stephen (1936), p. 1006.
[3] Stephen (1936), p. 100, and Fig. 69: cf. Beaglehole (1936), pp. 16–17. A Hopi throwing-stick may be seen at the Horniman Museum, London. Hopi to whom I have spoken are firmly convinced that the larger hawks, *buteos* in particular, kill a hare or rabbit on the ground by diving on it and striking it with the forward edge of their wing.

smallest—and fiercest—of the preying birds, of the Order *Falconiformes*, resident in Hopi country.

Regarding the red ochre used on the boy's face; red is the 'male' colour *par excellence*, associated with hunting and with warfare.[1] Lévi-Strauss, in his analysis of Pueblo origin myths (1958, p. 243–8), stresses the close conceptual link between hunting and warfare in the Southwest:

> la guerre, [he writes (p. 247)], apparaît, dans le processus dialectique, comme un *abus* de la chasse: chasse à l'homme, au lieu des animaux propres à la consommation humaine.

This link is amply confirmed for the Hopi, as we shall see later when we come to discuss Wü'wütçim initiation and the Soya'l. Indeed, a part of my interpretation of the Hopi evidence will be that *all* war attributes derive in origin from hunting, warfare—and the ceremonies which developed in response to warfare —being a relatively late event in pueblo history.

### DRESSING A GIRL'S HAIR

Stephen tells us[2] that, in the old days, younger girls were known as *naso'm-naiya*, and girls older but still unmarried, as *poli'in-naiya*. In this section, we have to see wherein the distinction lies.

According to Beaglehole,[3] when a girl was about 10 years old, it was time for her hair to be done up in *naso'me*, a miniature version of the traditional 'butterfly whorls'. For this purpose the maiden went to the home of her *so'o*, to grind corn for her for one whole day. In the evening, her *so'o* dressed her hair in *naso'me* for the first time, and she returned home.

About four years later, the girl's hair is put up in the full 'butterfly whorls', at a far more elaborate ceremony known as *poli'inte-vep'lalauwu*, 'butterfly-whorl making'. This takes place at the time her first period occurs.[4] On the evening of that day, the girl's mother takes her to the home of her *so'o*, i.e. of her father's eldest sister; and at the same time neighbouring women and female relatives of the girl also make their way there, bringing gifts of corn or other

---

[1] Stephen (1936), p. 1191. To what degree the 'maleness' of red is a native Hopi notion, I am not sure; it is possible that Stephen is drawing here on Tewa ideology.

[2] Stephen (1936), p. 143. On this whole section, see Hough (1918), pp. 248–9, and Fig. 20, E. and P. Beaglehole (1935), pp. 44–6, Parsons (1936), pp. 123–4, Stephen (1936), pp. 139–43, and Titiev (1944), pp. 203–4. There are a number of discrepancies between these reports, probably due to differences in practice between the three Mesas.

[3] E. and P. Beaglehole (1935), p. 44.

[4] The principal discrepancy between the various accounts turns on whether the ceremony co-incides with the onset of menstruation, and whether it was done singly or for a group of girls. Stephen, whose account I follow in the main, holds that the ceremony was performed for each girl singly, co-incident with her first period; Beaglehole, that it took place in June of each year, for all the girls in the village whose first menses had occurred during the previous twelve months; Titiev, that it took place, again in June of each year, but for an older group of girls (i.e. aged 16 or over), that it had no connection with the onset of menstruation, and that it should be regarded as a pre-marriage, not as a puberty rite. It may well be that these differences reflect differences in practice between the villages of the three Mesas.

food offerings (*no'bna*). The girl goes to her aunt's house to *ñüma'n va'ki*, 'grind inside (for her *poli'ne*)'. She sleeps there, and early the next morning begins grinding. Before sunrise the aunt hangs up a rug or blanket, so as to shield the girl from the sun's rays. For four days the girls grinds, on the first day white corn, on the second blue corn, on the third day red corn, on the morning of the fourth day yellow corn and in the afternoon black (i.e. deep purple) corn: stopping only at noon, and again at sunset, to eat some food (*pi'ki*, beans, and stewed peaches), and to sleep at night. During all this time, she may eat neither salt nor meat; she grinds in a darkened room; she may go out only before sunrise or after sunset; and if she wishes to scratch herself, she must use, not her fingers but a special head-scratcher, *na-ha'zri-pi*, prepared for her by her aunt's husband. She is 'like a baby'; and Hopi say, of a girl in this state:

| *Kü'yi* | *mana* | *ñüma'n* | *pa'ki* | *yü'tañwu*: |
|---------|--------|----------|---------|-------------|
| Kü'yi (her name) | maiden | meal-grinding | inside | hidden (from sun). |

Late in the afternoon of the fourth day, having now ground all the typical kinds of corn, the girl halts; and the feast, which the aunt and her friends have been preparing, is eaten. The girl joins in, eating freely of both salt and meat. Only women, who have themselves had their hair 'put up' in butterfly whorls, may attend the meal.

Very early the next morning, well before sunrise, the aunt washes the girl's head in yucca suds and water, using the ritual ear of corn; then she, and the girl's other paternal aunts, give the girl her new names.[1] The *so'o* rubs the girl's face with white corn-meal, brushes her hair, and dresses it in the traditional 'butterfly whorls', *poli'ne*.[2] Then the girl, accompanied by several of her friends and carrying in her hands a tray of corn-meal in which is set the head-scratcher, leads the way to the mesa edge. There she deposits the head-scratcher,[3] thrusting it well down in a crevice of the rock; as the sun rises, all the girls turn to the east, sprinkle meal towards the rising sun and pray, half under their breath, for:

| *ima'a yü'kala*: | *iho'kya yü'kala*: | *hü'mi ke'siwa*: |
|------------------|---------------------|-------------------|
| strong arms, | strong legs, | good growth of hair, |
| to grind meal: | to go up and down the mesa to fetch water: | to make fine hair whorls. |

Then they return to the house, and join in a breakfast of *pi'kami*, *nyö'kwivi*, piles of waferbread (*pi'ki*), and stewed peaches. Later in the day the girl grinds

---

[1] Stephen and Beaglehole agree that the head-washing takes place early on the morning of the fifth day, followed by the putting-up of the hair in butterfly whorls: Beaglehole (1935, p. 45) adds the detail of the giving of new names. Titiev (1944, pp. 203–4) states that the hair is 'put up' in whorls on the afternoon of the fourth day, prior to the feast given by the aunts.

[2] See Stephen (1936), Fig. 87, p. 141. Hough remarks (1918, p. 249) that the whorls are said to represent the squash flower, and to be 'significant of fertility'.

[3] According to Beaglehole (1935, p. 45), before the girl's hair is 'put up', the forelocks are cut off; the hair that is cut off is subsequently tied to the head-scratcher, which is then placed in the rafters.

some more corn, and bakes some *pi'ki* and *somi'viki*, for her aunts. In the evening she returns home, and resumes her normal life.

The essential feature of the *poli'inte-vep'lalauwu*—whether, indeed, it is a puberty (i.e. co-incident with the onset of menstruation) or a pre-marriage rite—is that it marks a change in the status of those who pass through it. The ritual, as Titiev points out,[1] lays stress on the fact that the girl is now ready to be married: in effect, the corn-grinding demonstrates that she is a competent housekeeper. This interpretation is confirmed by Edmund Nequatewa,[2] who says that, in the old days, 'a Hopi youth was not supposed to do any courting until he was able to raise a crop and be a good hunter; and a girl was not supposed to have any interest in a young man until she had gone through her "test ceremony" of grinding corn for getting her *poli'ne* (butterfly-wing whorls).'

The change of status, which accompanies the older girl's having her hair put up in *poli'ne* and is symbolised by her new coiffure, also marks the younger girl's obtaining her *naso'me*; for it is only after a maiden has had her hair dressed in that style, that she may be buried in the adult cemetery[3]—and so, I suppose, in the adult Hopi manner.

### COURTSHIP AND MARRIAGE

While much Hopi courtship is informal,[4] there are a number of occasions in the course of the year which offer definite opportunities for advances to be made by one party to the other: usually, in this case, by the girl to the boy, in the form of a gift of food.

The most formal of these occasions, in the old days, was known as *ove'knaiya*, a kind of picnic held on the day following a katçina dance or after the public performance of one of the more important rituals (e.g. the Flute, or Snake-Antelope, in August). The boys dressed themselves in their best clothes, smeared their faces with red ochre (*çu'ta*), and tied eagle feathers in their hair. The girls spent the early part of the day making *somi'viki*, 'maiden's cake', then dressed carefully in white moccasins and leggings, *manta* and ceremonial blanket, and put their hair up in the butterfly-wing whorls (*poli'ne*) required of unmarried girls. Late in the afternoon, both groups met at a selected spot outside the village, the boys having hunted rabbits on the way, the girls carrying the bundles of *somi'viki* which they had prepared earlier in the day. In the event of a girl having decided that she wished to marry one particular boy, she would prepare along with the other food a roll of *kwö'mi*; if the lad showed himself responsive, she handed him the *kwö'mi*—a proceeding equivalent to a formal proposal of marriage.

[1] Titiev (1944), p. 203.
[2] Nequatewa (1933), p. 42.
[3] E. and P. Beaglehole (1935), p. 13.
[4] On courtship, see especially E. and P. Beaglehole (1935), pp. 47–50, and Titiev (1944), pp. 31–6: also, on the food gifts that accompany courtship, Nequatewa (1933), pp. 49–50. On the sexual upbringing of Hopi children before puberty, see D. Eggan (1943), pp. 361–8.

This method of proposing, through the agency of a differential food gift, takes place on a number of other, less formal occasions. Several times during the early summer, and again in the fall, it was the custom to hold communal rabbit hunts[1] and for the unmarried girls to accompany the hunters into the field. On such occasions the young men presented the girls with the rabbits which they had killed, and the latter presented them with bundles of *somi'viki* in return; but any girl who wished to might take the opportunity to present the young man of her choice with a roll of *kwö'mi*. Again, at the conclusion of the Powamu night dance late in February, the dancers file out of the kiva passing the bench where the unmarried girls are seated; each of the girls has brought with her several bundles of *somi'viki*, one of which she hands to each performer as he goes by—but sometimes a girl has prepared a roll of *kwö'mi*, to hand in lieu of *somi'viki* to her boy-friend.

When a girl has decided that she wishes definitely to marry a young man, and provided her parents are agreeable, she proceeds to grind corn and to bake *pi'ki* to take to the boy's mother. In the evening, usually accompanied by her own mother, she goes to the house of the boy's mother, carrying a tray piled high with finely ground sweet-corn meal with five batches of *pi'ki* on top. When she reaches the house, she calls out: 'come, get this, and eat it'; if the boy's mother comes out and accepts the gift, it means that the boy's people are willing for the marriage to go forward. This constitutes *hä'si*, or betrothal; and both boy, and girl, now begin seriously to prepare for the actual wedding. The boy is busy getting firewood each day, and helping with the task of cleaning up and renovating his mother's house. The girl, meanwhile, grinds large quantities[2] of blue corn, white corn and sweet-corn meal.

Marriages usually take place either in the fall, during or after the harvest, or early in the spring: very rarely during the summer, when people are too busy in the fields, and never[3] during the 'dangerous moon', *kya' mü'iya*, i.e. December. On the evening of the day chosen,[4] the girl's *so'o* does her hair up in *poli'ne*,[5] and dresses her in *manta*, beads, and white ceremonial blanket with red border (*atö'e*). The girl's mother then takes a tray of white corn meal and accompanies her daughter to the house of the boy's mother; she presents the tray of meal to the latter and returns home, leaving the girl. From this time on,

---

[1] One such occasion was on the day after a girl first puts her hair up in 'butterfly' whorls, another on the day following the Nima'n dance late in July, and a third, towards the end of November, following the Wü'wütçim ceremony.

[2] It really is a lot. Parsons (1921*b*, p. 259) says that the girl, who may be helped by her female relatives, grinds enough meal to fill ten or twelve store-bought boiling cans, and that it may take her a month to complete the task; and Simpson (1953, p. 39), that it may amount to a thousand pounds of meal.

[3] Parsons (1921), p. 264, n. 15.

[4] The account that follows is based on reports by Voth (1900, pp. 238–46: 1912*b*, pp. 145–9): by Parsons (1921*b*, pp. 259–65): by Nequatewa (1933, pp. 41–54): by E. and P. Beaglehole (1935, pp. 46–59): and by Titiev (1944, pp. 31–8). Parsons' account refers to 1st Mesa; Nequatewa's, and Beaglehole's, to 2nd Mesa; Voth's, and Titiev's, to 3rd Mesa.

[5] Nequatewa says (1933, p. 49, n. 1) that this is only done if the bride is a 'maiden', i.e. if it is her first marriage.

the girl is addressed as *mö'wi*, instead of by her own name, by all the boy's kinsfolk—and often, also, by their near neighbours.

Early the next morning, before sunrise, the girl rises and starts grinding corn: for three days she grinds, white corn on the first day, blue corn on the following two days. The room in which she sits grinding is darkened; again, 'she is like a new baby', she must not see the sun, but she may eat salt and meat, and may scratch herself with her fingers. During these three days, the villagers bring presents of food; as each gift is delivered, the bride makes a return gift out of the corn-meal which she has ground.

On the afternoon of the third day, a mock battle takes place. As the bride sits grinding corn, the boy's paternal aunts enter in a group and attack her vigorously; they throw mud at her, accuse her of being a lazy good-for-nothing, who does not know how to cook properly and will not grind corn, and charge her with being their 'rival'.[1] The boy's mother and her sisters come to the help of the girl, insisting that she is an able and hard-working person, and protect her from the assault. Eventually the boy's aunts make off, taking with them most of the wood he has fetched over the last few days. They go home and use the fuel to bake a batch of *pi'ki*; later, in the evening, they return bringing the *pi'ki* with them, and give some to the boy's mother in return for the wood they have pinched, and some to the girl, 'to make friends with her again'.

Long before dawn on the morning of the fourth day, the bride's kinsfolk arrive, bringing with them the corn meal which the girl had prepared before she left home. The girl's mother, and the boy's mother, each prepare a bowl of yucca suds; they pour all the suds into one bowl, mix it thoroughly, then divide it again into two bowls. The boy's mother undoes the girl's *poli'ne*, and the girl's mother prepares the boy's hair; then each kneels in front of their respective bowl, the boy's mother washes the girl's hair, and her mother washes his hair; and when the hair of each has been washed singly, the hair of both is washed together in one large bowl, signifying[2] that they have 'become one'. When this part of the ceremony—*without which no wedding is considered binding*[3]—is over, the fires are lit in the house, and the bride and groom dry their hair. As the sun rises, they each take a pinch of corn meal and go together, silently, to the mesa edge. Standing close to the edge, they hold the meal to their lips, breathe a prayer (for long life and prosperity) over it, then sprinkle the meal towards the rising sun. They then return quietly to the house, being regarded henceforth as man and wife.

By now the fires are hot, and the bride bakes the first batch of *pi'ki*. When this is ready, her female kinsfolk serve breakfast—in the boy's mother's house—

---

[1] Parsons (1921*b*, p. 265, n. 18) interprets this as a relic of the custom of preferential cross-cousin marriage of a boy with his father's sister's daughter, i.e. with his *kya'a*. Cf. on this point, Titiev (1938), and (1944), p. 28, and Eggan (1950), pp. 121, 157.

[2] Voth (1912*b*), p. 148.

[3] Nequatewa (1933), p. 44. When both parties have been married before, the head-washing and the offering of meal to the sun is the only part of the ceremony that takes place.

to all the villagers, who come with gifts for the bride: corn, beans, and the like. She tastes the food first, 'because it is the end of her four days'. After the wedding breakfast, and the exchange of gifts, the boy's mother arranges the girl's hair in the matron's style, known as *tori'qui*; for this, she parts the hair in the middle and arranges it in two twists on either side of the head, the ends tied with wool so that they lie away from the face on either side. The dressing of the bride's hair in this manner symbolises her transition from the state of girl-hood to that of womanhood:[1] that is, from being a maiden, *mana*, to becoming a married woman, *wuh'ti*.

After the wedding breakfast is over, and the bride's hair has been 'put up' by the boy's mother, she sets to grinding more corn-meal. Meanwhile, the boy's kinsmen bring gifts of cotton to the house, for the weaving of the bride's wedding costume; and in return for these gifts, she fills the containers in which they have brought the cotton with corn-meal.

From now on, the bride stays on in the boy's mother's house until her wedding garments are ready. She continues to do most of the cooking for the household, in addition to preparing special dishes—usually *tçükü'viki*, and *somi'viki*, on alternate days—for the men who are weaving the costume.[2] This consists of one large white cotton blanket (*o'ba*), one small white cotton blanket, one plaited cotton belt with knotted fringe at either end, one pair of white buckskin moccasins, and one reed mat; one of the two cotton blankets (*o'ba*) will be worn as a robe on the day the bride returns home, and the reed mat is for carrying the other blanket and the belt. The work falls into a number of stages—spinning the cotton, setting up the warp, weaving the robes—and is chiefly done by the boy's father, assisted by the boy's maternal uncles, usually in the kiva to which his father belongs; the whole outfit may take four to six men, working steadily, from two to six weeks to complete.[3] All the time they are engaged on the work, the men who are doing the spinning and weaving are barred from salt, meat, and *lü'wa* (vulva, i.e. sexual intercourse).

When the weaving is nearly finished, the bride begins to grind corn-meal, to make *pi'kami*; and as soon as the last piece of her outfit is ready, she puts her *pi'kami* in the oven to bake. In the meantime, the men who have made the robes perform the final rite over them. First they make prayer-feathers for the happiness of the bride and for the souls of the children to be born to her, hanging these on each corner of the two *o'ba*; then, still in the kiva, they smoke silently

---

[1] Nequatewa (1933), pp. 50–2: for the hair styles (maiden's, and married woman's), see Stephen (1936), Figs. 490 and 491, p. 999. According to James (1903, pp. 68–9), the butterfly whorls in which the hair was previously dressed represent the squash blossom, Hopi emblem of maidenhood, while the two pendant rolls in which the hair is now done up represent the ripened fruit of the long squash, 'the Hopi emblem of fruitfulness'.

[2] The fullest account of the weaving of the wedding garments is given by Stephen (1936), pp. 270–4. Cf. Parsons (1921*b*), pp. 263–4: Nequatewa (1933), pp. 44–7: E. and P. Beaglehole (1935), pp. 53–5: Titiev (1944), pp. 37–8.

[3] This, according to Titiev (1944, p. 38, n. 26), is one of the reasons why Hopi marriages generally take place in the months between harvest and planting; at any other time, the men are too busy in the fields to help in the spinning and weaving of the wedding garments.

over the robes. Finally they carry the robes to the bride, and after presenting them to her, eat the *pi'kami* which she has prepared.

Early the next morning, before sunrise, the bride gets ready to 'go home' (*ni'man*, 'going home'). She puts on the smaller of the two *o'ba*, the boy's mother dresses her hair, and as the sun rises, carrying the other *o'ba* (wrapped in the reed mat) in front of her on outstretched arms and preceded for a short distance by the boy's father who sprinkles a path of corn meal before her, the bride sets off for her own home. On reaching it, she is received by her own mother, and the long drawn-out ceremony is at an end. Either the same day, or a few days later, the bridegroom joins her there: his first duty, on arrival, being to fetch firewood for the bride's mother, so marking the definite assumption of his new economic obligations.[1]

During the following weeks the bride, assisted by her female kinsfolk, is busy grinding corn, to 'pay for' the wedding costume:[2] the term employed is *si'sivi*, used nowadays for buying something in the store, but referring, in the old days, to the transfer of food in exchange for services of one kind or another. The bride is expected, with the help of her kinsfolk, to make some fifteen or twenty woven trays, and to fill them with as much corn meal as they will hold;[3] they are then taken in procession to the house of the boy's mother and presented to her, in 'payment' for the wedding outfit. If possible, this should be done by the time of the Niman dance following the wedding, that is, by the next July: otherwise, during the winter after the Niman. Should the bride die before the 'payment' has been made, her kinsfolk discharge the obligation on her behalf.

As to the significance of the various parts of the wedding ceremony, Hopi interest centres around the weaving of the wedding garments; and this, in turn, brings us to the edge of a whole complex of ideas relating to death and the after-life. For Hopi believe that the large blanket or *o'ba*, in particular, is needed by the girl both to reach the Underworld and, once there, to enter it. For this reason it is preserved with especial care, being only worn on a few select occasions, namely: at the Niman dance following the wedding, when all the girls who have been married since the previous Niman appear, late in the afternoon, arrayed in their full wedding costume;[4] at the birth of the girl's first child, when the mother—accompanied by her *so'o*—takes the infant to the mesa edge to greet the rising sun; on certain ceremonial occasions, such as, when a man returns from a salt expedition, his *so'o* goes out to meet him dressed in her *o'ba*; and finally at death, when as an old woman her body is wrapped in it, prior to

---

[1] E. Beaglehole (1937), p. 76. Illustrating the fact that where, in patrilineal societies, it is the *procreative* services of the girl that are exchanged in marriage, in matrilineal societies it is the *economic* services of the man.

[2] E. and P. Beaglehole (1935), pp. 55–6: on *si'sivi*, giving food in exchange for services, see E. Beaglehole (1937), pp. 76–7.

[3] Parsons (1921*b*) remarks that it may take a year or more to accumulate the necessary amount of meal.

[4] According to one old man, the appearance of the brides on this occasion helps to make rain: E. and P. Beaglehole (1935), pp. 54–6.

burial.[1] After four days in the grave, her 'breath' sets out on the journey to the Underworld, and when she arrives at the brink of the abyss, she spreads her white blanket, the *o'ba* which she received at her wedding, and floats down on it to the land of the dead.

This belief lies behind various practices in the manufacture of the wedding garments:[2] first, that they must be woven out of cotton, not wool; second, that those garments which require dyeing in any part must be dyed with a dye (e.g. indigo) that needs soaking only, not boiling, because—to enter the land of the dead—the woman must be wearing a garment of pure cotton (and boiling takes away from the purity). So deep-rooted is the belief in the need for wedding garments in the after-life—in that, without them, a woman cannot make a proper entry to the land of the dead—that, even when a young man dies early on in the course of the marriage rites, the girl may go through with her part of the ritual in order to obtain them. Titiev, indeed, holds[3] that this need is one of the compelling motives towards marriage, in Hopi society.

### SALT EXPEDITIONS, DEATH, AND BURIAL

It may seem strange, at first sight, to link salt expeditions with death and burial; but in Hopi thinking there is a close link between the two, as I hope to show in the course of this section.

Traditionally, salt was fetched[4] from near the floor of the Grand Cañon, some 80 miles to the northwest of the Hopi villages. As the deposit lies near the home of the dead, it is located in 'dangerous' territory; consequently, only men who have passed through the *Wü'wütçim* initiation may go there, the minimum number for such expeditions being three—namely, one man who acts as leader (*moñ'wi*), one man who (like the leader) has been at least once before, and a novice. Expeditions were commonly made in the fall, soon after the harvest had been gathered: the matter having been arranged at the conclusion of the previous Soyal, in December, and prayer-sticks for the undertaking made then.

Some days before the expedition is due to leave the village, each man goes to his *so'o*, or to one of his other paternal aunts (*kya'a*), and tells her that he is going to fetch salt for her. She prepares food for him to take on the journey. For four days beforehand, the men abstain from sexual intercourse, then they set out. The expedition takes six to seven days to complete, the salt being collected with due precautions and carried back to the village on the backs of burros. On their return to the neighbourhood of the village, the party makes an overnight halt at the wash below the village; and at sunrise the next morning,

---

[1] Stephen (1936), p. 1005: cf. Nequatewa (1933), pp. 48–9.

[2] Nequatewa (1933), p. 53, n. 18.

[3] Titiev (1944), p. 38: cf. E. and P. Beaglehole (1935), pp. 46–7.

[4] The account that follows is based on Titiev's relation (1937, pp. 244–58) of an expedition to Grand Cañon made in 1912, supplemented by Beaglehole's notes (1937, pp. 52–5); by the early 1930s, expeditions were no longer being made to Grand Cañon, but to a salt lake some 40 miles south of Zuñi, and it is to this kind of journey that Beaglehole's notes apply. See, also, Stephen (1936), pp. 497, 994.

the *so'o* of each man, dressed in *manta* and wedding blanket (*o'ba*), and accompanied by the other paternal aunts, go with the village chiefs (*moñ'mowitû*) to the point where the trail strikes the crest of the mesa. As the salt gatherers come up the trail, the chiefs sprinkle meal in their path; each *so'o* in turn steps forward, thanks her nephew, and sprinkles him with corn meal. Then all enter the village together, each *so'o* followed by her nephew carrying the salt for his aunt on his back.

The *so'o* leads her nephew to her house and, after sprinkling meal to the sun, conducts him inside. There, a white wedding blanket is spread on the floor, the salt emptied on to it, and the edges of the blanket folded over the pile of salt. Next, the *so'o* makes yucca suds and washes the man's hair. Then, *so'o* and *kya'a* together undress the man and wash his body: and each names him, according to the full naming ceremony, using the Mother Corn which the man carried while collecting the salt. 'We name him, because we are glad to have him back out of danger.'[1] The *so'o* now takes several large woven trays which she has made for the occasion. She fills them with blue-corn meal which she, and the other paternal aunts, have ground beforehand. On top of each tray, she places rolls of *pi'ki* and a large loaf of *kwö'mi*: 'this meal and food are to pay (*si'sivi*) for the salt that the man has brought back'. A procession is formed: the *so'o* leading, carrying the man's curved throwing-stick and other gear, then the man himself, then the *kya'a*(s), each carrying trays of meal. In this order they proceed to the man's own house, to deliver the trays of meal in return for the salt. The remainder of the salt, brought into the village on the back of his burro, the man divides between his own household and his kinsfolk.

The only point to which I wish to draw attention in this narrative, before passing on to consider death and burial, is the parallel between the man's return from a salt expedition and the woman's emergence from child-birth. Both are periods of 'danger': out of which the man passes by having his hair ceremonially washed and new names bestowed on him, and out of which the woman passes, again by having her hair washed, and by having her body 'fumigated' in juniper steam. In the rites surrounding death and burial, we shall find these two sequences brought into juxtaposition.

The belief in a continued existence after death is well defined in the religious conception of the Hopi, and finds expression in many of their rites and ceremonies. That part of man which they hold to be immortal, the Hopi call *hi'ksi*, 'breath'. At death, the *hi'ksi* leaves the body, i.e. it escapes through the mouth: as one Hopi put it,[2] 'the dead is like a corn husk, after the corn has been gathered —the breath has come out and gone to another world'; and it is by virtue of the survival of the *hi'ksi* that the dead continue their existence in the after-life. With this belief goes the Hopi theory of dreaming.[3] For Hopi believe that, in dreams also, the 'breath' leaves the body and makes its way elsewhere. In this

---

[1] E. Beaglehole (1937), p. 55.
[2] Parsons (1925), p. 77, n. 124.
[3] E. and P. Beaglehole (1935), pp. 15–16.

sense both sleeping and dreaming, and unconsciousness brought about by injury, are thought of as being equivalent to death, since in both states the 'breath' has left the body.

As soon, then, as it is certain that a person is dead, that is, that the 'breath' has left his body for good, his eldest surviving *kya'a* (father's sister) is sent for.[1] In the meantime, a white corn ear, a bowl of water and yucca suds are prepared. The body is stripped and the paternal aunt, assisted by other female relatives on the father's side, washes the dead man's hair and dresses it. She then washes the dead body, rubs it lightly with corn meal, and gives the corpse a new name: 'Now you have left us, set us aside. We give you a new name, that we may know you when we follow you.'

In the meantime, the dead man's father—or other male relatives on the father's side—prepare a number of prayer-feathers, and a *püh'tabi*, 'road'. The prayer-feathers are of turkey, or eagle, feathers;[2] one feather is tied to the corpse's hair, one is placed under each foot 'to take the body to the other world',[3] one is placed in each hand, and one over the navel, 'which is the place where the breath of a man lives'. The *püh'tabi* consists of a cotton thread about 3 feet long, with a feather at one end; the feather is laid over the dead man's mouth, and the string carried down over the chest to the navel. The father blackens the chin of the dead person with a piece of shale, dipped in water. Finally a mask, called 'white-cloud mask', is made out of raw cotton, teased into a mat about large enough to cover the upper half of the face, with holes for the eyes and mouth; this mask is laid over the dead man's face, without any fastening.

The underlying idea behind each of these ritual elements is the same: namely, that the 'breath body' may be light, not 'heavy' (*pe'te*), and so be enabled to go on its way to the land of the dead. Thus, Curtis remarks[4] that the downy eagle-feather, tied to the crown of the dead person's head, symbolises by its lightness the soul floating away to the home of the dead; and Stephen,[5] that the prayer-feathers, beside bearing prayers, are intended to make the 'breath body' light, that it may travel fast on its journey from the grave to the *si'papü*, the entrance to the Underworld. The cotton mask, again, is placed over the face of the corpse with the idea of making the 'breath body' light; while the *püh'tabi*, or 'road', represents that part of its journey which the 'breath', or soul, has yet to accomplish.

Next, some fragments of food—two or three rolls of *pi'ki*, a crust of *pi'kami*, and some dried meat—are placed either on the dead person's stomach, or in the pockets made by the flexion of the thighs against the body. The body is then

[1] The account of the mortuary rites given here is based on that given by Stephen (1936), pp. 824–8. Cf. Voth (1912*b*), pp. 99–103: Curtis (1922), pp. 39–40: E. and P. Beaglehole (1935), pp. 11–14.

[2] Voth (1912*b*), p. 101, n. 2.

[3] E. and P. Beaglehole (1935), pp. 11–12.

[4] Curtis (1922), p. 39.

[5] Stephen (1936), p. 825.

wrapped in several blankets (in the case of a woman, it is wound around with one of her two *o'ba*), tied round with ropes, and carried out to the place of burial on the backs of the male relatives of the deceased, the women following with vessels of water and small dishes of food. A round grave is dug, as deep as a man can stand in, and the body placed in it in a sitting posture, facing the sunrise (*ta'wa-t ahtai'ta*, 'looks towards the sun').[1] A vessel of water is placed between the feet of the corpse, together with a dish of food.[2] A rough structure of sticks and stones is then made over the dead person's head, and the grave filled in. The women who have brought the food dishes place them beside the grave, saying (or implying): 'You are no longer a Hopi, you are changed [*nih'ti*, grown into] a katçina, you are Cloud [O'mauwû]. You are to eat once of this food, i.e. accept this food offering, and when you get yonder, you are to tell the chiefs [i.e. of the six directions] to hasten the rain clouds here.' Finally, a planting stick (*so'ya*) is thrust into the mound of earth over the grave.[3]

Each of these ritual elements, again, is directed to a common end: namely, to hasten the 'breath body' on its journey to the Underworld. Thus, Curtis states explicitly that the gourd containing water, and the dish of food, are placed in the grave to give the spirit sustenance during the four days that it remains there, and during the four days of its journey to the home of the dead; while Beaglehole and Stephen explain the stick thrust into the earth, the one by saying that it serves as a ladder for the soul (i.e. the 'breath') to depart westward, the other that it represents the projecting end of the ladder leading down to the house of Masau'u, the deity who presides over the 'house' of the dead.[4] The speech of the women at the grave side introduces a further idea: namely that in the process of leaving the corpse, the 'breath body' undergoes some form of change, or metamorphosis, into katçina or Cloud. That idea we shall find developed later on; but we may note here that the idea has been foreshadowed in the covering of the face with the 'white-cloud mask', of which Parsons remarks[5] that 'it (i.e. the cotton mask) plainly identifies the dead with the kachina', and Beaglehole,[6] that it signifies 'its (i.e. the breath body's) future existence as a cloud'.

As soon as the rites at the grave side are concluded, all those present wash themselves with yucca suds and water, and then return to the village: the last man stopping at four points on the way, each time drawing four parallel lines ≣ across the trail with a piece of charred juniper. These marks are called

---

[1] Stephen (1936), pp. 826, 828: Beaglehole (1935, p. 12) says that the corpse is placed in the hole, in a sitting posture, facing *towards the west*.

[2] Curtis (1922), pp. 39–40.

[3] Stephen (1936), p. 825; cf. Parsons (1925), p. 77, n. 124: E. and P. Beaglehole (1935), p. 12.

[4] The grave is regarded as the entrance to *mas-ki*, the house of Masau'u. Masau'u was the first house-builder; this house was underground. It was from his house that people climbed on to the earth, and it is here that they return when they die. Stephen (1936), pp. 150–1.

[5] Parsons (1936), p. 825, n. 1.

[6] E. and P. Beaglehole (1935), p. 12: cf. Voth (1912b), p. 101. Also, dreaming about the dead is supposed to bring rain, sometimes: D. Eggan (1961), p. 23.

*Masau'u üh'ta,* 'closing-the-door to Masau'u', and are intended to close the trail to the deity. Outside the house, all the men who have taken part wash themselves in boiled juniper water, then enter the house and go through the exorcising rite known as *navo'tçiwa*: 'this is how all in the house are protected against the spirits'.

For three days following the interment,[1] bowls of food are set beside the grave. On the third day, either the father of the dead person, or his mother's brother or his own brother, makes the following prayer-offerings: one single black *pa'ho* (prayer-stick), one double green *pa'ho*, one *püh'tabi* ('road') consisting of an eagle breath-feather attached to a long cotton thread, and four or five *nakwa'kwosi(s)*. Towards evening he takes these to the grave, together with some corn meal and the bowl of food. The two prayer-sticks and the breath-feathers he puts on the grave, with the bowl of food; the *püh'tabi*, 'road', he lays on the ground to the west of the grave, the cotton thread pointing to the west. From this 'road', he sprinkles a line of corn meal, to show the deceased the path he has to travel. To make certain that the spirit does not return to the village, he stops four times on the way home and again draws the four parallel lines across the trail.[2] When he arrives at the house, all the members of the household wash their hair; juniper or piñon gum is put on the fire, and all present 'fumigate' their bodies and clothes in the smoke.

Early the next morning, according to Hopi belief, the 'breath body' (*hi'ksi ah'paa*) of the dead person rises from the grave, partakes of the 'breath' of the food, mounts the 'breath' of the single black prayer-stick, and then travels westward along the 'road' to the house of the dead, taking the 'breath' of the double green *pa'ho* with it as an offering to Masau'u.[3]

Certain of the basic ideas underlying the funeral rites we shall find elaborated in the ceremonial cycle, described in the succeeding chapters. Here I wish to point out the distinction, implied earlier, between washing of the hair followed by name-giving that accompanies any important change of status, and washing of the hair followed by some form of purification (e.g. 'fumigation' in juniper smoke) that accompanies emergence from any 'dangerous' state. The head of the deceased is washed in yucca suds prior to burial, and he is given a new name, because death is regarded by the Hopi as a major change of status,[4] comparable to birth or to initiation; the heads of those who have taken part in the rites at the grave side are washed, and their bodies 'fumigated', because death itself is a 'dangerous' state and those who have been attendant on it must purify themselves before they rejoin the community, in the same way as the mother has to purify herself after child-birth. In the washing of a man's head on his return from a salt expedition, there is a degree of mixing of these two

---

[1] The account of the final obsequies is based on that given by Voth (1912*b*, pp. 102–3): there are several discrepancies between Voth's account, and those of Stephen and of Beaglehole, chiefly regarding the days on which the events take place.

[2] E. and P. Beaglehole (1935), p. 13.

[3] Voth (1912*b*), p. 103: cf. Stephen (1936), p. 826.

[4] Titiev (1940), p. 499, n. 13.

notions. Clearly there is an element of 'danger' in the situation, in that the salt deposits are located near the home of the dead and to fetch salt requires special precautions (e.g. abstinence from sexual intercourse); but the fact that the head-washing is followed by name-giving indicates that the element of 'danger' is outweighed, in Hopi thinking, bv that of the change of status involved.

One further feature, common to the several *rites de passage* described in this chapter, may also be noted here: namely, the recurrence of the number *four*. Four parallel lines, marked on each wall, represent 'the house of the baby'; four parallel lines are drawn across the track to 'close the door' to Masau'u. A lad, in the course of his hunting initiation, observes a period of four days' abstinence, as does a girl grinding corn for her butterfly whorls; he is immersed four times in the water, and given four prayer-sticks to deposit on the four sides of the village spring. A man going on a salt expedition similarly observes four days' abstinence before his departure, and the 'breath-body' is believed to spend four days in the grave before setting out on its journey to the Underworld (which takes four days). This stress on *four*, the number of the cardinal points associated with the Sun's rising and setting at midwinter and midsummer, as the number of times for performing a ceremonial action and as the number of days in a ritual sequence (one for each cardinal point), will meet us again and again in the account of Hopi ceremonies that follows; to its significance, in particular for the light it throws on the origin of Hopi ceremonialism, I shall return in due course (see below, p. 434).

# 12

# *A pueblo liturgy*

The washing of the dead person's head, and the bestowing on him of a new name, indicate that the Hopi regard death as a change of status analogous to other changes that take place in the course of life; the covering of the face of the corpse with a cotton mask prior to burial—that they equate the dead, to some degree at least, with the katçinas and with the clouds. In the present chapter we pursue the latter notion a stage further, in following that segment of the ceremonial cycle which runs from early in January to the middle of March and is devoted to the katçina cult. As a preliminary, however, we have first to see how the Hopi conceive the katçinas, and by what channels they get in touch with them.

### UNDERLYING CONCEPTS OF HOPI RELIGION

According to Titiev,[1] belief in the continuity of life after death constitutes the most fundamental concept of Hopi religion. This belief is manifested in Hopi mythology, for example in the accounts of the Emergence from the underworld. These, and other, myths indicate that the dead Hopi live in villages like those on earth, have fields, plant and harvest their crops, conduct the ceremonial cycle in their own kivas, and generally behave much as people do on earth. The principal difference between life there and life on earth is that, where human beings consume material food, the dead eat 'only the odour or soul of the food' (Voth). And this distinction in turn gives rise to the further belief, noted above: that, because they eat only what may be called the 'essence' of food, the dead are 'not heavy'. They may, therefore, change into (*nih'ti*, grow into) Clouds or into katçinas; as such, they are potential benefactors to the living, and may on occasions revisit their former homes, bringing rain or other benefits to those left behind on earth.

Not all katçinas are the spirits of deceased human beings—some represent animals, some plants or other inanimate beings—but most are; and the common belief regarding their origin appears to be, in Kennard's words,[2] that 'the spirits of the dead go to the west where they become Kachinas and return to the village as clouds'. Yet the equation of katçinas with clouds is perhaps not quite as direct as that. The katçinas have definite 'homes', e.g. in the San Fransisco mountains, at the spring Kisiwu (about 40 miles N.E. of the Hopi villages), and

---

[1] Titiev (1944), p. 107. This account of Hopi religious beliefs is based on Titiev (1944), pp. 107–8, 171–3, and on Earle and Kennard (1938), pp. 1–12: with additional material derived from Stephen (1936), Nequatewa (1946), and Colton (1947*a*, and *b*).

[2] Earle and Kennard (1938), p. 2.

in other places, especially where spruce is to be found growing.[1] They live in these 'homes' for one half of the year; during the other half they reside in the neighbourhood of the Hopi villages, entering the villages on occasions to dance and sing. Each katçina is known by name, and can be readily recognised, not only by the painting and decoration of his mask and body, but also by his songs, his dance step, his call, and his bearing; and when they dance as a group in the open space at the centre of the village, they summon their 'cloud fathers' to come from the four (or six) directions and bring rain to the land. This suggests that the katçinas, rather than being themselves clouds, are spirits standing in very close relation to clouds.

Apart from the katcinas there are a number of supernatural figures, usually referred to as deities, who play a prominent part in Hopi mythology. Of these, the two most commonly met with are Masau'u and Mü'yiñwa. Where the katçinas are freely impersonated in group dances in the open air, the deities are only impersonated singly on special occasions, either at definite points in the agricultural cycle or in the course of the kiva ritual.[2] Thus Masau'u, the deity who first allotted the Hopi their lands and who has charge of the 'house' of the dead, is sometimes impersonated in spring and fall ceremonies, and again on the fourth night of Wü'wütçim when the novices undergo their initiation; while Mü'yiñwa, the deity who controls the growth of all plants sown or wild, is impersonated in the course of the Powa'mu ceremony in February, and again during the Oa'qöl rites in October. Each of the deities, like each of the katçinas, has his own distinctive appearance. Thus Masau'u wears no mask, his body is rubbed with ashes, in place of a kilt he wears a woman's discarded dress, he goes barefooted and carries in one hand a digging-stick and in the other a woven tray; whereas Mü'yiñwa wears an elaborate head-dress with two horns curving back from the forehead, has a single white line down the front of his arms and legs, wears a tanned buckskin kilt and moccasins, and carries a deer's horn in one hand and a stick in the other.[3] By their costume, mask, and body paint, any Hopi over the age of ten can at once recognise either deity or katçina.

Five principal colours[4]—yellow, blue-green, red, white and black—are used by the Hopi in ceremonial decoration. The first four colours correspond each

[1] Stephen (1936), p. 370. The 'spruce', referred to in accounts of many Hopi ceremonies, is *sala'vi*, Douglas fir; the appearance of its needles in the spring serves as a portent of the weather during the coming growing season: Whiting (1939), p. 63.

[2] This distinction between deities and katçinas among the Hopi appears to parallel the Zuñi distinction between *a·'wona·wi'lona*, 'the ones who hold our roads', and *uwanami*, the spirits of the ancestors who have become Clouds (and to whom the Zuñi pray for rain and other blessings); the former category comprehends the latter, but is not limited to it, i.e. the more important of 'the ones who hold our roads', namely Sun, the corn, prey animals, the war deities, are *a·'wona·wi'lona* but not *uwanami*. See, in particular, Bunzel (1932), pp. 483–6, and Parsons (1939), p. 171.

[3] This is Mü'yiñwa's costume as described by Edmund Nequatewa (Colton, 1947*b*, p. 11); but in each of the two ceremonies described by Voth in which Mü'yiñwa appears, i.e. the Powa'mu and the Oa'qöl, he is garbed differently.

[4] On the manufacture, use, and significance of pigments among the Hopi, see Stephen, (1898), pp. 260–5. Stephen, who had earlier worked as a prospector in Utah and Nevada,

to one of the four cardinal directions, black to the Above, and speckled (or 'all colours') to the Below: making six directions in all. The Hopi orientation is related, however, not to north and south, but to the points on the horizon which mark the places of sunrise and sunset at the summer and winter solstices. Asked to describe the ceremonial circuit, the Hopi begins by pointing to the place of sunset at summer solstice (N.W.), then to the place of sunset at winter solstice (S.W.), then to the place of sunrise at winter solstice (S.E.), and then to the place of sunrise at summer solstice: next to the Above (halfway between the points of sunrise and sunset at midsummer), and finally to the Below (halfway between the points of sunrise and sunset at midwinter). The names of these six directions, and their emblematic colours, are:

1. *kwini'wi*, yellow (*sikya*): 'because the anthropomorphic deity who sits there is yellow, wearing a yellow cloud as a mask which covers his head and rests upon his shoulders; a multitude of yellow butterflies constantly flutters before the cloud, and yellow corn grows continually in that yellow land'; i.e. northwest.

2. *te'vyüña*, blue-green (*sa'kwa*); i.e. southwest.

3. *ta'tyüka*, red (*pa'la*); i.e. southeast.

4. *ho'poko*, white (*kö'tsa*); i.e. northeast.

5. *o'mi*, black (*kü'mbi*); i.e. the Above.

6. *at'kyami*, all colours (*na'nalüña*): 'and here sits the deity regarded as the maker of all life germs. He sits upon a flowery mound on which grows all vegetation. He wears a mask of clouds of all these five colours, and before it flutter all the butterflies. Speckled corn and sweet corn grow there, and melons, cotton, beans, squash, etc.';[1] i.e. the Below.

The deity regarded as 'the maker of all life germs' is Mü'yiñwa. He first fashioned seeds, plants and fruits, especially the bean, by rolling them between the palms of his hands; and sends up beans, squashes, melons and seeded grasses for the Hopi to eat.[2] He is the deity who sits at the Below; he, and the chiefs of the other five directions, are the 'six directions' chiefs' (*na'nanivo moñ'mowitû*), or 'cloud fathers', to whom the prayers for rain—mediated through the katçinas —are addressed.

---

spent thirteen years in Hopi country before dying there, of tuberculosis, in 1894; he thus had unrivalled opportunities for observing the details of Hopi ceremonial. His *Hopi Journal*, edited in 1936 by E. C. Parsons, is one of the richest ethnographic sources ever published.

[1] Stephen (1898), pp. 261–2: cf. Stephen (1936), p. 333. Each of the six directions is associated with one of the six kinds of corn, and with one of the six other principal crops, grown by the Hopi: i.e. N.W. with yellow corn (+ water melon), S.W. with blue corn (+ muskmelon), S.E. with red corn (+ squash), N.E. with white corn (+ gourd), N. with black or purple corn (+ beans), S. with either speckled or sweet corn (+ cotton): cf. Parsons (1936), p. 1229, under *kawai'o*.

[2] Parsons (1936), pp. 1254–5. The bean pod, in Hopi belief, still bears the marks of Mü'yiñwa's palms on it.

Hopi recognise two distinct kinds of katçinas:[1] 'chief' (*moñ*) katçinas, and ordinary katçinas. *Moñ* katçinas are relatively few in number, perhaps thirty in all, compared with two or three hundred ordinary katçinas. *Moñ* katçinas never dance in groups like ordinary katçinas, but certain of them—the Soyal katçina, for example, and Eototo and Aholi—are impersonated in the course of the Soyal and Powamu ceremonies. Whereas ordinary katçina masks are made by their owners and redecorated each time a different katçina is to be represented, the masks representing *moñ* katçinas are permanent and are never duplicated; they belong to particular lineages, of which they are regarded as *wuya* or ancestors, are believed to possess great power, and are carefully kept and handed down within the lineages to which they belong. In general *moñ* katçinas are considerably more awe-inspiring than ordinary katçinas; they only appear at specified times during the year, and may be regarded as occupying a place in the katçina world analogous to that held by the chiefs (*moñ'mowitû*) in the village.[2]

The basis for all katçina impersonations is the mask, *kü'itü*. This is about 9 inches high, the shape of an upturned bucket, and is designed to fit right over the head and face, and down as far as the neck, of the wearer. In the old days it was made either of buckskin, or of white cotton cloth, stretched over a willow frame; to-day, it is usually made of leather. In preparing a mask for use, the mask is first scraped down and then painted. The decoration is very formal: the colours used, the kind and arrangement of feathers, and the designs themselves, being distinctive for any one katçina. In some, Eototo for example, the face is all of one colour, with just eyes and mouth indicated; in others, it is divided into two sections by a vertical line, with contrasting colours in each section. The sections in turn may be decorated with formal representations of corn, clouds, falling rain, lightning; these, as we shall see, are the common symbols used in all Hopi ceremonies, but their position, size and colour tend to become definitive on the mask of any particular katçina.

Prior to a katçina dance, the men who are to take part in it assemble in the kiva of the man who is sponsoring the dance. There, under his direction, they prepare their masks for the dance. Certain precautions are observed in the use of the pigments. The pigment is first rubbed down to a powder; then, instead of using water to liquefy it, the men sit round in a circle and chew melon seeds to generate saliva, which is then mixed with the pigment. Speaking secularly, Hopi say that the saliva causes the pigments to adhere to the mask; but the practice also has a religious significance of some kind.[3] Special attention is paid to the painting of the eyes of the mask. The word *po'shi*, in Hopi, refers to both

---

[1] On the distinction between *moñ* katçinas and ordinary katçinas, see Earle and Kennard (1938), pp. 4–5: Titiev (1944), p. 109: Colton (1947a), pp. 40–7.

[2] Earle and Kennard (1938), p. 5. At Oraibi, according to Titiev (1944, p. 224, n. 14), only Badger clansmen or those related to them may impersonate *moñ* katçinas.

[3] Stephen (1898), p. 265. Fewkes (1922, p. 272) says that, in the old days, the albumen of eagle's eggs was used for glazing masks.

eye and seed.[1] In preparing paint for the eyes, melon seeds are again chewed and the saliva mixed with the pigment; and when the dancers unmask at the end of the dance, the paint is always scraped from the eyes first.

Turning now to the significance of the mask: when a Hopi places the mask over his head so that it rests on his shoulders, and wears the appropriate costume and body paint, he—quite simply—becomes the katçina whom he is representing. 'When the mask is put over the head, the wearer becomes the same as one of the *Na'nanivak moñ'mowitû*, Chiefs of the Directions, the mask is the same as O'mauwû, Cloud, it is O'mauwû, i.e. the clouds that rest over the heads and upon the shoulders of the Chiefs of the Directions.'[2] And it is in this context that we have to interpret the designs painted on the mask, and the colours used in decorating the body. On any particular mask, part of the design is ornamental, and part symbolic; and that part which is symbolic may refer either to general or to specific symbols. When, for example, a Hopi paints a mask to represent an animal or plant katçina, no attempt is made at realism, because he does not aim to convey the object itself but its spirit, or 'breath'; some clue to the object is given, such as a bear track on the cheek, which tells the initiated that he is seeing a Bear katçina.[3] Certain katçinas, again, may appear with their limbs painted in different colours, representing the cardinal points. On one level, such use of colour simply indicates the direction from which the katçina has come, but on another: 'this pigmentary manifestation may be called chromatic prayer, as it is definitely regarded as a direct appeal to the clouds at the four directions to hasten with rain to the Hopi land'.[4] The use of feathers, to decorate the masks, also has its own symbolism: the principal feathers used for this purpose being those of eagle, owl, sparrow-hawk, crow and turkey.

Ordinarily, katçina impersonations take the form of group dances. A number of men rehearse the songs and steps for some days beforehand, and then perform from daybreak to sunset, with intervals for rest between the dances. Each man wears a kilt, woven out of white cotton and embroidered along the edge with coloured designs of clouds and falling rain,[5] a sash with woven designs at the end, buck-skin moccasins on the feet, on the right wrist a strand of yarn and a bracelet, and on the left a bow guard. Most katçinas wear a fox skin at their waist, with the tail dangling on the ground behind them. Exposed parts of the body are covered with paint, and the costume is completed by the donning of the mask.

In the usual katçina dance, a line of from twenty-five to sixty dancers, all dressed alike and masked alike, all singing and dancing in unison, performs

[1] Earle and Kennard (1938), p. 9: cf. Parsons (1936), p. 1206, under *bo'shi*.
[2] Stephen (1936), p. 1235, under *kü'itü*: evidently quoting Hopi informants.
[3] Earle and Kennard (1938), pp. 8–10.
[4] Stephen (1898), p. 265.
[5] On the costume of the dancers, see Earle and Kennard (1938), p. 9. Parsons (1936, p. 1280) adds that the meander pattern along the border of the ceremonial kilt represents the angles formed between the cotyledons and the stem of newly-sprouting bean plants: and the straight lines running through the embroidery, prayer-feather and corn-meal 'roads'.

in the village square before the assembled spectators. It is the effect of the line, rather than of the figures composing it, that impresses. The usual dance step consists of raising the right foot and stamping the ground, to the rhythm beaten out by a single figure seated at a drum. Tied to his right leg below the knee, each dancer wears a turtle-shell rattle, and usually carries in his right hand a gourd rattle, to re-inforce the beat. The body is held erect, with the arms close to the sides and the hands forward. The major variations on this pattern of dancing[1] occur in accordance with changes in the rhythm of the song. Sometimes the entire line will pause, at others two or more steps will be executed in quick succession, the change in tempo being marked by gestures of the arms and head; or the leader will twist his body, and the other katçinas follow suit, the movement flowing down the line and back. These differences in dance steps serve to distinguish one kind of katçina from another; they are, indeed, as essential characteristics as the painting and decoration of the masks— and just as formal.

Like the dances, the songs of the different katçinas help to distinguish them. About a dozen new songs are composed for each dance, the number of songs determining how many times the katçinas will come out to dance during the day.

> In a sense, [writes Kennard[2]], every song is a prayer, and the words express either the message of the Hopi to the clouds and the Chiefs of the Directions, or the message of the clouds and Kachinas to the Hopi. The same ideas, the same phrases are used over and over in all Kachina songs. In fact, it is really another medium in which the symbols for rain, corn, fertility, and growth are expressed:

> > Listen, my mothers,
> > > You have prayed that it would rain on your plants.
> > Listen, my fathers,
> > > You have prayed that it would rain on your plants.

> > When you look, after the rain,
> > > You shall see what you prayed for.
> > When rain falls among your plants,
> > > You shall see pools of water, my fathers,
> > > That is what you prayed for.

> > Listen, listen, my fathers,
> > > You prayed for us.

> > Yonder, to the west,
> > > At the house of Alosaka [= Mü'yiñwa] chief, we heard.
> > Happily we prepared. Many kinds of corn,
> > > Many kinds of clouds, we prepared.
> > Then we started to come, along the 'roads'
> > > Made by these old men,[3] the chiefs.

[1] On the dance steps, see Earle and Kennard (1938), pp. 10–11. Each complete dance usually lasts for some thirty to forty minutes.

[2] Earle and Kennard (1938), pp. 12–13.

[3] Refers to the sprinkling of corn-meal 'roads', by the katçina 'fathers'. At every katçina performance one man, usually an old man, acts as 'father' of the katçinas; he leads the

So, coming from each direction,
    We shall sprinkle rain.
That is what you prayed for, my fathers.

You start smoking your pipe,
    And hand it from one to another.
In the same way [as the clouds of smoke], the clouds
    Will approach with rain.
Aha ihi, aha ihi . . .

The element of prayer, implicit in the decoration of the masks and in the songs sung by the katçinas, is overtly demonstrated in the manufacture of prayer-sticks which accompanies every katçina performance: the *pa'ho*(s) being made in the sponsoring kiva on the day before the dance, and 'placed', on its conclusion, at katçina shrines near the village. And as, in the making of prayer-sticks, the religious ideas (which have been the object of our inquiry) receive their most complete outward expression, are indeed *epitomised*, I conclude with a brief account of their meaning to the Hopi.

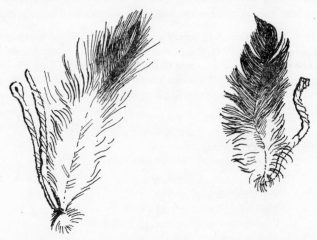

Fig. 30. *Nakwa'kwosi*, with cotton thread. Re-drawn from Voth (1903*b*), pl. vii e.

Prayer-offerings[1] are, in the main, of two kinds: *nakwa'kwosi*(s), 'breath' feathers, and *pa'ho*(s), prayer-sticks. The *nakwa'kwosi* is a feather, to which is attached a length of cotton twine: the *pa'ho*, either a single stick or two sticks tied together, 4 to 6 inches long, painted usually with either a blue-green or a black pigment, and bound around with twine in which is inserted a sprig of

---

dancers into the square at the commencement of the dance, and out again at the end; and at intervals during the dance he goes down the line, sprinkling the dancers with corn-meal. The 'father' of the katçinas does not wear costume.

[1] Prayer-sticks are made on all kinds of occasion in Hopi life: e.g. at planting a field, building a house, before a rabbit hunt, going on a salt expedition, etc. To-day, most Hopi drivers carry a *nakwa'kwosi* in the front window of their vehicles.

ma'övi (*Gutierrezia sarothrae*) or of kü'ñya (*Artemisia frigida*), a corn-husk packet containing corn-meal mixed with honey, and one or more feathers of various kinds. Perhaps the best description of a *pa'ho* is that given by Means:[1]

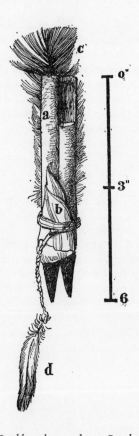

Fig. 31. *Double paho*, made at *Soyal*: *a.* pair of sticks, painted blue-green with black tips, one faceted; *b.* corn-husk packet, with herb sprig; *c.* black turkey feather; *d. nakwa'kwosi*, white feather with cotton thread. Re-drawn from Dorsey and Voth (1901), pl. xvi.

. . . a little bundle composed of two sticks, representing man and woman, seeded weed to stand for reproduction and growth, and a tiny packet of corn meal, folded into a corn husk. Attached to all this is a downy feather, to carry to the Hopi gods the prayer for rain and for increase.

[1] Means (1960), p. 121: but whether the two sticks represent man and woman, is an open question.

The *theory* of the prayer-stick, and breath-feather, is as follows:[1]

A man makes a prayer-stick because he wants something good, some benefit. O'mauwû (Cloud), Na'nanivak Moñ'mowitû (Chiefs of the Directions), Patü'shüñüla (Ice chief), Mü'yiñwa (Planting chief)—from these, and other chiefs, all benefits proceed.

Feathers are used in prayer-sticks and breath-feathers, because they are *ka-pü'tü*, 'not heavy', i.e. light; and Cloud, and all the other chiefs, desire them to make the fringe of feathers with which to decorate their foreheads.

The Hopi barters[2] his prayer-offerings with those chiefs for the benefits he desires to receive from them. He exchanges prayer-sticks and breath-feathers for material benefits. He places on his prayer-stick the prescribed feather and grass emblems, in accordance with the kind of material or other benefit that he may desire.[3] A turkey feather is tied to every prayer-stick. If a Hopi desires rain, he ties on yellow bird or duck feather; for hot weather in order to make a good peach harvest, owl feather; for game, the feathers of turkey and yellow bird are used, also *sö'hö*—the grass which deer and antelope prefer. The feather of bluebird is for snow and ice; this is addressed to Patü'shüñüla.

As Sun journeys over the earth, he sees the prayer-sticks and breath-feathers, and comes to them and inhales[4] their essence and takes them. He does not take up the material sticks and string and feathers, but their 'breath body', *hi'ksi adta ah'paa*, their *picha'ñ adta*, likeness. He places them in his girdle and goes in at the west to the Below (*at'kya*) and gives them, all that he has collected through the day's journey, to Mü'yiñwa. Mü'yiñwa knows all prayer-sticks and breath-feathers, and as he takes them up one by one and looks at each, he says to the other chiefs: 'this is for you, or you', according as the prayer-sticks are designed. Those that are ill made, or made by men of evil hearts, he casts away, saying: 'this one is from a bad man, *ka-ho'pi*,[5] a foolish one.' The chiefs thank Mü'yiñwa and the makers of the emblems, and decorate their foreheads with the feathers, and send the benefits that the prayer-maker desires.

### THE CEREMONIAL CYCLE

Describing, in *The Rainbow* (1915), the place held by the great festivals of the church in English rural life a hundred years ago, D. H. Lawrence spoke of them as providing 'a rhythm of eternity in a ragged, inconsequential life.' A com-

---

[1] Stephen (1936), pp. 1271–2, from which the following passage is taken nearly word for word; Stephen appears here to be following pretty closely in the steps of Hopi informants.

[2] The word used is *hu'hiyaiya*: root *he'ya-*, v. 'sells, barters, trades it' (Whorf, 1936, p. 1222). To be distinguished from: *na'hoiñwaiya*, v. 'exchanges it', referring to an exchange of gifts between two persons (Stephen, 1936, p. 375).

[3] Cf. Stephen (1936), p. 164: 'The prayer-feather carries the maker's desire . . .; the prayer-stick calls the attention of the deity. When Cloud or Sun or other deity sees the prayer-stick, he looks for the prayer-feather and there he reads what is in the Hopi maker's heart.'

[4] *Hüh'tü*, v. 'inhales essence as from prayer-stick, sacred object or person's hand': Stephen (1936), p. 1222.

[5] *Ka-ho'pi*, foolish. Thus, in Hopi myth, Coyote (who is a thief, and steals corn and watermelons) is *ka-ho'pi*, foolish, mischievous, rather than *ka-lo'lomai*, evil: Stephen (1936), pp. 1224–5.

parable rhythm the Hopi find in their festivals; and this we have to recapture, if we are to grasp the full meaning of the ceremonial cycle in pueblo life.

Seven great ceremonies—Wü'wütçim, Soya'l, Powa'mu, Nima'n, Snake-Antelope or Flute, Marau, Lako'n or Oa'qöl—fill the Hopi year.[1] The cycle begins in November with the Wü'wütçim, perhaps the most complicated of all the rites, in every 4th year of which novices were in the old days taken into the four men's fraternities. Two to three weeks after the conclusion of Wü'wütçim comes the Soya'l, the winter solstice ceremony; and early in the next moon but one, in the February moon, the Powa'mu is celebrated, during which beans are planted in the kivas to simulate the real crops that will be planted in the fields a few weeks later. The dates for the three principal winter ceremonies are established by watching the position of the setting sun, in relation to the San Francisco mountains.[2]

On the last afternoon of the Soya'l, the katçinas are re-admitted to the village and, from then until their departure in July, are believed to reside in the neighbourhood. During this period the katçina dances take place, at first in the kivas at night, and later, as the days lengthen, by day in the village square. Early in July, when the rising sun reaches a particular point on the eastern sky-line, the Nima'n (Home-going) Dance is announced; and sixteen days later the katçinas are formally 'sent home', in the final katçina dance of the season.

All Hopi ceremonies are, in a general sense, *for* rain, fertility, and growth of crops; and this aim is most overtly expressed in the ceremonies that take place in the late summer, when the need for rain is most acute. Early in August, every alternate year, the Snake and Antelope societies co-operate in carrying out the nine-day ritual which culminates in the public performance of the Snake dance; the following year, the Blue and Gray Flute societies undertake an analogous ceremony, culminating in a major rite at the village spring. Both ceremonies, according to Nequatewa, symbolise the entrance of the various clans into the pueblo; both enact prayers for rain, and both anticipate the ripening of the new crop.

Finally, in mid September and late October respectively, are staged the women's ceremonies: first, the Marau', then (in alternate years) the Lako'n or the Oa'qöl. The three ceremonies are similar in form, and may fairly be regarded as a kind of harvest festival, setting the seal to work in the fields. 'This

[1] On the ceremonial cycle, see in particular Nequatewa (1931), pp. 1–4. No single village still performs the complete cycle, and before its performance at Shungo'povi in November 1967, the Wü'wütçim had not been done for twenty years in any of the villages; but Soya'l, Powa'mu, Nima'n and the fall ceremonies are still celebrated annually in at least one village on each mesa.

[2] These mountains, known as *nüva'tükyau'ovi*, 'snow mountain sacred high place', lie on the western horizon and are clearly visible from all the Hopi villages. Middleton has pointed out (1958, p. 204) that a view of distant mountains, and their figuring in myth, may play a significant part in a people's conceptualisation of their society; I think that this is certainly the case for the Hopi in relation to the San Francisco Mountains, regarded (as we have seen) as the home of the katçinas.

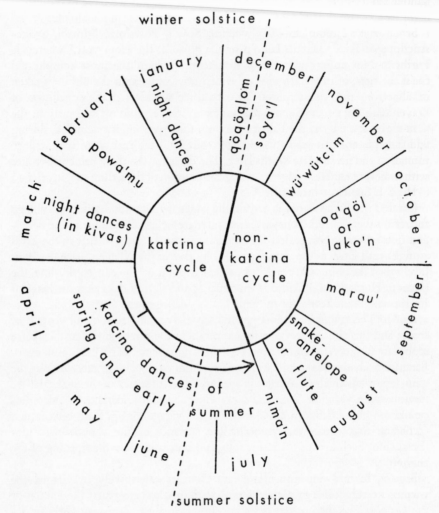

Fig. 32. Hopi ceremonial cycle. Re-drawn from Wright and Roat (1965), p. 28.

ceremony, like all others', writes Nequatewa,[1] referring to the Lako'n, 'is a prayer for health and prosperity, and brings to an end the year's cycle of sacred dramas.'

### OUTWARD FORM OF HOPI CEREMONIES

All the major ceremonies in the annual cycle have certain features in common.[2] Each is conducted by one or more leaders, whose offices are hereditary; each is

---

[1] Nequatewa (1931), p. 3.
[2] See, especially, Earle and Kennard (1938), pp. 3–4, and Titiev (1944), pp. 103–6.

announced a set number of days beforehand by the Village Crier, consists of eight days of secret rites conducted in the kiva which houses the ceremony, and is brought to a close by a public performance on the ninth day; each imposes strict prohibitions[1] on those taking part, and concludes with a discharming rite. Further, in the esoteric ritual carried out in the kivas, all ceremonies draw on the same range of ritual elements, namely: the making of prayer-sticks, erection of altars (*poñya*), consecration of medicine-water (*ña'küyi*), ritual smoking, prayer and songs.

In this section I discuss first the relation between kiva, ceremony and clan; and then describe the separate ritual elements out of which the complete ceremonies are built, as a preliminary to the detailed narration of the Powa'mu with which the chapter ends.

Hopi kivas are rectangular ceremonial chambers, built underground and orientated roughly north and south.[2] They are entered through a hatchway in the roof, by means of a stout ladder which projects a few feet above the opening and rests almost in the centre of the room beneath. The chamber itself is 12 to 14 feet wide, 24 to 28 feet long, and 6 to 8 feet high. The floor is built on two levels, the area south of the ladder being raised several inches above the northern portion. As a rule the raised southern part of the floor is smaller and is reserved for spectators, while the lower or main floor is the scene of the principal ritual activities. The kiva ladder rests on the raised section, near its junction with the lower level. On the main floor, just north of the ladder's base, there is a small scooped-out fireplace; and along the east, north and west sides, run stone banquettes about 2 feet high. To the north of the fireplace, in the middle of the main floor, there is a small square cavity, which is hidden under a wooden cover when not in use; this represents the *si'papü*, the opening through which mankind is believed to have climbed out upon the earth.

The Hopi kiva serves a dual function: namely, as ceremonial chamber, and as social club. Each kiva is owned by one particular clan, and is closely linked to the phratry of which that clan forms a part. Each of the principal kivas in the village is, further, the hub of the particular ceremony (*wi'mi*) of which its owning clan has charge. The ceremony itself is represented by a number of

---

[1] Specifically, prohibitions on the eating of meat and of food cooked with salt, and on sexual intercourse. Somewhere, in Hopi thinking, there is a link between these tabus and rain; thus Stephen, describing one of the katçina dances of early summer, writes (1936, p. 435): 'then (they) sing in Hopi, the *yoinapwûlshtawi*, song of no flesh nor salt eating, no venery, that rain may come'.

[2] Titiev (1944), pp. 103–4: for a detailed account of kiva construction, cf. Mindeleff (1891), pp. 111–37.

In fact, most of the kivas in the other pueblos, and all the twelve underground ones at Oraibi, are set on the N.W.–S.E. axis: probably, as Fewkes (1892b, pp. 33–4) suggests, because the clefts in the rock in which the kivas are constructed run from N.E. to S.W. As a consequence, the end (or 'north') wall of the kiva lies well to the west of pole-star north, and corresponds to the direction which the Hopi refer to as *kwini'wi* and with which they associate the colour yellow. When, therefore, in this account I speak loosely, e.g. of the 'north' end of the kiva, it must be borne in mind that this refers, strictly, to the northwest end, Hopi orientation being askew to ours.

C

ritual objects, essential to its correct performance; these are kept in the clan
house of the clan that owns the ceremony, in the care of its senior women, and
are only brought out at the time the ceremony is to be performed. Of these
objects the most important is the *ti'poni*, and it is ownership of its *ti'poni* that
marks the clan elder who has charge of the ceremony. This man may also act
as kiva chief, but more commonly the latter office is undertaken by another
elder, either of the owning clan or of one of the clans linked to it. As kiva chief,
it is his duty to represent the kiva, particularly in its relations with other kivas:
e.g. he takes the lead when his group puts on a katçina dance, smokes formally
with messengers who come to announce ceremonies in other kivas, and sponsors
the Nima'n in years when that obligation falls on his kiva. In addition, he
organises the various secular pursuits which are performed by kiva units, such as
communal rabbit hunts, and working parties for spinning and weaving cotton;
and he is responsible for seeing that the chamber is kept in good repair and well
stocked with firewood during the winter months.

At Oraibi before 1906, there were eight principal kivas in the village, each
associated with one or more of the great ceremonies in the annual cycle,
together with four 'common' kivas, of more recent origin and not associated
with any major ceremony. Each of the principal kivas was, further, linked to a
particular shrine outside the village, the shrine standing in a special ritual
relationship to the ceremony of which the kiva was the centre. These eight
kivas, with their owning clans, the ceremonies of which they had charge, and
their associated shrines, were as follows:[1]

1. *Sakwa'lenvi*, Blue Flute kiva:

owned by Spider clan, of phratry II $\left\{ \begin{array}{l} \text{Spider} \\ \text{Bear.} \end{array} \right.$

Spider clan controls the Blue Flute ceremony, which takes place in Sakwa'lenvi kiva.

Bear clan owns the Soya'l. In the old days, Sakwa'lenvi was the Chief (*moñ*) kiva of
Oraibi: the Soya'l was performed there, and it was, with Hawi'ovi kiva, one of the two
kivas for the main branch of the Wü'wütçim ceremony. But in 1896, as part of the
rupture between Bear and Spider clans (which eventually led to the split of the pueblo
in 1906), Bear clan leader withdrew from Sakwa'lenvi and moved his Soya'l to one of
the 'common' kivas, Tawa'ovi.

The shrine associated with Sakwa'lenvi is a katçina shrine in the San Francisco mountains. In the old days, when katçina dancers from this kiva sponsored the Nima'n, they
fetched spruce from the locality of this shrine, instead of from Kisi'wu.

2. *Hawi'ovi* kiva:

owned by Bow (phratry V), and Sand (phratry III), clans.

In the old days, Hawi'ovi was the kiva for the main branch of the Wü'wütçim ceremony, the most esoteric rites of that cult being held there. The Gray Flute ceremony,
owned by Pa'tki clan (phratry VIII), also took place in Hawi'ovi kiva.

[1] Titiev (1944), pp. 104, 241–7. The numbering of the phratries is that used on p. 11,
(above), n.1.

Its associated shrine is at Kisi'wu, a spring about 40 miles northeast of Oraibi, regarded as one of the main 'homes' of the katçinas; at the Nima'n, expeditions are sent to Kisi'wu to fetch spruce.

3. *Tao*, Singers' kiva:

owned by Parrot clan, of phratry I $\left\{ \begin{array}{l} \text{rabbit} \\ \text{katçina} \\ \text{parrot.} \end{array} \right.$

This is the kiva for the Singers (*Tao*) branch of Wü'wütçim; at Oraibi, Parrot clan controls the Singers' fraternity (Titiev, 1944, p. 138). Its associated shrine is located at Tü'wa-na'savi, the home of the germination deity Mü'yiñwa; after death, Tao men are believed to go to Tü'wa-na'savi.

4. *Na'savi*, central kiva:

owned by Bow clan, of phratry V $\left\{ \begin{array}{l} \text{greasewood} \\ \text{bow} \\ \text{reed.} \end{array} \right.$

Na'savi kiva is the kiva for the Horn (*Al*) branch of Wü'wütçim; at Oraibi, Bow clan controls the Al fraternity (Titiev, 1944, p. 137, n. 54). Its associated shrine is at a lake near the San Francisco mountains; after death, the spirits of deceased Al men are believed to go there.

5. *Kwan*, Agave kiva:

owned by one of the clans of phratry VI $\left\{ \begin{array}{l} \text{Masau'u} \\ \text{coyote} \\ \text{ko'kop.} \end{array} \right.$

This is the kiva for the Kwan or Agave branch of Wü'wütçim, controlled at Oraibi by Masau'u clan (Titiev, 1944, p. 134). Its associated shrine is at Kwanivi, whither the spirits of deceased Kwan men are believed to go.

All five of these kivas are associated with one of the branches of the Wü' wütçim: Sakwa'lenvi and Hawi'ovi with the main branch, Tao with the Singers branch, Na'savi with the Horn branch, and Kwan kiva with the Agave branch. We may note here[1] the distinction made between the main branch of the Wü'wütçim and the other branches; whereas the kivas housing the Al, Kwan and Tao fraternities are connected with special homes to which their members resort after death, the two principal kivas of the Wü'wütçim are associated with two of the best-known katçina shrines.

6. *Powa'mu* kiva:

owned by Badger clan, of phratry VII $\left\{ \begin{array}{l} \text{badger} \\ \text{gray badger} \\ \text{butterfly.} \end{array} \right.$

Badger clan controls the Powa'mu ceremony, which takes place in this kiva. Its associated shrine is a massive rock on the western edge of 3rd Mesa, known as *Oraibi*, which serves as a katçina shrine and from which the village is said to have taken its name.

[1] Cf. Titiev (1944), p. 247.

7. *Tçu*, Snake kiva:

owned by one of the three clans of phratry III $\begin{cases} \text{sand} \\ \text{snake} \\ \text{lizard.} \end{cases}$

This phratry owns the Snake ceremony, and the winter prayer-stick making of the Snake society is held in this kiva. At Oraibi, the Antelope society is controlled by Spider clan and meets in Na'savi kiva; the summer Snake/Antelope rites are celebrated jointly by the two societies, in these two kivas (Voth, 1903a, p. 274 ff.).

8. *Marau'* kiva:

owned by Lizard clan, of phratry III.

Lizard clan owns the Marau' ceremony, which takes place in this kiva. In the old days children were initiated into the Katçina fraternity, in the course of Powa'mu, in Marau' kiva (Voth, 1901, p. 94).

With this outline of the Oraibi kivas in mind, we may now turn to the ritual that is performed inside them.

All major rituals that are performed in kivas[1] are of nine days' duration. Certain ceremonies, however, are preceded by a preliminary meeting known as *pa'ho la'lauwu*, '*pa'ho* making', which usually takes place eight days before the main rites begin. On this occasion the society's officers meet together in the kiva where the ceremony is to be staged, smoke together, prepare *nakwa' kwosi*(s) and *pa'ho*(s), and arrange for the public announcing of their *wi'mi* (ceremony). At the conclusion of the *pa'ho la'lauwu*, some of the prayer-offerings are deposited at shrines outside the village; others are handed over to *tça'ak moñ'wi*, Crier chief. Early the next morning, *tça'ak moñ'wi* ascends to the roof-top from which announcements are made,[2] deposits the *pa'ho*(s) at a shrine there, and announces the forthcoming ceremony.

When the eight intervening days have gone by, the leaders assemble in the kiva which houses their ceremony and put up a standard (*na'atsi*), usually consisting of a bundle of four sticks to which eagle feathers are tied; this is erected just south of the entrance hatch, and serves to warn people that the ceremony is in progress. From now until the conclusion of the ritual, only members of the group that owns the ceremony may enter the kiva; and all those taking part must observe tabus on salt, meat, and sex.

The first day of the ceremony is known as *yü'ñya*, 'going in'; and the next four days are referred to, respectively, as '1st light' or '1st day', '2nd day', '3rd day', and '4th day'.[3] '4th day' is also named *ke'kel-kü-kü'yiva*, '*ke'le*(s) emerge', referring to the fact that initiation of novices into the society commonly takes

---

[1] On the form of Hopi ceremonies, see especially Titiev (1944), pp. 104–6.

[2] At Oraibi, this is the clan house of *ke'le* clan. From here *tça'ak moñ'wi*, acting as the 'mouth' of the Village chief, announces all major ceremonies except for katçina performances; the latter are never announced beforehand, as the katçinas are supposed to be resident in the neighbourhood of the pueblo and so not to need summoning.

[3] Stephen, in his description of the Nima'n, indicates (1936, p. 495) that each of these four days is devoted to one of the four cardinal directions.

place the night before. The final four days are referred to either by repeating the ordinal numbers, or by the special names given below:[1]

| day | 1. *yü'ñya* | 'going in' |
|---|---|---|
| | 2. *shüsh'tala* | '1st day' |
| | 3. *lüsh'tala* | '2nd day' |
| | 4. *paish'tala* | '3rd day' |
| | 5. *na'lüshta'la,* | '4th day', |
| | *ke'kel-kü-kü'yiva,* or *yü'ñya* | 'ke'le(s) emerge', or 'going in': |
| | 6. *shüsh'tala,* | '1st day', |
| | or *sosh-ka-hi'müi* | or 'all do nothing': |
| | 7. *lüsh'tala, pi'k toto'kya,* | '2nd day', '*pi'ki* providing', |
| | or *komo'k toto'kya* | or 'wood carrying': |
| | 8. *paish'tala, toto'kya,* | '3rd day', 'sleeps', |
| | or *pa'ho la'lauwu* | or '*pa'ho* making': |
| | 9. *na'lüshta'la, ti'hü,* | '4th day', 'impersonation', |
| | *ti'kive,* or *nüsh'ni-ca* | 'dance', or 'eats flesh'.[2] |

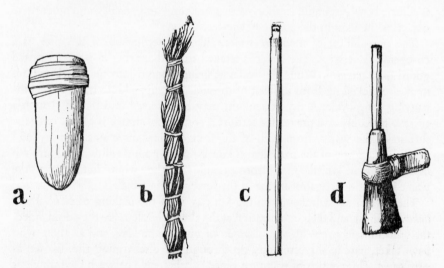

Fig. 33. *Smoking objects* used in *Soyal/Powamu: a. omaw'tapi,* cloud blower; *b. kopi'choki,* cedar-bark fuse used for lighting reed cigarette; *c. chono'tki,* reed cigarette, used for blowing smoke over certain katçinas; *d. sakwa'chono,* green-stone pipe. Re-drawn from Dorsey and Voth (1901), pl. iii.

[1] On the ceremonial day count, see Fewkes and Stephen (1893), p. 272, n. 2: Dorsey and Voth (1901), pp. 14–15, and p. 14, n. *: Voth (1901), p. 84, n. *: Parsons (1923), pp. 158–9, and (1936), p. 1041: Stephen (1936), pp. 162, 495: Titiev (1944), pp. 104–5.

[2] This refers to the end of the prohibition on eating meat, i.e. for all those except the leaders, who have to observe a further four days' abstinence.

As a rule, the first seven days are given over to esoteric ritual inside the kivas; the eighth day sees the making of *pa'ho*(s) and other prayer-offerings, the conclusion of the kiva ritual, and the discharming rite (by which those taking part are freed from the 'dangerous' contact of the spirits); the ninth day is the occasion for a public performance, commonly called a dance, followed by a feast—for the men in the kivas, and for the women and children in their own homes; and the 10th day is a holiday, *o'vekniwa*.

The greater part of the esoteric ritual that takes place in the kivas is devoted to smoking together, singing and praying to the accompaniment of gourd rattles, and the manufacture of prayer-offerings, which are subsequently deposited at special shrines outside the village. All major ceremonies, however, include three further elements: the setting-up of altars (*poñya*), the making of sand mosaics, and the preparation of medicine-water (*ña'küyi*). These three elements are generally combined in a single *ensemble*. The altar (*poñya*) consists of a wooden frame, some 2 to 3 feet high and about 4 feet wide, set in a ridge of sand. To the frame are fixed a number of wooden slats, carrying painted symbolic representations of corn, rain clouds, lightning, sacred animals, and deities. On the floor in front of the sand ridge is set out the sand mosaic; and on the ridge and the mosaic are arranged, in prescribed order, one or more *ti'poni*(s), medicine bowl, aspergill, feathers, variegated corns and pebbles, and other ritual objects to be used in the course of the ceremony.

The preparation of medicine-water,[1] like the setting-up of the altar, is a co-operative activity. The water is fetched from the spring in a special netted gourd (*moñ'wikuru*). While the water is being poured into the bowl, various items are picked up from in front of the altar and dipped into it, to an accompanying song cycle. A ray of sunlight may be reflected into the bowl with a crystal, probably as a prayer for fertility;[2] sometimes smoke is blown over the surface of the water, from each of the four cardinal directions in turn;[3] and nearly always one of the participants kneels on the gound and whistles into the liquid on a bone whistle, made from an eagle or turkey wing.[4] In these ways the water is sanctified, against its use in the forthcoming ritual.

The kiva ritual culminates on the 8th day with the making of *pa'ho*(s) and *nakwa'kwosi*(s), and their consecration at the altar. The altars are then dismantled, the sand mosaic swept up and disposed of outside the kiva, and all those who have taken part in the ceremony go through the discharming rite, known as *navo'tçiwa*. This consists of waving a pinch of ashes, held between the forefinger and thumb of the right hand, counter-clockwise ('widdershins') over the person

---

[1] *Ña'hü kü'yi*, 'charm water': Parsons (1936), pp. 1257. Fewkes (1892*b*, pp. 34–5) gives an excellent description of its preparation.

[2] Titiev (1944), p. 105, n. 24: several myths describe how women became impregnated when a ray of sunlight fell on their vulva. Cf. Stephen (1936), p. 332.

[3] 'Blowing smoke into water is interpreted as a direct appeal to the home of the Clouds': Titiev (1944), p. 105, n. 25.

[4] 'Blowing on a bone whistle is a means of summoning the deities': Titiev (1944), p. 106, n. 26.

(or object) to be discharmed, usually to the accompaniment of a special dis-charming song. Early on the morning of the ninth day, the prayer-offerings are deposited at the appropriate shrines or springs, the heads of those who have been initiated into the order in the course of the rites are ceremonially washed (and the initiates given new names), and later in the day the entire membership of the society, including the initiates, takes part in a public performance in the village square. After the dance is over, the leaders continue to sleep in the kiva for four more nights, the period of ritual abstinence from meat, salt and sex; they then return home and resume their normal secular lives.

THE KATÇINA CYCLE AT ORAIBI:
FROM THE 'OPENING OF THE KIVAS' TO POWA'MU

The 'opening of the kivas', which inaugurates the katçina season, falls into two stages: the arrival of the Soya'l katçina, followed some three to four weeks later—towards the end of December—by the actual 'opening' by the Qöqöqlom katçinas.

On an afternoon late in November, on the day after the termination of the Wü'wütçim ceremony, a figure is seen approaching the pueblo along the trail from the southwest.[1] He has the gait of an old man, and as he plods wearily up the mesa side, his clothes also are seen to be worn and ragged—a cotton shirt and leggings, of the kind formerly woven by the Hopi, a white cotton blanket with a skein of black wool over one shoulder, kilt, sash and belt of the sort commonly worn by katçinas, a length of black yarn tied around his right wrist and right ankle, and below his right knee a turtle-shell rattle; in his right hand he carries a gourd rattle, and in his left, a bag of corn-meal and four prayer-sticks. His gait, his costume and, above all, his mask—painted blue, with black slits for eyes and mouth, and surmounted by a tuft of red-dyed horse hair—proclaim him to be the Soya'l katçina, the first of the katçinas to visit the village since their 'going home' at the previous Nima'n.

He totters through the village, simulating the walk of one lately awakened from a long sleep, to Chief (*moñ*) kiva—to the kiva, that is, where the Soya'l will be celebrated in sixteen days' time; there, he deposits the four prayer-sticks beside the hatch, sprinkles a corn-meal 'road' from each of the four cardinal directions towards the hatch, then stands in front of the hatch and sounds his gourd rattle twice. At this point, the Village chief emerges from Chief kiva, bearing a tray of corn-meal with a number of *nakwa'kwosi*(s) resting on top; he gives the tray of prayer-offerings to the katçina, and takes from him, in return, his gourd rattle and the remainder of his corn-meal. Then the chief sprinkles a corn-meal 'path' to the southeast, for the katçina; the

---

[1] On the arrival of the Soya'l katçina, see Dorsey and Voth (1901), p. 14: Parsons (1936), p. 3, n. 5: Earle and Kennard (1938), pp. 15–16: Titiev (1944), p. 110.

latter sets out along the 'path' to the end of the street, then turns west and disappears over the lip of the mesa, making for a shrine where he deposits the prayer-offerings presented to him by *kik'moñwi*.

The visit of the Soya'l katçina to *moñ* kiva marks the first stage in the ceremonial 'opening' of the kivas. Twenty-four days later, on the afternoon of the last day of the Soya'l, the second stage is performed by the Qöqöqlom katçinas, a dance group of about twenty (ordinary) katçinas, accompanied by eight or ten *katçin-mana*(s), katçina maidens. While the Soya'l katçina is impersonated by a man of Bear clan, the sponsorship of the Qöqöqlom rotates annually with that of the Nima'n: whichever group is to put on the Nima'n in July, is responsible for the Qöqöqlom the preceding December. This gives unity to the katçina cycle, since it means that the same kiva has charge both of the first, and of the last, dance of the season.

The katçinas assemble[1] at Qowawaima, a shrine to the southeast of the village where all katçina dances begin. They put on their masks and walk in single file towards the village, the katçinas carrying various kinds of Hopi foods to distribute to the children, and the *katçin-mana*(s), woven trays containing corn meal, prayer feathers and seeds of all kinds. On the outskirts of the pueblo they are met by Powa'mu chief, the head of Badger clan (or his deputy), who (at Oraibi) has the care of the first half of the katçina cycle and who is to act as 'father' of the katçinas on this occasion. He leads them through the village, sprinkling a 'path' of corn-meal ahead of them, to each kiva in turn, so that in the course of the afternoon the katçinas visit all the kivas in the pueblo. At each kiva, two of their number detach themselves from the main body and go through the ceremony of 'opening the kiva'; first, they sprinkle corn meal down the kiva hatch, then they make four corn-meal 'paths' leading from the hatch in each of the four cardinal directions, while the other katçinas and the *katçin-mana*(s), ranged in two lines, carry out their dance under the supervision of Powa'mu chief. When the last kiva, Marau kiva, has been formally 'opened', the katçinas make their way back to Qowawaima, where they deposit the prayer-offerings which they have collected during their round of the kivas.

The Qöqöqlom ceremony represents the formal opening of the katçina season. From now on, until the Homegoing Dance late in July, the katçinas are supposed to reside in the neighbourhood of the pueblo and to visit it when they wish. Immediately after the conclusion of the Soya'l, each kiva begins to prepare for the series of night dances[2] which mark the first moon of the new year, *Pa'mü'iya*. On each occasion, every kiva in the village presents its own katçina dance, and in the course of the night its group of dancers make the round of all the other kivas in the pueblo, performing twice in each in the presence of the assembled spectators. As there are usually three or four such night dances, and

[1] For a description of the Qöqöqlom katçinas, see Dorsey and Voth (1901), p. 58: Earle and Kennard (1938), p. 16: Titiev (1944), pp. 111, 214–15.

[2] A vivid description of the night dances is given by Kennard: see Earle and Kennard (1938), pp. 16–18, and Titiev (1944), pp. 112–14.

each one takes several days to rehearse, the whole month is one of great ceremonial activity.

The first half of the katçina cycle concludes with the great ceremony known as Powa'mu. Ritually speaking, Powa'mu occupies the February moon, *Powa' mü'iya*, which takes its name from the ceremony. It is under the direction of the Powa'mu fraternity, the ceremony (*wi'mi*) being 'owned' by Badger clan; unless he is incapacitated by age or infirmity, the head of Badger clan acts as Powa'mu chief and has charge of the *ti'poni* belonging to the rite. Both the Powa'mu proper, and its introductory ceremony (*pa'ho la'lauwu*), take place in Powa'mu kiva owned by Badger clan; in carrying out the ritual, Badger clan chief is assisted by six or eight other members of the Powa'mu fraternity, and by the head of the Katçina fraternity. At root, the Powa'mu is a preparation of the forthcoming agricultural season; it begins with the sowing of bean seeds in boxes in the kivas, and concludes with a dance at which the freshly-harvested 'crops' are exhibited to the rest of the pueblo; in the course of the intervening rites, new members are initiated into the two orders, the Powa'mu fraternity and the Katçina, which share control of the katçina cult.

As soon as the February moon is sighted by Powa'mu chief,[1] he calls together the officers of the Powa'mu fraternity for the preliminary rite of *pa'ho la'lauwu*, or 'prayer-stick making'. At sunrise on the day chosen, the officers—Powa'mu chief, Katçina chief, and six or eight members of the order—assemble in Powa'mu kiva. They bring with them the feathers, sticks and various herbs needed for making prayer-sticks, together with some honey and a small bag of corn-meal each. After smoking together, Powa'mu chief and Katçina chief retire to the northwest corner of the kiva, to make the necessary number of *pa'ho*(s); they have to make enough to distribute one to each of the kivas that are to take part in the bean-planting, plus one for each of the four cardinal directions. Each *pa'ho* consists of two sticks, about $4\frac{1}{2}$ inches long, notched at the upper end and bound together with twine; one of the sticks is painted blue-green, and the other black. To the back of each pair is tied a small corn-husk packet, containing some corn-meal mixed with honey, a turkey feather, a small feather of a *tokotska* or cowbird, a spring of *kü'ñya* (mountain sage), and a sprig of *ma'övi* (snakeweed).

While the two leaders are making the *pa'ho*(s), other members are busy preparing the sand mosaic for the rite at which the *pa'ho*(s) will be consecrated. First, the coloured sands to be used in the mosaic are ground and pulverised, and set ready in five shallow trays: white (a white sandstone), yellow (an ochre), blue-green (a pale green clay), red (a deep red sandstone), and black (a black ferruginous sandstone). Then, sitting in a circle on the kiva floor, a number of the men together construct the sand mosaic shown in Figure 34,

[1] The following account of the Powa'mu, and of the prayer-stick making which precedes it, is based on the description by Voth (1901, pp. 73–158), supplemented by accounts by Kennard (Earle and Kennard, 1938, pp. 18–27) and by Titiev (1944, pp. 114–20). For the Powa'mu on 1st Mesa, see Parsons (1936), pp. 155–8, and Stephen (1936), pp. 159–257.

allowing the dry sand of different colours to run through their fingers on to the floor, so as to complete the design in the correct shades. Around the sand mosaic they arrange the various accessories, to complete the 'altar' shown in Figure 35.

Fig. 34. *Powa'lauwu Sand Mosaic*. Re-drawn from Voth (1901), pl. xlii. *a*. sun symbol, with blue-green face, on sand field. The four white lines with branch-like projections, and the twelve red lines emanating from the sun symbol, represent eagle feathers and bunches of red horsehair, both of which symbolise the rays of the sun; *b*. four circles— yellow, blue-green, red, white: representing the 'house' of the sun; *c*. 'blossoms' of the sun 'house': one in each of the four cardinal directions; *d*. sand field. For colour chart, see Figure 40, p. 78

Of these accessories the most prominent are the four clay stands, or *pa'ho* 'fields', placed around the sand mosaic one in each of the four cardinal directions.

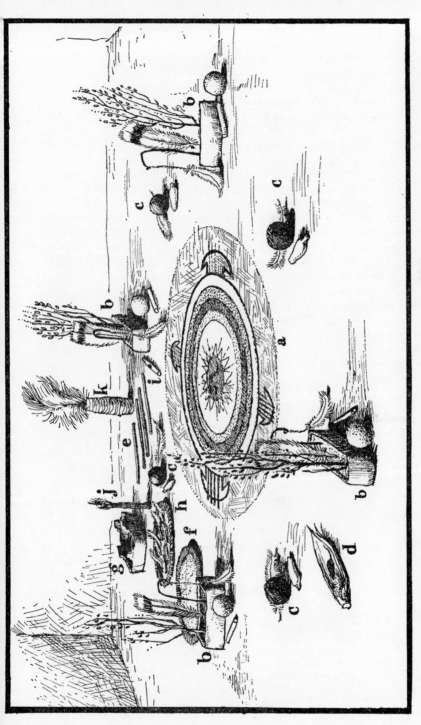

Fig. 35. *Powa'lawwu Altar. a.* sand mosaic; *b.* four clay stands, one at each of the four cardinal directions: in each stand is inserted a crook about 6″ long, to which a turkey feather is attached, a prayer stick, an eagle feather, and the sprig of one of four common herbs; *c.* four clay balls, painted black, with an eagle feather and a stone spear head; *d.* a corn husk, with some corn meal and a dead mouse; *e.* four reed tubes; *f.* a woven tray, with corn meal; *g.* medicine-water bowl; *h.* woven tray, with the prayer sticks to be distributed on the morrow; *i.* a bone whistle; *j. na'atsi,* emblem of the Powa'mu fraternity, consisting of four sticks about 18″ long with feathers attached. *k. ti'poni,* consisting of a corn cob wound around with white cotton, with feathers at the top. Re-drawn from Voth (1901), pl. xliii.

In these, [writes Voth[1]], are inserted at one end a small *ngölösh–hoya* (crook), to which a turkey feather is fastened. The crook is . . . the symbol of life in its various stages. Next to this stands one of the four *pa'ho*(s), . . . representing corn, the main subsistence of the Hopi. These double *pa'ho*(s) are sometimes called '*kaö*' (corn ears); and then [carry] a sprig of an herb to which four *qöqöpi*, chat (*Icteria virens*), feathers are tied. Sometimes *sikya'tsi* (fly-catcher) feathers are used instead. The herbs differ in the four stands. The one on the north side is a *siva'pi* [*Chrysothamnus*, or rabbit-brush]; the one on the west a *hovak'pi* [*Artemisia filifolia*, sand sage], on the south a *hö'novi* [*Cowania mexicana*, cliff rose], and on the east a *masi siva'pi* [another species of *Chrysothamnus*]. These four herbs, and especially the two varieties of *siva'pi*, are used in making the wind-breaks in the fields,[2] and their use here signifies a prayer or wish for protection of the plants and corn against the destructive sand storms for which these wind-breaks are made. Next to the herb is inserted an eagle feather, to which four *sikya'tsi* (fly-catcher) feathers are tied as a prayer for warm weather when the birds come. As the Hopi use the term *sikya'tsi* rather promiscuously for different small birds with yellow and greenish feathers, such as the flycatchers and certain kinds of warblers, it is very probable that feathers of any of these birds are used on this eagle feather. The last object inserted in this *pa'ho* stand is a short stick called *ta'ka pa'ho* (man *pa'ho*), pointed at both ends and made of the stem of *tu'mi* [*Cleome serrulata*, beeweed]. This stick is colored yellow in the stand on the north side, green on the west, red on the south and white on the east stand. To this stick is fastened a *yahpa* [mockingbird] feather. This *pa'ho* . . . is said to represent a *kaletaka* (warrior) standing at the end of the *pa'ho* stand, keeping watch over and protecting the various objects on the *pa'ho* stand.

Beside each clay-stand lie a single reed tube coloured yellow, containing corn pollen and a few small *tawamana* (oriole) feathers, and a dough ball, made from various sorts of Hopi meal; the dough balls, when deposited outside the village in the course of the ceremony, are said to serve as 'food' for the Clouds. Behind the sand mosaic, near the *ti'poni* of Powa'mu chief, lie four black reed tubes, each containing a small quantity of specular iron and a few small *tçoro* (bluebird) feathers.

About noon, the sand mosaic and altar are ready, and the participants arrange themselves around it. Tobacco chief lights a pipe at the fire and hands it to Powa'mu chief; all smoke silently together, handing the pipe from one to another in turn. Powa'mu chief utters a short prayer, and then, with all the men still seated on the floor around the 'altar', twelve songs are chanted in steady

---

[1] Voth (1901), pp. 76–7; certain of the items mentioned by Voth have been omitted from the drawing of the Powa'lauwu altar, for the sake of clarity. Also, Voth's cardinal points should read northwest, southwest, southeast and northeast.

[2] Voth is likely to be right on this point; other observers, however, report that grease-wood was the shrub chiefly used in the old days for windbreaks. Harry Masai'yamtiwa, with whom I farmed in the spring of 1966, told me that he made windbreaks of juniper, *siva'pi*, or *hö'novi*: not of greasewood, which (he said) was nasty to handle. In practice, the choice of shrubs may have depended on the locality of the fields: greasewood being used for fields on the alluvial flats, rabbit-brush and sand sage for those on the fans of tributary watercourses and on sand dunes, cliff rose and juniper for those sited near the mesa top.

succession. The first six are fairly straighforward, being addressed to the Cloud Deities in the six cardinal directions with a request for rain. In the course of the seventh, which treats of different kinds of seeds, Powa'mu chief takes corn-meal from the woven tray and sprinkles it, a little at a time, over the sand mosaic. In the course of the eighth, which treats of various herbs and of the wild foods used by the Hopi, he picks up the aspergill, stirs the contents of the medicine bowl, and then sprinkles the liquid, again a little at a time, over the sand mosaic. During the ninth song, Powa'mu chief's deputy picks up the bone whistle from the altar; he then takes the yellow reed tube from beside the clay stand on the northwest side of the mosaic, climbs halfway up the kiva ladder, and blows the corn pollen and the oriole feathers through the hatch to the northwest, following it with a few short notes on the whistle; he repeats the gesture with the yellow reed tubes in each of the other three cardinal directions. During the tenth song, the deputy goes through the same movements with the four black reed tubes, blowing the specular iron and the bluebird feathers in each of the cardinal directions.[1] He then takes the stone spear-head from each of the four directions in turn, puts some honey on it, climbs halfway up the ladder, licks the honey off the stone and then ejects it, first to the northwest, then to the southwest, then to the southeast, and then to the northeast.

In the course of the eleventh song, a messenger is despatched with the four clay balls, and the four *nakwa'kwosi*(s) lying beside them, to deposit them at four places on the trail leading to the village from the southwest. In the course of the twelfth song, four messengers each take a pinch of corn-meal from the woven tray beside the altar, then each gathers up the clay stand, the dough ball and the reed tube from one of the four cardinal directions, ascends the ladder in turn, and departs in his own direction. A few hundred yards from the village, the messenger halts, holds the corn-meal to his mouth, whispers a short prayer over it, sprinkles the meal in a line, places the clay-stand at the end pointing towards the village and the dough ball and reed tube at the end pointing away from the village, then makes his way back to the kiva. On their return, Tobacco chief relights the pipe and hands it to Powa'mu chief. All smoke in turn, exchanging terms of relationship as they pass the pipe from one to another. Powa'mu chief then picks up the tray with the *pa'ho*(s) on it, sprinkles a pinch of corn-meal over the *pa'ho*(s), holds the tray in front of him and prays over it. He hands the tray to Katçina chief; he does the same, then hands it back to Powa'mu chief, who places it on the banquette on the north side of the kiva. This completes the consecration of the *pa'ho*(s). The Powa'mu *ti'poni* is stored away, the sand mosaic swept into a blanket and carried outside, and food is brought into the kiva; for it is now late in the afternoon, and all eat together there before returning to their own homes.

At daybreak the next morning, Powa'mu chief begins a round of all the kivas in the village, taking with him the tray of *pa'ho*(s) consecrated the previous

---

[1] The yellow and blue feathers are blown through the hatchway as a wish or prayer for warm weather when the summer birds come: Voth (1901), p. 78, n. *.

afternoon.[1] At each kiva he smokes with the kiva head, only breaking the silence to exchange terms of relationship with him as they pass the pipe from one to the other. When the smoke is finished, he presents the kiva head with one of the *pa'ho*(s) and tells him that he may now start planting beans. As soon as Powa'mu chief has departed, the kiva head selects a few sturdy young men to go and fetch soil for the planting. The young men take with them the *pa'ho* left by Powa'mu chief; before beginning to dig, they partially bury it in the soil. They then sprinkle corn-meal over the ground and, loading their blankets with soil, carry it unobtrusively back to the kiva.

Within the kiva, each man fills a box with earth, plants from 50 to 100 seeds just under the surface, and waters his plot. From now until the culmination of the Powa'mu ceremony, a blazing fire is kept going day and night in each kiva, and in their spare moments all the members congregate to look after their 'crops'. The beans are said to be grown 'for' Eototo, the *wuya* of Bear clan, and Aholi, the *wuya* of Pikyas clan. Eototo is the spiritual counterpart of the Village chief, who is leader of the Soya'l, and Aholi of Pikyas chief, who assists Bear clan leader in its performance; both these two leaders, i.e. Village chief and Pikyas chief, also plant 'crops' of corn to be sprouted at the same time as the beans, as does Powa'mu chief himself.

While the plants are maturing, they are carefully tended and watered. Everyone is eager to have a good yield, not only as an indication of a successful farming season to come, but because a good crop is a sign that a person has a 'good' heart. Each night until the commencement of the Powa'mu proper, the kiva groups meet to practise their Bean Dance songs, and from time to time they hold informal (and unmasked) katçina dances, in order 'to help the beans grow'.[2]

At sunrise on the first day of Powa'mu, eight days after the *pa'ho la'lauwu*, Powa'mu chief and Katçina chief foregather in Powa'mu kiva, the former bringing with him the Powa'mu *na'atsi*, six ceremonial corn ears, some corn-meal, and a box containing feathers and other items needed for making *pa'ho*(s). The *na'atsi*, consisting of four sticks about 18 inches long, to each of which are attached four *nakwa'kwosi*(s) along the stem and an eagle feather at the tip, is set up at the hatch and sprinkled with corn-meal. This signifies that the ceremony is now in progress and that no one, other than those taking part, may enter the kiva. From now until four days after the ceremony ends, both leaders abstain from food containing salt or meat, and from sexual intercourse.

During the first four days of the ceremony, very little happens in the kiva. Each morning the *na'atsi* is erected outside the kiva hatch, and in the course of the day the two leaders meet there at intervals and smoke silently together.

---

[1] On this occasion he is said to represent the *tokotska*, whose feathers are on the *pa'ho*(s). When later this bird actually appears, the Hopi say: 'The *tokotska* has come, it is time to plant', and at once they begin to plant the earlier varieties of corn: Voth (1901), p. 83, n. ★.

The cowbird (*tokotska*) arrives in Hopi country, along with other north-bound migrants such as Red-winged and Yellow-headed Blackbirds, late in April or early in May.

[2] Titiev (1944), p. 115.

From time to time other members of the fraternity join them. In the other kivas the members are busy tending their bean 'crops', which are now several inches high, and preparing for the dance on the last night of Powa'mu.

The first half of Powa'mu culminates, on the fifth day (*na'lüshta'la*), in the initiation of novices into the Powa'mu fraternity. At sunrise, the *na'atsi* is put

Fig. 36. *Powa'mu Sand Mosaic. a.* The large round figure in the centre, as well as the four smaller ones in the four corners, represent squash 'blossoms'. They are set on a sand field; the vari-coloured dots, spread over the whole field, represent blossoms of herbs and grasses. *b.* The square, made of four wide stripes, represents a 'house': each side is called a *wona*, 'plank'. *c.* Each 'plank' is capped, at either end, with a cloud symbol: on each cloud symbol stand three turkey-feather *nakwa'kwosi*(s). Re-drawn from Voth (1901), pl. xlvii.

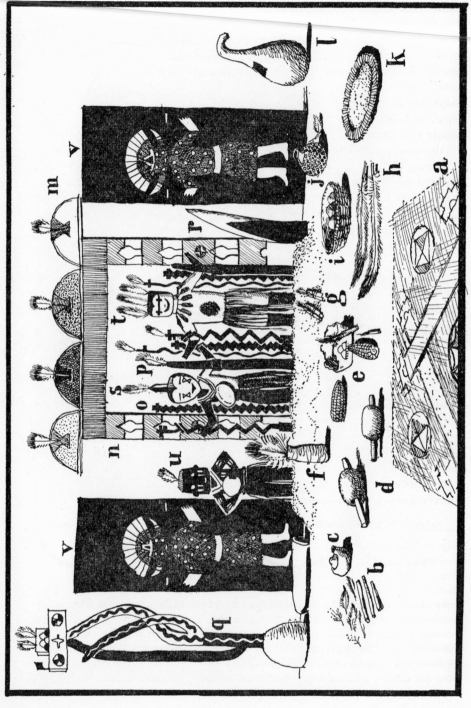

Fig. 37

up as usual outside Powa'mu kiva, but on this day not only the two leaders, but the other officers as well, foregather there. The greater part of the day is devoted to preparing and constructing the two 'altars', required for the initiation of children into the order that evening. Early in the morning, Powa'mu chief makes four *pa'ho*(s) to be placed in the sand ridge. In the meantime, a man of Sand clan has been sent down to the valley, to fetch sand for the sand ridge. He takes with him some corn-meal and two *nakwa'kwosi*(s); on arriving at the sand dune, he holds the *nakwa'kwosi*(s) and corn-meal to his lips, whispers a silent prayer over them, sprinkles the corn-meal and deposits the two breath-feathers on the dune, then fills his blanket with sand and makes his way back to the kiva.

During his absence the two leaders, assisted by the other officers, have constructed the sand mosaic shown in Figure 36. On his return, they use the sand he has brought to build up the sand ridge behind the mosaic, then set the feet of the wooden frame in the sand, arrange the painted slats on the frame, and place the other objects on either side and in front of the sand ridge, as shown in Figure 37. While they are doing this, other members of the fraternity are preparing the mask to be worn in the evening by the man who is to impersonate Tçowilawu, *wuya* of Badger clan, together with a peculiar object called the *po'ta*, to be used by him in his dance. This consists of a number of round discs, made of a kind of stiff canvas and sewn together in such a way that they can be opened and closed like a book; each 'page' carries representations of clouds, corn, sacred animals, etc., so that, as the 'pages' are turned, the spectator sees a succession of these images. Still other members of the order are busy making *nakwa'kwosi*(s), to be tied to the hair of the novices during the rites that evening.

About 3 o'clock in the afternoon, Powa'mu chief begins erecting the small altar shown in Figure 38, in the southwest corner of the deep part of the kiva, just west of the foot of the ladder. While this altar is being built and the main altar finished, the man who is to act as Tçowilawu katçina starts to get ready. Retiring to the southeast corner of the kiva, he daubs his body with white kaolin, all except for the forearms, front of his legs, upper lip, forehead, and two spots one on the back and one on the chest, which are painted black. He then puts on a new white breech cloth, a kilt made of red horsehair, and an old green

---

Fig. 37. *Powa'mu Altar and Sand Mosaic. Foreground: a.* sand mosaic. *Mid-ground: b.* pa'ho-making outfit, i.e. sticks and feathers; *c.* clay honey-pot; *d.* two gourd rattles; *e.* medicine-water bowl, with aspergill; *f.* ti'poni, of Powa'mu fraternity; *g.* pa'ho(s); *h.* eagle feathers; *i.* woven tray, containing lumps of dough; *j.* netted gourd water-vessel, with nakwa'kwosi; *k.* woven tray, containing corn meal; *l.* gourd vessel. *Background: m.* cloud symbols, representing the four cardinal directions; *n.* wooden frame, with blossoms and corn-ear symbols; *o.* plaque representing lightning; *p.* plaque representing corn ear, with nakwa'kwosi; *q.* cloud and lightning frame; *r.* clay stand, said to represent a bluff; *s.* figure of thunder deity; *t.* figure of Tçowilawu, wuya of Badger clan; *u.* figure of one of the two war deities; *v.* figures of the two Hu katcinas. Re-drawn from Voth (1901), pl. xxxviii.

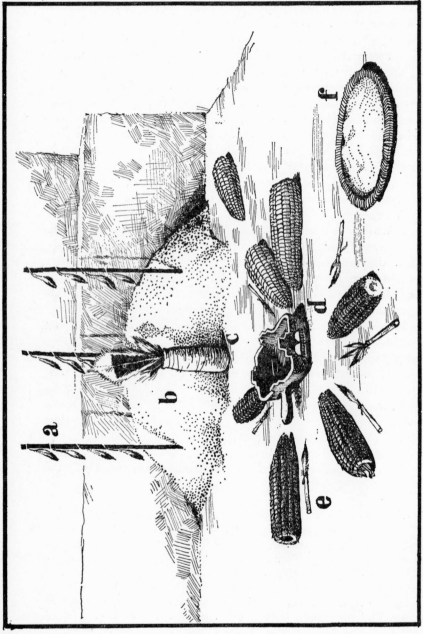

Fig. 38. *Powa'mu Small Altar. a,* three sticks, with *nakwa'kwosi(s)* attached; *b,* sand ridge; *c, ti'poni* of the Powa'mu fraternity: the *ti'poni* of the Powa'mu fraternity is temporarily borrowed from the main altar; *d,* medicine–water bowl, with cloud symbol; *e,* six ears of corn with their 'husbands', six old aspergills; *f,* woven tray, containing corn meal. Re-drawn from Voth (1901), pl. xlix.

leather belt from which is suspended, at the back, a grayish fox skin. When he is ready, he takes his mask under a blanket, and leaves the kiva.

While these preparations are going on, a number of women, also members of the Powa'mu fraternity, enter the kiva, each one carrying a small tray of corn meal. Soon after, by now late in the afternoon, the novices (*ke-kel'hoyamu*) begin to arrive, each accompanied by his ceremonial 'father'.[1] They are mostly aged from 6 to 10 years;[2] and in the years when Voth observed the ceremony, there were at Oraibi some thirty to forty novices at any one time.[3] As they enter, each novice is led by his 'father' first to the small altar, towards which each in turn casts a pinch of corn-meal, then to the large altar, towards which they do the same, and then to the banquette on the east side of the kiva, where the novices are seated in a row, their knees drawn up to their chins in the posture required of novices at all Hopi ceremonies.

At about 6 o'clock in the evening, when all are assembled, the officers of the fraternity arrange themselves around the small altar. They smoke together and then, after Powa'mu chief has uttered a short prayer, they begin chanting. The first song is directed to the Clouds at the six directions, and is clearly a prayer for rain. The second is directed to the birds associated with the six directions, the third to the coloured corn ears, and the fourth to the coloured stones, at the six directions. Each song follows the same pattern: an appeal, in the first stanza, to the deity of the direction in question (yellow, N.W.) to come to the Hopi land bringing the benefit desired (rain, full corn-ears, health), followed by a similar appeal to the deities in each of the other five directions. Each song is thus composed of six stanzas, identical except for the substitution of one colour, corn ear, bird's name, for another.

The fifth song is addressed, again, to the birds at the six directions; and, in the course of it, each novice has a small eagle feather *nakwa'kwosi* attached to his hair. The sixth is obscure. The seventh appears to be a response, on the part of the Cloud chiefs, to the prayers contained in the first six. At least, it turns on the word *yo'na*, 'to owe something, be indebted to';[4] and the meaning appears to be: 'we are indebted to the Powa'mu leaders, because they have made prayer-offerings for us, so let us go and bring them rain'.

At the conclusion of the seventh song, there is a short recess, during which the Powa'mu officers smoke together round the small altar. Powa'mu chief then dons his ceremonial kilt and sash, takes the medicine bowl and aspergill, and stands near the small altar. Next to him stands his deputy, also of Badger clan, holding a pinch of corn meal: then two old women, one of Badger and the other of Katçina clan, each holding the *ti'poni* associated with her clan: then two or three younger women, dressed in their white ceremonial blankets (*atö'e*)

---

[1] Parsons (1936, p. 199, n. 1) observes that a boy has the same 'father' as he will later have for his Wü'wütçim initiation.

[2] Earle and Kennard (1938), p. 19.

[3] Voth (1901), p. 90: thirty-nine in 1895, thirty in 1897, twenty-seven in 1901. Powa'mu initiation normally took place every third or fourth year.

[4] Voth (1901), p. 135.

and each holding a tray of corn meal. Katçina chief, who has also put on his ceremonial kilt and sash, now prepares to leave the kiva. Taking in his hands a tray with corn meal in it, and some *nakwa'kwosi*(s), he faces the northeast (the direction of Kisiwu) and calls out, first in a soft voice and then louder, summoning the *wuya* of Badger clan (who lives there) to come to the kiva. He then rushes up the ladder, followed by all the male members of the fraternity except Powa'mu chief. After a few minutes Katçina chief returns to the kiva, closely followed by the men in a body, and a moment later by Tçowilawu katçina, masked, with his kilt and sash on, and carrying in his hand the *po'ta* on which the symbols of rain, clouds, corn and lightning are painted.

The katçina goes to the north (N.W.) side of the sand mosaic. He begins a curious jumping dance, making his way round the mosaic in an anti-clockwise direction; four times he circles the mosaic in this fashion, constantly waving the *po'ta* in such a way that its leaves open and close at different places, exposing the painted images to the gaze of the audience (including the novices on their bench). During the dance Powa'mu chief, and the women with him, sprinkle the katçina with water and with corn meal, while the rest of the members keep up a continuous shouting. At its conclusion, both Powa'mu chief and Katçina chief hand the katçina a *pa'ho* and some corn-meal. Then Tçowilawu, accompanied by Katçina chief and followed by the same body of men as before, leaves the kiva and makes his way to the shrine on the N.E. side of the village from which he was fetched. There he deposits the prayer-offerings, and Katçina chief and the other men return to the kiva.

On his return to the kiva, Katçina chief takes off his ceremonial kilt and places his *ti'poni* beside the main altar. He then sweeps up the sand mosaic into a blanket, takes it out of the kiva and deposits the sand a few yards south of the kiva hatch. While he is doing this, Powa'mu chief dismantles the small altar, moving the paraphernalia to the large altar. He then addresses the novices, warning them that they must not reveal to anyone, not even to their own fathers and mothers, what they have seen and heard in the kiva; and, in particular, that they are not to speak of the Tçowilawu katçina under any form. By now it is about 8 o'clock in the evening; the novices are taken home by their 'fathers', while those taking part in the ceremony smoke together, have a meal and retire to sleep in the kiva.

At this point we may break our narrative of the Powa'mu ceremony, to inquire into the significance of initiation into the order.[1] The katçina cult is shared between two fraternities, the Powa'mu and the Katçina. Of the two, the Powa'mu fraternity is the senior, and (impliedly) the smaller; it has control of the first half of the katçina cycle, culminating in the Powa'mu ceremony. Initiation into the fraternity gives members the right to act as 'fathers' of the katçinas: that is, to lead the dancers on to the village square, prompt them in their songs and, above all, to sprinkle them with corn-meal and give them prayer-offerings to deposit at their shrines. A person, therefore,

[1] Voth (1901), pp. 93–4: cf. Earle and Kennard (1938), p. 18, and Titiev (1944), p. 116.

who wishes to sponsor a katçina dance, has to find a member of the fraternity to act as 'father' on his behalf, since he himself will be in the kiva concentrating his thoughts on the desired outcome of the ceremony.

Initiation into the Powa'mu fraternity takes place every third or fourth year, in the ritual we have just described. For four ensuing days, the novices must abstain from salt and meat; at sunrise on the ninth day of Powa'mu, their initiation is completed, when their hair is washed and they are given new names by the sister(s) of their ceremonial 'fathers'.

Fig. 39. *Katçina Initiation Sand Mosaic* (large). The two black figures represent the Hu Katçinas, who flog the children; the objects in their hands are yucca whips, and on their heads, eagle-tail feathers. The centre figure represents Hahai'i katçina, dressed in an embroidered *toi'hi*. The vari-coloured spots on the sand field represent blossoms of herbs and grasses. Re-drawn from Voth (1901), pl. lii.

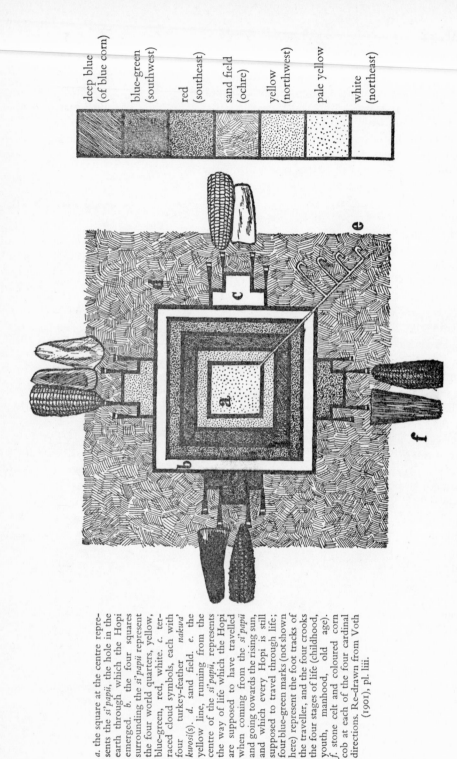

deep blue (of blue corn)

blue-green (southwest)

red (southeast)

sand field (ochre)

yellow (northwest)

pale yellow

white (northeast)

Fig. 40. *Katçina Initiation Sand Mosaic* (small).

*a.* the square at the centre represents the *si'papü*, the hole in the earth through which the Hopi emerged. *b.* the four squares surrounding the *si'papü* represent the four world quarters, yellow, blue-green, red, white. *c.* terraced cloud symbols, each with four turkey-feather *nakwa' kwosi(s)*. *d.* sand field. *e.* the yellow line, running from the centre of the *si'papü*, represents the way of life which the Hopi are supposed to have travelled when coming from the *si'papü* and going towards the rising sun, and which every Hopi is still supposed to travel through life; four blue-green marks (not shown here) represent the foot tracks of the traveller, and the four crooks the four stages of life (childhood, youth, manhood, old age). *f.* stone celt and coloured corn cob at each of the four cardinal directions. Re-drawn from Voth (1901), pl. liii.

In those years in which new members have been taken into the Powa'mu fraternity on the fifth day, the sixth is devoted to the initiation of all the remaining children (girls as well as boys) of the right age into the Katçina fraternity. This ceremony takes place, at Oraibi, in Marau kiva.[1] The essential features of the Katçina initiation are: the appearance of Powa'mu chief, in the rôle of Mü'yiñwa, followed by the whipping of the novices by two disciplinary katçinas, known as the Hu katçinas.

Early in the morning the *na'atsi* is put up, as usual, outside Powa'mu kiva, and a few minutes later Powa'mu chief erects a further *na'atsi* outside Marau kiva. At about 10 o'clock in the morning, several men from Powa'mu kiva begin to make the sand mosaic shown in Figure 39, on the floor in Marau kiva to the north of the fireplace. They first sift a layer of sand on the floor, $\frac{3}{4}$ to 1 inch thick, and then cover it with a layer of light-brown ochre. On this field they reproduce, in the appropriate colours, three figures, the one in the centre representing the Hahai'i katçina and the ones on either side the two Hu katçinas; the latter hold in their hands the bunches of yucca switches with which the (real) katçinas will whip the children in the course of the ceremony.[2]

Early in the afternoon, Powa'mu chief comes to Marau kiva and makes the smaller sand mosaic, shown in Figure 40, at the southeast corner of the larger one already made. This mosaic represents the *si'papü*, the hole through which people first emerged on earth, and the four crooks leading from the *si'papü* to the southeast, the four stages of life through which people (i.e. the Hopi, or perhaps, more specifically, the novices) must pass on their journey through life. On the four sides of the mosaic, he arranges the coloured corn ears, and the stone celts, shown in the figure. Meanwhile, in Powa'mu kiva, the three members of the fraternity who are to impersonate Hahai'i katçina, and the two Hu katçinas, assume the costume shown in the sand mosaic: in the case of Hahai'i katçina, a large embroidered robe (*toi'hi*), with knotted belt and moccasins, and green mask, and in the case of the two Hu katçinas, a kilt of dyed red horsehair, the body painted black all over with large white dots of kaolin, and black mask surmounted by two horns and a fringe of eagle feathers. When they are ready, the three katçinas leave the kiva, each carrying his mask under a blanket, and retire to a secluded spot outside the village to await their part in the ceremony.

Powa'mu chief, meanwhile, returns to Powa'mu kiva. He prepares a crook, about 3 feet long, to the upper end of which he fastens a cotton string and to the

---

[1] Voth (1901), p. 94. Titiev (1944, p. 116, n. 39) states that Hawi'ovi kiva was used for this purpose; Kennard (Earle and Kennard, 1938, p. 20), simply that it was a different kiva to the one used for the main Powa'mu rites. Seeing that the rite is owned by Katçina clan, one would have expected it to take place in the kiva owned by their phratry, namely *Tao.*

[2] On first Mesa, the Powa'mu novices are also whipped in the course of *their* initiation (Stephen, 1936, pp. 200–3); but this is not recorded in Voth's description of the ceremony at Oraibi, and Titiev (1944, p. 116, n. 42) says definitely that Powa'mu candidates are not whipped on 3rd Mesa.

lower end an eagle breath-feather; about midway along, he ties a corn ear and eight corn-husk packets, each containing corn-meal and honey; from each packet hangs a *nakwa'kwosi*. At the same time, Katçina chief and his deputy prepare three *pa'ho*(s), to be given to the three katçinas after the ceremony; and then put on their ceremonial costumes, the usual katçina sash and kilt, together with numerous strands of beads around the neck. Powa'mu chief sends one of the younger men, with a netted gourd vessel (*moñ'wikuru*) to fetch water from the spring; then prepares himself for the ceremony. Down the front of both legs and along both arms, from thumb to shoulder and down to the nipple, he makes a line of white dots; and under each eye, a white mark. Then he dons the white ceremonial blanket (*o'ba*), which—with the body markings, and the objects which he will carry—identify him to the initiated as Mü'yiñwa, the germination deity.

While these preparations have been going on in Powa'mu kiva, the preparations in Marau kiva have also been completed, and late in the afternoon the principal Village officers make their way to the kiva: *ki'k mon'wi*, the Village chief, followed by Crier chief, both carrying their chief's staffs (*moñ'kohü*), and later by War chief. All three take up position close to the wall to the west of the fireplace. Soon after their arrival, the novices begin to enter the kiva, each one accompanied by his ceremonial 'father'. As they enter the kiva, both 'father' and novice sprinkle corn-meal first on the *na'atsi* and then on the small sand mosaic. Next, each novice (*ke'le-hoya*, 'little sparrow-hawk') steps inside a ring, made of four lengths of yucca leaf tied together to form a wheel (with a hawk feather tied at each of the four knots) and held by two members of the Powa'mu fraternity; when the novice is standing inside the ring, the two men raise and lower it four times, at the same time praying that he may grow up and live to a happy old age. The novice is then led to one of the banquettes by his 'father', and seated there with his legs drawn up to his chin.

When all the novices have been brought in, Katçina chief and his deputy come over from Powa'mu kiva: the one carrying the Powa'mu *na'atsi* and a woven tray containing some corn-meal and one *pa'ho*, the other a tray containing corn-meal and the other two *pa'ho*(s) made earlier in the afternoon. Both take up position between the ladder and the fireplace. Village chief now lights a pipe and smokes silently with Crier chief and War chief. While they are smoking, Powa'mu chief enters the kiva, dressed in the simple white *o'ba*; in his left hand, he holds the *moñ'wikuru*, four corn ears, and a wooden implement (*wona'wikya*) used in the old days for hoeing, and in his right, the crook to which the eight corn-husk packets are attached.[1] He is Mü'yiñwa, and is supposed to have arrived by a long route from his home in the Below. He takes a stand to the east of the ladder. Deep silence prevails throughout the kiva. Presently one of the older men, addressing Mü'yiñwa, asks:

---

[1] For a drawing of Powa'mu chief, representing Mü'yiñwa, descending into Marau' kiva, see Voth (1901), pl. lvii.

'Well, now, and where have you come from?'

*Mü'yiñwa*: 'From yonder, below, from Tü'wa-na'savi[1] have I come.'

'Well, all right, but for what purpose do you wander around? tell us that.'

*Mü'yiñwa* (in a doleful, monotonous voice): 'Yes, all right. Those, there, at Tü'wa-na'savi, were all assembled, making a ladder. They set up the ladder, with strands of turquoise it was tied together. That was the way we came up and out [referring to the Emergence on earth].

Eastward we travelled . . .'

Then follows a long account[2] of their travels, of the katçinas they met on the way and of the crops and vegetables they (the katçinas) gave them, and of how, eventually, they reached Oraibi and settled there: ending with an exhortation to the three chiefs to see that the ceremonies are carried out and the children initiated, and to lead the people on a good 'road':

'. . . then may you fall asleep as old women and as old men.'[3]

As soon as Mü'yiñwa has finished his speech, he makes his way over to the novices, and sprinkles the head of each with a little water from his *moñ'wikuru*. Then he leaves the kiva and returns to Powa'mu kiva, where he takes off his costume, sits down near the fireplace and smokes.

Immediately Mü'yiñwa leaves Marau kiva, a member of the Powa'mu fraternity who has been keeping watch from a nearby rooftop signals to the three katçinas outside the village. Putting on their masks, they come running into the village, circle the kiva hatch four times, bang on the roof, then come tumbling down the ladder, to the accompaniment of much grunting and howling, rattling of bells and brandishing of whips. The novices are by now thoroughly scared,[4] as the katçinas take up their position on either side of the large sand mosaic. Suddenly one of the 'fathers' seizes his *ke'lhoya* and thrusts

[1] Tü'wa-na'savi, according to Voth (1901, p. 102, n. 1), is an imaginary place somewhere *atyaka*, 'down below', but is represented by a place about three miles south of Oraibi. Here the Badger clan is said to have lived for a time when coming from Kisiwu, before being admitted to the village.

In view of the fact that Mü'yiñwa is elsewhere referred to (Stephen, 1936, p. 592) as *Tü'wa At'kyamû moñ'wi*, 'Sand chief of the Below', the name itself is likely to mean 'the middle (*na'savi*) of the valley-sand (*tü'wa*).'

[2] For the full text of his recital, see Voth (1901), pp. 98–102. The events recounted run, *pari passu*, with what is represented graphically in the smaller of the two sand mosaics: i.e. the Emergence through the *si'papü*, visit to the four world quarters, and the following of a good 'road', marked by four stages.

[3] Not to 'die', but to 'fall asleep' of old age, is one of the fondest hopes of every Hopi: Voth (1901), p. 102, n. 10. The distinction is perhaps implied in the report (Stephen 1936, p. 140) of the death of Kü'yimana's elder sister in childbirth:

Kü'yi mana yükü'ka-adta   tih' talau'wu         mo'ki:

Kü'yimana her-elder-sister child-doing (bearing) died.

[4] Voth (1901, pp. 103–4) reports that, at this point, some of the children began to cry and scream; and that, during the whipping, some of the boys (who were naked) involuntarily passed water, and one or two even defaecated—'probably as a result of fear and pain'.

him forward on to the mosaic, where one of the two Hu katçinas whips the child, quite severely, across the back and buttocks, while the Hahai'i katçina looks on. As each child is flogged, another takes his place, until all have gone through the ordeal. Finally, the three katçinas whip each other thoroughly.

When the whipping is over, Katçina chief and his deputy hand one of their *pa'ho*(s) and some corn-meal to each of the three katçinas, who then leave the kiva. Outside, they circle the hatch four times as before, one of the Hu katçinas snatches the *na'atsi* from its stand, and then all three leave the pueblo on the trail leading to the north. Once outside the village they deposit the prayer-offerings at a shrine, disrobe behind a rock, and make their way back to Powa'mu kiva, carrying their masks and costume under a blanket. After the three katçinas have left the kiva, the three chiefs each speak a few words to the novices, charging them not to reveal anything of what they have seen and heard in the kiva. Katçina chief, his deputy and other members of the Powa'mu fraternity, then make their way back to Powa'mu kiva, while the rest—including the novices—return home.

Those who have undergone katçina initiation, completed—as in the case of Powa'mu initiation—by the washing of the hair of the novices and the bestowing on them of new names early on the last day of the Powa'mu ceremony, may now learn the katçina songs, be taught the traditions regarding the katçinas, and take part in katçina dances. But they may not act as 'fathers' of the katçinas: that privilege being reserved, as we have seen, for the members of the Powa'mu fraternity.

Resuming our narrative of the Powa'mu proper: the seventh and eighth days are taken up with further ritual in Powa'mu kiva, together with the fetching of spruce from Kisiwu and, on the afternoon of the eighth day, with the final dismantling of the main altar followed by the discharming ceremony. On both days, the *na'atsi* is set up at dawn outside the kiva hatch. Early on the seventh morning, after an initial rite in the kiva, a messenger is despatched to Kisiwu, the home of Tçowilawu katçina, to fetch the spruce required for the concluding dance in two days' time. He takes *pa'ho*(s) and *nakwa'kwosi*(s) to deposit at the spring, a netted gourd vessel to collect water in, and a bone whistle; he arrives at the spring that evening, blows on the bone whistle to announce his arrival to the spirits, fills the gourd vessel with water, collects the spruce and sets off home, getting back to the village early the next morning. On his way through the pueblo he stops at *moñ* kiva, where Bear chief and Pikyas chief are preparing the Eototo and Aholi katçina masks, and leaves some of the branches there; the remainder he takes to Powa'mu kiva.

On entering Powa'mu kiva, the messenger takes his stand to the east of the ladder, and Powa'mu chief receives from him the spruce, the netted gourd vessel containing the water from Kisiwu, and the bone whistle, placing them on the floor in front of the fireplace. He takes some ashes in his left hand, and from this a pinch between his right thumb and forefinger; standing before the messenger and humming a low tune, he circles his right hand several times over the messenger's head and then throws the ashes towards the hatch. He does this four times, taking a new pinch of ashes each time. Finally he gives the messenger a bowl of water containing an emetic, and all wait, in deep silence, until the young man is through vomiting.

Pipes are then lighted and all smoke together, Powa'mu chief smoking first and then handing the pipe to the messenger, exchanging terms of relationship with him as he does so. When they are through, Katçina chief sprinkles some corn-meal on the objects over which they have smoked, spits some honey over them, rubs some honey on the butts of the branches of spruce and some on the rim of the netted gourd vessel. The messenger is then called upon to recount his adventures on the journey to Kisiwu, and when he has finished, the objects are placed in front of the altar. After the messenger has told his story, the men return to their tasks. Powa'mu chief, in particular, is busy making prayer-offerings: a number of double *pa'ho*(s), one stick being green and the other black, for use the next morning, and a *püh'tabi* and eight *nakwa'kwosi*(s), to be taken to the spring that afternoon.

Early in the afternoon one of the kiva members is sent to the spring to the northeast of the village, to fetch water. He takes with him the *püh'tabi*, 'road', consisting of an eagle breath-feather attached to a long cotton thread: the eight *nakwa'kwosi*(s), made by Powa'mu chief during the morning: a netted gourd vessel, a bone whistle, and some corn meal. Arriving at the spring, he first blows the bone whistle four times. He then utters a short prayer, deposits four of the *nakwa'kwosi*(s) in a niche in the rock near the spring, sprinkles some corn-meal into the spring from each of the six directions, dips the netted gourd vessel six times into the water—to induce the Clouds to bring rain—and then fills the vessel. Turning back up the trail, he places the 'road' marker a few paces from the spring, together with the other four *nakwa'kwosi*(s), and sprinkles a line of meal from the spring over the *püh'tabi* towards the village—so that the rain, when coming to the spring, may also come to the pueblo and its fields. He then returns with the *moñ'wikuru* to the kiva, where Powa'mu chief places it and the bone whistle near the altar.

On his return the final ceremony, in the course of which the *pa'ho*(s) made by Powa'mu chief during the morning are consecrated, takes place at the altar. The altar is then dismantled, except for the sand ridge, the four *na'atsi* sticks, the *pa'ho*(s) and the medicine bowl, which remain until the following day; and all those who have taken part in the Powa'mu rites go through the discharming ceremony, *navo'tçiwa*. Each man takes off his left moccasin, and all present form in a semicircle around the fireplace. Each man takes some ashes in his left hand, and of this a pinch between the forefinger and thumb of the right hand. Powa'mu chief takes an eagle-wing feather in his left hand, and a pinch of ashes in his right. He sprinkles some of the ashes on the feather and beats time with it to the singing of the discharming song, in which all join. The song has six verses, one directed to each of the six cardinal directions. At the end of each stanza Powa'mu chief blows the ashes from the feather towards the hatch, while all the others cast theirs in the same direction; and at the end of the last verse they all rub their hands on their bodies, hold out their palms, and blow the ashes towards the hatch. They are now held to be purified of their 'dangerous' contact with the 'whip' of the Powa'mu. By now it is late in the evening. The members of the fraternity take a meal together, and then retire to sleep, in the kiva.

Very early the next morning, long before sunrise, the whole village is astir. In all the kivas where beans have been grown, the plants are pulled up and taken to the houses, to be used in the feast that takes place later in the day. In Powa'mu kiva, Powa'mu chief places on a woven tray four twigs of the spruce fetched from Kisiwu, four twigs of cottonwood, some leaves of the bean plants and of the corn grown in the kiva, four eagle-wing feathers, a bone whistle, a *moñ' wikuru*, and four of the double *pa'ho*(s) made on the previous day. After smearing some honey on the *moñ'wikuru*, he and the other officers smoke together over the tray and its contents. In the meantime, the member of the fraternity who is to impersonate the Hahai'i katçina puts on a large ceremonial blanket (*toi'hi*) in the form of a woman's dress, drapes another *toi'hi* over his shoulders, puts on his moccasins and knotted belt, and dons his fox skin; then, carrying his mask hidden under another blanket, he proceeds to a katçina shrine to the north of the village. A few minutes later Powa'mu chief follows him, carrying the tray—with the objects arranged on it—under a blanket.

Meanwhile in *moñ* kiva, the Eototo and Aholi katçinas, i.e. Village chief and the head of Pikyas clan, have also got themselves ready. Both have tied up several bunches of the young green corn grown in the kiva, to which they have added some twigs of the spruce brought from Kisiwu. They paint their bodies in the colours specific to the two katçinas they are to represent, then hiding their masks under a blanket, make their way to Kwan kiva, where they dress up fully and wait.

Arriving at the shrine (*pa'ho-ki*, 'pa'ho house') to the north of the village, Powa'mu chief deposits the four double *pa'ho*(s) there and sprinkles a corn-meal 'path', on which he lays a *nakwa'kwosi*, along the trail leading towards the village. He then hands the woven tray, containing the fresh green corn shoots and the beans grown in the kiva, to Hahai'i katçina, and makes his own way back to Powa'mu kiva. Hahai'i katçina, now dressed and masked, and carrying in her hands the tray on which lie the corn and bean sprouts and the twigs of spruce, slowly follows along the trail to the village, blowing the bone whistle and uttering a long-drawn 'hu hu hu-hu' as she goes. In this style 'she' enters the pueblo, makes her way to the village square, and then on to Powa'mu kiva; at intervals on the way, women and children approach the katçina, sprinkle her with a pinch of corn-meal, and take a sprig of the green corn or the spruce lying on the tray.

While Hahai'i katçina is waiting outside Powa'mu kiva, Eototo and Aholi emerge from Kwan kiva and slowly make their way there also. Eototo is dressed in the usual katçina sash and kilt, over which he wears an old shirt made of white cotton and embroidered, on the sleeves and lower border, with designs of cloud, plant and blossom symbols. His legs are dressed in white cotton leggings, and on his feet he wears green moccasins. The mask is very plain, made of cotton and painted white; to the lower edge a fox skin is attached, and to the crown a bunch of eagle feathers. In his right hand, Eototo carries a small bag of corn meal; in his left, his chief's staff, a netted gourd vessel, and some bunches of the green corn grown in the kiva. The Aholi katçina is likewise dressed in the costume appropriate to his identity.

About halfway between the Kwan and Powa'mu kivas, the two katçinas halt. Eototo makes a corn-meal cloud symbol on the ground, then waits while Aholi plants the butt end of his chief's staff on the symbol and, uttering a high-pitched cry, rotates the staff in each of the four cardinal directions in turn. Then, with Eototo leading the way and sprinkling a corn-meal 'path' for his companion, the two katçinas proceed on their way until they come to a spot just south of Powa'mu kiva where, during the night, a man of Bow clan has dug a hole about 10 inches square and 20 inches deep, to represent a *patni* (rock-cut cistern on the mesa top). At the *patni*, Eototo sprinkles a meal line from each of the six directions in turn, towards and into the 'cistern'; and then, again from each direction, he sprinkles a little water from the *moñ'wikuru* into the 'cistern'.[1] Aholi follows suit, then both katçinas proceed to Powa'mu kiva. They take up position beside Hahai'i katçina on the east side of the hatch; then first Eototo, and then Aholi, step forward, rub a handful of corn-meal on each of the four walls of the kiva hatch, and at the same time sprinkle a little water from their *moñ'wikuru* down the hatch itself.[2]

As soon as this rite is finished, the principal officers of the Powa'mu—led by Tobacco chief, Powa'mu chief and Katçina chief, and followed by the main body—emerge from the kiva: Powa'mu chief carrying the medicine bowl, aspergill, a *pa'ho*, and some corn-meal: Katçina chief, a *pa'ho* and some corn-meal: and the other members, *nakwa'kwosi*(s) and corn-meal; all arrayed in their ceremonial kilts. Tobacco chief smokes over the Hahai'i katçina, then hands her a *nakwa'kwosi* and some corn-meal. Powa'mu chief sprinkles water over the katçina, takes the tray containing the corn shoots from her and hands her, in return, a *pa'ho* and some meal. Katçina chief sprinkles corn-meal over her and hands her a *pa'ho*, and the other members do the same with their *nakwa' kwosi*(s). Then they re-enter the kiva. Hahai'i katçina makes her way to a katçina shrine about halfway down the mesa on the west side of the pueblo, where 'she' deposits the prayer-offerings; the man impersonating her then disrobes, wraps the mask and costume in a blanket and returns to Powa'mu kiva.

A few minutes after the dismissal of Hahai'i katçina, the Powa'mu officers again emerge from the kiva, and proceed to dismiss Eototo and Aholi in much

---

[1] Voth (1901), p. 113.

[2] Where it is caught in a bowl by a man standing on the kiva ladder. The sprinkling of water down the hatch signifies the bringing of much rain: Titiev (1944), p. 118.

the same way, i.e. by giving them *pa'ho*(s), *nakwa'kwosi*(s), and corn-meal. The two katçinas proceed to a number of houses of important persons in the village —first to the house of Soya'l chief,[1] then to the clan house of the Village chief, then to Pikyas clan house. Outside each, the two katçinas draw the cloud symbol on the ground and rotate the staff over it; Eototo then rubs four corn-meal lines on the wall of the house, and presents the senior woman of the household with a bunch of the recently-sprouted corn plants. After making their round, the two katçinas return to *moñ* kiva to disrobe. Later, during the after-noon of the ninth day, they take the *pa'ho*(s) and *nakwa'kwosi*(s) which they received in the morning and deposit them at the katçina shrine (Qowa'waima) to the southeast of the village.

The remainder of the forenoon is devoted to feasting. In *moñ* kiva, the mem-bers share a ceremonial meal of boiled beans, gravy and *pi'ki*, prepared without salt, and brought to the kiva in special trays and bowls by the Village chief's wife and other women relatives of the principal actors. In every household in the village, huge bowls of stew—made from the newly-sprouted beans and corn—are prepared, and copious portions are carried to all the kivas. During the afternoon, katçinas of all sorts perambulate the village, presenting the children with presents. All of these katçinas wear sprigs of the spruce brought back from Kisiwu. As they walk through the pueblo, pieces of spruce are broken off by members of the Powa'mu fraternity, are smoked over in the kiva, and later distributed to the households where they are placed upon the seed corn for the spring planting.[2]

On the night of the ninth day of Powa'mu, the Bean dance takes place. This follows the normal pattern of katçina night dances, in that each kiva puts on its own 'show' which it presents in all the other kivas in the village, with one exception: namely, that the dancers are *unmasked*. Two points may be noted here:

(*a*) The recently-initiated children, both those who went into the Powa'mu fraternity itself and those who were only inducted into the katçina cult, are taken for the first time into their own kiva (i.e. that of their ceremonial 'father') to witness a katçina dance. There they sit motionless on the east banquette, their knees drawn up to their chins in the position prescribed for novices at all initiations. As the katçinas are on this occasion unmasked, it does not take the children long to realise that the katçina impersonators are their own relatives and fellow villagers.[3]

(*b*) On the west bench of the kiva are seated the unmarried girls, wearing their hair—in the old days—in the traditional butterfly whorls. As the katçinas file out

---

[1] That is, of the man who impersonates Eototo; he may be the head of Bear clan, or he may be a deputy appointed by the head of Bear clan to act for him.

[2] Earle and Kennard (1938), p. 24.

[3] Titiev (1944), p. 119. The traumatic effect of this blow to the child's faith has been emphasised by Mrs. D. Eggan (1943, pp. 371–2); her remarks may well be read in con-junction with D. H. Lawrence's description, in Chapter 10 of *The Rainbow*, of the analogous process in our own society.

of the kiva after each dance, the maidens hand packages of *somi'viki* to each dancer. By custom, this is one of the occasions when a girl may offer a loaf of *kwö'mi* to her boy-friend, as a marriage proposal.

It is almost daybreak by the time the dancing comes to an end. The performers gather at their own kivas to feast on the *somi'viki* which they have collected from the girls in the course of the night. At the same time, the newly-initiated boys and girls are taken to the homes of their ceremonial 'father's' sister(s), where—as the sun rises—*their heads are washed and they are given new names.*[1]

In ordinary years, this concludes the Powa'mu ceremony; but in years when there has been a full Wü'wütçim ceremony (i.e. one that includes initiation) the previous November, the Powa'mu is extended by an extra day, to include the Patcava performance.[2] In anticipation of this event, each man plants two 'crops' of beans in his kiva instead of one: one of these, which usually consists of lima beans, being dedicated to the Patcava maidens.

The kivas most closely concerned with the Patcava rites are *moñ* kiva, together with the four—Hawiovi, Al, Tao, and Kwan—which conduct Wü'-wütçim initiation; all the kivas, however, play a part in the rites.[3] Sometime beforehand, the head of each kiva selects a maiden, usually his own niece or daughter, to act as Patcava maiden for his group; throughout the ceremony, the girls chosen for this rôle must abstain from sex, and from food containing salt or meat. All the young men initiated at the preceding Wü'wütçim are expected to sleep in the kivas and to observe the same tabus; and from their number each kiva head picks one youth, to look after the Patcava maiden's 'crops' and to act as her partner in the final ceremony on the tenth day.

The principal part of the Patcava ceremony takes place on the ninth, and tenth, days of Powa'mu. About noon on the ninth day, the Patcava *mana*(s) assemble at the katçina shrine to the north of the village. Each girl is dressed in the ceremonial costume prescribed for women, consisting of *manta*, *atö'e*, white moccasins and attached leggings, with the hair fashioned in the traditional butterfly-wing whorls; the girls are masked in the manner of Hemis katçina *mana*(s). At the shrine, they are met by four members of the Powa'mu fraternity representing *moñ* katçinas, together with one man impersonating Hahai'i katçina. The maidens form into a line behind the katçinas, and the whole body is led into the village by Powa'mu chief. The girls are supposed to be on their way to Tü'wa-na'savi, to harvest the bean crop with which they are to appear on the morrow. Near Wi'klavi kiva (one of the 'common' kivas, at Oraibi), the procession comes to a halt while the *moñ* katçinas chant a song, very long and extremely 'important', about plants which grow, ripen and are harvested. Then the group moves to the village square, where the song is repeated, and then on to

---

[1] Titiev (1944), p. 119.

[2] On the Patcava ceremony at Oraibi, see Titiev (1944), pp. 119–20, 222–6: cf. Earle and Kennard (1938), pp. 25–6, and Voth (1901), p. 123 ff.

[3] This is clear from Kennard's observation that there are twelve Patcava maidens, i.e. one from each kiva, in the procession into the village on the morning of the tenth day.

Sakwa'lenvi kiva for a third and final rendering. At the close of the song, Powa' mu chief dismisses the four *moñ* katçinas and Hahai'i katçina with prayer-offerings and corn-meal. The Patcava maidens he leads out to the katçina shrine known as Qowa'waima, to the southeast of the village, where the girls disrobe and are free to resume their normal occupations—and to attend the Bean dance that night—until the following day.

Early in the forenoon of the tenth day, the Patcava maidens go to the kivas which they are to represent, carrying special trays filled with baked sweet-corn meal which they have prepared beforehand. After delivering the trays to the kiva, they make their way out to Qowa'waima, to dress again in the ceremonial costume worn by Hemis katçina *mana*(s) and to await their partners. Within the pueblo, certain disciplinary katçinas perambulate the streets, driving all the women and children indoors. Inside the participating kivas, the partners of the Patcava maidens, assisted by the other kiva members, harvest the 'crops' dedicated to the girls. As the crops are 'harvested', they are arranged on the special trays brought to the kiva by the Patcava maiden. At the same time, bundles of bean sprouts are tied to greasewood branches, to the twigs of which are attached bunches of 'beans' fashioned out of dough (made from the baked sweet-corn meal brought by the Patcava *mana*, and suitably coloured); these branches, with their attached 'crops', are also laid on the trays, together with bits of the spruce brought from Kisiwu and vari-coloured ears of corn. When all is ready, the partners of the Patcava maidens put the finishing touches to their costumes, pick up their masks, and hasten to Qowa'waima; to be followed, more slowly, by the kiva heads, each one leading four members of his group carrying the loaded trays of produce.

As soon as they reach Qowa'waima, the Patcava maidens dress as on the preceding day. Then they are taken by Powa'mu chief to another shrine nearby, which represents Tü'wa-na'savi, the home of Mü'yiñwa,[1] to which they were supposed to have been on their way at the conclusion of the previous day's rites. After a brief rite there, Powa'mu chief leads them back to Qowa'waima, *as if they had just come from Tü'wa-na'savi*. There they are met by the principal officers of the pueblo (Village chief in the guise of Eototo, Pikyas head as A'holi, a deputy acting for Village chief, Crier chief, and War chief), together with the kiva heads, the assistants carrying the trays of freshly-harvested crops, and the youths who are to act as partners to the Patcava *mana*(s).

Going up to Eototo, Powa'mu chief asks four times for the right to enter the village, and requests permission to show what he can do.[2] Eototo eventually

---

[1] Voth (1901, p. 123) states that the place to which the Patcava maidens are taken is located *about a quarter of a mile south of the village* (i.e. on or near the mesa top), and that it is a duplicate of the 'real' Tü'wa-na'savi, located on the valley floor about three miles south of the village. Most of the places sacred to the Hopi have duplicates near the village where prayer offerings are deposited, to save going all the way to the real shrine.

[2] This is a dramatisation of the arrival of Badger clan at Oraibi in the time of Matçito, represented here by Eototo. The ceremony which the Badgers offered was the Powa'mu, including Patcava; and the crops to be carried by the maidens stand for the copious harvests which the ceremony will bring to the pueblo: Titiev (1944), p. 225, n. 20.

gives his consent, and the whole procession sets off towards the village: led by Powa'mu chief, then the village leaders in order of precedence, then the Patcava maidens with their partners on their right hand (each carrying one of the woven trays laden with the bean plants and their greasewood copies), followed by the other assistants carrying the remaining trays of 'crops', and joined, as they approach the village, by the whole body of disciplinary katçinas. As the procession enters the village, watched by the whole community crowded on rooftops and in doorways, Powa'mu leads the way to the special 'cistern' which was 'opened' by Eototo and Aholi on the preceding morning. Here a rite of 'closing' is performed, a lid is placed over the hole, and the procession circles the spot four times. Then the whole body moves on to Powa'mu kiva nearby and begins to circle the hatch four times. At the end of the fourth turn, the Patcava maidens hand the loaded trays to their partners, and as the fifth circuit draws to a close, Crier chief suddenly calls out: 'hide—cover up your children's heads!'. At once, all the uninitiated children who have been watching the scene are blindfolded, and the katçinas dash for their respective kivas. Two of the Patcava girl's attendants seize her tray and hasten with it to her home; the other two help her to unmask, then take her by the arms and hurry her down into their kiva. The village officers also take refuge in their respective kivas, all excepting Eototo and Aholi, who make their way slowly, and in full view of the spectators, to *moñ* kiva. Down in the kivas the katçinas disrobe, while the Patcava maidens, too, take off their costumes, wrap them in blankets, and eventually make their way home.

This ends the Patcava ceremony—and so the Powa'mu, except that all those who have taken part in the rites are expected to observe the ritual tabus for four more days before resuming their normal lives. In playing their part in it, the Patcava maidens are considered to have acted as 'mothers' of the whole village, and to have 'fed' the people with the crops which they brought back with them from Tü'wa-na'savi.[1] In exchange for their services, the girls keep the 'crops' grown for them in the kiva; and subsequently, when the planting season arrives, the kiva members sow and tend a special plot of corn for their Patcava *mana*, and when it ripens in the fall, they harvest the real crop for her and bring it to her house.

### SIGNIFICANCE OF THE POWA'MU

That the Powa'mu[2]—with its epilogue, the Patcava—is, primarily, a festival to promote the germination and early growth of the seeds to be planted in the

---

[1] Titiev (1944), p. 226.

[2] Voth (1901, p. 73, n. *) traces the name of the ceremony to a word used for 'putting (i.e. the fields) in proper shape, in order'. Parsons (1936, pp. 1283-4), on the other hand, derives it from the stem *po'wa-*, 'to be cured, healed (esp. by medicine man or sorcerer)', and refers to Powa'mu as 'a ceremony of exorcism', impliedly (p. 1284) with reference to the discharming rite which takes place on the eighth day; if Parsons is right, then perhaps the Powa'mu is an act of exorcism, for the pueblo as a whole, following the 'dangerous' moon, *kya' mü'iya*. This latter suggestion finds support in Fewkes' remark (1917, p. 150)

fields a few weeks later, is shown by three pieces of evidence: namely the rôle assigned in it to the planting of beans and, to a lesser degree, of corn; the meaning ascribed to the planting by Hopi themselves; and the part played in the ceremony as a whole by Mü'yiñwa, the deity who controls the germination and growth of plants. All three points are established, beyond reasonable doubt, by Stephen's notes on the subject.[1]:

the planting—and, by extension, the ceremony itself—is referred to either as *müzri ü'yi-lauwu*, 'beans plant-making', or simply as *ü'yi la'lauwu*, 'plant-making (for all cultivated vegetation)';

the Powa'mu leaders 'understand' (*na'twantota*) the omens of the coming season concerning the growth of corn, etc., as indicated by the height attained by the beans planted in the kivas:

cf. *na'twani*: n. collective, plants (in general), especially crop plants, vegetables, often equivalent to crop, harvest.

*na'twantota*: v. (a) makes trial, tries, tests, attempts to determine future, concentrates mentally on a hope to bring it to pass through meditative prayer, prays for something:

(b) makes trial of the prospective *na'twani* or general harvest, attempts to discover or assure the coming harvest.　　　　　　　　(Whorf, 1936, p. 1261)

the prayer-sticks made in the course of the ceremony are painted green, 'because it is vegetation that is asked for, prayed for';

all plants come from Mü'yiñwa; 'prayer-sticks are made and "placed" for Mü'yiñwa, and in exchange for these prayer-sticks he sends us vegetation.'

Interwoven with the germinative thread which runs through the whole ceremony, one can pick out other threads which receive emphasis at particular points in the ritual. Thus, as Titiev observes,[2] the Powa'mu stresses the rôle of the traditional pueblo leaders, particularly the Village chief, Pikyas chief, and other Soya'l officers: when, for example, these officers appear with their chiefs' staffs at the katçina initiation, when Eototo and Aholi 'bless' the houses on the ninth morning of the ceremony, and when, on the tenth morning, Powa'mu chief himself has to get Eototo's consent before he may bring his followers into the village; and it brings out, as do other Hopi ceremonies, the inter-dependence of the clans involved in its performance, e.g. Badger, Katçina, Bear, Pikyas, Bow and Sand.

Again, the Powa'mu stands in a definite relationship to the katçina cult as a whole, both structurally and with regard to the other parts of the katçina cycle. The first aspect is emphasised by the privilege, only accorded to members of the Powa'mu fraternity, of acting as 'fathers' to the katçinas; and by the

---

that the purpose of the ceremony is 'to purify the earth from the malign influences of a power which, through sorcery, is supposed to rule it in winter'. Stephen, however, holds (1936, p. 238) that its purificatory purpose is simply to exorcise the cold, *yo'hoo powa'nta.*

[1] Stephen (1936), pp. 160–2, 165, 238–42: cf. Nequatewa (1931), p. 2.
[2] Titiev (1944), p. 120.

induction of all the other children into the Katçina fraternity, as a concomitant to the Powa'mu observances. Regarding the second, the conclusion of the Powa'mu rites marks the mid point of the katçina season, in the sense that it ends the period of Badger control which began when Badger clan chief acted as 'father' to the Qöqöqlom katçinas, at the 'opening of the kivas'. Soon after the close of Powa'mu, the head of Katçina clan assumes the leadership of the katçina cult, holding it through the second series of night dances (in March and early April), and on through the *al fresco* dances of spring and early summer, until—late in July—the katçinas themselves are sent back to their 'homes' in the course of the fourth of the great ceremonies in the annual cycle, the Nima'n (Home-going) dance.

Finally, the Powa'mu ceremony with its ancillary rites gives a lead, which I propose to follow only a short distance here (deferring a more detailed study to Chapter 15), into the complex subject of Hopi symbolism and of Hopi ideas regarding the natural environment. As we have seen (above, pp. 47–8), Hopi recognise six cardinal directions (N.W., S.W., S.E., N.E., Above and Below), each identified with a primary colour. Each of these six colour-directions is further asssociated, in the several stanzas of the songs chanted during Powa'mu, with a series of objects in the natural environment: e.g. with a coloured stone or shell, a species of bird, a species of flower, a cultivated plant, and with one of the six principal kinds of corn grown. From these and similar associations elsewhere, it is possible to build up a kind of 'logical' classification of the natural world along the lines[1] shown on pp. 92–3.

A number of the associations in this list, particularly those of the birds and flowers, are simple colour associations: for example, the linking of a yellow flower and a yellow bird with the northwest (yellow). Behind others one may discern some form of geographical reference: thus, of the four principal game animals, deer were commonly hunted on the mesas to the north and northwest of the villages, mountain sheep on one particular mesa (*pañ-o'vi*) to the south-west of Oraibi, antelope on the flats down towards the Little Colorado River, and elk perhaps formerly in the Chuska mountains to the northeast, while the association of eagle with the Above, and of badger with the Below, clearly derives from their respective habitats. Others, such as those of the cultivated plants, appear to be arbitrary. Two general points may, however, be noted regarding the extent to which such a list constitutes a 'classification' of the natural world. In the first place, while the list certainly includes many of the animals, birds and plants that were of significance to the Hopi in their daily life, it still comprises only a tithe of the total number of species actually known to and named by the Hopi. In the second, we have absolutely no evidence even in the early reports as to the 'hold' which such a classification, if indeed it were a classification, exercised over traditional Hopi thinking. Did the ordinary Hopi,

[1] The list is compiled from Voth (1901), pp. 127–53, and (1903*b*), p. 29, in conjunction with Stephen (1936), p. 307, n. 1. It may be compared with that given by Lévi-Strauss (1962*b*), p. 56.

| *direction* | NORTHWEST | SOUTHWEST | SOUTHEAST |
|---|---|---|---|
| *colour* | *sikya*, yellow | *sa'kwa*, blue-green | *pa'la*, red |
| stone or shell | *naya'wuna*, a yellowish stone | *choshmuna*, turquoise | *wawuna*, a pink stone |
| bird | *ta'wa mana*, oriole | *tço'ro*, mountain bluebird | *kyaro*, parrot or macaw |
| flower | *he'si*, mariposa lily, a yellow flower common near the villages in spring | *tçoro'si*, larkspur, a blue flower common on sand slopes in spring | *mansi*, 'Indian paint brush', a bright red flower common on the mesas in the fall |
| cultivated plant | *homi ü'yi*, corn plant | *mori ü'yi*, bean plant | *pa'tña ü'yi*, squash plant |
| corn | *takuri*, yellow corn ear | *sakwa'pu*, blue corn ear | *pavala*, red corn ear |
| prey animal | *to'hoa*, mountain lion | *ho'nauwû*, black bear | *kwe'wûüh*, gray wolf |
| game animal | *sowi'ñwü*, deer | *pa'ñwü*, mountain sheep | *chü'bio*, antelope |
| bird of prey | *huñwikya*, Cooper's hawk | *kih'sa*, prairie falcon | *natüyauwu*, sharp-shinned hawk |
| tree or shrub | *kwi'ñvi*, mountain oak: hard wood, used for rabbit sticks, axe handles, digging sticks | *kaha'vi*, willow: used for hoe handles | *hö'novi*, cliff rose: used for arrow shafts |

| NORTHEAST | ABOVE | BELOW | direction |
|---|---|---|---|
| *kö'tsa*, white | *kü'mbi*, black | *ma'si*, gray or speckled: or *so'shü*, 'all (colours)' | colour |
| *shaatcina*, a white stone or shell | *aiwanga*, a black stone | *tçimotçima*, a grayish stone | stone or shell |
| *posi'wu*, magpie | *pa vau'kaiya*, swift or cliff swallow | *toposkwa*, canyon wren | bird |
| *poli'si*, evening primrose, a white flower common on talus slopes in late summer | *akau'wosi*, sunflower, yellow with black centre, common on sand dunes in the fall | *so'sosi*, 'all kinds of blooms' | flower |
| *pi'chin ü'yi*, cotton plant | *kawai' ü'yi*, watermelon plant | *so'shü ü'yi*, 'all kinds of plants' | cultivated plant |
| *qöyawi*, white corn ear | *koko'ma*, black corn ear | *tawa'kchi*, sweet corn ear | corn |
| *toko'chi*, wild cat | *kwa'hü*, golden eagle | *hona'ni*, badger | prey animal |
| *chai'zrisa*, elk | *so'wi*, jack rabbit | *ta'vo*, cottontail | game animal |
| *sowitoaya*, a bird of prey (unidentified) | (?) *kwa'hü*, golden eagle | *ma'si kwa'yo*, gray hawk (? Swainson's) | bird of prey |
| *ho'hü*, juniper: used for firewood | *siva'pi*, rabbit brush: used for wind-breaks | *tu siva'pi*, a smaller species of rabbit brush: also used for wind breaks | tree or shrub |

when he saw e.g. a mountain lion, instinctively think of it as in some way the 'same kind of thing' as a deer or an oriole, as we do when we group wolf, coyote and fox together as different kinds of dog? Or was it, rather, a far more *ad hoc* linkage, arising out of and giving emphasis to, but also restricted to, the ceremonial association between the six cardinal directions and the colours by which they were represented? Lévi-Strauss clearly inclines to the former view (1962b, pp. 55–6). I incline to the latter myself, on the ground that the real Hopi classification of the natural world is to be looked for elsewhere, in the grouping of objects and species represented by the clan-phratry system (see Chapters 15 and 16), and that the principle involved in that grouping is not a static but a dynamic one, arising not from accidents of external appearance but from close observation of the habits of the species linked together in each group. To show the kind of thing I have in mind, let us consider, briefly, the different feathers used in the course of Powa'mu.

In Voth's account of the preliminary prayer-stick making, the feathers of six different kinds of birds—apart from eagle and turkey, which are used in virtually all Hopi ceremonies—are referred to; these birds are *toko'tska*, cowbird (or, more probably, Utah Red-winged Blackbird), *qöqöpi*, yellow-breasted chat, *sikya'tsi*, 'yellow bird' or warbler, *ta'wa mana*, 'sun maiden' or oriole, *tçoro*, bluebird, and *yau'pa*, mockingbird. We have seen, further, that the *sikya'tsi* feathers are used 'as a prayer for warm weather when the birds come'; that the oriole and bluebird feathers are blown through the hatchway of the kiva 'as a wish or prayer for warm weather when the summer birds come'; and that Powa'mu chief himself, when he distributes the prayer-sticks which have been dedicated in the course of the ceremony, is said to represent the *toko'tska*, the subsequent arrival of which marks the time for planting early corn. Now all six of the birds referred to are, in point of fact, migrant species whose return in spring and early summer heralds the approach of warm weather; and it is this fact, I am sure, rather than a weak association of the colours yellow and blue with summer,[1] that accounts for the use of 'yellow bird' and bluebird feathers in this context. That this is the true interpretation, is borne out by one further piece of evidence: that bluebird feathers are *also* used, as we have seen above,[2] for snow and ice. This is the only case known to me, in Hopi symbolism, where a single feather has a double reference; and the reason lies in the special migratory habits of the mountain bluebird. Whereas the 'yellow birds' referred to, namely oriole, chat and warblers, are simple migrants, arriving in the Hopi region in spring and departing south in late summer, bluebirds are double migrants,

---

[1] Cf. the use of blue and yellow pollen on the arms and legs of the Marau' *mana*(s), in the course of the Marau' ceremony in September: see below, p. 190. Among the Rio Grande Tewa, the association of blue and yellow with summer, and of red and white with winter, is far stronger: see Ortiz (1969), pp. 34–6, 40, 94–5.

[2] Above, p. 54. Cf. the observation by Wallis (Wallis and Titiev, 1944, p. 529):

tco'ro: the feathers of this bird are affixed to prayer-sticks because, being from a winter bird, they ensure snow, which means that the ground will be well watered when it is time to sow the crops.

arriving early in the fall and staying until the weather turns cold (when they move on south), returning in the early spring and staying until the weather turns hot (when they move up into the high mountains). The appearance of bluebirds in the vicinity of the villages thus heralds the approach of cold weather in the fall, and of warm weather in the spring; hence, the double reference of bluebird feathers in Hopi ceremonialism. And it is on ecological observations of this kind, I maintain, rather than on accidents of external appearance, that the Hopi classification of nature is built.

# 13

# *Ritual fraternities of the Hopi*

We have seen, in discussing the Powa'mu, how that ceremony is linked to the Wü'wütçim: in that when the Wü'wütçim is celebrated in its full, initiatory form in November, the Patcava rite is added to the Powa'mu the following February. In the present chapter we go back four months in time, from the conclusion of Powa'mu to early in November, to follow that segment of the ceremonial cycle which fills the November and December moons; first, the Wü'wütçim—in Titiev's words,[1] 'the most complicated, and among the most vital of all Hopi ceremonies, the significance [of which] must be understood before we can hope to grasp the essential meaning of Hopi religion'—and then, the Soya'l.

## THE WÜ'WÜTÇIM CEREMONY

Soon after the onset of puberty, usually at the age of 15 or 16, every Hopi lad is expected to undergo initiation into one of the four fraternities of adult men, namely Wü'wütçim fraternity itself, Tao (singers), Al (Horn), or Kwan (Agave). These four fraternities together conduct the Wü'wütçim ceremony every November. In ordinary years the rites last five days and are directed, as we shall see, to specific agricultural ends; but about every fourth year, or whenever there are a sufficient number of youths of the right age to be initiated, the rites are extended to nine days to include the initiation of new members into the four branches.

This initiation constitutes a young man's 'coming of age' in Hopi society; it is probable, indeed, that the whole ceremony takes its name from this initiatory element in the ritual.[2] However that may be, the ceremony in its long form falls

---

[1] Titiev (1944), p. 130.

The last complete performance of the Wü'wütçim, at Oraibi, took place in the fall of 1912. Titiev's description (1944, pp. 130–9) is based on information obtained from men who had passed through the rites in that year, on observation of a part of the proceedings at Hotevilla in 1933, and on earlier accounts.

The earlier accounts, all referring to 1st Mesa, are those of Fewkes and Stephen (1892*a*, pp. 189–221), and of Stephen (1936, pp. 959–93), both referring to the full rites of 1891: of Fewkes (1900, pp. 80–138), referring to the abbreviated rite of 1898: of Parsons (1923, pp. 156–87), referring to the abbreviated rite of 1920: and Steward's very cursory description (1931, pp. 56–79) of the full rites in 1927.

The account that follows is based on that given by Fewkes and Stephen (1892*a*), supplemented by Titiev's description (1944, pp. 130–9).

[2] Dorsey and Voth (1901, p. 10, n.*) derive the word *wü'wütçim* from *wüwü'tani*, 'to grow up', and suggest that it indicates the fraternity of 'grown men' *wü'wüyom*.

into two, fairly clearly defined, parts: an initial period of four days, culminating in secret rites on the fourth night in the course of which the novices undergo their initiation; followed by five days of more public rites, during which agricultural (and fertility) *motifs* are emphasised. The account given here covers the ceremony in its long, or initiatory, form; but the reader will bear in mind, in following the events of the full nine days, that the second half of the long rite is, in substance, the abbreviated rite (as this is performed in ordinary years).

Of the four branches, the Wü'wütçim fraternity is the central one at Oraibi. It is controlled by Ke'le (sparrow-hawk) clan, and the head of Ke'le clan 'owns' the ceremony; novices into any one of the four branches are referred to, during the period of initiation, as *ke'le-hoyam*, 'little sparrow-hawks', and the November moon, during which the observances are held, is named *kel' mü'iya*. Not only does the Wü'wütçim fraternity control the Wü'wütçim ceremony at Oraibi; its membership there is by far the largest, and may well, indeed, exceed that of the other three branches put together. Five of the principal kivas at Oraibi are concerned with the Wü'wütçim, namely Hawiovi and Sakwa'lenvi, Tao, Na'savi and Kwan. Of these, the first two house the Wü'wütçim fraternity, Tao kiva houses the Singers fraternity, Na'savi the Horn (Al) fraternity, and Kwan kiva the Agave (Kwan) fraternity; while each fraternity performs its own share of the ritual in its own kiva, the esoteric part of the whole ceremony —at which all four branches are represented—takes place in Hawiovi kiva, under the direction of the leaders of the Wü'wütçim fraternity.[1]

Candidates for initiation into any one of the four branches are sponsored by their ceremonial 'father', who must already be a member of the particular branch which the lad wishes to join. In the normal course, the man who sponsors a lad at his Wü'wütçim initiation is the same man who, a few years earlier, put him into either the Powa'mu or the Katçina fraternity, at Powa'mu.

The Oraibi performance of the Wü'wütçim starts when the Sun Watcher announces that the sun has risen behind a point on the eastern sky-line known as Dinga'pi.[2] That evening the heads of the four branches meet together and hold a formal smoke, in the course of which they make various prayer-offerings;

---

Fewkes and Stephen (1892a, p. 189) call the extended rites *na-a'ç-naiya*, or head-washing, and the abbreviated rite *wü'wütçim*. But Hopi themselves, as Titiev points out (1944, p. 130, n. 4), refer to both as *wü'wütçim*; and in any case head-washing is a part of initiatory proceedings in *all* Hopi societies.

Parsons (1923, p. 156) states that the extended form of the ceremony is called *na'töña*, 'putting them in', and that the same term may be used for initiation into the Marau, the principal women's society. This is of especial interest, in view of the close link between the Wü'wütçim ceremony and the Marau: see Titiev (1944), pp. 164, 167-8.

[1] On 1st Mesa, the Wü'wütçim ceremony is controlled by Singers' society, Singers' leaders are in charge of the esoteric part of the ritual, and this takes place in Singers' kiva: Parsons (1936), p. 957.

[2] On or about 15–16 November. The full Wü'wütçim ceremony runs from about 20 to 28 November; on the afternoon following its conclusion, i.e. on 29 or 30 November, the Soya'l katçina appears; and sixteen days later, the Soya'l proper commences, extending over nine days—from about 15 to 23 December. The point on the sky-line, known as

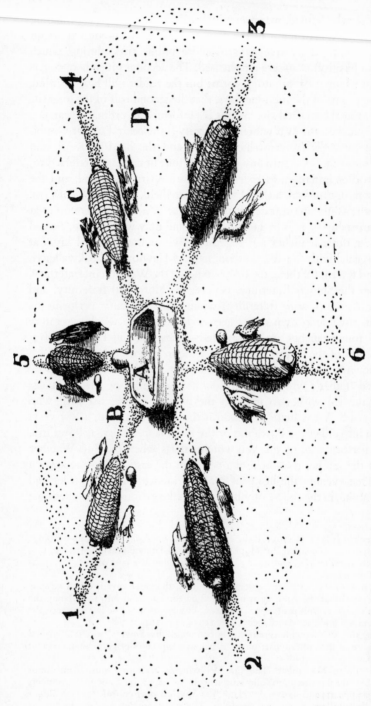

Fig. 41. *Six directions' Altar, made on the first morning of Wü'wütçim.* *a.* medicine bowl. *b.* intersecting meal lines (*tü'waha*). *c.* corn ear, with coloured pebble and two bird skins, for each of the six directions. *d.* sand field. The six ears of corn (*na'nanivo ka'ö*), and the identifiable bird skins, are as follows: 1. northwest: yellow corn, skin of oriole (*tawamana*). 2. southwest: blue-green corn, skins of jay (*d'a*) and of bluebird. 3. southeast: red corn, skin of red-shafted flicker. 4. northeast: white corn, skins of magpie and of night-hawk. 5. Above: black corn, skins of blackbird and of Western Robin. 6. Below: all-colours corn, skin of white-winged blackbird. Re-drawn from Stephen (1936), Fig. 483.

these they hand over to Crier chief. Early the next morning, Crier chief ascends to the roof of the Ke'le clan house, 'places' the prayer-offerings in the shrine there, sprinkles corn meal and corn pollen in each of the four cardinal directions, and then, facing the rising sun, calls out over the village that the Wü' wütçim will commence in four days' time.

Four days later, on the day known as *yü'ñya* ('going in')[1], the leaders of the four branches—accompanied by the other officers—enter their respective kivas at dawn and set up the *na'atsi* outside the hatch. The setting-up of the *na'atsi(s)* indicates that the ceremony has begun; from now until its conclusion, all those taking part observe the usual prohibitions on sexual intercourse and on eating meat or salt, no strangers may enter any one of the kivas involved, and the members of the different branches even take care not to see what is going on in the other kivas—except on those occasions when they enter Hawiovi kiva to take part in rites common to all four branches.

The principal events of the first day are: the erection of altars and invocation to the six directions, in the morning; and the making of new fire, followed by the introduction of the novices, in the afternoon and evening.

In the course of the morning, *ña'küyi po'ñya*, 'medicine-water altar(s)', are set up in each of the participating kivas by the fraternity head: who then, assisted by the asperser, carries out the 'invocation to the six directions', *na'nanivo tuñwa'inita*. Seated in the southeast corner of the deep part of the kiva, the fraternity head begins by sifting fine valley sand over the kiva floor, so that the sand covers the floor in an irregular circle, about 2 feet in diameter. Across the sand field he sprinkles three intersecting lines of white corn-meal, then puts a pinch of corn pollen into the bottom of a crenellate bowl, partly fills the bowl with water (fetched earlier from the spring), and places it at the intersection of the corn-meal lines. He then arranges the six corn ears, the coloured pebbles (*o'wa*) and the bird skins,[2] around the bowl in each of the six cardinal directions, as shown in Figure 41. Finally, into a tray of white corn-meal he sticks six triple bunches of pine needles, having first tied a short cotton string to the base of each; and sets the tray beside the 'six-directions' altar'.

The fraternity head and the asperser now sing a sequence of eight songs over the altar, in the course of which the asperser first sprinkles corn pollen into the bowl and then asperses in each of the six cardinal directions, taking up and

Dinga'pi, is so located (Titiev, 1944, p. 142, n. 10) that it permits just enough time to elapse for the climax of the Soya'l to be reached on or about 23 or 24 December, i.e. at the winter solstice.

On 1st Mesa (Parsons, 1923, pp. 158–9), and on 2nd Mesa (Nequatewa, 1931, p. 1), the dates of both winter ceremonies are ascertained by watching the position of the setting sun in relation to the San Francisco mountains.

[1] For the events of the first day of Wü'wütçim, see Fewkes and Stephen (1892a), pp. 191–8.

[2] Apart from *tawamana*, all these birds are—or, in the case of magpie, were—prominent fall migrants or winter residents in the Hopi region; the 'white-winged blackbird' must refer to the white patch on the wing of the male Yellow-headed Blackbird.

putting down the appropriate corn-ear as he comes to each direction. As the last song comes to an end, the asperser takes a quartz crystal from his bag and sends one of the younger men up the kiva ladder with it, to reflect a ray of sunlight into the liquid in the crenellate bowl (*ña'küyi-pi*). This concludes the 'invocation to the six directions'; the six ears of corn are tied together with a cotton string and hung on a peg on the west wall of the kiva, the woven tray with the corn-meal and the bunches of pine needles set on one side for use in the afternoon, and the sand field swept up and tidied away.

Late in the afternoon, the members of the other three branches file into *moñ* kiva[1] in three separate bodies, their leaders each carrying the tray of corn-meal in which are stuck the bunches of pine needles with cotton strings attached, and the other members a *kel' tsakwa*, i.e. a stick with sparrow-hawk feathers tied to it. Each group takes up position in one quarter of the chamber.[2] On the left of the fireplace, facing north, sits the Al (Horn) firemaker and his assistant. In front of him on the floor is his *pila'n kohü*, slab of willow about 18 inches long, and five spindles, for making fire: the spindles are made of bush clover, set in a handle of wild olive; over each end of the wood slab, several *nakwa'kwosi*(s) and lengths of cotton string are tied; corn pollen (*tala'si*) is used to increase the friction, in place of sand—used on secular occasions. Beyond the two Al firemakers, to the northwest of the fireplace, sit two Kwan firemakers with similar apparatus. The leaders of the ceremony[3] stand to the north of the fireplace, with *kel'tsakwa* in their hands.

For about five minutes, all stand in silence. Then, at a signal from one of the leaders, all four fraternities burst into song, each group chanting its own anthem to a different beat. After about ten minutes, all four groups cease singing at almost the same moment and then, in perfect silence, the two pairs of firemakers begin rotating their spindles[4] to make fire. Two or three minutes later, the flame springs up; it is fed with pieces of cedar bark, and then transferred to the fireplace. Next, the two leaders of the Wü'wütçim and Singers' groups take up position on either side of the fireplace, with their woven trays in their hands, and each in turn throws one of his pine-needle *nakawa'kwosi*(s) into the flames, until all are consumed. This rite is called:

> *Masau'u i'namu*            *so'çü moñ'mowitû    ano'ya* :
> Masau'u that-which-is-his    all    the-chiefs    have-put :

---

[1] i.e. Singers' kiva, at Walpi; probably, in the old days, Hawiovi kiva at Oraibi, since this was the kiva in which the main rites took place.

Throughout this account of the Wü'wütçim, I refer to the kiva in which the principal rites take place as the *moñ* kiva. But the reader must bear in mind that this applies, strictly, only to Walpi, where Singers' kiva served as *moñ* kiva for both Wü'wütçim and Soya'l; at Oraibi, in the old days, Hawiovi kiva served as *moñ* kiva for Wü'wütçim, and Sakwa'lenvi as *moñ* kiva for Soya'l (and so for the pueblo as a whole).

[2] For the position of the four branches in *moñ* kiva when the new fire is lighted, see Fewkes (1900), pl. iv, fig. 7.

[3] i.e. Singers at Walpi: *Wü'wütçimtu*, at Oraibi.

[4] Called *pi'lan-ta kü'hi-ma:* Fewkes and Stephen (1892*a*), p. 195, n. 1.

i.e. the chiefs have given to Masau'u that which belongs to him.[1] After the two leaders have thrown all their pine-needle prayer-offerings into the fire, a young Al (Horn) man is despatched to carry lighted whisps of cedar bark to each of the other kivas taking part; and the fires so lighted are kept going, with greasewood, throughout the nine days of the ceremony.

Meanwhile another Al man, who has been despatched earlier for the purpose, returns to the village from a nearby shrine, carrying—with great care and reverence—the wooden figure of *Ta'la-tüm'si*, 'dawn woman',[2] the patron deity of child-birth. He places the figure, facing westward, on the east side of the hatch of *moñ* kiva; during the next three days the image of *Ta'la-tüm'si* will be placed in a similar position, on succeeding days, outside the kiva hatches of the other three fraternities participating in the ceremony.

Just at sunset, a number of older men approach *moñ* kiva from their houses, each leading a lad aged from 12 to 17 years old. The lads are naked, save for a very scanty white kilt fastened round their loins with a string; their hair is loose, and before stepping on to the kiva hatch, each novice takes off his shoes. Each lad in turn casts a pinch of corn-meal down the hatch, then steps on to the first rung of the ladder; as he does so, one of the Wü'wütçimtu (or one of the Singers, at Walpi) climbs up the ladder from below, the lad clings round his neck and takes his feet off the ladder. The older man carries him down into the kiva and passes him into the arms of another; in this fashion the novices are carried across the kiva, one by one, some being set down on a blanket on the south side of the kiva and some on the north side. There they sit, with their knees drawn up to their chins, while one of the leaders fixes a woodpecker-feather *nakwa'kwosi* to the hair of each; while this is being done, each fraternity sings its own anthem again, and further prayers are offered by the leaders.

After further singing, the four fraternities leave *moñ* kiva, and proceed in order to the shrine of *Tü'wa-po'ñya-tüm'si*, 'sand-altar woman', outside the village, where their leaders deposit certain *pa'ho*(s) made during the morning. Then all return to their kivas, each body taking its own novices to the appropriate kiva. Later in the evening, the novices are rubbed all over with a yellow pigment, with two black marks down each cheek; and that night, as on the two following nights, they sleep in the kivas, wrapped in the same blanket with their ceremonial 'fathers'.

During the second and third days of the ceremony, relatively little happens. Each morning at sunrise, the *na'atsi*(s) are set up outside the participating kivas, and the figure of *Ta'la-tüm'si* is moved to another kiva hatch. All day the novices sit huddled in one corner of their kivas, naked except for their breech clouts. On their bodies, yellow ochrey clay is applied in bands around both legs, above

[1] Fewkes and Stephen (1892*a*), p. 196. According to Titiev (1944, p. 131), during this part of the ceremony the Kwan chief, impersonating Masau'u, is concealed behind blankets in the kiva. This is confirmed by Parsons (1925, p. 117, n. 178), who states that the man who impersonates Masau'u must be a member of the Kwan fraternity.

[2] *tüm'si*: a young married woman who has not yet borne a child: Fewkes and Stephen (1892*a*), p. 196, n. 3.

and below the knee, around their arms, and around the waist, with two smears down each side of their chest and back; their hair is tied around with a strip of yucca, and puffed out in front and at either side over a folded corn husk. In numerous different ways, the pretence is maintained that they are infants, or fledgling birds: they sit in the darkest corner of the kiva,[1] and a blanket is spread over the kiva hatch to prevent the sun's rays falling on them; they sit perfectly still, with their knees drawn up to their chins. They may only defaecate at night, when the Pleiades is halfway across the sky;[2] should they wish to relieve themselves during the day, an old vessel is brought into the kiva for their use. To scratch himself, each novice is provided with a small wooden scratcher by his 'father', which he uses as a bird does its claws. Whenever they are fed by their 'fathers', bits of food are held out to them and they have to move their arms with the motion of flapping wings and cry out shrilly, *'ke'le-le, ke'le-le'*,[3] the cry of the desert sparrow-hawk.

At daybreak on the morning of the 4th day, the *na'atsi*(s) are set up as usual; and on this day, the figure of *Ta'la-tüm'si* is set up outside Kwan kiva. Soon after the sun has risen, men of the Al and Kwan fraternities formally 'close' the trails leading into the village from the four cardinal directions, by drawing corn-meal lines across them and laying on each a whitened elk-horn; informants say[4] that, in former times, if any outsider were rash enough to venture within the proscribed limit, members of the Kwan fraternity inevitably put him to death. So far as the novices are concerned, the greater part of the fourth day is taken up[5] with a long journey, on foot, to a place some 15 to 20 miles distant from the village, to dig yucca root and to obtain *tü'ma* (white gypsiferous clay): the one to be used in the head-washing rite the next morning, and the other for personal decoration by the members of the Tao and Wü'wütçim fraternities later in the ceremony. They return to the pueblo about 6 o'clock in the evening, and are immediately taken down into *moñ* kiva[6]—for the culminating rite of their initiation.

No record exists of what actually takes place in *moñ* kiva on the fourth night of the Wü'wütçim ceremony. However, we have the following facts to go on:[7]

(i) From sunrise on the fourth day, until early the next morning, the main

---

[1] Stephen (1936), p. 967: cf. Fewkes and Stephen (1892a), p. 199.

[2] Parsons (1936), p. 1239.

[3] Titiev (1944), p. 133. Fewkes and Stephen (1892a, p. 198), and Stephen (1936, p. 973), say that, at Walpi, novices fast all through days 2, 3 and 4; Titiev (1944, p. 133, n. 23) states that, at Oraibi, ceremonial 'fathers' may bring their 'sons' food during these three days, provided that it is prepared without salt, meat or the use of blue corn meal.

[4] Fewkes and Stephen (1892a), p. 201, n. 1.

[5] Stephen (1936), pp. 975–6: Fewkes and Stephen (1892a), p. 205, n. 3.

[6] Not having eaten, nor drunk water, according to Stephen (1936, p. 976), since the evening they went down into the kivas. I find it hard to credit, even given the extraordinary physical toughness of the Hopi, that the novices can go without water for rather more than seventy-two hours.

[7] See Fewkes and Stephen (1892a), pp. 201–7: Stephen (1936), pp. 977–8: and Titiev (1944), pp. 135–7.

trails into village are barred. All that day, and most of the night, groups of Al and Kwan men patrol the village, to see that the proscription is observed.

(*ii*) In the course of the fourth day, the women of the village prepare large quantities of food. Towards sundown, the food is set out in bowls and on trays, and the doors are left wide open in all the houses on one side of an imaginary line dividing the village into two halves. At Oraibi, all those who live on that side of the line vacate their homes and take shelter for the night with friends or relatives who live on the other side; at Walpi, all the women and children leave the pueblo and find lodging in Sicho'movi or Hano.

(*iii*) Before sunrise on the fifth day, the ceremonial 'fathers' of the novices bring quantities of yucca root into the kivas and prepare to wash the heads of their 'sons'. After washing his own head first, the sponsor washes the novice's head and bestows a new name on him.

(*iv*) A little later, the members of the four fraternities assemble outside Kwan kiva and, as the sun rises, escort the figure of *Ta'la-tüm'si* back to the shrine from which it was fetched on the first afternoon. On returning to their kivas, all those who have taken part in the night's ritual drink from a basin of water, in which an emetic herb has been mixed, then go up on the roof of the kiva and vomit.

Titiev interprets[1] this sequence of events as follows:

(*a*) The food which is put out on the evening of the fourth day is put out for the spirits of the dead, who are believed to visit the pueblo during the night.

(*b*) In the course of the rites which take place in *moñ* kiva on that night, the dead are impersonated (Masau'u, the deity who presides over the 'house of the dead', being impersonated by the head of the Kwan fraternity), and in some manner the novices are ceremonially 'killed', i.e. their boyish lives are terminated, and they are reborn as men.

(*c*) The return of the image of *Ta'la-tüm'si*, 'mother of the novices',[2] to its shrine signifies that she has been 'delivered' of her children.

(*d*) The change of status which the novices have undergone is indicated by the washing of their hair and the bestowing on each of a new name.

Certainly this interpretation is borne out by the subsequent events on the morning of the fifth day (*na'lüsh-ta'la*). At about 8 o'clock, a feast is served in each of the participating kivas. At this feast the *ke'le*(s), novices, break their four-day fast and eat, for the first time, in company with the other members of

---

[1] Titiev (1944), pp. 135–6. Titiev's interpretation, of which only the gist is given here, appears to me incontrovertible.

[2] Cf. Stephen (1936), p. 973: 'Tala'tümsi is the mother of the novices. They are now [i.e. on the third day] in the depths of the underworld sea, in six days they will be elevated to the surface. They fast three days.'

the fraternity. From now on, they are known by their new names, no longer have to be protected from the sun, sleep apart from their sponsors during the remaining nights of the ceremony, and take part in the public performances put on by their fraternity.

Soon after mid-day,[1] about thirty Singers emerge from their kiva, naked save for a small loin cloth. Their bodies are entirely covered with a yellowish clayey pigment, with two broad stripes of red ochre running across their faces, one across the eyes from temple to temple, the other across the mouth from jaw to jaw, and phallic symbols, also in red ochre, crudely drawn on their back, chest and arms. In his right hand each man carries an ear of corn. Emerging from the kiva, the men arrange themselves in four lines and commence to dance and sing, while one of their number beats out the time on a small cottonwood drum. Using their ears of corn as pointers, the dancers gesticulate suggestively to the women gathered on the surrounding rooftops. The women shout back at them in anger, and throw down water and urine on them from above; now and then one of the older women runs in among the group and pours water from a gourd over individual dancers (this is called *ü'mi kü'ya*, 'thou I pour upon').

Singing and dancing, the whole body moves through the village, pausing in front of each group of houses, then moving on to the next, until finally they find themselves back at their own kiva again. Throughout their circuit of the pueblo, the dancers are escorted by two Al men, and in their ranks are the newly initiated *ke'le*(s).

This public dance by the Singers, in which the dancers display phallic emblems and gesticulate rudely at the women, and the women retaliate by dowsing them with water, sets the pattern for the dance by the Wü'wütçimtu later in the afternoon, and for the following two days' performances. Late on the same day, about an hour before sunset, the Wü'wütçimtu emerge from their kiva, each man carrying in his right hand an ear of corn and in his left a singular object, in the shape of the female genital organ, called *lü'wa* (vulva).[2] Escorted—like the Singers—by men of the Al fraternity, the dancers divide into two groups and proceed to the main square of the village. There, the larger group clusters round one of their number who beats out the time on a drum, while the smaller group forms in a rough circle and dances to the song chanted by the others. While they dance, women drench both parties with water and urine, screaming bawdy taunts[3] at them from the rooftops and occasionally running in

[1] For the subsequent events on the fifth day, see Fewkes and Stephen (1892a), pp. 208–10: cf. Stephen (1936), pp. 977–81.

[2] Fewkes (Fewkes and Stephen, 1892a, p. 209, n. 1) remarks, discreetly, that 'figures of this may be seen on consultation with the authors. They are too realistic for publication.' However that may be, the *lü'wa* is illustrated by Stephen (1936, Fig. 487, p. 979). It is made of sumac (*sö've*), wrapped around with cotton twine and pubic hair (*lü'wa hemi*); the handle is called 'its leg', *ho'kyadta*.

[3] Fewkes (1900, p. 98) points out that the obscene remarks, made by the W'üwütçimtu in the course of their dance, are directed principally at women of the Marau society, and that the same women retaliate in kind at the time of their own dance in the fall: cf., on this point, Fewkes and Stephen (1892a), p. 210, n. 2.

among the dancers and pouring liquid over them. After about an hour, both groups return to the kiva and the day's proceedings are at an end.

Early the next morning the Wü'wütçim fraternity repeat their public performance, under Al escort, and are again drenched with water by the women. Later, about 9 o'clock, the four fraternities leave the village in two separate parties, the Kwan men setting out to the east, the Wü'wütçim and Singers— under Al escort—to the west, to hunt rabbits and other game. Both parties return towards sunset, two of their members laden with the rabbits which the party has killed[1] and the rest carrying great loads of greasewood for the kiva fire. The game is carried down into the kivas, and later distributed among the households of the various members of the fraternity.

The following morning the Wü'wütçimtu again perform in public, and are again drenched with water by the women; but apart from this, there is no other public ceremony on the seventh day. Inside the kivas, however, there is considerable activity; the Wü'wütçim fraternity, in particular, being engaged in preparing *sikya'piki*, a yellow pigment, for use the next day—an activity which occupies the greater part of the day.

Early on the morning of the eighth day,[2] while it is still dark, the Wü'wütçimtu again perform their dance through the village, as on the previous two mornings, but on this day none of the women drench them with water. During the morning, in Al and Kwan kivas, the members of those fraternities are busy making *pa'ho(s)*—the Al men attaching hawk breast-feathers to sprigs of sumac (*sö've*), the Kwan men making ordinary $4\frac{1}{2}$-inch *pa'ho(s)* and painting them blue-green, while the Wü'wütçimtu and the Singers prepare for their public performance. Later, in Al and Kwan kivas, the six-directions' altars are again set up, as on the first morning, and the prayer-offerings which the members have made are consecrated there.

About an hour before noon, the Wü'wütçimtu emerge from their kiva, in brilliant costume: their bodies painted with a broad band of yellow pigment (*sikya'piki*) from shoulder to shoulder, with a band round the waist, three horizontal lines over the ribs at back and front, and both forearms (from elbow to wrist) and legs (from knee to ankle) painted. All wear white embroidered kilts, with a gray fox-skin hanging from the girdle; in their hair, parroquet feathers, and on their crown, a little to the right of centre, a multi-coloured 'blossom' cut in cardboard. With a Horn (Al) escort, they dance sideways through the village, at the same time singing 'a tuneful melody' to the beat of a drum. As they pass in front of the houses, the women express their admiration of the dancers. When they have completed the circuit of the village, the dancers return to their kiva. During the next three or four hours, the Wü'wütçimtu

---

[1] Stephen (1936, p. 983) reports that, in 1891, the Wü'wütçim and Singers' party brought back twelve to fifteen jack rabbits, seventy to eighty cottontails, and a dozen or more smaller game; and the Kwan party, twenty-nine cottontails and three field rats.

[2] For the events of the eighth day of Wü'wütçim, see Fewkes and Stephen (1892a), pp. 212–16; cf. Fewkes (1900), pp. 101–15, and Stephen (1936), pp. 986–90.

repeat their dance several times, returning in the intervals to their kiva where the members busy themselves making prayer-offerings of sumac. At about 3 p.m., the dancers return to their kiva for the last time, and disrobe.

In the meantime, in Singers' kiva, they have also been busy. Apart from making prayer-feathers of sumac, every man has moulded a lump of clay roughly in the shape of a cone, some 5 or 6 inches high, in which he imbeds corn kernels of various colours to form simple conventional designs of clouds, zigzag bands (lightning), etc. Each man has brought down into the kiva his own woven tray; on this, he now sprinkles corn meal, sets his *qa'ö to'kwi* (corn mound) in the meal, and arranges ears of corn around it on the tray. At about 4 p.m., the Singers emerge from their kiva and make their way to the village square, each man carrying his woven tray with the corn-decorated clay mould resting on it. On their way to the square the dancers are joined by members of the Al fraternity, emerging from *their* kiva, in such a way that members of the two fraternities alternate, one following the other. On reaching the square, the whole body divides into two lines, and there follows a highly elaborate performance in the course of which, to the rhythm of a solemn chant rendered by the two lines of dancers, two members of the Al fraternity — representing the Storm Cloud deities[1] — dash from one end of the line to the other, passing each other in the middle on the way. This *pas de deux* they repeat several times, as each stanza of the chant reaches an end. Finally, the whole double line of dancers moves sideways out of the square, and through the village, still singing; as they pass the houses, on the way back to their kivas, all the women come out and help themselves to the clay moulds and the ears of corn carried by the Singers on their woven trays.

Towards sunset, two young men from each of the Singers, Al, and Kwan fraternities, handsomely costumed and each carrying a large woven tray, leave their respective kivas and begin making a round of the village. Each pair of messengers goes right through the village, stopping at each house on the way; all the women are expecting them and bring out a double handful of meal, one half of which they cast into each tray. After completing the circuit of the pueblo, the young men carry the trays back to their own kiva, where they set them down to the left of the fireplace.

The night of the eighth day is passed by the different fraternities, in their respective kivas, grouped around their *ti'poni*(s) and singing. At some stage during the night, the Al men make their way to Kwan kiva, and a long ceremony takes place there in the course of which the *ke'le*(s), novices, who have been previously initiated, are aspersed from the six cardinal directions by the leaders of the two fraternities.[2]

---

[1] Particularly representing, according to Fewkes and Stephen (1892a, p. 214, n. 1), the nimbus clouds which frequently roll along the mesa summits, accompanied by lightning and heavy rains.

[2] Perhaps symbolising their 'emergence' from the depths of the underworld sea: cf. above, p. 103, n. 2.

As soon as the Al men have left their kiva,[1] the Kwan-tû commence decorating themselves, painting a line of white gypsum along the front of their arms and legs and renewing the other marks on their bodies. A number of songs are sung in the kiva; then the members put on their ceremonial kilt and sash, arrange feathers in their hair, and leave the kiva in line. In the meantime, Horn (Al) men have built three large fires in the village square. Around and over these fires, four Horn men—their helmets reversed, so that the horns curve forward—are bucking and jumping, miming the movements of mountain sheep. Beside the fires are piles of firewood, and over both wood-piles and fires the four 'sheep' career, stooping every now and then to throw more wood on the fires which cast a lambent glow over the courtyard.

First the Wü'wütçimtu, then the Singers, file into the square and take up their position. Finally the Kwan-tû enter, moving to the south side of the square where, facing the fires, they link arms with one another and begin to chant a solemn, impressive melody. Kwan leader is arrayed in a magnificent ceremonial blanket. He carries a bag of corn-meal; as the song begins, he steps forward and, starting at the west end of the line, sprinkles a broad path of meal in front of the singers, traversing the whole length of the line and back. He repeats this action three times in the course of the singing. Finally, as the last stanza draws to a close, he again traverses the line of singers, but this time—instead of sprinkling corn-meal—he takes his feathered stick (*kel'tsakwa*) and brushes the ground with it, from one side to the other, as if to obliterate the path he had previously made.

The Kwan-tû then return to their kiva, the other fraternities to theirs, and the people to their homes. It is still quite dark, and according to Stephen (1936, p. 992), piercingly cold.

At first light on the last day of Wü'wütçim, everyone in the pueblo—men and women alike—wash their heads in yucca suds; and many of the women do the same for their children.[2] As dawn breaks, certain of the Singers sprinkle broad trails of meal from their kiva to *moñ* kiva, from *moñ* kiva to the village square, from the square to Al kiva, from Al kiva to Kwan kiva, and from there back to their own kiva; using for the purpose[3] the corn-meal which the two messengers collected from the women of the village the previous afternoon. A few minutes later, six young men of Al, wearing the costume typical of their fraternity and carrying all the prayer-offerings from their own kiva, emerge from Na'savi kiva. They divide into pairs, and each pair follows the corn-meal 'path' to the kivas of the other three fraternities, where they are given the prayer-offerings of those fraternities, together with a considerable quantity of prayer-meal. The

---

[1] For the events of the last day of Wü'wütçim, see Fewkes and Stephen (1892*a*), pp. 216–17: Stephen (1936), pp. 990–2: and Titiev (1944), pp. 132–3.

[2] Fewkes (1900, p. 115) suggests that the general performance of head-washing at this time is due to the fact that, as virtually every adult male in the village belongs to one or other of the four fraternities which co-operate in the Wü'wütçim, all their families are also involved in the ceremony.

[3] Fewkes (1900), p. 108: Stephen (1936), p. 992.

three pairs of messengers then leave the village by three different trails, one pair making its way to Ta'wa-ki, the shrine of the Sun, one pair to the shrine of Ta'la-tüm'si, and one pair to another katçina shrine. As they leave the pueblo, the messengers sprinkle broad trails of corn-meal along the path; when they reach the respective shrines, they deposit the prayer-offerings there, then return to their kiva and disrobe.

In the meantime, each of the fraternities performs its own purificatory rite, *navo'tçiwa*.[1] In each of the participating kivas, every member takes a piece of water-melon rind and scoops into it a quantity of the ashes of the fire which was lit on the first day of the ceremony (and has been kept going ever since), taking care that all the ashes are finally removed from the fireplace. Each man then takes a handful of corn-meal in his left hand and, carrying the melon rind in his right, climbs the kiva ladder. Once outside, the whole group—led by the fraternity head—files through the village, and out to a point on the western edge of the mesa. There they stand in a line facing the west, each man holding the melon rind in his right hand and the corn-meal in his left. After sprinkling the corn-meal on the ashes, each man takes a pinch between his forefinger and thumb, circles his left hand four times over his head, and then casts it towards the west. He then throws the remainder of the meal, the ashes and the melon rind, over the cliff. After disposing of the ashes, the leaders of the several frater-nities vomit[2] over the cliff, then make their way back to the kivas, while the other members return to their homes.

So ends, substantially, the Wü'wütçim ceremony, though the leaders of the four fraternities must still sleep in their kivas, and observe ritual tabus, for a further four days after the *navo'tçiwa* rite. Later that same day, i.e. on the ninth day of the ceremony, first the Wü'wütçim group, and then the Singers, give their final performances in the village; and on the afternoon of the tenth day, the Soya'l katçina is seen approaching the pueblo from the southwest,[3] harbinger of the impending Soya'l.

In setting out to interpret the significance of the Wü'wütçim, we have to distinguish clearly between the two parts of the ceremony. In ordinary years the Wü'wütçim lasts five days, in place of nine in years when the full initiatory rites are performed. Of these five days, the concluding four correspond pretty closely, in their observances, to days 6, 7, 8 and 9 of the full ceremony; while the first day (*yü'ñya*, 'going in') corresponds, pretty closely again, to day 1 of the full ceremony. In other words, the principal events of day 1 (assembly in the kivas, setting-up of the six-directions' altars, lighting of the new fire, visit to the shrine of Tü'wa-po'ñya-tüm'si), the water-dowsing performances of the Wü' wütçim and Singers' fraternities on the afternoon of day 5 and on days 6 and 7, and the concluding observances of days 8 and 9 (public performances by Wü'wütçimtu and Singers, making and 'placing' of prayer-sticks, and *navo'*

---

[1] See Fewkes (1900), pp. 116–18.

[2] Having, one assumes, drunk a herb emetic for this purpose before leaving the kiva.

[3] For the arrival of the Soya'l katçina on 1st Mesa, see Stephen (1936), p. 28.

*tçiwa*), constitute one ceremonial sequence; while the later events of day 1 (fetching of the image of *Ta'la-tüm'si*, introduction of the novices into the kivas), the seclusion of the novices in the kivas on days 2, 3 and 4, and the initiatory proceedings that take place in the course of the fourth night and the morning of day 5, constitute another sequence.

So far as concerns the one sequence, its purpose is clearly and explicitly stated in the words which the village Crier uses to announce the ceremony, four days before it is due to begin. These run as follows:[1]

> All people awake, open your eyes, arise!
> 　Become *Ta'la-hoyam* (children of day), active and lively.
> Hasten, Clouds, from the four directions.
> 　Come, Snow, in plenty, that moisture may be abundant when summer comes.
> 　Come, Ice [? frost], and cover the fields, that after planting they may yield
> 　　abundantly.
> 　Let all hearts be glad.
> The Wü'wütçimtu will assemble in four days.
> 　They will go through the village, dancing and singing their songs.
> 　Let the women be ready to pour water upon them,
> 　That moisture may come in abundance and all shall rejoice.

In other words, the object of the ceremony—and, in particular, of the dowsing of the dancers with water—is to ensure good falls of rain and snow, to be followed by frosts, during the critical two to three months ahead.

Now it will be observed that the two fraternities which play the leading part in the dances of the latter part of the ceremony are the Wü'wütçimtu themselves, and the Singers. These two fraternities are linked to each other, in Hopi mythology;[2] they are also linked to the two leading women's societies, the Wü'wütçimtu to the Marau,[3] and the Singers to the Lako'n. It is on the members of these two fraternities that the women throw down water (and urine), and with them that they exchange taunts; and it is their representatives who paint their bodies with phallic signs, and who carry models of *lü'wa* (vulva). This fertility *motif*, explicit in the behaviour of the Wü'wütçim and Singers' dance-groups on the fifth, sixth and seventh days, is found—when we look more closely—to be implicit in two further aspects of the ceremony: namely, in the 'placing' of *pa'ho*(s) at the shrine of *Tü'wa-po'ñya-tüm'si* on the afternoon of the first day, and in the making of the special sumac prayer-sticks on the eighth day and their 'placing', early on the ninth day, at the shrine (among others) of *Ta'la-tüm'si*.

Regarding *Tü'wa-po'ñya-tüm'si*, 'sand-altar woman', we may note, first, that *tü'wa* refers to the brown sand of the valley, and that this sand has, as we have seen earlier (above, pp. 26-7), an especially close connection with child-birth:

---

[1] The words are given by Fewkes (1900), pp. 82-5.
[2] Fewkes (1900), pp. 124-5.
[3] Titiev (1944), p. 168. Singers' fraternity and Lako'n are linked in that, at Oraibi, both are 'owned' by Parrot clan.

it is 'the mother of babies', to which prayers are made 'for the fertility of women'. Of *Tü'wa-po'ñya-tümsi* herself, who is the sister of Mü'yiñwa,[1] we read as follows:[2]

> She is the mother of all living things, i.e. of all human kind, all animals, and all vegetation; plants suck from her breast a nourishing liquid, it passes up from their roots to their flowers and fruit, and animals and man eat of this vegetation, hence Tü'wa-poñya-tümsi is mother of all life. This liquid the bees suck from the flowers and make into honey.
>
> Bees (and butterflies) are the pets of Mü'yiñwa, knowing when melons, squash, flowers, all vegetation is to be plenty, and coming in great numbers to eat the pollen. When vegetation is to be scant they do not come.

This quotation, summarising as it does the Hopi view of Nature and of the life-process, conveys a clear idea of the significance ascribed to honey and pollen in Hopi ceremonies. The specific point to be noted here, however, is that the prayer-sticks offered at the shrine of Tü'wa-poñya-tümsi on the first afternoon of Wü'wütçim are likely, given the nature of the deity, to be in part certainly for 'fertility', but in part also—and perhaps in the major part—for the fertility of *women*.

And this interpretation receives support, to my mind, from the prayer-sticks made at the end of the ceremony. The majority of these are fashioned out of sumac (*sö've*, rhus trilobata), and this shrub, again, has an especial connection with child-birth; the cradle in which the new-born infant is laid is made of sumac twigs, the prayer-stick which girls carry throughout their initiation into the Marau is of sumac, sumac berries are used medicinally by women,[3] and the *lü'wa* (vulva) exhibited by the Wü'wütçimtu in their dances are made of sumac wood. Bearing in mind that these sumac prayer-sticks are deposited, on the ninth morning of Wü'wütçim, at (among others) the shrine of *Ta'la-tüm'si*, the deity who guards over child-birth, it seems fair to conclude that the fertility *motif* running through this sequence of the rites, also, is directed primarily to the fertility of women. If this conclusion is accepted, then we shall find, when we come to consider the Marau and the other two fall festivals, that the treatment of this *motif* in the Wü'wütçim ceremony is simply a variation on a theme already introduced and developed in the earlier ceremonies.

Turning now to the other (the initiatory) sequence, the rites that culminate in the initiation of novices into the four fraternities are chiefly controlled by the Al and Kwan fraternities; it is the men of Al and Kwan who kindle the new fire[4] on the afternoon of the first day, who patrol the village on the second and third nights and close the trails leading into it on the fourth morning, and who, by inference, play the leading rôles in the initiatory proceedings of the fourth night. An examination of the nature of these two fraternities, and in particular

---

[1] Stephen (1936), p. 261: Parsons (1936), pp. 1254–5.

[2] Parsons (1936), p. 1313: also p. 1252, under *mo'mo*, bumble bee.

[3] Parsons (1936), p. 1291: under *shü'bi*.

[4] The kindling of the new fire appears to play a part in both ceremonial sequences.

of the Kwan-tû, may then throw light on the purpose of the initiation itself.

There is no doubt, first, that a close link exists between the Kwan society and the cult of the dead. According to Nequatewa,[1] the Kwan-tû are regarded with great awe by the Hopi, for it is their duty to look after the dead; they are, in Hopi belief, in charge of the spirit on its journey from the grave to *Mas-ki*, the home of the dead. On 3rd Mesa, control of the Kwan fraternity rests in the hands of Masau'u clan, and normally the head of Masau'u clan is also head of the Kwan fraternity. Masau'u, as we have seen, is keeper of the home of the dead. He is also *wuya*, ancient, of Masau'u clan, and it was he who, in Hopi myth, first taught people the use of fire. Hence the kindling of new fire on the first day of Wü'wütçim, whatever other significance it may have, may be regarded as a dramatisation of one aspect of the Emergence story.

These two features, the link with the cult of the dead and the dramatisation of certain leading points in the Emergence myth, constitute—in Titiev's view[2]— the essential elements of the initiatory sequence. According to his interpretation, the four branches of the Wü'wütçim come together to enact the salient events of the Emergence, namely, the arrival of the first people on earth (recounted in the songs of the Tao society), their meeting with Masau'u, and his gift of fire to the Hopi, symbolised in the kindling of the new fire. At this point the novices are introduced; for three days they are kept in seclusion, then on the fourth night the dead return to the pueblo; they (or their impersonators) enter the kivas, the novices are brought face to face with them and, out of this confrontation, are 're-born' as men.

Regarding the actual form of the initiation, some light is cast on this by Voth's notes to the *Hopi Indian Collection at Grand Canyon, Arizona*.[3] Five items in that collection are of interest:

no. 303. *Tumoyi* (own food). A corn husk, containing some food, generally *piki*. This is given to the novice(s) on a certain day of the Wü'wüchim ceremony by his godfather or sponsor. Usually a sprig of juniper is attached to the roll, of which the sponsor chews a small quantity and spits it onto the novice at a certain time. During the long and complicated ceremony, there is usually a small stick attached to the object, which is to be used by the novice instead of the finger nails in case it becomes necessary for him to scratch his head.

no. 399. *Akua* (spoon, or pottery ladle). Spoons of this kind are given to the novices of the Wü'wüchim fraternity at their initiation into the order. At a certain time during the Ceremony, these spoons are fastened to a string which is tied around the neck of the novice in such a manner that the spoon is suspended on the breast.

[1] Nequatewa (1936), p. 104, n. 10.

[2] Titiev (1944), pp. 138–9. Titiev's interpretation is borne out, substantially, by Nequatewa's observation (1931, p. 2) on the Wü'wütçim: 'This ceremony portrays what happened in the Underworld before the Hopi people emerged and what they did to get out. Tradition says that the *Kwakwantû* played the most important part then, and that is why they still do in the ceremony.'

[3] Voth (1912c). These are the only notes of Voth's directly relating to the Wü'wütçim ceremony that have been published; by a series of 'accidents', none of the early observers (including Voth) appear ever to have been present in the kiva on the night that initiation took place.

no. 380, 481. *Tawiya* (gourd vessel). Used for getting water from springs for ceremonies [distinct from *moñwikuru*, netted gourds: no. 538]. In the Wü'wüchim ceremony, water is poured on the heads of the novices from these vessels, as part of the initiation ceremony, 'the rite resembling and practically being a baptism'.

no. 601. *Kel napna* (novice costume). These costumes are worn by the novices in the great Wü'wüchim ceremony, where they are initiated either into the Wü'wüchim (Ancients), Tao (Singer), Ahl (Horn), or Kwan (Agave) order. The novices of the first two of these societies put these costumes on early on the ninth day for certain ceremonies; those of the Agave society during the night following the eighth day.

no. 504. *Toho'pko* (Mountain lion animal). Given to the Wü'wüchim novices in their initiation ceremony and worn by them on the wrist as a prayer that these newly initiated members may be strong and courageous through life. (Similar fetishes occur archaeologically: sometimes near the wrist.)

The first two objects in this list imply special items of food, and special means of taking food or drink, preliminary to initiation; the third and fourth, some form of 'baptism' as a part of initiation and the assumption of special clothing as a consequence of it; while the fifth symbolises the purpose of the rite. To the significance of these details, I shall return later (see below, p. 488).

Whatever its precise form, Wü'wütçim initiation bestows, in Titiev's words, 'spiritual status' on those who have passed through the rites. This status is reflected in three particular respects:

(*a*) in the course of the initiatory proceedings, the novices are introduced to the 'fraternity of the dead', and thus made certain of occupying their proper places in the Underworld.[1] Each of the four branches of the Wü'wütçim has its own 'home', to which its members go after death. It is only after a young man has gone through the rites, therefore, that he is assured of going to the right quarter of the Underworld on his death.

(*b*) Only those who have been initiated into one of the four branches of Wü'wütçim may go on salt-gathering expeditions, 'which take men to the very brink of the home of the dead'.[2]

(*c*) Only those who have been initiated into one of the four branches of Wü'wütçim may take part in the Soya'l.[3]

The significance of this last aspect of initiation we shall be in a position to assess, when we have dealt with the Soya'l; and it is to this sequence of rites that I now turn.

---

[1] Titiev (1944), p. 136, and n. 48.

[2] Titiev (1944), p. 139. This, in turn, furnishes a further link with the Kwan fraternity: Fewkes (1900, pp. 117–18) reports that the horns on the Kwan head-dress are believed to be connected, 'in some occult way', with the stalactites found in the salt cave in the Grand Cañon.

[3] This is attested by all observers: e.g. Dorsey and Voth (1901), p. 9, n. †: Parsons (1936), p. 2: Titiev (1944), p. 142.

### THE SOYA'L, AT ORAIBI

From many points of view, the Soya'l is the key-stone of Hopi ceremonialism.[1] Control of the ceremony lies in the hands of Bear clan, its leader is the Village chief (or his deputy), its principal observances are held in *moñ* kiva (i.e. in Sakwa'lenvi kiva, up to 1896), and its supporting officers include the most important men in the pueblo, namely: Pikyas chief, who impersonates the Aholi katçina, Parrot chief, who (at Oraibi) controls the Singers' society, Crier chief, and War chief. These are the men who hold the 'chiefs' talk' at the close of the Soya'l, and who supervise the undertaking of major events, such as the sponsorship of the Nima'n or the planning of a salt expedition, that are to take place during the coming year. As Hopi say: 'everything branches out from the Soya'l.'

Apart from the general fact, noted above, that only men who have been 'put into' one of the four branches of the Wü'wütçim may take part in the Soya'l, the Soya'l is linked to the Wü'wütçim in two specific ways. Like that ceremony, the Soya'l has both a long, and an abbreviated, form: in the abbreviated form, lasting five days, the Soya'l centres around the making of prayer-sticks, which are deposited at special places on the last morning; in the full form, lasting nine days, the rites reach a climax in the Sun 'dance' on the last night of the ceremony, followed the next morning—as in the abbreviated form—by the 'placing' of *pa'ho*(s). In those years when Wü'wütçim initiation has been held in November, the Soya'l is celebrated in its long form the following month; and when the Soya'l is celebrated in its long form, those kivas associated with the four Wü'wütçim fraternities play a special rôle in the (extended) rites. In ordinary years, while the main rites are staged in *moñ* kiva, all the kivas in the pueblo take part and every adult (i.e. initiated) man is expected to go into his own kiva to make prayer-offerings. This is also true of the Soya'l in its long form; but in *that* case, the rites commence four days earlier, and the events of the first four days are restricted to those kivas which, the previous month, cooperated in the Wü'wütçim ceremony.[2]

Sixteen days after the advent of the Soya'l katçina, the Soya'l observances begin with the preliminary making of prayer-sticks, known as *Soya'l pa'ho la'lauwu.*

---

[1] Titiev (1944), pp. 142–3.

Descriptions of the Soya'l are to be found in Dorsey and Voth (1901), pp. 1–59: Fewkes (1898*b*), pp. 68–87, 101–9: Parsons (1936), pp. 1–6, and Stephen (1936), pp. 7–82: Titiev (1944), pp. 142–6. Of these, Stephen's account is based on observation of the abbreviated Soya'l of 1892 and 1893 (1936, pp. 30–82), and of the last night of the full Soya'l of 1891 (1936, pp. 7–28), and Fewkes', on observation of the abbreviated Soya'l of 1897: both on 1st Mesa. Dorsey and Voth's account is based on Voth's observation of the full Soya'l rites of 1893, 1897 and 1900, at Oraibi. The description that follows, of the Soya'l in its long form, is based on the account by Dorsey and Voth of the Soya'l at Oraibi.

[2] As is indicated by the fact that, in years when the Soya'l is celebrated in its long form, the *na'atsi*(s) are set up at *moñ* kiva, and at the Kwan, Tao and Al kivas, on the first day (*yü'ñya*) of the rites, and at all the rest on the fifth day (*na'lüsh-ta'la*).

This takes place, at Oraibi, in *moñ* kiva.[1] During the morning Soya'l chief, who is either the head of Bear clan or his deputy, makes five sets of prayer-offerings, each consisting of a *püh'tabi* and four *nakwa'kwosi*(s). Later in the day one set of these prayer-offerings is deposited at each of four shrines in the vicinity of the pueblo, one in each of the four cardinal directions. In the evening, the other five Soya'l leaders join Soya'l chief in *moñ* kiva. They seat themselves in a semi-circle around the fireplace, Soya'l chief having in front of him a woven tray filled with corn-meal and on the corn-meal the remaining set of prayer-offerings made that morning. The six leaders smoke together, then Soya'l chief takes the tray in his hands, utters a short prayer over it, takes a pinch of corn-meal from the tray, holds it to his lips, indicates each of the six directions with it, then sprinkles it over the *püh'tabi* and the *nakwa'kwosi*(s) on the tray. He hands the tray to the man on his left, who does the same, and so on until the tray, with the prayer-offerings, has made the complete round. The six leaders then smoke together again, and when they are through, Soya'l chief hands the tray to Crier chief. At day-break the next morning, Crier chief ascends to the roof of the Ke'le clan house, 'places' the prayer-offerings in the shrine there, sprinkles the corn-meal to the rising sun, and announces the forth-coming Soya'l.

At sunrise the next morning,[2] Soya'l chief sets up the main Soya'l *na'atsi* outside *moñ* kiva, sprinkling corn-meal over it and casting a pinch towards the rising sun. He then visits each of the other participating kivas—Kwan, Tao and Al, and sets up a *na'atsi* outside each, returning to *moñ* kiva when he has done so. The remainder of the day is spent by the leaders in the kiva, carding and spin-ning cotton to be used later in the ceremony for attaching to the Soya'l *pa'ho*(s) and *nakwa'kwosi*(s). The second and third days of the ceremony are spent in much the same way, the leaders sleeping in the kiva and, from the first day on, observing the usual ritual tabus.

At sunrise on the fourth day,[3] the *na'atsi*(s) are set up as before, but on this morning an additional *na'atsi*—a stick about 2 feet 6 inches long, with six flint spear heads and six arrow heads attached to it—is set up outside *moñ* kiva; this evidently belongs to War chief, and is put up in preparation for his dance later in the day. About 8 o'clock in the morning, all the Soya'l members return home and wash their heads in yucca suds; then return to their kivas, to prepare prayer-sticks and prayer-feathers. Lying on the east banquette in *moñ* kiva, are several bags containing pieces of root, sticks, herbs and feathers. While the other members continue to card cotton, the three principal leaders (Soya'l chief, Pikyas chief, and War chief) start making *nakwa'kwosi*(s), each consisting of an eagle, hawk, turkey or other feather attached to a cotton thread about 4 inches

[1] For description of *Soya'l pa'ho la'lauwu*, see Dorsey and Voth (1901), pp. 15–16. At Walpi, where Patki clan 'owns' the Soya'l, the preliminary smoke and prayer-stick making is held in Patki clan house.

[2] Or four days later, in years when the Soya'l is celebrated in the abbreviated form: Stephen (1936), pp. 30–1.

[3] For the events of the fourth day of Soya'l, see Dorsey and Voth (1901), pp. 18–27.

long; as each one is finished, the maker lays it down on the floor in front of him. War chief, having made four of these *nakwa'kwosi*(s) and a *püh'tabi* ('road'), takes these and a gourd vessel, leaves the kiva and makes his way down to Lenañva spring, at the foot of the mesa. Arriving there, he utters a short prayer, deposits the four *nakwa'kwosi*(s) beside the spring, sprinkles a little corn-meal over them and casts a pinch on to the water. Then he fills the gourd vessel, and starts back up the mesa, laying the *püh'tabi* on the footpath at a short distance from the spring.

On his return to the kiva, War chief makes a further *nakwa'kwosi*, which he attaches to a long black eagle feather; then he ties cotton strings to four shorter eagle feathers, smokes over them, and finally wraps them in a corn husk and lays them on the same tray on which the others have put their *pa'ho*(s) and *nakwa'kwosi*(s). In the meantime, Soya'l chief and Pikyas chief have made a number of *pa'ho*(s) of their own: Soya'l chief, a single black *pa'ho* (with a green band round the middle), about 14 inches long, to which are attached sprigs of four different kinds of herb (one of which is *sy'ovi*, salt-bush) and four corn-husk packets, and a single green *pa'ho*, about 16 inches long, with a stem of *kwa'kwi* grass, an eagle breath-feather and a corn-husk packet tied to it; Pikyas chief, a single long *pa'ho*, two *püh'tabi*(s) and four *nakwa'kwosi*(s). As they finish each one, they lay it on the woven tray and smoke over it in silence.

When all the prayer-offerings are ready, Soya'l chief and Pikyas chief seat themselves on either side of the tray and prepare to consecrate them. First, Soya'l chief takes a pinch of meal, prays over it, and sprinkles the meal over the *pa'ho*(s); then he takes some honey in his mouth and ejects it over them. Pikyas chief does the same, then both smoke silently over the tray. After sprinkling further corn-meal over the *pa'ho*(s), Soya'l chief takes the tray in both hands and moves it up and down in front of him, at the same time whispering a prayer lasting about twelve minutes; he hands the tray to Pikyas chief, who does the same, then both smoke together in silence, for about eight minutes. Finally, Soya'l chief takes the *pa'ho*(s) off the tray, wraps them in a blanket with the corn-meal, and hands the blanket to one of the Soya'l members. The latter takes the *pa'ho*(s) to a place called Sakwa'ska, where he buries them and brings back with him some white earth (kaolin), to be used later in the ceremony; Soya'l chief and Pikyas chief make their way to two other katçina shrines, to deposit the remaining *nakwa'kwosi*(s), and Tobacco chief goes down to the spring with a netted gourd vessel, to fetch water for use in the afternoon ceremony.

At about 3.30 in the afternoon War chief, having made certain preparations for the coming ceremony, puts about fifteen pieces of various kinds of roots in a woven tray, together with two pieces of a yellow clay. Then, sitting on the floor in the northwest corner of the kiva, he sprinkles three intersecting lines of corn-meal, places a corn-husk ring at the centre, lays a crenellate bowl on the ring, and arranges around the bowl, in each of the six cardinal directions, pebbles of the right colour, and beside each, a flint arrow-head and a black eagle feather. Taking the netted gourd fetched earlier from Lenañiva, he pours water into the bowl from each of the six directions, picks each of the roots out of the tray in turn, chews it, and spits the contents of his mouth into the bowl. Then follows a long and elaborate performance, in the course of which War chief puts on the body paint and costume of Pü'ükoñhoya,[1] the elder of the two War deities, 12 songs are sung and the medicine-water consecrated, and at the close of the last song, all those present take a sip of the consecrated water in their mouth, a pinch of the yellow clay in their hand, and run with these to their own houses.[2] There, they wet the clay with the water from their mouth, then smear it on the breast, back, arms and legs of each member of their household. This is 'to make their hearts strong', i.e. to make people brave and healthy; and so valuable is the rite considered, that members of households which lack Soya'l participants make it a point to visit more fortunate households in order to be included in the smearing.[3]

In the course of the fourth evening, the first 'hawk' impersonation takes place.[4] A pile of moist sand is prepared in the southeast corner of the deep part of the kiva (*moñ* kiva), and all the men take their places on the surrounding banquettes. Two wooden *tok'wi*(s), cones about 6 inches high, stand ready for use, together with two pointed sticks, 10 inches long, to one end of which several bunches of hawk feathers are tied; these are known as *masha'adta*, 'his (or its) wings'. At about 9.30 p.m., when all is ready, Soya'l chief puts a feather into the top of each of the two *tok'wi*(s). Then his deputy (also of Bear clan), who is to take the part of the Hawk impersonator, puts on his ceremonial kilt and daubs his shoulders, forearms, legs below the knee (with a band above), hands and feet, with the white kaolin fetched earlier in the day. All present take a sprig of cedar, crush it between their teeth, spit it into their hands, and rub their bodies with their palms.

Hawk man now takes a tray with some corn-meal on it, the two *tok'wi*(s), and an old *piwa'ni* (weasel) skin. Stepping to the southeast corner of the deep part of the kiva, he lays the skin on the sand pile, then sprinkles a path of corn-meal from the sand pile, diagonally across the floor of the kiva to within a few feet of the northwest corner: then south, to within a few feet of the step, where he sets one of the two *tok'wi*(s): then east, until the path cuts the diagonal path, at which point he sets the other *tok'wi*. He then resumes his seat. Tobacco chief hands cigarettes, made out of wild tobacco and prepared beforehand, to him and to War chief (seated, in full costume, in the northeast corner of the kiva), and all smoke together. Then a series of songs are chanted, lasting about two hours, and all smoke together again.

By now it is about midnight. The Hawk impersonator rises to his feet, takes the weasel skin off the sand pile, picks up the two *tok'wi*(s), and puts them all in

---

[1] The name is derived from the stem *püü'ka-*, v. strikes it, e.g. with a club: Whorf (1936), p. 1286.
[2] Dorsey and Voth (1901), pp. 25–6.
[3] Titiev (1944), p. 143, n. 13.
[4] Dorsey and Voth (1901), pp. 26–7.

the northwest corner of the kiva. Picking up the two *masha'adta*, he goes to the east side of the ladder, and waves them up and down for a few minutes in time to a melody sung by all present in a low humming voice. He then passes along the whole line of singers from right to left, touching the feet of each man with the *masha'adta*. Having touched the last one, he stands to the left (i.e. to the west) of the ladder, waves the *masha'adta* up and down to the same melody, then returns along the line of singers from left to right, drawing the *masha'adta* across the knees of each. This action he repeats, going from right to left, touching the shoulders of each man with the *masha'adta*, then back, brushing their faces, and finally, returning again, touches the crown of the head of each man with the hawk feathers. The Hawk impersonator then retires, with the *masha'adta*, to the northwest corner of the kiva. All present spit on their hands and rub their bodies with their palms, and the ceremony is at an end. The corn-meal path is swept off the floor, the *na'atsi*(s) taken in, and all who have taken part retire to rest in the kiva.

Early the next morning,[1] before sunrise, all the men from *moñ* kiva make their way to a rock about halfway down the mesa to the southeast of the village, and each man sprinkles a pinch of corn-meal towards the rising sun.[2] On their return, Soya'l chief makes a round of all the kivas in the pueblo, setting up a *na'atsi* at each kiva where he has not done so already; outside *moñ* kiva, he sets up the two *masha'adta* on either side of the main Soya'l *na'atsi*. On this day, all the adult men of the village are supposed to assemble in their respective kivas; from now until the morning of the ninth day, all those taking part sleep in the kivas, no meat or salted food is eaten,[3] and the greater part of the time is spent in carding and spinning cotton needed for making the Soya'l prayer-sticks.

During the fifth day, a number of different activities are pursued in *moñ* kiva. Early in the morning, the paraphernalia for the two Soya'l altars (to be erected on the eighth day) is brought into the kiva; and later, a man from Sand clan is sent to fetch valley sand, which is piled in the southeast corner of the deep part of the kiva. During the day, a great deal of cotton twine is spun, to be used later in the manufacture of *pa'ho*(s). In the meantime, Soya'l chief completes the sixteen short single *pa'ho*(s), on which he has been working for the last two days; these *pa'ho*(s) differ from ordinary prayer-sticks, in having only a sprig of *kü'ñya* (Artemisia frigida) tied to them, in place of sprigs of both *kü'ñya* and *ma'övi* (snakeweed), and they also have a bluebird-feather *nakwa'kwosi* attached—in place of the usual eagle, turkey, hawk or duck feather. During the morning some of the men, led by Tobacco chief, make four bunches of corn-husk packets, each packet being about 4 inches long and each bunch containing

---

[1] For the events of the fifth day (*na'lüsh-ta'la*) of the Soya'l, see Dorsey and Voth (1901), pp. 28–36.

[2] This sprinkling of meal towards the dawn, called *kuywa'to*, is performed in many Hopi ceremonies; it is done on this, and on the succeeding three mornings, of the Soya'l.

[3] The Soya'l leaders, in *moñ* kiva, eat only one meal in the twenty-four hours, late in the evening; this meal is brought to the kiva in special trays and bowls, and consists of corn-meal mush, boiled beans, and *pi'ki*: Dorsey and Voth (1901), p. 28, n. *.

ten or twelve packets; the packets are called *möçiata*, and are said to contain various kinds of seeds and pieces of different herbs and grasses. Other men make a number of 'blossoms', to be attached to the screen set up later in the ceremony; each 'blossom' consists of a cylinder of wood, about 2 inches long, into one end of which several radiating sticks[1] are fastened and the spaces between the sticks filled with twine, wound from one stick to another, and then dyed in different colours.

Late in the evening, in *moñ* kiva, there is a repetition of the hawk impersonation, this time in company with a maiden who plays the part of the Soya'l-*mana*. About 9.30 p.m., the Hawk man and his deputy paint their bodies and put on their ceremonial kilts; all present again chew a sprig of cedar, spit on their hands, and rub their bodies with their palms. About an hour later, Hawk man's deputy leaves the kiva, to return a few minutes later with the maiden who is to act as the Soya'l-*mana*, accompanied by two other women; the girl is dressed in an embroidered blanket (*toi'hi*) held by a knotted belt, worn over her usual dress, and in her hand she carries a white corn ear. The deputy now takes the weasel skin, the two *tok'wi*(s), and some corn-meal, lays the weasel skin on the sand pile, sprinkles the corn-meal path on the kiva floor and sets out the *tok'wi*(s), exactly as Hawk man himself did the previous evening. All smoke for a few minutes in silence. Then Hawk man's deputy leaves the kiva, carrying in his hand a dough ball about 2 inches in diameter. All wait, expectantly. Suddenly a screeching noise, like that of a hawk, is heard outside the kiva; it is made by the deputy, using a bone whistle concealed in his mouth, and is answered from inside the kiva by Hawk man himself. The two women call out: *yü'ñya*, 'come in'; a minute or two later, the same sound is heard close by, the deputy comes to the kiva hatch, throws the dough ball down the hatch (where it breaks into pieces on the kiva floor), then descends the ladder, carrying in his hands the two *masha'adta*.

It is now about 11 o'clock. There follows an extremely elaborate dance, lasting some two hours, in the course of which first Hawk man's assistant, then Hawk man himself, mimic the movements of a hawk, using the bone whistle to simulate the screeching of the bird and the pair of *masha'adta* to simulate its flight. In the course of the dance, to the accompaniment of tunes hummed by the other participants, each in turn makes his way along the corn-meal path, followed by the Soya'l-*mana* who, in turn, mimes the action of the leader—but with the white corn ear which she carries, in place of the *masha'adta*. The dance concluded, Hawk man again goes along the line of singers, touching each one on feet, knees, shoulders, face and crown of head with the hawk feathers, as on the previous evening. All present then spit on their hands, and rub their palms over their bodies.

Before sunrise the next morning, the men again make their way down the

---

[1] The sticks are made from hooks on the pods of a plant called *tomo'ala* (unidentified); they are claimed to have special influence over rain clouds: Dorsey and Voth (1901), p. 29, n. *. The plant also has certain efficacious properties: Wallis (1936), p. 63.

east side of the mesa and offer corn-meal to the rising sun. Then, the *na'atsi*(s) are set up outside the kivas. In *moñ* kiva, the greater part of the day is spent, by the leaders in preparing the 'blossoms', crooks and other pieces of equipment to be set on the altars, and by the other members in spinning and carding cotton. In the other kivas, also, men are busy spinning cotton; all those taking part are very devotional and serious throughout the day, and such talking as is done is carried on in whispers.

The seventh day of Soya'l is the great day for *pa'ho*-making. In *moñ* kiva, and in all the other kivas in the pueblo, after the erection of the *na'atsi*(s), the floor is swept, supplies of willow sticks, herbs and feathers are brought in, and the men seat themselves on the floor and set to making prayer-offerings.[1] These prayer-offerings are of two main kinds:

(*i*) Common double *pa'ho*(s):

These consist of two sticks, about $4\frac{1}{2}$ inches long, commonly painted green with black tips. All these double *pa'ho*(s) have a sprig of *kü'ñya*, and/or a sprig of *ma'övi*, tied to them, together with a corn-husk packet, a turkey feather, and a bunch of pine needles; they also have either a duck-feather or a hawk-feather *nakwa'kwosi*, attached. The prayer-sticks are distinguished as Soya'l *pa'ho*(s) by the triple pine-needles, attached to all prayer-sticks made at Soya'l.

In preparing the corn-husk packet, a pinch of meal is put in a strip of corn husk; the maker then dips his finger in honey, licks the honey off his finger, ejects the saliva over the feathers and herb sprigs, rubs a drop or two of honey on the meal, and finally spurts it on his hands and rubs his body with his palms. He then ties up the corn-husk packet and attaches it, with the feathers and herb sprig(s), to the *pa'ho* by means of a cotton thread wound tightly round the stick (or sticks).

Most of the common double *pa'ho*(s), made at Soya'l, are painted green with black tips; a few, however, are painted wholly black (? 'male'), a few wholly green (? 'female'), while a very few have yellow bodies. They fall into a number of different categories, i.e. *ka'ö pa'ho*(s), corn prayer-sticks, for putting in store-houses: *pa'sa pa'ho*(s), field prayer-sticks, for burying in the fields: house *pa'ho*(s), for putting in the rafters of houses, and on ladders to prevent accidents: horse, cattle and sheep *pa'ho*(s), for putting in corrals and stables for 'increase', and for burying in pastures where livestock graze: *ma'k pa'ho*(s), hunt prayer-sticks, either for depositing at special shrines or for burying in hunting grounds: miscellaneous *pa'ho*(s), e.g. for tying to peach trees for a good crop, or for placing in springs and cisterns to ensure an abundant water supply.

(*ii*) Sun (*ta'wa*) *pa'ho*(s):

These are substantially the same as the common double *pa'ho*(s), except that they are 6 to 7 inches long, in place of $4\frac{1}{2}$ inches: are painted white, except for

---

[1] On the making of Soya'l *pa'ho*(s), see especially Dorsey and Voth (1901), pp. 36–8, and p. 57, n. *: cf. for 1st Mesa, Stephen (1936), pp. 7–8, 39–47, 64–70, and for 2nd Mesa, Nequatewa (1931), p. 2, Beaglehole (1936), p. 24, and (1937), p. 50.

those made by Kwan men (theirs are painted black) : and have two eagle-feather *nakwa'kwosi*(s) tied to them.

Fig. 42. Bent *pa'ho* or crook, *nölösh'hoya*:

*a*. bent woodframe, tied with cotton.

*b*. corn-husk packet, with herb sprig.

*c*. long, black turkey feather.

*d*. two *nakwa'kwosi*, one black, one white.

Redrawn from Dorsey and Voth (1901), pl. xv.

The number of *pa'ho*(s) made by each man varies widely, but most men make from eight to twelve altogether. At the same time as the prayer-sticks are being made, a few *nölösh'hoya*, 'crooks', are also made. This is the first prayer-stick made for a lad; it is made for him, usually either by his father or his mother's brother, 'as a wish that the boy may thrive, be happy and live long', and symbolises the stages on the 'road' he is to follow in life.

When the double *pa'ho*(s)—and the *nölösh'hoya*(s)—are all finished, they are laid on trays against the north wall of the kiva, the floor is swept, and the men set to making hundreds of *nakwa'kwosi*(s) of all kinds—eagle, turkey, hawk, duck feathers being tied to willow sticks and to grasses of various sorts. These are the typical Soya'l prayer-offerings, in the sense that they are made at Soya'l and at no other time of the year, and will be deposited along the mesa edge on the ninth morning of the ceremony. As they are finished, the *nakwa' kwosi*(s) are hung in bunches from pegs on the kiva wall.

By the time all the prayer-offerings are ready, it is late in the afternoon. The trays containing the *pa'ho*(s) are set down on the floor near the fireplace, the members gather round them, each man takes a little honey in his mouth and spurts it over the prayer-offerings he has made, and all smoke over them together; then the *pa'ho*(s) are tied into bundles and hung on the kiva wall, in preparation for being deposited in the appropriate places on the ninth morning. Finally, the floor is swept, all the pieces are carefully gathered up, sprinkled with corn meal, taken out and thrown into a gully—to be carried down by the rains to the fields below.

There, for the moment, we may leave the *pa'ho*(s) and *nakwa'kwosi*(s); but, before doing so, it may be well to say a further word about the belief that underlies the making of them. According to Dorsey and Voth,[1] the common double *pa'ho*(s) and the willow-stick *nakwa'kwosi*(s), which constitute between them the great majority of all the prayer-offerings made at Soya'l, are offerings for the dead: but of two different kinds. The short double *pa'ho*(s), whether green-and-black, double-black or double-green, are said to be made for the dead *in general*, or alternately for the cloud deities, who are believed to reciprocate the kindness by sending the Hopi good crops, corn, increase of flocks, and the other benefits asked for. A *nakwa'kwosi*, by contrast, is made for *one* deceased; on this occasion, the *nakwa'kwosi*(s) are fastened to long sticks and set out along the mesa lip, and Hopi say that the dead come afterwards from their home and each one takes his own *nakwa'kwosi*, or rather the 'breath' or soul of it, and is grateful to the maker of it for remembering him thus.

The evening of the seventh day is devoted, in all kivas, to the making of *hihi'kwispi*(s), 'objects to breathe upon'. These are made in the following way. A cotton string is tied, first to the point, and then to the stub end, of a corn husk; about 12 inches away, on the same cotton string, another husk is fastened in the same way, then another, and another, making four in all. To the tip of each corn husk, an eagle-feather *nakwa'kwosi* is tied; and to the stub end of the last husk a cotton string, about 36 inches long, to the free end of which is attached a further eagle-feather *nakwa'kwosi*, together with six feathers representing the six cardinal directions. As each man finishes his *hihi'kwispi*, he folds the four husks together and puts it away, for use the next morning.

Early the next morning,[2] after the offering of meal to the dawn and the erection of *na'atsi*(s), Soya'l chief makes a round of all the kivas and leaves in each kiva one of the long black *pa'ho*(s) which he has made during the previous days (Fig. 43). Then, as the sun is rising, all the men who prepared *hihi'kwispi*(s) the evening before take them, sprinkle some corn-meal and corn pollen over the husks, and leave the kiva. Emerging from the kiva, each man holds the *hihi' kwispi* to the rising sun and says: 'breathe on this'; then he runs, first to his wife's house, then to his own (maternal) house, then to the houses of his clanswomen and of his ceremonial 'father's' sisters, calling on the women of each

---

[1] Dorsey and Voth (1901), p. 57, n.*.
[2] For the events of the eighth day of Soya'l, see Dorsey and Voth (1901), pp. 38-46.

E

household to breathe on the *hihi'kwispi*. When all have done so, he returns to his own kiva and hangs the *hihi'kwispi* on the wall, allowing the corn-meal and pollen to drip on to the kiva floor. When all have returned, one of the kiva members gathers all the *hihi'kwispi*(s) over his left shoulder, and proceeds with them to *moñ* kiva where he leaves them.

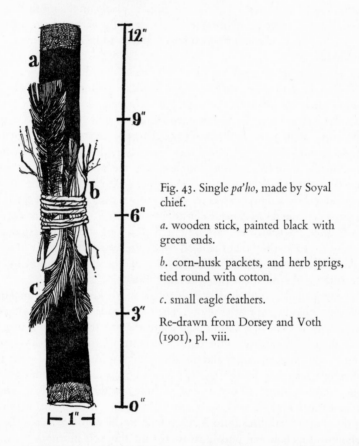

Fig. 43. Single *pa'ho*, made by Soyal chief.

*a.* wooden stick, painted black with green ends.

*b.* corn-husk packets, and herb sprigs, tied round with cotton.

*c.* small eagle feathers.

Re-drawn from Dorsey and Voth (1901), pl. viii.

The principal event of the eighth day is the setting up, in *moñ* kiva, of the two Soya'l altars, in preparation for the rites that are to take place that evening and during the night. Again, this is a solemn day; very little talking takes place in the kivas, and hardly anyone speaks above a whisper.

About 8 o'clock in the morning, all the Soya'l leaders go to their own houses and wash their hair thoroughly in yucca suds, then return to *moñ* kiva and smoke together, while their hair dries. To the north of the fireplace are lying the *moñ'kohü*(s), *ti'poni*(s), and other things to be set in front of the altar; to these, Soya'l chief adds a woven tray containing *pa'ho*(s) made by him the previous day. Crier chief and Pikyas chief make a number of *nakwa'kwosi*(s); and when these are ready, Pikyas chief takes his and goes down to Lenañva spring to fetch water in a netted gourd. In the meantime one of the other Soya'l members, of Sand clan, takes the other *nakwa'kwosi*(s) and fetches sand for the altars.

During the morning the main Soya'l altar is erected, in *moñ* kiva, under the direction of Soya'l chief assisted by Crier chief, Tobacco chief, and Hawk man. First, Tobacco and Crier chiefs make the four clay stands in which the legs of the wooden frame, and of the two *na'atsi*(s), are to stand; then they set up the wooden frame (see Figure 44). Hawk man makes a sand ridge, about 4 inches high, in front of the wooden frame; and then, in front of the ridge, lays out the sand field, some 32 inches from front to back. Over the field he makes a number of holes, into each of which he blows a puff of smoke and then closes up the hole.[1] After blowing smoke over the whole field, he hands the pipe back to Tobacco chief; then draws the four black semi-circles along the top edge of the field, representing rain clouds, and a number of black lines, representing falling rain, running back up the sloping surface of the sand ridge.

About an hour before noon, the two women who are to play the part of Soya'l-*mana*(s) enter *moñ* kiva: the one who is to play the leading part being dressed in an ordinary dress, tied with a white knotted belt, over which she wears the ceremonial blanket (*atö'e*) and over this, an embroidered robe (*toi'hi*), with moccasins on her feet.

About noon the Soya'l members, the leaders first, start bringing into *moñ* kiva bunches of corn cobs of different colours tied together with yucca fibre, from three to six cobs in a bunch: the cobs themselves being of the colours of the six cardinal directions. The bunches are stacked under, and behind, the wooden frame. Meanwhile, Soya'l chief is preparing the two *pa'ho*(s), and the crooks, which are to go on the sand field. Hawk man now places the quartz-crystal *ti'poni*, belonging to Soya'l chief, in front of the wooden frame in the centre, and on either side of it two *moñ'kohü*(s), belonging respectively to Village chief and Crier chief (on the left), and to Parrot chief and Tobacco chief (on the right). In front of the *ti'poni*, on the sand field, he puts the *moñ'wikuru*; and then, in a diagonal line running from the gourd vessel to the (southeast) corner of the field, alternately four flat, baked cakes, called *pika'viki*, and four clay stands— the first with a double *pa'ho* stuck in it, the second with a single green *pa'ho*, the third and fourth with crooks. In each instance, he first sprinkles corn-meal from the six directions, before setting the object in position. Finally, War chief sets the two *na'atsi*(s)[2] in place, on either side of the wooden frame; and Pikyas chief sprinkles corn-meal over their clay stands.

When the main altar is completed, Soya'l chief steps to the east side of it, with Parrot chief on his left, then Tobacco chief, then Crier chief, Hawk man and his deputy, and War chief. Each takes a pinch of corn pollen in his hand, holds it with great solemnity to his lips, and then each in turn, starting with

---

[1] Evidently a 'planting' of smoke: Dorsey and Voth (1901), p. 41.

[2] The herb sprigs tied to the *na'atsi*(s) are two bunches of *kü'ñya*, and two bunches of *ma'övi*, alternately; with two turkey-wing feathers tied to the top of each. Both mountain sage (*kü'ñya*), and snakeweed (*ma'övi*), grow on the mesas around the Hopi villages.

Fig. 44. *Main Soyal Altar.*
*Background. a.* wooden
frame, with blossoms.
*b.* sand ridge. *c. na'atsi,*
with sprigs of herbs.
*d.* pile of corn cobs. *e.* crystal *ti'poni,* set in wood.
*f.* pair of *moŋ'kohŭi,* set on
either side of the crystal
*ti'poni. g.* pair of corn-
cob *ti'poni,* with eagle
feathers attached.
*Foreground. h.* sand field,
with smoke holes in it.
*i.* semi-circular cloud symbols with black lines,
denoting rain. *j.* netted
gourd-vessel. *k.* flat baked
cake, with black lines on
top: four of these. *l.* clay
stand with double *pa'ho.*
*m.* clay stand with single
*pa'ho. n.* clay stand with
crook: two of these.
Re-drawn from Dorsey
and Voth (1901), pl. 1.

Soya'l chief, sprinkles it first on the *moñ'kohü*(s) and then along the line of cakes, *pa'ho*(s) and crooks. Pikyas chief, meanwhile, begins erecting the small altar in the southwest corner of the deep part of the kiva.

During the erection of the main altar, four young men have been busy in the south part of the kiva, putting on their costumes and daubing their forearms, legs and feet, shoulders and crown of head, together with a band around the waist and above each knee, with white kaolin. Each has on a katçina sash and kilt, fox skin dangling from his belt, ankle bands and moccasins, strands of beads round his neck, and bunches of feathers in his hair. Now they wait, as the leaders finish consecrating the main altar. As soon as they have done, the four young men set out, each carrying a large, flat woven tray. On emerging from the kiva, each takes one of the four Soya'l *na'atsi*(s) from beside the hatch; then they run through the pueblo, collecting from every household bunches of corn cobs tied up with yucca fibre.[1] These they bring back to *moñ* kiva, where the bundles are received by the leaders, carried to the main altar, and added to the pile already there. When all the bundles have been brought into the kiva and piled, the four young men disrobe.

At about 2 p.m., all the Soya'l members go to their houses and fetch a small tray of corn-meal. On returning to *moñ* kiva, they empty the meal into four large woven trays, set out by Soya'l chief in front of the sand field. In the meal in each tray, Soya'l chief sets a single black *pa'ho*, prepared the day before, together with a number of corn-husk packets; and beside each tray, on the floor, he lays the *hihi'kwispi*(s) in four separate bundles. The four messengers, who have been standing ready, now step forward, take up the four woven trays with the corn meal, sling the bundles of *hihi'kwispi*(s) over their left shoulder, and set off for Lenañva spring. Arriving there, they circle the spring four times, descend to a terrace[2] about halfway down, and again circle it four times, throwing the corn-meal against the stone walls as they do so. Then they thrust the *pa'ho*(s), together with the *hihi'kwispi*(s), into a niche on the north side of the spring: the corn-husk packets into another cavity on the west side: and then return back up the mesa side to the village, and so to *moñ* kiva.

All this time, i.e. from about noon onwards, Pikyas chief has been busy putting up the small altar in the southwest corner of the deep part of the kiva (see Figure 45). Now, at about 2.30 p.m., he and Soya'l chief, together with Hawk man and his deputy, gather round the small altar and commence a cere-mony, lasting about two hours and consisting in singing a sequence of songs, to the accompaniment of gourd rattles, and aspersing with water from the medicine bowl. While this is going on, men from the other kivas in the pueblo

---

[1] On the collection of the corn cobs on the eighth day of Soya'l, see Stephen (1936), p. 9, and Titiev (1944), p. 143.

[2] Lenañva was, in the old days, the principal spring of Oraibi; it is sited near the foot of the mesa, to the west of the village. The spring itself lies well below the surface of the ground, and the sides are built up in dry-stone walling at least 20 feet from top to bottom, and 20 to 30 feet across. To-day, the spring is buried under sand and only the top few feet of stone walling are visible, though it was still open and in use in the 1930s (Eggan, 1968).

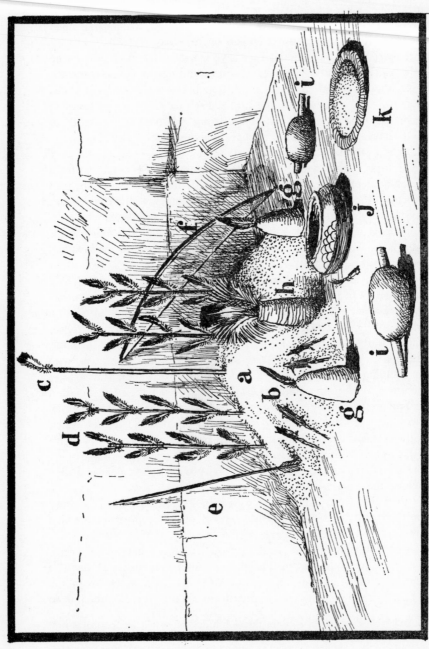

Fig. 45. *Small Soyal Altar. a.* sand pile. *b.* four weasel skins, lying on sand pile. *c.* stick, three feet long, with turkey feather at top. *d.* pair of sticks, with feathers attached. *e.* reed arrow. *f.* bow. *g.* pair of *to'kwi*, clay cones with feathers. *h. ti'poni* with feathers, belonging to Pikyas chief. *i.* pair of gourd rattles. *j.* medicine bowl with aspergill. *k.* tray with corn meal. Re-drawn from Dorsey and Voth (1901), pl. xviii.

have been bringing their prayer-sticks on woven trays to *moñ* kiva, and these have been arranged around the main altar. As the ceremony at the small altar draws to an end, Pikyas chief gets to his feet, takes the woven tray from in front of the sand pile and goes over to the main altar, where he sprinkles the corn-meal—which has evidently been consecrated in the course of the ceremony—over the *pa'ho*(s) brought from the other kivas. He then returns to the small altar, and the four leaders smoke together in silence.

Fig. 46. *Screen, ki'hü* (house), *used on the last night of Soyal.* The figure in the centre represents Mü'yiñwa, the deity of germination. He holds in his right hand a growing corn-stalk, and in his left, a *moñkohü* and a *moñwikuru.* Over his head are symbols of clouds, with falling rain and rays of lightning. Under the corn-stalk is the symbol of the moon, on the other side that of the sun.

The rectangle below Mü'yiñwa's feet represents a field, with planting holes; around the field are attached seeds of all kinds. Re-drawn from Dorsey and Voth (1901), pl. xxviii.

As sundown approaches, War chief again impersonates Pü'ükoñhoya, the war deity, as he did earlier—on the afternoon of the fourth day; and at the conclusion of his dance, medicine-water (*ña'küyi*) is again brewed. This is sprinkled over the *pa'ho*(s) set out around the main altar; then each man takes some of the water in his mouth, picks up a piece of the yellow clay which is lying on the kiva floor, and runs to his own house—where he again smears the moistened clay over the members of his household, 'to make them strong'. War chief, meanwhile, goes into the other kivas in the pueblo—where Soya'l *pa'ho*(s) are still being made—and asperses them with medicine-water from his bowl. He then returns to *moñ* kiva, disrobes, and washes off his body paint.

The sequence of rites that make up the Soya'l are now nearing their climax.[1] Late in the evening Hawk man and his deputy, painted and wearing their cere-monial kilts, prepare to repeat the Hawk impersonation. The Soya'l-*mana* again enters the kiva, the corn-meal path is laid on the kiva floor, the two *tok'wi*(s) set in position. Again, Hawk man's deputy leaves the kiva, and is re-admitted after screeching on the bone-whistle; and again the two Hawk men in turn, followed by the Soya'l-*mana*, make the circuit of the corn-meal path, waving the *masha'adta* in imitation of the bird's flight. One point, however, we may note here: that, at this performance,[2] the novices who were initiated in the course of the previous month's Wü'wütçim are present in *moñ* kiva, dressed in their ceremonial kilts and with white body decoration.

At the conclusion of the Hawk dance, Pikyas chief, accompanied by the Soya'l-*mana*, leave the kiva and make their way to Sun clan house. There, they both dress up for the forthcoming ceremony. While they are doing so, two Kwan men carry into *moñ* kiva a large painted screen of buck-skin, stretched over a wooden frame, representing Mü'yiñwa (Figure 46), and set it up in front of the sand field. Around the screen is fixed a frame of interlacing semi-circles, covered with cotton; to each side are fastened four 'blossoms', and a fringe of red horse-hair; and to the lower edge, a line of eagle feathers. To the lower half of the screen, below Mü'yiñwa's feet, are fixed seeds of water-melon, squash, cotton, and different kinds of corn; the seeds are arranged around a rectangular space, marked with four rows of parallel holes, eight holes to a row (probably representing a field, with planting holes).

Soya'l chief, Parrot chief, Tobacco chief and Crier chief, their *moñ'kohü*(s) in their hands, take their place on the raised floor of the kiva, the other members on the banquettes around the walls. Soon after midnight, Pikyas chief and the Soya'l-*mana* emerge from Sun clan house and make their way towards *moñ* kiva, Pikyas chief carrying the two *masha'adta* previously used in the Hawk impersonation, together with some corn-meal and four dough balls. Arriving near the kiva hatch, Pikyas chief screeches on the bone whistle, and after being answered from inside the kiva, throws the four dough balls down the hatch, then descends into the kiva, followed by the Soya'l-*mana*.

Stepping off the ladder on to the lower floor of the kiva, Pikyas chief pro-ceeds to circle slowly round the screen of Mü'yiñwa, waving the *masha'adta* up and down (and screeching on the bone whistle) as he goes, closely followed by the Soya'l-*mana*. When the two have completed the circle, Hawk man hands a woven tray containing two corn ears, some corn-meal and some *pa'ho*(s), to Soya'l chief; the latter takes the tray, and after he and the other four Soya'l leaders have smoked over it together in silence, he goes over to the screen of

---

[1] For the rites that take place on the last night of the Soya'l, see Dorsey and Voth (1901), pp. 48–59: cf. for 1st Mesa, Stephen (1936), pp. 11–28.

[2] Perhaps, also, at the earlier performances. Only Stephen (1936, p. 11 *et seq*.) specifically mentions the presence of the novices, and his account of the Soya'l in its long form only covers the events of the final night.

Mü'yiñwa, stoops down in front of it and, using one of the two corn ears as a tool, scoops the seeds off the lower half of the screen into the tray. At this point, Pikyas chief and the Soya'l-*mana* leave the kiva; and shortly after their departure, the two Kwan men remove the screen of Mü'yiñwa and take it to Wiklavi kiva (one of the 'common' kivas at Oraibi), where it is dismantled. In *moñ* kiva, meanwhile, Soya'l chief first picks up every seed that has fallen on the floor, then hands the tray with the seeds, the corn-meal and the *pa-ho*(s) on it to Hawk man, who places it near the main altar. Then all smoke together in silence: while, in Wiklavi kiva, the man[1] who is to impersonate the Sun in the final rite of the sequence gets ready for his part.

At about 3 a.m., War chief again puts on his things, takes his medicine bowl and goes over to Wiklavi kiva. There he asperses Star man, who is by now painted and costumed. Then War chief and Star man, preceded by four youths, and led by Pikyas chief sprinkling a 'path' of corn-meal in front of them, return to *moñ* kiva. On reaching the kiva hatch, Pikyas chief first sprinkles corn-meal from the six directions towards the hatch, then leads the way down into the kiva. In the kiva, all are standing: the principal act of the whole Soya'l is about to begin. War chief takes his stand beside the ladder, and asperses from his bowl; on the banquette on the west side of the kiva, a man beats a drum in a muffled tone, and around the drum the four youths group themselves. To the west of the fireplace stands Soya'l chief, holding a *pa'ho* and a tray of corn-meal, from which at intervals he sprinkles meal towards Star man; and on his left Pikyas chief, robed in a white blanket (*o'ba*).

Star man at once begins to dance back and forth[2] to the east of the fireplace, keeping step to the beat of the drum and singing to himself in a low voice. In his right hand he carries a long crook, to the middle of which is tied a black corn ear, and in his left, a bunch of corn ears, a *moñ'kohü* and a *moñ'wikuru*. His costume consists of the usual katçina kilt and sash, a turtle-shell rattle below each knee, ankle bands, green arm bands, a fox pelt around his waist, numerous strands of beads around his neck, but no moccasins. His body is un-painted, except for lines of white dots down the front of his legs below the knee, on both forearms, and on his chest and back. His head-dress is a leather skull-cap, with a large four-pointed star[3] in front and on each side a 'blossom'. All at once, Star man makes a leap towards Soya'l chief, hands him the crook, the *moñ'kohü* and *moñ'wikuru*, and the bunch of corn ears; and receives from Pikyas chief a flat woven disc, which the latter brought into the kiva concealed under his *o'ba*. The disc is about 12 inches across, with the face of the sun painted on one side and about a dozen eagle feathers, with a fringe of red horse-hair, arranged

---

[1] Referred to henceforth as Star man, after the four-pointed star which he wears on his forehead.

[2] For the dance of Star man on the last night of Soya'l, see Dorsey and Voth (1901), pp. 54-7: cf. for 1st Mesa, Stephen (1936), pp. 20-8.

[3] Perhaps representing *wu'yok so'hü*, 'broad star' or Aldebaran (Stephen, 1936, p. 860). Many Hopi ceremonies are timed by the rising, or setting, of Orion and the Pleiades; Aldebaran is a prominent star in that great constellation, in line with Orion's belt.

around its circumference. Impersonating now the Sun, and holding the plaque in front of him in both hands, he dances from side to side in front of the main altar; and as he dances, he twirls the plaque round and round in his hands, 'symbolising the going and coming of the sun'.[1] While he dances, War chief sprinkles him with water from his bowl, and at intervals Soya'l chief casts a pinch of corn-meal towards him.

Finally, as the chant ends, Star man again leaps towards Soya'l chief; the latter hands him the *pa'ho* which he has been holding in his hand, and Star man leaves the kiva, accompanied by Pikyas chief, and returns to Wiklavi kiva to disrobe. In *moñ* kiva, meanwhile, Soya'l chief places the crook, the *moñ'kohü* and *moñ'wikuru*, and the bunch of corn ears which he has received from Star man, behind the altar; and he, and the other Soya'l leaders, smoke over them there.

Soon after the conclusion of the Sun dance, each of the other kivas sends representatives to *moñ* kiva, to fetch the trays of *pa'ho*(s) taken there the previous afternoon. On their return, the trays are placed on the kiva floor, and smoked over; then a messenger, taking a prayer-stick (*ta'wa pa'ho*, doubtless) and a *nakwa'kwosi* from every man in the kiva, is despatched to *Ta'wa-ki*, 'Sun house', a shrine on the mesa top about 3 miles southeast of the village.[2] The messenger from *moñ* kiva also takes with him, besides the prayer-offerings from his kiva, the four flat cakes, the two *pa'ho*(s) and one of the two crooks from off the sand field in front of the main altar. All these he deposits at 'Sun house'. A few minutes after his departure, Soya'l chief, Crier chief and War chief put on their blankets—it is now about 4 a.m., and bitterly cold—and prepare to go out. Soya'l chief takes his *moñ'kohü*, together with the other crook from the sand field and a *püh'tabi*, 'road' prayer-feather, about 12 feet long; Crier chief also takes his *moñ'kohü*, War chief a stick, and all three some corn-meal. They set out on the trail leading down the mesa to the east. Stopping about halfway down, War chief digs a hole about 2 feet deep, and leading away from it to the southeast, a shallow trench the length of *püh'tabi*. Soya'l chief sprinkles corn-meal in the hole and along the trench, then places the crook upright in the hole and, while War chief holds it there, lays the *püh'tabi* along the length of the trench. All three then sprinkle corn-meal over the crook and along the *püh'tabi*, the earth is replaced, and after each in turn has walked along the covered 'road',[3] all three return to *moñ* kiva.

Towards morning[4], the men from the different kivas gather up all their *pa'ho*(s), i.e. all the *pa'ho*(s)—except the Sun *pa'ho*(s)—which they made on the

---

[1] Dorsey and Voth (1901), p. 55.

[2] Sited on the mesa top near Shungo'povi, across the main wash from Oraibi.

[3] Representing a wish or prayer that the Hopi may walk on the good road, that is, lead a straight, upright life, the corn meal being for life: Voth (1901), p. 102, n. 10, and Parsons (1923), p. 160.

[4] For the events of the ninth day of Soya'l, and in particular for the depositing of the Soya'l prayer-sticks, see Dorsey and Voth (1901), pp. 57–8, Nequatewa (1931), p. 2, and Titiev (1944), p. 144.

seventh and eighth days and which have been consecrated in the course of the night's rites in *moñ* kiva, and carry them to their own houses. Long before day-break, everyone in the pueblo washes his (or her) hair in yucca suds, and then, just as the sun is rising, the entire populace emerge from their houses; the women, many of whom are robed in their *atö'e*, and children carry handfuls, even armfuls, of willow-stick *nakwa'kwosi*(s) to the eastern lip of the mesa, where—as the sun lifts above the horizon—they thrust them into the ground,[1] while the men visit in turn chicken houses, sheep corrals, cattle byres, orchards, gardens, fields, hunting grounds, springs and distant shrines, to 'place' their prayer-sticks.

Meanwhile, in *moñ* kiva, Soya'l chief and the other leaders are busy dis-mantling the two altars. They sweep up the sand field, and dispose of it outside the kiva; then they tie the paraphernalia into bundles, for use the following year. Later in the morning, four Soya'l messengers gather together the bundles of corn ears from behind the sand ridge, and carry them through the village. Each woman carefully identifies and picks out her own bundle: the ears being stored away until the spring, *when they are planted with the rest of the seed corn*.[2] On the afternoon of the ninth day of Soya'l, the Qöqöqlom katçinas arrive in the village and formally 'open the kivas' for the new season; and three evenings later, while the members of the Soya'l fraternity are still sleeping in the kivas and observing ritual tabus, the next summer's Nima'n (Home-going) dance is announced.[3]

Early the next morning, the thirteenth of the complete rites,[4] every house-hold in the pueblo is busy baking and cooking, in preparation for the feast that is to bring the Soya'l to an end. In *moñ* kiva, about noon, the Soya'l leaders put on their costume for the last time; meanwhile, the space in front of the Soya'l-*mana*'s house has been swept, two large tubs of water put on the flat roof over-looking the street, and large trays of *somi'viki* prepared. Early in the afternoon, the Soya'l leaders—followed by the other members—emerge from *moñ* kiva, form in line and proceed to Soya'l-*mana*'s house, carrying a bowl of rabbit stew and trays of *wida'ka*. Arriving there, they climb up to the first storey and present the food; then, standing on the flat roof, they commence to throw down to the people waiting in the street below the packets of *somi'viki*, together with melons, squash and other kinds of food, which have been piled ready; at the same time, the women of the household throw water from the two tubs on the men of the Soya'l fraternity. Finally, when all the food has been distributed, the men run back to *moñ* kiva in twos and threes; there they dry themselves, and the celebra-tions conclude with a feast of rabbit stew in all the kivas, and in all the house-holds, of the pueblo.

[1] For pictures, see Dorsey and Voth (1901), pl. xxx, and Titiev (1944), pl. iii*a*.
[2] Titiev (1944), pp. 145–6.
[3] Titiev (1944), pp. 111–12, 144, 227–8.
[4] For the concluding rite of the Soya'l, see Dorsey and Voth (1901), pp. 58–9: cf. Titiev (1944), p. 144.

## SIGNIFICANCE OF THE SOYA'L

As in the Powa'mu, so in the Soya'l a number of different threads are inter-woven to make the complete design. Of these, the three dominant ones[1] are:

(a) prayer for snow and frost
(b) prayer for the fertility of livestock
(c) prayer to the Sun to turn in his path.

Regarding the first of these three threads, we have seen that intercession for snow and ice plays a leading rôle in the non-initiatory sequence of rites at Wü'wütçim. This thread, I believe, runs on into the Soya'l and finds overt expression in the two performances, one on the afternoon of the fourth day, the other on the afternoon of the eighth day, in which War chief impersonates Pü'ükoñ-hoya, the elder of the War twins. Regarding this deity, Stephen has the following entry in his *Journal* for 1894:[2]

> January 21. Full moon of Pa' mü'iyawû.
> When this next moon, Powa' mü'iyawû, goes, it takes the great cold with it. . . .
> Pyü'ükañhoya, his breath is ice cold, he understands the cold, hence appeals to him in the cold moons of *kya* and *pa* (December and January). During these two moons it is especially desirable to have plenty of rain or snow to permeate the land, then cold to make plenty of ice. If there has been little winter moisture and ice, when summer comes the fields get dry too soon, and little or no harvest is yielded.

In view of the link between Pü'ükoñ-hoya and snow-and-ice, may we not infer that the rite in which the deity is impersonated is one of the appeals for cold to which Stephen alludes?—an inference which gains support, when we look more closely at the prayer-sticks made in the course of Soya'l.

On the fifth day of the ceremony, as we saw above (p. 117), Soya'l chief puts the finishing touches to sixteen short single *pa'ho*(s), on which he has been at work for the last two or three days. These sixteen *pa'ho*(s)—which, by their number, are in all likelihood deposited on the afternoon of day 5 and of the three succeeding days at shrines in the four cardinal directions—differ from ordinary prayer-sticks in having only a sprig of *kü'ñya* tied to them, in place of sprigs of both *kü'ñya* and *ma'övi*, and also in having a bluebird feather attached—in place of the feathers, e.g. turkey, commonly used on prayer-sticks. Further, *all* the prayer-sticks made in the course of the seventh and eighth days of the ceremony are distinguished, as Soya'l *pa'ho*(s), by having a triple pine-needle attached to them. Now the bluebird feather, we know (above, p. 54), is for cold, but what of the pine-needles? Again, Stephen, describing the making of prayer-sticks on the penultimate day of the Soya'l of 1893, gives the answer:[3]

---

[1] A fourth thread, not sufficiently stressed in the text, is the consecration of the seed corn for the coming season; this is effected by the dance of Pikyas chief and the Soya'l *mana* around the screen of Mü'yiñwa on the last night of the Soya'l (Fewkes, 1898*b*, p. 108), the seed so consecrated being mixed with the other seed corn at the spring planting.

[2] Stephen (1936), pp. 238–9.

[3] Stephen (1936), pp. 76–8; the triple pine needles are almost certainly those of *Pinus ponderosa*, western yellow pine, the needles of which grow in bunches of three.

To all the prayer-feathers used . . . the triple pine needle is attached. All prayer-sticks have turkey-feather wrappers and *bam'navi* [= *ma'övi*] and sage [*kü'ñya*] as usual.

Each member, as he finishes a prayer-stick, prays silently upon it, holding it close to his mouth, then lays it on the tray. Each one also makes several additional prayer-feathers for horses, sheep, burros, etc., also owl-feather prayer-feather for peaches. The owl feather is used for this purpose because the owl feather is used at Powa'mu. No pine needles are fastened to the owl prayer-feathers, because the pine brings cold. Instead of the pine needle a sprig of *bam'navi* is fastened.

In other words the pine needle, like bluebird feather, is for cold; it is not attached to the peach-tree *pa'ho*(s) because, as Parsons remarks in a footnote to the above passage, 'spring frost damages the peach crops'. In place of the pine needle, a spring of *ma'övi* is fastened; *ma'övi*, then, is for warmth—hence its absence from the sixteen single *pa'ho*(s) completed by Soya'l chief on the fifth day, since these, as their bluebird feather shows, are for cold.

Turning now to the second of the three threads running through the Soya'l: the prayer-sticks that are made on the seventh and eighth days of the ceremony fall into two main categories, those made 'for the Sun' and the common double *pa'ho*(s); and of the latter, the majority are either *ma'k pa'ho*(s), 'hunt prayer-sticks', or *pa'ho*(s) for the 'increase' of sheep, cattle, burros, and other domestic animals. Apart from the Sun *pa'ho*(s), then, many of the prayer-sticks made at Soya'l are for the fertility of game and livestock;[1] and the reason why they are made at this time of year, and not at any other, must surely be that this is the mating season for both wild and domestic animals.[2]

Regarding the *pa'ho*(s) 'for the Sun', made on the seventh day of the Soya'l and 'placed' at Ta'wa-ki ('Sun house') early on the ninth, their purpose I take to be the same as that of the Sun 'dance' itself: namely, in Fewkes' words,[3] to induce the Sun to turn from his 'house', so as to approach the pueblos *and warm their fields for cultivation*. That this is, indeed, the true meaning of Star man's performance on the last night of the Soya'l is confirmed by that part of the Emergence myth, of which his dance is the overt dramatisation. According to the myth,[4] when the Hopi first emerged from the underworld and were allotted their land by Masau'u, it was still dark and freezing cold on earth, and the people had always to keep a fire burning near the fields, to see what they were doing and to warm the ground so that they could raise a crop. After a time, therefore,

---

[1] The importance of this element in Soya'l prayer-stick making has been noted by E. Beaglehole (1936, pp. 11–14, 24: 1937, p. 50), hardly at all by other observers.

[2] Traditionally, the December moon was a closed season for rabbit-hunting (Stephen, 1936, p. 387), to give the rabbits time to increase in numbers. Lambing, in Hopi country, takes place late in February (Beaglehole, 1937, p. 24); deer and antelope have their young with them in March and April, 'when the peach trees are in blossom' (Beaglehole, 1936, pp. 4–5).

[3] Fewkes (1898*b*), pp. 107–8. Cf. Titiev (1944), pp. 145–6: 'In other words, the main purpose of the Soyal is . . . that the sun may be induced to start back towards its summer home and thus bring suitably warm weather to permit the Hopi to plant their fields.'

[4] Voth (1905*c*), pp. 13–15.

and acting on Masau'u's advice, they cut out a round piece of cloth, stretched it over a ring, painted it with red oxide of copper and put a fringe of red horse-hair around the border—to represent the sun; then they placed the disc on a white cloth, directed one of the men to stand on the cloth beside it, and swung the cloth with its contents into the sky, where it kept twirling upward and upward towards the east. In due course the painted disc turned into the sun, while the man who was thrown up with it is believed to hold the sun in front of himself, turning it in his hands as the impersonator does in the dance.

The chief point to be noted in the myth, in relation to the dance, is the emphasis on the Sun as the source of warmth, and the importance of light and warmth for farming. And this theme we find further developed six weeks later at *Powa' lauwu*, 'prayer-stick making for Powa'mu', where the sand mosaic (above, Figure 34) portrays the Sun in his 'house', and in the course of which at least one of the sets of prayer-sticks made is for the Sun.[1] The Soya'l thus takes its place in a sequence of ritual events, that extends from early in November to the end of February and runs parallel to, and rather in advance of, corresponding events in the climato-agricultural cycle: Wü'wütçim forecasting the moisture and snow needed during the early part of the winter, Soya'l forecasting the frost—and the subsequent warming of the soil—required for planting, and Powa'mu, the further warming of the soil needed for the germination of the seed and its shooting above ground.[2]

This I regard as the primary place held by the Soya'l in the annual liturgy. But the Soya'l also holds a place in the initiatory sequence, and it is to this aspect of the ceremony that we may now turn. Just as intercession for cold finds overt expression in the performance of War chief as Pü'ükoñ-hoya, so the initiatory element finds expression in the three performances of the Hawk 'dance'; and in much the same way as the one represents the continuation of a thread that runs through Wü'wütçim, so I believe does the other.

In his account of the Soya'l at Walpi, Stephen notes[3] that the man who performs the Hawk dance is referred to as Kih'sha *ti'yo*, 'Kih'sha youth', and the girl who accompanies him as Kih'sha *mana*, 'Kih'sha maiden'. Kih'sha, or *ki'hsa*, in Hopi refers to the Prairie falcon, most efficient and ruthless predator found in the region, reputed to attain speeds of up to 150 m.p.h. when diving

---

[1] Stephen (1936), p. 165, and Fig. 97.

[2] A similar 'forecasting' element characterises the ceremonial cycle of the Rio Grande Tewa:

> One cannot help noticing, [writes Ortiz (1969, p. 100)], that each of the first four works in the traditional cycle actually comes about a month before the phenomena it is supposed to bring about.

The four works referred to are: (*a*) 'to lessen the cold', usually held early in February, (*b*) 'to bring the buds to life', later that month or early in March, (*c*) 'to bring the leaves to life', in late March or early April, and (*d*) 'to bring the blossoms to life', in late April or early May.

As Ortiz remarks, the ground often remains frozen for many weeks after the first work in the series, while the buds on even the earliest trees do not appear until late March or early April.

[3] Stephen (1936), pp. 17–18.

on its prey. Hopi, as we have seen (above, p. 32, n. 3), believe that the large hawks, including *ki'hsa*, kill their prey by striking them with the forward edge of their wing. Discussing Hopi warfare,[1] Stephen says that in the old days the Hopi were armed with spear, bow and arrow, and throwing-stick, 'a weapon that can be thrown so as readily to break an arm or a leg, and to kill if it strikes an enemy in the forehead'. Regarding the origin of the throwing-stick, he gives this account:

> Kih'sha was the first possessor of a *püch-ko'hü*. He carried it under his wing and hunted rabbits with it. It is modelled after the wing of Kih'sha, and referred to as his wing (*masha'adta*). Long ago the Hopi had bow and arrow, but no *püch-ko'hü*; a Hopi youth went to Kih'sha and from him got the *püch-ko'hü*. Kih'sha is the great hunter . . . he devised the *püch-ko'hü*.

The dance of the Hawk man during Soya'l, and the significance attached therein to his wing (*masha'adta*), is thus expressive both of hunting and of warfare, symbolised by the fierceness of the Prairie falcon and represented by the *püch-ko'hü*, an element common to both themes.

In the course of their initiation in November, the novices, as we have seen (above, p. 102), are treated as though they were fledgling birds; they are described as *ke'le-hoyam*, 'little sparrow hawks', their bodies are smeared with bands of yellow ochrey clay, and they have to mimic the sparrow-hawk's cry, and flap their 'wings', before being fed. Now *ke'le*, sparrow-hawk, and *ki'hsa*, prairie falcon, belong to the same ornithological series; both are falcons. It seems reasonable to conclude on this ground that the presence of the novices, painted (? as adult hawks) and costumed at the performance of the Hawk dance on the last night of Soya'l, marks the final stage in a sequence which began at their hunting initiation (see above, p. 32) and was carried a step further when they were brought into the kivas, on the first afternoon of Wü'wütçim, as fledgling birds; and that the 'growing-up', through which they have passed, marks their shouldering of adult responsibilities, namely hunting and fighting,[2] the essentially male duties of Hopi life.

Throughout the Soya'l, a very close link is established—in the minds of those taking part—between the living and the dead. Most of the prayer-sticks made in the course of the seventh and eighth days are offerings for the dead,[3] in return for which they send the benefits prayed for; and Titiev, who was living at Oraibi in the winter of 1933–4, writes:[4] 'The belief that at Soyal the dead come to the pueblo to get the "souls" of their prayer-offerings, is very vivid

---

[1] Stephen (1936), pp. 99–100, and for illustration of a Hopi throwing-stick, Fig. 69.

[2] This is in line with Titiev's assessment of the Kwan and Al fraternities as warriors, and hunters, respectively: Titiev (1944), pp. 137–8.

[3] Dorsey and Voth (1901), p. 57, n. *.

[4] Titiev (1944), p. 145, n. 22; and it is for this reason, i.e. because the dead are about, that the moon in which the Soya'l falls, *kya mü'iya*, is 'dangerous'. Cf. Parsons (1936), p. 1037, n. 1: 'Anyone out visiting at night should smear ashes on his forehead. Girls do not grind at night, lest the dead "come and do something to them".'

in the minds of the natives.' And it is this link with the dead that permits us, finally, to define more exactly the meaning of the 'spiritual status', bestowed on the novice by his Wü'wütçim initiation. For only those who have been initiated into one of the four fraternities may take part in the Soya'l; at the Soya'l, prayer-offerings are made for the dead; to make these offerings, on behalf of his own family, is the conspicuous office of the man who has been 'put into' one of the four fraternities; and only a man who has been 'put into' one of them can mediate in this way between the living and the dead, so securing for the living the benefits which only the dead can offer. In this sense, Wü'wütçim initiation is the gateway to manhood.

### THE NATURE OF HOPI FRATERNITIES

I propose now to touch briefly on two aspects of Hopi fraternities, not covered fully or—in the case of the second—not as yet covered at all: namely, their method of entry, and their curative powers.[1]

Each of the four Wü'wütçim fraternities (the Wü'wütçim itself, Singers, Al, and Kwan), the Soya'l fraternity and the Powa'mu, the other four men's societies (Blue Flute, Gray Flute, Snake, and Antelope), and the two leading women's societies (Marau and Lako'n), has its own sacred objects and has charge of its own ceremony (*wi'mi*); the most vital of a fraternity's sacred objects is its *ti'poni*, regarded as the 'heart' of the ceremony of which the fraternity has charge. The centrality of its sacred objects, to the Hopi notion of the fraternity, is reflected in linguistic usage.[2] The word *wi'mi*, 'ceremony', also refers to the ritual objects around which the ceremony is built, and members of the fraternity are known as *wi'wimkyamu*, 'those who know (the) *wi'mi*'. Thus where, referring to their clan membership, people say *i'tam Hona'n nyamü*, 'we-are Badger clan-people', referring to their fraternity membership they say *i'tam Powa'm wi'wikyamu*, 'we-are Powa'mu fraternity-people': a distinction that is pointed in the following sentence:

| hi'müi | nyamü | Soyal'üña | wi'mi | hi'müi | yüñ'wa: |
|--------|-------|-----------|-------|--------|---------|
| to which | clan | the Soya'l | ceremony | to which | does it belong? |

Each of the fraternities, further, has a particular illness or group of illnesses, which it controls. This is called its 'whip' (*wuvata*), and inheres in the sacred objects owned by the fraternity. Thus the 'whip' of the Soya'l fraternity is

---

[1] The literature, on either aspect, is extremely scanty. In the account that follows, I have drawn on Voth (1901), p. 109, n. 2, and p. 149, n. 1: Voth (1903*b*), pp. 44–5: Parsons (1923), pp. 181–2, (1933), pp. 9–16, (1936), p. 137, n. 3, and pp. 577–8: Stephen (1936), p. 371: Titiev (1944), pp. 106–7, 241.

Dozier points out (1965, p. 45) that curing plays a far smaller part in Hopi fraternities than it does in the fraternities of the eastern Pueblos; he relates this to the far *larger* part played in the Hopi fraternities by weather control, in response to the needs of flood-water farming. Perhaps, also, the greater exposure of the Rio Grande pueblos to imported diseases over the last 400 years has rendered curing more important there than farther west.

[2] Voth (1912*b*), pp. 133–4: cf. Parsons (1936), p. 1318, under *wi'mi*.

sore ears and ear-ache, of the Powa'mu rheumatism, of the Al a twisting and twitching of the face and neck (? tetanus), of the Kwan any disease in which the body is wasting away to a skeleton, of the Snake a swelling of any part of the body but especially of the abdomen, of the Wü'wütçim any disease that causes excruciating pain (and so makes a person 'twist' in agony[1]), of the Antelope epilepsy, of the Blue Flute lightning shock, and of the Marau facial sores.[2] The illness inheres in the sacred objects—and especially in the *ti'poni*—of a fraternity, in the sense that anyone who sees the objects, and is not a member of that fraternity, is likely to be struck by the disease.

In the ordinary course, as we have seen, a Hopi joins several of the fraternities in the course of his lifetime: Katçina or Powa'mu, when he is a boy, then as he reaches manhood, one of the four Wü'wütçim fraternities, and perhaps later one of the four fraternities (Blue or Gray Flute, Snake or Antelope) which conduct the great summer ceremonials. At each, he goes through the same process of inititiation—he must be introduced by a sponsor, his 'father', who already belongs to the fraternity in question; for three days he is kept in seclusion in the kiva, then he is admitted to the sacred objects which belong to the fraternity, his hair is washed in yucca suds, and he is given a new name; henceforth, he is free to take part with the other members in the ceremony of which the fraternity has charge.

Such is the ordinary course of events. A boy's parents choose a ceremonial 'father' for him from among their friends, and normally the lad will join that branch of the Katçina or Powa'mu fraternity, and that branch of the Wü'-wütçim, to which his ceremonial 'father' belongs.[3]

However, there are two other, less voluntary ways of joining a fraternity:[4] due to trespass, and to sickness. Where a boy, or man, is caught looking into a kiva while its ceremony is in progress, he is forced to join the fraternity whose sacred objects he has espied; and the man who catches him acts as his 'father' at the initiation. Again a person who contracts the ailment controlled by one of the fraternities may call upon its head man, or other leading member, to cure him.[5] This is generally done by circling ashes over the patient's head, at the same time as the discharming song belonging to that fraternity is chanted. As a rule, the sick person then joins the order which cured him,[6] either permanently or for a number of years.

Each of these two involuntary modes of entry is the outcome of the Hopi

[1] Parsons (1936), p. 869, n. 1: clinically, this would cover e.g. angina pectoris, renal calculi, gall stones, strangulated hernia, gout even (do the Hopi get gout?).

[2] Probably, also, venereal disease: Parsons (1936), pp. 864–5. The Lako'n, also, may cure for venereal disease: Parsons (1936), p. 830.

[3] Stephen (1936), pp. 137–8) observes that brothers are usually initiated into different branches of Wü'wütçim, so—if there are four brothers—there will be one in each fraternity.

[4] Parsons (1923), pp. 181–2: (1939), pp. 112–13, and p. 113, n. 1 and 2: Titiev (1944), p. 106.

[5] Since the 'whip' of that fraternity is thought to have hurt him: Voth (1901), p. 149, n. 1.

[6] For example, a person shocked by lightning is initiated into the Flute society: Parsons (1936), p. 137, n. 3.

belief in the power, the 'dangerous' (*kya*) quality, of the sacred objects owned by the fraternity. And this belief is reflected in one final aspect of Hopi cere-monialism: the fact that, at the conclusion of any major ceremony, all those who have taken part in it must undergo the rite known as *navo'tçiwa*, 'purifi-cation'. This is performed, as is the curing rite for sickness, by circling a pinch of ashes (held between the forefinger and thumb[1]) above the head, at the same time as the fraternity's discharming song is chanted; and has the effect, as the ety-mology of the word shows,[2] of 'separating' the person so purified from the 'dangerous' thing with which he has been in contact:

> *navo'tçiwa*:  v. 'exorcises oneself, separates oneself from supernatural person or thing by making passes with a feather or other object, usually casting or blowing powder, meal, ashes, from feather . . . .'
> (Whorf, 1936, p. 1262)
> n. 'cleansing, purification, exorcism, separating oneself from the supernatural person or thing': used for *navo'tçiwa* are crow, buzzard, and eagle feathers.     (Parsons, 1936, p. 1262)

[1] I am unable to reconcile the conflicting evidence (above, pp. 62–3, 83–4, 108), as to whether this action is performed with the left or with the right hand; the fact that the ashes are held in the palm of one hand, and a pinch taken between the forefinger and thumb of the other, may have been a source of confusion to the early observers. Alter-natively, it may depend on whether the rite is done with *corn meal* or with *ashes*: the left hand being used for corn meal (below, p. 142), and the right for ashes (above, pp. 62–3, 83–4).

[2] On *navo'tçiwa* as an act of separation, see Stephen (1936), p. 371. The word *powa'ta* may also signify 'purification' or 'exorcism', but in origin refers to 'curing, healing, especially by medicine man' (Whorf, 1936, p. 1283); where *powa'ta* signifies exorcism, it refers to a rite where two are engaged, *navo'tçiwa* to a rite where many are engaged (Parsons, 1936, p. 1284). *Powa-*, as we shall see later (below, p. 219, and n. 3), is the general Shoshoni stem for 'supernatural power'.

# 14
# *A pueblo liturgy (concluded)*

I return now to conclude the account of the ceremonial cycle, resuming where we broke off at the end of Chapter 12. In that chapter I described the first half of the katçina cycle: the part, that is, that runs from the 'opening of the kivas' and the first series of night dances (in January), through the Powa'mu in February, and on to the second series of night dances (early in March). The latter half of the katçina cycle covers the four moons of spring and early summer (April to July), in the course of which the fields are prepared for planting and the crops sown; ceremonially, these months are marked by a sequence of day-long katçina dances, held in the different villages in turn and culminating in the great Nima'n (Home-going) dance, late in July, when the katçinas are despatched to their homes.

Early in August the first crops ripen; and late August, September and early October constitute the harvest season in Hopiland. These three months, also, are marked by their own festivals: August by either the Flute ceremony or the Snake-Antelope, held in alternate years in the various pueblos, September by the Marau, and October by either the Lako'n or the Oa'qöl, depending on the year and on the village. Of these festivals of the summer and fall, the katçina dances (including Nima'n) are primarily—as we shall see—for rain, the Flute and the Snake-Antelope for rain and for the ripening of the early crops (sweet corn, beans and other vegetables), and the three women's ceremonies—Marau, Lako'n and Oa'qöl—for the main corn harvest and for fertility.

Of these festivals I describe, first, the katçina dances of spring and early summer, and the Nima'n; then the Snake-Antelope, as representative of the two ceremonies of *pa'mü'iya* (the August moon); and finally the Marau, which sets the pattern for the other two 'harvest' festivals. Our narrative of the ceremonial cycle will then be complete, and we shall be in a position to assess the rôle which the cycle plays in Hopi life.

KATÇINA DANCES OF SPRING AND EARLY SUMMER

During the spring and early summer, the great day-long katçina dances take place.[1] No one village is likely to put on more than three such dances a season, but as every village usually puts on two or three, there are about twenty such

---

[1] The account that follows is based on the accounts given by Earle and Kennard (1938), pp. 29–33, and by Titiev (1944), pp. 126–8. For comparative material from 1st Mesa, see Parsons (1936), pp. 350–3, and Stephen (1936), pp. 353–492.

dances between mid-April and mid-July. Each dance is put on by one particular kiva in the village, and is sponsored by an adult member of the kiva group. A man who wishes to put on a dance for some special purpose, such as recovery from an illness or a child's birthday, approaches the Village chief some weeks beforehand and, provided his 'heart is good', usually gets his consent.[1]

For sixteen nights before the dance, the men who are to take part go to the kiva every night to practise the steps, learn the songs, and prepare their masks. As a rule there are some thirty to forty dancers, anyone who has been through the katçina initiation at Powa'mu being eligible to dance. For several days before the dance day, *ti'kive*,[2] the womenfolk related to the man who is sponsoring the dance are engaged in grinding meal, making *pi'ki*, and preparing other kinds of food; and for the last two days, every household in the pueblo is busy preparing dishes for the feast that invariably accompanies a katçina dance.

On the last night, all those who are to participate in any way meet in the sponsoring kiva for an all-night session devoted to smoking, praying, and rehearsing. The members of the Powa'mu fraternity, who will lead the katçinas to the village square the next day and sprinkle them with corn-meal while they dance, are busy now making prayer-sticks and *nakwa'kwosi*(s) for them; some of these they deposit at katçina shrines just before daybreak, the remainder are given to the katçinas when they are dismissed. In the early dawn the dancers put on their costumes and, with mask in hand, proceed to Qowa'waima, a shrine to the southeast of the village (i.e. of Oraibi). There they form into two lines and rehearse the first song, un-masked; then, as the sun is about to rise, they put on their masks and start for the village in single file. As they reach the outskirts of the pueblo, they are met by the man who is to act as 'father'[3] to the katçinas, who leads the way to the village square sprinkling a 'path' of corn-meal for them as he goes.

Entering the village square the dancers take up position, usually (in the first position) facing towards the east and north, the 'father' sprinkles the leader with corn-meal, and gives the sign to start; during the singing he walks down the line and back, two or three times, casting a pinch of corn-meal over each dancer as he passes him. At the end of about ten minutes the song comes to an end, and the 'father' sprinkles a further corn-meal 'path' to lead the dancers to their second position, facing towards the north and west. There they sing their second stanza, and then the 'father' leads them to the third position, facing

---

[1] Titiev (1944), pp. 126–7. Kennard (Earle and Kennard, 1938, p. 16) says that the big katçina dances are arranged in the course of the preceding Soya'l; this certainly applies to the last dance of all, the Nima'n, but it is likely that most of the others are arranged on a more *ad hoc* ground.

[2] The four days before the dance day, and the dance day itself, are named as for the concluding five days of any nine-day ceremony, i.e. from *yü'ñya* ('going in') to *ti'kive* ('dance'): Stephen (1936), p. 375.

[3] There may be more than one 'father', as in the Nima'n. The man, or men, who act as 'fathers' to the katçinas are quite separate from the man who sponsors the dance; they *must* be members of the Powa'mu fraternity, he need not be.

towards the south. Finally, as the last stanza of the song comes to an end, he leads the katçinas out of the village square and back to the shrine from which they started; there they rest for half an hour or so, before returning to the square for their second dance.

From daybreak until just before sunset the katçinas perform, the length of their rests depending on the number of songs they have prepared. Eight or ten different songs are usually rendered in one day; sometimes, indeed, so many have been composed that it takes two days to sing them all. By early afternoon, all the rooftops overlooking the square are packed with people; and now, as the katçinas file into the square, they are laden with presents—katçina dolls for the small girls, bows-and-arrows for the boys, baskets of peaches, rolls of *pi'ki* dyed yellow and red, melons, sweet corn and other foods. As they enter, they set their gifts down in the centre of the square and begin to dance. At the end of the first movement, the dancers step out of line, pick up their presents and distribute them to the children, and adults, for whom they are intended. Then they return to their places and complete the dance.

Each time they come back, the katçinas sing a different song, reiterating their prayer for rain; during the dance, their 'father' answers the words of their song, and shouts to encourage them. A typical katçina song, given by Kennard,[1] runs as follows:

> Aha ihi, aha ihi . . .
> At last we came there, to our houses.
> > Blue-green prayer-sticks you offered us.
> The chiefs-of-all-directions prepared the good life.
>
> Those living in each direction have asked us:
> > 'Our fathers, what do they say?
> > How shall our fathers send them there?'
> Yes, yes, we shall soon visit them with rain.
> > Yes, yes, we shall soon come to them with rain.
>
> Indeed, they said, you should go yonder.
> > With that shall we start with rain
> From all directions, falling upon their plants.
> > aha ihi, aha ihi . . .
>
> Listen, my fathers, listen, listen, my friends.
> > Do not lose faith in me.
> Pray to me. And I, in return,
> > With water downpouring will keep you alive.
>
> So, go yonder to the west.
> > On the wings of male turkeys,[2] the clouds will appear.

---

[1] Earle and Kennard (1938), pp. 32–3.

[2] i.e. prayer-sticks. On the use of the breast feather of turkey for making *pa'ho*(s), Fewkes and Stephen (1892b, p. 228, n. 1) write: 'Its speckled colour is said to indicate the all-colour of the below; its white tip the foaming water at one of their early deluges, prior to which the whole tip of the feather was black. It is a very general moisture emblem.'

This way, my animals[1] will bring rain
On their flapping wings.

After the katçinas have danced for the last time, their 'father' thanks them, then passes down the line from man to man, placing in the left hand of each a *nakwa'kwosi* and a pinch of corn-meal; he then leads them out of the village and back to the katçina shrine. There they deposit the prayer-offerings which they have just received,[2] and then un-mask. Each dancer removes the mask from his head with his left hand, sprinkles it with a little corn-meal, and then bids his mask (i.e. the katçina) farewell, at the same time praying *him* to send the rain-clouds for which he has been singing and praying all day:[3]

> *ikwa'chi,      yu'pa ni'manaa . . .*
> 'my friend, you are going home. Send us rain clouds, all the things we have asked you for with these prayer-feathers.'

Each dancer then performs the *navo'tçiwa* rite, circling his head four times with a pinch of corn-meal held in the left hand and then casting it away; in this way he separates himself from the katçina whom he has *been*. Each man then puts on his ordinary clothes, rolls his mask in a blanket and makes his way back to the kiva. A four-day period of abstinence concludes the entire performance.

### THE NIMA'N, OR HOME-GOING DANCE

The Nima'n, or Home-going dance, which I propose now to describe,[4] is the last and the greatest of the all-day katçina dances of spring and early summer. It takes place late in July, 'when corn is knee high',[5] and its purpose is to despatch to their homes in the San Francisco mountains, Kisiwu and elsewhere, the katçinas who have been residing in the vicinity of the Hopi villages since their 'return' six or seven months previously. But where, in the earlier dances, the emphasis lies on the dance itself and the proceedings that lead up to it are in the minor key, in the Nima'n the rôles are reversed. There are thus two sequences of events to follow: the sequence of esoteric rites—manufacture of prayer-sticks, setting-up of the altar, despatch of messengers to Kisiwu to

---

[1] i.e. eagles. I suppose the word used to be *pok'adta*, 'their animals (or pets)', referring to the particular species associated with the several deities: see Stephen (1936), pp. 306–7, and p. 307, n. 1.

[2] Titiev (1944, p. 128) states that they keep some of these to deposit in their fields.

[3] This very important part of the ritual is fully recorded only by Stephen: (1936), pp. 369–71, 386–7. According to Kennard (Earle and Kennard, 1938, p. 33), the dancers un-mask *before* depositing the prayer-offerings.

[4] The account that follows is based on the accounts by Earle and Kennard (1938), pp. 35–8, and by Titiev (1944), pp. 128, 227–35. For accounts of the 1891 Nima'n at Walpi, see Fewkes (1892a), pp. 69–103, and of the 1893 Nima'n, Stephen (1936), pp. 494–540.

[5] Stephen (1936), p. 374. Titiev's statement (1944, p. 128), that 'the rites take the form of a sixteen-day ceremony, beginning four days after the summer solstice and culminating about mid-July', is not easily reconcilable with the observed dates of the dance: e.g. for 1st Mesa, on 27 July in 1891, 22 July in 1892, 23 July in 1893.

fetch spruce—which is carried out by the leaders of the Powa'mu fraternity and takes place in (and from) *their* kiva, and the sequence of (less secret) preparations—rehearsal of dance steps and songs, painting of masks, making of prayer-sticks—which goes on co-evally in the kiva that is sponsoring the dance. As we have seen, the privilege of sponsoring the Nima'n rotates among the different kivas in the pueblo; the esoteric rites, on the other hand, always take place in Powa'mu kiva under the direction of the leaders of that fraternity.

As with other nine-day ceremonies, the Nima'n festival is preceded by prayer-stick making and a formal announcement. This takes place about the end of the first week in July. Katçina chief, who is in charge of the Nima'n, and Powa'mu chief meet in the Katçina clan house, on the morning of the day chosen, to make the necessary *pa'ho*(s) and to smoke and pray together. Late in the afternoon a further meeting is held in the house of the Village chief, at which Village chief, Crier chief and War chief, as well as the two leaders of the ceremony, are present; at this meeting more prayer-offerings are made, and final arrangements are discussed for the staging of the Nima'n.

Early the next morning, as the sun is rising, Crier chief goes to the house of Village chief, collects the tray of prayer-offerings made the evening before, ascends to the roof of Ke'le clan house and deposits them there. Then, facing northwest and speaking in a low voice so that only the Cloud-people can hear what he is saying, he announces the Nima'n:

> You, who live in the northwest, loom up. . . .
> In sixteen days from now, these katçinas, our friends, are to be 'put up' as we have planned. So you, people [i.e. of the pueblo], must be kind to each other and help one another with happy hearts.

This announcement he repeats in each of the four cardinal directions, then descends from the roof. In the meantime, Katçina and Powa'mu chiefs take the prayer-sticks which they made the previous morning and 'place' them at katçina shrines to the west and north of the village.

Eight days later, Katçina and Powa'mu chiefs, together with the men who are to act as 'fathers' to the katçinas, go into retreat in Powa'mu kiva; from now on, the rites in that kiva are only open to members of the Powa'mu fraternity. On the afternoon of the 4th day, the six-directions' altar (*poñ'ya*) is set up in Powa'mu kiva, with the *ti'poni*(s) of the Powa'mu and Katçina fraternities disposed near it; and medicine water (*ña-küyi*) is consecrated, by sprinkling corn-meal and pollen into the water from each of the six directions[1] in turn. In the course of the next three days, i.e. days 5, 6 and 7 of the ceremony, a great many prayer-offerings are made, the *pa'ho*(s) being painted with pigments mixed by Powa'mu chief with water from the medicine bowl.

---

[1] Asked why by Stephen (1936, pp. 517–18), Powa'mu chief replied: 'These are the beneficial things from the six directions. They make the water no longer water but *ña'küyi*, and with this I mix the pigments with which we paint the prayer-sticks calling all the katçina to hasten the clouds with rain to this place.'

Immediately after breakfast on the sixth day, Katçina chief, Powa'mu chief and the 'fathers' of the katçinas make a special set of prayer-sticks for the spruce-gatherers, who are about to leave for the spring at Kisiwu, some 40 miles to the northeast of the village[1]; at the same time, in his own kiva, the man who is sponsoring the Nima'n also makes a set. When they are ready, Katçina chief takes the *pa'ho(s)* made in Powa'mu kiva over to the sponsoring kiva, the two sets are put into a sack, together with a *moñ'wikuru*, an eagle-bone whistle, a pipe and tobacco and some corn-meal, and handed—with other *nakwa' kwosi(s)*—to the leader of the spruce-gathering party.

The party sets out, taking the trail leading out of the village to the east, and then turning northeast up the valley. On their way, they deposit a number of prayer offerings beside the trail. Reaching the vicinity of the spring about sun-down, they camp for the night about half a mile away. Early the next morning they make their way to the spring, naked except for a loin cloth and with their hair loose. As they approach the spring, the leader halts at four separate places and blows on the eagle-bone whistle—to warn the katçinas of their arrival. On the last occasion they are almost at the spring. Choosing a relatively dry spot near the spring, the men set out their prayer-sticks in a row; then they squat down for a formal smoke, and when they have finished, the leader fills the *moñ'wikuru* from the spring. As soon as the gourd vessel has been filled, the men return to their camp to dress. Later, they go back to the spring for a careful inspection of the row of *pa'ho(s)*; if some of these have in the meantime collected dew, this is a good sign, i.e. for rain.

After a light meal of *pi'ki* and water, the party begin to gather spruce, the principal object of their expedition. The leader and his deputy each cut a complete shrub, the one regarded as male, the other as female, while the other members break off branches and stuff them into sacks which they have brought for the purpose. In return, they deposit the remaining *nakwa'kwosi(s)* at the base of trees from which they have taken branches. When all the sacks are full, they set out for home, reaching the village towards dusk the same evening (day 7). Just outside the village, the men deposit their sacks in a convenient hiding-place, the leader breaking off a few sprigs of spruce, keeping some himself and giving some to his deputy. Then the leader, carrying the *moñ'wikuru* and the other ritual objects, makes his way to Powa'mu kiva, while the other men proceed to the sponsoring kiva. In each, a formal smoke is held to mark their return, and then 'a detailed, circumstantial account of the journey' is related, the leader speaking in Powa'mu kiva and his deputy in the sponsoring kiva. After this is over, the spruce gatherers go to their own homes to rest and eat.

Throughout these three days the members of the Powa'mu fraternity have been engaged in making a very large number of different kinds of prayer-sticks. By the eighth morning Stephen counted some 387 set out in twenty-four woven trays around the six-directions' altar, in Powa'mu kiva; at noon these

---

[1] The spring at Kisiwu is located near the head of the Oraibi wash, at an elevation of 7,200 feet, where the pinyon gives way to Douglas fir.

*pa'ho*(s) are consecrated in a brief ceremony around the altar,[1] after which (in Stephen's words) Powa'mu chief and the other leaders 'briefly prayed for rain to come and vivify the growing crops'. Meanwhile, in the sponsoring kiva, the dancers are busy finishing their costumes, preparing the katçina dolls (*ti'hü*) and the bows-and-arrows to be distributed to the children on the morrow, and putting the final touches to their masks.[2]

Late in the evening, all those who are to take part in the Nima'n, including the 'fathers' of the katçinas, assemble in the sponsoring kiva. Only Powa'mu chief is absent, for he has to maintain a long, solitary vigil, smoking and praying all night in Powa'mu kiva. In the sponsoring kiva, after a complete rehearsal of the morrow's dance followed by a ritual smoke between the leaders, the spruce gatherers are sent to fetch the loaded sacks from their cache. By now it is around midnight, and on their return the entire group leaves the kiva and moves across to the village square. While the dancers line up on one side of the square and rehearse their first song, Katçina chief and the 'fathers' of the katçinas are busy at the northwest corner, planting the two spruce shrubs—referred to as 'brother' and 'sister'—on either side of the small katçina shrine which is located there. After planting the two shrubs, they attach *nakwa'kwosi*(s) to their branches, then sprinkle a corn-meal 'path' from the shrine (*pa'ho-ki*) towards the east, the Hopi path of life.

The Nima'n sponsor and his deputy now retire to *their* kiva, to smoke and pray. But in the square Katçina chief and the 'fathers' of the katçinas take up position to sprinkle the dancers, as they will do on the morrow, and a further rehearsal takes place. By the time this is finished, it is nearly dawn. Katçina chief and the 'fathers' join Powa'mu chief in his kiva; the dancers hurry to the sponsoring kiva, tie the spruce twigs to their belts and to the collars of their masks, put on their dance costumes, take up their masks and proceed to Qowa' waima, there to await the sunrise. While they are waiting, Katcina chief and the 'fathers' of the katçinas emerge from Powa'mu kiva and make their way to the edge of the village—in the direction from which the katçinas will come.

Sometime very early in the morning of the ninth day, a number of men go down to their corn fields in the valley below and uproot plants of sweet corn. This is the sweet corn that was specially planted early in April,[3] for the Nima'n; the whole plant is uprooted, and bundles of the corn—ears, leaves, stalks— carried back up the mesa. At some stage these bundles of corn are given to the dancers waiting at Qowa'waima: for, as the sun rises, the latter put on their masks, form into line and set off towards the village, and as they draw near, every man in the line is seen to be carrying a bundle of the freshly uprooted corn stalks.[4] As they reach the outskirts of the village, Katçina chief takes the lead and, followed by the 'fathers' of the katçinas, leads the way through the

---

[1] See Stephen (1936), pp. 526–9.

[2] For the method of painting the masks, see Fewkes (1892*a*), p. 79, n. 2.

[3] On the planting of the Nima'n sweet-corn in April, see Stephen (1936), p. 373.

[4] Stephen (1936), pp. 530–1: confirmed by Kennard (Earle and Kennard, 1938, p. 35).

village and into the square, sprinkling a path of corn-meal as he goes. As they enter the square, the katçinas lay down the bundles of corn and the other gifts they are carrying, take up their positions and commence their first song. At the conclusion of the first movement, the dancers step out of line, distribute the bundles of sweet corn to the women of the pueblo, and the katçina dolls and bows-and-arrows to the girls and boys respectively, then move to their second position and proceed with the dance.

So begins the Homegoing Dance, the last of the great katçina dances of spring and early summer. All day long, with intervals for rest, the dance goes on, Katçina chief and the 'fathers' of the katçinas leading the dancers into the square, sprinkling them with corn-meal and encouraging them as they dance, then leading them out again as each performance comes to an end, while down below in his kiva Powa'mu chief sits alone, smoking and praying.

Towards evening, the katçinas are led into the square for the last time and begin their final dance. At about the same time, the two senior women of Katçina and Badger clan enter Powa'mu kiva, accompanied by Tobacco chief (usually the head of Rabbit clan, of the same phratry as Katçina) and a number of members of the Powa'mu fraternity. After the first two movements of the final song have been sung in the village square, Katçina chief and the 'fathers' of the katçinas pull up the 'brother' and 'sister' spruce shrubs and carry the shrubs with them as they lead the dancers to an open space just west of the hatch of Powa'mu kiva, for the last movement of the final song.

While this movement is still in progress, the two shrubs are carried down into the kiva, and a minute or two later the leaders who have been waiting there come out to bless the katçinas in various ways. First Katçina chief, followed by the 'fathers' of the katçinas, goes down the line, casting a pinch of corn-meal over each performer; then Powa'mu chief asperses each dancer with *ña'küyi*, medicine water; Tobacco chief follows, blowing a puff of smoke over each man; then the 'mother' of Katçina clan, followed by the 'mother' of Badger clan, each carrying concealed under her ceremonial blanket the *ti'poni* of the fraternity associated with her clan, walks down the line, making a gesture with the *ti'poni* (still concealed under her garment) towards each man as she passes him. Their blessings concluded, Powa'mu chief, Tobacco chief and the two clan 'mothers' re-enter the kiva to dispose of their ritual objects; Powa'mu chief gathers from around the altar the prayer-sticks and prayer-feathers which have been made and consecrated during the previous four days, distributes them among the leaders and other members of the fraternity, and all emerge again from the kiva.

Above ground, the dance is still in progress; and as the final verse begins, first Katçina chief, then the 'fathers' of the katçinas, then Powa'mu chief, Tobacco chief, the two clan 'mothers', and finally the ordinary Powa'mu members, go down the line sprinkling the dancers with corn-meal.

When the song at length ends, the distribution of prayer-offerings begins. First, Katçina chief gives prayer-sticks, prayer-feathers and meal to the men at the head of the line until he runs out of *pa'ho*(s), whereupon he gives the remaining dancers only *nakwa'kwosi*(s) and meal. The katçina 'fathers' give *nakwa' kwosi*(s) and meal to the first few men, then prayer-sticks to those who have not yet received any; when their supply runs out, they too distribute only prayer-feathers and meal. Each succeeding leader, and then the other members of the fraternity, do the same, until at the close every performer has at least one prayer-stick and several sets of *nakwa'kwosi*(s).

By now the sun is low on the horizon and it is almost time for the katçinas to be dismissed to their homes. Before they are led out of the village for the last time, however, the 'fathers' of the katçinas each in turn makes a farewell speech to them:[1]

> Now we have finished the day. This morning I told you that we were to have a good time here this one day, but at sunset you must go home to your parents as I promised you. Now the time has come, the sun has reached its place and I am tired, and you too may be tired.
>
> When you go home and get to your parents and sisters and the rest of your relatives who are waiting for you, tell them all the words that I am going to tell you. Tell them that they should not wait, but let them come at once and bring rain to our fields. We may have just a few crops in our fields, but when you bring the rain they will grow up and become strong. Then if you will bring some more rain on them we will have more corn, and more beans, and more water-melons, and all the rest of our crops. When harvest time comes we will have plenty of crops to gather, so we shall have plenty of food for the whole winter.
>
> So now, this will be all. Now go back home, happily, but do not forget us. Come to visit us as rain.[2] That is all.

As each katçina 'father' finishes his speech, he sprinkles the katçinas with corn-meal. Then Katçina chief leads them out of the village,[3] sprinkling a path for them as he goes. He leads them down the mesa to the southwest of the village, to a katçina shrine where each dancer in turn deposits his prayer-feathers and meal—but not his prayer-stick.[4] When all have done so, Katçina chief makes his way back to the pueblo and rejoins the group in Powa'mu kiva. The dancers, meanwhile, unmask, perform the *navo'tçiwa* rite,[5] then disrobe,

---

[1] For the form of words used, see Titiev (1944), pp. 233–4: cf. the version given by Earle and Kennard (1938), pp. 37–8.

[2] The actual words are:

| üm | i'tamü | poptai'yani | yo'yangwai | ak'wai |
|----|--------|-------------|------------|--------|
| you | us | may-you-visit | raining | with , |

and this phrase, as Titiev observes (1944, p. 234, n. 19), clearly identifies the katçinas with clouds. The stem *yo'wi-*, in Hopi, signifies 'rains, is raining': Whorf (1936), p. 1322.

[3] As they leave the village for the last time, the people pluck spruce from the dancers to plant in their fields: Stephen (1936), p. 535.

[4] Titiev (1944), p. 234: confirmed by Stephen (1936), p. 535.

From the fact that the prayer-stick is included in the blanket which is taken to his home, not (with the mask) in the one which the man himself carries back to the kiva, it seems likely that the *pa'ho* is later deposited by the man in his field.

[5] Stephen (1936), p. 535.

wrap all their things (except the mask) in a blanket which each man hands to his wife or sister to take home, wrap their mask in a second blanket, and then return, carrying the mask wrapped in the blanket, to the sponsoring kiva. There they deposit their masks, smoke together, and then make their way home.

Meanwhile in Powa'mu kiva, as soon as Katçina chief returns, all those who have taken part in the ceremony begin to break pieces off the 'brother' and 'sister' spruce; and when everyone has his share, the group disperses, Katçina chief and the 'fathers' of the katçinas taking the shrubs to their own homes. The next day all those who have acquired bits of spruce, prayer-offerings (from the branches), or the shrubs themselves, take them to their fields[1] and 'place' them there with prayers for good crops.

So, virtually, ends the Nima'n festival. Early on the following morning, the leaders of the Powa'mu fraternity visit the katçina shrine to the southwest of the village and further prayer-offerings are deposited there.[2] Later in the day the altar, which was set up in Powa'mu kiva on the afternoon of the fourth day, is dismantled; and, some time subsequently, the *navo'tçiwa* rite performed in the kiva. For the next three days the customary tabus on salt and meat, and on sexual activity, are observed; and during this time the Nima'n sponsor and his assistant continue to sleep in their kiva, as do Powa'mu chief and his in theirs. Finally, on the fourth evening after the dismissal of the katçinas, all the members of the Powa'mu fraternity assemble in Powa'mu kiva to smoke and pray, for rain and crops.[3]

Of all the major Hopi ceremonies, the katçina dances of spring and early summer, and the Nima'n festival which represents their *finale*, are the simplest in form and the most direct in purpose. The dances, including the Nima'n, form a series which runs from late April, when the newly planted corn is just sprouting, until late in July, when it is knee-high in the fields and the ears are forming. The first two months of this period, as we saw earlier, are the time of crucial rain-lack in the Hopi calendar; the third, in a good year, sees the end of the spring drought and the onset of the summer rains. The purpose of the katçina dances and of the Nima'n is, quite simply, to hasten their onset and so to moisten the parched fields: 'As the katçinas are rain makers and promoters of crops, they are naturally appealed to at the season of planting and when rainfall is needed, in spring and early summer.'[4]

This simplicity of form and purpose enables us to isolate, very clearly, the essential elements in the transaction between the Hopi and the katçina spirits.

---

[1] Titiev (1944), p. 234, n. 22.

[2] Titiev (1944), pp. 234–5: cf. for 2nd Mesa, Fewkes (1892a), pp. 99–103. At Shungo' povi, and perhaps elsewhere, a further ceremony has taken place in the kiva in the course of which the katçinas are formally 'sent home' for the last time: Eggan (1968).

For subsequent events on this day, see Fewkes (1892a), pp. 71–8: Parsons (1925), p. 100: and Titiev (1944), p. 234, n. 21.

[3] Parsons (1936), p. 495, n. 2.

[4] Parsons (1936), p. 350. I am inclined to think that the indeterminacy of the katçina calendar, apart from the Nima'n itself, is a direct response to the uncertainty of the rainfall during the period when the dances are performed.

For six to seven months, from their 'return' late in December until the Home-going late in July, the katçinas are believed to reside in the neighbourhood of the Hopi villages; at intervals during this period they come into the pueblo to dance, for rain. The katçina 'father', *kachinûm na'amû*, 'uncostumed and shabby, . . . offers the katçinas prayer-stick and prayer-feathers in exchange for clouds and rain'.[1] The prayer-stick and *nakwa'kwosi*(s) are placed in the left hand of each dancer with a pinch of meal, at the conclusion of the ceremony; at that moment the dancer *is* still the katçina. He takes the prayer-offerings, which carry the wishes of their makers, to the katçina shrine (*pa'ho-ki*) and deposits them there. Then he un-masks, and as he does so, he bids farewell to the katçina whom he has *been*, at the same time reminding it (him) to send the 'rain clouds, all the things we have asked you for with these prayer-feathers'. In this way the dancer mediates between the katçina 'father', representing the people and offering on their behalf the prayer-sticks carrying their desires, and the katçinas, who are able to gratify those desires, i.e. by sending the objects prayed for.

### CONCEPT OF THE YEAR'S DUALITY

The departure of the katçinas, on the last evening of the Nima'n festival, marks their journey back to the Underworld. For six to seven months they have been living in the vicinity of the Hopi pueblos; now they return to their 'homes', where they are believed to 'sleep' until they are summoned again at the conclusion of the next Soya'l. This division of the year into two, nearly equal halves, during one of which the katçinas are 'locked away' in their homes and during the other are resident in the neighbourhood of the villages, reflects one of the fundamental frames of Hopi thinking: what Titiev has called, the 'concept of the year's duality'.

Very briefly, Hopi believe[2] that, whatever is happening in the upper world, its opposite is happening in the Underworld: when it is day here, it is night there, when it is summer here, it is winter there. This belief is extended to the naming of the moons, and lies at the root of the Hopi calendar; for while the upper world is experiencing a particular month of the winter season, the lower world is thought to be going through the corresponding month of the summer. Thus, when it is winter *kya mü'iya* (December) on earth, it is summer *kya mü'iya* (July) in the Underworld; when it is winter *pa'mü'iya* (January) here, it is summer *pa' mü'iya* (August) there; when it is winter *powa'* and *ö'sö mü'iya* (February–March) here, it is summer *powa'* and *ö'sö mü'iya* (September–October) there. As Stephen, evidently quoting a Hopi informant, puts it:[3]

> When Powa' mü'iyawû shines in the Above, its counterpart, Nasha'n mü'iyawû [harvest moon] is shining in the Below, at the house of Mü'iyiñwa. Summer is

---

[1] Stephen (1936), p. 371: cf. pp. 361–2, 373–4.
[2] See Titiev (1944), pp. 173–6: with references given there.
[3] Stephen (1936), p. 239.

yonder, winter is here. All vegetation is mature, fruits all ripe, in the Below. When the Nasha'n shining now in the Below comes to the Above, next September, it will bring just the same harvest as that it is now shining on in the Below.

This notion of the duality of time and place is extended to the ceremonial cycle. Since life in the other world is supposed to reflect life on earth (with the seasons reversed), when a major ceremony is being held here, a minor ceremony will be held there to co-incide with it; and when a major ceremony is being held there, a minor one will be held here at the same time. Thus, at Oraibi, the Snake-Antelope, Flute, Marau and Lako'n societies—all of which give their major performances in the summer or fall—hold brief winter meetings about six months earlier,[1] in the course of which they manufacture, consecrate and deposit prayer-offerings having the same purpose as the far more numerous ones which they make in the course of the summer ceremony. Thus the head of the Snake fraternity at Walpi, asked by Stephen[2] why they made prayer-sticks in the winter, replied: *pa'ho la'lauwû püt yo'kivani*, 'prayer-sticks made that rain may come'; adding that, while prayer-sticks were made during winter *pa' müi'yawû*, the dance itself was celebrated during summer *pa' müi'yawû*.

With this brief introduction I turn now to the two great festivals of August and September: namely, the Snake-Antelope and the Marau.

### SUMMER CEREMONIES: THE SNAKE-ANTELOPE

In the old days, according to Voth,[3] the summer ceremony of the Snake-Antelope fraternities took place every alternate year at the five pueblos of Oraibi, Shungo'povi, Sipau'lovi, Mishong'novi and Walpi: in even years at the first three, in odd years at the latter two. In years when the Snake-Antelope ceremony was not held, its place was taken by the Flute ceremony. Every August, therefore, each of the five pueblos celebrated either the Snake-Antelope, or the Flute, festival.

The date of the Snake ceremony is regulated, partly by watching the sunrise, but chiefly by the state of the crops.[4] Ordinarily, the *pa'ho*-making session takes place about August 6th, and the first day of the ceremony (*yü'ñya*) falls eight days later; but if the drought is very severe and the crop is suffering, the date of the ceremony may be put forward. Thus Voth records that, in the very dry year of 1898, pressure was brought to bear on the old Snake chief to hasten the ceremony and so secure for the crops the much-needed rain. It was also

---

[1] The Snake-Antelope and the Flute during the January moon, the Marau and Lako'n during February or early in March. The three winter ceremonies (Wü'wütçim, Soya'l, and Powa'mu), on the other hand, have no summer correlates: cf. Titiev (1944), p. 175.

[2] Stephen (1936), p. 713.

[3] Voth (1903a), p. 274. This account of the summer ceremony of the Snake-Antelope fraternities, at Oraibi, is based on the accounts given by Voth (1903a), pp. 262–358, and by Titiev (1944), pp. 149–54. For descriptions of 1st Mesa rites, see Fewkes (1894a), pp. 1–126: Parsons (1936), pp. 577–80: and Stephen (1936), pp. 590–718 (the ceremonies of 1891 and 1893, at Walpi).

[4] Particularly, according to Parsons (1936, p. 577, n. 1), of the melons: cf. Stephen (1936), p. 667.

believed, however, that if the concluding dance of the Snake ceremony were held too early, then it would freeze early, too.[1]

The ceremony itself, like all major Hopi ceremonies, extends over nine days; and the rites take place in two separate kivas, being carried out jointly by two independent fraternities, the Snake and the Antelope. At Oraibi, Spider clan (which owns the Blue Flute ceremony) also owns the Antelope *wi'mi*; and the preliminary meeting of the Snake and Antelope leaders takes place in Spider clan house, where the sacred objects of both the Blue Flute and the Antelope fraternities are stored. The Antelope fraternity itself meets in Nasavi (Al) kiva, and its esoteric rites are performed there, while the Snake society—as the name implies—meets in Tçu (Snake) kiva.[2]

Early in the morning of the day chosen, Antelope chief (who is ordinarily the leader of Spider clan) with his three assistants (of Coyote, Pat'ki and Rabbit clans), and Snake chief with his three assistants (all three from his own clan), assemble in the clan house of Spider clan. The two leaders have brought with them pipes and tobacco, corn meal, and all the paraphernalia needed for making *pa'ho*(s)—feathers, sticks, pigments, herb sprigs, cotton thread. They smoke together; then set to making prayer-sticks. Antelope chief makes four ordinary double-green *pa'ho*(s), one *püh'tabi* ('road'), and four *nakwa'kwosi*(s) stained with red oxide (*çu'ta*); Snake chief makes three double-green *pa'ho*(s), one *püh'tabi*, and four *nakwa'kwosi*(s) similarly stained red; and the other members make six ordinary *nakwa'kwosi*(s) each.

As soon as the prayer-offerings are finished, they are placed on a tray, then all smoke together, blowing the smoke over the tray. Corn meal is sprinkled over the prayer-offerings, which are then disposed of in the following way: Antelope chief sends one of his assistants to Lenañva spring, and another to a shrine on the east side of the mesa, each taking one of his and one of Snake chief's *pa'ho*(s), together with a *nakwa'kwosi* from each member; Antelope chief himself takes one of his own and one of Snake chief's *pa'ho*(s), his own *püh'tabi*, two of the red *nakwa'kwosi*(s) made by himself and two of those made by Snake chief, together with one *nakwa'kwosi* from each member, and sets off for the shrine of *Kokyang wuh'ti* ('Spider woman'), *wuya* of his clan, where he deposits them. The remaining *pa'ho* made by Antelope chief, the *püh'tabi* made by Snake chief, the two red *nakwa'kwosi*(s) made by each of the two leaders and the ordinary *nakwa'kwosi*(s) made by the other members, are left on the tray and taken, by Snake chief, to the house of Crier chief.

In the evening, Snake chief and his deputy, Village chief and Crier chief, meet in the Village chief's house. The tray containing the prayer-offerings is placed on the floor, and all four smoke over it together, handing the pipe solemnly from one to the other. Then each in turn takes the tray in both hands, and holding it in front of him, utters this prayer:

---

[1] Parsons (1925), p. 101.

[2] At Walpi, the Antelope fraternity—which plays the leading part in the rites—meets in *moñ* kiva, and the Snake society in Wikwa'lobi kiva: Fewkes (1894*a*), pp. 9–13.

Now we have for these different chiefs [*moñ'mowitû*, Cloud deities], our fathers, clothed (dressed up) these prayer-offerings. So now you have them, do not tarry on the way, but quickly have pity on us with rain. Sixteen days from to-morrow, these Snakes and Antelopes, if their hearts are good, will do the ceremony together. So, from now on, we must live in harmony (and not quarrel).

If some chief [i.e. Cloud deity] have pity on us[1] with falling rain, then shall we subsist, . . . and our people henceforth be happy, strong.

After all have smoked together again, Crier chief takes the tray with the prayer-offerings to the clan house of Pat'ki clan, where it remains overnight. Early the next morning, as the sun is about to rise, he ascends to the roof of the *ke'le* clan house, deposits the prayer-offerings in the shrine there and then, addressing the Cloud people, announces the forthcoming ceremony:

You, who live to the northwest, loom up! You to the southwest, loom up! You who live to the southeast, and you to the northeast, loom up!

In sixteen days from now, these Snakes and Antelopes, if they keep their hearts good, will conclude (their ceremony). So, for that many days, may we live at peace with one another. Then may some chief have pity on us with falling rain. On that shall we subsist, . . . and our people live happily, and be strong.

Eight days later, early in the morning of the first day of the ceremony (*yü'ñya*),[2] Antelope chief and Snake chief repair to their respective kivas, the one to Nasavi kiva, the other to Tçu kiva: taking with them the *na'atsi*(s) of their respective fraternities, together with pipes and tobacco, and corn meal. After sprinkling corn meal to the rising sun, each leader sets up the *na'atsi* outside the hatch of his kiva, then sweeps the kiva floor and lights the fire. Other members come in, and all smoke. Having finished their smoke, the men in Snake kiva make some eagle-feather *nakwa'kwosi*(s), staining them with the red *çu'ta*. Each man ties one of these in his hair, where it is worn throughout the ceremony; it is called *omau' nakwa'*, 'cloud wish (or prayer)'. Then they prepare the special sticks used for digging up the snakes, and the small buckskin bags for carrying them in. At about 6 a.m., Snake chief goes over to Nasavi kiva where he and Antelope chief smoke together, exchanging terms of relationship. After breakfast, the members of the Snake fraternity gather in Tçu kiva, preliminary to the snake hunt. Each man combs his hair, paints his body, puts on his ceremonial kilt and moccasins, and all smoke together. Then they set out, taking the trail *to the northwest*, each man carrying—beside his snake stick and bag—a bag of corn meal, some *nakwa'kwosi*(s), and some sticks of *hoho'ya öñga* (bladderpod), a root used for discharming purposes; Snake chief also carries a pipe and tobacco.

In Nasavi kiva, nothing of importance takes place all day. Antelope chief himself spends the greater part of the day in the kiva, carding cotton and smoking; and from time to time other members of the fraternity drop in. But the

---

[1] It is clear, from Titiev's account (1944, pp. 251-2) of an inter-pueblo council of chiefs, that 'to have pity on' their people is one of the principal functions of Hopi chiefs. In the prayer here cited, this attitude is translated to the Cloud deities, who are also *moñ'mowitû*.

[2] For days one to four of the ceremony, see Voth (1903*a*), pp. 285-95.

majority spend their time in the fields[1] or fetching wood, only returning to the kiva late in the afternoon to eat and sleep there. In the evening, about 6 p.m., the Snake men return from the snake hunt, carrying in their bags the snakes they have caught; these are put in two or three large earthenware jars against the south wall of the kiva. Then the men smoke together, and eat their evening meal. After supper, while the men prepare to sleep in the kiva, Snake chief again repairs to Nasavi kiva—as he did in the morning—and smokes there with Antelope chief. Then all retire for the night.

This pattern of events is followed, substantially, on each of the three succeeding days of the ceremony: except that, on the second day, the snake party takes the trail *to the southwest*, on the third the trail *to the southeast*, and on the fourth day the trail *to the northeast*. Morning and evening, Snake chief makes his way over to Nasavi kiva, to smoke there with Antelope chief; and while the latter continues to spend most of the time in his kiva, the other members of his fraternity are busy working in their fields[2] during the day.

At sunrise on the fifth day[3] a new *na'atsi* is set up outside each of the two participating kivas, beside the old one; this *na'atsi* is called a 'bow' *na'atsi*, and consists of an old bow to the string of which are tied several bunches of red horsehair and some eagle feathers. On this day the rites become more complicated, especially in Antelope kiva (Nasavi). Indeed, while up to this point events in Snake kiva have held the stage, from now on—at least until the evening of the eighth day—our attention will be principally directed to Antelope kiva; during these four days a great many prayer-offerings are made in that kiva, the main altar (*poñya*) is set up, and elaborate night ceremonies are performed.[4] Throughout this period, from the morning of the fifth day until the evening of the eighth, Antelope chief and his assistants fast during the day-time.

After setting up the new *na'atsi*(s), the two leaders carry into the kivas the paraphernalia needed for setting up their respective altars. Soon after breakfast, Antelope chief makes his way over to Snake kiva. There he smokes, with Snake chief and a number of the Snake men, around the fire. After they have smoked, each man utters a prayer, and Antelope chief prepares to go; stopping at the foot of the ladder, he turns and announces that the singing will commence in his

---

[1] Much weeding of the crops has to be done at this time of year, especially if the July rains have been good.

[2] But not in fields lying in the direction towards which the snake-hunters have gone. No Hopi, not a member of the Snake fraternity, must see the Snake men hunting; were he to do so, his abdomen would swell up and burst: Stephen (1936), p. 612.

[3] For the events of day five, see Voth (1903*a*), pp. 296–313.

[4] A similar division of activities occurs in the 1st Mesa rites, but there the timing of events is different. On 1st Mesa, the main altar and sand mosaic are set up, in Antelope kiva, on day one (Fewkes, 1894*a*, pp. 13–24: Stephen, 1936, pp. 590–6 and pl. xvii); and on day two, prayer-offerings are made, consecrated at the altar and then 'placed' at shrines (Fewkes, pp. 25–37: Stephen, pp. 599–605). Days three, four, five and six are given over, in Antelope kiva, to the making of further *pa'ho*(s): and in Snake kiva, to the four days of the snake hunt (Fewkes, pp. 37–52: Stephen, pp. 622–36). And it is not until day seven, on 1st Mesa, that the sand mosaic and altar are set up in Snake kiva (Fewkes, pp. 52–61: Stephen, pp. 639–41 and Fig. 350).

kiva that evening. Then he leaves the kiva. After his departure, Snake chief and his assistants set to making the sand mosaic and altar,[1] in the deep part of their kiva. The mosaic consists of the usual sand field, with—superimposed upon it—four squares, the inner one yellow, the next blue-green, the next red, and the outer one white. Inside the inner square are drawn the figure of a mountain lion, and around it, four snakes in different colours. A line of crooks and sticks is set, in clay stands, on either side of the same mosaic, and behind are ranged wooden effigies of Pü'ükoñhoya (war deity) and of Tü'wa-poñya-tümsi,[2] two lightning frames, and the jar(s) containing the snakes.

Meanwhile, in Antelope kiva,[3] the officers of the fraternity are busy making prayer-offerings. Antelope chief himself makes six double-green *pa'ho*(s), with black tips, each about 4½ inches long: one short double-green *pa'ho*, about 2 inches long: and *nakwa'kwosi*(s), twelve of large turkey feathers, four of small turkey feathers, and four of small eagle feathers, all of which he stains red. He also makes a *püh'tabi*, 'road', i.e. a long cotton string to one end of which he ties a large eagle breath-feather and six smaller feathers, representing the six cardinal directions, and to the other end the short double-green *pa'ho*. His chief assistant, of Badger clan, makes four *chocho'kpi*(s), two about 14 inches long and two about 4½ inches long. A *chocho'kpi* is a single black prayer-stick, pointed at one end, with a facet—painted white—at the other end; to the faceted end is tied a sprig of *kü'ñya* and one of *ma'övi*, a turkey feather, and a corn-husk packet, containing meal and honey; these are tied to the stick with cotton thread, wound tightly round to a width of about 1½ inches. Meanwhile the asperser, of Pat'ki clan, brings into the kiva the medicine bowl, four netted gourd vessels, six corn ears of different colours, and other items for use at the six-directions' altar; and Antelope chief's deputy, of Spider clan (like himself), prepares the crooks for use on the main altar. Around mid morning a man of Sand clan is despatched, with corn meal and *nakwa'kwosi*(s), to fetch sand from the main valley; on his return, the deputy begins erecting the main altar in Antelope kiva (Figure 47).

First, he makes the sand ridge on the floor against the north wall of the kiva, about 3 feet long, 8 inches wide and about 5 inches high. In the centre, leaning against the ridge, he places an old medicine bowl, along the crest of the ridge a row of buzzard feathers, and at either end a *ti'poni*, consisting of a stone celt set in a piece of cotton-wood root. In front of the ridge, he draws the sand mosaic, the four squares of which represent the four world quarters; the space inside, the Hopi land;[4] the semi-circles at the base, clouds; and the zigzag lines emanating from the clouds, flashes of forked lightning (? striking the land).

---

[1] For description, see Voth (1903a), pp. 298–300 and pl. clxi.

[2] Since she is described as the sister of Mü'yiñwa, this deity must be Tü'wa-poñya-tümsi, 'Sand altar woman'. Voth's spelling of her name has gone awry.

[3] Voth (1903a), pp. 301–8, and pl. clxii.

[4] Stephen (1936, p. 639), speaking of the sand mosaic in Snake kiva, says that 'the lines enclose all the Hopi land (*tü'chkwa*)'; and when, in the course of the ceremonies at the altar, the asperser sprinkles the mosaic with water from the medicine bowl, 'his aspersions are the rain falling from the rain clouds' (Stephen, 1936, p. 687).

Fig. 47. *Altar made in Antelope kiva*, on 5th day of summer Snake ceremony.

*Background.* *a.* sand ridge. *b.* two *ti'poni*(s), made of cottonwood root with a stone celt inserted in the upper end. *c.* old rectangular medicine-bowl. *d.* four *chocho'kpi*(s), black sticks with white facets, with sprigs of herbs, turkey feather and corn-husk packet attached. *e.* row of buzzard feathers. *f.* short double-green *pa'ho*, with cotton-thread 'road' leading diagonally across the sand mosaic to the east. *g.* old pottery vessel, containing corn stalks, bean plants, squash and watermelon vines.

*Mid ground.* *h.* sand mosaic, with cloud symbols and four 'lightning snakes' emerging from the clouds. *i.* four ordinary double-green *pa'ho*(s). *j.* row of alternating crooks and straight sticks, set in clay stands. *k.* breath-feathers, scattered over sand field. *l.* bunch of feathers representing the cardinal directions, with a single eagle feather, at farther end of 'road'.

*Foreground.* *m.* woven tray, with corn meal. *n.* medicine bowl, at intersection of corn-meal lines, with a single corn-ear and aspergill radiating in each of the six cardinal directions; the yellow corn-ear at 12 o'clock represents the northwest. Redrawn from Voth (1903), pl. clxii.

On either side of the mosaic, he sets a row of crooks and straight sticks, the crooks representing life in its various stages, and the sticks, deceased members of the fraternity. Finally, in front of the mosaic, he makes three intersecting lines of corn meal, places the medicine bowl at the intersection, pours water into it from a netted gourd brought from Lenañva by the asperser, and casts some corn pollen into it; then places the corn ears around the bowl, radiating from it in each of the six cardinal directions, and finally lays an old aspergill[1] beside each.

Of the prayer-offerings made by Antelope chief, one of the six double-green *pa'ho*(s) has already been taken to the shrine of Spider woman, one he now thrusts into the sand ridge near the *ti'poni* on the right, and the remaining four are laid on the floor to the left of the sand mosaic; the short *pa'ho* with 'road' attached he sticks into the sand ridge near the *ti'poni* on the left, laying the cotton thread diagonally across the sand mosaic. The four *chocho'kpi*(s), made by his assistant, he sticks upright into the sand ridge just behind the medicine bowl; and the *nakwa'kwosi*(s), he scatters over the sand field.

About noon, one of the members of the fraternity is despatched, with corn meal and *nakwa'kwosi*(s), to fetch water from a spring to the east of the village; while another goes down to his garden to fetch bunches of green corn-stalks, bean plants, squash, musk-melon and water-melon vines, all with their leaves and roots still on them. On his return these are put into an old earthenware pot, called *pat'ni* (cistern), and then set in the N.E. corner of the kiva,[2] behind the sand ridge.

Late in the afternoon of the fifth day, the girl who is to act the part of Antelope *mana* in the ceremony that evening, is brought into the kiva. On entering, she sprinkles a pinch of meal towards the altar, then sits down on the banquette in the S.E. corner of the deep part of the kiva. First, her hands and feet are daubed with white kaolin (*dü'ma*), her chin is smeared with mud from the bottom of a well, and a black line drawn across the upper lip from ear to ear. She is then arrayed in her costume: first, a ceremonial blanket (*toi'hi*) arranged in the form of a dress, then a kilt (*pit'kuna*), and around her waist a knotted belt, to the right side of which is fastened a bell. In her ears she wears turquoise pendants, and around her neck, many strands of white and red beads; her hair is loosely combed, and a small white downy eagle-feather tied to the crown. Finally, a drop of honey is placed in the *mana's* mouth. In the meantime, the man who is to play the part of Antelope *ti'yo* (youth) is dressed in the usual ceremonial kilt and sash, with a fox skin trailing from the sash behind. In his hair he wears a bunch of white eagle-feathers.

When all is ready, a messenger is sent to notify the Snakes, and a few minutes later they enter the kiva. As each man enters, he sprinkles a pinch of corn meal towards the altar, then takes his seat on the east banquette or on the floor. In the N.W. corner of the kiva, sits Antelope chief. Behind the sand ridge stands

---

[1] Referred to as the 'husbands' of the corn ears. In many Hopi songs, the corn ears are represented as being female: Voth (1903a), p. 303, n. 3.

[2] Cf. on the vines in the *pat'ni*, Fewkes (1894a), pp. 43–6: Stephen (1936), p. 623.

Antelope *ti'yo*, holding in his left hand some corn meal and, in his right, the *ti'poni* from the west end of the sand ridge; next to him stands Antelope *mana*, holding in her left hand some corn meal and, in her right, the *pat'ni* containing the green corn, bean plants, squash and melon vines. The other Antelope leaders are grouped in the N.E. corner of the kiva. Present also at the ceremony, for the first time, are novices (*kele'hoyam*) entering either of the two fraternities.[1]

As soon as the Snakes have taken their seats, all—except the novices—smoke together and exchange terms of relationship. Antelope chief now takes from their stand the crooks and sticks on the left-hand side of the sand mosaic, and his deputy takes those on the right-hand side, all excepting the last crook at the south end of each row, and hands one to each of the officers of the fraternity and one to each of the novices. Snake chief takes a live snake from the bag which he has brought with him, and hands it to Antelope *ti'yo*; the latter transfers the *ti'poni* to his left hand, grasps the snake in his right hand behind the neck, and holds it there throughout the ceremony.

The ceremony that follows lasts between one hour and two hours. In the course of it, a series of sixteen songs is chanted, and while the songs are being chanted, Antelope youth—carrying the live snake in one hand, and the *ti'poni* and corn meal in the other—and Antelope *mana*, carrying the *pat'ni* in one hand and corn meal in the other, keep step to the singing, constantly moving from one side to the other behind the altar. At the same time, the asperser asperses water from the medicine bowl over the sand mosaic, and later lights the *omau' tapi*, 'cloud blower', and blows clouds of smoke over it. When the last song comes to an end, the crooks and sticks are replaced in their stands beside the mosaic; all smoke together, and exchange terms of relationship. Snake chief then takes the live snake from the *ti'yo* and puts it back in the bag. Antelope chief takes the *ti'poni* and corn meal from him, stands in front of each novice in turn and waves the *ti'poni* towards his head, face, neck and chest, saying to each one:

> May your life be long, and may you grow to old age. . . .

He then steps back to the N.W. corner of the sand ridge, carrying the *ti'poni* diagonally across the mosaic along the line of the *püh'tabi* as far as he can reach. He does this four times, then holding the *ti'poni* in front of himself, utters a short prayer:

> Now, we have performed this (ceremony) in the right manner. So, since we have performed it rightly, we shall surely benefit by it [i.e. attain the object sought]. . . .

He hands the *ti'poni* and corn meal to Snake chief, who goes through the same performance, first in front of the novices, expressing the same wish, and then beside the altar, uttering a similar prayer. When he has finished, he hands

---

[1] Fewkes (1894a, pp. 61–5) speaks of the Snake novices being initiated, i.e. introduced to the *ti'poni* and other sacred objects of the fraternity, in the course of a ceremony in Snake kiva, on the seventh day. He observes, further (p. 65), that novices may choose either of the two societies; but that a person initiated into one does not, except in the case of illness, join the other. Membership of the two fraternities is thus exclusive.

the *ti'poni* and corn meal back to Antelope chief, and the Snakes file silently out of the kiva. When they have gone, Antelope chief sprinkles the corn meal over the sand field, replaces the *ti'poni*, takes the *pat'ni* and corn meal from the *mana*, again sprinkles the corn meal over the altar, and puts the *pat'ni*—with its bunches of vegetation—on the sand mosaic.[1] The *ti'yo* and *mana* then disrobe, and go through the discharming rite. The girl leaves the kiva, the *ti'yo* joins the other men, and later they all take supper together—with no meat or salt—and sleep in the kiva.

Early on the morning of day six, Antelope chief emerges from Nasavi kiva and takes over to Snake kiva a tray containing the four double-green *pa'ho*(s) and the four *chocho'kpi*(s), which were consecrated in the course of the previous evening's ceremony: also, some of the *nakwa'kwosi*(s). During the morning, these prayer-offerings are deposited by Snake man at shrines outside the village, in each of the four cardinal directions.

During these three days,[2] a definite pattern emerges. Each morning, in Antelope kiva, Antelope chief and his deputy make the four double-green *pa'ho*(s) and four *chocho'kpi*(s); in the evening, these prayer-offerings are consecrated at the altar, in the course of the rites in which the *ti'yo* and the *mana* take part. Early the next morning, Antelope chief takes the prayer-offerings over to Snake kiva; and they are deposited by Snake men, later in the morning, at shrines outside the village—the shrines being located nearer and nearer to the village on succeeding days.

In addition to the four sets of prayer-sticks to be 'placed' in the four cardinal directions, a great many other prayer-offerings are made in both kivas during these three days. In Antelope kiva, on the morning of the sixth and seventh days, Antelope chief and his deputy make two special prayer-sticks called *mü'in kü'ña toki*(s), 'stream-ball sticks'. These prayer-sticks consist of a short thick stick, about 2 inches long, painted black with green ends, with an eagle-feather *nakwa'kwosi* tied to the middle; they represent the small clay balls (*kü'ña*) formed by the water (*mü'in*, flow of water) in the beds of arroyos, and are considered to be a special prayer that the washes may rise and flood the fields. When these are finished, they are laid beside the sand mosaic with the other *pa'ho*(s). Antelope chief also makes two rain 'wheels' out of the leaves of the *wi'po* rush, about 3 inches in diameter and painted black, to each of which he attaches a number of duck-feather *nakwa'kwosi*(s); and the other leaders, a number of double-green *pa'ho*(s).

In Snake kiva, the members are busy carding cotton and spinning thread; and on the seventh morning,[3] they also set to making prayer-sticks. Snake

---

[1] Cf. Fewkes (1894*a*), pp. 67–71. On 1st Mesa, Antelope *ti'yo* and *mana* only take part in the sixteen-song ceremony on the eighth and ninth days of the festival.

[2] For days six, seven and eight, see Voth (1903*a*), pp. 313–28.

[3] On this day, on 1st Mesa, the sand mosaic and the altar are set up in Snake kiva; following this, the Antelopes file into Snake kiva, and a long ceremony takes place, in the course of which the novices are introduced to the sacred objects of the fraternity: Fewkes (1894*a*), pp. 52–65: cf. Stephen (1936), pp. 639–47.

chief himself, assisted by two or three others, makes a set of ten *püch'ko pa'ho*(s), 'flat-wood prayer-sticks'. Each of these consists of a chunk of cottonwood root, about 7 inches long and 2 inches wide; they are first painted white, then one half green and the other half yellow, both sides of the slab being painted alike; the two colours are separated by a black line, running down the middle of the *pa'ho* itself marked with several elongated white dots. About an inch from either end of the slab, a pair of notches are cut, about ½ inch apart; and into each end is thrust a small eagle feather. Meanwhile, the other leaders are busy making a number of ordinary double-green *pa'ho*(s), and the members, *nakwa'kwosi*(s). When all these are ready, they are placed in front of the altar, and the leaders smoke over them. Later, during the afternoon, Snake chief takes the tray containing the prayer-offerings over to Nasavi kiva, together with some corn meal and honey. There, he and Antelope chief smoke over them; then they are divided into two sets, one set being handed over to Antelope chief's deputy to take with him when he goes to fetch water for the race, while the other set Snake chief takes back with him to his own kiva.

Late in the afternoon of the seventh day, Antelope chief's deputy is despatched to a spring some miles to the southeast of the village, to fetch water for the race early the next morning. He takes with him a netted gourd vessel (*moñ'wikuru*), a long *chocho'kpi* with one of the rain 'wheels' and one of the 'stream-ball sticks' tied to it, an eagle-bone whistle, a whirrer (to simulate thunder),[1] some corn meal, corn pollen and honey, a number of the *pa'ho*(s) made in Antelope kiva, and the set of prayer-offerings brought over from Snake kiva. The prayer-sticks, etc., he carries wrapped in an old blanket over his left shoulder, the netted gourd vessel he carries in his right hand. He leaves the village by the trail leading down the mesa to the southeast. At four points on the way, as he crosses the main valley, he stops; at each point he twirls the whirrer, then deposits one of the double-green *pa'ho*(s) and a number of *nakwa'kwosi*(s). Arriving near the spring, he blows four times on the eagle-bone whistle, to warn the spirits of his presence, approaches the spring, deposits the remainder of the prayer-sticks, and facing the spring, utters these words:

> Now, then, these [prayer-offerings] I have brought for you. With them [i.e. by their agency] have I come to fetch you. So, being arrayed in them [refers to the Cloud deities putting the feathers in their hair], may you rain on our crops! Then will our corn stalks grow up by that rain. When they ripen, we shall ... be fed, be happy. When you, of your bounty, provide lush grass, we shall rejoice; and our animals, eating it, will rejoice also.
>
> For this [purpose], do we go to the trouble of assembling. Hence it must happen this way. Therefore have pity on us. Let us go now ... you [addressing the Clouds] all follow me!

---

[1] Cf. Stephen (1936), pp. 637–8: and for the instrument itself, Fig. 348. The act of whirring, or whizzing, is *ümü'motoya*; Stephen says that its purpose is to induce the lightning to strike the fields, which then become fertile; *ii'mü-* is the root for 'thunders, is thundering'.

He then enters the water and, after sprinkling corn meal into it from each of the six cardinal directions, fills the *moñ'wikuru*. Carrying the *moñ'wikuru*, he sets off towards the village; but when he reaches the point near the main wash where the race is to start the next morning, he breaks his journey and sleeps the night there.[1]

Long before sunrise on the eighth day,[2] the village is astir. In Snake kiva, the two men who are to act as *kaletaka*(s), 'warriors', paint their bodies and put on their kilts, and each takes a whirrer, together with a number of the prayer-sticks from the tray in front of the altar. Then they set out to the southeast, on the trail taken by the water-fetcher the afternoon before. At each point on the trail where he deposited *pa'ho*(s), they deposit theirs; and when they reach the point where the race is to begin, they deposit the remainder there.

Meanwhile, all those (men and boys) who intend to take part in the race—i.e. who are *not* members of either of the two fraternities—are making their way down to the starting-point. Others, including members of the two fraternities, go down to their corn fields in the valley and pull up armsful of fresh green corn and squash vines; others, again, line the course. In Antelope kiva, Antelope youth and maid are dressed up and waiting; Antelope chief and his assistants are ready, and the prayer-sticks are set out beside the sand mosaic. At about 5 a.m., the Snake leaders are summoned; they enter the kiva and take their places, and all wait expectantly, ready to start the ceremony directly the signal arrives.

Soon after 5 a.m., the water-fetcher arrives at the starting-point, carrying the *moñ'wikuru* filled with water, a *püh'tabi*, and the long *chocho'kpi* with rain 'wheel' and 'stream-ball stick' attached. When all are assembled, he rubs a little clay into the hand of each man who intends to take part in the race, lays the *püh'tabi* on the trail pointing to the village, then facing the men, who are ranged in a line across the trail, addresses them:

> Now, let us race joyfully. So, you young men, do not tarry on the way. Whoever comes out ahead, on his account[3] shall we drink[4] when the sun has not yet reached half-way.[5] Being concerned (about this) to these our mothers, our fathers, to the village let us ascend, let us enter it happily. Now let us go!

The water-fetcher then sets off along the trail towards the village. A minute or two later, the two *kaletaka*(s) follow. When the latter reach a certain point on the trail, they make a signal. At this, all the men give a yell—which is the signal

---

[1] On 1st Mesa, Antelope chief and his three assistants go together to Sun spring on the night of day seven; they deposit their *pa'ho*(s) there, sleep the night near the spring, and return to the village early the next morning: Fewkes (1894*a*), pp. 65–7, cf. Stephen (1936), pp. 647, 651.

[2] See Voth (1903*a*), pp. 321–8.

[3] Because he receives the water, which is supposed to bring rain: Voth (1903*a*), p. 324, n. 5.

[4] He speaks here on behalf of the thirsty crops, for which he is sent to fetch the clouds, and which are eagerly awaiting the expected rain: Voth (1903*a*), p. 324, n. 6.

[5] Indicating that the clouds should not procrastinate, but come quickly: Voth (1903*a*), p. 324, n. 7.

for the leaders in Antelope kiva to commence singing—and the race begins. To the first man who overtakes him, the water-fetcher hands the *moñ'wikuru* and the long *chocho'kpi*; whoever overtakes *him*, then takes them over, and so on.

As the runners reach the foot of the mesa, they are met by those who have been to collect corn stalks and squash vines from the fields. The runners struggle up the mesa side, followed by the men and boys carrying the vegetation. As they reach the top, the runners are sprinkled with corn meal by some of the Snake leaders waiting there; but they surge past them and on into the village, to Antelope kiva. As the men and boys carrying the vegetation reach the out-skirts of the village, the women and girls dash out to meet them, and snatch the corn stalks and squash vines from them; these they bear off to their own homes, and lay them on the corn piled in their storehouses.

The runners, meanwhile, pass through the crowds to Antelope kiva. On reaching the kiva, the first man—the *moñ'wikuru* and *chocho'kpi* in his hands—stops just to the east of the kiva hatch, and announces his arrival by stamping with his foot on the kiva roof. The asperser emerges, takes the *moñ'wikuru* and *chocho'kpi* from the runner, sprinkles some corn meal over them, and re-enters the kiva. There, he hands them to Antelope chief. The latter takes the *moñ' wikuru* and *chocho'kpi*, adds one of the double-green *pa'ho*(s) from beside the sand mosaic, utters a prayer over all three, then hands them—with some corn meal and a digging-stick—to the asperser, who emerges again from the kiva and hands the objects back to the lad who 'won' the race. He goes down to the valley to one of his fields, digs a hole in the ground with the digging-stick, casts a few pinches of corn meal into it, sprinkles the water from the *moñ'wikuru* into the hole, sets the long *chocho'kpi* (with rain 'wheel' and 'stream-ball stick' attached) upright in the hole, and refills it with earth, so that the tip of the *chocho'kpi* protrudes a little above the ground[1]. The double-green *pa'ho* he thrusts into the ground close by; later, he takes the gourd vessel back to Antelope kiva.

In the meantime, in Antelope kiva, the singing ceremony is carried to its conclusion, the Snakes return to their own kiva, Antelope *ti'yo* and *mana* disrobe and go through the discharming rite, all present smoke together and then take breakfast, still avoiding meat and salted food.

The forenoon of the eighth day is devoted, in both kivas, to the making of prayer-sticks of various kinds.[2] In Antelope kiva, all the leaders make six or eight ordinary double-green *pa'ho*(s); in addition, Antelope chief makes two *püh' tabi*(s) and nine *chocho'kpi*(s), and all the members make a number of *nakwa' kwosi*(s). At about noon, each man takes off the small red feather, which he has so far worn in his hair, and ties a cotton thread to it; these *nakwa*(s) are later deposited by the owners at fields, melon patches, etc., outside the village. In

---

[1] 'These offerings', writes Voth (1903*a*, p. 327), 'are considered a special blessing to the field and augur a good crop not only at the approaching harvest, but in coming years.'

[2] See Voth (1903*a*), pp. 328–34. On the making of prayer-sticks on the eighth day, on 1st Mesa, cf. Stephen (1936), pp. 651–3.

Snake kiva, Snake chief makes four *püch'ko pa'ho*(s), 'flat-wood *pa'ho*(s)', and one *püh'tabi* of a special kind, while others of the leaders make a number of *na'alüñü pa'ho*(s), 'all-colours prayer-sticks'; these consist of a pair of sticks about 4½ inches long, one painted green and the other black,[1] bound together with cotton thread, with the usual corn-husk packet and sprigs of *ma'övi* and sage attached. Each member of the fraternity, besides making six or eight *nakwa' kwosi*(s), makes a special willow prayer-stick, about 16 inches long, painted black and pointed at one end, to the butt of which he ties an eagle-wing feather, corn-husk packet, and sprigs of *ma'övi* and sage;[2] farther down the stem four black lines are incised, and a single red *nakwa'kwosi* tied to each prayer-stick. As each man finishes his set of prayer-offerings, he smokes over them, then places them on a woven tray with the others; when all are finished, the woven tray is laid in front of the altar and the leaders smoke together over all the prayer-offerings, in silence. Later, around noon, one of the members brings an armful of corn stalks, bean plants and melon vines into the kiva, and places it on the floor behind the altar.

In the meantime several of the younger members of the Snake fraternity have been sent to fetch cottonwood branches, to make the shelter (*ki'si*) in the village square. On their return early in the afternoon, they take the branches straight to the village square and set up the shelter in the northwest corner; this is similar in construction to the shelters which Hopi make near their fields for sleeping in during the harvest, 5 to 6 feet high, the open side being covered with an old blanket. When the shelter is ready, Snake chief emerges from the kiva, carrying a *pa'ho*, a *nakwa'kwosi* and some corn meal, and proceeds to the square. In front of the entrance to the *ki'si*, he digs a shallow pit about 10 inches square and 6 to 8 inches deep, lays the prayer-offerings in the pit, sprinkles them with corn meal, and utters a short prayer, addressed to the cloud deities and calling on them to send rain; then he covers the pit with a plank of wood,[3] and returns to the kiva. Later, before the dance begins, another of the Snake men makes his way to the *ki'si*, carrying the bunch of vines and other vegetation from the kiva, and conceals himself inside the shelter.

At about 4.30 p.m., the Antelopes begin to get ready in their kiva.[4] Their chin, hands and feet are painted black; they wear embroidered sash and kilt, a hank of dark blue yarn over the right shoulder, a strand around each leg below the knee, ankle bands, strands of beads around the neck, and in their hair, a white eagle feather. Antelope chief carries in his left hand the *ti'poni* of the order, a netted gourd vessel and bag of corn meal, and in his right, a rattle; the asperser, the medicine bowl and aspergill; and all the members, in their

---

[1] Stephen (1936, pp. 497–8) states that the *na'alüñü pa'ho*(s), made at Nima'n, are painted green and *yellow*, and that these prayer-sticks are a prayer for flowers and all cultivated vegetation.

[2] Cf. Fewkes (1894*a*), pp. 70–1, with illustration.

[3] The pit represents the *si'papü*: Fewkes (1894*a*), p. 71.

[4] For the 'vine dance', see Voth (1903*a*), pp. 334–6: cf. Titiev (1944), p. 151, and for 1st Mesa, Fewkes (1894*a*), pp. 71–4.

left hand, one of the sticks from beside the altar, a netted gourd vessel and bag of corn meal, and in their right, a rattle. Leaving the kiva, the Antelopes make their way to the square, shaking their rattles as they go. Arrived there, they circle in front of the shelter four times, in an anti-clockwise direction,[1] each time sprinkling the plank with corn meal and stamping their right foot on it as they pass. Then they line up, with their backs to the *ki'si*, and wait for the Snakes.

The Snakes, meanwhile, their bodies painted, dressed in kilt and moccasins, each man carrying his snake whip and a bag of corn meal, emerge from their kiva and proceed to the village square. There, they too circle four times in front of the *ki'si* in similar fashion, then line up, facing the Antelopes and about 6 feet away. Antelope chief steps forward and sprinkles a line of corn meal in front of the Snakes, and then another in front of his own men; he places the *ti'poni* at one end of this latter line, the asperser lays the medicine bowl on the ground, and the other men their netted gourds. After a number of songs rendered in unison by the two groups to the accompaniment of the gourd rattles, the Antelope man who is to play the part of the 'vine dancer' and the Snake chief leave their respective lines. Four times they dance between the two lines, the 'vine dancer' leading the way, the Snake chief following with his left hand on the other's left shoulder. Approaching the *ki'si* for the fourth time, the 'vine dancer' leans forward and receives, from the man concealed inside, the bunch of vines; putting it between his teeth and holding both ends in his hands, in exactly the same manner as the Snake men will do—with live snakes instead of vegetation—on the morrow, he again dances the length of the two lines, followed by Snake chief.[2] Having done this four times, he returns to the *ki'si*, lays down the bunch of vines, and the two dancers resume their places in the line. One of the Snake men picks up the bunch of vines, which he later takes down to the valley and puts on his field; then both parties, in turn, circle four times in front of the *ki'si*, and return to their own kiva. This completes the day's events; and that evening, in Antelope kiva, the leaders break their four days' fast and all the members of the fraternity eat together.

Early the next morning,[3] around sunrise, almost exactly the same sequence takes place as on the previous morning. The Antelopes assemble in their kiva, Antelope *ti'yo* and *mana* put on their things for the last time, and the Snake leaders are admitted. Down in the valley the race begins, in the same manner as before, and at that moment the ceremony of sixteen songs begins in Antelope kiva. The 'winner' of the race is again presented with the *moñ'wikuru* and the *chocho'kpi*, and with a prayer-stick from the altar, and again takes them down to his field and buries them there. After the ceremony is over, the novices[4] are

---

[1] See Voth (1903*a*), pl. clxxxi.

[2] In Stephen's account of the dance (1936, pp. 653–4), the Antelope man first takes corn stalks in his mouth and goes the whole length of the line; then Snake chief takes vines in his mouth, and does the same; then Antelope man repeats with corn stalks, and Snake chief with vines.

[3] For the events of the ninth day, see Voth (1903*a*), pp. 336–49, and Titiev (1944), pp. 151–2; cf. for 1st Mesa, Fewkes (1894*a*), pp. 74–95.

[4] Fewkes (1894*a*), p. 81: cf. Stephen (1936), pp. 665–6.

taken to the house of their ceremonial 'father's' sister, where their heads are washed in yucca suds, each novice is given an ear of corn, his face is smeared with corn meal, he is given a new name, and a *nakwa'kwosi*, dyed red, is tied to his scalp lock; this feather he wears until the conclusion of the festival.

Soon after breakfast, the altar in Antelope kiva is partially dismantled. The buzzard feathers are taken out of the sand ridge, the crook and sticks from their clay stands, and the contents of the *pat'ni* strewn over the sand mosaic. In fact, everything is removed, except one *ti'poni*, one prayer-stick, the medicine bowl, the tray with corn meal, one netted gourd vessel, one corn ear, and the long black eagle feather required for the discharming rite. During the morning, the long *püh'tabi*, 'road', is deposited by Antelope chief on the trail to the east of the mesa; the four *chocho'kpi*(s) from the sand ridge are taken by his deputy and buried in one of his (the deputy's) fields; and all the 'field' *pa'ho*(s) and *nakwa'kwosi*(s), made the previous day, together with the water in the gourd vessels, are taken by the various members to their corn fields, peach orchards and melon patches; there, each man deposits his prayer-offerings and pours the water from the gourd vessel on the ground nearby. Other prayer-sticks, made on the eighth day and known as *pü'vüva-ta pa'ho*, 'arroyo prayer-sticks', are taken by older members of the two fraternities down to the valley, together with mud balls (with willow twigs stuck in them) which dissolve when the rain comes; these are laid in watercourses there, with the prayer (*ho'moya*): *i'ich yo'kivani, i'ich mü'invani*, 'hasten rain, hasten flowing water'.[1]

On their return there takes place, in Snake kiva, what Voth describes[2] as 'one of the most weird and unique rites' in the whole ceremony: namely the washing, or baptising, of the snakes.

Ever since their capture, the snakes have been kept in a number of jars near the altar in Snake kiva. Now, just before noon on the last day of the ceremony, Snake chief scatters sand over an area about 5 feet square to the east of the fireplace; over the sand, he sprinkles corn meal; then places two bowls, one containing yucca suds and the other clear water, on the west side of the field. Precisely at noon, one of the Snake members is sent to announce that all in the village must retire into their houses, as the washing of the snakes is about to begin.[3] The men in the kiva are very solemn. When all is ready, the older men squat down on the north side of the field, some of the younger men on the south side, and the three who are to handle the snakes on the west side; all are

---

[1] Stephen (1936), pp. 651–2, 706–7, and Fig. 382: the name of these *pa'ho*(s) is derived from *pü'va*, to be eroded into a gully by rains (Whorf, 1936, p. 1286). 'Formerly,' writes Stephen (1936, p. 709), in his Journal for 14 August, 1893, 'great rains fell at this observance and the arroyos ran brimming full, now but little rain falls.'

[2] Voth (1903*a*), p. 339, and for account of the whole rite, ibid. pp. 339–42: cf. for 1st Mesa, Fewkes (1894*a*), pp. 81–7, and Stephen (1936), p. 659.

[3] The washing of the snakes is considered to be one of the most sacred and solemn rites of the whole ceremony (Voth, 1903*a*, pp. 342–3). It is especially forbidden to women to witness the rites; Hopi say that women are especially obnoxious to the snakes (cf. Stephen, 1936, p. 709). Throughout this day, the Snake members fast until the evening; and during the morning, before the washing of the snakes, they wash their own heads in yucca suds.

naked, their bodies rubbed with red *çu'ta*, with a red-dyed feather in their hair. Each snake in turn is taken out of the jar by the man sitting nearest to it, handed to the second who passes it through the bowl of yucca suds, and on to the third, who passes it through the clear water and then lays the snake on the corn meal on the sand field. Meanwhile, the men sitting round the sand field smoke uncon- cernedly,[1] puffing smoke over the snakes as they writhe on the field, handing the pipe from one to another and exchanging terms of relationship as they do so.

About 2 p.m., when all the snakes have been washed and smoked over, they are gathered up and put in a bag, in preparation for the dance that is to follow. The men who bathed them wash their hands, while Snake chief sweeps up the sand and corn meal and carries it outside the kiva. Throughout the ceremony, absolute silence prevails in the village.

Early in the afternoon, the Antelopes begin preparing for the final perfor- mance. First, they cover their bodies all over with a thin coat of black; then, a white line is drawn from ear to ear across the upper lip, and the legs from knee to ankle, and the forearms, are painted white; finally, from the shoulder to the waist, on chest and back, and also on the upper arms and on the thighs, are drawn bold white zigzag lines, 'called lightning marks, because they represent lightning'. Their costume, which they put on next, consists of the usual kilt and sash, with fox skin dangling behind, a hank of dark blue wool over the shoulder, moccasins, beads, and feather headdress. While they are getting ready, Snake chief takes the bag of snakes to the square and puts it on the ground inside the *ki'si*.

Towards sunset,[2] Antelope chief, carrying—as on the previous afternoon— the *ti'poni* and bag of corn meal in his left hand, and in his right the medicine bowl and a rattle, leads the way into the village square, followed by the members of the fraternity each carrying a rattle. There they repeat the circling in front of the shelter, then line up and await the arrival of the Snakes. A few minutes later the Snakes file into the square, each man carrying his snake whip in one hand, circle four times in front of the *ki'si*, and line up facing the Antelopes. Antelope chief again sprinkles the two lines of corn meal on the ground, one in front of each party, and a number of songs are chanted in unison.

As soon as the singing ceases, the Snakes arrange themselves in pairs, the man in front tucking his snake whip into his sash, the man behind placing his left hand on the left shoulder of the man in front and stroking his back with his snake whip;[3] to each pair, a third man attaches himself, to pick up the snakes

---

[1] The reader must bear in mind, throughout this account of the washing of the snakes and of the subsequent snake 'dance', that the majority of the snakes are lethal: Fewkes (1894a, p. 101) reckoned that, of the sixty snakes used in the 1891 dance, not less than forty were rattlesnakes.

[2] Fewkes (1894a, p. 87) states, specifically, that the dance itself takes place as the sun is going down. For account of this, the concluding performance of the whole ceremony, see Voth (1903a), pp. 344–7: cf. for 1st Mesa, Fewkes (1894a), pp. 87–95.

[3] Titiev (1944, p. 152, n. 64) observes that the man behind is usually the ceremonial 'father' of the one in front.

when they are put on the ground. Each pair in turn then moves, with a slow dancing step, toward the *ki'si*; there the leader kneels down and is given a snake from inside the shelter, which he places between his teeth (as the 'vine dancer' did the bunch of vines, on the day before), grasping its body in both hands. Both men then move slowly round in front of the *ki'si*, in an anti-clockwise direction, stepping in time to the rattling kept up by the Antelopes. After a few minutes, the leader drops his snake in one of the four cardinal directions, and then gets another, until all are gone. As the snakes are dropped on the ground, they are gathered up by the snake gatherers, who first throw down a pinch of corn meal and then pick up the snake; by the end of the 'dance', each gatherer may have four or five snakes in his hand.

As soon as the last snakes have been picked up from the ground, Snake chief moves a few yards away from the *ki'si* to where a group of women and girls are waiting, holding in their hands woven trays filled with corn meal.[1] Snake chief sprinkles a corn-meal circle, about 20 feet across, on the ground, and within the circle six lines representing the six directions.[2] The women and girls cast their meal into the circle, whereupon all who hold snakes throw them down on the meal; then each Snake member makes a dive for the pile, seizes a handful of the reptiles, and dashes out of the village to release them, either in his own fields or at distant shrines located in the four cardinal directions.[3] After releasing the snakes, they take off their ceremonial things, wrap them in a blanket and make their way back to the kiva: the Antelopes, in the meantime, having circled four times in front of the *ki'si*, return to *their* kiva.

Soon after returning to their kiva, each Snake man comes out again, drinks about a pint of the emetic which is standing in a jar by the hatch, goes to the mesa edge and vomits, and then returns to the kiva. Then the *navot'çiwa* rite is performed in each of the two kivas. Finally, in each kiva, the dismantling of the altar is completed, and the altar paraphernalia wrapped up in bundles: that of the Snake fraternity being taken to the clan house of Snake clan, and that of the Antelopes to the clan house of Spider clan, where the things are stored until the next ceremony. Before the sand mosaic is swept up in each kiva, the members take pinches of sand from each of the different coloured clouds and from the four lightning snakes;[4] early the next morning, they take them to their corn fields in the valley and sprinkle them there, the different coloured sands symbolising the directions from which the rain and the lightning are to come.

[1] See Voth (1903*a*), pls. ccxii–ccxiii: the trays are decorated with zigzag, i.e. lightning patterns.

[2] Voth (1903*a*), p. 347: but pl. ccxiv (*b*) shows five lines, and Titiev (1944, p. 152) states that Snake chief marks the corn-meal circle 'into quadrants'. Fewkes, however, describes (1894*a*, p. 94) a ring of corn meal, with six radial lines 'corresponding to the cardinal directions'.

[3] Titiev (1944), p. 152. Fewkes (1894*a*, p. 95) says that they run with the snakes out of the village, along the trails leading in the four directions from which the snakes were gathered, and release them in the valley; Stephen (1940, p. 211), that they put them in the fields.

[4] Fewkes (1894*a*), pp. 95–6: cf. Stephen (1936), pp. 664–5.

Turning now to the significance of the Snake-Antelope rites: Fewkes, in 1894, summed up the purpose of the ceremony in the following words:[1]

> The Snake Dance is an elaborate prayer for rain, in which the reptiles are gathered from the fields, entrusted with the prayers of the people,[2] and then given their liberty to bear these petitions to the divinities who can bring the blessing of copious rains to the parched and arid farms of the Hopi.

Three years later, in 1897, he wrote:[3]

> That the ceremony is a rain-making observance can not be doubted . . . [To this] must now be added corn or seed germination, growth and maturity . . . a dominating influence in every great rite of Tusayan. I am inclined to believe that the Snake dance [i.e. the whole ceremony] has two main purposes, the making of rain and the growth of corn . . .

And he goes on to point out that, of the two elements which are interwoven in the ceremony, rain-making is more prominent in the work of the Snake fraternity, and corn growth in the work of the Antelopes.

Of the rightness, in broad terms, of Fewkes' interpretation, there can to my mind be no question. Numerous items in the ritual—e.g. the cloud and lightning symbols on the sand mosaics, the prayer before the race on the eighth and ninth mornings, the race itself and its aftermath, the placing of prayer-sticks in the beds of watercourses—attest the rain-making thread that runs through the festival;[4] and numerous other items, e.g. the holding of the *pat'ni* filled with vegetation by Antelope *mana* during the ceremony of sixteen songs, the pulling-up of corn stalks and vines at the time of the race, the 'vine dance', the placing of prayer-sticks in fields and gardens on the last morning, testify to the vegetative thread. Indeed, the two threads are run together in the final song sung by the Antelopes, at the conclusion of the Snake 'dance' and just before the snakes are taken out of the pueblo to be released:[5]

> All of us here,
> Our breath-feathers and our *pa'ho*(s) are placed.
> Look, O clouds, from the four quarters.
> Our fathers! listen to your children singing.

---

[1] Fewkes (1894*a*), p. 124: on the snake as a symbol of water, and so more generally of rain, see Fewkes (1891), p. 131.

[2] Earlier (1894*a*, p. 103), Fewkes notes that, during their captivity, the snakes are treated with the greatest gentleness and care, 'almost amounting to reverence'.

[3] Fewkes (1897*b*), p. 307.

[4] An elderly Hopi, quoted by Titiev (1943), deprecated the ceremony on the ground that it *failed to bring rain*.

[5] Stephen (1940), p. 211. Stephen remarks (ibid. p. 212, n. 1) that in 1891, while the Antelopes were still chanting their prayers for rain, copious showers fell upon the corn fields and gardens around the foot of the mesa.

*Ta'wa* (Sun) comes to us with the heat from the south.
  From the four quarters let the heavy rains come,
  Till the land with water flows.[1]
Let vegetation be abundant, let the corn grow large.
  Let the corn ripen . . .
  Let the thunder-clouds come . . .

Nevertheless, while in broad terms I am sure Fewkes is right, I believe that he is mistaken in detail: namely, in saying that the vegetative thread which runs through the rites is devoted to *corn* growth. Much of the evidence indicates, rather, that it is directed to the growth of crops other than corn: that is, of beans, sweet corn, squash and melons. The date of the festival is determined primarily, according to Parsons, by the state of the melon crop; beans, squash and melon vines—as well as corn stalks—are set in the *pat'ni* carried by Antelope *mana*, are distributed among the women of the village on the morning of the eighth and ninth days, and are used in the 'vine dance' itself; and Voth, describing[2] the 'placing' of the prayer-offerings on the morning of the ninth day, states specifically that these are put in water-melon patches, as well as in fields and peach orchards. If, for 'water-melon patches', we substitute 'gardens', I believe we have the key we require.

Apart from irrigated gardens (of which there are not more than 15 acres in the whole region, and in which special vegetables such as onions, chilis and sunflowers are grown) and orchards, the farm lands of the Hopi fall into two main categories: the large fields, ranging in size from 3 to 12 acres, which lie on the fans of tributary watercourses—and in the old days, before its dissection, on the flood plain of the main wash; and the small fields, usually not more than one to two acres in extent, to be found in the gullies and around the foot of the mesas below the villages. Fields of the first kind are used chiefly for growing corn, fields of the second kind chiefly for growing vegetables; the latter, consequently, may better be termed 'gardens' than fields. Now the crops that are grown in these 'gardens' ripen a month to six weeks earlier than the main corn crop: sweet corn late in July and early in August, early beans late in August, other beans, squash and melons at the beginning of September[3]—whereas the main corn crop is not usually ready until late in September. It seems likely, therefore, that the emphasis on vines and beans in the Snake-Antelope rites is deliberate, not fortuitous; and reflects the fact that the festival is primarily a 'garden' festival, having as its main purpose, beside rain-making, the promotion of garden crops. If this is indeed the case,[4] then we may expect to find that the

[1] Cf. Forde (1934, p. 224): 'The lower-lying parts of the flats receive a number of inundations during late June, July and August. The land is temporarily drenched or even flooded to a depth of six inches or more . . .'.

[2] Voth (1903a), p. 345.

[3] For rough dates of the ripening of the various crops, see Forde (1934), pp. 230–1.

[4] The interpretation put forward above receives support from one unexpected source: according to a Hopi informant (Parsons, 1936, p. 817, n. 1), in the race on the ninth morning of the Flute ceremony, the runners carry *green corn or chili or onions*, i.e. the special crops of

Marau and its analogues, the Lako'n and the Oa'qöl, have as *their* main purpose the promotion of the principal field crop, namely corn.

In addition to these two elements in the Snake-Antelope rites, the one of rain-making and the other of crop-growth, there is—as Titiev points out[1]—a third: the mortuary. This aspect is emphasised in the making of the altars, and in the ceremonies which take place around them. In both kivas, a line of crooks and sticks is ranged on either side of the sand mosaic, and in the course of the ceremony of sixteen songs in Antelope kiva—and perhaps, also, of analogous rites in Snake kiva—these are distributed among the leaders, and to the novices, for them to hold while the songs are chanted. Of these crooks and sticks, Stephen writes:[2]

> The crooks (*ñülü'kpi*) represent the old men bent with age, the *wü'wüyomo*, the wise, thinking old men, who have passed away. The crooks at the Antelope altar represent those of the Antelope society; those at the Snake altar represent those of the Snake society. The long straight prayer-sticks (*wu'pa pa'ho*) represent the younger men who yet walked erect when they died.

And later, evidently referring to the placing of the sticks and crooks in the clay stands beside the sand mosaic, he says:[3] 'It is analogous to the placing of a planting stick at the grave.'

To the significance of this aspect of the Snake-Antelope rites, I shall return later, when we come to discuss the meaning of Hopi religion. In the meantime the Marau, the last of the great festivals I propose to describe, awaits our attention.

### FALL CEREMONIES: THE MARAU

All three of the fall ceremonies—Marau, Lako'n and Oa'qöl—are in the hands of women's societies, although the more esoteric part of the ritual is carried out by men on their behalf. All three are, primarily, 'harvest' festivals: the Marau being celebrated in mid September in odd years, the Oa'qöl late in October, also in odd years, and the Lako'n in late September or early October, in even years.[4] At Oraibi, when the ceremonies were still being observed, the Marau was held in the Marau kiva, 'owned' by Lizard clan, while the Lako'n and Oa'qöl societies used Hawiovi kiva for their rites.

---

*irrigated* gardens, while the children who come out to meet them carry corn and water-melons. 'All this, the race and the chasing, means that the crops must hasten to mature.'

[1] Titiev (1944), pp. 152–4.

[2] Stephen (1936), pp. 673–5.

[3] Stephen (1936), p. 709.

[4] The practice varies from mesa to mesa. On 3rd Mesa, in the old days (*pace* Voth 1903*b*, p. 6), both Marau and Oa'qöl were celebrated in odd years (1893, 1895, 1897 . . .), and Lako'n, by inference, in even years. On 1st Mesa (Stephen, 1936), Marau and Lako'n were celebrated every year (1891, 1892, 1893 . . .), and Oa'qöl omitted.

On the ninth day before the Marau ceremony[1] is due to begin, the preliminary prayer-stick-making session is held in Marau kiva, attended by Lizard clan chief, his sister (the senior woman of the society) and her deputy, and the six other women who are to play a leading part in the ceremony. Lizard clan chief makes six double-green *pa'ho*(s), six single black *pa'ho*(s), and six *nakwa'kwosi*(s), one for each of the six cardinal directions, together with one *pa'ho* for the Sun and two for the Thunder deity; while the women prepare a set of *nakwa' kwosi*(s) for each of the six directions. When they are ready, the prayer-offerings are placed on a tray, some corn meal is sprinkled over them, and Lizard clan chief blows smoke over them; late in the afternoon, he takes the prayer-offerings and deposits them at different places outside the village. Early the next morning, the forthcoming ceremony is announced:

| *pü'ü* | *tala'vaiyi* | *chaa'k-moñ'wi* | *chaa'lauwú* |
|---|---|---|---|
| early | (this) morning | crier chief | announced |
| *nana'l* | *to'ki* | *Mamzrau* | *yü'ñini.* |
| (in) eight | days (hence) | Marau society | will-assemble. |

Eight days later,[2] at sunrise, Lizard clan chief and the senior women of the society again assemble in Marau kiva. The Marau *na'atsi* is set up outside the kiva hatch, and corn meal sprinkled towards the rising sun. During the morning a number of prayer-sticks are made, and after these have been consecrated in the usual manner, they are given—with a handful of corn-meal—to four of the younger women who deposit them at shrines sited in each of the four cardinal directions. Around noon, sand is brought into the kiva, and Lizard clan chief proceeds to set up the Marau altar.[3] This consists of a sand ridge, with (in front of it) the usual six-directions' arrangement of medicine bowl and corn ears. In the sand ridge he fixes three large white slabs of wood, representing corn stalks, four or five zigzag plaques representing lightning, and a row of straight sticks, representing deceased members of the order. Near the ridge, on the left, stands the Marau *ti'poni*—an ear of corn, wound round with cotton thread, with a bunch of different kinds of feathers stuck in the top.

Early in the afternoon, two of the women are sent to fetch water in netted gourd vessels, one to Lenañva spring, the other to the spring on the east side of the mesa. On their return, all take part in a ceremony of nine songs around the altar. During the concluding song, Lizard clan chief hands to one of the

---

[1] The account that follows is based on the accounts given by Voth (1912*a*), pp. 41–69, and by Titiev (1944), pp. 164–8: with comparative material, for 1st Mesa, drawn from Fewkes and Stephen (1892*b*), pp. 217–45, and Stephen (1936), pp. 865–911.

[2] At Oraibi, the first day (*yü'ñya*) of the Marau fell in 1893 on 4 September, in 1895 on 15 September, in 1897 on 10 September, and in 1901 on 20 September.

[3] See Voth (1912*a*), pl. v: cf. for 1st Mesa, Fewkes and Stephen (1892*b*), pl. 1. On 1st Mesa, the sand ridge, with two *ti'poni*(s) and some other objects, is set up on day one; and the medicine bowl and six corn ears placed in front of it the next morning. It is not until the afternoon of day four that the wooden plaques are set in the sand ridge, and a sand mosaic drawn in front of it; subsequently, the vertical altar (*poñ'ya*) is hung with corn-stalks, melon and squash vines, brought up from the fields by two girls.

women one of the straight sticks from the sand ridge, and she beats time with the butt end of the stick on the kiva floor; thus announcing to the deceased members in the nether world that a ceremony is in progress.[1] When the song comes to an end, Lizard clan chief takes the stick back and replaces it in the sand ridge.

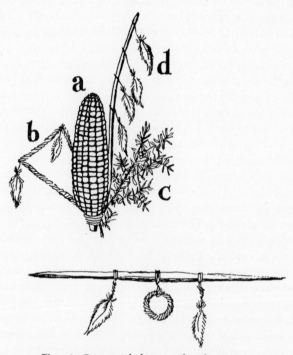

Fig. 48. *Ceremonial objects used in the Marau.*

*Upper. Ke'le pa'ho*, novice's prayer-stick. *a.* white ear of corn. *b. lü'wa* (vulva), a triangle of *sö've* wound around with cotton, with two feathers one at each corner. *c.* sprig of juniper. *d.* twig of *sö've*, with four feathers attached.

*Lower. Yo'yu-ñü'la pa'ho*, 'rain-ring' prayer-stick. Made out of a piece of willow, sharpened at both ends and scraped, with an annulet of cat-tail rushes (*wi'po*) tied with cotton twine to the centre, and on either side a hawk-wing feather. Re-drawn from Fewkes and Stephen (1892*b*), pl. ii.

Towards sunset, the senior woman of the Marau starts making *ke'le pa'ho*(s), one for each *ke'le* (novice) who is to be initiated into the society. For each one, she takes a twig of sumac (*sö've*), bends it into a triangle, wraps it round with cotton twine, and fastens a bluebird feather to the two angles; this triangle is called *lü'wa*, 'vulva'. Next, she makes four *nakwa'kwosi*(s), and fastens them along a straight twig of sumac. She then takes a white corn ear, ties the *lü'wa*

[1] Voth (1912*a*), p. 23.

(by its 'open' end) to the stub with a strip of yucca fibre, adds the straight stick with the four *nakwa'kwosi*(s) attached, and finally a sprig of juniper. This completes the *ke'le pa'ho* (Figure 48, upper). Next, she makes a yucca-fibre ring, about 18 inches in diameter, called *ki've*, 'womb', which she hangs on a peg on the wall; then taking a tray of corn meal, she sprinkles a ring of corn meal on the kiva floor just east of the ladder, from the ring a 'road' of meal leading to the altar, and from the altar a further 'road' to the banquette on the south side of the kiva. When all is ready, the Marau principal takes the *ke'le pa'ho*(s), one for each of the girls who are to be initiated, and leaves the kiva.

A few minutes later, the Marau principal returns to the kiva, followed by the novices (aged about 12 years old) each carrying her *ke'le pa'ho*.[1] She takes the yucca-fibre ring ('womb') from its peg on the wall, and lays it on the floor over the ring of corn meal; each novice in turn jumps inside the ring, the Marau principal raises the ring up and down four times as high as the girl's waist, at the same time 'muttering an almost inaudible invocation to Mü'yiñwa . . . to make the girl a fruitful mother'; then leads her along the meal 'road' to the altar and from the altar to the banquette on the south side of the kiva, where the girls sit huddled up, side by side, in the manner of fledgling birds.

On this and the succeeding three days, all the usual restrictions of Hopi ceremonialism are observed. The leaders fast each day until late in the evening; the other members abstain from salt and meat; and they, with the novices, sleep each night in the kiva. Each day begins with the setting-up of the Marau *na'atsi*, and the offering of meal to the rising sun. During the morning, a number of prayer-sticks are made;[2] later these are given to the four younger women, who distribute them, as on the first day, at shrines outside the village. Throughout the second and third days, the novices sit—huddled up and silent—at the south end of the kiva; they are given food, but are not allowed to leave the kiva except at night, even to relieve themselves. Early on the fourth morning, before the sun is up, they are taken to a house across the way from the kiva, where they grind corn all day.[3]

The fourth day, which the novices spend grinding corn, is one of the two key days in the whole ceremony.[4] Very early one of the Marau women is despatched, with *nakwa'kwosi*(s) and corn meal, to a shrine some miles west of the village; this shrine is located on the trail taken by the spirits of the dead on their journey to the Underworld; according to Hopi informants,[5] the mes-

---

[1] The description of the initiation of novices is taken principally from Fewkes and Stephen (1892b), pp. 220–1, 223, 226, 229–33.

[2] Fewkes and Stephen (1892b, pp. 227–8) distinguish between the ordinary *sakwa' pa'ho*(s), blue-green *pa'ho*(s), which are taken out and placed at shrines in the four cardinal directions; and *kü'yi pa'ho*(s), water *pa'ho*(s), single long prayer-sticks painted black with a green tip, which are placed only at the various springs. To the significance of the latter kind, I shall return in due course.

[3] Fewkes and Stephen (1892b), p. 226.

[4] For the events of the fourth day, see Voth (1912a), pp. 51–6: and, especially of the fourth night, Fewkes and Stephen (1892b), pp. 230–3.

[5] Titiev (1944), p. 166, n. 19.

senger deposits the prayer-offerings there, at the same time inviting the spirits ('breaths') of departed Marau women to come and join in the rites that are to take place that night. During the morning, a great many *pa'ho*(s) and *nakwa' kwosi*(s) are made, and subsequently consecrated at the altar. In addition to the sets of *sakwa' pa'ho*(s) and *kü'yi pa'ho*(s), made as on the previous three mornings, the ordinary members of the society make numbers of *nakwa'kwosi*(s)—mostly of turkey feathers—for their departed relatives and friends, while the two leaders (i.e. the Marau principal, and her deputy) each make a *yo'yu-ñüla*, 'rain ring': a straight stick of willow about 8 inches long, painted black, to the centre of which is attached a ring of rushes about 2 inches in diameter, also painted black, and farther along the stem, two *nakwa'kwosi*(s)—see Figure 48, lower. At the same time, two other s of the senior women are busy making a peculiar object called *ka'ö tuk'wi*, 'corn mound', consisting of a cone of clay, about 10 inches high and 6 inches across at the base; into this soft cone are pressed kernels of corn, arranged in four stripes, one yellow, one blue, one red and one white, running from the base to the apex of the cone; into the apex itself, a bunch of feathers is inserted. The cone is then placed on the kiva floor, to the east of the altar, where it remains until the last day of the ceremony. After they have been consecrated at the altar, the prayer-sticks—but not the *nakwa'kwosi*(s)—are taken out and deposited, in the course of the afternoon, at various shrines and springs in the vicinity of the village: the two 'rain rings' being thrown into the principal spring of the village, as an offering to Mü'yiñwa.[1]

Early in the afternoon, all the Marau members—except the Marau principal and her deputy—leave the kiva and go to their own homes, to collect food. While they are absent, the Marau principal puts a large bowl, containing some *pi'ki* and cooked beans, on the raised part of the kiva floor near the ladder, and beside it a tray with corn meal, together with a tray containing the *nakwa' kwosi*(s) prepared by the women for their departed relatives and friends. The other women now begin to re-enter the kiva, carrying the various dishes of food for the evening meal. As each one enters the kiva, she puts a share of each kind of food that she has brought into the large bowl; then sets the vessel down on the floor near the fireplace. When all have made their contribution, they stand in a circle round the dishes, and begin to sing. Meanwhile, the Marau principal and her deputy kneel on either side of the large bowl and, all at once, dump the meal from the tray into the bowl, make a dough of the mixture, and then knead it into about sixteen balls, which they place on the tray with the *nakwa'kwosi*(s).

As soon as the singing ceases, four of the women step forward; the Marau principal gives to each a share of the meal balls and of the *nakwa'kwosi*(s), placing them in a corner of the blanket which the women wear over their dress. The four messengers then leave the kiva, and each one takes the trail out

---

[1] Fewkes and Stephen (1892*b*), p. 229. It is clear, from Fewkes' discreet indications, that these two prayer-sticks bear—in addition to their rain-making purpose—a physiological (i.e. fertility) 'charge'.

of the village in one of the four cardinal direction. Once outside the village, each turns to her left and runs one quarter of the way round the pueblo, throwing away the food balls and *nakwa'kwosi*(s) as she runs, as an offering to the dead; for it is supposed, as Voth puts it,[1] 'that the spirits of the departed come and get the food and the prayer-feathers, or rather the *hi'ksvi* (breath, essence, soul) of those objects'. On their return to the kiva, all join together in eating the evening meal; and some time now, the novices are brought back into the kiva.

About nine in the evening, the kiva begins to fill with women; each one, on entering, casts a pinch of meal towards the altar, and each also brings an ear of corn which she lays down near the altar, in a pile. For two hours or so, the women join in singing a number of songs: the general tenor of which, according to Fewkes and Stephen, 'is a harvest thanksgiving, the same strain being frequently repeated with the substitution of a different word or two describing the various field and garden products'. They sing of the beauty of the far-stretching rows of corn and the pleasant task of gathering and husking it, together with some songs of a broader turn. Some time after midnight, when Orion and the Pleiades are high overhead, the leaders of the society group themselves around the altar and perform the ceremony of sixteen songs.[2] This lasts about two hours. At its conclusion, all the women rise; the Marau principal takes the *ti'poni* from beside the sand ridge, her deputy takes the *moñ'wikuru*, and each of the senior women takes one of the other objects until none is left. Lizard chief, who has been present throughout the ceremony, now pulls up the straight sticks from the sand ridge, and as the women circle the altar four times before leaving the kiva, he thrusts one of the sticks into the rolled-up blanket on the back of each woman. The women then file out of the kiva and proceed to their own homes, leaving the Marau principal, her deputy and the novices, alone in the kiva.

By now it is nearly sunrise. The women return to the kiva, carrying bowls of water and yucca roots which they set down around the fireplace. After they have beaten the roots into foaming suds, the senior women proceed to wash the heads of their 'god-daughters', afterwards rubbing their face, neck, breasts, arms and legs, with corn meal. Meanwhile, the Marau principal herself washes the heads of the novices, using the girl's *ke'le pa'ho* for the purpose; then each of their respective 'god-mothers' rubs their face, neck and breasts with meal, takes the *ke'le pa'ho*, passes it up and down four times in front of the girl's face (repeating a short prayer as she does so), and gives her a new name. Finally, as dawn is breaking, Marau principal leads the novices to a shrine to the northwest of the village, where they deposit their *ke'le pa'ho*(s).

So ends the initiation of the novices; from now on, they are free to come and

---

[1] Voth (1912a), p. 55.

[2] At least one of the songs is for copious rains and an abundant harvest, and during the singing of another, the Marau principal and her deputy beat time on the floor with their sticks. This, according to Fewkes and Stephen (1892b, p. 232), is to inform Mü'yiñwa that they are assembled and are calling him to listen.

go in the kiva as they wish. The next three days (days 5, 6 and 7 of the ceremony) are relatively quiet. On the mornings of the fifth and sixth days, the women bring piles of ripe peaches into the kiva and later eat them there; and on the morning of the seventh day, they husk large quantities of corn, and tie up bundles of beans with chili, subsequently taking these to their own homes. No prayer-sticks are made on these three days; but each afternoon a number of the women emerge from the kiva, their bodies smeared with mud, and proceed to the village square where they perform various, more or less obscene, dances.[1] In the course of these performances (in which some of the women are disguised as men), they taunt the men, who retaliate by dowsing them with water and stale urine.

Day 8 is the second of the two key days in the Marau ceremony.[2] At dawn, the *na'atsi* is set up outside the kiva as usual, and at about 6 o'clock Lizard clan chief begins to make prayer-sticks: he makes one light-blue double *pa'ho*, with two eagle-feather *nakwa'kwosi*(s) attached, for the Sun, four ordin.iry double-green *pa'ho*(s), and two single black *pa'ho*(s) to be taken to the two springs later in the day by the women who are sent to fetch water. At about 8 a.m., one of the younger women brings in an armful of green corn stalks, some bean plants, squash and melon runners, and a peach branch with some peaches on it; these she places on the floor near the altar.

In the course of the morning, a number of men come into the kiva and prepare things for use on the morrow. One man takes a bunch of the corn stalks and vines, ties them into a bundle with four strands of yucca fibre, and attaches a *nakwa'kwosi*—two of hawk feather, one of eagle and one of turkey—to each strand. Another man, of Bow clan, prepares two sets of bows and arrows, together with two 'lances' and two fibre rings, or 'wheels', about 7 inches in diameter. Others, meanwhile, refurbish an old shield, about 16 inches long and 12 inches broad, called *pavai' yoyi'kyashi* (the name refers to copious rains), which will be worn by the Marau principal, on her back, the following day; the shield is made of a frame of osiers, over which an old cloth is stretched; the frame is fringed with small red feathers, the upper half of the cloth is painted green, the lower half red, and in the centre is depicted a figure with a human face but otherwise resembling an eagle, said to represent Mü'yiñwa, the germination deity.[3] Four head-pieces, made of a ring of tightly twisted yarn into which three sticks are fixed to form a kind of pyramid, are also prepared, and decorated with various feathers, dyed horse-hair and red wool.

While these activities are going on, Lizard clan chief has been engaged in reconstructing the Marau altar in the deeper part of the kiva. Around noon, he again arranges the medicine bowl and the six corn ears in front of the sand

---

[1] On these dances, analogous to the men's dances in the course of Wü'wütçim, see Voth (1912a), pp. 56–7: Fewkes and Stephen (1892b), pp. 233–4: Stephen (1936), pp. 895–6, 899–900: Titiev (1944), p. 165, and n. 12.

[2] For the events of the eighth day of Marau, see Voth (1912a), pp. 57–63: cf. Fewkes and Stephen (1892b), pp. 234–7, and Stephen (1936), pp. 900–7.

[3] Voth (1912a), p. 59.

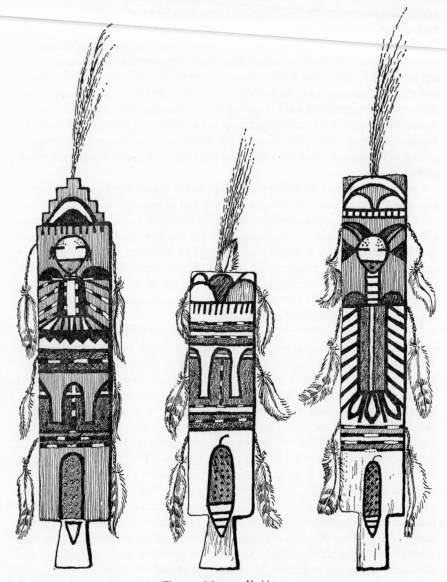

Fig. 49. *Marau pa'ho*(s).

*Left.* The terraced upper end represents a cloud, with rain falling from it. Below this is a picture of Mü'yiñwa, perched on a rainbow. Under the rainbow are three towering clouds, also on a rainbow; and at the bottom, an ear of corn.

*Middle.* Cloud symbol above, three towering clouds in the middle, with rainbow above and below, and at the bottom, an ear of corn.

*Right.* Similar to the one on the left.

Redrawn from Voth (1912a), pl. xviii.

ridge; all the objects which have been prepared are then set out around the altar. Early in the afternoon, the old Marau *pa'ho*(s) are brought out and re-painted, and new ones made; these are flat wooden boards (see Figure 49), about 12 inches long, with a handle at the base, corn tassels attached to the top and *nakwa'kwosi*(s) to the sides, and painted 'with a great variety of corn, germination, rain, and cloud symbols'.[1] Later, two of the members of the order are sent to fetch water from two of the springs below the mesa, and on their return the ceremony of nine songs is again performed around the altar, as on the first day. Towards sunset, a number of the women emerge from Marau kiva, their bodies smeared with mud, and proceed to the village square; in the course of their performance there, they again taunt the men who reply, as before, by dowsing them with water and urine from the surrounding roof-tops.[2] The women then return to their kiva, where they take the evening meal.

That night, when the Pleiades has reached the zenith, the leaders of the Marau again gather round the altar, and perform the ceremony of sixteen songs for the last time. When this is finished, all the painted slabs are taken out of the sand ridge, tied in bundles, and taken to Lizard clan house to be stored; but the sand ridge itself, the sand field in front of it, the Marau *ti'poni* and some other objects, are left in place. Bowls of water and yucca roots are then brought into the kiva, and all present wash their heads in the suds.[3]

Very early in the morning, on the ninth day,[4] about twenty youths go down to the corn fields in the valley and shortly before sunrise return to Marau kiva, carrying bunches of corn stalks with the young ears on them. At the kiva hatch, several of the women receive them and stack them against the hatch. At about the same time, the cooking pits are opened throughout the village, in preparation for the feast to be served later in the morning. Meanwhile, the four women who are to play the part of Marau 'youths' make their way to *moñ* kiva, to paint their bodies and put on their costume. While they are doing this, the other members of the society assemble in Marau kiva, wearing their white ceremonial blankets with embroidered borders, their faces smeared with corn meal. As each woman enters the kiva, she takes a bunch of the corn stalks from beside the hatch, then joins the other women around the altar. Finally, the four Marau 'youths' arrive from *moñ* kiva, each dressed in the traditional blue woollen shirt (normally worn only by men), and take their place in the circle.

As the sun rises, the women line up to leave the kiva. First comes the Marau

---

[1] Titiev (1944), p. 166. For a full description of the Marau *pa'ho*(s), see Fewkes and Stephen (1892b), pp. 240–1, and pl. iv. All the *pa'ho*(s) carry a representation of an ear of corn, rising out of the handle, with cloud symbols above and frequently a representation of Mü'yiñwa in between.

[2] Fewkes and Stephen (1892b), pp. 235–6.

[3] Fewkes and Stephen (1892b), pp. 236–7. In Voth's account (1912a, p. 64), it is now that the novices have their heads washed by the Marau principal.

[4] For the events of the ninth day of Marau, see Voth (1912a), pp. 64–9: Titiev (1944), pp. 166–7: cf. Fewkes and Stephen (1892b), pp. 237–41, and Stephen (1936), pp. 907–11.

principal, wearing a man's ceremonial kilt and sash with fox skin dangling behind, on her back the rain 'shield', on her head an elaborate head-dress covered with white feathers, and in her left hand her *moñ'kohü*. Next come the four Marau 'youths', each wearing sash and kilt with fox skin dangling behind, blue woollen shirt, and pyramid-shaped head-dress: the first pair carrying bow-and-arrows and the bundle of vines (from beside the altar), the second pair carrying the two 'lances' and the two 'wheels'. Behind them follow the other women, dressed in their ceremonial blankets and each carrying under her left arm a bundle of corn stalks. As they leave the kiva, Lizard clan chief asperses each woman from the medicine bowl.

Outside the kiva, the four Marau 'youths' stand to one side, while the Marau principal leads the main body of women to the village square. There, the women throw the corn stalks in a pile on the ground, all except one stalk which each woman keeps to beat out the time; then form in a circle around the pile of corn stalks and begin chanting a low chant, at the same time swishing the ground with the single corn stalk held in their right hand.[1] As they dance, first the two 'archers', then the two 'lancers', make their way from the kiva to the village square: the first two throwing the bundle of vines on the path ahead of them and shooting their arrows into it,[2] the second two throwing down the two 'wheels' and casting their 'lances' at them. In this manner the two pairs of Marau youths proceed towards the ring of dancers, the two 'archers' circling round and then entering the ring, the two 'lancers' remaining outside and flinging their 'lances' and 'wheels' over the heads of the dancers into the ring. The two 'lancers' then go to a nearby house[3] and fetch bowls, one containing sweet-corn meal and the other water, which they carry inside the ring of dancers. Kneeling on opposite sides of the two bowls, they pour the water onto the meal and knead it into a dough; this they fashion into balls, about the size of a duck's egg,[4] and when all the dough has been made into balls, the two 'lancers'—assisted by the two 'archers'—go round the inside of the ring, throwing the balls of dough over the heads of the dancers to the spectators, who scramble for them from all sides. When all the dough balls have been distributed in this way, the four Marau 'youths' leave the square and make their way to *moñ* kiva, followed soon after by the Marau principal; there, they change into the same costume as the other women and then proceed to Marau kiva. A few minutes later the dancers end their chant, throw their corn stalks on the ground, and also repair to the kiva; as the last of the women file out of the square, the younger

---

[1] The chant is singularly beautiful; I was present when the women sang it at Hotevilla, soon after sunrise, on 7 October 1967.

[2] The act of shooting at the bundle (*ko'pi*) of vines is called *kop' mümü'itiwa*, from *mü'a*, to hit the mark with an arrow: 'It is said to typify lightning striking in the cornfield, an event which is regarded as the acme of fertilisation' (Fewkes and Stephen, 1892b, p. 239).

[3] The house of the Village chief: Voth (1912a), p. 66, n. 1. At 1st Mesa, the dough balls have been prepared in the kiva beforehand, and are fetched from there.

[4] These are balls of *qömi* (Titiev, 1944, p. 167); the kneading of the dough is called *qöm' lalauwû*, '*qömi* making'.

men and the boys dash forward and gather up the corn stalks, bearing them off to their own homes.

When all the women have returned to the kiva, they form in a circle around the fireplace, together with Lizard clan chief; each takes a pinch of ashes in her hand, and they perform the *navo'tçiwa*, purification rite.[1] During the course of the day, six or eight further performances take place in the village square. These are essentially the same as the one in the morning, including the kneading and throwing of the dough balls, except that the women taking part now carry the Marau *pa'ho*(s) in place of corn-stalks; each dancer carries a pair of these, grasping one in each hand by the handle, and as they chant, they move them up and down in time to the melody. Between the dances, the women return to their kiva; and each time they withdraw, a different trio of women dress up, one to act as Marau principal in the next dance, the other two to act as 'lancers'[2] and so to distribute the *qömi* balls.

Shortly before sunset, after the last performance, the women return to the kiva for the last time, carrying their Marau *pa'ho*(s). The Marau principal gathers up the remaining objects from the sand ridge and wraps them in a bundle, then sweeps the sand into a pile on the kiva floor. Finally she takes the *ka'ö tuk'wi*, 'corn mound', which has stood beside the sand ridge since it was made on the fourth day, breaks it into pieces and gives a small piece of the cone, with a few grains of corn stuck into it, to each of the women who have taken part in the ceremony. All stand around in deep silence for several minutes, holding the piece of the 'corn mound' in one hand and covering it with the other, while they utter a silent prayer. Then, taking their piece with them, the women depart to their own homes, where they take the evening meal.

Turning now to the significance of the Marau—and of its analogues, the Oa'qöl and the Lako'n,[3] three threads are readily discernible in the ritual:

(a) *for rain.* This aspect is brought out in the making of prayer-sticks on days 1 to 4 of the ceremony, and their 'placing' at shrines in the four cardinal directions: in the dowsing of the women on the afternoons of days 5 to 8: in the invocation to the deities of the six cardinal directions during the songs chanted

---

[1] Why the *navo'tçiwa* rite takes place in the morning after the first dance, rather than in the evening after the last dance, I do not know. It may be just a matter of convenience; for Voth remarks that, by the afternoon, several of the women have left the dancing and resumed their domestic duties, e.g. looking after small children.

[2] On 1st Mesa (Fewkes and Stephen, 1892b, pp. 238–9), the two act as 'archers', and there are no 'lancers'; on 3rd Mesa, according to Titiev's informants (1944, p. 167, n. 26), only the 'archers' appear at the first dance in the morning, and only the 'lancers' at the later ones. At the ceremony I attended at Hotevilla, there were neither 'archers' nor 'lancers'; the Marau principal herself carried in a woven tray with a cake of dough on it, and laid it on the ground inside the ring of dancers; at the conclusion of the dance, one of the older men stepped forward and quietly removed the tray.

[3] In Titiev's view (1944, p. 170), the Marau represents the basic women's observance, while the other two 'are hardly more than imitations of it'. The fullest account of the Oa'qöl is that given, for 3rd Mesa, by Voth (1903b, pp. 1–46): and of the Lako'n, that given —for 1st Mesa—by Fewkes and Owen (1892, pp. 105–29).

around the altar on the first, fourth and eighth nights:[1] and in the rain symbols displayed on the altar and on the Marau *pa'ho*(s).

(b) *for corn growth*. In interpreting the Snake-Antelope rites, I have argued that their primary purpose, apart from rain-making, is to promote the growth of the bean, squash and melon crops due for harvesting in a few weeks' time; and that we may expect to find a similar concern for *corn* growth, in the Marau and the other two 'harvest' festivals. This concern is evidenced, in the Marau, by the making of the 'corn mound' on the fourth day and the distribution of the pieces on the ninth, by the use of corn-stalks at the opening dance on the ninth morning,[2] and by the representation of corn cobs on the Marau *pa'ho*(s) used in the later dances; in the Lako'n, again by the making of a 'corn mound' covered

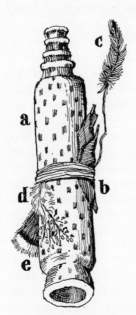

Fig. 50. Corn-ear *pa'ho*, used in the *Oa'qöl. a.* wooden body, painted green with black dots. *b.* corn-husk packet. *c. nakwa'kwosi. d.* herb sprigs. *e.* turkey feather. Re-drawn from Voth (1912*b*), pl. lvii.

with corn, melon and squash seeds;[3] and in the Oa'qöl, by the making of special 'corn-ear *pa'ho*(s)', which are later consecrated at the altar and then 'placed', by the maker, either in the stacks of corn in his storehouse or in his fields.[4]

In the Marau, the concern for corn growth is further evidenced by the words of at least one of the songs sung by the women in their kiva on the fourth night of the ceremony:[5]

---

[1] For the words of some of these songs, see Voth (1912*a*), pp. 69–88.
[2] Stephen (1936, p. 937) states specifically that the motive of the prayer sung with the corn stalks is to hasten the ripening of the corn, *i'ich ü'yi tü'ksini*.
[3] Fewkes and Owen (1892), p. 115.
[4] On these *ka'ö* (corn-ear) *pa'ho*(s), see Voth (1903*b*), pp. 31–4, 37, 46.
[5] Stephen (1936), p. 889.

> To-morrow when it (i.e. the day) comes,
> We will gather in our corn.
> My heart is glad, to look upon the bounteous fields.
> We will husk the corn, we will shell it,
> And bring it home, rejoicing.
> My heart is glad ...

And it is to be found again, I believe, in the part ascribed to Mü'yiñwa in all three of the harvest festivals. In the Marau, Mü'yiñwa is depicted on the 'rain shield' worn by the Marau principal, and on the Marau *pa'ho*(s) carried by the women dancers, on the ninth day; in the Lako'n, one of the four effigies ranged in front of the sand ridge[1] is that of Mü'yiñwa, and he appears again on the sand mosaic; in the Oa'qöl, the same deity is represented (Figure 51) on the central plaque of the altar, holding in his right hand a growing corn stalk, and in the course of the rites on the fourth night of the ceremony when the novices are initiated,[2] he is impersonated by the brother of the Oa'qöl principal.

The other ceremony where Mü'yiñwa plays a leading rôle is the Powa'mu, in February. In the course of that ceremony, as we have seen, bean plants are grown in the kivas as an omen of the coming season, and on the fourth night— as on the fourth night of Oa'qöl—Mü'yiñwa is impersonated by one of the senior men of the fraternity. The word used for 'discovering the future harvest' is *na'twanta*; and this word is related to another, *na'twani*, a collective noun referring to 'plants (in general) especially crop plants, vegetables: often equivalent to crop, harvest.'[3] Mü'yiñwa is undoubtedly regarded by Hopi as the deity controlling germination; thus Stephen, evidently quoting a Hopi informant, writes:[4]

> All plants come from Mü'yiñwa; prayer-sticks are made and 'placed' for Mü'yiñwa, and in exchange for these prayer-sticks he sends us vegetation.

Nevertheless, two pieces of evidence suggest that Mü'yiñwa, as well as controlling germination (in general), is especially linked with corn (in particular): first, he is often represented, as on the central plaque of the Oa'qöl altar, holding a growing corn plant in his right hand; second, Sand clan chief (who impersonated Mü'yiñwa in the Oa'qöl ceremonies at Oraibi in the 1890s), explaining to Voth[5] the meaning of the six corn ears and the six different kinds of shrub referred to in the chants, said that while the growth of (all) plants is controlled by Mü'yiñwa, he 'owns' the corn.

---

[1] Of the other three figures, the two central ones appear to represent Lako'n youth and Lako'n *mana*, and the one on the left, Pü'ükoñ-hoya: Fewkes and Owen (1892), pp. 114–16, and pl. ii.

[2] See Voth (1903*b*), pp. 22–9.

[3] Whorf (1936), p. 1261: cf. p. 90, above.

[4] Stephen (1936), p. 239: cf. on Mü'iyiñwa as deity of germination, Haeberlin (1916), pp. 22–3.

[5] Voth (1903*b*), p. 29.

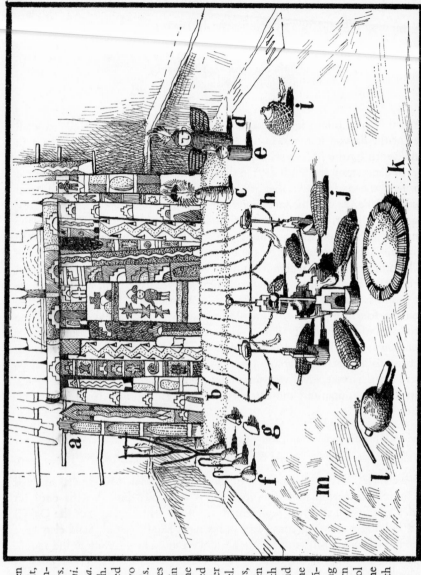

Fig. 51. *Oa'qöl altar.* *a.* wooden frame, with plaques fixed to it, representing Mu'yiñwa, cloud symbols, lightning, corn ears, rainbows. *b.* sand ridge. *c.* Oaqöl *ti'poni.* *d.* wooden effigy of Oa'qöl *mana.* *e.* wooden effigy of Oa'qöl youth. *f.* four clay stands, two with forked sticks, two with crooks. *g.* two wooden objects, representing birds. *h.* cloud symbols, with straight lines representing falling rain, traced in black shale on the sand field: at the apex of each cloud symbol is traced the outline of a turkey-feather *nakwa'kwosi.* *i.* netted gourd vessel. *j.* medicine bowl, with six corn ears, six aspergills, and four wooden cloud symbols. *k.* woven tray with corn meal. *l.* gourd rattle. *m.* sand field. The central plaque on the wooden frame represents Mu'yiñwa, the germination deity, holding in his right hand a growing corn stalk; above his head is the symbol of clouds, beneath his feet that of the rainbow. Re-drawn from Voth (1903*b*), pl. 1.

If this is so and there is a special link between Mü'yiñwa and corn, and if the Powa'mu is concerned with 'foretelling'—as the root of the word *na'twanta* indicates—the prospect for those crops, i.e. vegetables and early corn, to be planted a few weeks later (the harvest of which is subsequently anticipated in the Snake-Antelope rites), then we may expect to find an analogous ceremony in which corn will be planted in the kivas (in place of beans) and in which Mü' yiñwa will again play a prominent part, taking place about a month after the first and 'foretelling' the prospect for those crops, i.e. the main corn crop, to be planted a few weeks later still (the harvest of which is duly anticipated in the Marau and Lako'n rites). That ceremony is the *Uñ'kwa-ti*, celebrated late in February or early in March;[1] and it stands, I suggest, in the same relation to the Marau and the Lako'n as Powa'mu stands to the Snake-Antelope rites. In each pair, the earlier ceremony anticipates the planting of the crop, and the later ceremony its harvesting: the one pair referring primarily to vegetables and early corn, the other pair to the main field crop, i.e. corn.

(c) *for fertility of women.* This aspect of the Marau is brought out in the design of the *ke'le pa'ho*(s) made for the novices, in their stepping inside the yucca ring (or 'womb') on entering the kiva for the first time, and in their initiation on the fourth night. It is probably represented symbolically, also, in the actions of the 'archers' and 'lancers' during the opening dance on the ninth morning,[2] and perhaps practically in the distribution of *qömi* balls,[3] then.

However, while for the purpose of analysis we may separate these three threads in the ceremony, they are so closely interwoven in the ritual, and in Hopi thinking, that any such separation must be largely artificial. Thus, the 'corn' and the 'fertility' elements are intimately linked: corn is referred to as 'mother'; the *ke'le pa'ho* is based on a corn ear; when the novice steps inside the yucca ring, Mü'yiñwa is called upon to make her a fruitful mother, and prayers are again addressed to that deity when the two 'rain ring' *pa'ho*(s) are cast into the main spring on the afternoon of the fourth day. Even the rain-making element is assimilated to the fertility *motif*; the action of the 'archers', in shooting at the bundle of vines on the last morning of the Marau, is said to typify lightning striking in the corn field, and the striking of a field by lightning is believed to impart fertility to the field.[4] In the Oa'qöl, the link is still more

---

[1] *Uñ'kwa-ti*, the second or following dance, i.e. the dance following the Powa'mu: from *uñ-ki*, second or follower, *ti-ki-ve*, dance. The planting of the corn, *ü'yi la'lauwu*, takes place in the kiva(s) four days before the new moon, *ü'shü mü'iyawu*, and the first day (*yü'ñya*) of the five-day ceremony falls thirteen days later, e.g. on 13 March in 1894. After the planting the corn is watered assiduously, 'for thus we hope rain will come copiously after our corn is planted in the fields'. The fullest account of the ceremony, also known as *Pa'lülükonti*, after the water serpents which figure in it, is that given by Fewkes and Stephen (1893), pp. 269–84: cf. Stephen (1936), pp. 289–341.

[2] The symbolic link between shooting an arrow, and sexual intercourse, is certainly recognised by Hopi themselves: cf. Titiev (1938), p. 108.

[3] Since loaves of *qömi* serve as courtship gifts (above, pp. 23, 35–6, 86–7), the distribution of balls of *qömi* at the Marau' festival may have originated in a custom of this kind.

[4] Stephen (1936), pp. 637–8.

explicit: there[1], in place of a bundle of vines, the Oa'qöl *mana*(s) roll two netted wheels on the ground ahead of them and shoot at them with feathered 'arrows', consisting of a corn cob with a pointed stick at one end and two eagle-wing feathers in the butt (see Figure 52).

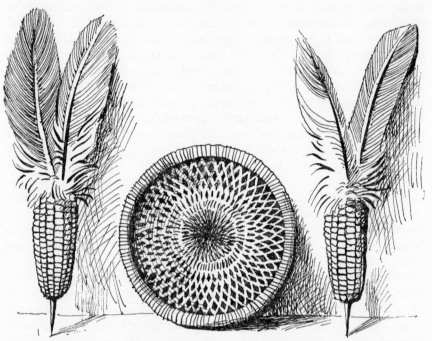

Fig. 52. *Netted wheel, with two corn-cob arrows:* used by the Oa'qöl *mana*(s). Re-drawn from Voth (1903*b*), pl. xv.

As to the idea underlying the link between rain, corn growth and fertility, an old Hopi explaining the mysteries to Stephen seventy years ago, said:[2]

> all these ceremonies are for rain to fall to water the earth, that planted things may ripen and grow large; that the male elements of the Above, the Ye, may impregnate the female earth virgin, the Naasun.

Finally, in the Marau—as in the Snake-Antelope and, to some degree, in all Hopi ceremonies—a mortuary element is present. Early on the fourth morning, the dead are invited to attend the proceedings that are to take place that night in the kiva; during the morning numerous *nakwa'kwosi*(s) are made for them by their relatives and friends, and later in the day these *nakwa'kwosi*(s), together with specially-made dough balls, are distributed around the periphery of the village; at the ceremony of sixteen songs that night, as at similar rites on the first and eighth nights, sticks representing dead members of the order are

[1] See Voth (1903*b*), pp. 42–3, and pls. xx and xxi.
[2] Stephen (1936), p. 626.

disposed on either side of the altar and used for beating on the floor, to acquaint those below that the rites are in progress.

## THE MEANING OF HOPI RELIGION

In discussing the significance of the Soya'l, I have argued that the Soya'l may be regarded as one in a sequence of ceremonial events that runs parallel to, and rather in advance of, corresponding events in the climato-agricultural cycle: Wü'wütçim forecasting the rain and snow needed during the early part of the winter, Soya'l forecasting the frost and the subsequent warming of the ground needed in the later part of the winter and early spring in preparation for planting, Powa'mu forecasting the germination of the seed and its shooting above ground. That sequence we may now complete, as follows:

| month | ceremony | primary 'purpose' | sequent agricultural or climatic event |
|-------|----------|-------------------|----------------------------------------|
| February | Powa'mu | germination | planting of vegetables and early corn (late April–early May) |
| March | Uñ'kwa-ti | germination | planting of main corn crop (late May–early June) |
| April | katçina dances | | period of drought (April to |
| May | of spring and | RAIN | June), followed by onset of |
| June | early summer, | | summer rains in July: corn |
| July | Niman katçina | | knee-high by late July |
| August | Snake-Antelope Flute | rain, and ripening of early crops | vegetables and early corn ripen in August and September |
| September | Marau Lako'n | ripening of main corn | main corn crop ripens late in September, harvested during |
| October | Oa'qöl | harvest | October |

The gist of the interpretation offered is a very simple one: namely, that each ceremony in the calendar takes place a few weeks before the agricultural or climatic event with which it is concerned, and has as its primary purpose, apart from a substratum of intent common to *all* Hopi ceremonies, the influencing of that event into a favourable course. In support of this thesis I bring two final pieces of evidence, before passing on to discuss the means by which this aim is achieved.

The first concerns the fertility element in the Marau and its analogues, the Lako'n and the Oa'qöl. That this element is specifically directed to *human* fertility, is indicated by the words and ritual used at the initiation of girls into each of the three societies, and by the rôle ascribed, at least in the Oa'qöl, to Tü'wa-poñya-tümsi, 'sand altar woman'.[1] In interpreting the Soya'l, I have suggested that the making of prayer-sticks for 'increase' of domestic (and wild)

---

[1] For the initiation of girls into the Oa'qöl society, on the fourth night of the ceremony, see Voth (1903b), pp. 22–9.

G

animals takes place then, because this is the time of year when the animals are mating or are about to mate. Much the same applies to the interpretation of the fertility element in the three fall ceremonies: the fall is the principal time of the year for the celebration of Hopi marriages,[1] and it is surely no co-incidence that the three 'harvest' festivals are in the hands of women's societies and are characterised by a strong human-fertility thread running through the ritual—thus introducing the theme that will be further developed in the course of Wü'wütçim, a month to six weeks later.[2]

The second piece of evidence concerns the Flute ceremony, and requires a digression on the water supply of the Hopi villages. The villages are dependent[3] for their domestic water on two sources: on *pat'ni*, or cisterns, cut in the rock on the mesa top, and on a few powerful springs at the mesa foot. On the mesa top in the neighbourhood of Old Oraibi, there are some forty to fifty *pat'ni*, each with its own small catchment area of bare rock off which the rain runs into the mouth of the cistern; the cisterns themselves are about 8 feet deep,[4] and probably hold from 1,000 to 1,500 gallons each when full. These *pat'ni* are filled with water by the snow melt of late winter and the rains of early spring, and for two to three months, say to about the middle of June, they provide the chief source of domestic water for the pueblo. From then on, until the summer rains commence and re-fill the *pat'ni*, the people are dependent on the springs at the foot of the mesa. In the old days, I was told, the women and girls used to leave the village long before dawn each morning, in the summer, to fetch water in their pots; and as July passed into August, if there had been no rain, the flow in the springs gradually became weaker and the pots took longer to fill—so that often there was a long queue of women waiting their turn at each spring.

Now we have seen how, on the ninth morning of Powa'mu,[5] the Eototo and Aholi katçinas—on entering the village—ceremonially 'open' a miniature *pat'ni* cut in the pathway, by sprinkling water into it from each of the six cardinal directions: an act clearly intended to 'forecast' (*na'twanta*) the rains which it is hoped will fall during the spring and fill the real cisterns on the mesa top. Far more significant, however, is the analogous rite which takes place on the ninth afternoon of the Flute ceremony, six months later. On that occasion the two societies assemble at the main spring[6] of the village, the Gray Flutes gathering

---

[1] 'Formerly', according to Wallis (Wallis and Titiev, 1944, p. 531), 'marriages were held only in January and September. In the latter month there was always abundant food.'

[2] See above, p. 110.

[3] i.e. they were, up to about fifteen years ago. Now, most of the drinking and cooking water is obtained from taps in the settlements at the mesa foot and carried up, in sixty-gallon drums, in the back of pick-ups.

[4] Most of them are disused and half filled with silt now; but I was told that in the old days, after the cisterns had been cleaned, a man needed a ladder to climb out again.

[5] See above, p. 85.

[6] Lenañva at Oraibi, Toreva below 2nd Mesa, Tawa'pa (Sun spring) below 1st Mesa. Titiev (1944, pp. 147–8) witnessed the ritual at Toreva spring, below 2nd Mesa, during the Mishong'novi performance of 1932; Fewkes (1894b, pp. 285–6) was present, at Tawa'pa spring, at the Walpi rite of 1892 (cf. Stephen, 1936, pp. 815–16). Titiev, in his account, does not mention the 'placing' of the *pa'ho(s)* in the bed of the spring.

on one side and the Blue Flutes on the other. After a ritual smoke and the chanting of various songs, one of the Flute members, naked except for a breech
clout, enters the water and wades some way towards the middle, while the men
on the bank continue singing and rattling; he takes a lighted pipe and blows
four puffs of smoke, one in each of the four directions, over the surface of the
water; he then hands the pipe back to one of the men on the bank, receives a
*pa'ho* from the heads of each of the two fraternities, and wades farther into the
pool; he circles it four times, then wades right to the middle and dives under
the surface, plants the *pa'ho*(s) in the bed of the spring and emerges a moment or
two later,[1] just as the singing and rattling stop, 'holding aloft in either hand a rod
to which are attached several netted gourds full of water. All the participants
thank him heartily, *because his actions symbolise the manner in which the pueblo's
main spring supplies the inhabitants with water.*'[2]

Flute man's mime, like that of Eototo and Aholi in 'opening' the *pat'ni*, is
clearly an act of *na'twanta*, 'forecasting'; and in this context we may consider
the *kii'yi pa'ho*(s), made on days 1 to 4 of the Marau ceremony. Fewkes describes
these prayer-sticks as 'water *pa'ho*(s)'; but he misses, I think, their real significance. In Hopi, as Fewkes points out,[3] there are two words for water: *pa'hii*,
meaning water as a natural phenomenon and an element of wild life (as in
*pa'mii'iyawu*, 'water' or 'moisture moon'), and *kii'yi*, water in human use, as in a
vessel. The *kii'yi pa'ho*(s), then, are to ensure the supply of water in vessels, that
is of drinking and cooking water. And their 'placing' at various springs in the
vicinity of the village, in the course of the Marau ceremony in mid September,
has the same object (I suggest) as the culminating rite of the two Flute societies
at the main spring a month earlier: namely, to ensure the domestic water
supply of the village at a time when, in the event of the failure of the summer
rains, the flow of those springs has reached a critically low level.[4]

If, then, we may regard the Hopi liturgy as a 'cycle', revolving in the year,
and the Hopi themselves, in performing the ceremonies of which the liturgy is
made up, as people putting their shoulder to the wheel and assisting it to turn in
its course, there yet remains the question: what forces they call on to help them
in their task, and how they invoke the aid of those forces.

The heart of Hopi religious practice lies, I believe, in its simplest elements;
and if its meaning is to be grasped, it will be through an understanding of these
elements—or not at all. The elements I have in mind are: the use of corn meal
(and pollen), the use of feathers, the making, consecration and 'placing' of

---

[1] In the Walpi rite, the Flute man emerges from the water *with a handful of black mud*,
which he smears on certain prayer-offerings.

[2] Titiev (1944), p. 147: my italics.

The alternative interpretation, also advanced by Titiev (1944, p. 148), that the performance at the spring 'enacts the bringing of rain (water) from the very home of the clouds
(the spring)', does not explain why the rite should particularly take place in August.

[3] Fewkes and Stephen (1892*b*), p. 228, n. 2: cf. Whorf (1936), p. 1237.

[4] Cf. Voth's photograph (1903*a*, pl. cliv) of Lenañva spring, showing the water vessels
left to be filled as soon as enough water should have run into the spring.

prayer-sticks, and the dance. And I propose to approach each of these in turn, by way of the Hopi word used to describe it.[1]

> *ho'moya*, v. sprinkles with meal as a religious rite, makes a prayer by such sprinkling
> (Whorf, 1936, p. 1220):
>
> *ñü'mni*, n. meal: hence,
> *hom'ñümni*, prayer-meal, as in
>     *hom'ñümni püh'tabi*, prayer-meal road.

In the old days every Hopi woman, on rising in the morning, went to the mesa edge and sprinkled corn meal to the rising sun, praying at the same time for health and for long life. The rite of sprinkling corn-meal in this manner is *ho'moya*; and the various other instances of the use of the word, cited in Stephen's *Hopi Journal*, show that it is applied equally to the sprinkling of corn meal on prayer-offerings at the time of their consecration in the kiva; to the sprinkling of corn meal to the Sun by mothers after the birth of their child and by novices after their initiation; to the sprinkling of corn meal on the katçina dancers by their 'fathers' in the village square; and to the sprinkling of corn meal at shrines, at springs or in the fields, when prayer-sticks are deposited. Stephen, in 1892, was taught (by Si'mo, the old head of the Flute society at Walpi) how to pray, in the following words: 'Taking the pinch of meal and carrying it to (the) mouth, pray that [the Chiefs of the Six Directions] . . . may not forget us, their children, but hasten here with rain.' And later, in the course of the Lako'n, when two of the girls are given prayer-feathers and corn meal and sent down to the fields to collect corn stalks and other vegetation, one of the senior women of the society explained: 'they (the maids) will pray upon the meal (*ho'moya*) that the clouds from the four corners will come overhead and rain fall (*yo'kova*) upon the corn fields in the east valley where they go to gather corn, beans and melons to decorate the altar.'

The essential elements in the act of prayer are thus the formulation of a wish, the taking of a pinch of meal (in the left hand), the carrying of it to the mouth, the breathing on it of the wish formulated, and its casting away (from oneself). In this sequence, the physical acts (i.e. the taking of the pinch of meal, carrying it to the mouth, and throwing it away) are covered by the word, *ho'moya*. There remain two elements not yet accounted for, namely the formulation of the wish, and the 'breathing' of it onto (or into) the corn meal. Taking the latter first, the word for 'breathes' is *hi'kwse*, and for 'breath', *hi'kwsi*: whence comes *nakwa'hikwsi* (usually transliterated *nakwa'kwosi*), 'feather-breath', commonly rendered 'prayer-feather'; but *hi'kwsi ad'ta*, 'its breath', may be used alone for the feather attached to a prayer-stick, while *hi'kwsi a'pa*, literally 'breath bed', refers to the 'breath road, by which your breath goes to the spirit'. The road, *püh'tabi*, may be of corn meal, or of cotton twine with breath-feather attached; feathers are used because they are *ka-pü'tü*, not heavy, light, corn meal and

[1] The rest of this section is mainly based on the Glossary to Stephen's *Hopi Journal* (1936, pp. 1201–1326), under the appropriate Hopi words.

cotton perhaps for the same reason. But in either case the idea is the same: 'the *püh'tabi* (Si'mo speaking) is the trail over which travel all the prayers of all the people, old men and young, women and children.'

The word for the wish itself is:

*na'wa*, stem of *na'wakna*, v. wants, desires, needs, lacks.

In other words, the act of prayer (*ho'moya*) begins in a need that is felt; this is translated into a wish, the wish is 'breathed' onto (or into) the material object, feather or corn meal, to be conveyed by it to the particular spirit to which the prayer is addressed—and which is believed to be capable of answering the prayer, in the sense of making good the need.

*pa'ho*, n. prayer-stick (etymology unknown: perhaps from *pa-*, water).

The making and consecration of prayer-sticks constitutes, to my mind, the core of the work done in *all* Hopi ceremonies. The leaders of the fraternity assemble in the kiva *in order to* make *pa'ho*(s); and the altars are set up, and the ceremonies performed around them, *in order to* consecrate the *pa'ho*(s) before these are taken out and 'placed' at their ultimate locations. Like corn meal and breath feathers, prayer-sticks carry the wishes of their makers; and each piece in the ceremonial—the blowing over them with smoke, the sprinkling with medicine water, the singing of prayer songs over them—serves to concentrate these wishes on the objects that are to carry them. But where prayer-sticks differ from corn meal and breath feathers as a vehicle for prayer, is in the elaborateness of their symbolism: *pa'ho*(s) may be single or double, of various lengths, and made of different kinds of wood: the majority are painted blue-green with black tips, but some are painted wholly black, and a few special ones are painted with yellow, red, or white pigment: commonly, prayer-sticks are 'clothed' with a corn-husk packet containing corn meal and honey, together with sprigs of *kü'ñya* and *ma'övi*, bound to their middle with cotton thread—on occasions, however, one or other of the herbs is omitted, while bunches of pine needles or pieces of grass may be put in their place; all prayer-sticks have one (or more) breath-feathers attached to them, selected from eight or ten different kinds of feather used for the purpose.

For certain of the elements in this symbolism I have offered interpretations earlier in the narrative. Thus the use of sumac (*Rhus trilobata*) wood in prayer-sticks, e.g. in those made for the novices at Marau, appears to have a special link with the female; and I suspect that the use of *moñ'pöhövi* (*Fallugia paradoxa*), in many of those made at Soya'l,[1] has an analogous link with the male—this wood having been in common use, in the old days, for making arrows, and arrows being especially associated, as in the cutting of the boy's umbilical cord, with boys and men. The omission of the sprig of *ma'övi*, the substitution of a bunch of pine needles and the use of a bluebird feather, in a number of the prayer-sticks made at Soya'l, is evidently *for* cold, while the use of an owl

---

[1] See Stephen (1936), pp. 39, 41, 1252.

feather in some of those made at Powa'mu is *for* warmth; of the other feathers in common use, that of yellow bird is said to be for hot weather or for rain, that of duck for rain, and that of turkey either for rain or for game. Regarding the pigments used in painting the prayer-sticks, interpretation is still more uncertain: thus, of the two commonest colours, Stephen[1] says that blue-green is used because it is the colour of vegetation, and it is vegetation 'that is asked for, prayed for'; Fewkes,[2] that blue-green indicates the southwest from which the rain clouds come, and black the Above, especially the black rain-cloud; Voth,[3] that blue-green represents the female, and black the male. So hard is it, at this late stage, to unravel Hopi symbolism. But the fact that it is hard for us to unravel does not mean that it is so for those who are brought up to it, any more than a foreign language is difficult for those who speak it as their native tongue. In this sense the various elements in the form and decoration of prayer-sticks represent a code, or language, each element of which carries its own meaning prescribed by tradition;[4] the completed prayer-stick conveying a message which is 'read', by the spirit to whom the prayer-stick is addressed, in much the same way (as Hopi told Stephen) as we read a letter.

That the message which it carries, rather than the stick itself, is the essential root—in Hopi thinking—of the *pa'ho*, is shown by two curious extensions of the use of the word. Ko'peli, head of the Snake fraternity at Walpi, explaining to Stephen (1936, p. 715) the rôle of the snakes in his ceremony, said:

> For the snake head washing I alone make the medicine water, *chü'a ña'hü*. None other knows how. When the snakes' heads are washed in the water they become *pa'ho* (prayer-sticks), that is why I wash them. On the evening after the dance the snakes are distributed (*ta'bi*, placed) for this same reason. They are prayer-sticks and they are placed so that Cloud may see them and hasten with rain. As the bearer lays them down, he casts meal upon them and prays (*ho'moya*)—*i'ich yo'kavani*, hasten rain!

Again, at the public performances on the last day of the Marau, each of the women who is to play the part of the Marau *mana* smears corn meal over her face and decorates her legs and forearms, the one with blue pollen and the other with yellow pollen. The women's decorated leg is called[5] *ho'kya pa'ho*, 'leg prayer-stick', and her arm *ma'a pa'ho*, 'arm prayer-stick'; rain is expected to fall on this day, and the following morning the women should go down to the fields and wash their legs, arms and faces in the rain pools and pray (*homo' yüñwüh*), then plant their rain (*yo'ki*) and other prayer-sticks in the field shrine, *pa'smi pa'ho-ki*. Clearly, in the one case the snakes themselves are regarded as the bearers of a message to the Cloud deities, and in the other the decorated

---

[1] Stephen (1898), p. 265: (1936), p. 165.

[2] Fewkes and Stephen (1892b), p. 227.

[3] Voth (1901), p. 108.

[4] 'A man makes a prayer-stick as prescribed, because the thinking old men of the old time knew and said make it thus or thus': Parsons (1936), p. 1271.

[5] Stephen (1936), p. 928. Yellow (corn) pollen, according to Stephen (1929, p. 39), symbolises both fruitful field and fruitful women.

arms and legs of the women are deemed to carry a similar message; it is in this sense that both are referred to as *pa'ho*(s).

I said above that, in my estimation, the making and consecration of prayer-sticks constitutes the core of the work done in the kivas and that the other elements in the ritual, in particular the setting-up of altars and the ceremonies that take place around them, are subordinate to that end. I do not mean by this that the ritual has no significance. Nor is the observation itself wholly true, at least so far as concerns the two spring ceremonies, the Powa'mu and the Uñ'kwati; for in those two ceremonies, much of the time and care of the kiva members is spent in planting and tending the 'crops', in the one case beans and in the other corn, which they are to 'harvest' on the concluding day. The success or failure of their 'crop' is a matter of great concern to those taking part in the ceremony; and the linguistic usage by which this concern is expressed throws light on the significance, not only of the 'crop'-raising ritual, but also of the ritual employed in those other ceremonies where attention is primarily focussed on the making and consecration of prayer-sticks:

> *na'twanta*, v. (*a*) makes trial, tries, tests, attempts to determine future, concentrates mentally on a hope to bring it to pass through meditative prayer, prays for something:
>
> (*b*) makes trial of the prospective *na'twani*, or general harvest, attempts to discover or assure the coming harvest.
>
> *na'twampi*, n. instrument of *na'twanta*, any object used to aid one in praying for something which is held in mind as an image and concentrated upon meanwhile, especially a prayer-pipe used in this way, the concentrating being done while exhaling the smoke.

(Whorf, 1936, p. 1261).

Now it is commonly stated that the growing of 'crops' in the kivas, in the course of Powa'mu and Uñ'kwati, is a piece of 'mimetic magic'. If we mean by this that the practice is rooted in a notion of causality which supposes that like in some way *induces* like, then certainly this element is present; it *is* believed that the height reached by the plants grown in the kivas influences the growth of the real crops soon to be planted in the fields—just as it is believed that the dance of Star man on the last night of the Soya'l will help the Sun to turn in its course and bring warm weather more quickly to the land, and that the races run in the course of the Flute and Marau ceremonies will hasten the ripening of the crops. This mimetic element, which is present in other aspects of Hopi life, e.g. in the use of a weasel skin during labour that 'the child may come out quickly',[1] also has a place in the ritual by which the prayer-sticks are conse-crated—e.g. in the use of the smoke pipe, *na'twampi*: 'If a large dense cloud is made, then copious rain will come; if a thin cloud only, then little or no rain' (Parsons, 1936, p. 681, n. 1). But we do not do full justice to the quality of Hopi religious experience if we take this element to be the only, or even the prin-cipal, one involved; for *that*, I feel sure, lies in the concurrent meaning of the

---

[1] Dorsey and Voth (1901), p. 34, n.*: cf. above, p. 26, n. 3.

verb *na'twanta*, namely 'concentrates mentally on a hope to bring (something) to pass through meditative prayer'. It is this mental (or spiritual) element that furnishes the force needed to bring about the change desired, of which the mime is the outward sign.

In any particular piece of ritual, one or other of these two elements is likely to be predominant. The predominance of the mental (or spiritual) element in the consecration of *pa'ho*(s) is largely responsible for the solemnity with which the consecrating rites are carried out, the other factor here being that, at this point, the dead are called in to add their prayers to those of the living; and it is this element, again, which lies behind the notion, emphasized by all Hopi informants, that—for rites to achieve their desired end—the hearts of all those taking part must be 'good'.

To give a single instance: the summer of 1892 was one of prolonged and terrible drought in the region of the Hopi villages; from midsummer until late in October, no rain fell on the parched fields. In that year the Flute ceremony was celebrated at Walpi, from August 5 to 13, by which time the summer rains were already long overdue. On the evening of the fourth day of the ceremony, Si'mo (the old head of the Flute fraternity on 1st Mesa) said to Stephen:

> I know not why the rain does not come. I have been thinking much. Some Hopi hearts and thoughts (inside of heads) must be bad.

Later the same evening, towards the close of the ceremony around the altar, one of the older men broke into violent sobbing and weeping: 'there is more emotional speaking to-night', wrote Stephen in his *Journal*, 'than I ever heard among these folks before. The subject, of course, is the delayed rain and its cause; whose heart is bad, whose thoughts are bad, whose words are leaving the straight path.' And finally, on the last evening of the ceremony, Si'mo again confided to Stephen:[1]

> I know not why rain comes not. I have been asking my heart and my head. I have been thinking much, but we have foolish youths in the village whose thoughts are crooked and whose speech lies far from the straight trail. Unless our thoughts and speech be straight, we can not expect Cloud to listen.

This dual emphasis, on hearts being 'good' and thoughts (and speech) following the straight path, is found in all Hopi accounts of their religious mysteries. Si'mo, explaining the significance of the prayer-offerings and their distribution to Stephen, said:

> We have no streams [i.e. running water] in our valleys, yet we have corn, etc. Cloud sends rain enough because we are a peaceable people; because we do not quarrel; all our hearts beat together; all our speech is straight and travels in the same direction; all our prayers (*homo'ita*) converge upon the same object at the same

[1] For these three quotations, from Stephen's account of the Flute ceremony of 1892, see Stephen (1936), pp. 793–6, 811–12; and for the next two, the one from the Flute and the other from the Lako'n, ibid. pp. 779–80, 847–8.

time (all are in unison). We make the prayer-feathers and we breathe our prayers upon them. We place them at the altar and sing our prayers upon them, that the Cloud chiefs may send rain, clouds.

And later Stephen himself, evidently following closely his Hopi informants, writes: 'The prayer-songs are not for a general distribution of rain, not for Ko'honino [Havasupai], Navajo, or Zuñi, but for themselves, for the Hopi. Each must pray for himself; all must pray together. Without unison in thoughts and action, prayers are nearly always ineffectual, the prayer-sticks are not looked at nor the song-prayers listened to, by the deities.'[1]

The unanimity of heart and mind of those taking part in any ceremony is one of the central tenets of Hopi religious doctrine, and finds expression in many aspects of the ritual. To take a single instance, again: that of smoking together around the altar. We have seen already that this rite has both a *mimetic* element, in that the clouds of smoke 'are', or stand for, rain clouds; and a *mental* (or spiritual) element, in that those taking part concentrate their mind, while they are exhaling the smoke, on the rain clouds which they are praying for. It also has a *social* (or moral) aspect: for, as they sit in silence passing the pipe round from one to another, the men exchange terms of relationship—'my father', 'my son', or 'my elder brother', 'my younger brother'—with each other. Various explanations of this custom have been put forward[2]: for example, that it reflects the respective ages of the man who hands the pipe and of the man he hands it to, or that it reflects their actual kin or clan relationship, or that it reflects their ceremonial relationship. My own view is that, while the usage may indeed on particular occasions reflect any (or all) of these alternatives, its real significance is quite other: namely, that *the words have to be taken in some moral sense, as a way of behaviour—being loving or peaceful or considerate.*[3] If this is accepted, then the use of kinship terms in the ritual is simply an outward sign of the requirement that those taking part should be at one together, inwardly: a requirement that is dramatically expressed, for all to see, in the public performance (*ti'hü*, dance) with which every major ceremony ends.

[1] Given this attitude, we can understand the terrible strain to which social relations were put when prayers were *not* answered. The drought of 1892 initiated a series of thirteen lean years—clearly reflected in tree-ring growth over the whole of the Colorado and San Juan drainage—which led up to, and was, I have argued elsewhere (Bradfield, 1971), ultimately responsible for, the split of Old Oraibi in 1906. What I did not know when I wrote that paper was that a similar interpretation had been put forward thirty-five years earlier by A. E. Douglass, who himself visited the pueblo in 1898 and again in the 1920s:

> In 1906, [wrote Douglass (1935, p. 24)], dissensions arose among the Indians of Old Oraibi. Although the Indian Bureau attributed this trouble to difficulties connected with school attendance, a highly educated Indian told me it was a religious dispute over methods of bringing rain. And this perhaps suggests an important factor, namely, food supply; for the ten years preceding 1906 had been severe drought years, destroying much farm area, and causing crops to fail.

[2] Cf. Stephen (1936), p. 782: Parsons (1936), pp. 1050–2: Titiev (1937b), pp. 10–11.

[3] The sentence is quoted from a quite different, but I think analogous, context in S. Isaacs, *Social Development in Young Children* (London, 1933), p. 216—whence came the idea put forward above. I feel that this is, ultimately, why the Hopi refer to themselves as *Hopi'tü*, the 'peaceable people'—that they see themselves as a religious community.

I remarked above that the co-adjutant reason for the solemnity of the rites at which prayer-sticks are consecrated is the presence of the dead. The dead are represented, as we have seen, by the crooks and sticks stuck in the sand ridge or ranged on either side of the sand field; certainly in two of the ceremonies (Wü'wütçim, and the Marau), and perhaps in others, they are summoned beforehand and food is set out for them; and in the course of the prayer-songs around the altar, one or other of the leaders beats on the kiva floor to tell them that the rites are in progress. This association of the dead with the living in their prayers is the outcome of two notions: the fundamental Hopi belief in the continuity of life after death, and the idea, noted by Stephen,[1] that 'it is seemly also for a strange people to help their friends in their prayers; it displays kindness, a good heart ...' Conversely, when the dead are celebrating *their* ceremonies, the Hopi make prayer-sticks to assist *them*.

Regarding the tabus that are observed during the celebration of all major ceremonies, the prohibition on eating food cooked with salt is perhaps traceable to the near presence of the dead; while the prohibition on sexual intercourse is ascribed by Hopi themselves to the fact that the 'smell' of women is displeasing to the clouds, 'and hence no rain will fall if people have intercourse during the performance of sacred rituals.'[2] The *navo'tçiwa* rite with which the kiva ritual ends is similar, in principle, to the elaborate exorcising rites performed at the termination of burial,[3] and evidently has the same purpose: to separate those taking part from the spirits, both of the dead and other spirits, with which they have been in touch.

As to the deities whose help is invoked, I take these to be primarily those for whom prayer-sticks are made, namely Cloud and the Chiefs of the Six Directions (perhaps the same persons), Mü'yiñwa (who controls germination and growth of all cultivated plants, but especially of corn), Pü'ükoñhoya (who controls ice and cold), Tü'wa-poñya-tümsi (who controls animal fertility, beside that of women), and Ta'wa, Sun (who controls the return of warm weather). 'A man makes a prayer-stick because he wants something good, some benefit ...... from these and other chiefs all benefits proceed.' It is to these deities that Sun carries the prayer-sticks he has seen, the 'breath' of which he has inhaled (*hüh'tü*), on his daily journey across the Hopi land; to them, again, the katçinas carry the prayer-offerings[4] which they have been given, e.g. at the Nima'n, and the dead man the prayers with which *he* has been entrusted before setting out on his journey from the grave. That the deities are regarded as

[1] Stephen (1936), p. 848.
[2] Titiev (1944), p. 206.
[3] See above, pp. 43-4.
[4] This is in line with Stephen's description (1898, p. 260) of the katçinas as 'beneficent intermediaries'; other accounts, however, imply that the katçinas themselves are the deities from whom the benefits come. The contradiction in the evidence reflects, I think, a basic inconsistency in Hopi thinking; as Kennard observes (Earle and Kennard, 1938, p. 2): 'the feeling for organisation so characteristic of their life is not reflected in their thought'. Professor Eggan suggests (1968) that, the katçinas being a relatively new (perhaps 14th century A.D.) introduction, the Hopi have not yet resolved the contradiction.

'chiefs', *moñ'mowitu*, we have seen already; beyond that, we can hardly go.

Yet this relatively simple, and in itself consistent, interpretation of Hopi religious practice—namely, that certain material objects (corn meal, feathers, prayer-sticks, and the like) are charged with the prayers of the people and then despatched to particular deities who are able to 'read', and if made by men of good heart, to grant the wishes which they carry—while it may indeed correspond closely to the way in which Hopi themselves regard their own practice, does not cover the whole range of their religious experience. Any religion which has developed over the course of many generations—and there is archaeological evidence to show that e.g. corn meal, cotton and feathers, have been of religious significance in pueblo life for some twelve to fifteen centuries —is likely to have, imbedded in its practice, survivals from earlier layers of belief. I said above that there is a strong *mimetic* element in certain aspects of the kiva ritual; also, that the separate items in the manufacture of prayer-sticks represent a code. Now there is no need for the items in a code to be mimetic; yet a number of the separate items in the decoration of prayer-sticks clearly *are* mimetic. For example, regarding the use of yellow-bird feathers for rain, Si'mo explained to Stephen (1936, p. 782): 'the yellow bird is used because this yellow bird constantly scatters the fructifying pollen, its colour shows that, and when there is no rain, there are no yellow birds; when there is plenty of rain, there is plenty of grass seeds and multitudes of yellow birds are seen eating the seeds and scattering the life-giving pollen over the land'. Similarly, duck feathers are used, 'because ducks swim in ponds of water through the land after rain'.

The current notion of the prayer-stick, the one (that is to say) that seems generally to have been put to Stephen by the Hopi of his acquaintance, is that the prayer-stick carries a message to the deity to whom it is addressed. The transaction is thought of in *social* terms; the prayer-stick is 'bartered' against the benefit desired, the deities who control, e.g. rain, being conceived as 'chiefs'. The *mimetic* element appears, then, to be a survival from an earlier and partially submerged layer of belief, springing (as I have said above) from a notion of causality which supposes that like induces like, or that things act directly on things, compulsively. Certainly, the compulsive strain is strong elsewhere in Hopi ritual, for example in the katçina dances of spring and early summer; anyone who has spent a long summer day in a Hopi village, watching the dancers file into the square and listening to the rhythmical re-iteration of their plea for rain, will have experienced this; by late afternoon one feels that the clouds must, are *bound to*, start rolling up from beyond the San Francisco mountains. What I am suggesting is that the emergence of personalised deities, controlling such natural forces as clouds, germination, ice and cold, is a fairly late development in pueblo thinking; that this arose on an older ground of belief, based on the notion that things act directly on things due to a common element in their nature, e.g. the water which the asperser sprinkles on the sand field *is* the rain falling on the Hopi land; and that what has become, in the manufacture of prayer-sticks (e.g. the use of different woods, herbs, grasses, feathers), a code to be 'read' by the deities to whom the prayer-sticks are addressed, originated in a choice of materials where each kind of wood, herb, grass, feather, stood directly for the thing required. For, in the beginning, 'the whole universe was endowed with the same breath, rocks, trees, grass, earth, all animals, and men. The flesh of all human kind and of all animals had the same breath at the first.' And, in the Below, 'all grasses, herbs, and trees had speech; all rocks had speech; they spoke Hopi. They cannot speak to us now, but they had thought and speech once.'[1] What the Hopi are asserting here, surely, is that there was, once, communion between men, animals and (what we call) things, based on a common element in their nature: a communion, the interruption of which has necessitated the use of prayer-sticks charged with a message (prayer) to the deity to whom the prayer-stick is addressed.

I put these ideas forward, not as affording any cut-and-dried schema for the development of Hopi religious practice, but as showing that no simple explanation is likely to do full justice to the complexity of the material or to accommodate all the facts of which we have knowledge.

Regarding the end, as distinct from the means of pueblo religion, Fewkes pointed out many years ago[2] how closely the Hopi ritual, with its emphasis on rain-making and growth of crops, reflects 'the arid climatic characteristics of north-eastern Arizona' and the status of the people themselves as agriculturalists. More recently, Titiev has taken up and developed this theme.

> In its broader aspects, [he writes[3]], the religion of the Hopi can be understood only with respect to other manifestations of their culture. For about two thousand years they and their immediate ancestors have occupied a semi-arid zone, despite which, for the greater part of that time, they have relied on agriculture as their principal source of food. During many centuries they have dwelt in fairly large pueblos, but with a decentralised social organisation which contained within itself an ever-present threat of collapse.

After listing the dangers—chiefly disease, and external attack—to which the pueblos were exposed, Titiev goes on:

> Under such conditions, life was far from easy for the Hopi. Lack of rain, failure of crops, internal strife, onslaughts of disease, and enemy attacks, all combined to threaten the very existence of their society. To offset these dangers they took whatever material measures they could, but finding these inadequate to guarantee the permanence which every social group requires, they resorted to supernatural means to give them assurance that they would not be destroyed. Against each of the perils which endangered Hopi society, their ceremonial system opposed a comforting buffer. . . . Shorn of its elaborate superstructure of costumes, songs and dances, the entire complex of Hopi religious behaviour stands revealed as a unified attempt to safeguard Hopi society from the danger of disintegration or dissolution.

[1] Stephen (1936), p. 706: pp. 1254–5, under Mü'iyiñwa: and p. 1308, under *to'zri*.
[2] Fewkes (1898*b*), p. 183.
[3] Titiev (1944), pp. 177–8.

With this conclusion I am in agreement; the Hopi ceremonial system does, I believe, perform the integrative function which Titiev ascribes to it. But this, to my mind, is only one side of the coin. To guarantee 'the permanence which every social group requires', a community must not only protect itself against attack from outside and disintegration from within; it must also strike a balance between its own needs and the natural resources available to it. In an environment as marginal as that in which the Hopi villages lie, the balance is necessarily a delicate one[1]; that the Hopi have survived there for so many generations, implies that they early reached a stable relation between their own needs and the ability of the land to satisfy those needs—without a gradual drain on its resources. In striking such a balance, the Hopi, in effect, set a *voluntary* limit[2] to their own use of the resources available to them; and the maintaining of this limit was, as I hope to show in the course of the two chapters that follow, the other major service rendered by their ceremonial system.

[1] The abandonment of many pueblo sites farther north during the late 13th century A.D. may well have been due to a tilting of the balance, brought on by a run of abnormally dry years.

[2] The idea of a *limit* is implicit in the Hopi attitude to nature, whether expressed by Hopi themselves (Whiting, 1939, pp. 6–7) or inferred from their behaviour towards plants and animals (Beaglehole, 1936, pp. 23–4).

# 15

# *Thought-world of the Hopi*

So far, in this account of Hopi life, we have been concerned primarily with
what the Hopi *do*: in the first two chapters, with what they do in relation to
subsistence and the life cycle, and in the latter three, with what they do in their
ceremonies and festivals. In this chapter and the next, we shall be concerned with
what the Hopi *think*: that is to say, with the notions on which their action is
based, and with the underlying patterns according to which the notions themselves are organised. This is a very difficult subject, and one that requires great
care on the part of the writer and close attention on the part of the reader: but
once the effort has been made and the main lines of Hopi thinking have been
established, we shall be in a position to grasp the essential character—the 'Hopi-
ness'—of Hopi society.

We shall begin with the Hopi classification of nature, as mediated through the
clan-name system, and pass on from there to the representation of time, with
the object of seeing, first, how each of these aspects of their thinking is correlated
with the notion of causation which we considered at the close of the last chapter;
and of seeing, then, how all three aspects combine to present a coherent view of
the universe in which the Hopi find themselves.

## THE CLASSIFICATION OF NATURE

The root problem we have to resolve in this section turns on the relationship
between clans and phratries; for, as Titiev noted twenty-five years ago, there are
two contradictory aspects to this relationship. On the one hand, as he observes
(1944, p. 201), 'the social structure of the Hopi is made up of a number of
phratries, each of which contains two or more clans. There are strong bonds
uniting the people within the respective clans, but the ties between clans in
the same phratry are often very weak.' On the other hand (ibid. p. 58), 'if the
phratry is an unnamed unit, and the clan has a name, why should natives rarely
err in assigning people to their proper phratries, but make frequent mistakes
with regard to clan membership?'

That they do so, there is no doubt. Thus Lowie, writing of his own principal
informant, says (1929, p. 336):

> In first speaking of his clan affiliation, Lewis Le'hungwa described himself as an
> *uma'ö* (Cloud) and a *qa'ö* (Corn) individual, but subsequently he preferred to use
> the term *pa'tki* (Water-house) in preference to the former. In referring to his father,
> Lewis spoke of him as an *a'sa-wüñwa* (Mustard individual) but also as a *hu'çpu-wüñwa*
> (Chapparal cock). Lewis's father-in-law is both a Rabbit and a Tobacco man.

Herein lies the contradiction: if the clans are, as all the evidence indicates they are, the main structural units of Hopi society, how is it that Hopi themselves may put the same person into two, or even three, different clans?[1]

Now earlier, in discussing the linkage of clans into phratries, Lowie had himself provided a clue to the puzzle. 'In this connection,' he wrote (ibid. p. 331), 'it is essential to distinguish between actual clans, present or known to have become extinct within the memory of men still living, and mere clan *names* associated together by native theorizers.' And it is this clue that I propose to follow.

In an earlier section (see above, p. 8 *et seq*), we have treated the clans of Old Oraibi (before 1906) in the first sense of the distinction drawn by Lowie: that is, as actual bodies of living (or recently dead) kinsfolk, owning corn fields, house sites, cisterns, and ceremonial office. In this section we shall approach the Hopi clans in the second sense of the distinction drawn by Lowie: that is, as clan *names* associated together by native theorizers. But not as *mere* clan names. For we shall approach them on the assumption that the clan names linked together by native theorizers represent fundamental associations of ideas (so fundamental that they dictate, in the persons of those who stand for them, who shall not marry whom); that these associations of ideas are how the Hopi classify nature and their own place in nature; that this classification lies at the root of the ceremonial system, the one being the outward form and *affirmation* of the other; and that the links established between certain bodies of related persons (i.e. the clans) and certain associated elements of nature (i.e. the elements represented by the clan *names*) furnish the means by which, in their ceremonial, the Hopi community brings the communal *will* to bear on the environment at the point where physical action, e.g. digging the fields, cleaning the springs, setting traps for game, ends. In other words I shall propose, as answer to the problem posed by Titiev, that where the clans are *actual* bodies of related kinsmen, to do primarily with the owning and inheriting of property rights, the phratry groupings represent *conceptual linkages*, to do primarily with ceremonial functions.[2]

As first step in this approach, let us consider the twelve phratry groupings as reported for the villages of 1st, 2nd, and 3rd Mesa:

---

[1] Mrs. Barton Wright, who is engaged on a study of Hopi silverwork and silversmiths, tells me that this is sometimes a source of confusion in identifying the work of individual craftsmen even today: at Shungo'povi, for example.

[2] The germ of the idea developed here is to be found in F. Eggan (1950), pp. 80–9; indeed, the whole section represents a variation on a theme by Eggan, although at a number of points I have gone beyond Professor Eggan's own interpretation. The principal sources used, apart from F. Eggan (1950, pp. 80–9), are: Lowie (1929, pp. 337–8), Parsons (1922a, p. 289: 1933, pp. 21–4, and 36–41), Stephen (1936, *passim*), and Titiev (1944, pp. 55–8); cf. also, for Zuñi, Kroeber (1917), especially pp. 166–8.

As the argument stands or falls on the evidence adduced to support it, I have adopted the expedient of citing all relevant references in the text, and of setting the more detailed material in small print.

| Walpi-Sicho'movi, ca. 1890–1: Stephen (1936), pp. 1068–73 | Walpi-Sicho'movi, ca. 1893–6: Fewkes (1900b), pp. 582–4 | Walpi-Sicho'movi, 1929: Forde (1931), p. 400 | Mishong'novi, 1916: Lowie (1929), p. 332 |
|---|---|---|---|
| I. BEAR, *ho'nau* spider, *ko'kyañ* *püiküsh*, bear-skin rope | BEAR, *honau* spider, *kokyan* | BEAR, *huni* spider, *kokyañ* | BEAR, *hu'ni* spider, *qu'kyañ* carrying-strap, *piaqö's* |
| *mü'i*, field mouse | | | a digging animal, *mö'yi* |
| *cho'sro*, bluebird *wi'kois*, fat of the eye *toko'chi*, wild cat | *tcosro*, bluebird *tokotçi*, wild cat | | bluebird, *tco'çi* bear's eye, *wi'qosi* |
| II. KACHINA, *katcina* *gy'azro*, parrot *añwü'si*, raven *hek'pa*, spruce (fir) *sala'bi*, Douglas fir (Whiting, p. 63) | KATCINA, *katcina* *gyazru*, parrot *añwuçi*, crow salab, spruce *sühüb*, cottonwood *sikyatçi*, yellow-bird *tawamana*, bird | KATCINA, *katcina* parrot, *kyac* *qöhö'vi*, willow (Whiting, p. 72) | PARROT, *kyaci* kachina, *qatci'n* raven, *añwö'çi* |

I have included virtually *all* the clan names found in the eight main lists, i.e. Fewkes, Stephen, Lowie, Forde (2), Parsons (2), and White. It is not suggested that this number of clans has ever existed among the Hopi: only that these are the names which would be given to clans in the various phratries, if that number of names were ever required.

The numbering of the phratries (I, II, III . . .) follows Eggan's scheme (1950, Table 2, pp. 65–6), rather than Titiev's (see above, p. 11, n. 1). The leading clan of each phratry grouping, i.e. the one from which the phratry as a whole takes its name in *that* village or group of villages, is set in capitals.

| Mishong'novi, 1929: Forde (1931), p. 401 | Shungo'povi, 1921: Parsons (1922b), p. 295, and Nequatewa (1936), p. 112, n. 73 | Oraibi, 1905–6: White, 1932 (in Titiev, 1944, p. 49) | 3rd MESA (Oraibi-Hotevilla-Bakabi), 1921: Parsons (1922b), p. 288 |
|---|---|---|---|
| BEAR, *honö* spider, *kokyan* strap, *piaqös* | BEAR, *hon* spider, *kokyañ* carrying strap, *piqwösi* | BEAR, *ho'nau* spider, *ko'kyañ* carrying strap, [*piqö'sha*, raw-hide strap: Voth, 1905b, p. 80] | BEAR, *huna* spider, *kokyañ* |
| | gopher, *mü'i* [N] | | |
| bluebird, *tcosi* | bluebird, *chosh* greasy hole, *wi'kösiñ* | bluebird, *tço'ro* bear's eye-ball | bluebird |
| PARROT, *kyæ* katcina, *katcina* | KACHINA, *katcina* parrot, *kyash* crow, *añwü's* [N] | KATCINA, *katcina* parrot, *ky'aro* crow, *añwü'si* spruce, *hek'pa* | PARROT, *kyash* kachina, *katcina* |
| *qöhövi*, willow | | | |
| | | jack rabbit, *so'wi* cottontail, *ta'vo* tobacco, *pi'va* pipe, *cho'ño* | rabbit, *tab* tobacco, *pi'p* wild tobacco, *chi'p* |

Names marked [N], in the Shungo'povi list, are taken from Nequatewa (1936); some additional clan names, given by Voth (1905b), have also been inserted into the Oraibi list compiled by White in 1932. Neither Nequatewa, nor Voth, gives the phratry grouping of the clans to which he refers.

| Walpi-Sicho'movi, *ca.* 1890–1: Stephen (1936), pp. 1068–73 | Walpi-Sicho'movi, *ca.* 1893–6: Fewkes (1900*b*), pp. 582–4 | Walpi-Sicho'movi, 1929: Forde (1931), p. 400 | Mishong'novi, 1916: Lowie (1929), p. 332 |
|---|---|---|---|
| III. SNAKE (rattlesnake), *chü'a* | SNAKE, *tcüa* | SNAKE, *tcö* | LIZARD, *qö'qötçi* |
| *lülü'koñ*, house snake | | | sand, *töva* snake, *tcö'i* |
| *hü'wi*, mourning dove | *hü'wi*, dove | dove, *höwi* prairie dog, *dökya* | |
| *tü'wa-chü'a*, sand snake *ta'ho chü'a*, sinew snake | | | |
| { *ü'shü*, cholla cactus (Whiting, p. 86) | *uçü*, cactus | | |
| { *püna'ñ*, its fruit *ka'chi*, sage wren | | cactus fruit, *pöna* | |
| { *ü'yüñü*, prickly pear (Whiting, p. 85) | *yuñü*, opuntia (cactus) | | |
| { *na'vwü*, its fruit *to'hoa*, mountain lion | *nabovú*, — *tohoú*, puma | | |
| SAND, *tü'wa* | SAND, *tüwa* | SAND, *töwa* | |
| lizard, *kü'küchi* | LIZARD, *kükütç* | lizard, *qöqöts* | |
| *mana'ñüya*, another kind of lizard | | | |
| *ma'chakwa*, horned toad | | | |
| *choro'si*, larkspur | | blue flower, *tcojo'si* | |
| *ka'tsi*, blue gilia | *si'hü*, flower | | |
| *man'si*, painted cup | | red flower, *man'si* [Parsons, 1933, p. 21, n. 78] | |
| *he'si*, mariposa lily | | yellow flower, *he'si* | |
| IV. EAGLE, *kwa'hü* | *kwahu*, eagle | SUN, *tawa* | EAGLE, *qwa'* |
| *ta'wa*, sun | *tawa*, sun | eagle, *kwa* | |
| *pala'kwayo*, red hawk | | | |
| *masi'kwayo*, gray hawk | *kwayo*, hawk | | gray hawk, *masi' qwa'yi* |
| *kih'sa*, prairie falcon | | | |
| *koyo'ño*, wild turkey | *konoña*, turkey | | wild turkey, *qoyu'ñ* |
| REED, *pa'kabi* | REED (or arrow), *pakab* | REED, *paqap* | |
| *te'be*, greasewood | | *tep*, greasewood [Lowie, 1929, p. 332] | |
| *moñ'wú*, owl | | | |
| *mo'chini*, shrike | | | |
| *yau'pa*, mockingbird | | | |
| *sho'hü*, all stars | *çohu*, — | star, *ço* | |
| *Püükoñhoya*, elder of the War Twins | *Püükoñ*, war god *Palaña*, war god | | |
| *ke'le*, desert sparrow hawk | | | |

| Mishong'novi, 1929: Forde (1931), p. 401 | Shungo'povi, 1921: Parsons (1922b), p. 295, and Nequatewa (1936), p. 112, n. 73 | Oraibi, 1905–6: White, 1932 (in Titiev, 1944, p. 49) | 3rd MESA (Oraibi-Hotevilla-Bakabi), 1921: Parsons (1922b), p. 288 |
|---|---|---|---|
| LIZARD, *qöqötsi* | — | SAND, *tü'wa* | SNAKE, *chü* |
| | sand, *teu* [N] | snake, *tçü* | sand, *tuwa'* |
| | | prairie dog, *tü'kya* burrowing owl, *ko'ko* [Voth, 1905b, p. 88] | |
| | | lizard, *gü'gütsi* | |
| | | horned toad *tükya'msi*, 'prairie-dog flower', larkspur [Voth, 1905b, p. 91] | |
| EAGLE, *kwa* | SUN, *tawa* eagle, *qwa'* [N] | SUN, *ta'wa* eagle, *kwa'hü* star | EAGLE, *kwa* sun, *tawa* |
| gray hawk, *masi kwa* | | gray hawk, *masi'kwa'i* hawk (another kind) | |
| wild turkey, *koyun* | sun's forehead, *kalang* | turkey, *koyu'ño* sun's forehead | |
| | reed, *pakab* | V. REED, *ba'kavi* | V. REED *paqab* |
| | | greasewood, *te've* | greasewood, *te'be* |
| | | { bow, *a'out* { arrow, *ho'hü* | bow, *a'wat* |
| | | | { sparrow hawk, *ke'le* { crane, *ato'k* |
| | | roadrunner | |

| Walpi-Sicho'movi, ca. 1890–1: Stephen (1936), pp. 1068–73 | Walpi-Sicho'movi, ca. 1893–6: Fewkes (1900b), pp. 582–4 | Walpi-Sicho'movi, 1929: Forde (1931), p. 400 | Mishong'novi, 1916: Lowie (1929), p. 332 |
|---|---|---|---|
| VI. *KO'KOP*, fire spindle, or cedarwood (Stephen, 1929, p. 40, n. 2) *tuve'e*, piñon *ho'ko*, juniper | *KOKOP*, firewood *tuvoú*, piñon *hoko*, juniper | COYOTE, *i's* cedar wood, *kokop* (*h*)*och'ki*, cedar tree (Parsons, 1933, p. 30) | CEDARWOOD-FIRE, *qo'qop* |
| *te'büq*, live embers [= *te've*, fire] | | *koyühi*, fire | |
| *Masau'u*, Masau'u *kwe'wûüh*, gray wolf *isau'wu*, coyote *zroho'na*, (?) mountain coyote *le'taiyo*, gray fox *sikya'taiyo*, yellow fox | *Eototo*, Eototo *Masi*, Masau'û (death-god) *kwewû*, wolf *isau'û*, coyote *zrohono*, — *letaiyo*, gray fox *sikyataiyo*, yellow fox | *masau*, 'redhead man' (corpse) | red-headed man, *ma'çi* coyote, *i'çi* |
| *a'wat*, bow *sikya'chi*, small yellow bird *tüvü'chi*, small red bird | *awat*, bow *sikyatçi*, yellow bird *tüvatçi*, bird | | |
| VII. BADGER, *hona'ni* *bo'li*, butterfly *masi'boli*, moth *po'boli*, moth all colours *ña'hü*, medicinal root, herb *mü'iñyauwü*, porcupine *wi'shoko*, turkey vulture | BADGER, *honani* *buli*, butterfly *muiyawu*, porcupine *wiçoko*, turkey vulture | BADGER, *hona'ni* medicine, *ñahü* porcupine, *manyau* | BADGER, *hona'ni* butterfly, *puli* moth, *po'wuli* porcupine, *möñya'ü* |
| VIII. TOBACCO, *pi'va* *cho'ño*, (tobacco) pipe *so'wi*, jack rabbit *ta'vo*, cottontail | RABBIT, *tabo* *piba*, tobacco *sowi*, hare | RABBIT, *tap* tobacco, *pi'ip* butterfly, *puli* | tobacco, *pi'p*, *pi'va* cottontail rabbit, *ta'vi* |

| Mishong'novi, 1929: Forde (1931), p. 401 | Shungo'povi, 1921: Parsons (1922b), p. 295, and Nequatewa (1936), p. 112, n. 73 | Oraibi, 1905–6: White, 1932 (in Titiev, 1944, p. 49) | 3rd MESA (Oraibi-Hotevilla-Bakabi), 1921: Parsons (1922b), p. 288 |
|---|---|---|---|
| FIRE, *kokop* | | *KOKOP*, (?) fire spindle | KOKOB |
| | | piñon, *tuve'e* juniper, *ho'hü* [Voth, 1905b, p. 78] | |
| | | fire, *to'vü* Agave, *kwa'ni* yucca, *mo'hu* yucca (another kind) | Agave, *kwan* |
| red-headed man, *masau* | | Masau'u, *masau'u* | Masau' |
| coyote, *is'* | | coyote, *i'sauwu* | coyote |
| | | fox, *le'taiyo* yellow fox, *sikya'taiyo* [Voth, 1905b, p. 105] Püükoñhoya millet, *le'* | |
| BADGER, *honani* butterfly, *povoli* | badger, *honan'* [N] butterfly, *povul* [N] | BADGER, *hona'ni* butterfly, *po'li* gray badger, *ma'si hona'n* | BADGER, *honani* butterfly, *poli* |
| porcupine, *monya* | | porcupine, *mu'ñawu* [Voth, 1905b, p. 80] | |
| | | VIII. — (see under II, above) | VIII. — (see under II, above) |
| tobacco, *pip* | tobacco, *bif* [N] | | |
| rabbit, *tap* | rabbit, *tav* [N] | | |

| Walpi-Sicho'movi, ca. 1890–1: Stephen (1936), pp. 1068–73 | Walpi-Sicho'movi, ca. 1893–6: Fewkes (1900b), pp. 582–4 | Walpi-Sicho'movi, 1929: Forde (1931), p. 400 | Mishong'novi, 1916: Lowie (1929), p. 332 |
|---|---|---|---|
| IX. PA'HÜ, moisture, or PA'TKI, water house | PATKI, rain-cloud | WATER, patki | CORN, pi'kec water house, pa'tki |
| yo'ki, rain | | rain, | |
| | | yoyuñ (Parsons, | |
| süv'wü yo'ki, fine misty rain | | mist or 1933, | |
| | | fog, p. 30) | |
| | | pa'müsi | |
| ka'ö, corn | kaii, maize | corn, qaö | |
| pikya'sh, young corn plant | | sprouting corn, pikyec | |
| tüwa'kchi, sweet corn | | | |
| omau'wu, cloud | | cloud, omau | cloud, omau' |
| nü'vwa, snow | | snow, növa | |
| lemo'wa, hail | | | |
| ta'ñaka, rainbow | tanaka, rainbow | | |
| ta'lawi'piki, lightning flash | talawipiki, lightning | | |
| pa'kwa, frog | pakwa, frog | frog, pakwa | |
| pa'wikya, wild duck | pawikya, duck | | |
| | pavatiya, tadpole | | |
| pa'tsro, water bird, snipe | | | |
| pa'lülükoñ, water snake | | | |
| siva'pi, rabbit brush | sivwapi, rabbit brush | sage, sibap (Parsons, 1933, p. 30) | plant with yellow blossom, siva'fi |
| | kwan, agave | | |
| X. SQUASH, pa'tañ (Lowie, 1929, p. 332) [extinct] | SQUASH, patuñ [extinct] atoko, crane kele, pigeon-hawk | SQUASH, patañ [extinct] | SQUASH, pa'tañ crane, ato'q sparrow hawk, qel |
| pü'çovi, Hopi cotton (Lowie, 1929, p. 336) tü'bish, sorrow-making (Stephen, 1936, p. 108) | tubiç, sorrow-making | | |
| XI. HORN, al | HORN, ala | HORN, ali | — |
| sowi'ñu, deer | sowinû, deer | deer | |
| pañ'wu, mountain sheep | pañwû, mountain sheep | | |
| chü'bio, antelope | tçübio, antelope | antelope, tcöp | |
| chai'zrisa, elk | tcaizra, elk | | |
| le'na, flute or le'hü, millet | leleñtû, flute | millet, le'h (Lowie, 1929, p. 326, n. 2) flute, le'na | |
| a'nü, various kinds of black ant | anu, ants of various kinds | ant, a'n | |
| pala' a'nü, red ant | wuko anu, big ant | | |

| Mishong'novi, 1929: Forde (1931), p. 401 | Shungo'povi, 1921: Parsons (1922b), p. 295, and Nequatewa (1936), p. 112, n. 73 | Oraibi, 1905–6: White, 1932 (in Titiev, 1944, p. 49) | 3rd MESA (Oraibi-Hotevilla-Bakabi), 1921: Parsons (1922b), p. 288 |
|---|---|---|---|
| SPROUTING CORN, *pikyec* | WATER HOUSE, *pat'ki* | PIKYAS, young corn water house, *pa'tki* rain, *yo'i* | WATER HOUSE, *pat'ki* |
| corn, *qaö* | corn, *ka'e* [N] young corn-ear, *pihkash* | corn, *ka'ö* | young corn-ear, *pihkash* |
| WATER, *patki* cloud, *omau* | cloud, *omaw* [N] | cloud, *omau'wu* [Voth, 1905b, p. 94] | |
| snow, *növa* mist, *pa'möç* | snow, *növya* | snow, *nü'va* | |
| frog, *pa'kwa* | | rainbow lightning frog, *pa'kwa* | |
| | | tadpole | |
| | rabbit brush, *sivaf* [N] | rabbit brush, *siva'pi* | rabbit brush, *siva'pi* |
| SQUASH, *patañ* | — | SPARROW HAWK, *kel* squash, *pa'tña* crane, *ato'ko* [Voth, 1905b, p. 74] | SQUASH, *pa'tña* [extinct] (for sparrow-hawk and crane: see under V, above) |
| — | HORN, *ahl'i* [extinct] | — | — |
| | millet, *leh* [extinct] | (for millet: see under VI, above) | |

| Walpi-Sicho'movi, ca. 1890–1: Stephen (1936), pp. 1068–73 | Walpi-Sicho'movi, ca. 1893–6: Fewkes (1900b), pp. 582–4 | Walpi-Sicho'movi, 1929: Forde (1931), p. 400 | Mishong'novi, 1916: Lowie (1929), p. 332 |
|---|---|---|---|
| XII. MUSTARD, *a's* or wild tansy | MUSTARD, *asa* | MUSTARD, *as* | — |
| *kwiñ'üvi*, mountain oak | | acorn, *kwiñyap* | |
| *püch-ko'hü*, throwing-stick | *pe towa*, stick [Parsons, 1925, p. 91, n. 142] | rabbit-stick, *pötskoho* | |
| *po'siwu*, magpie | *poçiwû*, magpie | magpie, *pushiwûh* [Parsons, 1933, p. 26] | |
| *ho'shboa*, roadrunner, chaparral cock | *hosboa*, roadrunner | *hu'çpuw*, chaparral cock [Lowie, 1929, p. 336] | |
| *Cha'kwaina*, name of a katcina | *tçakwaina*, a katcina | *tcakwena* | |
| *chi'sro*, bird | *tcisro*, bunting | | |
| *pochi'lüwa*, meadow lark | | | |

The only point I wish to draw attention to, at this stage, is the dominance—in the villages of all three mesas—of *the same pattern of phratry grouping*. Roughly 120 clan names have been recorded for the different villages, by six independent field workers; with certain minor anomalies, and two major exceptions, these 120 clan names are put in the same phratry groupings by informants from all three mesas. The minor anomalies I shall discuss when we come to deal with the separate phratry groupings, where we shall find that several of them, for the very reason that they are anomalous, throw light on the principles governing the groupings. The two major exceptions concern Phratry III, and Phratries IV and V, respectively.

On 1st Mesa, the Reed-Greasewood-Püükoñ people 'go in' with the Sun-Eagle people, to form a single phratry referred to either as Eagle or Reed; at Mishong'novi, the Reed grouping is not represented; at Shungo'povi, as on 1st Mesa, Reed people 'go in' with Sun; on 3rd Mesa, Sun-Eagle people form one phratry grouping (IV), and Reed-Greasewood-Bow another (V). Now Forde, in his 1929 survey of the clans of Walpi-Sicho'movi, while he lists Sun-Eagle-Reed as a single phratry, shows it as two separate land-holding groups, namely Sun-Eagle people (owning four pieces of land), and Reed people (three pieces). The only other phratry that Forde divides in this way is Snake-Sand-Lizard, where he reports Snake people as owning two pieces of land and Sand-Lizard people as owning one piece. Now the situation regarding Snake-Sand-Lizard is precisely the reverse of that regarding Sun-Eagle-Reed; for where the Sun-Eagle-Reed grouping is combined into one phratry on 1st Mesa (and at Shungo'povi) but divided into two phratries on 3rd Mesa, the Snake-Sand-Lizard grouping is combined into one phratry (III) on 3rd Mesa (and at Mishong'novi), but divided into two phratries on 1st

| Mishong'novi, 1929: Forde (1931), p. 401 | Shungo'povi, 1921: Parsons (1922b), p. 295, and Nequatewa, (1936), p. 112, n. 73 | Oraibi, 1905–6: White, 1932 (in Titiev, 1944, p. 49) | 3rd MESA (Oraibi-Hotevilla-Bakabi), 1921: Parsons (1922b), p. 288 |
|---|---|---|---|
| — | *A's*, tansy mustard [N] | — | — |
|  |  | *po'siwuu*, magpie [Voth, 1905b, p. 101] (for roadrunner: see under V, above) |  |

Mesa. In other words, Forde's land-holding evidence bears out an incipient division of Snake-Sand-Lizard phratry into Snake people and Sand-Lizard people (as found on 1st Mesa, but not on 2nd and 3rd Mesas), and a further division of Sun-Eagle-Reed phratry into Sun-Eagle people and Reed-Greasewood people (as found on 3rd Mesa, but not on 1st and 2nd Mesas).

The identity of the phratry groupings is preserved by two devices, one social, the other *noumenal*. In the first place, a person may not marry within the phratry grouping of which his own clan forms a part; and in the second, the linkage between the clans making up a phratry is validated by reference to myth. The general pattern of Hopi 'historical' myth is set by the following extract from the Oraibi version of the Emergence myth (Voth, 1905c, pp. 23–5), recounting how, after various wanderings and adventures, the several clans reached the village:

When the Bear clan arrived at Na'tuwanpika [a place a mile or two west of Oraibi], Skeleton [Masau'u] came to meet them there. 'We have arrived here', the Hon'wungwa [Bear clan leader] said, 'we would like to live here with you, and we want you to be our chief. Now, what do you think about it? Will you give us some land?' But Skeleton replied, 'No, I shall not be chief. You shall be chief here . . . I shall give you a piece of land and then you can live here.' Hereupon he stepped off a large tract of land [the boundaries are given, in detail] . . . this piece of land he allotted to the Bear clan.

The Bear clan brought with them the Soya'l cult, the E'ototo, and the Soya'l katçinas. Soon other clans began to arrive. When a clan arrived, usually one of the new arrivals would go to the village and ask the village chief for permission to settle in the village. He usually asked whether they understood anything to produce rain and good crops, and if they had any cult [i.e. either a ceremony, *wi'mi*, or a katçina dance], they would refer to it and say, 'Yes, this or this we have, and when we assemble for this ceremony, or when we have this dance, it will rain. With this we have travelled, and with this we have taken care of our children.' The chief would then say, 'Very well, you come and live in the village.' Thus the different clans arrived: first, the Hide-strap clan, the Bluebird clan, the Spider clan, etc. When a new clan arrived, the village chief would tell them: 'Very well, you participate in our cult and help us with the ceremonies', and then he would give them their fields according to the way they came. And that way their fields were all distributed.

One of the first clans to arrive was the Bow clan, which came from the south-west. When the village chief asked the leader of this clan what he brought with him to produce rain, he said, 'Yes, I have here the Sha'alako katçinas[1] . . . When they dance, it usually rains.' 'Very well', the village chief said, 'you try it.' So the A'out-wungwa arranged a dance. On the day before the dance it rained a little, and on the last day when they had their dance it rained fearfully. All the washes were full of water. So the village chief invited them to move to the village and gave them a large tract of land. He told them that they should have their ceremonies first. This was the Wüwütçim ceremony, the chief of the Bow clan being the leader of this ceremony. So this ceremony was the first one to take place.

Then followed the Soya'l ceremony, in charge of the village chief. And then in the Ba'ho month[2] the Snake and the Flute ceremonies, which change about every two years. The Snake cult was brought by the Snake clan, the Antelope cult by the Bluebird clan,[3] and the Flute cult by the Spider clan. The Lizard, which also arrived from the north-west, brought the Marau' cult, and the Parrot clan the Lako'n cult. Others came later. Small bands living throughout the country, when they heard about the people living in Oraibi, would sometimes move up towards Oraibi and ask for admission to live in the village. In this way the villages were built up slowly.

Now this account of the building-up of the villages, by the arrival of successive clan-groups previously resident in the surrounding country, probably reflects actual conditions around 1150 to 1300 A.D.[4] The area in the immediate vicinity of the Hopi villages still awaits detailed archaeological investigation; but studies carried out to the north and west respectively, in the region to the north of the Klethla Valley centred on Kiet Seel and Betatakin, and to the west of the Little Colorado river around Wupa'tki, show that, while both areas were relatively heavily settled by sedentary agricultural communities from *c.* 1050 to 1250 A.D., the majority of the settlements were abandoned, perhaps

[1] These katçinas figure prominently in the two spring festivals, Powa'mu and Uñ'kwati: Stephen (1936), pp. 1147–8.

[2] i.e. the January moon, when the winter prayer-stick making of the Snake-Antelope and Flute societies takes place, in alternate years. The words *ba'ho*, and *pa'ho*, are interchangeable in Hopi.

[3] Controlled now, on 3rd Mesa, by Spider clan: Eggan (1950), p. 103.

[4] For the crystallisation of mesa-top pueblos in the Zuñi River drainage over the same period, cf. Woodbury (1956), especially pp. 558–60.

as a consequence of arroyo cutting, in the latter half of the thirteenth century.[1] Similarities in kiva- and house-building styles, in methods of agriculture, in corn-grinding techniques and in social structure,[2] suggest that groups of their inhabitants moved across to the vicinity of the present-day Hopi villages and joined up there with the resident population, already established in village-settlements along the principal washes since about 1050 A.D. Out of this amalgam, perhaps with further influences from Cañon de Chelly in the east, emerged—around 1300—the definitive Hopi culture, the final phase of which was observed by Stephen, Fewkes and Voth 600 years later.

The archaeological evidence enables us to set the Hopi 'world view' in a geographical and temporal frame. The natural environment which it reflects is the tract of plateau country bounded to the west by the San Francisco mountains, to the north by the Tsegi Canyon area, to the east by the line of the Chuska mountains and to the south by the Little Colorado river, with all the plants and trees, insects, reptiles, birds and mammals, indigenous to that area, also the soils and rocks under-foot and the celestial bodies overhead, as seen through the eyes of a primarily agricultural people who have lived in a state of close ecological dependence on that environment for the past six to eight hundred years.[3] And with this introduction, we may turn to the twelve phratry groupings which comprise Hopi society and in which, as I hope to show, their view of the natural world is embodied.

### PHRATRY I. BEAR–SPIDER

| | | |
|---|---|---|
| *hon'au*, bear | *ko'kyañ*, black spider | |
| *püikü'sh*, hide-strap | *mü'yi*, gopher | *toko'chi*, wild cat |
| *wi'qösi*, fat of the eye | *tço'ro*, bluebird | |

*Myth:* Wanderings of the Spider people (2nd Mesa: Voth, 1905c, pp. 39–41).

So the people travelled on. All at once one party came upon a bear that had died. They were called the Bear (*hon'au*) clan. Right after them came another party, who cut straps from the skin of the bear and were called *püikü'sh* clan, the name given by the Hopi to this particular strap. Another party followed and found the cadaver covered

---

[1] Dean (1967), pp. 674–7. Dean puts the maximum population of the thirteen dated sites in Tsegi Canyon, around 1275 A.D., at about 700 persons.

[2] Dean (1967, pp. 139–51) produces convincing evidence, based on tree-ring dating of individual rooms at Betatakin and Kiet Seel, that the basic unit in the Tsegi Canyon villages was the 'room cluster' consisting of one, or more, living rooms each with its own storage chambers, opening on to a courtyard; this grouping of rooms around a courtyard almost certainly represents a multi-family household, engaged in co-operative economic activities; and Dean suggests (pp. 151–2), by analogy with Hopi social organisation, that these multi-family households were based on matrilineal descent and a rule of matrilocal residence. Certainly, the examples he cites (e.g. pp. 272–3), of the 'budding' of new rooms on to existing clusters, are highly suggestive of Hopi practice.

[3] This is what Mauss, referring to the Eskimoes, calls (1968, pp. 437–8) the 'mental volume' of a community, as distinct from its geographical volume:

Le *volume géographique*, c'est l'étendue spatiale réellement occupée par la société considereé; le *volume mental*, c'est l'aire géographique qu'elle parvient à embrasser par la pensée.

with spider web, from which they were called Spider (*ko'kyañ*) clan. A fourth party found blue-birds sitting on the cadaver and they were called the Blue-bird (*cho'ro*) clan. A fifth party found that maggots had eaten out the eyes, leaving the cavities bare with a little fat attached to the bone; from this they were called Fat Cavity clan (*wi'qös-nyamü*). A sixth migrating party came upon the scene and found that a mole had dug his way up under the place where the cadaver had been lying, and hence they were called Mole (*mü'yi*) clan.

(for alternate version of myth, see Nequatewa, 1936, pp. 30–4)

*Natural observation, and ceremonial referents*

*hon'au*, bear. This is the black bear (*Ursus americanus*), still fairly common in Mesa Verde National Park (Douglas, 1961, p. 59), a rare visitor to the Navajo Mountain and Tsegi Cañon region (Navajo informant), and still occasionally found in the general area of the San Francisco Peaks (Lincoln, 1961, p. 49). Eighty years ago, bears were 'quite numerous' in Navajo country (Stephen, 1893, p. 357).

Regarding their habits, Hallowell observes (1926, pp. 31–3) that bears do not usually den until after the first fall of snow; they invariably den singly, and emerge in early spring when snow is still lying on the ground. Regarding Hopi views on the bear, Eggan writes (1950, p. 82): 'The bear is considered a strong animal, with powerful 'medicine'; in aboriginal times he was the only animal that the Hopi could not handle. Since he hibernates in winter, he is associated with seasonal changes.'

*püikü'sh*, hide-strap or carrying strap. This was originally made from bear skin, and was used for carrying loads; the loads were carried on the back, usually in deep baskets, and were held in place by a strap running around the forehead. The principal loads carried in this way were the corn harvest and firewood, corn in late September and October, firewood in November and early December.

*wi'qösi*, fat of the eye. *wi*- is the general Shoshoni root for 'fat'; fat (*wi'hü*), and salt (*ö'ñga*), were the two items of food abstained from by participants in all major Hopi ceremonies. Beyond that, the significance of this clan name remains obscure.

*ko'kyañ*, black spider. It seems likely, from its habit (referred to in the myth) of weaving its web out-of-doors in the open that the spider in question belongs to the *Epeiridae* family of Arachnids (? *Epeira umbricata*); these spiders are active from the spring through to the fall, retiring in winter to crevices in the rock and other hiding places.

Spider woman, *ko'kyañ wu'hti*, is *wuya* (ancient) to this phratry. She is a powerful deity, on the whole well disposed towards the Hopi (Nequatewa, 1936, p. 104, n. 7); she helped them at the time of the Emergence (Stephen, 1929, pp. 5–6), and subsequently on their wanderings; in one version (Cushing, 1923, pp. 165–6), she span a mantle of pure white cotton which became the moon, and Eggan says (1950, p. 82) that she taught the Hopi how to spin and weave. However, she is a deity to be careful of: as one version of the Snake myth puts it (Stephen, 1940*b*, p. 3), 'She has a good breath, bad breath, and a breath. She can cause good or evil to happen, or she can remain passive. She knows everybody in the world. . . .'

Titiev's statement (1942, p. 549) that Spider woman was the first witch is a calumny, based on a recent version of the Emergence myth slanted so as to discredit Spider clan of which she is the particular *wuya* (see further, on this point, Goldfrank, 1948, especially pp. 249–52). In all other versions (e.g. Voth, 1905*c*, pp. 10–11, 19–20: Cushing, 1923, pp. 166–8), the first witch on earth was an un-named girl who slipped out of the *si'papü* at the time of the Emergence; from her all later witches are descended, and to her all the misfortunes which befall the Hopi can ultimately be traced.

What the precise significance of spider was to the Hopi, is hard to determine. There are two possible lines of enquiry:

(*a*) Cushing suggests (1892, pp. 313–14) that, at least among the Zuñi, spider was associated with *hunting*, and that its chief power was that of snaring invisibly, a power symbolised in the Zuñi spider knot (ibid. p. 302, Figure 30); this was tied in yucca fibre and laid on a game trail, to 'ensnare the heart of the game'. Yucca-fibre nets, designed for catching deer and antelope, are commonly found in pueblo ruins of the twelfth to the thirteenth century A.D. (museum collections at Mesa Verde and Aztec). Made from the bark of mountain dogbane (Steward, 1938, p. 312), such nets are also found widely among the Great Basin Shoshoni; among the Gosiute, to the south of the Great Salt Lake, the same word (*wana*) is used both for a game-trap of this kind and for spider's web (Reagan, 1935*a*, p. 37). The suggestion put forward here receives support from an unexpected source. In a cabinet displaying *Ritual Objects from the Southwest* in the Field Museum of Natural History at Chicago, item no. 260985, a miniature string trap about $4\frac{1}{2}$ inches across, is an almost exact replica of the large fibre traps of the Anasazi period on show in the museums at Aztec and Mesa Verde; it is ascribed 'Prayer offering representing Spider goddess', and dated to about 300 A.D.

Since life is represented, in Hopi animal-drawings, by a 'breath-line' running from the heart to the mouth, the association between spider and hunting perhaps explains why the Hopi offer prayers to Spider woman for long life, i.e. she has the power to give and to take away life.

(*b*) There is certainly some association of ideas between *spider, cotton weaving, clouds,* and *dew.* Cotton was widely grown in the San Juan basin in the Anasazi period (ninth to thirteenth century A.D.)[1], and woven cotton fabrics of high quality are found in the ruins of that period. 'When you plant cotton', said Wallis's 2nd Mesa informant, speaking in 1912 (Wallis and Titiev, 1944, p. 542), 'you should tell Spider: "I wish this cotton to grow".' The cotton

---

[1] For example, on the low canyon floors (elevation, 4,000 feet) draining into Glen Canyon and the lower San Juan river: Lipe (1970), pp. 92–3.

mask laid over the face of the dead is known as a 'white-cloud mask' (above, p. 42); and Spider woman is believed, according to some reports (e.g. James, 1903, p. 108), to weave the clouds which in turn bring the rain. Finally, the old Antelope chief at Walpi explained the purpose of his ceremony to Stephen (1940b, p. 21) in these words:

> We sing to our ancestors . . ., we petition them to ask Cloud to send rain, that we may have water to drink; that the clouds may lie upon the mountains and cause the grass to grow and game to be abundant; to send rain upon our cornfields and gardens that we may have food in plenty; to send rain upon the valleys and cover them with grass, that our flocks may increase.
>
> On the seventh day, before the dance, I prepare my *pa'ho*(s) and breath-feathers . . . Preparing myself to receive that which they [the deities to whom the prayer-offerings are addressed] have to give, I ask that the answer to our petitions be brought on the clouds; that *the element which is contained in the spider* may be a beautifier to our possessions.

If we take 'our possessions' to refer to the corn and other crops growing in the fields, then it appears to be the dew hanging on the spider's web which has caught the eye of the Hopi observer.[1]

These diverse attributes of spider or of the deity Spider Woman, *ko'kyañ wu'hti*, evidently characterise her, in Lévi-Strauss's terms (1958, pp. 248–50), as a mediator between opposites—*'maîtresse de la rosée et des animaux sauvages, associée à la nielle,*[2] *détentrice de vêtements . . .'*

*mü'yi*, gopher. This animal has been variously identified as field mouse, as 'a corn-eating burrowing animal smaller than the rat' (Lowie, 1929, p. 333), as 'little animals who use hair or wool for their nests or burrows' (Voth, 1905c, p. 37), as mole, and as gopher (Nequatewa, 1936, p. 32: and my own 3rd Mesa informants). The word (*mü'yi*) is common to all the Great Basin Shoshoni languages, in addition to Hopi.

Beaglehole, discussing Hopi observation of nature, writes (1937, pp. 34–5):

> Observation of sun, moon, animal and bird life is used to predict seasonal and weather change. . . . The return of birds and small winter hibernating game to the fields shows that summer is coming.

*tço'ro*, mountain bluebird. As we have seen (above, pp. 94-5), the arrival of bluebird in the fall signals the approach of cold weather, and their return in the spring, the approach of warm weather. The first bluebirds I saw, in the fall

---

[1] This would also furnish an ecological link between Spider woman and snakes (see below, p. 232). Snakes, like most other animals, lose moisture by evaporation through the skin; to replace it, they are able to collect dew with their tongues from the leaves of plants (L. Appleby, 'The Sun-worship of the Adder', in *Country Life*, vol. cxliii, for 21 March, 1968, pp. 693–4).

[2] Corn smut, *na'naha*, is used as a body decoration, particularly in the course of the Snake-Antelope ceremony, as a chromatic prayer for rain (Stephen, 1936, p. 708): because, when rain is plentiful, corn smut abounds in the corn. In the absence of corn smut, soot is used instead (ibid. p. 412).

of 1970, were two flocks (of four, and nine birds, respectively) on the mesa top near Old Oraibi on October 14th; on 4 March, 1892, Stephen observed 'two or three flocks' of bluebird in greasewood on the main valley floor east of 1st Mesa, and remarked (1936, pp. 348–9) that this was unusually early for them.

Regarding both *mü'yi* and *tço'ro*, I have no doubt that these are two of the birds and small winter hibernating game referred to by Beaglehole, the return of which to the fields 'shows that summer is coming'.

The common thread running through these four sets of animal observations is evidently that of *seasonal change*: in particular, of retirement into—and emergence from—hibernation in the case of bear, spider and gopher, and of arrival of fall—and return of spring—migrants in the case of bluebird.[1]

### Actual ceremonial duties

In the Oraibi version of the Emergence myth (above, pp. 209–10), Bear clan brought the Soya'l, and Spider clan the Blue Flute ceremony. And in fact, at Oraibi (i.e. before the split of 1906), the Soya'l has remained in the hands of Bear clan, and the Blue Flute in the hands of Spider.

Now there is a wealth of evidence for a strong conceptual tie between the Soya'l and the Flute observances, and this tie centres on the theme of *seasonal change*. One of the principal elements in the Soya'l, symbolised in the dance of Star man on the last night of the ceremony (see above, pp. 129–30), is *to induce the Sun to turn from his winter 'house'*, so as to warm the fields for cultivation; and an analogous motif runs through the various ceremonies conducted by the two Flute fraternities. These two fraternities are the Blue Flutes and the Gray Flutes, the one controlled (at Oraibi) by Spider clan and wearing 'sun shields', the other controlled by Pa'tki clan and wearing 'moisture tablets'.[2] Early in the new moon following the conclusion of the Soya'l (i.e. in *pa' mü'iyawu*, the January moon), the two fraternities hold a special session, known as *ta'wa paho'lauwû*, 'sun prayer-stick making', in the course of which *pa'ho*(s) are made for the sun and later deposited at a shrine to the southeast of the village, located in the direction of the sun's mid-winter rising point. At Powa'lauwû, the initial prayer-stick making of the Powa'mu ceremony held early in the February moon, one of the songs sung, known as *natwa'n ta'wi*, 'planting song', runs as follows:

> . . . *ü'yühi yuyaha*, the plants are being clothed,
> *tahawaha wiki'müyiwa*, the sun he is bringing,
> *tahawaha wuni'müyiwa*, the sun he is watching. . . .

---

[1] Cf. on the swallow as the bringer of spring and summer in European folk-lore, Halliday (1933), pp. 85–6. Halliday observes, later (ibid. p. 92, n. 7), that the belief that swallows hibernate is due to a misunderstanding of the facts of migration; it is possible, though I think not very likely, that a similar misunderstanding on the part of the Hopi led to the inclusion of *tço'ro* in this phratry grouping. Hopi are aware that some poor-wills *do* hibernate.

[2] Titiev (1944), p. 146, n. 26.

In the latter two lines, according to Voth (Dorsey and Voth, 1901, p. 151, n. 4), reference is made to the watching of the Sun and the influencing of his return by the [Flute] 'priests'. It is said that especially the Flute priests are here meant 'because from January, when the Flute priests make *pa'ho*(s) especially to the sun, until the summer solstice, when they do so again, it is their business to see that the sun receives his prayer offerings; while from the summer to the winter solstice the sun is under the "care" of the Soya'l priest, who also controls the Soya'l ceremony by which the sun is supposed to be induced to return from his southward course.'

A few days before the summer solstice, a further set of prayer-sticks is made for the Sun and deposited at his summer 'house', to the northeast of the village; by this ceremony, writes Parsons (1925, p. 95, n. 147), 'the Sun is turned back towards winter'. The major observances of the two Flute fraternities are held in August, in alternate years, and are primarily (as I have argued above, pp. 186–7) for rain to replenish the village springs. But Titiev holds (1944, p. 146, n. 35, and p. 149) that these rites also complement the Soya'l:

> Both groups, [he writes, referring to the Soya'l and Flute fraternities], are deeply concerned with the sun's progress. . . . If the Soya'l is supposed to start the sun on its journey from its winter to its summer home, it is the Flute performance [i.e. the main rites in August] that sends it on the return trip from its summer to its winter home.

Now, bluebird feathers figure in the prayer-sticks made during the Flute ceremony, and locust is represented prominently (Stephen, 1936, pl. xxii, p. 796) seated on clouds beside a reed, playing on his flute. In the Emergence myth (Stephen, 1929, pp. 5–6), locust (*ma'hü*) climbed the stalk of the reed out of the underworld, and was the first to emerge through the opening: 'locust carried a flute, slung on his back, he drew it out and began to play upon it . . .'.

> Flute performances, [writes Titiev (1944, p. 149)], are invariably associated with warm weather, for the Hopi believe that the flutes represent the sounds of locusts, who are regarded as harbingers of summer.[1]

Returning to natural observation: locust is important, according to Eggan (1950, p. 341, n. 90), because he comes out of the ground at a definite time. And Beaglehole writes (1937, p. 35): 'To hear many cicadas (*ma'hü*) singing in the trees means a hot summer and little rain.' Whether, then, the *ma'hü* of Hopi myth and ceremony is in fact locust or cicada, there can be no doubt that he is closely associated in Hopi thinking with the long, hot summer.

One further point may be noted here. It is the Spider-Bluebird fraction that is primarily responsible, conceptually, in myth, and in ceremonial practice, for the *seasonal change* and *return of hot weather* theme that lies at the heart of this

---

[1] On the link between locusts and warm weather, and between their song and flutes, see further, Voth (1905*c*), pp. 217–20. Locust is also associated with the melting of the snow in the spring: Parsons (1939), p. 192, n. 2.

phratry grouping. The Bear fraction is associated with it at Soya'l and Powa'mu; but, as the Hopi say, 'everything branches out from the Soya'l'. What they mean by this, we shall see as we go along; the essential point is that *seasonal change* is only one element in Bear's associations.

### Association of ideas

The ideas associated with this phratry grouping run, I suggest, along the following lines:

. . . Bear hibernates—spider, emerges from crevices in the spring—*mü'yi*, likewise—change of season—sun 'returns from his house'—bluebird, harbinger of summer—weather gets hotter—chirping of locusts, or cicadas—summer solstice—Flute ceremony—sun turns again—bluebird, harbinger of winter—carrying in crops and firewood . . .

### Anomalies, and comments

*toko'chi*, wild cat. This is the bobcat (*Lynx rufus*), still fairly common in the Hopi region to-day. Stephen (1936, p. 390, n. 1) notes the bobcat as raiding sheep pens; and Anderson reports (1961, p. 62) that, in Mesa Verde National Park, mountain lions, coyote and bobcat are the three principal predators of porcupine.

In the Hopi directional system, bear and bobcat are two of the six prey animals, 'pets' of Pyü'ükoñ-hoya (Stephen, 1936, p. 307, n. 1), associated with war. To the significance of this observation, I shall return later (below, p. 269).

At this point I must introduce the reader to the major difficulty that faces us in attempting to work out the Hopi view of nature, namely that of *double reference*: the fact, that is to say, that a single plant or animal (or object of material culture) may stand for more than one set of ideas, each corresponding to a different level of Hopi cultural development. When I first approached the Hopi thought-world, I did so with the idea that the Hopi were, first and foremost, a corn-squash-and-bean-growing people, who incidentally practised some hunting, chiefly of rabbits, and some gathering of seeds and roots. I expected to find the primacy of agriculture reflected in their world-view, as indeed it is at many points, and with this notion in mind, the chapter was first drafted. Gradually, however, under the influence of the material presented here, my own thinking changed, and I came to regard the Hopi, both in point of historical development and in the image which they hold of themselves in relation to their environment (in so far as that image can be inferred from the evidence furnished by their clan names), primarily as a hunting-and-gathering people who incidentally practise some agriculture. In short, I came to realise the truth of Mauss's remark—'*L'agriculture, c'est un cas de l'ethnobotanique*'—as applied to the Hopi. This change in attitude was completed when I found how closely many aspects of the hunting-and-gathering side of Hopi life, as reflected in the grouping of clan names, are foreshadowed in the culture of the Great

H

Basin Shoshoneans. To illustrate this dichotomy, I take the case of bear, since it was in relation to bear and its place in Hopi thinking that I first became aware of the problem.

There is no doubt that bear (*hon'au*) has, or once had, vital associations for the Hopi, both with the return of spring and with war. The association of bear with *war* has been specifically noted on 1st Mesa: there, according to Parsons (Hallowell, 1926, p. 77),

> it was customary after killing a bear, to treat the animal like a dead human enemy, the slayer of the bear being called war chief (*kahletaka*) for the time being. Beads were strung around the dead bear's paws and there was formerly a war dance. Eaters of bear meat had to paint their faces black.

The holding by the Hopi of a war dance to mark the killing of a bear, calls to mind the Bear Dance itself, practised at one time by all the Shoshonean-speaking tribes of the eastern half of the Basin-Plateau area, and peculiar to them. Steward, who observed the remnants of the dance among the Uintah Mountain Utes in 1931, wrote (1932, pp. 263–4):

> The Bear Dance was, in the past, a spring festival that preceded the breaking of winter camps and migrations in search of food and game. In the old days, small bands of Ute, probably numbering 50 to 100, took up winter quarters in the coniferous forest of the foothills along the southern slope of the Uintah mountains. Early in spring, probably about February, came the dance as a signal to break camp and move about in the pursuit of game.

The Uintah Ute myth, of the origin of the Bear Dance (Mason, 1910, p. 363), specifically links the Bear Dance with the melting of the snow and the emergence of bear from his winter hibernation. And Reed, who observed the Bear Dance some forty-five years before Steward in southern Colorado, remarked (1896, pp. 238–41) that it had as its main purpose to assist the bears to recover from hibernation and to find food; the drumming that accompanies the dance, he wrote, is intended to simulate the thunder in the mountains, 'which, it is believed, wakes the bears from their long winter sleep'.

Now let us consider some linguistic evidence. An analysis of the Shoshonean words for *bear* discloses three distinct 'bear' territories in the Basin-Plateau region:

(*a*) The central and northwestern area, embracing the main body of the Western Shoshoni and the central and northern groups of the Northern Paiute, where the common word for bear is *wüda*,[1] and the word for grizzly, also applied to shamans who were able to transform themselves into bears (Steward, 1938, p. 278, n. 3), *padoa*.

---

[1] Also given as *tokawidja*: I take it that -*widja* is a local form of *wüda*, and *toka*- an ellision of *tu'kwa*, the common Shoshonean stem for black.

(*b*) The southeastern area, embracing the Pahvant and Uintah Mountain Utes and the Southern Paiute of Kaibab plateau, where the word for bear, including the grizzly impersonated in the Bear Dance, is *kwi'yan* (or *qwiya'ts*).

(*c*) The southwestern area, embracing the Northern Paiute of Owens Valley, the Western Shoshoni adjoining Owens Valley and the western group of Southern Paiute, where the ordinary word for bear is *pa'havits*.[1] In the southern half of the Owens Valley, however, *pa'havits* is replaced by *unu'ᵘ* (Steward, 1938, p. 274, n. 1). Discussing shamanism among the Northern Paiute of Owens Valley, Steward writes (1933, p. 309):

> Some 'doctors' [i.e. shamans] got power from the bear. . . . They could transform themselves into bears.

And adds the footnote (*ibid.* p. 309, n. 180: cf. p. 253):

> Ordinary bears were called *pahavitci*; transformed doctors were called *ünü*.

*Unu'ᵘ* (or *ünü*) appears then to be the analogue, among the Northern Paiute of the southern half of Owens Valley, to *padoa* (or *baduo*) among the Northern Paiute farther to the north and among the main body of the Western Shoshoni; like *padoa*, it refers both to the bear and to the shaman who derives 'power' from, and is transformed into, the bear; like *padoa*, also, the word may refer specifically to the grizzly, the grizzly being especially feared by the Owens Valley Paiute and credited by them with supernatural power (Steward, 1934, p. 431, n. 27). And this is where the Hopi come in, for *unu'ᵘ* is the only 'bear' root in the other Shoshonean languages corresponding to the Hopi word for bear, *hon'au* (or *hu'ni*); and the association of the latter, in the remote past, with Great Basin shamanism furnishes, we may suppose, the original source of the spiritual authority of the Hopi *ki'k moñwi*.[2]

The rôle attributed to bear in Hopi thinking appears, then, to arise from a layer of associations widespread among the Shoshonean-speaking peoples of the Basin-Plateau area. This suggests that the Hopi Powa'mu, in which Bear clan leader plays a prominent part, may be the analogue to the Bear Dance, a suggestion that finds support in Eggan's observation (1968) that *powa'* is the general word for 'ceremonial power' among the tribes to the north,[3] and in his further observation that, among the Hopi, badger (*hona'ni*) may well have replaced bear (*hon'au*) as the main curing animal. This, in turn, would explain why the head of Bear clan, as keeper of the *hon wöye* or Bear mask (Parsons,

---

[1] Among the Southern Paiute (Ash Meadows), the word is *papau'h*: I take this to be a reduplicated form of *pa'ha-*, the stem of *pa'havits*, *-its* (or *-vits*) being the classifying suffix for animate nouns in Shoshonean. The same word, transcribed *par-pow*, is also found among some of the Utah Shoshoni (Reagan, 1935*a*, p. 30).

[2] On the transformation undergone by shamanism in the course of being *pueblo-ised*, see Benedict (1928), pp. 577–8: cf. Parsons (1939), p. 63.

[3] Cf. among the Southern Paiute, Sapir (1931), p. 622: under *poa*, or *pu(w)a*, supernatural power.

1933, pp. 36–7, and n. 147), is traditionally *ki'k moñwi* of the Hopi village: since on him, we may suppose, fell the duty of impersonating Bear when he 'emerged' on the ninth morning of the Bear Dance.[1]

PHRATRY VII. BADGER–BUTTERFLY

*hona'ni*, badger
*ña'hü*, medicine root          *mü'iñyauwû*, porcupine
*po'li*, butterfly             *wi'soko*, turkey vulture

*Myth*: Wanderings of the Badger people, *honan' nyamü* (1st Mesa: Parsons, 1933, p. 27).

> After they came up, they found a man at work digging. 'What are you doing, our uncle?', they said to him. 'My brothers and nephews and my sisters, where are you going?'—'We are going to a place called Si-tü'kwi ['flower mountain': 1st Mesa, or Walpi], to make our home there.'—'Is that where you are going? well, you are my relatives.'—'What kind of a man are you?'—'I am a Badger. I am like a person, but when I put on my skin I go around like a badger. Well, my nephews and brothers, I had better go with you.' As they went, they found a butterfly [*po'li*]. . . . As they travelled on, a child became sick. They asked Badger, 'What can we do to help the child?' He began to dig weeds [*ña'hü*, roots dug by the badger] for medicine. He gave the medicine to the child to cure it. . . .

In another myth (1st Mesa: Stephen, 1936, p. 860, n. 1):

> . . . Badger (*hona'ni*) came up in the centre of the field, from the Below (*at'kyaa*), carrying a bundle on his back which contained all medicines (*ña'hü*), and in his left hand he carried wing feathers of the buzzard (*wi'shoko pü'hü masha'adta*). He said, 'I know all medicinal charms, and I have the feather for *navo'chiwa*, to drive away all bodily ills . . .'—'An'chai [thanks],' they all said, 'now we shall change into Badger clan people (*hona'ni nyamü*) and you shall be chief.'

*Natural observation, and ceremonial referents*

*hona'ni*, badger (*Taxidea taxus*). Badger is fairly common in the region of the Hopi villages, digging his burrows in dunes on the main valley floor and in tamarisk thickets on the floor of the main wash. Sometimes he raids the corn-fields and, if his depredations become too severe, is trapped by the Hopi farmer. He likes meat, too, and will dig out e.g. a cottontail, if he sees one go down a hole. He is quite a good hunter, Hopi say.

Regarding the Hopi view of this animal: 'The badger', writes Eggan (1950, p. 84), 'is the medicine animal *par excellence*, and through his digging ability controls all roots; through the latter control he is also responsible for the early growth of wild plants.' He is also the animal especially associated with the Below (*at'kyaa*), as the myth relates.

---

[1] It may be noted, too, that among the Deep Creek Gosiute, who performed the circle dance as part of their spring festival, the dance was directed by the valley chief, called *Unu'*. And the circle dance, in Steward's view (1938, p. 139) a borrowed form of the bear dance, was 'to make seeds grow'.

*ña'hü*, medicine root. The particular roots identified (Stephen, 1936, pp. 711, 1220) are *hohoi'yaña*, bladder-pod (*Lesquerella intermedia*), *momo'ña*, 'bee root' (? an *Astragalus*), *hü'yaña*, a plant with a yellow flower and finely divided leaves (*Hymenopappus lugens*), and *hon'ña-pi*, 'bear root' or white aster (*Aster leucolene*).

*po'li* or *po'voli*, butterfly. Fewkes observes (1910, p. 583) that there are two Hopi words for butterfly (or moth), *hoko'na* and *po'li*; of these, *hoko'na* is applied to any large butterfly, and *po'li* to any small one.

Regarding their significance: 'Bees and butterflies are the "pets" (*po'komatü*) of Mü'iyiñwa, knowing when melons, squash, flowers, all vegetation is to be plenty, and coming in great numbers to eat the pollen. When vegetation is to be scant, they do not come. They and wasps (*tañai'ya*) eat pollen only.' (Stephen, 1936, p. 1252).

There is also an association (ibid. p. 684) between butterflies, particularly *hoko'na*, and rain.

The link between butterflies and Mü'iyiñwa is important, because Mü'iyiñwa is *wuya* to the Badger people. He is the deity associated with the Below, and controls the germination and growth of plants. In the Emergence mythology (Stephen, 1929, pp. 8–10: Wallis, 1936, p. 10), Mü'iyiñwa is especially linked with corn, water-melons and other vegetables, of which he gave the seeds to the Hopi.

*mü'iñyauwû*, porcupine (*Erethizon dorsatum*). Porcupines are certainly to be found on the mesas around the Hopi villages, as dogs return from time to time with porcupine quills stuck in their faces. They evidently feed on young piñon trees: Anderson (1961), pp. 55–7.

Their quills were traditionally used for katçina anklets: Stephen (1936), p. 1254.

*wi'soko*, turkey vulture (*Cathartes aura*). This magnificent bird is to be seen soaring over the cliffs and valley floor near the Hopi villages, either singly or in two's or three's, at any time from mid April to late in September. Vultures, like crows, are scavengers (*charognard*); both, therefore, in Lévi-Straussian terms (1958, pp. 249–50), are *mediatory*.

Vulture wing feathers, sometimes called 'buzzard' feathers, are used in the rite of exorcising (*navo'chiwa*) at the end of a ceremony, commonly in association with ashes, another intermediary substance.

### Actual ceremonial duties

On 3rd Mesa Badger clan controls the Powa'mu ceremony, the primary purpose of which, as we have seen (above, pp. 89–90), is to promote the germination and growth of the crops that are to be planted a few weeks later. In this control Katçina clan is closely associated with Badger, katçina initiation—as Eggan remarks (1950, p. 342, n. 96)—being concerned in part with ceremonial knowledge relating to the growth of plants; and on all three mesas both fraternities, Powa'mu and Katçina, are in the hands of either Badger, Katçina or Parrot clans.

Badger clan's control of Powa'mu clearly reflects the dominant strand in the underlying ideas linking this phratry grouping, namely a line of thought running from germination, through the early growth of corn and other crops, to butterflies, pollen and rain. As to the Hopi notion how the desired effect is mediated, we may recall the first line of the planting song sung at Powa'lauwu:

> . . . *ii'yühi yuyaha*, the plants are being clothed . . .;

the idea, according to Voth (Dorsey and Voth, 1901, p. 151, n. 3), is that the seeds and plants are being 'clothed' or dressed in the ground, probably with moisture and the power of germination, so that they can grow. 'When asked by whom, informants said that they did not know, but thought by Mü'iyiñwa, the God of Germination, who is supposed to live *atyaka* (below). The husks on a corn ear are called its clothes, and the putting on of feathers and herbs on a *pa'ho* is called 'clothing' or dressing it, and of clouds it is said that they are clothed with *balaye* (rain water).'

Apart from control of Powa'mu, Badger clan has two other important ritual functions. Since the Badger people understand medicines, one of their senior men should prepare the medicine water (*ña-kü'yi*) for all major ceremonies, e.g. Soya'l, Flute, Snake-Antelope, Marau' (Voth, 1905c, p. 29: cf. Parsons, 1933, p. 28, n. 110), and act as asperser during the rites (Parsons, 1925, p. 100); and for the same reason, when the ceremony is over, the rite by which those who have taken part in it are 'discharmed', should be performed by a member of Badger clan (Nequatewa, 1936, p. 112, n. 67). This aspect of Badger clan's ceremonial duties reflects the subsidiary strand in the ideas linking the phratry grouping: namely, the line of thought running from badger's digging activity, through medicine roots and the use of buzzard feathers, to curing.

### Association of ideas

The conceptual linkage represented by this phratry grouping we may, then, summarise as follows:

. . . badger digs—herbs and roots, for curing—*atky'a*, the below—Mü'iyiñwa—corn and vegetation—germination—growth and ripening—flower pollen—bees, butterflies and wasps—rain—katçina dances—porcupine-quill rattles—exorcising rite . . .

### Anomalies, and comments

Fewkes (1900b, pp. 582–4) lists Katçina clan both under Katçina-Parrot phratry, and under Badger; this simply illustrates the close conceptual and ceremonial link between the two groupings, noted independently by Stephen (1936, p. 1072, n. 4).

At Mishong'novi, the Tobacco-Rabbit people 'go in' with Badger; on 3rd Mesa, they 'go in' with Katçina-Parrot. To this point I shall return, when we come to discuss that phratry grouping.

## PHRATRY II. KATÇINA–PARROT

*katçina*, katçina

| | |
|---|---|
| *ky'aro*, parrot, macaw | *söhö'vi*, cottonwood |
| *añwü'si*, crow, raven | *qaha'vi*, willow |
| *hek'pa*, spruce, fir | *sikya'tsi*, yellow bird, warbler |
| *sala'vi*, Douglas fir | *ta'wa ma'na*, 'sun maiden', oriole |

*Myth.* The myth of the Wanderings of the Katçina people (1st Mesa: Parsons, 1933, p. 34) tells how, after the Emergence, the people came to a big lake (*patü'bha*): there they met one of the katçinas, living under the water; later they found a parrot (*ka'ro*), he could speak their language; he said that he was their uncle and was waiting for them: 'If you take me with you, you may use my feathers on your head when you dance.'

Another myth (1st Mesa: Parsons, 1933, p. 35) tells how the Cottonwood people (*sühüp' nyamü*) found a crow (*awü'shi*) sitting, and later met a katçina, who became their guide.

And a third myth (2nd Mesa: Nequatewa, 1936, pp. 79–83) links Crow clan with the katçinas living on the San Francisco Mountains.

### Natural observation, and ceremonial referents

*ky'aro*, parrot, macaw. The Hopi word refers either to the Thick-billed Parrot (*Rhynchopsitta pachyrhyncha*), to the Red-blue-and-yellow Macaw (*Ara macao*), or to both. Neither bird is found in the region of the Hopi villages to-day, but far to the south. However, bones of four thick-billed Parrots were found in the ruins of the twelfth to thirteenth century pueblo at Wupa'tki, leading Hargrave to the conclusion (1939, p. 208) that *Rhynchopsitta* 'may or may not at one time [i.e. prior to 1250 A.D.] have been indigenous to the pine forests of San Francisco Mountain', the archaeological evidence being insufficient to establish whether the bird was ever native as far north as that. The bones of the single Macaw (*Ara macao*) found at Wupa'tki, he attributes definitely to trade.

In the old days, *ky'aro* feathers were highly valued, and were got by barter from the settlements on the Gila river and from Sonora (Fewkes, 1900c, p. 692: cf. Beaglehole, 1937, p. 85). Ceremonially, *ky'aro* is the bird associated with the south-east; and it may be that its feathers, like the fringe of red horse-hair tied to the Flute *na'atsi* (Fewkes, 1892a, p. 111), symbolise 'the warm rains of the south', which sweep up from the Gulf of Mexico during July and August. As the myth indicates, the feathers form an integral part of katçina costume.

*añwü'si*, crow, raven. These birds, ravens in particular, are common permanent residents of the Hopi region, and according to Eggan (1950, p. 83, and p. 342,

n. 93), are associated with storm clouds, 'since they come in flocks an hour or two before a storm'. Lévi-Strauss, however, points out (1962*b*, p. 76):

> Les Indiens du sud-ouest des États-Unis, qui vivent de l'agriculture, considèrent le courbeau surtout comme un pilleur de jardins. . . .

This is certainly my impression. Ravens will strip a corn field, given the chance, and are especially mischievous at pecking holes in ripening watermelons. Bourke (1884, p. 98), Fisher (1903, p. 35) and Wallis (Wallis and Titiev, 1944, p. 527), all pay reluctant tribute to their destructive powers.

*añwüs' katçina*, crow-wing katçina. While this phratry grouping is, as Eggan observes (1950, p. 83), in general charge of the katçinas, the close link established in the 2nd Mesa myth between crow (*añwü'si*) and the Katçina people indicates that the particular katçina with whom they have a special relation is *Añwüs' katçina*, 'Crow-wing katçina', and that she is *wuya* to the whole phratry. She acts as 'mother' of the katçinas during the katçina initiation. And this, in turn, is reflected in the purpose of the initiation: since, in the traditional Hopi economy, the two principal tasks of small boys were (*a*) to herd sheep and goats, and (*b*) *to keep the crows from the ripening corn* (Bourke, 1884, pp. 98, 233). The conceptual link thus established between crow and the katçinas extends to *double entendre*: 'the crows are wearing blue moccasins' meaning, to Hopi children, that the katçinas are coming to dance.[1]

*hek'pa*, spruce, fir. Found growing on the higher slopes of the San Francisco Mountains.

*sala'vi*, Douglas fir. Also found on the higher slopes of the San Francisco Mountains, occasionally in canyons at lower altitudes (e.g. in the canyon above Betatakin), and around the spring at Kisi'vu, some 40 miles northeast of the Hopi villages. Both kinds of spruce (or fir) are associated with the katçinas (Stephen, 1936, pp. 220, 324, 370, 439); also, according to Stephen (ibid. p. 395), the state of the branches gathered for katçina purposes in the spring foretell the summer weather: if the branches are glossy green, there will be good rains, but if the spruce is dull (*ma'si*), it is a bad sign.

*söhö'vi*, cottonwood. This tree, as also the willow (*qaha'vi*), is associated with springs and water, and so with the katçinas. A branch of cottonwood, brought from the spring at Bakabi, is placed on the Powa'mu altar (Voth, 1901, p. 108); according to Hopi tradition (Parsons, 1922*a*, p. 288, n. 13), the cottonwood growing at Bakabi was originally transplanted from the spring at Kisi'vu. Prayer-sticks for rain are made of cottonwood, as are the katçina dolls carved at Powa'mu.

*sikya'tsi*, yellow bird, warbler:
*ta'wa ma'na*, 'sun maiden', oriole.

---

[1] E. C. Parsons, in *Journal of American Folk-Lore*, vol. 49 (1936), p. 173.

The return of birds and small winter hibernating game to the fields shows that summer is coming. If a yellow bird (*sisü'kyadzim* = *sikya'tsi-m*) ... comes back when peach trees are in blossom, this forecasts a good summer. If the red-headed bird (*ta'wa ma'nau*) comes back early, this means that the sun flowers will blossom early too, and there will be much pasturage for the stock. When the black bird with red on its breast (*doko'dzka* = *toko'tska*) returns, it is time to plant corn.

Beaglehole (1937), pp. 34–5.

The name *sikya'tsi*, in Hopi, is applied to all warblers with more or less yellow on them, e.g. Yellow Warbler, Wilson's Warbler, Western Yellowthroat. The Orange-Crowned Warbler is called *ta'wa sikya'tsi*, 'sun *sikya'tsi*', indicating an orange or red element associated with the sun (as in the use of red horse hair around the sun disc: above, p. 129).

*ta'wa ma'na*, 'sun maiden', is commonly rendered oriole. But the *ta'wa* component in the name leads us to expect some red or orange in the bird, and this is confirmed by Beaglehole's designation of it as 'the red-headed bird'. The bird must be the Western Tanager (*Piranga ludoviciana*), the male of which—but not the female—has red head and throat in the breeding season, but not in September (when I saw many of the birds, feeding on olive 'cones' in the Oraibi wash). Both warblers and Western Tanagers are migrants, arriving in April–May and departing south in late September.

*toko'tska* is the Utah Red-winged Blackbird (*Agelaius phoenicius*); the red patch, only carried by the male, is on the shoulder, not the breast. Birds pass through the Hopi region, on their fall migration, early in October, and return early in May.

Ceremonially, both *sikya'tsi* and *ta'wa ma'na* are associated with the return of warm weather, as the use of their feathers in Powa'mu (above, pp. 68, 94) confirms. Further, in the course of the winter prayer-stick making of the Gray Flutes at Oraibi, late in January 1898, one of those taking part brought in a small ball of snow, about three inches in diameter, into which he thrust four oriole [*ta'wa ma'na*] feathers; he did this, he said (Voth, 1912*b*, p. 126), 'so that the snow should melt and make the fields wet'.

### Actual ceremonial duties

There is a close link, ceremonially, between the Katçina and Badger phratry groupings. On all three Mesas, the Katçina fraternity and Nima'n are in the hands either of the Katçina clan alone or of Katçina-Parrot; on 1st Mesa and at Mishong'novi, these clans control the Powa'mu ceremony, while at Oraibi Badger and Katçina clans jointly control the Powa'mu. On 1st Mesa, Badger and Katçina clans are traditionally linked (Stephen, 1936, p. 1072, n. 4). The ceremonial linkage between the two phratries, expressed (on 3rd Mesa) in joint control of the Powa'mu ceremony, reflects the conceptual linkage between them: where the Badger grouping is organised around the idea of seed germination and growth of the young plants, the Katçina grouping is organised around that of the rain needed to 'clothe' them with moisture. And this conceptual linkage is further reflected in myth: for Mü'iyiñwa, *wuya* of Badger clan, is regarded—at least on 1st Mesa (Stephen, 1936, pp. 1254–5)—as mother's brother to the katçinas, all of them.

Apart from control of the Katçina cult, the clans of this phratry grouping have other, major ceremonial functions. Thus, at Oraibi, Parrot clan furnishes one of the principal officers of the Soya'l (Titiev, 1944, p. 63), 'owns' the Lako'n ceremony, and controls the Singers' branch of Wü'wütçim. With regard to the first of these functions, it will be remembered that Bear clan, besides controlling the Soya'l, 'owns' the Eototo katçina, and the Eototo katçina, as the myth below recounts, 'has' the water and rain: further, that on the last morning of Powa'mu (see above, p. 85), Eototo—accompanied by the Aholi katçina—proceeds through the village, opening on his way the *pa'tni* (cistern) dug in his path by a member of Bow clan. In Eototo's opening of the cistern at Powa'mu, we may see an exchange for Parrot clan leader's part in the Soya'l: and in both, a further thread—a thread representing moisture, this time—in the strands branching out from the Soya'l.

### Association of ideas

Just as the ceremonial functions of the clans in the Katçina phratry grouping dovetail in with those of the Badger grouping, so the ideas associated with the Katçina grouping complement theirs:

... snow melts—return of yellow birds in the spring—warm weather— katçina dances—spruce—cottonwood—parrot feathers—(?) warm rain from the south: crows—katçina initiation—bird-scaring in the corn fields—Nima'n katçina ceremony—rain ...

### PHRATRY IX. PIKYAS–PA'TKI

| | | |
|---|---|---|
| *pa'tki*, water house | | *pikya's*, young sprouting |
| *pa'hü*, moisture | *pa'wikya*, wild duck | corn |
| *yo'ki*, rain | *pa'tsro*, water bird | *qa'ö*, corn, all kinds |
| *omau'wû*, cloud | *pa'kwa*, frog | *tüwa'kchi*, sweet corn |
| *nü'va*, snow | *pa'lülükoñ*, water snake | *siva'pi*, rabbit brush |

*Myth.* The myth of the Origin of the Bear clan (3rd Mesa: Voth, 1905c, pp. 28–30) links Bear clan and Pikya's closely together:

> The Bear clan were the first to arrive at Oraibi. Their chief, Matçito, had brought the Soya'l altar and cult with him. They also had with them the Eototo katçina; he 'has' (i.e. owns, controls) the water and rain. The Pikyas people, who joined the Bear people on their wanderings, had the Aholi katçina, and the screen (O'mauwû) now used in the Soya'l and the Corn ceremonies. Later the Spider people arrived, bringing the Blue Flute ceremony.
>
> The Pa'tki clan came from where the sun rises; they had with them the Gray Flute ceremony. They came to the village of Oraibi and arranged a contest at Muyi'ovat-ki where each planted corn, the Blue Flutes sweet corn, the others *wu'pa qö'o* ('tall corn'), over which they played all day [i.e. on their flutes]. The sweet corn grew first, and so the Blue Flutes to this day go to the village in procession, first closing the well (*pa'tni*) on the village square.[1]

[1] Moñya'ovi, where the corn-growing contest referred to in the myth took place, is a ruin,

The Mishong'novi myth of the Origin of the Clans (Voth, 1905c, pp. 47–8) records that the Pa'tki people brought with them mud, grass, and water in a *moñ'wikuru*, and put it into the spring [Toreva] to increase the flow of water. 'Before the Pa'tki people came, the corn was very small. They made it rain and so it grew large. The Pikyas clan brought better and larger corn with them.'

And another myth (Cushing, 1923, p. 168) relates how corn seed was given to the Corn people by the god of Dew [? Mü'iyiñwa].

### Natural observation, and ceremonial referents

The clan names of this phratry grouping fall into two well-defined classes, one to do with springs and natural precipitation (clouds, rain, snow), the other to do with corn and corn-growing. The names in the first group comprise:

*pa'tki*, water house. The word evidently refers (Eggan, 1950, p. 85) either to the clouds themselves as sources of water, or to the springs and cisterns (*patni*) upon which the Hopi were formerly dependent for their domestic water supply; melting snow fills the cisterns, in the spring.

*pa'hü*, moisture, water. The Hopi word refers to water as found in nature, as distinct from water in domestic use, *kü'yi*: Whorf (1956), p. 142, n. 4.

*omau'wû*, cloud. Hopi distinguish various different kinds of cloud, e.g. *wisi' o'mau*, high stringy cloud (cirrus), *mutsinho' o'mau*, fluffy cloud, non-rainy (cumulus), *toko' o'mau*, towering rain cloud (cumulo-nimbus), *hiyupau' o'mau*, the low cloud that accompanies heavy rain (nimbus).

*yo'i*, *yo'ki*, rain. A distinction is drawn between *sü'vwü yo'ki*, small drop rain, fine and gentle, regarded as female, and *wü'wükava*, great drop rain, regarded as male: Stephen (1929), p. 17.

*pa'wikya*, 'scoops the water', duck. The term is applied to all the ducks that migrate through the Hopi region in spring and fall, e.g. mallard, pintail, gadwall, cinnamon teal, shoveler.

*pa'tsro*, 'water bird'. The term refers, primarily, to long-legged shore birds, principally sandpipers and yellowlegs, which poke about at the water's edge, leaving their foot-prints in the mud. These are the birds referred to by Beaglehole (1937, pp. 34–5):

> Again, should the water bird with white markings on its wings (*ba'dyo* = *pa'tro* or *pa'tsro*) be seen in spring, this signifies a wet summer; should one hear these birds flying northward at night before the *niman katçina* dance, it will rain hard before the katçinas leave the village.

*pa'kwa*, frog: *pava'tiya*, tadpole. These, with *pa'wikya* (duck), *pa'tsro* (water bird), *pa'lülükoñ* (water snake) and *yüño'sona* (turtle), are regarded as 'pets' of Cloud (Stephen, 1936, p. 307); as such, they are associated with clouds and with rain.

---

sited on the mesa top to the east of the main wash; the farm land at the mesa foot, and the eagle-nesting cliffs above, traditionally belonged to Pikyas clan.

In the old days turtles were caught, in early summer, in a tributary of the Little Colorado river (Beaglehole, 1936, pp. 22–3); before anyone might take a shell, it had to be smoked over and prayers offered by Pa'tki clan chief (Parsons, 1933, p. 21); the shell was then carefully cut off, and the flesh returned to the stream. Turtle shells were used as dance rattles, attached to the right leg, at dances held during the Pa'lülükoñ-ti ceremony early in March (Stephen, 1936, p. 335), and at the Nima'n festival.

Conceptually, *pa'tüsaka*, the grasses that grow near water (Titiev, 1943*b*, p. 428, n. 10), are also linked to this group of clan names.

*pa'lülükoñ*, water snake, chief 'pet' of Cloud. This creature plays a major part in Hopi mythology and ceremonialism. 'Every spring and water hole', writes Titiev (1943*b*, p. 428, n. 9), 'is thought by the Hopi to harbour a *pa'lülükoñ*, a reptile ranging in size from a worm to a serpent, from which water is supposed to issue.' And *The Tale of the Stolen Spring* (ibid, pp. 425–30) recounts how a Shungo'povi man 'stole' one of the Oraibi springs by catching the *pa'lülükoñ* which lived in it and carrying him back to Shungo'povi in a bottle; a few months later, the Oraibi spring dried up. In another myth (Stephen, 1929, p. 55), *pa'lülükoñ* tells the Hopi where, and how, to dig for water.

In serpent form, two huge *pa'lülükoñ* inhabit the underground sea (*patü'bha*) upon which the world is floating, waiting to cause earthquakes and to turn the land over (Nequatewa, 1936, p. 103). It is these serpents that are represented in the Pa'lülükoñ-ti ceremony (below, pp. 229–30); and there can be no doubt, in the light of the dream material collected by Mrs. D. Eggan (1966, pp. 242–9), that the Water Serpent deity has entered deeply into the Hopi imagination.

The second group of clan names in this phratry centre around corn and corn-growing:

*pikya's*, young corn plant. The term refers to the plant when it is about knee-high, i.e. around the time of the *nima'n katçina* dance, when the ears are just beginning to form (Parsons, 1933, p. 30). Eggan (1950, p. 85) refers to it as the 'milk' stage in the ripening of corn.

*qa'ö*, corn. Refers particularly to the ears of corn when they are fully formed: Whorf (1936), p. 1229.

*tüwa'kchi*, sweet corn. Also known as *katçina* corn (Stephen, 1936, p. 1071), because it is planted especially early in order to ripen in time for the Nima'n dance.

*siva'pi*, rabbit brush. A yellow-flowering shrub, common on the fans of tributary watercourses; where it grows well, corn grows well, too. Branches of the shrub were also used, in the old days, for making wind-breaks to protect the young corn plants (above, p. 68: cf. Fewkes, 1892*a*, p. 152).

### Actual ceremonial duties

Conceptually, and ceremonially, two separate threads are interwoven in the Pa'tki—Pikya's grouping: a *cloud-and-rain* thread, represented by Pa'tki clan and its analogues, a *corn-growing* thread, represented by Pikyas, corn and

*siva'pi.* The latter thread is expressed, at greatest intensity, in the dance of
Pikyas clan chief around the screen of Mü'iyiñwa, on the eighth night of the
Soya'l; prior to that dance, it will be remembered (see above, pp. 127–8)
seeds of all kinds of corn, melons, squash and other vegatation have been
attached to the lower half of the screen below the feet of Mü'iyiñwa, while
behind the altar are stacked bundles of corn, collected from all the households
in the village—bundles which will subsequently be retrieved by the households which brought them, stored until the spring, and then mixed in with the
other seed corn for planting.[1] Now the main element embodied in the dance of
Pikyas clan chief and the Soya'l *ma'na* is, in Fewkes' view (1898b, p. 108), a
dramatisation of the fructification of the earth and *of imparting virility to the
seeds of corn*: in this way, he writes, 'the stack of corn on the altar is endowed
with a vitality which it otherwise would not have'. Here, then, in the imparting
of virility to the seed corn to be used in a few weeks' time, we have another of
the strands branching out from the Soya'l.

Regarding the *cloud-and-rain* thread represented by Pa'tki clan and its
analogues, this finds expression in part in the act by which, on the ninth morning
of Powa'mu, the Eototo and Aholi katçinas—the latter represented, at Oraibi,
by the head of either Pikyas or Pa'tki clan—open the main cistern of the
village (Titiev, 1944, pp. 62–3), and in part by Pa'tki's ownership of the Gray
Flute ceremony. But still more is it expressed, I believe, in a ceremony in
which the two themes meet and receive their consummation: namely, the
Uñkwa'ti, the 'following ceremony' or Pa'lülükon-ti.

This ceremony is now extinct on 2nd and 3rd Mesas, and has not been
performed on 1st Mesa for many years, but there is no doubt that it once filled
an important place in the Hopi ceremonial calendar. The ceremony takes
place early in the moon following Powa'mu, that is in *ü'shü mü'iyawu* (late
February—early March), and combines two principal *motifs*: the growing of
corn in the participating kivas, and the representation of Pa'lülükoñ, water
serpent. A number of kivas take part in the growing of corn, but the representation of Pa'lülükoñ is restricted to the controlling kiva. Four days before
the new moon,[2] the leaders assemble in their kivas for *ü'yi la'lauwû*, 'plant
doing'; sand is brought in, seeds of the eight different colours of corn are planted
in boxes, and during the following days the boxes of plants are carefully
watered—'for thus we hope rain will come copiously after our corn is planted
in the fields'. Twelve days later, the leaders again assemble, for the main
ceremony which extends over five days (24-28 February, in 1893). On each of
the first three evenings a special screen is erected in the controlling kiva, and
ingenious representations of Pa'lülükoñ, slipped over a man's arm and thrust

---

[1] According to Miss Freire-Marreco's Tewa informants (1914, pp. 281–2), 'to consecrate
our seed-corn and make prayer-sticks for us all at the Winter Solstice' is one of the chief
duties performed, on behalf of the women of the clan, by their mother's brother(s).

[2] For an account of the Pa'lülükoñ-ti of 1893, on 1st Mesa, see Stephen (1936), pp. 289–
324; cf. for some references to the ceremony of 1921, Parsons (1925), pp. 43, 56–9.

through holes in the screen, imitate the writhings of the serpent, to the sound of trumpeting said to be the speech (voice) of the water, *pa'hü lavai'yita*. On the morning of the fourth day, prayer-sticks are made by the leaders of the ceremony, and late in the afternoon they all, carrying prayer-sticks and corn meal and accompanied by other men bearing the effigies of Pa'lülükoñ, and others again bearing trumpets, proceed to the main spring of the village; there they deposit the prayer-offerings, smoke and pray together, then lay the effigies of Pa'lülükoñ at the water's edge and gently dip the head of each into the water. Then all together make their way back to the controlling kiva. In the meantime, in all the kivas taking part, the corn 'crop' has been harvested. In the controlling kiva, the harvested 'crops' are set up in clay stands arranged in rows on the floor, 'like corn growing in a field', and that evening the representation of Pa'lülükoñ is performed for the last time; towards the end of the final song, the 'mother' snake knocks all the corn in the cones flat—'this knocking the corn stalks flat on the floor typifies ripeness, abundance, a field of corn with ears so heavy as to break down the stalks' (Stephen, 1936, p. 322). Late that night the fallen stalks are collected together, and distributed to the women of the village.

I have found no direct evidence as to which phratry grouping 'owned' the Pa'lülükoñ-ti—beyond the fact that, on 1st Mesa, its leader in 1893 was called *U'üwa*, 'corn just forming roasting ears', therefore a 'child' of Pikyas-Pa'tki. But just as the underlying ideas expressed in the Powa'mu would allow us to infer, if we did not know it from other sources, that the first of the two great spring ceremonies was in the hands of Badger-Butterfly and Katçina-Parrot groupings, so the combination of ideas expressed in the Uñkwa'ti—namely, the growing of corn *plus* the flow of water in springs[1]—permits us to conclude that the second or 'following' ceremony was originally owned by clans of the Pikyas-Pa'tki grouping: and that Pa'lülükoñ, the deity especially associated with it, was their *wuya*.[2]

Apart from ceremonies in which they play a leading rôle, both Pikyas and Pa'tki clans bear a part in all other major ceremonies in the calendar; for at every major kiva rite it is the duty of Pikyas clan chief to sprinkle the corn-meal 'road' for the leaders of the ceremony (see Freire-Marreco, in Robbins *et al.* 1916, p. 98; cf. Parsons, 1925, p. 37, n. 62, and p. 121, n. 185), and of Pa'tki clan chief to fetch the spring water for making *ña-kü'yi*, medicine water. As Parsons' 1st Mesa informant remarked (1925, p. 110, n. 170):

---

[1] An analogous juxtaposition of corn and moisture motifs is found in the course of Lako'n: there, the corn mound (*qa'ö tü'kwi*) is placed beside the water jar (*pat'kiñ*), 'because plenty of moisture brings plenty of corn—they go together' (Stephen, 1936, p. 849). On 1st Mesa, the Lako'n ceremony is handed down within the *Pa'tki-Pikyas* phratry grouping, probably (Parsons, 1936, p. 830) within the Pikyas clan.

[2] This conclusion finds support in mythology: one myth (Stephen, 1929, pp. 60–3) relates how Pa'lülükoñ sent the rain-and-corn phratry their *ti'poni*. The supposition, that the Pa'lülükoñ-ti ceremony was brought by Pa'tki clan, is also confirmed by a careful reading of Fewkes (1900*a*, pp. 134–6).

'*pa'tki*, Coyote and Tobacco clans have to be represented in every ceremony, because of their relation [conceptual and ritual] with clouds, fire, and smoke.'

### Association of ideas

The basic ideas associated with this phratry grouping have been delineated by Eggan, thus (1950, p. 85):

> The Pa'tki-Pikyas-Corn-Cloud-Rain phratry is concerned primarily with the growth cycle of corn. As one informant said: 'The clouds come, the rain falls, the corn grows and forms ears which feed the Hopi.'

Following the pattern adopted for the other phratry groupings, we may summarise the lines of thought that runs through the grouping as follows:

... *pa'tki*—clouds—snow, hail, thunder, lightning—springs and cisterns—*pa'lülükoñ*—frogs, tadpoles—grasses growing by the water—turtle-shell rattles—rain: *pikya's*, corn plants growing—*siva'pi*, wind breaks and corn fields—sweet corn—*Nima'n katcina*—rain—*qa'ö*, corn ears filling and ripening ...

### Anomalies, and comments

The 3rd Mesa myth, of which a composite version is given above, accords separate origins to the two leading clans in this phratry, Pa'tki and Pikyas; and this separation corresponds to the conceptual dichotomy we have noted above, i.e. between *cloud-and-rain* and *corn-growing*. At Mishong'novi (Forde, 1931, p. 401), the separation is recognised in actuality; there, *pa'tki*-cloud form one phratry grouping, and *pikyas*-corn, another separate grouping.

The inclusion of *Kwan* in this phratry grouping by Fewkes (1st Mesa: 1900b, pp. 582–4) is clearly an error,[1] as we shall see when we come to discuss the ideology underlying the Ko'kop-coyote grouping. Whiting (1939, p. 47) puts greasewood in this phratry, as well as with Reed: probably because land that carried greasewood, like land that carries *siva'pi*, grows corn well—and greasewood, also, is used for wind breaks.

### PHRATRY III. SNAKE–SAND–LIZARD

| | | |
|---|---|---|
| *tçü'a*, rattlesnake | *hü'wi*, mourning dove | *tü'wa*, sand |
| *lülükoñ*, non-poisonous snake | *ü'shü*, cholla cactus | *gü'gütsi*, lizard |
| *ta'ho tçü'a*, sinew snake | *ü'yüñü*, prickly pear | *mana'ñüya*, horned lizard |
| *tü'kya*, prairie dog | *ka'chi*, sage wren | *macha'kwa*, horned toad |
| *ko'ko*, burrowing owl | *to'hoa*, mountain lion | *si'hü*, various flowers |

[1] Ideologically, that is; practically, it is no doubt due to the same cause as Stephen's inclusion of Sho'tokünuñwa, the deity associated with lightning, in this phratry grouping—namely, that leadership of the Kwan or Agave fraternity, on 1st Mesa, has passed into the hands of Pa'tki clan: Stephen (1936), p. 1071, n. 3.

*Myth.* The Oraibi myth of the Origin of the Clans (Voth, 1905c, pp. 28–30) distinguishes between Lizard clan, 'to which the Sand clan is related', and Rattle-snake (*tçu'a*) clan. 'The Lizard people were also asked what they knew and when they said the Marau cult, they were also permitted to stay, but were requested to co-operate in the Soya'l ceremony. For that reason the village chief, who is of the Bear clan, now makes the *pühü* (road) in the night of the Marau ceremony from the *na'tsi* at the south end of the kiva towards the rising sun.'

The Mishong'novi myth of the Origin of the Clans (Voth, 1905c, pp. 47–8), links Sand clan with Pa'tki in their wanderings:

> When travelling, the Sand clan would spread sand on the ground and plant corn; the lizards and snakes would come into the sand, and hence these names are also applied to the Sand clan. The Pa'tki clan would cause it to thunder and rain (by singing), the crop would grow in a day and they would have something to eat. They [i.e. the Sand people] brought with them . . . the Lako'n cult. . . . [on arriving at the village] they were asked what they knew to produce rain and crops. They spread the sand, made corn grow, etc., whereupon they were welcomed. . . .

The 1st Mesa myth (Stephen, 1929, pp. 35–40: cf. 1940b, pp. 2–8), relating the origin of the Snake cult, links rattlesnake (*tçü'a*) with turtle dove, yellow-flowered cactus and red-flowered cactus. A prominent part is played in this myth by *Ko'kyañ wuh'ti*, Spider woman; she also figures prominently in the 2nd Mesa myth (Voth, 1905c, pp. 30–6) of the same event.

*Natural observation, and ceremonial referents*

*tü'wa*, sand. This is the brown sand of the valley (Stephen, 1936, p. 592), of which the sand ridge, e.g. in the Marau altar, is made; the personal names bestowed by women of this clan (Voth, 1905b, pp. 110–11) demonstrate the close conceptual link between sand (*tü'wa*) and altar (*poñya*). *Tü'wa*, as we have seen earlier (above, pp. 26–7, 109–10), also has a close relation to child-birth.

*tçü'a*, rattlesnake, 'he of the earth' (Stephen, 1936, p. 1211).

The snakes of the snake myth are rattlesnakes (*tçü'a*), and the myth (Voth, 1905c, p. 34) refers to them specifically as living in the fields and *in the sand*; it may be that *tçü'a*, too, has some link with child-birth—the snake myth refers to the girl becoming pregnant 'quickly, like snakes' (ibid. p. 34, n. 1).

*tü'kya*, prairie dog. These rodents dig their 'towns' in sand dunes on the main valley floor. The ecological link between snakes, prairie dogs and burrowing owl (*ko'ko*), is furnished by the following observation of Stephen's (1936, p. 277):

> The rabbit and hare frequently run down prairie dog holes for safety when pursued by men or hawks, then the snakes get them. The rattlesnake, the house snake (*lülükañüh*), the constrictor (*ta'ho*), all snakes frequent the dog hole; they lie there in ambush for rabbit and hare. The snakes also prey upon the young prairie dogs (*tü'kya*) and owls. The burrowing owl (*ko'ko*) lays its eggs and hatches its young in the prairie dog house (*tü'kya-ki*), hatches four or five young ones. . . .

*hüwi*, mourning dove (*Zenaidura macroura*). This bird is a summer resident of sand dunes, of peach orchards, and of fields on the fans of tributary water-courses, commonly found in pairs or in small flocks near water; doves arrive in late April and early May, and depart south late in September.

> If the dove (*hŏ'wi*) comes early, [writes Beaglehole (1937, pp. 34–5)], this forecasts a good summer. If this bird, and other birds, come late, it will be a bad summer, there will be no rain and the frosts will come early.

*ka'chi*, sage wren. Identified by Stephen as sage (or cactus) wren, a bird unknown as far north as the Hopi region, *ka'chi* is almost certainly Bendire's Thrasher (Fisher, 1903, p. 35); the latter is a summer resident of sand slopes, nesting in bushes or peach trees there, and departing south late in August.

*ü'shü*, cholla cactus: *ü'yüñü*, prickly pear. Both these cacti grow on the flats below the Hopi villages (Whiting, 1939, pp. 85–6); the fruits of both are edible.

*gü'gütsi*, lizard. Late in September, I heard a Hopi woman say that it would not turn cold yet awhile, the lizards were still out around her house. Lizards are, in fact, extremely sensitive indicators of seasonal change, their emergence from hibernation being directly dependent on warming of the ground in the spring, and their retirement into hibernation, on its progressive cooling due to the declining angle of the sun's rays during September and October (Douglas, 1966, pp. 722–8, 742); in Mesa Verde National Park, the two common varieties of lizard—*Sceloporus graciosus*, Sagebrush Lizard, and *Sceloporus undulatus*, Northern Plateau Lizard—are commonly 'out' from mid April until late September, exact dates depending on the season and on location.

*mana'ñüya*, horned lizard. There appears to be some relation between lizard and love-making (Eggan, 1950, p. 83). Stephen writes (1929, p. 30, n. 1):

> To the vivid hued lizard called *mana'ñaya*,[1] aphrodisiac power is ascribed. When an amorous Hopi youth encounters this lizard, he addresses it as his friend and asks it to help him with his sweetheart.

Several of the personal names bestowed by women of the Lizard clan refer to the lizard emerging from its skin when shedding it; and I think it probable, in the light of the part played by the Lizards in the Hopi myth of the Toothed Vagina (Stephen, 1929, p. 28–30) and particularly of the reference there to the young men drawing back their foreskins, that lizard is associated conceptually with the male sex organ (*kwashi*, penis).

*si'hü*, flowers of various kinds. Sand slopes and dunes carry a rich *flora*; the flowers, which are linked to snake and sand in myth and which furnish additional clan names for this phratry grouping, are common members of the sand slope *flora*.

---

[1] Identified by Voth (1905c, p. 176) as horned lizard; I was told, at Oraibi, that it is a black-and-white striped lizard.

*tü'saka*, the rustling grasses of sand slopes, are also linked conceptually with this phratry grouping: Stephen (1936,) p. 706.

### Actual ceremonial duties

The primary ceremonial function of this phratry grouping centres on control of the two great fall ceremonies, Marau' and Lako'n, with their emphasis—as we have seen earlier (above, pp. 180–4)—on the corn harvest and on the fertility of women. Thus, at Oraibi, the Lizard people brought—and still control—the Marau', while at Mishong'novi the Sand-Lizard people brought, and still control, the Lako'n. A further ceremonial function of the grouping is the duty laid on Sand clan to fetch the valley sand (*tü'wa*), needed for making the sand ridge and sand field at all major kiva rites (Parsons, 1925, p. 103); in certain of the villages, e.g. Mishong'novi, the man to whom this duty falls is referred to as *tü'wa moñwi*, 'sand chief': Stephen (1936), pp. 736, 745. Now the deity especially associated with the Marau' and Lako'n ceremonies is Tü'wa-poñya-tumsi, 'Sand Altar Woman'; the sand or earth, as Eggan observes (1950, p. 83), is regarded as a 'mother' who feeds the Hopi by producing crops; all vegetation is the offspring of the earth personified as Tü'wa-poñya-tumsi, fertilised by rain and warmed by the sun (Wallis, 1936, p. 15), while Sand Altar Woman is also closely linked conceptually, not only with fertility in general, but with sex desire (*cho'va*) and copulation, in particular (cf. Stephen, 1936, p. 261). It seems reasonable to conclude, therefore, that Tü'wa-poñya-tumsi, the patron deity of childbirth, is *wuya* to this phratry grouping—*or at least to the Sand-Lizard fragment of it.*

Turning now to the Snake fragment of the phratry grouping: Snake clan controls the Snake cult on all three mesas. The principal purpose of the summer ceremony of the Snake-Antelope fraternities is, as we have seen above (pp. 167–8), to bring rain to the growing crops. But there is another, quite distinct, thread present in Snake ideology: that of war. Thus, in the Snake myth from 1st Mesa, a clear distinction is drawn between the two groups represented in the summer ceremony: the Antelopes—'through you shall come rain, and snow, and green grass . . . from you shall the songs proceed, to you shall the songs return'; and the Snakes—'only those of strong hearts can sit at the altar of the Snake . . . the celebration of the Snake ceremony is to instil courage' (Stephen, 1929, pp. 38–9: cf. 1936, pp. 636–7, and 1940b, pp. 6–7, 21). The distinction was elaborated to Stephen by Kopeli, the old head of the Snake fraternity at Walpi, in these words (1936, p. 714):

> In the old time the Snake society were actual warriors, and when they went on the war trail (*tü'oviita*), they carried neither spear nor bow and arrow. They had the battle axe (*kala'pikya'iñwa*) and the nodule club (*pü'vwülshoñni*). They knew no fear and marched up to the enemy and seized him by the throat (as we seize a snake) and knocked him on the head with axe or club. The Antelope society were old men, they remained in the kiva and sang and prayed while the Snakes were fighting.

There is no connection between Antelope society and Antelope clan. The society is so called because long ago they used scapulae of antelope strung together for rattles, antelope rattle, *chüb'aya*. It is also distinct from the Snake society. An Antelope never becomes a Snake, nor vice versa.

The Antelope fraternity, then, which belongs to the Bluebird-Spider fragment of Bear phratry, is primarily *for* rain and the growth of vegetation:[1] the Snakes, primarily *for* war. Ceremonially, the war aspect of Snake ideology is expressed in the winter *pa'ho*-making of the Snake fraternity, held late in January, last of a sequence of rites (Wü'wütçim, Soya'l, and the winter ceremony of the warrior society) through which the same thread runs. Symbolically, it is expressed by the presence of *to'hoa*, mountain lion, among the clan names related to Snake; while the prominent part given to Spider Woman in the Snake myth may be ascribed to the same source, *Ko'kyañ wuhti* being grandmother to the Twins and an associated War deity. On a different level again, we may note that Hopi themselves designate the six fraternities chiefly responsible for preserving the integrity of the pueblo, as the concentric walls of a house (Stephen, 1940*b*, pp. 18–20): the two outer 'walls' being formed by the Kwan and Al fraternities, the next two by the Wü'wütçim and the Singers, and the two inner 'walls' by the Snakes and by the Warrior society.

## Association of ideas

The dominant thread in the ideology of this grouping we may, then, characterise along these lines:

... Sand—corn fields—snakes (*tçü'a*), prairie dogs, burrowing owl—ripening corn: Sand, 'mother of all babies'—Tü'wa-poñya-tumsi, Sand altar woman —ripe corn ears—corn 'mother'—child-birth—*lü'wa*—Marau and the fall ceremonies—lizards—sex desire (*cho'va*)—'birth, copulation [and death] ...'

## Anomalies, and comments

*to'hoa*, mountain lion (*felis concolor*). Mountain lions range more widely than bears both in their daily and seasonal activities. They are still fairly common in Mesa Verde National Park (Anderson, 1961, p. 61), are rare visitors to the Navajo Mountain and Tsegi Canyon area (Benson, 1935, p. 449, confirmed in 1969 by Navajo informant), and are occasionally reported from the area of the San Francisco Peaks (Lincoln, 1961, pp. 48–9). It is possible that they are still to be met with on rare occasions in Hopi country; thus, a man who

---

[1] The 'peaceful' character of the Antelopes is borne out by the prayer-sticks made by them during the Snake-Antelope ceremony: of the seven sets of *pa'ho*(s) made by Antelope chief at the ceremony of 1892 (at Sipau'lovi: Stephen, 1936, p. 744), one set was for Sun, one set for *ü'yi* (vegetation), one set for *kü'yi* (spring water), and one set each for the Cloud chiefs (*o'mauwú moñwi*) at the four cardinal directions.

On 2nd and 3rd Mesa, and probably until recently also on 1st Mesa (Eggan, 1950, p. 343, n. 137), the Antelope ceremony has remained in the hands of Bear-Spider phratry grouping: Eggan (1950,) p. 103, cf. Voth (1905*b*), p. 88.

dreamed (D. Eggan, 1957, p. 47) that his flock of sheep was savaged by a wild animal, assumed that they had been attacked by a mountain lion.

*To'hoa* is one of the four prey animals, 'pets' of Pyü'ükoñhoya, war deity, and is especially associated with war (Stephen, 1936, p. 307, 766). The sand mosaic, made in Snake kiva on the seventh day of the Snake-Antelope cere-mony, depicts *to'hoa* inside the four squares of coloured sand (Stephen, 1936, pp. 639–40: cf. 1940b, p. 31); the area inside the inner square represents the Hopi land, and lion is watcher chief (*tü'wala moñwi*), guarding the land. At his Wü'wütçim initiation (above, p. 112), a lad is given a mountain lion emblem to wear, that he may be courageous and strong.

On 1st Mesa, Snake clan with its related clans has remained distinct from Sand-Lizard and *its* related clans; on 2nd and 3rd Mesa, the two groups are merged in a single phratry grouping. The cause of this merging—or, alternatively, of Snake clan never having broken away from Sand-Lizard—is to be looked for, I suggest, in the part played by war in pueblo history. The Snake cult reached the Hopi, from Zuñi and the eastern pueblos, fairly late in their history; and it seems likely that its introduction co-incided with the arrival of the nomad marauders (Apache, Comanche, Navajo, mounted Utes) in the Southwest, and its florescence with their dominance there. As the threat from external enemies declined in the latter half of the nineteenth century, the war aspect of the Snake fraternity fell into desuetude, and the way lay open for the *conceptual* unity underlying the Snake-Sand-Lizard grouping to re-assert itself.

### PHRATRY IV. SUN—EAGLE

| | | |
|---|---|---|
| *ta'wa*, sun | *kwa'hü*, eagle | *kih'sa*, prairie falcon |
| *kala'ñ*, sun's forehead | *kwa'yo*, hawk, buteo | *koyu'ñ*, wild turkey |

*Myth.* The principal, relevant myth (Stephen, 1929, pp. 15–18) relates how the Twins, Pyü'ükoñ-hoya and his brother, seek their father, Sun, and how they slay the giant bird, Kwa'toko. The Twins make their way to the house of their father, Sun, who is described as the 'father of the hawks'; after various adventures, and with the help of Eagle (*kwa'hü*) and Hawk (*kwa'yo*), they kill Kwa'toko. 'After this, Sun, who was the first maker of bow and arrow, gave them to Pyü'ükoñhoya so that he might hunt antelope and deer.'

In another myth (Stephen, 1929, p. 51), the Twins use the wing feathers of hawk to fletch their arrows.

### Natural observation, and ceremonial referents

*ta'wa*, sun. In the old days, every Hopi woman went out at dawn to the mesa's edge and sprinkled (*ho'moya*) corn meal to the rising sun, at the same time praying for health and long life for herself and her family. *Kala'ñ* refers to the 'brow' of the sun, as it appears above the horizon.

*kwa'hü*, golden eagle (*Aquila chrysaëtos*). A permanent resident of the Hopi region, nesting in eyries along the cliffs near the villages and on the buttes to the south; eggs are laid early in March, and the young birds are ready to leave the nest by mid June.

Eagle feathers are used for a variety of ceremonial purposes. The smaller feathers, from the breast and under the wing, are used for *nakwa'kwosi(s)* and, with a long cotton thread attached, for 'road' (*pü'hü*) prayer-feathers. The larger feathers, from the wings and tail, are used on masks, standards (*na'atsi*), and altars (*poñya*).

In all major kiva rites, whistles (*tütyü'kpi*) are used to summon the deities, and these are made from the wing bones of either eagle or turkey; at the Nima'n katçina, the whistling into the medicine bowl (*tütyü'klauwû*) is 'a calling to the six directions for clouds to come' (Stephen, 1936, pp. 514–15).

There is a close conceptual link, as the myths indicate, between eagle and Sun. The typical Hopi sun symbol is profusely decorated with eagle tail feathers, representing the rays of the sun (Voth, 1912*b*, pp. 108–9: cf. Stephen, 1936, p. 791); in the Flute ceremony, in August, each of the leaders wears such a sun symbol on his back as part of his ceremonial costume (see Voth, 1912*b*, Pl. xlviii).

*kwa'yo*, large hawk, buteo. The two species resident in Hopi country are the Western Red-Tail (*Buteo jamaicensis*), *pa'la kwa'yo*, and Swainson's Hawk (*Buteo swainsoni*), *ma'si kwa'yo*; the Western Red-Tail is fairly common and nests along the cliffs, Swainson's I have never seen.

*kih'sa*, prairie falcon. The prairie falcon (*Falco mexicanus*) is not often seen in the vicinity of the Hopi villages; it may be more common on the flats down towards the Little Colorado river. *Ma'si kih'sa*, peregrine falcon (*Falco peregrinus*) or duck hawk, is rarer still, though Fisher saw one on his visit to Keam's Cañon in July, 1894 (Fisher, 1903, p. 34).

There is a close conceptual link between the large hawks (*kwa'yo*, *kih'sa*) and hunting, especially rabbit hunting. *Kih'sa*, as we have seen (above, p. 135) gave the Hopi the throwing-stick: 'all the preying animals have bow and arrows so also has *kih'sa*, but he alone devised the *püchko'hü*. He carried it under his wing and hunted rabbits with it.'

In the old days, bow and arrow were used chiefly for hunting deer and other large game (Stephen, 1936, p. 277); and arrows were fletched with hawk feathers, the triple feathering being wrapped on with sinew (Hough, 1918, p. 288). Rabbits were chiefly hunted with two kinds of throwing stick, the straight throwing-stick (*müzri'ko*) and the curved throwing-stick (*püchko'hü*); and of the two, the latter in particular was associated with Kih'sa, the great hunter.

In the *Tale of Siti'yo* (Titiev, 1943*b*, pp. 431–7), the lad Siti'yo, who has been unable to kill any rabbits for the forthcoming Soya'l, sets out on his own, on the flats down towards the Little Colorado river; there he meets Spider woman, who promises to help him, and then Tih-kü'yi-wuhti, who 'owns all the game'. The next morning he goes out hunting: he sees a jack-rabbit, but before he can throw his stick, hawk (*ki'sa*) swoops down and kills it 'with one jab of its powerful sharp-pointed wing'; rabbit after rabbit is killed in this way, then Ki'sa flies back to the cliff where he lives, and Siti'yo returns to the village, carrying the rabbits.

*koyuñ'*, wild turkey (*Meleagris gallopavo*). Turkeys still run wild in the forests around the San Francisco Peaks, but no longer on Black Mesa. Numerous turkey bones, found in the ruins at Kiet Seel pueblo, indicate (Hargrave, 1939, p. 208) that turkeys were under domestication there in the later thirteenth century. Jean Pinkley has recently argued (1965, pp. 70–2), on the basis of experience gained at Mesa Verde National Park, that the birds may have needed no domesticating: from the time the Pueblo people first began farming (in Basketmaker II), it must have been a battle to keep the turkeys *out of* the fields, and they probably solved the problem by allowing them *into* the villages.

In the old days, turkeys were kept in the Hopi villages and their feathers used extensively for *pa'ho*(s); Stephen records (1936, p. 605) that, by mid August, so many of their feathers had been used for prayer-sticks that the birds were plucked bare. The turkey feather, particularly the breast feather, is 'a very general moisture emblem' (Fewkes and Stephen, 1892, p. 228, n. 1), the speckled colour and white tip symbolising the foaming water after a deluge.

### Actual ceremonial functions

The Sun-Eagle phratry grouping appears to have two important ceremonial functions. The first of these concerns the Sun's progress. On the last night of the Soya'l, as we have seen (above, p. 129), Star man performs the dance in which the twirling of the Sun shield in his hands symbolises 'the going and coming of the sun', or the return of that luminary from his winter 'house'. Now this dramatisation of the Sun's progress, considered by all who have observed it to be the culminating point in the Winter Solstice ceremony, is played—at least on 3rd Mesa—by a leading member of Sun clan;[1] and from the fact that the Sun shield itself is fringed with eagle tail-feathers, I infer that this is a joint Sun-Eagle responsibility (or privilege). It is balanced by a brief ceremony at midsummer (June 22), in the course of which the members of Sun clan make prayer sticks for the Sun and deposit them at his 'house' sited to the north-east of the village, i.e. at his midsummer rising place.

The second function of this phratry grouping refers to the use of eagle feathers, and requires a digression on the subject of eagle-hunting among the Hopi.

---

[1] By Talaskwaptiwa, in the ceremony observed by Voth. The important rôle, which Don Talai'yesva refers to in his autobiography (Simmons, 1942) as being his in the Soya'l, may have been that of taking the part of Star man on the last night of the ceremony; Don Talai'yesva was also of Sun clan, and later held the office of Sun watcher, *ta'wa otaima*, at Oraibi. At Sipau'lovi, in the old days, the office of Sun watcher was hereditary in Sun clan: Stephen (1936), p. 723.

The territory around the Hopi villages where eagles are to be found is, and has been for a long time past, divided into portions or allotments, which are controlled by particular clans and lineages.[1] Every spring, in May or early June, hunting expeditions set out to procure young birds at the nest, both of eagles (*kwa'hü*) themselves and of the larger kinds of hawk (especially *pa'la kwa'yo*, western red-tail). When captured, the young birds are tied to wooden racks and carried back to the villages; there they are kept on the flat roof tops,[2] tied by one leg to a beam or stone to prevent their escape, and fed daily on rabbits, field rats and other small rodents; by late July, the young birds should be full grown. During the nine days of the Nima'n katçina festival, they are treated with special care and attention, then—early on the morning of the tenth day—all the birds in the village are ceremonially killed. The killing of the eagles is done in a special, prescribed manner: while one man holds the thong attached to the bird's leg, another throws a cloth or a blanket over its head, pulls the bird to the ground and kills it by pressure exerted on the heart and throat. No eagle is killed by any other method (Voth, 1912*b*, p. 108); and each bird is killed in this way—'that its breath may mount to Cloud with the Hopi prayers for rain, that its breath-body may return to its real home' (Stephen, 1936, p. 569).

When life is extinct, the large feathers are plucked and carefully sorted; the body is then flayed, and the skin with the remaining feathers carefully dried and preserved. Five prayer-feathers (*nakwa'kwosi*) are tied to the corpse, one to the beak, one to the tip of each wing, and one to each leg just above the claws: this is done, so that 'the eagles should not be angry but hatch young eagles again next year' (Voth, 1912*b*, p. 108). Some rolls of blue *pi'ki*, corn meal and a woven tray are prepared, then the carcass, prayer-offerings and a pointed stick are taken to the graveyard especially devoted to eagles; a hole is dug with the pointed stick, and prayers offered that the soul ('breath body') of the eagle may fly back to the buttes, there to be born again; then the body of the bird, with the food, is buried in the eagle grave, *kwa'hü tü'ami*.

Now while, in recent times, a number of different clans (e.g. at Oraibi, Bear, Spider, Reed, Pikyas, Bow, Lizard, Burrowing Owl and Badger, as well as Eagle) have controlled their own eagle territories, Voth is of the opinion (1912*b*, p. 107) that originally the Eagle clan, and later also clans related to the Eagle clan, were the only ones that 'owned' the eagles; and that it was by a later development that other clans outside this phratry grouping came to share the privilege. If Voth is right, and the restriction of analogous 'rights' to other phratry groupings furnishes a close parallel to what he holds to have been the

---

[1] In this summary of eagle-hunting among the Hopi, I follow closely Voth's account (1912*b*, pp. 105–9), with further details taken from Fewkes (1900*c*, pp. 690–707), Beaglehole (1936, pp. 18–22), and Stephen (1936, pp. 568–9).

[2] Beaglehole states (1936, pp. 20–1) that, as the birds come from clan-owned cliffs and buttes, they are considered to be 'children' of the clan; and that, on the return of the hunting party to the village, the women of the clan should assemble, wash the head of each eagle, and ceremonially name it with an appropriate clan name.

case with regard to eagles, then control of eagles—with all that that implies, having regard to the symbolic significance of their feathers in Hopi ritual— constitutes the second major ceremonial function of the Sun-Eagle phratry grouping.

### Association of ideas

Two threads, again, are interwoven in the ideology underlying this phratry grouping: one of *seasonal change*, running from the dance of Star man on the last night of Soya'l, through the representation of the sun on the sand mosaic at prayer-stick making for Powa'mu, to the wearing of the sun shield on the backs of the leaders at the Flute ceremony, parallelled—in those villages where the office of Sun watcher is vested in Sun clan—by the daily watching of the sun on the eastern horizon; the other of *rain and moisture*, informing the use of turkey feathers for *pa'ho*(s) made during the spring and early summer, culmi- nating in the choking of the young eagles on the tenth morning of Nima'n, that their breath 'may mount to Cloud with the Hopi prayers for rain', and parallelled, this time, by the blowing of turkey and eagle-bone whistles in the course of the Powa'mu, Nima'n, Flute, and Marau' ceremonies (Stephen, 1936, pp. 229, 514–5, 774, 891, 918). The ideas associated with the Sun-Eagle phratry grouping we may, then, summarise as follows:

. . . Soya'l—eagle feathers on the sun disc—Sun turns from his winter 'house'— return of warm weather—*ta'wa otaima*, Sun watcher—planting of crops— turkey feathers—rain—eagle- and turkey-bone whistles—Nima'n katçina festival—killing of the young eagles—eagle feathers at Flute ceremony—Sun turns from his summer 'house' . . .

### Anomalies, and comments

Conceptually, the linking of Sun-Eagle phratry grouping with Reed-Grease- wood on 1st Mesa is due, I suggest, to the mediation of Pü'ükonhoya. The Twins are, to a degree, common to both groups; their images are in the keeping of Reed-Greasewood, while, their father being Sun, they figure prominently in the myths attaching to Sun-Eagle.

Practically, the merging of the two phratries was no doubt due to the fact that the clans of the Sun-Eagle fragment were already, in the 1890s, on the point of extinction: Lowie (1929), pp. 309–17, cf. Parsons (1936), p. 1067, n. 6.

# 16

# *Thought-world of the Hopi (concluded)*

The six phratry groupings we have considered so far are rather clearly differentiated, ceremonially and conceptually. Each grouping has its own ceremonial functions, peculiar to the clans within that grouping; and the clan names linked together within each phratry represent a fairly coherent body of phenomena, actual or symbolic—*phenomenal* or *noumenal*. Singly, the primary emphasis of each of the six groupings centres on one aspect of the return of warm weather, rain and growth of crops; taken together, they inter-relate to cover all the main events of the agricultural cycle, from the clearing of the fields in early spring to the corn harvest in the fall.

The six remaining phratry groupings are less clearly differentiated one from another. And this is due, I think, to the fact that all six of them are involved in one way or another in the performance of the Wü'wütçim ceremony, each individual grouping being primarily concerned *either* with the main theme of the Wü'wütçim, *or* with war, *or* with hunting. The complexity of the phratry groupings is thus related to the complexity of the Wü'wütçim ceremony in which they all share, and the interweaving of conceptual threads represented by the groupings reflects the various ideational strands knitted together in that complex ceremony. This complexity we have now to unravel; much of it, as I hope to show, derives from the many-sided nature of Masau'u, the deity most intimately involved in the Wü'wütçim.

### PHRATRY V. REED–GREASEWOOD–BOW

| | | |
|---|---|---|
| *pa'kab*, reed | *te've*, greasewood | *mo'tsni*, shrike |
| *a'out*, bow | *sho'hü*, all the stars | *yau'pa*, mockingbird |
| *ho'hü*, arrow | *Pyü'ükoñ-ho'ya*, War deity | *moñwû*, owl |

*Myth.* The 1st Mesa myth, of the Origin of the Reed people (Parsons, 1933, pp. 31–2), describes how the Reed people got their name from the reed (*pa'kab*) inside which the people climbed to emerge from the Underworld; how, after the Emergence, they saw the Sun (*ta'wa*), and met the Eagle (*kwa'*); and how the Twins (*Pyü'ükoñ*), their 'brothers', became their guides (*kaletaka*).

Other versions of the Emergence myth (Wallis, 1936, pp. 3–7: cf. Voth, 1905c, p. 10) relate the prominent parts played by *mo'tsni*, shrike, and *yau'pa*, mockingbird, at the Emergence; the former found the hole by which the people came out[1], while mockingbird taught them the songs sung in the Below.

The 3rd Mesa Emergence myth, given above (pp. 209–10), states that the Wü'wütçim ceremony, or at least *that part of it which has to do with rain,* was brought by Bow clan.

### Natural observation, and ceremonial referents

*pa'kab*, reed. Both among the Basin Shoshoni (Steward, 1938, p. 312), and among the Hopi (Voth, 1905*b*, p. 76), reeds were at one time used for the shafts of arrows. Personal names bestowed by women of both Bow and Reed clans (Voth, 1905*b*, pp. 74–6) refer to arrows (*ho'hü*); but some Reed clan personal names refer simply to the reed as a plant, e.g. Loma'hongioma, 'standing up nicely'.

*a'out*, bow. Bows were traditionally made either from oak wood (*kwi'ñvi*), or from shadblow (*tawa'vi*), a species of wild apple. Arrows (*ho'hü*) had a reed shaft and a wooden foreshaft: Whiting (1939), p. 23. Woods used for arrows include cliff rose (*hö'novi*), Apache plume (*moñpö'hovi*), and greasewood (*te've*); all these shrubs are found growing near the Hopi villages.

*te've*, greasewood. Greasewood grows in pure stands, where the land has not been cleared for agriculture, on the alluvial flats below the villages. Both among the Basin Shoshoni (Steward, 1938, p. 312), and among the Hopi (Stephen, 1936, p. 608: cf. Hough, 1918, pp. 236–7), greasewood was the wood traditionally used for digging-sticks; and among the Hopi a man's digging-stick was set upright in his grave (Stephen, 1936, pp. 709, 825), as a ladder for his 'breath' to climb at the beginning of its journey to the land of the Dead.

*sho'hü*, all the stars. When the people first emerged on earth, it was dark and cold; the stars were made by Coyote to give light to the Hopi at night (Beagle-hole, 1937, p. 34). The stars are associated with war (Parsons, 1936, p. 84, and p. 87, n. 1); on 3rd Mesa, the War chief (*kaletaka*) is drawn from Coyote clan.

*po'ko* dog. Although *po'ko* does not appear among the clan names of this phratry, dogs are closely associated, conceptually, with the Reed people. 'All the Reeds are warriors . . .' (Stephen, 1929, p. 33, n. 4); and the chief of Reed clan, who on 1st Mesa is chief of the warriors, is also chief of the dogs—'all dogs belong to him. The dogs are (were) warriors, hunters and watchers' (ibid. p. 34, n. 2). And at the end of the myth relating why dogs belong to Reed clan, we read (ibid. p. 34):

> The dogs were hunters of rabbits, deer, and even of antelope. They caught the legs of the antelope. The dogs also guarded the houses . . . watched the fields, and drove away the coyotes who came to steal corn and melons. In the night time they yelped and barked . . .

[1] I have been told, however, that it was *Ko'kop-hoya*, black-throated sparrow (*Amphispiza bilineata*), who found the hole after shrike had failed to find it. This little bird is *tühi'sa*, wise, knowing; he 'belongs to' the Ko'kop people, *ko'kop nyamü*.

*mo'tsni*, loggerhead shrike (*Lanius ludovicianus*). This bold, black-and-white-faced bird is to be seen all the year round in the vicinity of the Hopi villages, perched on the top of bushes, posts and boulders, guarding its territory, and swooping down to the ground to take grasshoppers, beetles, lizards, mice. With the desert Sparrowhawk, it is the commonest predator in the region.

*Mo'tsni* appears on a Hopi war shield (Wallis and Titiev, 1944, pl. iii), where he is described as 'a watchman' (*tü'wala*); the only other birds so represented are owl (*moñwû*), night hawk (*ho'otsko*), and eagle (*kwa'hü*). *Mo'tsni* 'belongs to' the Agave (Kwan) fraternity: Stephen (1936), p. 1251.

*yau'pa*, mockingbird (*Mimus polyglottos*). A summer resident in Hopi country. There is no ecological reason why the bird should be included in this phratry; its black and white colouring, however, relates it to Shrike.

*moñwû*, owl. This is the Great Horned Owl (*Bubo virginianus*), a permanent resident of the region nesting along the cliffs in the vicinity of the Hopi villages.

*Moñwû* appears on a war shield (Wallis and Titiev, 1944, pl. vii), and is described there as 'a scout with piercing eyes who goes about by night to reconnoitre the foe'. The calls of owls and night hawks were used for sending secret messages at night.

Regarding the clan names listed above, three points may be noted. First, they include two (*a'out*, bow, and *ho'hü*, arrow) of the four artifacts that serve as clan names, the other two being *ko'kop*, fire spindle (Phratry VI), and *püchko'hü*, throwing stick (Phratry XII). Second, all the objects named, and the birds (apart from *yau'pa*), have a 'war' aspect. Thirdly, all the objects named, like those of the next two groupings, represent items that are important in Great Basin ecology. *A'wat* and *hu'* are the basic stems, in all the Shoshonean languages, for bow and arrow; bows were commonly made either of juniper or mountain oak, arrow shafts of reed. Greasewood occurs abundantly on valley flats throughout the Great Basin; the wood was used for the foreshaft of arrows, and for digging sticks, required chiefly in late summer and fall for digging roots, bulbs and tubers (Steward, 1933, pp. 244–5). Dogs, associated with this phratry in Hopi myth, were used in all parts of the Great Basin for hunting larger game.

*Pyü'ükoñhoya*, War deity, elder of the Twins. The 1st Mesa myth, given above (p. 241), records the close association between the Reed people and the Twins; in the myth, the Twins become their guides (*kaletaka*). On 1st Mesa, the office of *kaletaka* (scout, warrior) is filled by a Reed man; he acts for the Twins, 'takes their place' (Parsons, 1933, p. 31). And on 1st Mesa the Reed clan, or one of its maternal lineages, has in its keeping the images of the Twins (Stephen, 1929, p. 50), and makes *pa'ho*(s) for them (Parsons, 1925, p. 14): from which I infer that Pyü'ükoñhoya, the elder of the Twins is their *wuya*.

But Pyü'ükoñhoya has two other aspects, beside that of war. He 'understands', as we have seen earlier (above, pp. 132–3), the cold. And the Twins have some relation, not so much to land as cultivated but to land in its basic form, i.e. to its physiography. Thus, in one version of the Emergence myth (Stephen, 1929, p. 6), after the Emergence the Twins 'made all the rocks, and the mountains, everything that is of stone; they made the cañons (*tüb'ka*), and through these the water flowed away.' And another myth (Stephen, 1929, pp. 50–1) records how the Twins drained the land and created vegetation:

> On the morrow Pyü'ükoñhoya and Pa'luñhoya went to the mountain top and pulled out their hairs . . . and, pulling out their hairs, they cast them to the winds, calling each handful by the name of something growing out of the ground, as pine, piñon, cedar, oak, the grasses, etc. . . .

Now this latter aspect of Pyü'ükoñhoya furnishes an important link with greasewood (*te've*). The Wü'wütçim ceremony, brought by Bow clan, falls in November; and of the November moon, Parsons writes (1936, p. 1036)—

> November, *ke'le mii'iyawû*: *ke'le*, sparrow-hawk, novice, initiate. In this *ke'le* moon, the fields for the following year's planting are cleared of brush, etc.

This clearing of brush refers, I suggest, not to the ordinary tidying-up of fields for planting which takes place in February and March (Beaglehole, 1937, pp. 23–4), but to the clearing of *new* land, i.e. for making *new* fields; if we take this meaning, then such land will have been cleared in November, and left over the winter for snow and frost to do their work, prior to planting in the spring. For the arduous work of breaking new land, the greasewood digging-stick was in the old days, i.e. before the introduction of metal tools, the chief implement.

Before discussing the actual ceremonial functions of the Reed-Greasewood-Bow phratry grouping, I propose to deal with the Ko'kop-Coyote grouping. This will entail an analysis of the nature of Masau'u, *wu'ya* of that grouping. We shall then be in a position to discuss the actual ceremonial functions of the two groupings together, and to delineate the principal conceptual threads underlying each.

### PHRATRY VI. KO'KOP–COYOTE

| | | |
|---|---|---|
| *ko'kop*, fire spindle, or cedarwood | *Masau'u*, Masau'u | *isau'wû*, coyote |
| | | *kwe'wûüh*, gray wolf |
| *ho'ko*, juniper | *tüvü'tsi*, a black bird | *zroho'na*, (?) mountain |
| *tuve'e*, piñon | with red on it | coyote |
| *kii'hi*, fire | *kwan*, agave, or mescal | *le'taiyo*, gray fox |
| *tü'vü*, live ember | *mo'hü*, yucca | *sikya'taiyo*, yellow fox |

*Myth.* 1st Mesa myth of the Origin of Coyote people (Parsons, 1933, p. 30):

> After they came out, they came to a place where a man was sitting by the road-side. The man said, 'How are you, my sisters and brothers? Where are you going?' —'We are going to Si-tü'kwi'—'I heard you were coming, so I waited to go with

you. I am your uncle, but they call me Coyote.' He put on his skin and he was a coyote. They went along with him. They came to a place where there were cedar trees [*och'ki*, juniper] ..., they built a fire [*koyühi*], they used the cedar wood [*koh'kup*] for their fire. They said they would have Fire in their clan. Then they came to this place [i.e. 1st Mesa]. They saw a tall man standing by the trail.

They asked him, 'Are you a man who lives here?' He did not speak, but he nodded his head yes. He held out his hand as if to say, 'Everything in this world belongs to me. I am chief of this world.'—'What are you called?' Then he said he called himself Masau'u. So they called him their uncle. He does not go around in the day time, only in the night time, watching the world. He sleeps in the day time.

The 3rd Mesa myth (Titiev, 1944, pp. 155–6) relates how the Ko'kop people, who claim Masau'u as their *wuya*, arrived at Oraibi from the northwest and how, at first, they were refused admission to the pueblo: how, subsequently, when Oraibi was threatened by a large party of raiders, two of their members dressed themselves in the guise of Masau'u, with gourds full of ashes in their hands, and saved the pueblo by throwing the ashes in the face of the enemy: and how, on their return to the village, Matçito (head of Bear clan) welcomed them and gave them land in return for their services.

When they settled in the village, the Ko'kop people are supposed to have brought with them, as their *wuya*, Masau'u and the War Twins (Pyü' ükoñhoya); as the latter are considered to be grandsons of Spider Woman, the Ko'kop people also entered into a partnership with Spider clan, helping them to direct the warrior society known as the *Mutç-wi'mi*: Titiev (1944), pp. 155–6.

*Natural observation, and ceremonial referents*

*ko'kop*, (?) fire spindle. No one knows precisely what *ko'kop* means, nor its etymology (Whorf, 1936, p. 1232). The word has been variously rendered as fire spindle (Parsons, 1936, p. 1067, n. 4: Stephen, 1936, p. 1068), as cedarwood (Stephen, 1929, p. 40, n. 2: Parsons, 1933, p. 30), and as cedarwood-fire or charcoal (Lowie, 1929, p. 332).

In the old days, fire was made by quickly rotating a stick in one of a set of holes in a flat board, known (in Hopi) as *pila'n ko'hü*, until the friction produced a spark which set light to shredded bark placed around the hole. In historic times (Stephen, 1936, pp. 1279–80), the board has been made either of willow or a flat piece of mescal root, and the spindle of dried cottonwood. Fire boards from twelfth to thirteenth century pueblo ruins,[1] however, appear to be made from a resinous wood (? pine, or piñon), and the spindles from sharpened reeds, while the bark used for tinder was 'cedar' or juniper.

---

[1] Specimens in the museums at Mesa Verde National Park, and at Aztec pueblo, New Mexico. The National Parks Service *Notes*, beside a juniper tree near the Betatakin overlook, states specifically, referring to the thirteenth-century cliff-village below, that fires were started with *juniper* fire-drills, the shredded bark being used for tinder, and the wood for fuel. A specimen of a Hopi fire-board figures in the H. R. Voth Hopi Indian Collection at Grand Canyon: Voth (1912c, item 418). Cushing refers (1896, p. 369) to the roots of the juniper and the cedar, 'from which fire is kindled with the fire drill'.

It seems likely, on this ground, that *ko'kop* refers either to the fire spindle used in the new-fire ceremony on the first afternoon of Wü'wütçim, or to the cedar-bark fuse (*kopi'choki*) used for conveying the new fire to the other kivas: cf. Stephen (1936), p. 965. The verb *pi'la*, in Hopi, means 'makes fire' (Whorf, 1936, p. 1280). The same word, according to Voth (1912c, item 418), is applied to the ritual officer in charge of fire; and Voth states further (1905b, p. 79):

> The Cedar or Juniper clan controls the apparatus with which in the Wü'wütçim and New Year's ceremony the new fire is produced. . . .

*ho'ko* or *ho'tcki*, juniper (*Juniperus utahensis*), often referred to as 'cedar'. Juniper grows extensively on the mesas around the Hopi villages, and is one of the two principal firewoods used by the Hopi.

Juniper ashes have a number of ceremonial uses; they are used for the purification of the mother after child-birth and of those who return to the house after a burial, and as a prophylactic against witches (Titiev, 1942, p. 554).

*tuve'e*, piñon (*Pinus edulis*). Piñon also grows on the mesas in company with juniper, and is the other main source of firewood; piñon wood burns hotter than juniper, but juniper is preferred for some purposes, e.g. for baking and *pi'ki* making. Piñon nuts ripen in the fall, and are still gathered by Hopi; the nuts are roasted with salt, and stored for the winter.

Piñon gum is smeared on an infant's forehead and chest, as a prophylactic against witches (Parsons, 1936, p. 1037, n. 1); it is also put on the fire, to 'fumigate' those who have taken part in a burial.

*kü'hi*, fire: *tü'vü*, live ember. In the Emergence myth (Voth, 1905c, pp. 12–13: cf. Nequatewa, 1936, pp. 25–6, and p. 105, n. 11), Masau'u gave fire to the Hopi. In another myth (Stephen, 1929, p. 55), Masau'u gave the Hopi both the secret of fire and the uses of wood.

*Masau'u*, Masau'u. To the complex nature of Masau'u, I shall return presently. Here, we may take note of the following observations. On 1st Mesa, Masau'u figures in the clan myth of Coyote clan; he is *wuya* to Coyote clan (Parsons, 1936, p. 995). On 3rd Mesa, Ko'kop and Coyote clans are closely linked in myth,[1] Masau'u figures in the clan myth of Ko'kop clan, and the man who impersonates Masau'u must belong either to Masau'u or Ko'kop clan (Voth, 1905b, pp. 93–4), or to one of the other clans in this phratry grouping (Titiev, 1944, p. 140, n. 81). On both mesas, as also on 2nd Mesa (Nequatewa, 1936, p. 22, and n. 10, pp. 104–5), there is a close conceptual relation between Masau'u, the deity who gave fire to the Hopi and who controls death, and the

---

[1] Voth (1905c), p. 9. It is clear, from the list of personal names he gives for Ko'kob clan (1905b, pp. 88–9), that Voth has confused *ko'kop* (fire spindle, cedarwood) clan with *ko'ko* or *ko'kob* (burrowing owl): of the nine names he gives, the first four and the last apply to burrowing owl clan, and numbers five to eight to *ko'kop* (cedarwood) clan. In the myth cited above, although Voth translates *ko'kop-wüngwa* as 'burrowing owl clan member', the context makes clear that *ko'kop* (cedarwood) clan member is meant.

Agave fraternity, who strike the new fire at Wü'wütçim and who act as guards on the road to the Underworld.

*tüvü'tsi*, a bird with red on it. The name is, surely, derived from *tü'vü* + *-tsi*, 'live-ember bird'. Stephen describes *tüvü'tsi* as a black bird (1936, p. 962), and also (p. 1071) as 'a small red bird'. Western Robin (*Turdus migratorius*) is the only bird that fits the bill, though the head and back are gray, not black.[1] Robins arrive with the cold weather, usually in late October or November, and stay for the winter.

At Wü'wütçim, a skin of *tüvü'tsi*, a skin of *toko'tska* (cowbird, or Utah redwing) and a black corn (*ko'koma*) ear, are placed on the Agave altar facing to the north, i.e. to the Above: Stephen (1936), pp. 961–2. As the black corn ear is especially associated with Masau'u, being carried on his back and called his *na'atsi* (Voth, 1905*b*, p. 93), it is likely that *tüvü'tsi* also has a special link with Masau'u.

*kwa'ni*, agave, mescal or century plant (*Agave parryi*). Agave does not grow in Hopi country, but far to the south in the Gila river region, and to the northwest in the lower reaches of Grand Canyon, whence it was traded to the Hopi by the White Mountain Apache and the Havasupai. The plant is especially associated with the Kwan fraternity; its stalk is placed on top of the Agave kiva during the Wü'wütçim ceremony, and appears to 'stand for' the single horn of the order.

*mo'hü*, yucca. Yucca is fairly common in Hopi country. The roots are crushed with stones, then mixed with water and lathered into a foam; the hair is washed in the suds thus formed, prior to all naming rites, to all major ceremonies, to marriage, to burial, and on entry to the Underworld.

Kwan clan 'owns' the yucca plant, and several of its personal names refer to the yucca: Voth (1903*b*), p. 93.

In parts of the Great Basin, a small mescal plant, *Agave utahensis*, grows in abundance on the hill-sides; formerly, the buds of this plant were gathered in the spring, then roasted in pits dug on the hillside and lined with smooth pebbles. According to Coville (1892, pp. 355–6), the cooking of the mescal took place late in April and was accompanied by certain ceremonies. In regions where no mescal grows, the Shoshoni used the buds of the tree yucca, *Yucca brevifolia*, in a similar manner; the flower-buds were collected in April, and roasted on hot coals. The tissues of the yucca buds, like those of mescal, are sweet and highly nutritious, being full of sugar and other carbohydrates. The Hopi word for sugar is *kwang'wa ö'ñga*, 'sweet salt'; the link with salt may explain the ceremonies which, among certain Shoshoni, accompanied the cooking of mescal.

*ö'ñga*, salt. Conceptually, *ö'ñga* should go in with this phratry grouping, since the salt deposits lay in Grand Canyon and the Agave fraternity were the guardians of the route leading there. I have found no reference to a salt clan,

---

[1] The identification is confirmed by Mearns (1896, p. 403), who gives Western Robin as (*p*)*tu-we-wurtz'ē* [= *tüvü'tsi*].

but a Hopi man remarked one day at lunch: 'If we had no salt (*ö'ñga*) clan, how should we have got the salt?'

*isau'wû*, coyote (*Canis latrans*). Coyote are still found in Hopi country; they come round the fields, especially at night, Hopi say. Examination of coyote dung, carried out in Mesa Verde National Park, shows that their summer diet consists of deer and porcupine meat, *ribes* berries, birds and insects, roughly in that order. Anderson (1961, p. 58) regards coyote as a major regulator of the deer population; now that wolves have gone, he says, coyote and mountain lion are the only sizeable predators that remain.

*kwe'wûüh*, gray wolf (*Canis lupus*). In the 1850s and 1860s, when travellers first entered the drainage of the Little Colorado river, they reported numerous signs of bear, mountain lion and wolf. The wolf is known to have occurred near Wupa'tki as late as 1937 (Lincoln, 1961, p. 49); it is believed to be extinct now, i.e. south of the San Juan river. Like coyote, wolf is regarded by Hopi as a wily hunter.

*zroho'na*, '(?) mountain coyote, in size between fox and coyote': Stephen (1936), p. 1325. Kennard, who made special enquiries among the Hopi regarding this animal (White, 1943, pp. 439–40), reports:

> It is a small animal, like a coyote in appearance but smaller, that lives in the San Francisco Mountains; it is a great hunter, particularly of deer and antelope, and is a night prowler.

Among the Keres (Acoma-Laguna), White identifies *roho'na* as jaguar (*felis onca*), an animal fairly common in Mexico but very rare as far north as the Pueblo region. He holds, further (1943, p. 442), that

> the Hopi have borrowed both the word and the idea of a hunting animal from the Keres, and have identified it with the swift fox (*Vulpes velox*) or perhaps the desert fox (*Vulpes macro'is*).

Jaguars, however, though rare, still occur north of the Mexican border; one is reported (Hoffmeister, 1971, p. 85) to have been killed near the south rim of Grand Canyon in 1907. And the accounts of the early Spanish explorers indicate that, at that time, jaguars were common in those parts of the Southwest to which the Spaniards penetrated (Olin, 1954, p. 30). On these grounds it seems probable that the Hopi, too, originally applied the term *roho'na* to the jaguar, and that it was only as the animal retreated from the region that they transferred the name to a smaller predator: perhaps, as White suggests, to the desert or Kit fox, one of which was taken in the Wupa'tki area in 1961 (Lincoln, 1961, p. 49).

*le'taiyo*, gray fox: *sikya'taiyo*, yellow fox. Both kinds are resident in the region of the Hopi villages. In the old days, both coyote and foxes were trapped by means of fall traps, weighted with a heavy stone (Beaglehole, 1936, pp. 17–18); Pyü'ükoñhoya was the first to make these traps (Stephen, 1936, p. 188).

Different clans, according to Eggan (1968), 'owned' different trapping areas in the vicinity of the villages.

Both kinds of fox pelt are used for ceremonial purposes, the pelt being attached to the wearer's belt by its head, with the tail dangling down behind him as he walks.

Regarding the clan names in this phratry grouping, we may note, first, a general association of the objects and animals named with fire and hunting. There is, further, an affinity of certain of the animals, notably wolf and coyote, with witchcraft. Both coyote and wolf are regarded as sources of *duhisa*, witch power (Titiev, 1942, p. 549). Coyote is the 'pet' of witch (Parsons, 1936, p. 1281), he follows him 'as a dog does a man' (Stephen, 1929, p. 9); frequent references in myth (e.g. Wallis, 1936, pp. 6, 12, 16) confirm the close link between coyote and witchcraft. Finally, the 3rd Mesa myth relates how the ancestors of this phratry grouping arrived *from the northwest*. The principal clan names of the group support such an origin, i.e. they all represent plants or animals that are important in Great Basin ecology. *Cedar* branches were used by the Shoshoni for building winter shelters; *piñon* nuts furnished their main source of winter food; *juniper* provided firewood, and the berries were eaten when other supplies failed; both *yucca* and *agave* were special plant foods; and, throughout the Great Basin, *coyote* and *wolf* figure prominently in myth—'we are coyote children', say the Owens Valley Paiute (Steward, 1933, p. 235).

To each of these points I shall return later. In the meantime, preliminary to elucidating the character of Masau'u, we have briefly to consider Hopi warfare.

### PRACTICES AND BELIEFS RELATING TO WAR

(a) *Actual war practices*[1]

The principal weapons used by the Hopi, in the old days, were: bow (*a'out*) and arrow (*ho'hü*), nodule club (*pikyai'ñwû*), edged-stone club (*ka'la pikyai'ñwû*) or stone axe, straight stick with fire-hardened point (*la'nsa*), straight oak throwing-stick (*müzri'ko*) and curved throwing-stick (*püchko'hü*). A typical method of fighting (Stephen, 1936, p. 99) was to throw the *püchko'hü* at the enemy as he was drawing his bow; the *püchko'hü* was thrown so as to strike the bow, the Hopi then rushed in and either clubbed, or speared, the enemy before he could recover.

When preparing to fight, warriors wore their ordinary clothes, with the addition of caps made from mountain lion or wild cat skin to which eagle feathers were attached, and bear-skin moccasins. Prior to their departure, the men made *nakwa'kwosi*(s) and prayed to ancient deceased warriors and to Masau'u, who was asked to move in spirit among the enemy and to touch them with his club so that they might be easy victims for the Hopi. The village War chief (*kaletaka*) led the men into battle, dressed in the character of Pyü'ükoñhoya

---

[1] See, particularly, Titiev (1944), pp. 155–6, 160–1: cf. Stephen (1936), pp. 95–100.

and carrying in his hand a stone club, emblem of that deity; after him came the *real* warriors, and after them the rank-and-file. Returning warriors were not allowed to say that they had killed anyone, but were expected to attribute all deaths to the *wuya* of their clan; thus in the Ko'kop clan myth, as the men were returning to Oraibi after the battle and began to count those whom they had slain, if anyone said 'Who killed this enemy?', the answer would be: 'My ancient (*wuya*) killed this one.'

### (b) Ceremonies relating specifically to war

There appear to have been, in the old days, two ceremonies specifically directed to war: the *Mutç-wi'mi* ceremony, and the warrior prayer-stick making (*kaletak-pa'ho la'lauwû*) ceremony, the one held in the fall and the other at midwinter.

The *Mutç-wi'mi* ceremony, which is only reported for Oraibi (Titiev, 1944, pp. 156-9), took place annually, in Wiklavi kiva, not long after the close of the Marau: i.e. late in September. The ritual paraphernalia was owned by the Spider and Ko'kop clans. The rites lasted two days; they took the usual form of the setting-out of an altar (*poñya*) and the making of medicine-water (*ña-kü'yi*) on the first day, followed by a public performance at sunrise on the second day. In the kiva ritual, the Ko'kop head impersonated Pyü'ükoñhoya, and Spider chief impersonated Spider woman; effigies of Spider woman, of the War Twins and of Masau'u, were present on the altar; and during the preparation of the medicine water, special prayers were addressed to the preying animals at each of the four cardinal directions, and to Kwato'ko, the savage bird representing the Above. Other deities prominent in this cult, according to Titiev, were Sho'tokünuñwa, the principal sky deity, represented either by a single star or by a lightning frame; the Sun (*ta'wa*); and the stars (*so'hü*) forming the Milky Way, *soñwuka* (cf. Stephen, 1936, p. 87, Fig. 63).

Turning now to the winter prayer-stick making of the warrior fraternity (*mom'tçitu*): at Oraibi, this was incorporated in the Soya'l and took place on the 4th day of that ceremony (Dorsey and Voth, 1901, p. 18 *et seq*); on 1st Mesa it was celebrated four days after the conclusion of the Soya'l, and it is the latter ceremony that will be described here.[1] The ceremony, on 1st Mesa, belonged to Reed (*pa'kab*) clan, and was performed, not in kiva, but in the clan house of the Reed people. Each of the four walls of the room in which the ceremony took place was decorated with a mural painting of one of the four preying animals (Fewkes, 1902, pp. 485-6, and Pl. xxii):

> northwest . . . *to'hoa*, mountain lion: outline in black, the body brown; its eye a fragment of haliotis shell, and a red line running from the mouth to the heart to represent the breath-line.
> southwest . . . *ho'nau*, bear: coloured brown.

[1] Principal source, Fewkes (1902), pp. 482-91: cf. Parsons (1936), pp. 83-4, and Stephen (1936), pp. 85-100.

southeast ... *toko'tçi*, wild cat: its belly white, the legs margined in black,
  its back yellow and dotted; above, a circle enclosing a five-pointed star.

northeast ... *kwe'wû*, wolf: painted white, the colour symbolic of this
  direction; behind, a disc representing the Sun. Each of the four animals
  about three feet long, with a breath-line emerging from its mouth.

The deities principally involved in the ceremony were, again, Pyü'ükoñhoya
(the Twins), their grandmother Spider Woman, and Masau'u. The ceremony
lasted two days. On the first day, prayer-sticks were made for these three deities
(Stephen, 1936, p. 90); this was followed by an all-night session of songs, in the
course of which medicine-water (*ña-kü'yi*) was brewed, and on the afternoon of
the second day, by the public performance known as *kaletak-pa'ho la'lauwû
ti've*, 'warrior *pa'ho*-making dance'.

Regarding the purpose of the two war ceremonies: rather surprisingly (at
first sight), *two* threads are present, not one. The medicine-water, which was
brewed during the night of the midwinter ceremony and given to the younger
boys (aged from 7 to 9: Stephen, 1936, p. 91), was given to them *to make them
brave*: Parsons, 1936, p. 84. But the all-night session of songs that accompanied
the brewing of the *ña-kü'yi* had as its purpose, not only 'to be brave', but '*to
make the ground freeze*': Parsons, 1936, p. 94, n. 3. The latter thread is confirmed
by one further observation: early on the second morning of the midwinter
ceremony, the Tobacco-Rabbit man (who acts as Crier chief for the winter
ceremonies) calls out[1] that the women are not to grind corn that day, nor the
men to sing katçina songs. Grinding, as Parsons points out (1925, p. 16, n. 14),
is associated with crops, and katçina songs are primarily *for* rain; and both are
forbidden, 'for the ceremony is not for rain or crops, *but to make the ground freeze*'.

To the significance of this thread in the war ritual, I shall return when we
come to discuss the actual ceremonial functions of the Reed phratry grouping.
In the meantime, we have to unravel the complex nature of Masau'u.

### MASAU'U AS GUARDIAN OF THE CROPS

So far, we have seen that there is a close conceptual link between Masau'u
and death (in that he is the owner of Mas-ki, the house of the dead), between
Masau'u and fire (in that he gave fire to the Hopi, and is impersonated in the
course of the Wü'wütçim ceremony), and between Masau'u and war (in that
he is one of the principal deities whose aid is invoked, both in the war ceremonies and before setting out on a war party). I turn now to a quite different
aspect of Masau'u, his relation to crops and to the land.

In all the leading versions of the Emergence myth,[2] it was Masau'u whom the
people first met when they emerged on earth, and it was he who gave them
their first crops and allocated land to the clans. Thus the Oraibi version states

---

[1] On 1st Mesa, that is: Parsons (1925), p. 16. Titiev also remarks that, according to his
informants, no corn meal was used in the *Mutç-wi'mi* ceremony at Oraibi.

[2] Cf. Voth, (1905c), pp. 12–13, 23–4: Cushing (1923), p. 166: Stephen (1929), pp. 52–3:
Wallis (1936), pp. 3–4, 16–17: Nequatewa (1936), pp. 25–6.

(Voth, 1905c, p. 13) that, after the people met Masau'u and had collected wood and made a fire, he gave them 'roasting ears, and water-melons, melons, squashes . . ., and they ate and refreshed themselves'. The Shungo'povi myth (Wallis, 1936, p. 3) says, specifically, that Masau'u 'had watermelon, musk-melon, pumpkin and squash to eat', and later (pp. 4, 16) refers to him as owner of the land: 'I shall give you my land . . . the whole earth is mine'. According to the Walpi myth (Stephen, 1929, p. 10): 'the Hopi obtained from Mü'iyiñwa all their typical plants except the squash and koko'm ka'ö (black corn), and these Masau'u gave them.' This link between Masau'u on the one hand, and squash and black corn on the other, is confirmed from other sources; Masau'u, as we have seen, carries a black corn-ear on his back (Voth, 1905b, p. 93), and in one account of him (Nequatewa, 1936, p. 25) his head 'was . . . like the biggest squash, and there was no hair on it'.

Now it is in keeping, as Titiev observes (1944, p. 184), with the belief that Masau'u was the original proprietor of the earth and one of the principal owners of all Hopi crops, that in former times it was customary for someone to impersonate Masau'u whenever a communal working party went into the fields, whether at planting time or at harvest. Titiev himself has described (ibid. pp. 184–7) one such impersonation, at harvest time, on 3rd Mesa. Four days before the working party is announced, the man who is to take the part of Masau'u and his assistant—both of them members of the Ko'kop-Coyote phratry grouping—retire into the Ko'kop clan house, to prepare themselves by fasting and sexual abstinence. Two days before the event, all the men who are to help in the work go out on a rabbit hunt: they take care to kill the rabbits by tossing them high in the air so as to keep the blood within the carcass, for only fresh blood may be used in Masau'u's costume; all the rabbits are brought to Ko'kop clan house. Early on the morning of the appointed day, the working party (so'hkyañ) goes out to the field and starts work. Towards noon, Masau'u and his assistant make their way to a cave or other secluded spot on the mesa side overlooking the field, and there Masau'u dresses. First, his entire body is rubbed with ashes; then an old, shabby, woman's garment (manta) is put on in reverse fashion, so that the right shoulder is exposed instead of the left. A strip of yucca is bound round the ankles and the wrists, and another strip around the waist, into which is tucked, on the left side, an ear of black corn. A hood, made out of the skins of the rabbits killed two days earlier, is drawn tightly over his head, the fur inside and the smooth surface outside, and gathered in around the neck with fibres of yucca; the face is painted like a skull—'it fits so tight that it doesn't look like a mask at all' (Mrs. B. Aitken: quoted by Forde, 1931, p. 397) —with big eye-holes, big mouth, and no nose. Finally, the man's head is dowsed with fresh rabbit's blood, which is left to dry on the mask.[1]

[1] This description of Masau'u's costume is a composite picture, taken from Titiev (1944, pp. 185–6), Mrs. B. Aitken (Forde, 1931, pp. 396–7), Stephen (1936, pp. 994–5), and Beaglehole (1937, pp. 46–7); the four accounts are in substantial agreement. The reader will note the emphasis on ashes, yucca, black corn, and the tight-fitting mask (like a big squash), all associated in one way or another with Masau'u.

Late in the afternoon as the working party is drawing to a close, the Masau'u impersonator stalks down to the field where the work is in progress. Apart from the old, shabby *manta* draped over his left shoulder, he is naked, his head and body covered with blood; in his left hand he carries a planting stick, and in his right a club, about a foot long, covered with an inverted rabbit skin and dowsed in blood. On reaching the field, Masau'u runs among the people, brandishing his club and threatening to strike anyone whom he catches. Then he rushes over to the piles of corn, stacked ready for carrying back to the village, and pats them with the palms of his hands, 'to indicate his ownership of the entire crop' (Titiev, 1944, p. 186). Then all return to the village. There, about sunset, the Masau'u impersonator disrobes, his assistant peels the rabbit-skin mask from his head and buries it, and later that evening all those who took part in the working party share in a rabbit stew, prepared from the rabbits which they killed earlier.

The 'purpose' of the Masau'u impersonation, whether this is performed at planting time or at harvest, is much the same in either case. At planting time, Masau'u goes through the motions of digging a few holes in the field with his digging-stick, and dropping a handful of seeds in each (Forde, 1931, pp. 396–7: cf. Beaglehole, 1937, pp. 46–7); at harvest, he goes out to the fields to overlook *his* harvest (Stephen, 1936, pp. 994–5), patting the piles of corn with the palms of his hands to indicate that they are his.[1] In either case, he is re-asserting what the myths say: namely, that he (Masau'u) was the original 'owner' of the land, that he first gave the farm lands to the Hopi, and that they are indebted to him for the crops which their fields yield.[2]

Now this aspect of Masau'u, i.e. as guardian of the crops and 'owner' of the land, is (I believe) the most fundamental in his nature, to which the others, i.e. as giver of fire, as deity in control of death, and as war leader, are subsidiary. To delineate in what sense this is so, I propose now to consider certain aspects of Hopi thinking regarding the nature of the world, with the object of seeing how Masau'u fits into the scheme of things as conceived by the Hopi.

[1] The whole mime finds a striking parallel in an impersonation of Masau'u, reported by Fewkes (1917, pp. 156–8) as taking place in one of the kivas at Hano on the night of 15–16 February 1900, as part of the Powa'mu. There, the two impersonators each wore on his head a large hollow gourd, painted black and spattered with glistening haematite, and carried in his hand a planting stick. The ceremony began with prayers and songs, 'the intent throughout were prayers to fertilise the fields that corn might germinate and grow' (p. 157); the two men then entered the kiva, put on their gourd head-pieces, and, *assuming the kneeling posture which the Hopi take when they are planting on their farms*, went through the motions of planting the corn seed, manipulating their planting sticks in rhythm with the songs (p. 158).

[2] Masau'u's 'ownership' of the land is further expressed, concretely, on a boundary stone that used to stand about halfway between Shungo'povi and Oraibi, the upper end of which was roughly carved in the shape of a human head, with round shallow holes for eyes and mouth, representing Masau'u: Stephen (1889), p. 214, and (1936), p. 390, n. 1, and Fig. 220. In the fall of 1967, on the day of the Lako'n dance at Shungo'povi, I walked home from that village to Oraibi via the old trail, hoping to see the stone; but either the stone has gone, or I missed the track, because I did not see it.

HOPI COSMOGNOSIS[1]

The three aspects of Hopi world-knowledge that I propose to consider, are: the Six Directions system, with particular reference to the Above and the Below; the balance of the world, with particular reference to its remaining in being; and the notion of time, as a process of becoming or unfolding. These three aspects I shall take in turn; then, bearing each of the three in mind, we shall be in a position to weigh the rôle ascribed to Masau'u in the Hopi world view.[2]

### (a) the Above and the Below

The Hopi orientate their countryside, not—as we do ours—by reference to North and to the pole star, but by reference to the points on the horizon which mark the places of sunrise and sunset at the summer and winter solstices. This gives them, as we have seen above (pp. 47–8), a primary grid of four points, corresponding roughly to our northwest, southwest, southeast, and northeast, each of which is named and each of which is associated with its own particular colour—yellow, blue-green, red, and white, respectively. At these four points, the four Cloud chiefs are believed to sit, sending the clouds which bring rain to the Hopi fields. This primary grid we may represent as follows:

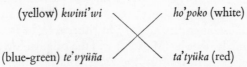

(yellow) *kwini'wi*      *ho'poko* (white)

(blue-green) *te'vyüña*      *ta'tyüka* (red)

Two further points bring the cardinal directions of the Hopi from four to six. The first of these lies between *ho'poko* and *kwini'wi*, in the direction of our North, and is referred to as *O'mi*, or *o'vi*, the Above; its associated colour is black. The second lies between *te'vyüña* and *ta'tyüka*, in the direction of our South, is referred to as *At'kyami*, the Below, and its associated colour is either all colours' or speckled. At all major ceremonies these six cardinal directions are represented by corn-meal lines on the sand field in front of the altar, corn cobs of the appropriate colours (yellow, blue, red, white, black or purple, and sweet corn) are set in each of the six directions, and prayers addressed to the deities who reside there to send rain and other benefits. For the lay-out of such an altar, the one made for the *Yasang'lauwû* ('making the year') ceremony at

---

[1] I use this word, rather than the more familiar *cosmography*, to indicate that the Hopi approach to the world, while it makes use of much clear-sighted empirical observation, is primarily *intuitive*: and that the body of knowledge consequent on this approach is more akin to a work of the imagination than to a scientific construct. Like a work of the imagination, it is internally consistent, follows its own logic, and does not depend for its verity on an appeal to fact—nor can it be overturned by such an appeal.

[2] The *traditional* world-view, that is; how far this view is held—even by older Hopi—to-day, is another matter. Further, the traditional world-view itself has been under pressure from outside influence, at least since Catholic fathers reached the Hopi villages in the early seventeenth century; thus a part of the trouble in reaching a just estimate of the character of Masau'u is due, I believe, to his having acquired—or been invested with—elements that rightly belong to the Devil (as portrayed in late medieval Doom paintings).

Oraibi[1] furnishes a nice example—except that, as this is an altar of the Kwan fraternity, the sixth corn-ear points not in the direction of the Below (south), but in the direction the 'breath body' takes when it leaves the grave (i.e. west):

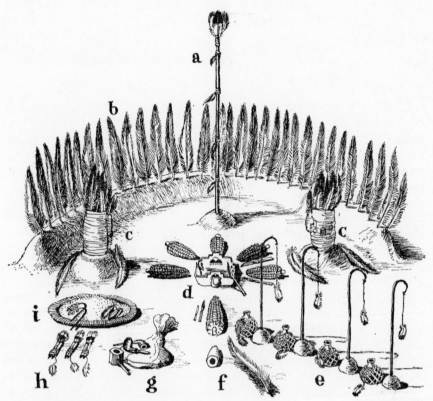

Fig. 53. Altar of *Yasang'lauwû* ('making the year') ceremony. *a. na'tsi*, standard. *b.* 32 eagle-feathers, set in sand ridge. *c. ti'poni*(s) of the Kwan fraternity. *d.* bowl and aspergill, with six corn ears. *e.* four *moñwikuru* (netted gourds), and four crooks (symbols of life) set in clay cones, leading to the east. *f.* cloud blower. *g.* bag of tobacco, with pipes. *h.* three prayer-sticks. *i.* woven tray with corn meal, with two shell rattles and two *nakwa'kwosi*(s) lying on the meal. Re-drawn from Voth (1912b), pl. li.

Schematically, then, we may represent the two final directions thus, with the 'path of life'—and the route taken by the 'breath body' after death—cutting their axis at right angles:[2]

---

[1] This ceremony, which formerly took place in September and ushered in the new ceremonial year, is only known for Oraibi, in a single description by Voth (1912b), pp. 115–19; like the Wü'wütçim, it involved the making of 'new fire' (above, p. 246).

[2] On the road taken by the dead and leading to the west, see Parsons (1925), p. 66, n. 109; and on the 'path' of life leading towards the rising sun, ibid. pp. 97, 113, 115.

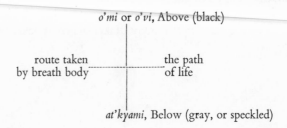

*o'mi* or *o'vi*, Above (black)

route taken
by breath body

the path
of life

*at'kyami*, Below (gray, or speckled)

Clearly, *o'vi* and *at'kya* represent a pair of opposites. Just as *kwini'wi* and *ta'tyüka* form one pair, and *te'vyüña* and *ho'poko* another, so *o'vi* and *at'kya* form a third pair; whatever the one is, the other is opposite to it. Now, in everyday speech, *o'vi* and *at'kya* have three simple referents. The first is architectural. Hopi houses were traditionally built on two or three floors,[1] one above the other, the upper floor being reached by an internal stair coming up through the floor; many are still built on two floors; when the weather turns warm around May or June, the whole family moves *o'vyak*, upstairs, for the summer, the upper floor being cooler and getting any breeze that may blow; and when the nights turn cold in late September or October, they move *at'kya-k*, downstairs again, for the winter. This, then, is one common meaning of the *o'vi/at'kya* pair, i.e. up(stairs)/down(stairs).

Now, if a Hopi announces at breakfast that he is going *o'vyak*, he means simply that he is going up onto the mesa, e.g. to collect firewood; if he says that he is going *at'kyamy-ak*, he means that he is going down into the valley, usually down to his fields below the village or to herd sheep near the wash. Due to the physiography of Black Mesa and the siting of the Hopi villages on the southwesterly spurs of the plateau, *o'vyak*, 'up', also signifies towards the north; while *at'kyamyak*, 'down', also signifies towards the south, i.e. down towards the Little Colorado river. Thus a Hopi woman, referring to bird migration (in which I was interested), spoke of the birds as going *at'kyamy-ak*, i.e. *down* south, in the fall, and *o'vyak*, i.e. *up* north, in the spring. Here, then, we have two further meanings of the *o'vi/at'kya* pair: namely, up (on the mesa top)[2]/down (in the valley below), up (towards the north)/down (towards the south).

Turning from everyday speech to myth: in Hopi mythology, *At'kyami* (or *At'kyabi*) has a specific reference, it is the Underworld or the Below, where people first lived and from which they emerged, through the *si'papü*, on to the

---

[1] A feature common to pueblo ruins throughout the Southwest, e.g. at Wupa'tki, Tsegi, Chaco Canyon. A more specific architectural feature linking the Hopi villages to the Tsegi Canyon sites is the use of T-shaped doors and windows, very common at Kiet Seel and Betatakin, and extensively used by the Hopi in the old days (Simpson, 1953, p. 60).

[2] Hence the suffix *-ovi* in many Hopi place names, e.g. Shungo'povi, Mishong'novi, Sicho'movi, Nü'va-tü'kya-o'vi (San Francisco Peaks).

surface of the earth (*tü'wa ka'tsi*, 'earth lies flat'). Thus, one version of the Emergence myth (Stephen, 1929, p. 10) runs:

> In bygone times all people lived in the Below, in the lower house; after a time they passed up to another house; after another lapse of time they passed up to a third house, and after more time had elapsed they again passed upward, by means of the reed, and emerged from the *si'papü* upon this fourth or upper house, this *tüwa'ka'chi*, land (earth) surface, upon which they now live. The four houses rest above each other . . ., being called the *na'liyûm ki'hü naach'vi*, the four houses situated above each other.[1]

When the people emerged on earth, it was dark there; after a time they met Masau'u; Masau'u 'owned' the earth, and it was he who gave them both fire and land. Regarding himself, he told them (Shungo'povi Emergence myth: Nequatewa, 1936, p. 26): 'he was their god—the god of the upper world, and it all belonged to him; although he was the god of the upper world, he could not walk about in the day time, but only at night by the light of the fire'. In another version of the Emergence myth (Stephen, 1929, p. 7), Masau'u actually stood over the *si'papü*, helped the people out, and thanked them for coming. In yet another version (Stephen, 1929, pp. 51–5), Mü'iyiñwa and Masau'u are specifically contrasted, as deities of the below-ground and of the above-ground, respectively; the 'place below', *At'kyabi*, is located 'far away in the South, just where no one knows'; and Mü'iyiñwa is characterised as having given the Hopi the secret of the rocks and the art of house building, Masau'u as having given them the secret of fire and the uses of wood.

Thus, in myth, we find a specific link between Mü'iyiñwa and the Below, located somewhere in the south, and between Masau'u and the Above, i.e the earth surface (*tüwa ka'tsi*) of which he was first owner. Masau'u is further associated with darkness, i.e. with the original darkness on earth; and this latter association furnishes the necessary link between Masau'u and the ceremonial direction, *o'mi* or *o'vi*, since black is the colour associated with the Above. Here then, in myth, we find a further extension of the *o'vi/at'kya* polarity; namely, up (on the earth surface)/down (in the Below), represented respectively by Masau'u and Mü'iyiñwa.[2]

But this polarity, clear in the myths, has been obscured by the character attributed to Masau'u as deity in charge of death. Thus Nequatewa, in a footnote (1936, p. 105, n. 11) to the Shungo'povi myth quoted above, states:

---

[1] The metaphor, here, is evidently that of the multi-storied house with a terrace on the roof, as constructed in some of the twelfth and thirteenth century pueblos; the *si'papü* derives from the stair well in the floor, and the reference to reed suggests that house ladders may at one time have been made from their stems.

[2] The antithesis between Mü'iyiñwa and Masau'u is confirmed, independently, by Fewkes. Speaking of the former, Fewkes writes (1917, p. 151):

> The breath bodies of men pass to their future home, the underworld, a realm of the departed, presided over by the supernatural being called the God of Germs [i.e. Mü'iyiñwa].

Five pages later (p. 156), he refers to Masau'u, as 'the god of planting, also known as the supernatural of the "surface of the earth" '.

'Masau'u is the owner of all the Hopi world. He also represents death, for he controls the fate of the departed spirit in Mas-ki, the underworld.' And in another footnote, describing the duties of the Agave (Kwan) fraternity of which he was a member, he writes (1936 p. 104 n. 10):

> ... it is the duty of these priests to look after the dead. They are in charge of the spirit upon its journey from this world into Mas-ki, the underworld or spirit world of the Hopi. These priests serve Mü'iyiñwa, the Germ God, owner of the underworld, and Masau'u, God of the earth and of death.

Much the same blurring of the distinction between the Above and the Below occurs in Stephen's notes on the subject (1936, pp. 150-1). Masau'u, says Stephen, was the first house builder[1], he has a two-storey house underground; the grave is the entrance to this house (*Mas-ki*), of which we see only the roof of the second storey—the interior we will not see until we die; the dead go to the lower storey where the houses are like those we live in, and what is called dying is a return to the early house, i. e. *Kibvuñ'kani*, 'the house they return to'.

The source of the confusion lies, I think, in this: Masau'u is 'owner' of the land, and consequently the grave, *tü'ami*, 'belongs' to him. But neither the grave nor the underworld is, in a strict sense, Mas-ki: *that*, as Mrs. Colton points out (Nequatewa, 1936, p. 105, n. 12), is held to be Grand Cañon, thought of as a long passage through which the 'breath', or spirit, has to make its way on the journey from the grave to the underworld. On its way through the cañon, the spirit comes to a fork in the road, one branch of which leads to the fire pits where witches are burned, and the other to the land of the dead. Now the Cañon, being on the earth's surface, even though it is 'down below' (*at'kyamy-ak*) in a geographical sense, is 'up above' (*o'vyak*) in relation to the Below; and so it still 'belongs' to Masau'u, while the Below, the realm of Mü'iyiñwa, lies beyond. But due, I think, to a false association[2] between Masau'u, death, the fire pits, darkness, and the after-life as a place of punishment (a notion alien to Hopi thinking, except in the single case of witches), Masau'u has mistakenly been invested with control of the underworld—and has even come to be regarded *primarily* as the deity having charge over death and the after-life, whereas *primarily* (and aboriginally) *he is the deity in control of the earth and of crops*, as his association with the Above witnesses.

## (b) The balance of the world

In the preceding section we have delineated four axes of the Above/Below polarity, namely, as an architectural referent, up(stairs)/down(stairs): as a locational referent, up on the mesa top, down in the valley: as a geographical referent, up towards the north, down towards the south: and as a referent to

---

[1] Simpson notes (1953, pp. 58-9) that in the old days, on completion of the building of a new house, prayer-sticks to Masau'u were placed among the rafters.

[2] Almost certainly taken over from Catholic dogma: cf. on this point, Parsons (1936), p. 150, n. 1.

the ordering of space in myth and ceremonial, up on the earth's surface, down in the Below. I turn now to the final axis of the Above/Below polarity, that between the sky (*to'kpela*) and the waters under the earth (*pa'tübha*).

In the Hopi theogony Sho'tukünuñwa, the sky deity, is the most powerful of the supernaturals; he created the world and assigned separate regions and powers to the other deities (Stephen, 1940*b*, p. 16: cf. Nequatewa, 1936, p. 104, n. 7), but he has remained remote from the world he created. In most versions of the Emergence myth, as we have seen, it was Masau'u who gave the Hopi their land and certain of their crops (notably squash, and black corn), and Mü'iyiñwa who gave them their other crops (chiefly corn, sweet corn, and beans). But in some myths (e.g. Stephen, 1929, pp. 50–5), Sho'tukünuñwa himself is credited with having allotted the first (Hopi) chief his domain, given him the seeds of corn, melons and edible vegetation, and instructed him to plant them in the valleys—'for of these things no one but Sho'tukünuñwa understood'. Subsequently the deity withdrew into the sky, where he is known by two natural features: the star Aldebaran, which is the 'eye' of Sho'tukünuñwa and is represented in certain ceremonies (cf. Stephen, 1940*b*, p. 19, Figure *e*), and forked lightning, which he controls—represented, again, by the lightning 'frame' used in certain of the kiva rituals.

Opposed to the sky (*to'kpela*), are the great waters (*pa'tübha*) under the earth; on them, the earth rests. And in control of the waters is Pa'lülükoñ, the great serpent: 'Underneath is Pa'lülükoñ . . . All underneath us is water. He shakes the earth and then we have an earthquake. He lives in every spring and stream . . . [if we do not act rightly], Pa'lülükoñ will rise up and shake the whole world, and it will turn upside down. In one day, we shall all be turned upside down.'[1] Pa'lülükoñ also, as we have seen, is represented in certain ceremonies, notably in the Uñkwa'ti ceremony, or Pa'lülükoñ-ti, held in March and characterised by the planting of corn in the kivas and by the representation of water serpents at the village spring.

On a balance between these two forces, the forces of the sky (or the Above) represented by Sho'tukünuñwa, and those of the Below represented by Pa'lülükoñ, the Hopi universe rests. Symbolically, the two elements are brought into contact in the making of medicine water, where the ray of sunlight flashed into the bowl signifies the Above, and the water itself (Stephen, 1936, p. 711), the Below. A similar imagery lies behind those myths, e.g. the Emergence myth from Shungo'povi (Wallis, 1936, p. 15), which treat the forces of the sky as male and the earth itself as female:[2]

> Now, Mü'iyiñwa lives in the earth. He has a sister who lives with him. The Earth is a female. Now . . . So'teknani [Sho'tükunuñwa], who sends the rain, married the earth. When they have intercourse, we get rain, for that is the fertilizing

[1] Wallis (1936), p. 12: cf. Stephen (1929), p. 7, and Nequatewa (1936), p. 103.
[2] Pa'lülükoñ, also, may be represented as female, i.e. 'as a crested one-horned serpent of great size and most prodigious power, possessing mammae which are the source of the blood of all animals and of all plant-life': Stephen (1940*b*), pp. 46–7.

fluid. All the vegetation is the offspring of the earth (Tüwa'poñtümsi, Sand Altar Woman). So'teknani puts grass seeds inside of hail-stones.[1] When these melt, the seeds go into the earth, the sun shines with heat, and soon they spring up.

And finally, the two elements—Above (sky, rain, lightning, sun rays), and Below (earth, water in pools, springs and cisterns)—are brought together, corporeally, in the conceiving of the Twins. According to the myth relating their birth (Stephen, 1929, pp. 13-14), a Hopi maid lay out on the Mesa and was fertilised first by the rays of the sun, and then by drops of water, falling on her vulva; she conceived, and in due course gave birth to the Twins. 'Like the antelope, she gave birth to two upon the same day; the first born was the child of the Sun, Pyü'ükanhoya, the other twin was also the child of the Sun, but is called the child of the Water, Pa'lüñahoya.'

Now, I have referred earlier (above, pp. 149-50) to what Titiev calls the 'concept of the year's duality': namely, the Hopi belief that whatever is happening in the upper world, its opposite is happening in the Underworld—when it is light here, it is dark there, when summer here, winter there, and when *we* are celebrating a major ceremony, *they* are celebrating an analogous minor one. This duality extends, I believe, not only to the *timing*, but also to the *content*, of the ceremonies that make up the ceremonial cycle. For, in studying the sequence of ceremonies which runs from the *Mutç-wi'mi* ceremony, through Wü'wütçim, Soya'l and the winter prayer-stick making of the warriors, to the winter session of the Snake fraternity, and which covers the months from late September to the end of January, we get the impression that these are 'male' ceremonies, having to do with 'male' activities (ice and cold, war, hunting), and that the deities chiefly involved in them (Sho'tukünuñwa, Pyü'ükoñhoya, Masau'u) are 'above' deities: in contra-distinction to the sequence of ceremonies running from Powa'mu and Uñkwa'ti, through Nima'n and the summer ceremony of the Snake-Antelopes, to the Marau' and Lako'n, which are essentially 'female' in character, having to do with the earth, rain, and the growth of crops, and the deities chiefly involved in which (Mü'iyiñwa, Pa'lülükoñ, Tüwa'poñtümsi) are 'below' deities.

## (c) Time, *as a process of becoming*

I turn now to a more difficult problem, namely, how the Hopi handle aspects of time in their everyday speech.[2] I shall begin with some simple observations on how the Hopi record temporal events, then consider what kind of notion of time their method of recording temporal events reflects, and finally consider what light the Hopi notion of time throws on the character

---

[1] As Parsons observes (Wallis, 1936, p. 15, n. 2), hail occurs in connection with lightning storms and So'teknani is a Lightning spirit.

[2] This is the problem that exercised Benjamin Lee Whorf throughout his work on Hopi linguistics. In this section I present only a handful of his salient conclusions on the Hopi time-sense, in so far as these bear on the matter in hand, and refer the reader to Whorf's own writings for a full exposition of his views.

of their deities—chiefly, since it is his character with which we are concerned here, of Masau'u.

Let us begin with the ceremonial day count. This runs, as we have seen earlier, *yü'ñya, shüsh ta'la, lüsh ta'la, paish ta'la, na'lüsh ta'la . . .*, 'going in, first day, second day, third day, fourth day . . .': *-ta'la*, used for marking the passage of days, derives from the stem, *ta'la*, adj. v. '(is) bright, light', hence *ta'la*, n. 'light, a day'. So, the literal meaning of the ceremonial day count is: ' . . . is light (i.e. dawns) the first time, is light the second time . . .'. An alternative method of reckoning is 'by night': using the stem *to'ki*, v. 'a night elapses', hence *to'ki*, n. 'a night'. But while both *ta'la*, and *to'ki*, may be used on their own as nouns, referring respectively to a single 'day' and a single 'night', in reckoning the passage of time they are used in what is essentially a *verbal* not a noun form, with *ordinals* not with cardinals. Thus, each dawning ('is light for the first time', 'is light for the second time', . . .) is seen as a further stage in the process of 'getting later and later'—the immediate and subjective awareness of which constitutes, in Whorf's view, the sensory experience at the root of *all* notions of time. Where, with us, this awareness has been dulled by the linguistic usage which enables us to cut time into segments, to set them one beside another, and to imagine a 'length of time' as so many of these units (minutes, hours, days) set out in a row like bottles, with the Hopi it has been dulled by no such usage. For, in Hopi, plurals and cardinals are used only for entities that form or can form an objective group, e.g. six men. There are no imaginary plurals; such an expression as 'ten days' is not used. Instead, the day in question is reached by a suitable count: 'they stayed ten days' becomes 'they stayed until the eleventh day', or 'they left after the tenth day'. In other words, our 'length of time' is not regarded as a length, but *as a relation between two events in lateness* (Whorf, 1956, p. 140).

Much the same applies to the words used for cyclic events and time periods (see Whorf, 1946, pp. 165, 180: 1956, pp. 142-3), except that these are not verbal in form, but *adverbial*. Words denoting points and periods in natural cycles, like morning (and other times of day), summer (and other seasons of the year), the moon's phases, the Hopi months, etc., are not nouns—that is to say, they cannot be used as the subject or object of sentences—but a kind of adverbs. They mean e.g. 'when it is morning' or 'while morning-phase is occurring', 'when it is summer', 'while the harvesting moon is on the wane', etc. One does not say, in Hopi, 'it is a hot summer', or 'summer is hot'; summer is not hot, summer is only *when* the sun draws near and the crops ripen, just as winter is *when* the sun withdraws and the ground freezes.

One of my own early attempts at speaking Hopi ran as follows. We were crossing the bridge over the Little Colorado river and, observing that there was little or no water in the bed of the river (it was summer) and remembering that the Hopi word for water in its natural state is *pa'hü* (as distinct from water in domestic use, *kü'yi*), I hazarded the remark, *ka pa'hü*. The Hopi, to whom the remark was addressed, looked down into the wash to see what on earth I could be referring to, then replied: *ka'e, ka mü'na,* 'no, (it) does not flow'. His correction points one of the fundamental differences between Hopi, and by inference the other languages of the Uto-Aztecan family, and English: namely, that where English tends to analyse reality in terms of *things,* Hopi tends to analyse it in terms of *events* or *happenings.* To see how this mode of analysis is tied to Hopi syntax requires a brief *excursus* on the structure of the Uto-Aztecan languages, of the northern or Shoshonean branch of which Hopi forms the southeasterly outrider.

The central fact of this structure, writes Whorf (1935, pp. 600–2), is a stem of the form CVCV (consonant-vowel-consonant-vowel) with a verb-like meaning, modified by certain changes in the second stem vowel, by several types of reduplication, and to a relatively small extent by prefixes.[1] The basic meaning of the stem is typically that of a verb, denoting a class of event rather than a class of thing; and from this meaning nouns, names of things or qualities, are derived in various ways, e.g. Hopi *ñü'lü,* v. 'is in the form of a loop or curve', *ñülü'kpi,* n. a crook: Tübatulabal *yühpa,* v. 'shuts', *yühpal,* n. a door. This fundamental situation is not altered by the fact that a given verbal stem may, without change of form, also serve as a noun, as in Hopi *ta'la,* v. 'is light', n. a day, *to'ki,* v. 'is dark', n. a night, *mü'na,* v. '(water) flows', n. stream, river, *pü'va,* v. 'is cut into an arroyo', n. arroyo, wash; nor by the fact that a given verbal stem may be represented *only* by its noun derivative. Thus, in each language of the family, the greater part of the noun-vocabulary is elaborated independently from the language's own stock of verb stems.

In addition, however, there is a common stock of nouns, belonging to the ancestral speech before its separation and fragmentarily preserved by the daughter languages. This common stock includes most animal, plant, anatomical and kinship terms, many nouns of topography and the world of nature, and a few nouns of material culture. These archaic nouns are also of the form CVCV or else clearly derived in the usual way from such stems, with the exception of some which are monosyllabic. For, along with the main stock of CVCV stems, the Uto-Aztecan languages contain another set of stems, much fewer in number but extremely common, of monosyllabic form CV. Some of these are verbs, some nouns like *ma,* 'hand', *pa,* 'water', *hu,* 'arrow'. Although at first sight one might suppose these must be out-and-out nouns, *names of things,* yet many of them appear on closer examination to be merely derivative meanings, become extremely common, of terms that *primarily denote classes of events or of relationships,* and are on the whole verb-like. Thus, in both Aztec and Tübatulabal the stem *ma* is a verb, meaning in the one language 'catches', and in the other 'touches', and only with nominal affixes does it serve as a noun (Aztec *i·ma,* Tübatulabal *ma·n,* 'his hand'); further, such CV stems may themselves be reduplicated, and then may yield CVCV stems, like Aztec *mama,* 'carries'.

If the first fundamental character of Hopi speech is to analyse reality in terms of events rather than things, the second is to classify the events themselves by *duration types.* Events of necessarily brief duration cannot be anything but verbs. If the root denotes a transitory event, leaving no effect or an effect that rapidly vanishes: if, so to speak, the ground or field returns to its original

---

[1] In certain languages of the group, the first consonant (C′) may be zero, but this C′ is derived from a Uto-Aztecan consonant (', *h, p, w,* or *y*).

state after the momentary 'happening' (a flash, a wave, a splash), then the root is a pure verb. Thus, in Hopi, a flash of lightning, a wave, a flame, a shooting star, a puff of smoke, are verbs, not nouns; and there can be neither original nor derived nouns meaning 'a flash', 'a spark', 'a wave', a 'nod', 'a blow' (Whorf, 1946, p. 164). At the other end of the scale come the true nouns, words (that is) referring to *whatever gives the visual appearance of closed (or nearly closed) and lasting outlines*, including not only tangible objects (*ki'hü*, house) but also inaccessible ones like clouds (*o'mau*) and heavenly bodies (*sho'hü*, star), certain clear-cut configurations of landscape (*tükwi*, hill), masses of material such as water (*pa'hü*), plants, animals and parts of the body (*kü'tü*, head). In between the out-and-out verbs and the out-and-out nouns come a large class of words, the ambivalents, which may be verb at one minute and noun the next (i.e. they can take *either* inflectional system), but in which 'the verb nature is paramount and the verb system preferred' (Whorf, 1946, p. 163). These words refer, in particular, to events or happenings which leave durative shapes and outlines which are, nevertheless, subject to change (and which may, therefore, alter their shape or outline as the result of a further event of the same kind). Examples of such ambivalents are: *mü'na*, v. '(water) flows', n. stream, river, *pü'va*, v. 'is cut into an arroyo', n. arroyo, wash, *ti'va*, v. '(they) dance', n. dance, ceremony, *tso'ki*, v. 'is perched, planted, set up (on something)', n. bush, tree. The ambivalents include all words denoting shape or outline, e.g. *wü'tsi*, v. 'is flat', *nü'lü*, v. 'is round or curved'; the only true adjectives are words that denote colour (*si'kya*, yellow), figureless percepts (*wu'ko*, big, *wu'pa*, tall, high), or intellectual concepts (*lo'lomai*, good).

Whether a Hopi word is a verb, an ambivalent or a true noun, i.e. whether it takes verb inflections only, may take verb or noun inflections, or takes noun inflections only, thus depends, in large measure, on the effect that the event to which it refers has on the field where it operates; where the effect is transitory, the word will be a verb, where permanent a noun, and where temporarily stable but subject to change, an ambivalent. 'Cloud' and 'storm' are at about the lower limit of duration for pure nouns, and 'puff of smoke', by inference, at about the upper limit for pure verbs, while a bird perched on a branch or a katçina dance configuration, both of which present outlines that are temporarily stable yet subject to change, will be delineated by ambivalents.

The most abstract or intellectual words are usually verbs, expressing various kinds of thinking, desiring, mystical experience (Whorf, 1956, p. 61). And this leads on to a further, fundamental character of the language: its treatment of time. In place of our three-fold division of the passage of events into past, present and future, Hopi imposes a two-fold division, into 'earlier' and 'later'. The 'earlier', which is roughly equivalent to our present-past, Whorf calls[1] the *manifested* or objective, and the 'later', the *manifesting* or subjective. The root of the distinction between the two categories lies in this: that, in the ceaseless

---

[1] In his paper entitled 'An American Indian model of the Universe', reprinted in Whorf (1956), pp. 57–64.

process of 'becoming later and later', there is a point ('now', 'at this moment') at which certain relations between things are changed in an irreversible manner. Everything that lies on the 'near' side of this point is *manifested*, that is how it is, the form it has taken; the *manifested* or objective category, therefore, comprises everything that is accessible to the senses (what we are seeing, touching, hearing, smelling), together with everything that has happened in the past and is accessible to memory or recounted in myth. The other category, the *manifesting* or subjective, comprises the realm of belief, intuition, and uncertainty, all that has not yet taken final shape and between the elements of which relations may still change (or be changed): in other words, what we call the 'future', plus all that we call *mental*—'everything that appears or exists in the mind, or as the Hopi would prefer to say, in the *heart*, not only the heart of man, but the heart of animals, plants, and things, and behind and within all the forms and appearances of nature, in the heart of nature and ... of the Cosmos itself' (Whorf, 1956, pp. 59–60).

This latter realm, the *manifesting* or subjective, we may speak of as the realm of *hope* or *hoping*; and an analysis of the Hopi word used for this activity throws light on the distinction between the two categories outlined above:

> *tüna'tya*, v. 'is in the action of hoping, hopes, is hoped for, thinks or is thought of with hope ...': (Whorf, 1936, p. 1311: 1956, p. 61).

The verb *tüna'tya* contains in its idea of hope something of our words 'thought', 'desire', and 'cause', which sometimes must be used to translate it. But, at root, its meaning is set in a bed of ideas which are peculiar to Hopi culture; it refers, in Whorf's words, to the state of the subjective, un-manifest, vital and causal aspect of the universe, and the fermenting activity towards fruition and manifestation with which it seethes—an action of *hoping*, i.e. mental-causal activity, which is forever pressing upon and into the manifested realm. The Hopi see this burgeoning activity in the growing of plants, the forming of clouds and their condensation in rain, the careful planning-out of the communal activities of agriculture, and in all human *hoping, wishing, striving*, and *taking thought*, and as most especially concentrated in *prayer*—'prayer which conducts the pressure of the collective Hopi thought and will out of the subjective into the objective' (Whorf, 1956, p. 62).

Now Hopi has an aspect of the verb, the *ingressive* (-*va*), which refers to this edge of emergent manifestation, the edge where subjective becomes objective, marking the passage from the latent—and, as yet, unrealised—form of the activity to which the verb refers, to the manifested form. It is most often used (Whorf, 1946, p. 175) on a stem denoting an activity that lasts some time, such as *to'kya*, '(they) sleep', to denote entry into the state referred to, as *to'kva*, '(they) begin to be sleeping, go to sleep'. But on verbs denoting causal power, like *tüna'tya*, it denotes beginning, not of the activity itself, but of its fruition. The root meaning of *tüna'tya* is that of subjective force or activity, 'hopes', 'is hoped for', or, better, 'uses hoping', the subject being either the person who hopes or the thing hoped for, and the outcome being dependent, in some measure at least, on the amount of hoping 'power' that the one can bring to bear on the other; the ingressive is then the terminus of such activity, hence the form *tüna'tyava*, v. 'comes true, being hoped for'. And if the simple form *tüna'tya*, 'hopes for, is hoped for', be regarded as corresponding to the realm of the *manifesting* or subjective, then the ingressive form *tüna'tyava*, 'comes true, being hoped for', may be regarded as equivalent to the realm of the *manifested* or objective.

The Hopi thought-world, then, as mediated by the Hopi language, analyses reality largely in terms of events (or better, 'eventing': Whorf, 1956, pp. 147-8); the events referred to are classified by the effect they have on their field of operation, whether transitory, temporarily stable yet subject to further change, or permanent; and the sequence itself is cut at the point where events that are yet to come (and are, in consequence, still subject to the influence of 'hope' or prayer) take their final form, so passing out of the *manifesting* or subjective realm, into the *manifested* or objective.

Within this framework, the primary vehicle for the reporting of events is the verb; and the Hopi verb, as Whorf demonstrates (1946, pp. 173-5: 1956, pp. 51-6), is very rich in the development both of aspects and voices to denote variations in meaning on the basic theme represented by the root. As example, let us take one voice, the *eventive*, and two aspects, *punctual* and *segmentative*, of one class of verbs, the k-class. k-class verbs have CVCV roots, and commonly refer, in their root meaning, to a distinctive visual outline left in the field, either transiently or lastingly, by a prior happening. The *eventive* is the zero form of k-class verbs and of all ambivalents, that is to say, it is the 3rd-person singular intransitive voice, punctual aspect, present-past tense—'it declares an event; its subject is that part of the ground or field to which something happens, or has happened, whereby a new or altered configuration manifests, either fugitively or with lasting effect' (Whorf, 1946, p. 174), e.g.

ha'rü, v. is bowed, crooked, bent over, making a rounded angle:
pü'va, v. (of land) is broken into a gully or arroyo.

The segmentative aspect is formed by final reduplication of the root, plus the durative suffix *-ta*, and converts the single figural image of the k-class stem, shown in the punctual aspect as operating about a single point, into a repeating pattern over the whole (or at least a wider) field:

harü'rüta, v. lies in a meandering line, makes successive rounded angles (referring to meander patterns in decoration):
püva'vata, v. extends in successive gullies, is broken into arroyos (said of eroded ground on the main valley floor).

In these and similar cases, where the phenomenon denoted by the root requires a rigid field to operate in, the segmentative aspect exhibits the resulting outline as a static tableau disposed in space. But in other cases, where the phenomenon denoted by the root either operates in a mobile substance such as water or refers to disturbance about a point in a subtle medium such as air, the segmentative aspect of the verb refers, more nearly, to pulsation in time:[1] e.g.

| | |
|---|---|
| *wa'la*, v. (of water) makes one wave, gives a slosh: | *wala'lata*, v. is tossing in waves, is kicking up a sea. |
| *rü'pi*, v. gives a flash: | *rüpi'pita*, v. (of light) is sparkling. |
| *'ü'wi*, v. flares up: | *'üwi'wita*, v. (of fire) is flaming. |
| *'ü'mü*, v. booms, thunders: | *'ümü'müta*, v. is thundering. |

The punctual and segmentative aspects of the verb thus provide two means of reporting events, or of referring to phenomena, falling within the *manifested* or objective realm.

The *manifesting* or subjective realm comprises events which, already potentially in being, have yet to take their final form: the final form that any event will take being in part dependent on the nature of the event itself, and in part on the amount of hoping 'power' that can be brought to bear on it (to direct it into the desired course). For in the Hopi world-view, as evidenced by the Hopi language (Whorf, 1956, pp. 147–8),

> existents do not 'become later and later' all in the same way; but some do so by growing like plants, some by diffusing and vanishing, some *by a process of meta-morphosis*, some by enduring in one shape till affected by violent forces. In the nature of each existent able to manifest as a definite whole, is the power of its own mode of duration: its growth, decline, stability, cyclicity, or creativeness. Everything is thus already 'prepared' for the way it now manifests by earlier phases; and what it will be later, partly has been, and partly is in act of being so 'prepared'.

This concludes our account of Hopi modes of reporting events, and to illustrate the difference between the Hopi way of seeing things and our own, I propose now (following closely in Whorf's footsteps: 1946, pp. 182–3) to analyse a single clause of a single Hopi sentence:

*yowya'ñ löqö'tsoki-t mü'a* . . ., 'upon lightning striking the pine tree . . .'.

'Lightning', being a momentary event, cannot be a noun or an ambivalent. The verb *ta'lawipi*, composed of *ta'la*, 'light', and *wi'pi* (k-class verb), 'lashes once (like a whip-lash)', denotes the occurrence of a lightning flash; the derived noun, *ta'la-wi'piki*, denotes the outline of lightning as capable of being fixed, hence a lightning design; neither is applicable here, if we are to refer to the blasting of the tree by making 'tree' the object of a transitive verb. English treats 'lightning' as an actor, acting upon the tree, but in Hopi *ta'lawipi* is a verb and cannot be an actor. But *yowya'ñ*, 'rain-storm', denotes a long-enduring event, is a noun, and can be a subject; it is treated here as the 'real' or

---

[1] An example of the influence of linguistic form on imagination may be seen in this account of the Underworld (Stephen, 1929, p. 4):

> At that time, at sunrise the sky was wide, the horizon was far around, but at noon the sky vibrated, it alternately compressed and distended. The horizon was not so far around as it is in this world. In the daytime, in the Underworld, it was beautiful, there was bubbling water in commotion, all around the landscape. . . .

In both cases, of the sky *vibrating* and of the water *bubbling*, I suppose the segmentative aspect of the verb to be employed, the availability of the linguistic form having pre-disposed to the choice of image.

objective agent (i.e. with transitive verb). From the Hopi view-point, 'rain-storm' is the common source of all the varied phenomena experienced at such a time—lightning flashes, thunder, falling drops, blasting of trees, and so on. The verb is a special use of *mü'a*, 'deals it a swift penetrating blow, stings, shoots at (with arrow)';[1] *löqö'tsoki*, 'pine tree', is a compound of *lö'qö*, 'pine', and *tso'ki*, 'tree, bush', occurring free as a k-class ambivalent, '(thing) perched up or on'; *-t*, objective case.

And now let us return to the nature of the Hopi deities: first, to Sho'tokünuñwa, associated with the stars and with lightning. But lightning, to the Hopi, is an event not a thing, 'lashes once (like a whiplash)', and is gone. So Sho'tokünuñwa must either be the spirit-person associated with the momentary 'lightning-flash' happening, or with the durative storm-cloud from which the flash emanates. He cannot be, in any sense that *makes sense* to Hopi, the 'god of lightning', because Hopi does not conceive lightning as a thing at all, but as an event or happening.

Much the same applies to the description of Masau'u, as 'god of death'. We recall the sentence:

Kü'yi ma'na     yükü'k-aadta   tih-talau'wü       mo'ki:
Küyimana ('s)   elder-sister   (in) child-bearing   died;

*mo'ki*, v. 'dies, is dead', is a k-class verb, punctual aspect: 'it declares an event . . . its subject is that part of the field to which something happens, or has happened, whereby a new configuration manifests, either fugitively or with lasting effect.' If Masau'u is especially associated with death, then it is not with death as seen through the eyes of Bunyan's pilgrim:

death, where is thy sting? grave, thy victory?

but with dying as a (momentary) event whereby a new configuration manifests. Now the dead, as we have seen (above, pp. 42–3: cf. Parsons, 1925, p. 75, n. 121), is washed by his aunt and given a new name, 'to use in the other world where he becomes like a baby'; he is no longer a Hopi, he is 'changed (*nih'ti*, grown into)' a katçina, a Cloud. Dying, objectively an event whereby certain relations between things are changed in an irreversible manner, for the person concerned is conceived *as a metamorphosis*. And it is this fact, I believe, that furnishes the key to Masau'u's character.

Let us enumerate his attributes: he is especially associated with the event of dying; he is present at the striking of the 'new fire', and is sometimes referred to (Stephen, 1936, p. 704) as *kü'hi moñwi*, 'fire chief'; he is impersonated in the course of the Wü'wütçim ceremony; the Kwan clan, of which he is *wuya*, 'owns' the yucca plant, used in the taking of all ceremonial steps (birth and naming, katçina initiation, entry into fraternities, return from salt expedition, death and burial); the growing crops and the harvest 'belong' to him. Each of these aspects involves *metamorphosis*, or change, in some degree: the *social* metamorphosis of birth, initiation, marriage, death, the *physiological* metamorphosis of plant growth, the *physical* metamorphosis of fire, flaming up and

---

[1] Old stone arrow-heads, found in the fields, are believed to come from lightning: Stephen (1936), p. 137.

turning into ashes. *Metamorphosis*, as Whorf stresses, is one of the processes by which things manifest themselves in the ceaseless 'becoming later and later' that constitutes the Hopi awareness of time. And it is the juxtaposition of these attributes of Masau'u, with the place ascribed to the process of change in the Hopi view of the world, that confirms (to my mind) Stephen's early characterisation of that deity as 'god of the metamorphoses of Nature':

> *Masau'*, the one whose touch destroys ... presides over the surface of the earth. When his child is sick, the Hopi prays Masau' to come and look upon it and pass by without touching it. To come and look upon his cornfield and garden, and pass by without touching them. Portions of his field products are specially planted for Masau', and, after harvest, are deposited as offerings at Masau's rock. His special attribute is *the power of causing all the metamorphoses of Nature*. (Stephen, 1940*b*, pp. 8, 16–17: my italics).

One further metamorphosis we have noted earlier, that of the *po'aka*, or witch; a Hopi 'merely turns over and *becomes* a coyote or a crow', and later transforms himself back into his human form.[1] Now, there is evidence for some affinity between Masau'u and witchcraft. Coyote and wolf, two of the animals conferring witch power (*duhisa*), are among the clan names of the phratry grouping of which Masau'u is *wuya*; the time of year when Masau'u is abroad in the villages, November and December, is a particularly 'dangerous' (*kya*) one so far as witches are concerned; and Mrs. Eggan, in her interpretation of Hopi dream material,[2] has linked the frequent occurrence of dreams figuring Masau'u with the 'ever-present fear of witchcraft' on the part of the dreamers. If Masau'u's special attribute is, as Stephen says, 'the power of causing all the metamorphoses of nature', then we can understand the nature of the affinity between that deity and witchcraft.

### PHRATRIES V AND VI (CONCLUDED)
*Actual ceremonial duties of Reed-Greasewood-Bow, and of Ko'kop-Coyote*

The Bow clan, according to the Oraibi myth quoted above (pp. 209–10), 'brought' the Wü'wütçim ceremony, i.e. that part of it which is concerned with the inducing of rain, snow and ice, while clans of the Ko'kop-Coyote grouping 'own' the making of the new fire, which takes place on the first afternoon of the ceremony. Clans of the latter grouping also control the Kwan fraternity, one of the four fraternities concerned in the initiatory sequence of Wü'wütçim. The distinction between the two parts of that ceremony, drawn in the account given earlier (see, especially, pp. 108–11), is recognised by Hopi

---

[1] Wallis (1936), pp. 12, 16. It is possible that 'crow', in this context, does not refer to *añwü'si* at all, but simply means 'any black bird', as in Stephen's description of the Agave altar (1936, p. 962): 'north, black corn (*ko'koma*) ear: skin of *tokiichka*, crow, blackbird (?) ...'. If this is the case, it establishes a further link between Masau'u and witchcraft.

[2] D. Eggan (1952), p. 476. For examples of dreams figuring Masau'u, see D. Eggan (1957), pp. 58–9, 80, 86, 96, 119: (1961), pp. 10, 13, 23–4, 64.

themselves; thus Luke, Lowie's 2nd Mesa informant, describing his own part in the ritual (as a Badger person, he was connected with tobacco and had the privilege of 'offering smoke' in it: Lowie, 1929, p. 334), refers specifically to the Kwan fragment of the rites, the _kwa'kwantu_, 'which is the property of the Cedarwood-Fire clan', and is _performed at the time of the wü'wütçim-tu_. In other words, Cedarwood-Fire clan(s), owning the fragment of the rites that has to do with fire and initiation, and Greasewood-Bow, owning the fragment that has to do with rain, snow and ice, 'go in together' every fourth November to perform the complete ceremony.

Regarding Reed clan, its principal ceremonial function (on 1st Mesa) is charge of the effigies of Pyü'ükoñhoya, filling of the office of _kaletaka_ (war chief), and ownership of the winter prayer-stick making ceremony of the warrior society; on 3rd Mesa, these 'warrior' duties were discharged by clans of the Ko'kop-Coyote grouping.

Clearly, there is a close link between the clans of the Ko'kop-Coyote grouping, and those of Reed-Greasewood-Bow. The clans of the two groupings share control of the Wü'wütçim ceremony in November, and of the warrior observances in late September and again at the time of the Soya'l; the _wuya_ of the two groupings are Masau'u, and Pyü'ükoñhoya, respectively, both associated—directly or indirectly—with war; and effigies of the latter deity are placed on the altar in the course of Soya'l (Parsons, 1925, p. 122, n. 187: cf. Stephen, 1936, p. 40, Figure 22). At first sight, this linkage appears to represent strands in a 'war' theme, running from the _Mutç-wi'mi_ ceremony in late September, through the Wü'wütçim, Soya'l and winter prayer-stick making of the warrior society, to the winter prayer-stick making of the Snake fraternity towards the end of January. In support of this interpretation, we may note that the special 'pets' of Pyü'ükoñhoya (Stephen, 1936, p. 307, n. 1) are: mountain lion (N.W.), bear (S.W.), wolf or jaguar (S.E.), and wildcat (N.E.); these are the four preying animals to which songs are addressed, and which are represented on the four walls of Reed clan house, in the course of the two 'war' ceremonies. Of the four, mountain lion 'belongs to' the clans of the Snake phratry grouping, bear and wildcat to the clans of the Bear-Spider grouping, wolf and _zroho'na_ to the clans of the Ko'kop-Coyote grouping; while Pyü'ükoñhoya himself 'belongs to' Reed clan, and Spider Woman, also prominent in the 'war' cult, to Bear-Spider grouping. Further, the association of bear with _war_ has been specifically noted on 1st Mesa (see above, p. 218).

At first sight, therefore, it appears that we have here a nexus of ideas centred around war and village defence, embodied mythically in the figures of Masau'u, Pyü'ükoñhoya and Spider Women, mediated through the four preying animals, dramatised in the course of the principal ceremonies of late fall and early winter, and represented socially by the clans of the four phratry groupings: Ko'kop-Coyote, Reed-Greasewood-Bow, Bear-Spider, and Snake.

But a closer look at the evidence indicates, I think, that while perhaps over the last 300 to 400 years—the period, that is, of increasing nomad pressure against the settled agriculturalists of the Southwest—the 'war' thread has indeed been a principal one running through the fall and winter ceremonies of the Hopi, this 'war' thread itself is a late embroidery on an older ground: namely, the inducing of ice and snow. That the need for ice and snow in late fall and winter, and its correct timing, were believed to be of paramount import to the agricultural cycle, is shown by the following references to cold weather:

The precise timing of the Snake ceremony in August has an influence on the occurrence of the first frosts: 'sometimes, if the Snake chief does not watch the sun right, they dance early, then it freezes early too' (Parsons, 1925, p. 101). On the other hand, at the winter prayer-stick making of the Snake fraternity, 'everybody smokes *to bring rain and snow*' (ibid. p. 37). Several other references in the *Pueblo Journal* (Parsons, 1925) refer to smoking in the course of the fall and winter ceremonies, to bring rain and snow; thus, on 31 October, the Village chief and the head of Bear clan have to stay up all night and smoke, to ask for snow and rain 'in order to have more crops next year' (ibid. p. 115).

The Wü'wütçim announcement, early in November, appeals (above, p. 109) for snow and ice to come and cover the fields 'that after planting they may yield abundantly'. This aspect of Wü'wütçim is brought out forcefully in a Hopi dream, recorded by Mrs. D. Eggan (1957, pp. 97–9). In the dream, the dreamer is returning from herding his sheep on the flats below the village; it is still summer, and he is surprised to see cold clouds rising from the north and large snow flakes begin to fall. When he reaches the foot of the mesa, he finds that the path is blocked and that the Wü'wütçim ceremony is already in progress. He meets his brother; they agree it is strange to have Wü'wütçim so early, *since it will bring frost.* They go to the house of the Snake people for the night, and there one of the old men sitting by the fire remarks: 'My friends, your people are having Wü'wütçim so early that it will bring cold weather. Your crops will freeze.' This remark so perturbed the dreamer that he woke up immediately.

The pine needles attached to many of the *pa'ho*(s) made at Soya'l are specifically, as we have seen earlier (above, pp. 132–3), *for* cold. Prayer-sticks made in the course of the winter meeting of the Warrior society similarly have pine needles tied to them (Stephen, 1936, p. 91); and the songs sung during the all-night session that follows their making are of two kinds (Parsons, 1925, pp. 15–16), songs 'to be brave' and songs 'to make the ground freeze'.

Finally, regarding Pyü'ükoñhoya, Stephen writes (1936, p. 239):

His breath is ice cold, he understands the cold, hence appeals to him in the cold moons of *kya* and *pa* (December and January). During these two moons it is especially desirable to have plenty of rain or snow to permeate the land, then cold to make plenty of ice. If there has been little winter moisture and ice, when summer comes the fields get dry too soon, and little or no harvest is yielded.

*kya mü'iyawû*, the December moon, is also known (Stephen, 1940*b*, p. 23, n. 1) as 'snow moon'; and I suppose that the appeals to Pyü'ükoñhoya, referred to here, are appeals for ice and cold, made in the course of Soya'l and of the winter prayer-stick meetings of the Warrior and Snake fraternities.

These scattered references witness to a recurrent pre-occupation with the advent of cold weather, running from late summer to the winter solstice and beyond: an interest which is the obverse of the interest in the return of the sun and advent of warm weather, running from Soya'l to the Nima'n katçina festival in late July. The need for ice and snow, stressed in the ceremonial, is recognised also on a practical level by Hopi. Thus Stephen has the following entry (1936, p. 939) in his *Journal* for 22nd September, 1892: 'Late fall rain is desirable, to make ice when the real cold comes. Ice is very desirable, but just why I can not discover. . . .'

In answer to my query on this point, Professor E. W. Russell (of the Department of Soil Science, University of Reading) suggests three possible links between winter ice and the following season's crop-growth. First, clay soils are nearly always improved by frost, if the clay is moist, for the frost breaks down the clay clods into a friable crumb structure from which a seedbed can easily be made; but if the snow comes first, and the frost comes when the soil is already covered with a few inches of snow, then the frost is unlikely to penetrate far into the soil. Second, it may be that, if the soil remains frozen for some length of time, there will be a larger flush of nitrification when the spring comes than if the soil lay moist (and unfrozen) all winter; as maize is a crop that responds well to nitrogen, quite a small increase in the nitrates present in the soil in the spring might give an appreciable percentage increase in yield. Third, a long spell of frost may well kill insect pests when over-wintering; as maize is attacked by quite a range of insect pests, this factor too might give a further increase in yield.

The interesting point, arising out of these observations by Professor Russell, is that they confirm the order in which the Hopi desire these events to occur: namely, late fall rain to saturate the ground, followed by frost and snow to freeze it.

The interpretation I am proposing is that the winter ceremonies of the Hopi, in particular the Wü'wütçim, the Soya'l, and the winter prayer-stick making of the Warriors and of the Snake fraternity, while presenting—in the form in which they have come down to us—a strong 'war' aspect, were in origin ceremonies for ice-and-cold; as such, they formed an integral part of the climato-agricultural ceremonial cycle, corollary and complementary to the return-of-the-sun-and-warmth theme represented by the Powa'mu ceremony, the summer observances of the Flute fraternity, and the Nima'n katçina; and that it was only under the growing pressure of the nomad raiders (i.e. Apache, Navajo, and later, mounted Utes), from *ca.* 1500 on, that the winter ceremonies were transmogrified and their original purpose subordinated to the over-riding needs of village defence. If this is true and if the vestiges of the ice-and-cold theme, which still survived in the rites when these first became subject to outside scrutiny in the '90s, represent the original *raison d'être* of the winter ceremonies, then we may expect to find that those deities (Masau'u, Pyü'ükoñhoya, and Sho'tukünuñwa) chiefly associated with the ceremonies, and commonly referred to by the early observers as *war* deities, are in fact primarily ice-and-cold deities—or at least have strong ice-and-cold elements in their character.

Regarding Masau'u, the association appears fairly clear. Masau'u has a general link with cold and darkness, in that, when the Hopi emerged on earth, it was cold and dark there, and the only light was given by the stars; Masau'u showed the first people how to make fire, and by its light (and warmth) they were

enabled to plant and harvest their crops. More specifically, Masau'u is associated
with cold by the pine needles thrown on the fire after the kindling of the new
fire (above, p. 100), returning to him 'what is his'.

To establish the relation between Pyü'ükoñhoya, Sho'tokünuñwa and cold,
requires a brief digression on the rôle of the stars in Hopi thinking. Stephen,
in his *Journal*, makes frequent reference to the careful observation by the
leaders of the two principal winter ceremonies, Wü'wütçim and Soya'l, of the
exact position in the night sky of Orion and the Pleiades for the timing of the
kiva rituals; this is confirmed, for the Soya'l, by Parsons' 1st Mesa informant
(1925, p. 122, n. 187), and Stephen refers to similar observations in the course
of the Flute ceremony in August, and of the Marau' in September. The night
sky over north-eastern Arizona is brilliantly clear, and Orion is a great constellation, only rivalled at this latitude by the Plough turning around the pole star
to the north and by Scorpion lying low on the southwesterly horizon; but when
Orion is up, it dominates the sky over the Hopi villages, both by its scale and
by the magnitude of its individual stars. During the last thousand years, the
period with which we are concerned here, Orion has been at its most prominent during the months of November and December, as the following table of
its (current) rising times shows:[1]

| Date | Last star of Orion visible above the horizon (2nd Mesa) | Orion crosses the meridian |
|---|---|---|
| September 18 | 1 a.m. | 5.30 a.m. |
| October 18 | 11 p.m. | 3.30 a.m. |
| November 18 | 9 p.m. | 1.30 a.m. |
| December 18 | 7 p.m. | 11.30 p.m. |

Now *sho'hü*, the stars ('all of them'), is one of the clan names of Reed–Greasewood–Bow phratry grouping, of which Pyü'ükoñhoya is *wuya*; and Pyü'
ükoñhoya, as we have seen, 'his breath is ice cold, he understands the cold . . .'.
Sho'tokünuñwa, also, is associated with Reed clan (Stephen, 1936, p. 96), and with
the stars: in that his name, evidently derived from *sho'hü*, star, *to'kpela*, sky,
*ünu'ñwa*, heart, probably refers to the four-pointed star by which he is often
represented. This star is, in point of fact, Aldebaran (Stephen, 1940*b*, p. 19,
Figure *e*), regarded as the 'eye' of the deity; and Aldebaran, the red-tinged
star, is one of the prominent stars in the outer ring of the constellation Orion,
and the first to rise above the horizon. On this ground it seems a reasonable
guess that the stars (*sho'hü*), which figure among the clan names of this phratry
grouping, are not the stars in general, but refer specifically to the stars of the
Orion constellation, 'all of them', and perhaps also to the Pleiades.

The stars themselves are generally considered (cf. Parsons, 1936, p. 84, and
p. 87, n. 1) to be associated with war; but no *prima facie* reason is to be found,

[1] Observations made at Oraibi in the fall and early winter, 1969–70. The Pleiades rises,
and crosses the meridian, about one hour ahead of Orion.

either in natural observation or in myth,[1] why they should be so associated. But there is an excellent reason, in natural observation, why they should be associated with the advent of cold weather. Looking back to the table of Orion's rising times, it will be seen that the constellation first becomes visible a few days after the summer solstice, when it appears shortly before dawn above the eastern horizon; during the next four months, as it rises earlier and earlier (four minutes earlier each night), the constellation becomes more and more prominent in the night sky, until, during the months of November and December, it is visible virtually all night long. Now these six months are precisely the period over which the Hopi evince a keen interest in the approach of cold weather; and it is surely not far-fetched to suppose a conceptual link between the waxing of Orion and the Pleiades, and the return of cold weather? Nor to suppose a more specific link between the cold, glittering stars of the night sky in November and December, and the glittering frost and ice with which those stars co-incide?[2]

I conclude then, on the evidence before us, that the principal ceremonial function of the Ko'kop-Coyote and of the Reed-Greasewood-Bow phratry groupings is control of those ceremonies, namely the Wü'wütçim ceremony and the winter prayer-stick making of the Warrior society, the primary purpose of which during the historic period has been war and village defence; that the *original* purpose of these ceremonies, before they altered their character under the pressure of the nomad marauders, was climato-agricultural, i.e. to induce the ice, cold and snow[3] required for the growth of the next season's crops; and that it was in response to the change in the purpose of the ceremonies, that the deities associated with them changed *their* character.

### Association of ideas

The complex of ideas associated with the *Ko'kop-Coyote* phratry grouping I suppose to be centred around notions of cold weather and fire: of being initiated, going on salt expeditions, and dying, all forms of *social* metamorphosis or becoming; of witchcraft, coyote and wolf being two of the animals into which witches commonly change or are turned: of prophylaxis against witchcraft, piñon gum and juniper ashes being commonly used for the purpose, and December being the 'dangerous' moon for witches; of crop growth, Masau'u being linked with squash and black corn, with ownership of the land

---

[1] With one exception—Parsons, referring to the observation of Orion and the Pleiades by the Hopi at the time of the winter ceremonies, states (1926, p. 212, n. 12): 'Orion's belt is thought of as a bandolier (*to'zriki*), for the constellation is a war chief (*kahletaka*).' But this may well be a late gloss.

[2] Or used to co-incide; in recent years, November–December has been relatively mild, and the real cold has not set in until January or even early in February.

[3] The link between ice-and-cold, and war, is also recognised by the Tewa of Hano. In the old days the Tewa used to hold a war ceremony in January, and a ground-freezing ceremony in February; the two were linked in some way (Parsons, 1926, p. 216). In the course of the latter, those taking part 'used to whip each other, so the ground would freeze and then be wet, likewise so men would be brave and hardy' (ibid. p. 220).

and with the harvest; and of hunting, Masau'u having some link with wild animals, and wolf, coyote, *zroho'na* and fox being renowned for their cunning and for their skill in hunting.

The *Reed-Greasewood-Bow* grouping is evidently associated with the fall, with the waxing of Orion and the Pleiades in the night sky, with the onset of cold weather, with hunting (through the use of bow and arrow, and the link with dogs), and, secondarily, with war.

Clan names of both groups show a close link with successive stages of the Emergence myth, as might be expected since both play a major rôle in the Wü'wütçim ceremony. It was *mo'tsni* (shrike) who found the hole through which the people were to emerge, *pa'kab* (reed) by which they climbed out of the Underworld, *yau'pa* (mockingbird) who taught them their languages, and *sho'hü*, the stars, which first gave them light when they emerged on earth; after their emergence on earth, the people met Masau'u, who gave them fire (*kü'hi*) to warm themselves by and who also taught them, according to one version (Stephen, 1929, p. 55), the uses of wood and the habits of wild animals.

Both groups, again, exhibit an affinity with witchcraft. Wolf and coyote, as we have already noted, are sources of *duhisa*, witch power. So also are dogs (*po'ko*), and owls (*moñwû*), both of which figure among the clan names of Reed-Greasewood-Bow.

### Anomalies, and comments

The inclusion of owl (*moñwû*) in the Reed-Greasewood-Bow grouping is, at first sight, puzzling. Apart from the association of owl with war (above, p. 243), owl feathers were attached to prayer-sticks made at Soya'l, at the winter prayer-stick making of the Flute society, and at Powa'mu (Stephen, 1936, pp. 78, 91, 109), to bring warm weather needed for the early growth of the peach crop. The usage appears to run counter to the general emphasis on cold, represented by the other clan names of the phratry. However, according to Edmund Nequatewa,[1] owl feathers have influence over *cold weather*; they are tied to peach trees during Soya'l, *to keep the trees from freezing*. Peach trees having been introduced into the region by the Spaniards in the early or mid seventeenth century, owl feathers—previously associated with cold—were evidently put to a new purpose.

The inclusion of Bow clan in the Ko'kop-Coyote phratry grouping on 1st Mesa, rather than in the Reed-Greasewood grouping, and the inclusion of Pyü'ükoñhoya in the Ko'kop-Coyote grouping on 3rd Mesa, are both readily explainable in terms of the close ceremonial (and conceptual) linkage between the two phratries.

The inclusion of an Eototo clan in the Ko'kop-Coyote grouping, on 1st Mesa, is ascribable to the fact (Parsons, 1925, p. 98, n. 150: 1933, p. 31, n. 121) that at Walpi the mask of Eototo, normally vested in Bear clan, has passed into the keeping of the Coyote people.

[1] I am indebted to Dr. A. F. Whiting for this piece of information.

PHRATRY XI. HORN–MILLET

| | | |
|---|---|---|
| *Ahl*, horn | | *le'hü*, Indian millet |
| *sowi'ñwû*, deer | *pa'ñwû*, mountain sheep | *a'nü*, ant (various kinds) |
| *chü'bio*, antelope | *chai'zrisa*, elk | *pa'la a'nü*, red ant |

*Myth.* The 1st Mesa myth of the origin of the Horn people (Parsons, 1933, p. 34) recounts how, after they came out from the Underworld, they found a deer, and how they took its name, together with those of the other horned animals.

Another myth (Stephen, 1929, pp. 67–70) tells how the ancestors of the Horn and Mountain Sheep clans met with the Masau'u on their wanderings, how he showed them a cave to build their 'great house' in and a valley where they could grow their crops, and how a man of Wolf clan guided them on their subsequent journey to the south.

*Natural observation, and ceremonial referents*

*Ahl*, horn. The word probably refers to the horns of the mountain sheep (*Ovis canadensis*); according to Fewkes (1900a, pp. 131–2), the two horns worn by men of the Ahl fraternity were those of mountain sheep.[1] Of the four game animals formerly hunted by the Hopi, deer were found on the mesa top, antelope on the flats to the south of the villages, and mountain sheep either in the canyon heads to the northeast, where they were once very abundant (Bourke, 1884, pp. 134–5), or on 'mountain-sheep mesa' (*pa'ñ-o'vi*) to the southwest. Elk (*Cervus canadensis*) were probably always rare in the Black Mesa region, since their chosen habitat is in the higher mountains (Anderson, 1961, p. 63); but Mearns records (1896, pp. 392–3) the killing of one by Hopi hunters, some years earlier.

Mountain sheep were hunted in September,[2] after the Marau'; deer and antelope in October after the Lako'n, when the animals were at their fattest, or in December, when snow made their tracks readily discernible. Deer and antelope were run down, usually by two men carrying water and provisions for two or three days; they followed the trail all day, slept beside it at night, then took it up again in the morning; when they eventually came up with the exhausted animal, they either shot it with bow and arrow, or else threw it to the ground and smothered it by pressing the head into the sand. The latter was the preferred method, for it was believed that smothering the animals enabled their 'breaths' to go to their home and so to be born again on earth. Mountain sheep were hunted by a communal party, with the help of dogs; they aimed either to drive the sheep into a *cul de sac*, or to drive them over a mesa lip in

---

[1] The single horn of the Kwan fraternity, on the other hand, was associated 'in some occult way' (Fewkes, 1900a, p. 117) with *lepe'na*, the stalactites in the salt cave at Grand Canyon; the same word, *lepe'na*, is also used for icicle (Voth, 1905b, p. 95).

[2] The following notes on Hopi hunting practices are based on Beaglehole (1936), pp. 4–11, 23–4, with additional material taken from Stephen (1936), pp. 149, 277–9.

such a way that they would be killed or severely injured by their fall; the cornered or injured animals were then lassoed with ropes of braided wool, hauled to the top of the cliff, and either choked to death or shot with bow and arrow.

Certain rites preceded a communal hunt, in the old days. Four days before the hunt was due to begin, the hunt chief—*ma'k tüna'tyaita*, 'the one who desires a hunt, plans it, sets his thoughts hopefully on it'—makes a number of prayer-sticks, usually a set of six: one for Masau'u, one for Tih-'kü'yi-wu'hti, the 'mother of all (game) animals', one for wolf and one for coyote, one for Kih'sa, the hunting deity, and one for either Sun (*ta'wa*) or eagle (*kwa'hü*). These he takes to Badger clan chief, 'because Badger clan owns all the animals';[1] they smoke together over the prayer-sticks; early the next morning, Badger chief announces the forthcoming hunt, and later places the *pa'ho(s)* at the shrine of Tih-kü'yi-wu'hti outside the village. On the morning of the hunt, a further set of prayer-sticks is offered to the two deities, Tih-kü'yi-wu'hti and Masau'u, chiefly concerned.

On returning to the village after the hunt, each man wipes off with his hands —and blows away with his breath—the odour of the animals he has killed, that their 'breaths' may not return to trouble him.[2] He then fumigates himself over a bowl of lighted juniper, as an aid to purification.

*le'hü*, Indian millet (*Oryzopsis hymenoides*). *Le'hü* is one of the two common grasses found growing on the valley slopes in the vicinity of the Hopi villages, the other being *sü'hü* (*Hilaria jamesii*). *Sü'hü* is attached to prayer-sticks made at Soya'l, for the increase of deer and antelope; the seeds of *le'hü*, Indian millet, have excellent food value and were collected by the Hopi in the old days, especially in times of famine (Hough, 1898, p. 142).

*a'nü*, ant (various kinds). These, I take it, are the different kinds of ant the hills of which, often colonised by Mormon tea (*Ephedra torreyana*), are common on the valley slopes where *sü'hü* and *le'hü* form the main vegetal cover.

The clan names of this phratry, like those of Ko'kop-Coyote, support the northern provenance postulated by its origin myth. Throughout the Great Basin area, deer, antelope, mountain sheep, and an occasional elk, furnish the principal large game animals. Indian millet or Indian rice-grass, *Oryzopsis hymenoides*, is one of the chief grasses whose seeds were gathered, and ground into flour on stone metates, by all the Shoshonean-speaking peoples of the Great Basin (Steward, 1933, p. 244, and 1938, pp. 26–7). Ants, too, were an important

---

[1] At Mishong'novi, that is: Beaglehole (1936), p. 5. Horn-Millet phratry not being represented in the villages of 2nd Mesa, it seems likely that Badger clan has taken over functions belonging to that grouping, just as—at Mishong'novi—it has taken over certain of the functions belonging to Rabbit-Tobacco.

[2] There is a distinction, in Hopi, between those animals which have 'breaths' and so have to be propitiated, and those which do not (Beaglehole, 1936, pp. 17–18). Included in the former group are the principal game animals, eagle and the larger kinds of hawk, and all the preying animals down as far as coyote and fox: perhaps, also, jack rabbit and cottontail.

source of protein; among the Gosiute, for example, Reagan reports (1934, p. 54):

> In the Deep Creek country, there is a large red ant that makes a large bushy mound for a home. In the old times the Goshutes used to go to these ant hills and collect the ants and the ant eggs in a basket, take them home and boil them into a soup. . . .

They also made soup out of fly larvae, and roasted grasshoppers for eating. *A'nü* appears, therefore, to 'stand for' the various winged insects, and *le'hü* for the various seed grasses, once utilised as food sources.

### Actual ceremonial duties

There seems little doubt that originally the Ahl fraternity, the 'two-horned' society whose duty it is to act as guards at the Wü'wütçim ceremony, 'belonged to' the clans of the Horn-Millet phratry grouping. The Ahl fraternity is especi- ially associated with hunting; four men of this fraternity take the part of mountain sheep in the dance on the eighth night of Wü'wütçim (see above, p. 107). Also, it is a man of the Ahl fraternity who takes the prayer-sticks to the springs, and starts the men and boys on their race up the mesa side, on the ninth morning of the Snake-Antelope ceremony; and Parsons' 1st Mesa informant stressed (1925, p. 103) that the object of that ceremony, as well as being for rain and crops, is for plenty of grass 'so that all the animals have good feed and get fat'.

Now the three deities especially associated with hunting are Pyü'ükoñhoya, Masau'u, and Tih-kü'yi-wu'hti. Pyü'ükoñhoya is *wuya* to Reed-Greasewood- Bow phratry; he taught the Hopi the use of bow and arrow for hunting deer and antelope (Stephen, 1929, p. 18), and how to fletch their arrows with the feathers of hawks' wings (ibid. p. 51); the four preying animals (mountain lion, bear, wolf, wildcat) are his 'pets', they 'have' bow and arrow (Stephen, 1936, p. 100), and they are especially associated with hunting (Stephen, 1936, p. 1248: under *ma'kto*). Masau'u is *wuya* of the Ko'kop-Coyote phratry group- ing; in the myths (Stephen, 1929, p. 55) he taught the Hopi the habits of wild animals, and at the winter solstice special prayer-sticks are placed at his shrine for their 'increase'. There is also some link between hunting and fire: before a hunt a special fire (*ma'k kü'hi*) is ignited by means of the fire drill, a handful of dry grass is thrown on it together with pellets of hare or antelope dung, and each hunter passes his club or throwing-stick through the smoke (Stephen, 1936, pp. 1006, 1024). Stephen further records (1936, p. 278) the use of fire, again ignited by means of fire drill and board (*pi'lan ko'hü*), for hunting antelope;[1] and it is this use of fire, I think, that explains why the kindling of the

---

[1] This use of fire may well lie at the root of the link between Masau'u and hunting, and may explain his title of *kü'hi moñwi*. The use of fire for driving game was widespread among the western Shoshoni and the Northern Paiute: Steward (1933), pp. 252–4, and (1938), p. 39, cf. Lowie (1924), pp. 198–9.

new fire at Wü'wütçim (see above, pp. 100–1) is done by two men of Ahl fraternity, as well as by the two men of Kwan fraternity.

Tih-kü'yi-wu'hti is the 'mother' of antelope, deer, mountain sheep, and of both kinds of rabbits (Stephen, 1936, p. 1006: cf. Parsons, 1936, p. xli, and Titiev, 1943*b*, pp. 431–4); she gave birth to two antelopes (hence the notion that twins *are*, in some sense, antelopes), and there seems no doubt that her name refers to the bursting of the 'bag of waters', a striking feature of mammalian parturition. Prayer-sticks are made for her prior to every hunt; and just as Tü'wa-ponya-tümsi—conceptually linked with Mü'iyinwa—is referred to as 'sister' to that deity, so Tih-kü'yi-wu'hti is linked with Masau'u and referred to (Stephen, 1936, p. 1006) as his 'sister'. While I have found no specific evidence on this point, I have no doubt that Tih-kü'yi-wuhti is—or was originally—*wuya* of the Horn-Millet phratry grouping; and I think it probable that the deity known as Ta'la-tümsi, 'Dawn Woman', whose effigy is fetched from its shrine on the first afternoon of the Wü'wütçim ceremony (see above, pp. 101–2) and who is especially associated with the Horn fraternity (Parsons, 1925, p. 119, n. 182), is to be identified with Tih-kü'yi-wuhti.

The three phratry groupings associated with the three hunting deities, i.e. Reed-Greasewood-Bow, Ko'kop-Coyote, and Horn-Millet, are the three groupings especially involved in the performance of the Wü'wütçim ceremony in November. The primary motif of that ceremony, I have suggested above, is *for* ice and cold. The remaining deity associated with the cold-weather theme is Sho'tukünuñwa, and he is credited, in myth, with the sowing of the wild grasses and the trees. According to one myth (Stephen, 1929, p. 55), Sho'tukünuñwa gave the seeds of grasses and trees to the first leader of the Hopi and directed him to take them to the mesa top, so that he could cast them by the handful over the entire country (he also taught them how to build the walls of their houses in stone, and how to make roofs of wood and grass); according to another myth (Wallis, 1936, p. 15), he puts grass seeds into hail stones, and when these melt, the seeds go into the earth, the sun shines with heat, and the grasses soon spring up.

Earlier in this account (above, p. 217), I pointed out that one of the difficulties in working out the Hopi view of nature is that of *double reference*, i.e. that any particular plant or animal may stand for more than one set of ideas, each corresponding to a different level of Hopi cultural development. That difficulty is especially acute with regard to the clan names of the phratries involved in Wü'wütçim, and to the ideas represented by them. I have already suggested that, underlying its superficial 'war' aspect, Wü'wütçim is a ceremony for ice-and-cold and, as such, takes its place in the climato-agricultural cycle of Hopi farming festivals. But the nature of the deities associated with Wü'wütçim, namely Pyü'ükoñhoya, Masau'u, Tih-kü'yi-wu'hti and Sho' tokünuñwa, indicates that, underlying its agricultural aspect, lies a substrate of ideas centred on hunting.

The Hopi, it will be remembered, are the most westerly of the pueblo Indians, they live in high plateau country and speak a Shoshonean language, their nearest linguistic congeners being the Shoshoni of the Great Basin some 300 to 400 miles to the northwest. When first encountered by European travellers in the early nineteenth century, these Shoshoni were still primarily gatherers, their habitat a high semi-arid steppe, consisting of a monotonous succession of long, sage-covered valleys separated by lofty mountain ranges which run north and south. The valleys yielded only sparse crops of brush and grass seeds; the mountains, receiving more rainfall, supported juniper and pine-nut trees and various species of edible roots and berries. Game, everywhere scarce, consisted of rabbits and antelope in the valleys, deer and mountain sheep in the mountains. Throughout this region (in area, the size of France), from early spring to late in the summer, individual families—or, at most, two or three related families—wandered at large foraging for food. Only in the fall, when the pine-nut harvest in a given area was sufficiently abundant to attract a number of such groups to camp together in one locality, was anything approaching a village community established; communal rabbit drives and a fall festival followed the gathering and storage of the pine nuts, and the group so formed commonly stayed together until the spring, when its component families set out on their travels once more.

> The most stable group among Nevada Shoshoni, [writes Steward (1937*b* pp. 629–30)], was, therefore, the small winter village with its somewhat shifting population and its informal headman. But even village cohesion was loose and the head man had little authority except to arrange minor, local dances and to decide when people should go to collect seeds and pine nuts. He might direct hunts, though often a special man led rabbit drives and perhaps some other man took charge of deer or mountain sheep hunts.

The interpretation I am proposing is that it was piñon-nut gatherings, of the kind still practised among the western Shoshoni half a century ago, that formed the germ from which the Hopi villages developed, in a not dissimilar environment, a thousand years earlier: a development, the origin of which lay at the point where the families that came together in the fall to collect the nuts and to hunt large game together, instead of dispersing the following spring to gather seeds and berries, to dig roots and to hunt smaller game, stuck together and took to cultivating the fertile soil in the valleys below their winter camping grounds[1]; and further, that the Wü'wütçim ceremony represents the original fall ceremony, or dance, of the hunting and gathering groups out of which the villages were to emerge. Before ever it was found to be

---

[1] A point that is nicely illustrated, in the regional archaeological record, by the White Dog (Basketmaker II) sites in the Glen Canyon area, dated to 200–300 A.D. Located near the canyon heads, these sites afforded easy access both to the canyon floor where the inhabitants grew corn, and to the mesa top, where they gathered piñon nuts and wild grass seeds and hunted deer and rabbits: see Lipe (1970), pp. 93–104.

beneficial for agriculture, snow-and-frost was required for hunting,[1] and fire, to abate the dreadful cold of winter on the wind-swept mesas. Of the three phratry groupings especially associated with the ceremony in the form in which it has come down to us, and of the elements surviving (we may suppose) from the ceremony in its original form, the *Ko'kop-Coyote* grouping is linked with the piñon nut, with the hunters, coyote and wolf, and with fire; *Reed-Greasewood-Bow* with bow and arrow, with dogs and, through the stars, with cold; and *Horn-Millet* with wild grasses (*le'hü*) and their seeds, and with game animals. The hunting and gathering theme represents, then, the oldest, pre-agricultural layer in the Wü'wütçim rites; and it is this fact that explains why, where katçina initiation is concerned in part with ceremonial knowledge relating to the growth of plants (Eggan, 1950, p. 342, n. 96), Wü'wütçim initiation is concerned primarily with *hunting*.[2]

Besides the hunting of deer, antelope and mountain sheep, the holding of communal rabbit drives and the gathering of piñon nuts in the fall, vestiges of nearly all the salient features of Basin-Plateau ecology are to be found in Hopi culture: *viz.* the gathering of wild vegetables or 'greens' in the spring (Titiev, 1944, pp. 140–1, and n. 78), of the seeds of herbaceous and other plants in early summer (Simpson, 1953, p. 54), and of berries and edible roots in late summer (for the various kinds, see Fewkes, 1896, pp. 14–21, and Hough, 1898, pp. 142–4); the use of twined baskets for collecting seeds and berries, of metates and manos for grinding the seeds, and of simple digging sticks for digging roots; the relative importance of small game, particularly of rodents, as a source of food (cf. among the Hopi, the baking of rabbit, squirrel, prairie dog, porcupine and other small game: Stephen, 1936, p. 354); the inclusion of certain insects, notably grasshoppers or crickets (Bourke, 1884, p. 252) and locusts (Voth, 1912*b*, pp. 141–2), in their dietary; the occasional employment of fire as a means of hunting game (Stephen, 1936, p. 278); and the use, not only of deer skin for clothing (Hough, 1918, pp. 242–3), but also of rabbit-skin blankets for warmth in winter (Stephen, 1936, pp. 273–4, 1022).

*Association of ideas*

The Horn-Millet phratry grouping is primarily associated with game animals and their reproduction, and with the seeds of edible grasses and their harvesting. There is, also, a link with witchcraft; black ants, included in this phratry, are a prime source of *duhisa*, witch power, and in one myth (Parsons, 1933, p. 33), the Millet people (*le'h nyamü*) are particularly suspected of being witches.

In Hopi belief (Titiev, 1942, pp. 549–51), certain animals, credited with possessing witch power, are made use of by witches as their familiars, *dualang'mosa*; in animal shape the witch, *po'aka* (or *powa'ka*), is thought to prowl

---

[1] Light falls of snow enable the hunter to track game more readily (Beaglehole, 1936, pp. 4–5); Parsons (1925, pp. 22–4), Wallis (1936, p. 61) and D. Eggan (1961, p. 4), all refer to hunting rabbits after falls of snow.

[2] See above, pp. 134–5. It may also have been concerned, formerly, with knowledge of wild plants; during the spring following Wü'wütçim initiation at Oraibi, perhaps also at Walpi (Parsons, 1939, p. 508), a wild-plant or seed-gathering ceremonial was held, in the course of which Masau'u was at one time impersonated.

about by night doing mischief. As to the nature of the transformation, one myth (Wallis, 1936, p. 12) puts it thus:[1]

> You do not believe it because you do not know. But a Hopi merely turns over and *becomes* a coyote or a crow; if you observe their features carefully, you will be able to see the nose or beak of the animal pressing under the skin of the man's forehead when in human shape.

The animals believed to be a source of witch power, in addition to coyote and crow, are dogs (and cats), wolf, owl, and black ants. Each of these animals, apart from crow, is also associated with one of the three 'winter' phratries, Ko'kop-Coyote, Reed-Greasewood-Bow or Horn-Millet; and the time of year when these three phratries are active ceremonially, i.e. November–December, is a 'dangerous' (*kya*) one for witches, being the season especially when they are out and about at night. Now the only parallel to the process by which the witch is believed to 'turn over and *become* a coyote or a crow', is that other process whereby the shaman or doctor *becomes* a bear:

> Some 'doctors', [wrote Steward (1933, p. 309) of the Owens Valley Paiute], got power from the bear; their songs imitated grunts, their dance was a slow bear-like step. *They could transform themselves into bears.*

The word for the 'power' which the shaman or doctor got from the bear is, in all the Shoshoni languages, *po'a* or *po'wa*;[2] and I have suggested above (pp. 219–20), in connection with Powa'mu, that the origin of Bear clan leader's spiritual authority among the Hopi is to be traced back to the *po'a* of the Great Basin bear shaman. We now see the other side of the coin: the Hopi word for witch (*po'aka*, or *powa'ka*) being derived from the same root, the witch evidently draws on the same source of supernatural power as the shaman. But where Bear clan leader, as *ki'k moñwi* of the village, taps this source for the common good, the ends for which the *powa'ka* taps it are individualist, anti-social and malevolent.

*Anomalies, and comments*

On 3rd Mesa, Millet clan 'goes in' with the Ko'kop-Coyote phratry grouping; this is readily explainable in terms of the ceremonial and conceptual linkage between the two groupings (cf. Parsons, 1933, p. 33, nn. 130 and 132).

---

[1] The linking of coyote and crow in the myth is surely due to the ambivalent ecological status of the two animals, emphasised by Lévi-Strauss (1958, pp. 248–9). Coyote lives on meat, but will also raid corn fields, crow lives on vegetables—but will also eat carrion; coyote eats meat that he has not killed, crow eats corn that he has not grown; coyote stands to hunting (the fall and winter activity), as crow stands to farming (the spring and summer activity). And Hopi have responded, we may suppose, to the dis-ease induced by their ambivalence by endowing both animals with witch-power (*duhisa*)—in rather the same way as, on a social plane, they respond to homosexuals, with dislike.

[2] Eggan (1968): cf. Sapir (1931), p. 622, Steward (1933), pp. 311–12, and for the Hopi, Whorf (1936), pp. 1283–4, under *po'wa*.

On 1st Mesa, a Flute clan, *le'n nyamü*, is reported. Parsons is surely right (1933, p. 33, n. 131: 1936, p. 769, n. 1) in regarding this as a mistake for *le'h nyamü*, millet clan, particularly in view of Lowie's remark (1929, p. 326, n. 2) that the same man was designated to him on one occasion as of Flute clan, and on another as of 'grass clan' (*le'tüñwa*). The mistake no doubt arose because, on 1st Mesa, the Blue Flute ceremony has passed into the hands of Millet clan.

## PHRATRY VIII. TOBACCO–RABBIT

*pi'va*, wild tobacco          *ta'vo*, cottontail rabbit
*cho'ño*, tobacco pipe         *so'wi*, jack rabbit, hare

*Myth.* The myth of the origin of the Rabbit people (1st Mesa: Parsons, 1933, p. 28) tells how, after they came out from the Underworld, the people came to a place where a rabbit (*ta'vo*) was sitting: 'he was a rabbit, yet he was a man'. He greeted them, and asked them where they were going: to Si'tü'kwi, they said. Then, 'he put on his skin and became a rabbit'. So they took his name for their clan. Later, they found some weeds and pulled them up. Rabbit told them that the weeds were tobacco (*pi'va*), 'to pray with for what they wanted, to smoke and give them rain'. They took the weeds with them. Thus they got tobacco for their ceremony.

*Natural observation, and ceremonial referents*

*pi'va*, wild tobacco (*Nicotiana attenuata*): an annual, described by Bourke (1884, p. 259) as 'a low, squatty plant, with thick, broad, dark-green leaves, which have an acrid taste'. It grows wild on the mesa slopes, and was also cultivated, in the old days, in small patches in the gardens below each village (Stephen, 1936, p. 1278). The leaves are gathered in the fall, put out to dry, and later smoked, either in a ceremonial pipe (*cho'ño*) or in the form of corn-husk cigarettes, as an essential part of all major kiva rituals. In general, as Whiting remarks (1939, p. 90), 'the smoke is associated with clouds, and hence has the power to bring rain. Smoke is also said to carry the prayers of the people to the gods.' In one myth (Stephen, 1929, p. 55), it was Cloud himself who gave tobacco to the first chief, telling him to smoke whenever he wanted rain; and a special mixture of wild tobacco with the young leaves of spruce and fir, also used for smoking in the kivas, is known as *o'mau vwi'va*, 'Cloud tobacco': Stephen (1936), p. 599, n. 1.

*ta'vo*, cottontail: *so'wi*, jack rabbit. Both kinds are common in the region of the Hopi villages, cottontail on the mesa slopes and in sand dunes, jack rabbit in greasewood stands on the main valley floor. In the old days communal rabbit hunts were held at intervals throughout the year (see Beaglehole, 1936, pp. 11–14), especially in early summer when there were eagles to be fed, around harvest time, and in connection with certain of the winter ceremonies, notably Wü'wütçim and Soya'l; the principal weapons used were the straight and the curved throwing-stick, both made of oak.

Rabbits, with deer, antelope and mountain sheep, constitute the principal game animals hunted by Hopi. The following list (Lincoln, 1961, Table 3) of animals whose bones were found at eight twelfth to thirteenth century sites in the Wupa'tki region, indicates their relative importance in pueblo dietary 700 years ago:

| | |
|---|---|
| jack rabbit (*Lepus californicus*) .. .. .. .. .. .. .. | 401 |
| cottontail (*Sylvilagus auduboni*) .. .. .. .. .. .. .. | 277 |
| pronghorn antelope (*Antilocapra americana*) .. .. .. .. .. | 124 |
| *larger rodents:* | |
|   prairie dog (*Cynomys gunnisoni*) .. .. .. .. .. 64 | |
|   antelope squirrel (*Citellus leucurus*) .. .. .. .. .. 8 | |
|   pocket gopher (*Thomomys bottae*) .. .. .. .. .. 8 | |
|   kangaroo rat (*Dipodomys ordi*) .. .. .. .. .. 6 | |
|   rock squirrel (*Citellus variegatus*) .. .. .. .. .. 5 | |
|   cliff chipmunk (*Eutamias dorsalis*) .. .. .. .. .. 1 | |
|   — | 92 |
| mule deer (*Odocoileus hermionus*) .. .. .. .. .. .. | 17 |
| bighorn sheep (*Ovis canadensis*) .. .. .. .. .. .. .. | 1 |
| | — |
| | 912 |

As Lincoln points out (1961, pp. 55–7), the two most important food animals consumed by the prehistoric inhabitants of Wupa'tki were jack rabbit and antelope, followed by cottontail, the larger rodents, and deer.

All four of the clan names in this phratry represent items common to Hopi and to Shoshoni culture. *Tav-* is the Shoshoni stem for the cottontail, found throughout the Great Basin area. Jack rabbit was the object of the communal rabbit drives, held by all Shoshoni groups in the fall. Wild tobacco (*Nicotiana attenuata*) grows on mountain sides throughout the Great Basin (Steward, 1938, p. 313); the leaves were gathered in late summer, dried, and stored. Among the Owens Valley Paiute (Steward, 1933, pp. 294, 319–20), the tobacco was smoked in pipes made from hardwood or steatite, chiefly by the older men, and generally in the sweat house; a young man smoked for the first time, and began to sleep at the sweat house, after killing his first deer.

### Actual ceremonial duties

The first of the ceremonial functions exercised by this phratry grouping has to do with hunting, and belongs to the Rabbit people. There can be no doubt, I think, that in the old days Rabbit clan chief had major ceremonial duties relating to communal rabbit hunts.[1] On the day before the hunt, the man who 'desires the hunt, sets his mind on it', *m'ak tüna'tyaita*, made sets of prayer-sticks for Masau'u and for Tih-kü'yi-wu'hti; in the evening he took these to the

---

[1] Lowie (1929), p. 338: cf. Parsons (1933), p. 21, and (1936), p. 1081, and Titiev (1943*b*), p. 430. On 2nd Mesa (Beaglehole, 1936, pp. 12–13), where Rabbit clan 'goes in' with Badger phratry, these duties have been taken over by Badger clan chief.

house of Rabbit clan chief, they smoked together over them, and early the next morning Rabbit clan chief announced the hunt; later, he 'placed' the *pa'ho*(s) at the shrine of Tih-kü'yi-wu'hti outside the village. These duties of Rabbit clan chief may, at one time, have extended to deer hunts also. Jack rabbit (*so'wi*) and deer (*sowi'ñwŭ*) are considered by Hopi to be closely related (Stephen, 1936, p. 277). As Lowie puts it (1929, p. 338): 'the Rabbit clan has the privilege of heralding a rabbit hunt, because the Rabbit people own the rabbits. But they were also considered owners of the deer, and accordingly heralded a deer hunt also.'

The second ceremonial duty exercised by this phratry grouping belongs to the Tobacco people. It is their responsibility to furnish the man who fills the pipe (*cho'ño*) with tobacco and lights it, prior to its being handed round and smoked, at all major kiva rituals (Parsons, 1933, p. 29); at Oraibi, the man who takes this rôle is referred to as *pi'p moñwi*, 'tobacco chief'. As Hopi themselves say (Parsons, 1925, p. 110, n. 170): '*pa'tki*, Coyote and Tobacco clans have to be in every ceremony, because of their relation with clouds, fire, and smoke.'

Ceremonially and conceptually, then, we can distinguish two distinct threads within the Tobacco-Rabbit grouping: a hunting thread, represented by the Rabbit people, and a thread to do with smoking and prayers for rain, represented by the Tobacco people. It remains for us now to unravel the relation between these two threads.

Discussing the ceremonial use of tobacco among the Tewa of 1st Mesa (Robbins *et al*, 1916, pp. 103–7), Miss Freire-Marreco observes that, at Hano, the Tobacco clan is one of the three leading clans in the village, the other two being Bear clan and Corn clan; the chiefs of these three clans are, in effect, head men of the whole village. In ceremonies affecting the whole village, Tobacco clan chief brings tobacco, while Bear clan and Corn clan chiefs bring medicine and corn-meal; and when a party of katçinas, e.g. from the neighbouring Hopi villages, visits the chiefs' kiva (*moñ kiva*), Tobacco clan chief smokes over them. This smoking of tobacco, writes Miss Freire-Marreco, is connected with the 'thought' or 'intention' of a chief: adding that until recently (i.e. 1912–13), among the Tewa, boys were forbidden to smoke *until they had killed deer, jack rabbit, and coyote*.

Now the Tewa lack the Wü'wütçim ceremony (Parsons, 1926, p. 227); nor have they any procedure analogous to that employed by the Hopi, for initiating young men into manhood. The Hopi, on the other hand, have the Wü'wütçim ceremony, on to which is tacked, every fourth year or so, the initiatory process we have described earlier (above, pp. 101–4); and this process itself forms part of a sequence running through both Wü'wütçim and Soya'l, and having to do primarily with hunting (see above, pp. 134–5). Among the Hopi, hunting (*ma'k*) refers especially to rabbit hunting; the deity associated with the hunting sequence running through Wü'wütçim and Soya'l is Kih'sa, the prairie falcon, whose principal prey is rabbits; and he it was who gave the Hopi the curved throwing-stick, modelled on his own wing, to hunt rabbits with. In other words, what among the Tewa of Hano is a general hunting *rite de passage* (except that there is no *rite*), among the Hopi has been epitomised in rabbit hunting, and formalised in Wü'wütçim initiation.

The stress on rabbit hunting, as an essential ingredient of the two great winter ceremonies, has entered deeply into the Hopi imagination. In the *Tale of Sitiyo and the Hawk* (above, pp. 237–8: Titiev, 1943*b*, pp. 431–7), we are brought to feel, not simply the practical need of meat required for the Soya'l feast, but the *emotional* need of the young man to kill his fair share of rabbits, *in order to prove himself a man*. More strongly still is this emotional need conveyed in a Hopi dream, recorded by Mrs. Eggan (1952, p. 472), dreamed some *thirty years after* the events with which it deals:[1]

The dreamer dreams that he goes hunting with some white men and secures several deer. He takes a load of venison to a clan relative, who is an old war chief in another village. The people there are very grateful for the rare delicacy. The old chief invites the dreamer to replace a man, now ill, who was to lead a religious dance. After the dance, the dreamer is highly praised for his performance by three men—the old war chief, the sick dance leader, and the leader's brother. While this is going on, a runner tells these men that the village is about to be attacked by enemies. The three men are in a panic and begin to cry, but the dreamer swallows the lump in his own throat and, rebuking their cowardice, says: 'I'm only a common man, but *I* can stand on my feet and fight. Stand on your feet and fight like men!' The dreamer then wakes from his dream sweating, and says it wasn't a very good dream.

'Nor was it', writes Mrs. Eggan (1952: pp. 472–3) in her commentary on the dream, '—but it would have been far worse if his waking mind had remembered the dream thoughts which had helped to construct the dream. The facts are these: some thirty years before this dream occurred, the dreamer was a candidate for tribal initiation into manhood [i.e. at the Wü'wütçim, held at Oraibi in 1912]. He was afraid of this initiation, and the old war chief of his dream was prominent among those who forced him into it. One requirement for tribal initiation was the killing of a large number of rabbits. Being an incredibly poor hunter, the dreamer failed to get even one rabbit after hunting for two days. The sick dance leader whom he replaced in the dream and the leader's brother, who with the war chief became *three incompetent cowards in this dream thirty years later*, patted the neophyte on the back in a condescending manner and offered to hunt for him. They secured forty rabbits for him in one day, which allowed the initiation to proceed.

The entire dream handles this old hurt in a healing manner; the dreamer hunts with white men, which gives him status in his own eyes; he returns quantities of venison for the lowly rabbits of his boyhood; and he angrily shames the cowardice of all three men who contributed to his former humiliation. But, even so, the dream was not as effective as it needed to be [i.e. in relieving, or disguising, the inner tensions which arose out of the original, unpleasant experience], and the dreamer awakened in sweating discomfort.'

Turning back, now, to the significance of smoking: we have seen (Whiting, 1939, p. 90) that 'smoke is associated with clouds, and hence has power to bring rain. Smoke is also said to carry the prayers of the people to the gods.' In the myth quoted above (p. 282), the people are told that the weeds they

---

[1] For these events, see Simmons (1942), p. 157.

pulled up are tobacco, 'to pray with for what they wanted, to smoke to give them rain'. Among the Tewa, Miss Freire-Marreco reports, the smoking of tobacco is connected with the 'thought' or 'intention' of a chief. This calls to mind a Hopi word which we came across earlier:

> *na'twanpi*, n. 'instrument of *na'twanta*, any object used to aid one in praying for something which is held in mind as an image and concentrated upon meanwhile, especially a prayer-pipe [*cho'ño*] used in this way, the concentrating being done while exhaling the smoke': Whorf (1936), p. 1261.

The aspect of smoking incorporated in *na'twanta*, meditative prayer, is reflected in a remark of one of Mrs. Eggan's informants (1961, p. 31), who, speaking of her old uncle (her own mother's mother's brother), said: 'he has power to smoke for rain, . . . like many of the old men.' Now, the old men of Hopi society, those who particularly have power to 'smoke for rain', are the *wü'wüyom*, the 'wise, thinking old men' (Stephen, 1936, p. 1321); initiation to manhood, symbolised by the ability to hunt (and kill) rabbits, is *wü'wütçim*; and what constitutes tribal initiation among the Hopi—and on this point, it seems to me, the evidence is conclusive—is joining the body of those who 'smoke for rain',[1] this being at the same time the simplest, and the most fundamental, activity of Hopi religious practice.

If, then, ability to hunt rabbits is the sign of a young man's fitness to assume adult responsibilities, and if the assumption of those responsibilities is marked by the conferring on him of the right to 'smoke for rain', we may expect to find the phratry grouping which controls both rabbit-hunting and tobacco-smoking, namely Tobacco-Rabbit, playing a crucial rôle in the ceremony whereby adult status is bestowed, i.e. the Wü'wütçim.

Now we have seen, in the myth quoted above (p. 282), how the Rabbit people found some weeds and pulled them up, and how these turned out to be tobacco (*pi'va*): 'thus they got tobacco for their ceremony.' Assuming that the word used is *wi'mi*, we ask: what ceremony? And the answer, fairly conclusively, is Singers' branch of the Wü'wütçim. For some thirty years, from the time that Stephen was living on 1st Mesa in the early 1890s until Parsons' visit there in 1921, one of the most influential and ceremonially important men in Walpi-Sicho'movi was Ha'ni, Tobacco clansman and chief of the Singers' society; he played important rôles in both Wü'wütçim and Soya'l (see, especially, Parsons, 1936, pp. 1094–5), as well as in the Snake-Antelope and Flute ceremonies; and when eventually he died in 1921, he was succeeded as head of the Singers' society by Ña'muqi, of Rabbit clan (Parsons, 1933, p. 29, n. 112). The Wü'wütçim ceremony, as we have seen earlier, comprises two parts: a climato-agricultural ceremony, originally 'brought' by Bow clan and

---

[1] See further, on smoking, and 'thinking' for rain, Mrs. B. Aitken—*née* Freire-Marreco—(1930), pp. 372–6. Among the Owens Valley Paiute (above, p. 283), a lad smoked for the first time after killing his first deer; among the Navajo (Hill, 1936, p. 7), on joining his first war party. The Navajo case is of interest, since the Navajo probably borrowed the custom, i.e. of smoking tobacco, from the pueblos.

performed every year, and an initiatory ceremony, tacked on to the front of the other and performed every fourth year (or when there are enough boys to be initiated). Now it is quite clear, from the scattered references made by Parsons[1] to Ha'ni's varied activities, that it is the chief of the Singers' society who decides when the long form of Wü'wütçim is to be observed: that it is he who summons the men of the other three fraternities (Wü'wütçim, Al and Kwan) to the fire-drilling rite on day 1 of the ceremony: and that, of the four fraternities involved in the Wü'wütçim, Singers is 'the one thought of, in some ways, as paramount'. Further, a distinction is to be drawn (Parsons, 1936, p. 972, n. 1) between the Tobacco-Rabbit man who serves as head of the Singers' fraternity at Wü'wütçim, and another man of the same phratry, his brother or sister's son usually, who serves as tobacco chief, *pi'p moñwi*, in the same ceremony.[2]

The evidence from 1st Mesa shows, then, the crucial rôle accorded to Tobacco-Rabbit phratry in the initiatory sequence of Wü'wütçim in that, as 'owners' of the Singers' fraternity, they are in charge of the timing of the whole ceremony. This conclusion is borne out, in an oblique way, by the evidence from 3rd Mesa: there, the Tobacco-Rabbit people 'go in' with Katçina-Parrot phratry grouping, and it is this phratry (Eggan, 1950, p. 103) which controls the Singers. At Mishong'novi, where Rabbit and Tobacco 'go in' with Badger phratry but where no members of either clan are now living (Lowie, 1929, p. 334), the smoke-offering function of the Tobacco people is exercised by Badger clan,[3] while control of the Singers' fraternity has passed into the hands of Katçina-Parrot.

The rôle played by clans of the Tobacco-Rabbit grouping in the initiatory sequence of Wü'wütçim, through their control of the Singers' fraternity, thus bears out the conceptual rôle ascribed to rabbit-hunting and tobacco-smoking in the rites themselves; and this fact, in turn, confirms the interpretation advanced in the previous section regarding the aboriginal nature of that ceremony. Among the Great Basin Shoshoni,[4] communal rabbit hunts were held in the fall, November being 'the proper time'; before setting out on the hunt, the people held a Rabbit dance, *qamu' nö'qa*,[5] extending over five days; the hunt itself was directed by a 'head man of the hunt', and each morning a fire was made and all the men gathered there to get their instructions from him. May we not conclude, then, that the Hopi Wü'wütçim ceremony is

---

[1] Parsons (1923), pp. 156–60, and p. 156, nn. 2, 3 and 4: (1925), pp. 16, 116–17, and n. 177: (1926), p. 219: (1933), p. 29, and n. 112: (1936), pp. 3, 957–8. Cf. on Hani's position in the 1st Mesa Wü'wütçim, Lowie (1929), p. 345.

[2] Luke's function in the Wü'wütçim at Mishong'novi, inherited from his mother's brother, was clearly that of tobacco chief: Lowie (1929), p. 334.

[3] As are the hunting functions of Rabbit clan chief: Beaglehole (1936), pp. 5, 9–10, 12.

[4] Lowie (1924), pp. 196–8, 305. Steward also refers frequently (1938, pp. 53–4, 105–6, 112–13, 138–9) to the fall festival of the Shoshoni, held in connection with communal rabbit drives, after pine-nut gathering, and lasting for five or six days.

[5] *Qam* (or *kam*) is the general Shoshoni stem for jack rabbit, as distinct from cottontail.

lineal successor to the fall festival of the Great Basin Shoshoni, and that the emphasis laid in the rites on the hunting of rabbits goes back to a time when their meat was the principal source of animal protein in the diet of those who hunted them?[1] And if further, Masau'u, the deity especially associated with that ceremony, is indeed—as his place in the Hopi imagination suggests that he is—an aboriginal deity, then we can readily understand why a communal rabbit hunt is the necessary prelude to his appearance (e.g. at Wü'wütçim, at Soya'l, at the spring planting, and at harvest), and why rabbit skin and rabbit's blood enter so prominently into his costume (above, p. 252).

The northern and aboriginal nature of Masau'u is confirmed, I believe, by the evidence of circum-polar shamanism. Masau'u, it will be remembered, besides having general charge of the dead, is himself Skeleton (above, p. 13); he controls fire; and he has a special relation to wild animals, especially game animals. All these are specific attributes of the Siberian and north American shaman: the shaman, too, is Skeleton, 'un mort qui est ressuscité' (for further details, see Eliade, 1968, pp. 66–7, 137–44); he conducts the spirit on its journey to the underworld (ibid. pp. 154–6); he is 'maître du feu' (ibid. p. 369); and he is intimately associated with wild animals, knowing their language (ibid. pp. 88–93). This linkage, in turn, confirms Stephen's characterisation of Masau'u as 'god of the metamorphoses of Nature' (above, p. 268): since the quality peculiar to a shaman, differentiating him from other men, is the ability to transform or metamorphose himself into an animal (Eliade, 1968, p. 90).

### Association of ideas

The ideas represented by this phratry grouping we may characterise, very simply, as follows:
... rabbits—hunting—initiation of young men—tobacco smoking—prayer and mental concentration, *na'twanta*—rain and snow ...

### Anomalies, and comments

The anomaly that requires explaining is why, on 2nd Mesa (Mishong'novi), the Tobacco-Rabbit people 'go in' with Badger phratry, and why, on 3rd Mesa with Katçina-Parrot. To this question I shall return presently (below, p. 295), when we have dealt with the two remaining phratries, Squash-Sparrowhawk-Crane and the Mustard-Roadrunner grouping.

### PHRATRY X. SQUASH–SPARROWHAWK–CRANE

*pa'tña*, squash
*ke'le*, sparrowhawk                    *tü'bish*, sorrow-making
*a'toko*, crane                         *pü'çovi*, Hopi cotton

### Natural observation, and ceremonial referents

*pa'tña*, squash. Corn and squash were the two staple crops of early pueblo

[1] It is possible that there is also a symbolic link with the onset of winter, in that, in the mountain ranges of the Great Basin (but not in the Hopi region), jack rabbits turn white in winter: Reagan (1935a), p. 11.

agriculture; their cultivation goes back at least 1700 years in the San Juan basin area. Masau'u is credited (Wallis, 1936, p. 3) with having given the Hopi 'watermelon, muskmelon, pumpkin, and squash to eat', as well as black corn; and in one account (Nequatewa, 1936, p. 25), his head 'was . . . like the biggest *squash*, and there was no hair on it'.

*ke'le*, sparrowhawk (*Falco sparverius*). This is the commonest hawk, also the smallest, found in the vicinity of the Hopi villages. It is a permanent resident of the region, nesting in the cliffs along the valley and hunting from poles, bluffs and prominent bushes; its call is a sharp *killy, killy, killy* (hence the Hopi name), and its diet consists mainly of lizards, grasshoppers and beetles. Sparrowhawks also, however, take small birds; and their numbers, at least in the Oraibi valley, are considerably augmented during September and early October when the migrant warblers and other small birds are passing through on their way south. Eggan writes (1950, p. 86):

> The *kele* or chicken hawk is a symbol of bravery, since it attacks birds larger than itself; novices in the Wü'wütçim initiation are *kelehoya*, 'little chicken hawks', getting ready to leave their nest.

I have myself twice seen sparrowhawks attack a Western Red-Tail.

*a'toko*, crane or heron. The Hopi word refers to any long-necked, long-legged wading bird that migrates south in September–October, usually in flocks, and that lives by spearing frogs and small rodents, usually in shallow water or marshes; more specifically, it probably refers to the Sandhill Crane (*Grus canadensis*). Bones of the latter bird were found at Wupa'tki pueblo (Hargrave, 1939, p. 208).

Beaglehole, in his notes on Hopi bird and animal observation, writes (1937, pp. 34–5):

> Finally, when the wild duck (*a·a'dok*) flies southward in flocks at peach-drying time, cold weather and frosts will soon come and harvesting should be hastened.

Clearly, this observation refers to crane, not wild duck. Of the three personal names listed by Voth (1905b, p. 74) as belonging to this clan, two refer to cranes flying in a line across the sky. According to James (1903, p. 86), hawk and crane feathers were used for the *na'tsi* on two of the kivas at Walpi, at the New Fire (i.e. Wü'wütçim) ceremony in 1898.

*tü'bish*, 'sorrow-making'. The word evidently derives from *tü'bish lato'to*, vituperation[1], and refers either to the taunting songs (Stephen, 1936, p. 1086), sung by the men of the Wü'wütçim fraternity and the Singers in the course of the Wü'wütçim ceremony and by the women of the Marau' society in the

---

[1] Since writing this, I find that among the Luiseño Indians, distant linguistic congeners of the Hopi, *tuvish* is the name given to the mortuary rites that occupy the night following death (Kroeber, 1925, p. 675); this may well be its meaning in Hopi, so furnishing a link with the cotton mask laid over the dead person's face.

course of their ceremony, or to the rude jests exchanged between the two groups (Fewkes, 1900a, p. 125).

pü'çovi, Hopi cotton (*Gossypium Hopi* Lewton). Hopi cotton, a much-branched shrub growing to a height of about two feet, was formerly cultivated on the valley floor near Moencopi; it was also grown, as late as 1912 (Lewton, 1912, p. 6), in non-irrigated gardens near Oraibi. There was some link (above, p. 213) between the growing of cotton and Spider Woman; and it was that deity who first taught the Hopi how to weave cotton (Eggan, 1950, p. 82).

Cotton thread was prepared by placing the fibre-enveloped seeds on a bed of sand, then whipping them with a bundle of pliant rods (Hough, 1918, pp. 252–3); this process removes the seeds and leaves the fibre in a fluffy mess, which is then rolled into thread by hand. Cotton thread was needed for prayer-sticks and prayer-feathers, for wrapping around the *ti'poni*(s) of the several fraternities, for weaving the wedding blanket (*o'va*) for every Hopi maiden; raw cotton, for the cotton mask laid on the face of the dead.[1]

### Actual ceremonial duties

The principal ceremonial function of this phratry is, or was until recently, control of the Wü'wütçim fraternity. On 1st Mesa, this phratry grouping had been extinct for some decades even when Stephen resided there in the 1890s, and control of the Wü'wütçim fraternity had passed into the hands of Mustard clan; but Squash clan was remembered (Stephen, 1936, p. 1086) as having owned both the Wü'wütçim *wi'mi*, and the Marau'. At Mishong'novi, the Wü'wütçim fraternity was owned by Coyote and Squash clans (Eggan, 1950, p. 103); on 3rd Mesa, it was owned by the *ke'le* fraction of Squash-Sparrow-hawk-Crane phratry grouping.

### Association of ideas

As Eggan observes (1950, p. 86): 'the Kele-Squash-Crane group is traditionally associated with the Wü'wütçim ceremony.' Squash furnishes a link with Masau'u, in his aspect as 'owner of the crops'; *ke'le*, with the initiatory sequence and with hunting; *a'toko*, with the southward migration of cranes at peach-drying time and the approach of cold weather; *tü'bish*, with the slopping of water and urine, symbol of rain-and-snow, over the dancers in the course of the Wü'wütçim ceremony[2]; and cotton, through the 'cloud' mask, with the

---

[1] Cotton appears to be *mediatory*, par excellence, in Lévi-Straussian terms (1958, pp. 249–50); the plant grows *wild* in the Arizona mountains (Parsons, 1939, p. 18, n. 3), yet has been taken into cultivation since around 900 A.D.; *raw* cotton is used for the mask for the dead, mediatory between life on earth and life in the underworld; *woven* cotton for clothing, mediatory between un-culture and culture, and for the wedding blanket, mediatory between maiden (*ma'na*) and married woman (*tü'msi*); and cotton *thread* for prayer offerings, mediatory between the social order and the powers that control nature (of which the social order is a part). Tobacco, *pi'va*, is clearly another such intermediary, i.e. between wild and cultivated, between boy and man, between people and deities.

[2] Or with the deceased, if the word refers to mortuary rites.

recently dead and with the ancestors, so completing the sequence (noted above, p. 235) of 'birth, copulation and death', which runs through the Marau' and Wü'wütçim rites.

### Anomalies, and comments

The inclusion of Sparrowhawk and Crane clans in the Reed-Greasewood-Bow phratry grouping, in Parsons' 1922 list for 3rd Mesa, gives evidence of the close conceptual tie between these two clans and Bow clan, credited in myth with having 'brought' the Wü'wütçim ceremony to Oraibi. On 1st Mesa, Stephen puts *ke'le* into the Eagle-Reed phratry grouping.

PHRATRY XII. MUSTARD–CHAKWAINA–ROADRUNNER

*a'sa*, mustard, wild tansy
*püchko'hü*, throwing stick
*kwi'ñvi*, mountain oak
*posi'wû*, magpie

*Cha'kwaina*, a female katçina
*ho'spowi*, chaparral cock, roadrunner
*tçi'ro*, small bird, snowbird
*püchi'lüwa*, western meadowlark

*Myth.* Between the Mustard-Cha'kwaina phratry grouping and Ko'kop-Coyote, there is a close link (Parsons, 1925, pp. 77–8: 1933, p. 26, n. 104, and p. 35, n. 140); on their wanderings the Mustard people (*A's nyamü*) acted as 'watchers' for the Coyote people—if anything came to hurt them (the Coyote people), then the Mustard people had to fight for them, 'they must mind [look after] Coyote clan'.

### Natural observation, and ceremonial referents

*a'sa*, tansy mustard (*Sisymbrium canescens*). In the old days the Hopi picked the young leaves and shoots of the Tansy Mustard, which they boiled and ate as greens (Bartlett, 1931, p. 3). According to Stephen (1929, p. 60, n. 5), the plant was used for making a red dye; among the Tewa (Ortiz, 1969, p. 34), the colour red is especially associated with warfare and with hunting.

*püchko'hü*, throwing stick. This is the curved throwing-stick, used chiefly for hunting rabbits, but also in warfare (above, p. 249).

*kwi'ñvi*, Gambel's oak (*Quercus gambelli*). Gambel's oak does not grow in the vicinity of the Hopi villages, but in canyon heads some miles to the northeast, near the edge of Black Mesa, from where the Hopi used to procure the wood. Throwing-sticks, bows, arrows, clubs and digging sticks, were all made from the wood of Gambel's oak (Hough, 1918, pp. 287–8).

*posi'wû*, magpie (*Pica pica*). At one time, according to Mearns's 1st Mesa informants (1896, p. 400), magpies were common about the Hopi villages; they are no longer found in the region to-day, though they are still common farther north, e.g. in Mesa Verde National Park (where I saw seven in one morning, early in October 1969). The bird is a scavenger, as its Hopi nickname *no'kswa* (= *no'va si'kwi*), 'eats meat', indicates. In the old days, the men of the warrior society (*momchitû*) are said to have worn head-dresses of magpie feathers: Voth (1905*b*), p. 101.

*Cha'kwaina*, a female katçina, restricted to 1st Mesa and 'belonging to' Mustard clan. She is a warrior katçina (Stephen, 1936, p. 44, 122, and Figure 29), carries bow-and-arrow (Parsons, 1925, p. 78, n. 126), and figures in the Soya'l at Walpi-Sicho'movi.

*ho'spowi*, chaparral cock, roadrunner (*Geococcyx californianus*). A sparse summer resident on the grass flats below the Hopi villages, noted for the speed with which it runs, and for its skill in hunting snakes and lizards. According to Stephen (1936, p. 950), the flesh when eaten 'makes those who partake of it swift and tireless'.

*tçi'ro*, bird, snowbird. *tçi'ro* is the general Hopi word for bird (of any kind); more specifically, it refers to small birds. Fewkes (1900*b*, pp. 582–4) gives *tçi'ro* as 'bunting', Voegelin (1957, p. 18, A7.4) as 'bird, snowbird', while a folk tale recorded by Voth (1905*c*, pp. 201–2) describes *tçi'ro* as going about in flocks. In his *Journal* (1936, p. 1025), Stephen has the following entry for 29 October, 1893:

> I saw snowbirds (*nüva'to'cha*) for the first time this year on the mesa top near Tüki'novi. They understand cold and snow. They bring snow.

And Parsons, in the glossary to the *Journal* (1936, p. 1265), renders *nüva'to'cha*, 'snowbird, snow bunting'. Almost certainly, the bird referred to is the Oregon Junco (*Junco oreganus*), a common winter resident around the Hopi villages.[1]

*püchi'lüwa*, western meadowlark (*Sturnella neglecta*). This conspicuous, yellow-breasted bird, to-day a sparse permanent resident of the grass flats below the Hopi villages, was common there seventy to eighty years ago. Since meadow-larks require rich grass cover to feed in (their decline in numbers throughout the region has gone *pari passu* with the over-grazing of the last seventy years), they may well have served as indicators, in the old days, of where antelope were to be found.

### Actual ceremonial duties

The Mustard-Cha'kwaina-Roadrunner phratry is only found on 1st Mesa; it was probably brought by the Tewa, when they settled there around 1700 A.D.

---

[1] The only other serious contenders are Horned Lark (*Eremophila alpestris*) and McCown's Longspur (*Rhynchophanes mccownii*). Seventy to eighty years ago, McCown's Longspurs were still fairly common winter residents in north-eastern Arizona; in winter, they are 'gregarious birds of open grasslands', while Horned Larks 'are gregarious among themselves, but flock with no other species save McCown's Longspur' (*Birds of Arizona*, pp. 93–5, 212).

That the *tçi'ro* referred to in the clan name is one or other of these three birds is put beyond reasonable doubt, to my mind, by the following observation. Kluckhorn, who used Whorf's 2nd Mesa word list on his visit to Moenkopi in 1937, adds this note (Kluckhorn and Macleish, 1955, p. 153):

*tci'ro*, 'said to refer only to small birds, *especially winter birds that come while the snow is on the ground*'.

Its chief ceremonial function at Walpi-Sicho'movi is control of the Wü'wütçim fraternity, which passed to the Mustard people on the extinction of Squash clan (Stephen, 1936, p. 958). It also has care of the Cha'kwaina katçina, a warrior deity, prominent in the Soya'l on 1st Mesa.

### Association of ideas

The ideas associated with this phratry grouping are mainly centred on war, and on the 'war' thread running through the Wü'wütçim and Soya'l ceremonies: and, to a lesser extent, on hunting and on the return of cold weather.[1] The Cha'kwaina katçina, whose mask is exposed in kiva in the course of the Soya'l (Stephen, 1936, p. 44) and again in January (ibid. pp. 120–2), is a war katçina, closely associated with Masau'u (Parsons, 1925, p. 78, n. 126); *posi'wû*, magpie, is a scavenger and meat-eater; *püchko'hü*, throwing stick, furnishes a link both with rabbit hunting and with war; *kwi'ñvi*, mountain oak, as the wood used for making throwing-sticks, bows and arrows, and clubs, a further link with war or with hunting; and *ho'spowi*, roadrunner, with the speed and endurance needed for running down deer and antelope. Finally *tçi'ro*, Oregon Junco (or, possibly, Longspur), signalises by its return the onset of cold weather and the season for performing the ceremonies necessary for success in those pursuits.

### Anomalies, and comments

The inclusion of Roadrunner in Reed-Greasewood-Bow phratry, on 3rd Mesa, may be attributed to the war and hunting element common to both groupings.

The six phratries we have been considering are inter-related, in that they all play a part in the Wü'wütçim ceremony; and that ceremony, I have suggested (above, p. 279), is lineal successor to the fall festival of the Great Basin Shoshoni. Now the memory of the original linkage between the several clans and the four fraternities which participate in the Wü'wütçim ceremony is preserved, I believe, in a myth recorded by Stephen,[2] the myth of 'How the Katçina brought the *ti'poni* to the Rain phratry':

> Long ago, runs the myth, the Hopi lived far away in the south, where the rocks and the earth are red. . . . Each clan had its own house with a store room attached, into which was placed the whole harvested crop as a common store. At that time there were four phratries (*nato'lyya*), and the clans (*nyamü*) which composed them were these:
>
> Eagle (*kwa'hü*): eagle, Sun, turkey, hawk, greasewood . . .

---

[1] Actually, the hunting element is a lot stronger than I realised when I wrote this: at Zuñi, the Cha'kwaina deity is patroness of hunting and, as Rabbit Mother, controls the fertility of rabbits as well as of girls (Parsons, 1917, pp. 380–1). The Cha'kwaina's control of hunting and of rabbits accounts for her link with Masau'u, and for the phratry's link with Wü'wütçim and with the Soya'l, much better than the (probably late) war *motif*.

[2] Stephen (1929), pp. 60–3: the notes in square brackets are my own gloss on the myth. Also, there are many inconsistencies in the myth, most of which I have omitted in the shortened version given here; the interested reader should consult the original.

Rain (*yo'ki*): rain, corn, badger, butterfly, bear, Katçina, parrot, rabbit, tobacco, mustard, oak . . .

Deer (*sowi'ñwû*): deer, antelope, mountain sheep, antelope grass (millet).

Snake (*tçü'a*): rattlesnake, yellow cactus, red cactus, coyote.

Each phratry had a large house (kiva) where the men would congregate, relate personal experiences, do odd jobs of labour, or listen to the teachings of the chief.

After living here a long time, certain misfortunes befell the Hopi, and they determined to leave that bad land and go to the north. They gathered their goods together and journeyed north, living on seeds and roots of many plants, carrying water with them, and travelling at night time so as to escape the heat of the sun and avoid their enemies. At length they came to the basin of the Little Colorado where, finding good grass and water, they determined to stop. They planted, and built houses, and resumed their former habits of life. The people were greatly pleased over the prospect of a continued place of residence and the men all came together and sang and danced [Wü'wütçim]. After the men had finished singing and dancing, the women said that they also would dance . . ., so when the corn, melons, squashes and other crops were gathered and stored away, the women had their dance [Marau']. Many things which the Hopi have now forgotten were then done, but the festival in the main and its object have been preserved, *viz. the song and prayer asking for children, to replace those removed by death.*

Eventually two old men, who proved to be katçinas, came from the west from the house of Pa'lülükoñ, one of them bearing the *ti'poni* which he gave to the chief of the Rain phratry, 'in the middle of this *ti'poni* a small hole was made, in which corn meal was placed, typical of its being the chief support of life'; and the other bearing a small sack of white meal, so finely ground that it could hardly be felt between the fingers, 'this meal was given to the woman chief [i.e. of the Marau'] whose duty it then became to see that the sack should never become empty'. After the *ti'poni* had been set up in front of the altar, these katçina selected eight men who were to be known as singing men [Singers' fraternity], whose duty it should be to sing to the chief [Pa'lülükoñ] on the days of the sacred feast or whenever the katçina returned. They were taught many songs, and instructed how to move in the dance. The women were also instructed in this.

The people lived in that country for a long while . . ., then troubles broke out among them, they moved from one place to another on the Little Colorado, until eventually they moved over the mesas to the north and came to the places where they now live. This region was selected 'because of the abundance of wood and the great number of springs and because grass was plenty'.

In the myth the harvesting of 'corn, melons, squashes and other crops', which preceded the women's ceremony, has evidently been transposed in time. Apart from that anachronism., I take it that the four *nato'lyya* represent the four fraternities co-operating in the aboriginal fall ceremony, Eagle-greasewood-hawk representing the Wü'wütçim fraternity, Rain-tobacco the Singers, Deer-millet the Ahl, and Snake-coyote the Kwan fraternity, and that the women's ceremony is the Marau'; that the bringing of the rain-and-corn *ti'poni* marks the change from a gathering-and-hunting economy to an agricultural one; and that the 'setting up of the *ti'poni* in front of the altar' refers to the whole complex of agricultural rites embracing the Powa'mu, Pa'lülükoñ-ti, Nima'n katçina and Flute observances, the primary object of which is rain and corn growth. In keeping with this interpretation, we may note that all four of the phratry groupings which have charge of these rites, namely Badger-Butterfly, Pikyas-Pa'tki, Katçina-Parrot and Bear (-Spider), have in the myth been tacked on to the Tobacco-Rabbit grouping, whose function— to 'smoke for rain'—most nearly approximates to their own.[1]

Now the conceptual linkage which the myth reveals between the clans included in the Rain *nato'lyya* explains why, on 2nd Mesa (Mishong'novi), Tobacco-Rabbit people 'go in' with Badger phratry, and why, on 3rd Mesa, with Katçina-Parrot. Very briefly we may say that, as agriculture replaced gathering-and-hunting as the main source of food in pueblo economy, the practical importance of rabbit hunting (embodied in the Rabbit fraction of Tobacco-Rabbit phratry) waned, at the same time as the ritual importance of smoking-for-rain (embodied in the Tobacco fraction) waxed. The phratry grouping as a whole thus slewed away from its hunting function and towards its smoking-for-rain function, away from being a fall-and-winter grouping to being a spring-and-summer one, eventually on 2nd and 3rd Mesas 'going in' with phratries, Badger in one case, Katçina-Parrot in the other, whose *raison d'être* is germination, rain and growth of crops.

Earlier (above, p. 197) I argued that, beside its integrative function, the ceremonial cycle serves to maintain the limit which the Hopi have voluntarily set to their own use of the resources available to them. We can now see how that limit is maintained. Every relation, or at least every *critical* relation, between community and environment is watched over by one of the phratries; each of these, in turn, 'owns'—or is closely associated with—one or more of the major ceremonies, the purpose of which is to promote the harmony of the relation in its care. This watchful care alone may have sufficed to keep the balance between people's needs and the capacity of the land to satisfy them; but behind it, in case it were not enough, lay the 'whip' (*wuvata*) which inheres in each ceremony, ready to be exercised on the communal behalf by the fraternity responsible for carrying out its rites.

### SIGNIFICANCE OF THE PHRATRY GROUPINGS

Our account of the twelve groupings which make up Hopi society being now concluded, it remains for us to assess their significance.

One point is clear, at the outset. Nearly everything in their environment has been remarked and given a name by the Hopi. To take a single instance, plants: take a cutting of any of the many grasses, herbs or shrubs growing around the villages and present it to a Hopi, at least to one of the older generation, and, unless it is an especially rare or obscure one, he will be able to put a name to it

---

[1] On 1st Mesa, where Tobacco-Rabbit has remained an independent grouping, *po'li*, butterfly, still (Forde, 1931, p. 400) 'goes in' with that phratry.

at once. Insects (spider, bee, wasp, butterfly, grasshopper, locust), aquatic animals, snakes and lizards, birds, small rodents, game animals and animals of prey, all are recognised and named. Yet, out of the whole range of natural objects (or beings, in Hopi view) observed and named by the Hopi, only certain ones have been selected to serve as clan names. Thus, out of eighteen larger mammals (cottontail and bigger) listed in the Glossary to Stephen's *Hopi Journal* (1936), all but two, skunk (*pü'cha*) and weasel (*piva'ni*), serve as clan names; but of ten smaller mammals (ground squirrel, wood-rat, chipmunk, etc.), common around the fields and villages and named by the Hopi (Fisher, 1896, p. 174), only two, prairie dog (*tü'kya*) and gopher (*mü'yi*), have been chosen. Of fifty-six distinctive Hopi bird-names,[1] twenty-four serve as clan appellations. Of trees and shrubs, seven of the eight conspicuous trees found growing within seventy-five miles of the villages, i.e. spruce, Douglas fir, piñon, juniper, cottonwood, willow and mountain oak, are numbered among clan names, only ponderosa pine (*lö'qö*) being absent; but of twenty-four woody shrubs that grow in the immediate vicinity of the villages,[2] only two, greasewood (*de've*) and rabbit-brush (*siva'pi*), have been chosen, and of six grasses, only one (*le'hü*).

Now, while it would be possible to argue that all the objects that *are* so chosen as clan names are of significance, either by their use or ceremonially, to the Hopi, one could not reasonably argue that the objects not chosen to serve as clan names are of *no* significance. For example, of the shrubs, snakeweed (*ma'övi*), fourwing saltbush (*sy'ovi*), Apache plume (*moñpö'hövi*), and mountain sage (*kü'ñya*), each has important uses, practical, culinary or ceremonial, yet none serves as a clan name; of cultivated crops, beans (*mori'vosi*) figures more prominently than squash in the Hopi dietary,[3] yet is not used as a clan name. Of birds, crow (*añwü'si*) and magpie (*posi'wû*) are used, but piñon jay (*a'a*) and red-shafted flicker (*wari'ñyau*) are not; yet both the latter birds are common, both raid the corn fields in the fall, and the feathers of both are used ceremonially. And of insects, spider, butterfly and ant have been selected, but not locust, bee or wasp, though all three of these are significant in relation to warm weather, honey and pollen.

A further point, also, may be noted. The classification represented by the phratry groupings is independent of, and in no sense usurps the place of, the primary classification of things based on language. To take a simple example, again: the Hopi make a clear linguistic distinction between *pa'wikya*, 'scoops the water' or duck, comprising birds which swim on the surface of the water

---

[1] Listed in a paper of my own (1970). This is not to say that Hopi only recognise fifty-six species of birds; in fact they recognise more, as some of the Hopi names cover more than one of our species and Hopi may then distinguish further between different species covered by a single name, e.g. *pa'la* (red) *kwa'yo* and *ma'si* (gray) *kwa'yo*.

[2] Listed in Bradfield (1968), pp. 63–9.

[3] Beans, however, were a relatively late addition to the list of crops grown. Linton holds (1940, p. 36) that it was the introduction of beans into the San Juan basin that provided the nutritional basis for the development of classical Pueblo culture.

and forage under the surface for food, *pa'tçiro*, 'water bird', comprising long-legged birds which poke around at the water's edge leaving their footprints in the mud, and *a'toko*, crane or heron, birds which stalk about in shallow water or in marshland spearing frogs and mice with their beaks. It so happens that birds of the first two kinds are included, along with other aquatic animals, in Pikyas-Pa'tki phratry grouping, and those of the third kind, in Squash-Sparrowhawk-Crane grouping; but the subsuming of the three categories under two different phratry groupings is independent of the primary linguistic distinction between them.

With these two qualifications, namely, that the clan names represent only a proportion—varying in each main category—of the phenomena actually observed and named by the Hopi, and that the similarities and distinctions implicit in the groupings are independent of the primary categorisation embodied in the language, I find myself in agreement with Eggan in his conclusions regarding the Hopi phratry groupings. These groupings, he says (1950, p. 300), need to be looked at from two stand-points: as a classification of people for social purposes, and as a classification of the world of nature in its important aspects. Throughout the western Pueblos, we find a common set of clan names:

> In my opinion, [writes Eggan (1950, p. 301)], the common set of clan names must be viewed in terms of the relationship between man and nature. The aspects of the natural world which have social or ritual value for the Pueblos are similar, and the clan names reflect these aspects; the division of each village into segmentary units, and their association with particular aspects of nature, is a widespread technique for establishing such relationships.

Looked at objectively, the system of clan names, and their grouping into a number of distinct phratries, appears to represent, *not* a 'scientific' classification in the sense that every object is allotted its place in a set of over-riding categories (as, for example, in the classification of plants according to the Linnaean system), but *rather* the emergence within the environment—upon which a rough-and-ready classification has precedingly been imposed by the language itself[1]—of a number of *foci* of interest, around which cluster sets of related phenomena: the *foci* of more intense interest, the moisture-corn focus for example, attracting larger clusters of related phenomena, and the *foci* of less intense interest, smaller clusters.[2] These clusters of related phenomena appear to be, as Eggan remarks

---

[1] Cf. Whorf's words (1956, pp. 55–6), written at the time (1936) he was working on the Glossary to Stephen's *Hopi Journal*, clearly with Hopi in mind:

> We are inclined to think of language simply as a technique of expression, and not to realise that language first of all is a classification and arrangement of the stream of sensory experience which results in a certain world-order. . . . In other words, language does in a cruder but also in a broader and more versatile way the same thing that science does.

[2] Some months after completing this section, I found that the interpretation offered in it comes very close to that put forward, though without reference to the Hopi, by Goldenweiser nearly sixty years earlier (1910, pp. 274–6). *Totemism*, a term I have avoided as begging the question I was seeking to answer, Goldenweiser regarded essentially as the

(1950, p. 73) of the moisture-corn complex, 'indefinitely expandable, as far as clan names are concerned, everything connected with rain or water or corn, as well as useful plants such as *siva'pi* (rabbit-brush), being considered to belong to this phratry'. And up to a point, this is true: not only of the moisture-corn complex, but of each of the other clusters. But there are, in fact, two limits to the extent of a cluster. The first limit is where that cluster meets another; for example, the moisture-corn cluster could *not* include greasewood (*pace* Whiting, 1939, p. 47), although greasewood has certain associations with corn-growing, because—its other associations being stressed—greasewood has already been pre-empted into the Reed-Greasewood-Bow grouping. The second limit is implicit in the purpose which the groupings serve; for the groupings are essentially, as I propose now to show, *action* groupings, designed to serve as means of acting on the environment, and for this purpose, to get a leverage so to speak, they need to be concentrated, not too diffuse.

The overt means by which the phratry groupings act on the environment is through their *wöye*. The word *wöye* (or *wuya*), pl. *wü'wüyom*, means in the first instance 'old man, old men'. Thus Parsons' 1st Mesa informant, describing the races that take place in March, refers (1925, p. 61, n. 101) to the oldest man of each clan as *wöye* of that clan. Again, once in a while every clan has a meeting, held in the house of the matrilineage where the ancestral mask is kept, at which all the members of the clan are present and the oldest man talks to them, 'telling them where they came from and how they came here';[1] traditional knowledge of this kind is referred to as *wü'wüyom lavai'yi*, 'old men talk' (Stephen, 1929, p. 33: 1936, p. 713). In addition to its primary meaning, the word *wöye*, pl. *wü'wüyom*, has two major extensions of reference. It is used to refer to those old men of a clan, or of a fraternity, who have passed on to the next world; thus the crooks (*ñülü'kpi*), arranged beside the sand field in front of the Antelope altar (above, Figure 47, p. 155), 'represent the old men bent with age, the *wü'wüyomo*, the wise, thinking old men, who have passed away. . . . The long straight prayer-sticks (*wu'pa pa'ho*) represent the younger men, who yet walked erect when they died' (Stephen, 1936, pp. 673–5). Finally, the word *wöye* (or *wuya*) is used to refer to the ancestral or mythical being with which each clan or phratry grouping is especially and intimately linked in myth and sentiment, the mask of which—also referred to as *wöye*—is kept in the house of the senior matrilineage of the clan to which it belongs (cf. Parsons, 1922, p. 289: 1926, p. 212, and p. 219, n. 24: 1936, p. xxxviii).

---

process whereby objects in the natural environment, *which are of emotional value*, become socialised by being associated with definite social units (descent groups, commonly). The totem itself he consequently defined (ibid. p. 276, n. 1) as being *an object or symbol of emotional value referring to a definite social unit*; since an animal, a plant, or an object, is a totem on account of its definite social relations, it cannot, in the absence of such relations, be one—as, for example, the guardian spirit of the Plains Indians is not.

[1] See Parsons (1925), p. 77, for an account of such a meeting of the Mustard clan, on 1st Mesa.

Now we have seen, in our account of the twelve phratry groupings, that each of the main phratry groupings has as its principal *wuya* one of the leading figures of the Hopi spiritual world: thus, Badger-Butterfly phratry has Mü' iyiñwa as its *wuya*, Bear-Spider has Kokyañwuhti, Ko'kop-Coyote has Masau'u, and Reed-Greasewood-Bow has Pyü'ükoñhoya as *wuya*.[1] The link between the phratry grouping and its *wuya* is established in myth; the mask representing the 'ancient' is kept in the clan house of that clan to which it specifically belongs, to which also belongs the right to impersonate the 'ancient' ceremonially; certainly every phratry, and perhaps, also, each of the leading clans within the phratry,[2] has its own *wuya* and its own ancestral mask. So close, indeed, is the link between *wuya* and social group that, in native philosophy, it is the ancestral mask (*wöye*) which holds the group together (Parsons, 1922, p. 289), is regarded as the 'heart' (*ünü' ñwa*) of the clan which owns it, and may even lend its name to the whole phratry—Ko'kop-Coyote, for example, being referred to on occasions as *Masau' nyamü*, 'Masau' people', and Mustard clan as 'Cha'kwaina people': Parsons (1933), p. 38, n. 151.

The link established in myth between the phratry grouping and its principal *wuya*, and validated by possession of the mask representing the 'ancient', has certain practical manifestations. The *wuya* is regarded, in a very special sense, as 'partner' to the phratry grouping to which it belongs; it may be referred to as 'our grandfather', or as 'our mother's brother'; only members of the grouping to which it belongs may impersonate the *wuya*, e.g. the impersonation of Masau'u by a man of Ko'kop-Coyote grouping, at harvest-time; during the Soya'l, each clan makes prayer-sticks for its own, and associated, *wuya* (Eggan, 1950, p. 81); and the particular ceremony, designed to promote the climatic or agricultural event over which the *wuya* is believed to exert a beneficent influence, is commonly found to be in the hands of the phratry grouping to which the *wuya* belongs, e.g. Powa'mu ceremony, *wuya*—Mü'iyiñwa, 'owned' by Badger-Butterfly phratry. Whence one might conclude, simply, that prayers are made to the *wuya*, for the benefit desired. Such an interpretation, however, while it contains an element of truth, is not (I think) the whole truth. For *that*, we must return again, and for the last time, to the Hopi view of the world.

We have seen earlier that Hopi view the cosmic process as one of 'becoming

[1] I have adopted the spelling *wuya*, in an endeavour to keep distinct the different senses in which the one Hopi word is used: i.e. when referring to the principal mythical being associated with each phratry (e.g. Mü'iyiñwa, Masau'u), to use the spelling *wuya*; and when referring either to the eponymous animal or plant (e.g. bear, badger) with which each clan is associated, to the mask by which it is represented, or to the clan ancestor(s), to use the spelling *wöye*. *wuya* is Titiev's spelling, *wöye* is Parsons'.

[2] Thus, at Hano (and, by inference, at the neighbouring Hopi villages), a man of Bear clan is guardian of the Hon *wöye*, Bear clan mask: Parsons (1933), p. 36. The whole matter is confused by one's never being quite sure, in reading Dr. Parsons' various accounts, whether she is referring to clan or phratry: for example, in her remark (1936, p. 1078), 'it is probable that every clan has a clan mask or *wöye*, but Stephen does not enumerate them.' Parsons habitually refers to the phratry as a clan and to the clan as a lineage, but she is not consistent even in this; for confusion confounded, see her footnote (1936), p. 1087, n. 1.

later and later', in the course of which existents, hitherto un-manifest (and to that extent malleable), manifest themselves in the form in which they become perceptible to the senses. Each existent manifests itself in its own way, and in the nature of each existent able so to manifest itself, is the power of its own mode of duration—its growth, decline, stability, etc. Everything is thus already 'prepared' for the way it now manifests by earlier phases; and what it will be later, partly has been, and partly is in act of being, so 'prepared' (Whorf, 1956, pp. 147–8). In such a view of the universe, the unfolding of events —the succession of the seasons, for example, or the growing of crops to fruition—is not *dependent* on will, since each existent carries within it the seeds of its own development or metamorphosis. Nevertheless to the extent that, in the manifesting or subjective realm, relations between things are still reversible and the forms which they will finally assume still malleable, the unfolding of events is *susceptible to* the influence of will, since the manifesting or subjective realm—besides comprising the realm of uncertainty or, as we call it, the 'future' —is also the field of action for all human *hoping, wishing, striving* and *taking thought*. The manifesting realm is thus the meeting ground, where events unborn or, as we might say, 'in the womb of time', are impinged upon by human will.

One aspect of this impingement is expressed by the word *tüna'tya,* v. '(it) hopes, is hoped for, thinks or is thought of with hope'; and we may note here, as example of this aspect, that the man who makes the prayer-sticks preparatory to a hunt is referred to as *ma'k tünai'tyaita,* 'the one who desires a hunt, sets his thoughts on it', while the two leaders who plan a katçina ceremony are called *tüna'tyamü,* 'thought-desires theirs', referring to their hopes being centred on the forthcoming dance (Stephen, 1936, p. 423). A further aspect is expressed by the word *na'twanta, -tota,* v. 'concentrates mentally on a hope to bring (something) to pass, holding it in your heart, putting your mind on it, earnestly hoping'; from this word, as we have seen earlier (above, p. 90; cf. Whorf, 1936, p. 1261: 1956, p. 149), comes the word *na'twani,* n. 'crops, harvest', i.e. that which is tried or hoped for. To understand the intimacy of the link between hoping and harvest, we have to bear in mind that, to the Hopi, one's desires and thoughts influence not only his own actions, but *all nature as well.* The Hopi thought-world, writes Whorf (1956, pp. 149–50), has no imaginary space, as ours has; when he thinks concentratedly about e.g. a corn plant in the field,

> a Hopi would naturally suppose that his thought (or he himself) traffics with the actual corn plant that he is thinking about. The thought, then, should leave some trace of itself with the plant in the field. If it is a good thought, one about health and growth, it is good for the plant; if a bad thought, the reverse.

Further, Hopi emphasise (ibid. p. 150) the intensity factor of thought. Thought to be most effective should be *vivid in consciousness, definite, steady, sustained,* charged with *strongly felt good intentions*; and it is this aspect that finds expression in the word *na'twanta.*

'Thought-power' is thus the force that runs through all Hopi religious action, from the simplest act of *ho'moya* or sprinkling of corn meal, through ritual smoking and prayer-stick making, to the most complex dances and ceremonies. In an earlier section (above, pp. 188–9), we analysed the act of sprinkling with corn meal, and found that it comprised three stages: the formulation of a wish, the 'breathing' of the wish on to (or into) the corn meal, and the sprinkling of the corn meal to the deity from whom the benefit is desired. To the physical act of sprinkling (*ho'moya*) corresponded, we saw, the mental act of wishing or desiring, *na'wakna*. Now this latter word also means, as Kennard has pointed out (1937, pp. 491–2), 'wills' or 'prays'; and he goes on:

> Thus, it is often said that it is unnecessary to speak one's prayer, since mere willing or transfer of the wish by means of the breath of a prayer stick or prayer meal has the same effect. The essential idea seems to be that by concentration the collective will is projected so that the powers are compelled to obey.

It is clear, from the context, that Kennard is referring here to the concentration of the collective will in the course of ceremonies, but the same question remains: what 'powers', precisely, are compelled to obey? My own view, formed in the light of Whorf's exposition of the Hopi thought-world, is that the collective will, or concentrated prayer-force, acts *directly* on things or rather on *events*, in their un-manifest and so malleable form, influencing them in the right direction (in rather the same way as on a practical level the Hopi farmer, seeing a rain-storm in the hills, will hasten to dig shallow run-ways in his field to divert the approaching flood around the roots of his corn plants); that the *wuya* are appealed to for their help, not because they *control*, but because they are believed to have a special intimate link with, and so be able— if so 'minded'—to exert an especially powerful influence on, the event or natural phenomenon which it is hoped to direct into the right channel; and that that section of the community, whose collective will is more potent than any other in directing a particular event or natural phenomenon into the right channel, is the phratry grouping whose clan names betray their affinity with it.

This interpretation seems to me to be the only one capable of reconciling the 'determinism', implicit in the Hopi view of the world, with the scope accorded to will and prayer in their ceremonies and especially in their notion of *na'twanta*. By it, the phratry groupings associated with particular clusters of related phenomena in the natural world are so associated *in order that*, affinity established between the social group and the natural, the collective will of the one may act the more effectively on the *event* which forms the nucleus of the other;[1] while the principal *wuya*, associated with the various phratry groupings, appear not so much as deities who have it in their power to bestow benefits,

---

[1] Conversely, anyone who withdraws his will affects the event adversely. Thus, a person sleeping at a katçina ceremony is apt to retard the growth of corn: Stephen (1936), p. 437, n. 1.

as 'partners' who are appealed to by their Hopi associates to add their will to their own, with the object of influencing events yet un-manifest into a good course, in the ceaseless process of 'becoming later and later' that is the Hopi version of 'time'. Whence comes, in the first place, the need for concentratedness in the cluster of related phenomena represented by any one phratry grouping, in order that the traffic between the social group and its counterpart in the natural order may be direct and to the point; and, in the second place, the special affinity which exists between each group and its *wuya*.

Regarding the precise nature of the affinity between the social group and its *wuya*, I doubt whether anyone not born and bred a Hopi will ever grasp this wholly. However, we have certain clues to go on; and perhaps the most fruitful line of approach is by way of the eponymous animal, plant, or other natural object, with which each clan is especially associated. These, also (i.e. beside the principal, mythical being associated with each phratry), are known as *wöye*, e.g. *Hon wöye*, 'bear ancient', and may be represented by masks or figurines. Besides being applied to old men of the clan who are still living, to the recently dead and to the long dead (i.e. ancestors) represented by crooks beside the altar, the word *wöye*, pl. *wü'wüyom*, refers, then, to the being—whether animal, plant or natural object—represented by the clan name; and between each group and its *wöye* in the latter sense, there is, as Titiev noted (above, p. 9), 'a strong feeling of empathy and kinship'.

Now the essence of the Hopi notion of 'causal power' or latency is, as we have seen earlier (above, pp. 263–5), that while events are yet in their subjective and un-manifest state, their final state being still malleable, they may be acted upon and directed into certain courses by the power of thought and will: that is, by the act of *na'twanta* or concentrating mentally on what is desired, epitomised in the act of ritual smoking. Smoking tobacco, among the Tewa, is connected with the 'thought' or 'intention' of a chief; and it seems clear, from the remark of Mrs. Eggan's Hopi informant (above, p. 286) regarding her old uncle—'he has power to smoke for rain . . . like many of the old men'—that the efficacy of one's smoking increases, or may increase, with age. In the myths of origin, e.g. of the Rabbit people and of Badger people, the eponymous being associated with the clan is commonly referred to as 'uncle' (i.e. mother's brother), or as 'grandfather'; at one moment he is a man, and at the next, an animal—in Hopi words, 'he was a rabbit, yet he was a man' (Parsons, 1933, p. 28). Finally, in two out of a series of fifteen of Don Talai'yesva's dreams recorded by Mrs. Eggan (1949, pp. 181–96), one of the characters in the dream changes into his own eponymous animal, without the dreamer showing any marked surprise at this event: in one dream, it is the old Village chief (of Bear clan) who changes himself into a bear, and in another, the dreamer's own uncle—who had been dead some years at the time of the dream—turns himself into an eagle.

Taking Titiev's observation in the literal sense of the words, the feeling of kinship between clan and *wöye* stems from the fact that, in his human form (cf. the myths), he is their elder clan relative, i.e. mother's brother, or grandfather; while the empathy that is felt between the living members of the group, and their *wöye* in his animal form, stems from the fact that they *are* in a sense, or may readily become (cf. Don Talai'yesva's two dreams), their own epony-mous animal.[1] As to the *efficacy* of the relation, that stems from the nature of the Hopi thought-world; when a Hopi thinks concentratedly about e.g. a corn plant in the field, he 'naturally supposes that his thought (or he himself) traffics with the actual corn plant that he is thinking about' (Whorf, 1956, p. 150). His thought, therefore, will be the more effective if he himself already stands in a special relation of 'empathy and kinship' to (all) corn plants: that is, if he is a member of Pikyas clan.

One final question remains to be answered, that from which we set out: namely, why is it that, while there are strong ties uniting the people within the respective clans and only weak ones between clans in the same phratry, Hopi 'rarely err in assigning people to their proper phratries, but make frequent mistakes with regard to clan membership'? And the reason is to be looked for, I suggest, in the different functions which the two groupings serve. The clan is, primarily, the unit for the transmission of rights—rights over house sites, fields, cisterns, eagle-nesting cliffs, political and ceremonial office, esoteric knowledge; it takes its name from an object (or being) in the natural world, with which the members of the clan are held to have an especial affinity. The phratry, on the contrary, has no property rights, except to the extent that it 'owns' the particular ceremony with which, as a whole, it is associated; but through the affinities of its several clans with particular *objects* in the natural world, the phratry as a whole represents a grouping of natural phenomena, or conceptual category, *via* which its members exert an influence on the *event* that lies at the core of that grouping. Where the clan is a body for the ownership of *things*, the phratry is a body for the control of *events*; and the fact that Hopi 'rarely err in assigning people to their proper phratries, but make frequent mistakes with regard to clan membership', is due to their according precedence, in their habitual thought (cf. Whorf, 1956, pp. 147-8), to the latter aspect of reality over the former.

To illustrate, this point, let me end with a simple analogy. Imagine a university, let us say Cambridge, where the dons *live* in their own colleges, but go out to *work* in a number of different faculties: where, to put it in a rough-and-ready way, the colleges are *for* the transmission of rights, e.g. rooms, fellowships, 'chairs', and the faculties *for* knowledge of—and so control over—the natural world. Suppose, further, that groups of two or three colleges

---

[1] There is no suggestion of witchcraft in this affinity. However, the lability of state evidenced by the myths (and by Don Talai'yesva's two dreams) may have been the original soil in which witchcraft beliefs took root: see Parsons (1927). It would be interesting to know, also, whether people who are believed to assume the form of animal familiars (*dualang'mosa*), in fact take on the form of their own eponymous animals, or not; the fact that Millet people are suspected (on 1st Mesa) of being witches, and that black ants are the most potent source of *duhisa*, suggests that they sometimes do.

specialise in related subjects, one group, say, in biochemistry-physiology-medicine, another in mathematics-physics-astronomy, and perhaps a third in agriculture and soil science. [In the analogy, colleges are the Hopi clans, and groups of related colleges the phratries, while faculties are the major Hopi ceremonies, representing the phratries in their *active* aspect.] Now, if we are thinking primarily in terms of residence and the transmission of rights, we shall often find ourselves saying: 'Well, I know Jones belongs to Trinity, but I'm not sure whether he's a biochemist or a physiologist'; alternately, if we are thinking primarily in terms of knowledge of the natural world, we shall find ourselves saying: 'Well, I know McPherson is an astronomer, but I'm not sure whether he comes from St. John's or Peterhouse'.

The fact that Hopi frequently put people in the wrong 'college', but are nearly always right with regard to 'faculty', implies (I suggest) that they habitually think in terms of control over the environment rather than of transmission of rights. In other words, they 'place' a person as member of a body exerting an influence on the course of *events*, before placing him as member of a body standing in a particular relation to (i.e. 'owning') *things*.

That this is the right way of regarding the matter, is borne out by one final piece of evidence: the Hopi system of naming. As we have seen, each phratry grouping is organised conceptually around one set of ideas, and is associated ceremonially with one or more ceremonies *via* which the ideas find expression. Further, each clan within the grouping has at its disposal a stock of personal names which bear, in one way or another, upon the leading ideas around which the phratry is organised. Now the principal offices pertaining to any particular ceremony are handed down within the phratry to which that ceremony belongs: e.g. the offices relating to the Powa'mu ceremony, within Badger and Katçina phratry groupings. But outsiders are also admitted to membership of the various fraternities, as in the initiation of young men into, say, the Wü'wütçim or Snake fraternities, and of girls into the Marau' or Lako'n; and whenever a person is so initiated into a fraternity, his head is washed in yucca suds and a new name bestowed on him by his sponsor—the name bestowed on a young man at his Wü'wütçim initiation being the one by which he is commonly known for the rest of his life. Since his new name is one of the names belonging to his ceremonial 'father's' clan (and so refers, directly or indirectly, to the animal or plant after which the clan is named), and since that clan is likely to be one of those in the phratry[1] owning the ceremony (*wi'mi*), the novice is in this way associated conceptually with the objects for which the fraternity stands.

It is as though, to return to the analogy, when a person takes his degree in our imaginary university, he were first given a new name to *mark* his calling, then smoked together with the members of the faculty, exchanging kinship

---

[1] It seems reasonable to suppose that, originally, *only* members of the 'owning' calns could act as ceremonial 'fathers' in any given fraternity.

terms with them 'to unite their hearts': with us, to *know* the natural world more thoroughly,[1] with the Hopi to *act upon it* more effectively.

### Postscript to Chapters 15 and 16

Long after completing these two chapters, I read for the first time John Livingston Lowes' study of the origins of *The Rime of the Ancient Mariner*, in which he traces the sources of the Mariner's fateful voyage in the exploration literature of the 16th, 17th and 18th centuries, and delineates the process whereby the many diverse strands that went to its making were woven into order by the shaping power of Coleridge's imagination: the imagination which, 'out of the chaos of elements or shattered fragments of memory, puts together some form to fit it'. The process itself bears striking resemblance to the one by which, I believe, the imagination of the Hopi brought order out of the chaos of sensory impressions streaming into *their* consciousness; and on that ground I would urge any reader who has followed the argument so far, and who wishes to pursue it still farther, to go to that perceptive study[2] the sub-title of which betrays its affinity with the matter discussed above.

[1] H. A. Krebs, in a recent address on 'The Making of a Scientist' (*Nature*, vol. 215, pp. 1244–8), has stressed the rôle of 'kinship' and 'genealogy' in scientific work, and has shown how deeply indebted to their sponsors (ceremonial 'fathers') many of the great chemists and biochemists of the last 150 years have been.

[2] *The Road to Xanadu: a Study in the Ways of the Imagination* (London, 1927: 2nd ed. 1951), by John Livingston Lowes. For the quotation in the text, see there pp. 56, 403; for the centres or nuclei within the mind (the *foci of interest* of the Hopi, above pp. 297–8), upon which 'cluster points on cluster points' of associations converge, see pp. 132–3, 137, 187, 192, 254, 305–6, 387, 397; and for the coherence and 'inner congruity' of a work of the imagination as of a dream (and as of the Hopi thought-world, above p. 254, n. 1), see pp. 299–303, 339, 410–13.

# 17

## *The meaning of community*

> He [Hegel] saw . . . that large parts of the world in which we live, in fact our whole environment so far as it is social and even some aspects of it so far as it is natural, are penetrated by mind because constructed by mind: not indeed by my mind or yours, but by a mind common to generations of human beings. Institutions, social practices, the sciences, language itself, are examples of such common achievements. But to comprehend things of this kind we need a different sort of concept from those which are in place in the description of the natural world. We need the idea of . . . a continuant whose phases are related not mechanically, but rather as are the phases of a piece of music or a novel, one arising out of another as its natural development. In such cases we have to do with what can properly be described as identities in difference; in Hegel's own language, we have to do with concrete universals.
>
> quoted from 'Was Hegel a great philosopher?',
> anonymous, in *Times Literary Supplement*, no. 3512 (1969), pp. 649–51: p. 650.

So. But these *concrete universals* (of which I take the Hopi categories, represented by the clan names of the twelve phratries, to be an example), how then, if they are not imbibed (like the maternal antibodies) with the mother's milk, are they absorbed and incorporated into the structure of the child's thought?

In the last chapter of Part II and in the chapter preceding this one I have endeavoured to show, taking the Banks Islanders and the Hopi as example, how every society has certain *techniques du corps* by which its members may be identified, its own language (imposing certain modes of handling experience on those who use it as their natal tongue), and its own body of conceptual categories, or thought-world, to which they all subscribe and assent *simply by virtue of being members*. It remains for us now to see how the child, born into such a society, acquires the patterns of bodily movement and the techniques of speech which are preliminary to its taking the final step to full membership of his (or her) own community: preliminary, that is to say, to entry into the thought-world of the community. For I shall argue that one does not, except in a purely physical sense, enter one's society at birth, and leave it at death; *rather*, one enters it at the time that one grasps its essential notions, an event which, in certain societies (but not in all), receives overt expression, e.g. in a change in name or mode of address, in an initiation ceremony, or a change in mode of burial; nor does one leave it at death, but only when the memory of oneself is no longer held in the minds of its living members.

As first step in the enquiry, let us consider the work of the great Swiss *savant*, Jean Piaget, on the development of children in our own culture, particularly as it bears on four, related aspects of child growth: namely, the acquisition of motor skills, the uses of language, the handling of conceptual categories, and the development of the personality.[1]

### MENTAL DEVELOPMENT IN SMALL CHILDREN
### (SIX MONTHS TO SIX YEARS)

At birth, Piaget argues, the infant is essentially ego-centred: that is to say, he refers everything back to himself or, more precisely, to his own body, and mental life consists simply in the exercise of reflex mechanisms, such as that of sucking. Very early on, however, these mechanisms become refined with exercise; thus, a new-born child sucks better after a week or two than during the first few days. Subsequently, he learns to discriminate what he is sucking; then, to co-ordinate other movements with his sucking, so that he can, for example, suck his thumb, or pick things up and suck them. Simple co-ordinated actions of this kind form the starting-point for new patterns of conduct, acquired with the aid of experience; between the ages of three and six months, the infant begins to seize hold of whatever catches his attention, and this capacity for prehension, and later for manipulation, increases enormously his ability to acquire new skills.

The next great advance takes place around the age of 12 to 18 months, with the development of directed action. At this age the child learns to get hold of an object which he wants, e.g. by pulling towards himself the table cloth or other support on which the object is resting, or, later still, by manipulating a stick to the same end. Actions of this kind clearly display intelligence; but an intelligence which is, as yet, wholly practical. It has to do, as Piaget stresses, with the manipulation of objects, and in place of words and concepts, it makes use only of perceptions and of movements linked together into 'schemes of action' which yield the desired result. This kind of intelligence Piaget calls 'sensory-motor', and parallel with its development, there takes place a revolution in the child's relationship to the external world. To begin with, i.e. in infancy, there is no real differentiation between the *me* of the child, and the external world; the impressions that crowd in upon the infant are referred neither to a personal consciousness felt as a 'me', nor to objects themselves conceived as external to the self; they are simply *data* in an undissociated mass. Consequently, everything that is perceived is centred on the infant's own activity, and consciousness has its origins in an ego-centredness that is both unaware of itself and all-embracing. With the growth of directed action, however, two poles emerge, that of the self which directs the action and that of the object which is acted upon; and this, in course of time, leads to the construction of an objective

---

[1] The gist of what follows is to be found in Piaget (1964), pp. 15–75, itself a *résumé* of a whole corpus of work carried out by Piaget himself and his colleagues at Geneva over the last forty years. I give certain of Piaget's insights in considerable detail, since—apart from their bearing on the central theme of this study—they throw a flood of light on some of the matters discussed by the way, especially in the latter half of Chapter 9.

universe, within which the child's own body figures as one element among many, and over against which stands the interior life, localised in that body.

This development, in turn, has profound effects on the affective life. To begin with, before the elaboration of an external universe, the affective states of the small child (joys, sadnesses, etc.) remain bound to his own activity, without any precise demarcation between those which have their origin specifically in himself and those which are attributable to other possible sources of activity. With the construction of an external universe, and in particular with the elaboration of more or less clearly defined 'objects', external to the self and independent of it, the situation is radically altered. On the one hand, and closely related to the elaboration of objects, the consciousness of the 'me' begins to assert itself, in the sense of an internal pole of reality in contrast to the external pole represented by the object. On the other hand, objects themselves are conceived at first, by analogy with this *me*, as active, alive and conscious; and this is particularly the case with those objects, exceptionally unpredictable and interesting, *people*. The elementary feelings of e.g. joy and sadness, initially bound to the child's own activity, are experienced now with reference to those persons who stand in close and intimate proximity to him—his mother, first, then his father, then other near relatives; and it is from this experience that the earliest inter-individual sentiments, the sympathies and antipathies which will play so prominent a part in the child's later development, derive.

With the use of language, from the age of two onwards, these early patterns of behaviour are profoundly modified. For some months before this, the child has been learning to imitate the movements and gestures of those around him; now he begins to mimic the sounds they make. The association of the sounds he learns to reproduce, with particular actions and objects, leads eventually to the acquiring of speech itself; at first elementary word-phrases, then nouns and verbs on their own, and finally whole phrases. Now the first and most obvious consequence of the acquiring of speech is to permit an exchange and a process of communication between the child and those around him. But how far is this possibility realised during the early years of childhood? To answer this question, we must go to what small children actually say to one another, when they are together in a group. Here is one example:[1]

Pie, aged 6½, is sitting at a table, drawing, in company with Ez, his special friend, and three or four other children:

23. Pie (to Ez, who is drawing a tramway with a line of carriages): *Mais ils n'ont pas de pavillons les trams qui sont accrochés derrière.*          (no reply.)

24. (speaking of his own tram): *Ils n'ont pas de wagons accrochés . . .* (addressing no one in particular. No one answers.)

25. (to Béa): *C't un tram qui a pas de wagons.*          (no reply.)

26. (to Hei): *Ce tram a pas de wagons, Hei, tu comprends . . .*          (no reply.)

[1] Piaget (1923), pp. 16–18: the numbering of the sentences is that given in the original.

27. (Lev says out loud: *Un monsieur qui est drôle*, from across the room and without addressing Pie or anyone else in particular.) Pie: *Un monsieur qui est drôle!* (he goes on drawing his tram).

28. *Le tram je le laisse blanc.*

29. (Ez, who is drawing on his own, says: *Je le fais jaune.*) *Non, y faut pas le faire tout jaune.*

30. *Je fais l'escalier, regarde* (Béa replies: *J'peux pas venir cette après-midi, j'ai le cours de rythmique.*)

31. *Qu'est-ce que tu dis?* (Béa repeats the phrase.)

32. *Qu'est-ce que tu dis?* (Béa does not answer. She has forgotten what she said, and gives Ro a shove.)

33. (to Béa): *Mais laisse-le.*

34. (Mlle B. asks Ez if he wishes to come with her): *Ez, viens, c'est pas fini . . . Ez a pas fini, mademoiselle.*

35. (without addressing anyone): *Je fais des cailloux noirs . . .*

36. (as before): *Jolis . . . ces cailloux.*

37. (to Ez): *Mieux que toi, hein?* (no answer: Ez has not heard the preceding sentence.)

This example was chosen, in the first place, because it shows Pie engaged in the most *social* activity of which he was capable at his age, namely drawing, in company with his friends. And we might reasonably expect, in a situation of this kind, that the primary function of what he says would be to communicate thought. But this is not, in fact, the case. When Pie says: '*Ils n'ont pas . . .*' (24), or '*Je fais . . .*' (35), he is not addressing anyone in particular; rather, he is thinking out loud in front of his drawing, just as some people mutter to themselves when they are working. Here, then, we have one category of speech, which we may call *monologue*. When Pie says to Hei or to Béa: '*C't un tram . . .*' (25), or '*Ce tram . . .*' (26), it certainly looks, at first sight, as if he is trying to make himself understood; but, on a closer examination, it is clear that it doesn't really matter to him who he is speaking to, or even whether that person is listening. He thinks that somebody is listening, that is all that is required. Similarly, when Béa gives an answer that shows absolutely no connection with what he himself has just said (30), Pie makes no attempt either to make himself understood or to understand her. They each remain tied to their own line of thought, and are perfectly happy. The person spoken to acts simply as a stimulant. Pie speaks for himself alone, as in a monologue, but with the satisfaction of believing himself to be an object of interest to the others. Here, then, we have another category, which we may call *collective monologue*. Finally, there is a third category, represented by (23) and the second half of (34), where actual information or thought is exchanged. Here, the child addresses a particular person, rather than anyone who happens to be handy, and speaks with the intention that the person addressed should hear and understand him. In this category, also, we may place exchanges such as (33), which convey orders or instructions to others.

From these facts, and others of the same kind, Piaget draws a number of general conclusions. In the first place, the speech of children of this age (two to six or seven years) remains closely bound to physical action:[1] the child

[1] For the extent to which, even among adults, this is still the case, cf. Malinowski's analysis (1923, pp. 310–12) of the verbal exchanges that accompany a fishing expedition in the lagoon at Kiriwina.

soliloquises to himself as he goes along, explaining to himself (rather than to others) what he is about. Even when children of this age appear to be talking to each other and to be exchanging ideas and information, in fact, for much of the time, they are simply carrying on a 'collective monologue', each throwing out his own assertions without any attempt to reconcile them with those of the others; up to the age of 6 or 7, consequently, they find it very hard to discuss things among themselves, as distinct from doing so with a grown-up. This characteristic of their speech is also found in their games; in a game of marbles, for example, where older children are ready to accept a single set of rules and adjust their own play to that of the others, younger children play each one for himself, without troubling about the rules of his neighbour.

In short, Piaget concludes, the analysis of spontaneous speech among small children, like that of their behaviour in collective games, shows that these earliest forms of *social* behaviour still remain only halfway towards true socialisation. In place of getting outside his own point of view and co-ordinating it with that of others, the child remains centred on himself and his own activity, and this ego-centredness in face of the social group reproduces and prolongs that which we have already noted in the face of the physical world. In both cases, it derives from a lack of differentiation between the *me* and external reality, here represented by other individuals and no longer by objects alone; and in both cases the same kind of initial confusion, i.e. between the me and the not-me, entails the primacy of the viewer's own view of things.

Nevertheless, while in practice much of the spontaneous speech of small children remains bound to their own physical action, the acquisition of language opens the way, not only to exchanges between individuals, but also to the emergence of thinking itself, by way of the interiorisation of speech. And this in turn produces, between the ages of two or three and six or seven, a transformation of the intelligence; from being wholly 'sensory-motor' or practical as it was at the outset, intelligence develops now, under the double influence of language and of the process of socialisation, new powers of comprehension. Language, first of all, by providing the child with the means of recounting his own actions, furnishes him both with the power to reconstruct the past, and so to evoke it in the absence of the objects to which his own previous actions referred, and, by the same token, to anticipate actions not yet carried out, i.e. the future. To this must be added the socialising effect of language; for the acts of thought which the child undertakes no longer belong exclusively to the *me* which engenders them, but are sited now on a plane of communication which enormously increases their range. Language itself conveys concepts and notions which are widely shared; and it is to this system of collective thought that the child acquires a key, when he learns to speak.

To begin with, however, the child finds it hard to adapt himself to the new realities which he is discovering through his growing command of language, and much of his early thinking, like much of his behaviour at this age, retains a strongly ego-centred bias. This comes out clearly in the kind of play characteristic of this phase of childhood, namely, symbolic play: that is, games of imagination or of imitation, such as playing with dolls, playing 'shop', etc. While it is clear that games of this kind involve a real exercise of thought, it is equally clear that the thought involved is essentially ego-centred. Their function consists, in effect, in satisfying the *me* by a transformation of the real world in terms of the subject's own desires; the child who plays at engine-driving, or dolls, goes over his own life again, but re-fashions it according to his own notion of what it should be; he re-lives all his pleasures and all his conflicts, but resolves them in his play; above all, he calls fiction to his aid, to make good the deficiencies of reality. In short, says Piaget, the symbolic game is not at all an attempt by the subject to come to terms with the real world; on the contrary, it assimilates the real world to the *me*, and distorts it in the process. Further, even though language plays a part in this kind of imaginative thinking, its chief tool is the image or symbol—the image which, like the word, is a sign, but which, unlike the word, is a private and individual sign, elaborated by the child out of his own personal experience and frequently only understood by him. It is in this double sense, that it assimilates the real world to the *me* and that its principal tool is the private (i.e. non-collective) image, that symbolic play stands at the ego-centred pole of thought.

At the opposite pole stands the kind of thinking most nearly adapted to the real world that the child of this age if capable of, namely 'representational' thinking. The intelligence of the very small child (up to, say, two or three years) is, as we have seen, essentially practical or empirical; he is able to carry through courses of action requiring forethought and application, such as opening a matchbox to get out some beads that are inside it, long before he is able to verbalise such actions. And this practical intelligence widens its scope throughout the period we are now considering (from two or three, to six or seven years of age), at the same time as the child is busy acquiring new skills and techniques. But alongisde it there develops now a kind of thinking which marks a real advance on the pre-verbal acts of comprehension hitherto available to the child. This kind of thinking, employed increasingly from the age of four to five years in such exercises as matching a set of red counters against a set of blue counters, makes use of the 'schemes of action' characteristic of empirical intelligence, but transposes or *interiorises* them as representations. In this sense, therefore, the re-presentative images which form the tools for thinking of this kind extend the range of mind, in relation to the external world, beyond that attainable by empirical intelligence on its own; on the other hand, since these images are not yet capable of being generalised and made consistent with one another, they fall far short of the logical operations which will develop in the course of later childhood (i.e. from the age of six to seven on).

Parallel with these changes in intelligence go equally profound changes in the affective life of the small child. From the time that communication first becomes possible between the small child and those who surround him, a subtle play of sympathies and antipathies develops between them, a play that becomes richer when language furnishes the means for the explicit transmission of values from the one to the other. Among these relationships, one kind is especially remarkable: namely, the respect which the small child pays to those whom he regards as superior to himself, i.e. to certain grown-ups, and particularly to his own parents. This respect, itself a mixture of affection and fear, is the source of the first sentiments of morality. For those beings who are respected have only to give orders to the one who respects them, for such orders to be felt as binding upon him and so to give rise to the sentiment of duty; the child's earliest morality is thus one of obedience, and his primary criterion, the will of his parents.

The characteristic feature of the morality of early childhood is, then, that it is *heteronomous*, i.e. attached to an external will, either that of the parents or of other beings to whom respect is paid. And this feature comes out clearly, in a fairly simple and well defined area of morality like that of lying. For the small child readily accepts the rule of conduct that imposes veracity on him, well before he understands in himself the value of truth or even the nature of a lie— when, indeed, his own habits of play and of imagination constantly lead him to distort reality and to bend it to his own desires. While, however, he accepts the rule of telling the truth, at least to grown-ups (since it is they who 'mind'), and sees it as quite right that he should be blamed, or even punished, for telling lies, his lack of grasp of the true nature of a lie is shown by his evaluation of different untruths: for he equates the degree of 'naughtiness' involved in telling a lie, not with the motives of the person telling it, but with the distance that the untruth departs from reality—i.e. the 'bigger' (and more incredible) the lie, the worse.

The age of six to seven marks, in Piaget's view, a decisive turning-point, alike in social relationships, in mental development, and in affective life. The changes that take place in the social behaviour of children at this age are perhaps best illustrated by the games they play: in particular, by the advent of the collective game or game of rules. The period from six or seven to eleven marks the efflorescence of this type of game. Now a collective game such as marbles, or prisoners' base, pre-supposes a body of rules: rules defining the exact manner of rolling the marbles, the order which the players are to follow, the rules for winning, etc. This body of rules, together with the legal theory (*la jurisprudence*) required for applying it, constitutes an institution which is virtually confined to children of this age-group, and which is handed down from one generation of children to the next with an extraordinary power of conservation.[1] Previous to this, as we have seen, children of from four to six years of age when they play a game certainly try to observe some of the rules, learned by watching older children; but in practice no one of them knows all the rules, and each plays for himself without caring a fig for the rules which his neighbour is observing. From the age of six or seven, all is changed. Children

[1] Cf. Opie and Opie, *The Lore and Language of Schoolchildren* (Oxford, 1967), pp. 1-3, *et passim*.

of this age, while they still may not know all the rules by heart, make sure at least that the rules observed at any one sitting are all the same, and keep a careful eye on one another to see that all are treated alike according to a single law. Further, the term 'to win', more or less meaningless to younger children (since, in their games, several or all the players may win), now acquires a recognised, collective sense; it means to succeed as the outcome of a competition controlled by rules, and clearly the recognition of the victory of one player over the others implies ordered discussion, leading to conclusions that all are prepared to accept.

This 'socialisation of behaviour', as Piaget calls it, is only one aspect of the whole process by which the child of seven begins to break free from the ego-centredness of early childhood: a process which extends to, and eventually transforms, both intelligence and affectivity. So far as the first is concerned, the process involves the initial stages of constructing a logical system of thought. Where the distinctive tool of representational thinking was the re-presentative image, that of logical thinking is the rational 'operation'; such 'operations' may be of several kinds, e.g. arithmetical operations (adding, subtracting, etc.), temporal operations (arranging events in sequences, and the sequences in their right order). To illustrate what Piaget means by 'operation', let us take a particular case, the operation by means of which objects are grouped together to form 'classes', and again, let us begin with a concrete example:

The child is given an open box containing about twenty brown beads and two or three white ones, all the beads being made of wood; when he has had time to establish these facts for himself by handling the beads, he is asked, quite simply, whether there are in the box more wooden beads or more brown ones. Before the age of seven, the great majority of children say: 'there are more brown'; because, to the very extent that they dissociate the whole (i.e. 'all wooden ones') into two parts, they are no longer able to compare one of these parts to the whole that has been thus destroyed mentally, and so can only compare it to the other part. Around the age of seven, this difficulty is overcome, at a step: the whole is seen to be comparable to any of its parts, and each part is conceived from now on in terms of the whole itself (i.e. a part = the whole less the other parts).

Much the same applies to the elaboration of number. During early childhood (i.e. up to the age of six or seven), the child can only handle the first few numbers, since these are grasped intuitively, like the shapes of objects or their colour, as the result of direct perception. The full sequence of numbers and, above all, the operations of adding (and its inverse, subtracting), and of multiplying (and its inverse, dividing), only become accessible to him, in the great majority of cases, after the age of six or seven: because, number being in reality a combination of certain other operations that are precedent to it, it is dependent on their prior elaboration.

What, precisely, do such 'operations' consist in? An operation, says Piaget, is a mental act of some kind (e.g. grouping together individuals in a class), the source of which is always either a motor or perceptual experience, or the re-presentation of such an experience. In other words, those events which serve as the starting point for 'operations', are themselves rooted either in the actual

L

doing of things, or in their perception; before ever they become 'operational', they constitute the raw material for sensory-motor, and subsequently for representational, intelligence to work on. Representational thinking develops, as we have seen, by creating re-presentative images of events that were previously only experienced directly (i.e. lived); and these processes, in turn, transform themselves into rational operations when they come to constitute unitary systems, the parts of which both combine together to make a working whole *and are freely reversible*. In short, mental acts become operational when two acts of the same kind can be combined together into a third, still of the same kind, and when each stage of the process can be reversed: thus, the act of bringing things together in the mind (either in logical grouping, or in arithmetic adding) is an operation, because to add one thing to another, then another to that, is the equivalent of a single act joining them all together (the sum of the various additions), and because each phase of the exercise can be reversed and the things temporarily brought together dissociated again. Piaget concludes, on this ground, that the child's thinking becomes logical to the extent that it becomes capable of building up unitary systems, or 'groupings', out of mental 'operations' of the kind we have been considering; and the outward sign of this power is the ability of the child to group things into their correct classes, an ability which itself requires a grasp of the 'whole' and of the 'parts'.

As a concrete example, again, of the difficulty experienced by small children in classifying things, in grasping the underlying principle on which any particular classification is based, and consequently in using correctly *general* words (i.e. words grouping a number of objects into a single class), here are four remarks of a single child, aged 6 years and 7 months,[1] concerning mushrooms, the houses in a village, butterflies, and birds:

J: *Les champignons, c'est le nom de tous, n'est-ce pas? Les lycoperdons* (which we were out collecting in the meadows) *sont des champignons?*

J (the same day): *Ça* (a hamlet of four or five houses), *c'est un village? — Non, c'est encore La Sage* (name of the village nearby) *— Alors c'est une partie de La Sage?*

J (the same day): *Les papillons bleus ils aiment l'humide? — Oui — Et les bruns? — Le sec — Alors pourquoi il y en a ici avec les bleus?*

J (the next day): *Les corbeaux ont peur de nous. Ils se sauvent — Oui — Mais les merles n'ont pas peur — Non — C'est la même famille, les merles et les corbeaux, alors pourquoi ils ont peur s'ils sont de la même famille?*

Turning now to affective life: the co-operation with others, which characterises this age-group (from six or seven, to eleven years of age) and is particularly prominent in collective games and in work undertaken in common, and the 'grouping' of rational operations, which permits a far more coherent view of things than hitherto, are both conducive to the emergence of new moral sentiments. The moral sentiments of early childhood are the outcome of the respect

[1] Piaget (1945), pp. 244–6. The child was Piaget's own daughter, Jacqueline; many of Piaget's observations were made on his own three children, as they grew up.

in which the small child holds his own parents and other grown-ups; being based on obedience, they are, in Piaget's term, *heteronomous*. The morality which develops from the age of six or seven on is no longer based on obedience, but increasingly on mutual respect. This comes out very clearly in the collective games which are so marked a feature of this age-group, and in the attitude adopted to the rules controlling those games. Regarding the rules, younger children, though in practice they often play with complete disregard for the rules, yet regard them as having existed for all time and as unchangeable: in short, as sacrosanct. Older children, by contrast, increasingly come to look upon the rules of any particular game simply as the expression of a common wish or of an agreement between those taking part: rules are seen now, not as having been laid down from above, but as originating in some kind of contract between the players. And this change is reflected in the attitude taken, by older children, to the game itself. Rules are obeyed, no longer because they are imposed from outside, but because they are the outcome of an agreement, explicit or tacit, between those playing that particular game; and they are compelling to the very extent that the individual gives his consent, *of his own free will*, to the agreement which now binds him. In this process, mutual respect plays a growing part, and the growth of mutual respect, particularly between one child and another, brings with it a range of moral sentiments not previously experienced: honesty between players, which excludes cheating, no longer simply because it is 'forbidden' but because it violates the agreement which all have freely entered into; *camaraderie* between those of the same age; 'fair play', and so on. It explains, further, why it is only now that the lie begins really to be understood;[1] and why it is that, at this age, deceitfulness between friends comes to be thought of as worse than lying to grown-ups.

A further outcome of the growth of mutual respect is the sentiment of justice, very strong in children of this age (seven to eleven or twelve years). Among younger children, obedience takes precedence over justice, or rather, to begin with, the notion of what is just is confused with what is imposed from above; 'wrong' is equated simply with the breaking of rules, regardless of the intentions or state of mind of the actor; so their idea of what is just is both arbitrary, and absolute. Older children, by contrast, believe strongly in a justice which is the same for all and which, while it exacts penalties for wrongs committed, takes more account of the intentions and circumstances of the wrongdoer than of the substance of what has actually been done. These new notions of justice, while they certainly derive in part from the experience of injustice at the hands of adults and from the consequent dissociation between justice and obedience, derive still more from the experience of co-operation with other children, both in collective games and in work undertaken together, and from the growth of mutual respect which such co-operation engenders.

We may say, then, that the mutual respect which develops in the course of

[1] The French psychologist, Janet, held that the discovery of the lie 'marked one of the great intellectual advances of mankind': Piaget (1945), p. 247. Note the word *intellectual*.

later childhood leads to a new organisation of moral values, the principal characteristic of which is that the values themselves derive from the child's own experience, rather than being imposed upon him from outside; in this sense they are *autonomous*, in contrast to the *heteronomous* values of the preceding stage. The whole system which these values represent, Piaget compares to the system of rational operations which also develops at this stage; honesty, the sense of justice, and the other sentiments arising from co-operation and reciprocity, constitute in effect a consistent system of personal values, comparable to the 'grouping' of relationships which lies at the root of logical thinking: the only fundamental difference between the two being that values are arranged according to a scale and not simply, as is the case in logical groupings, according to objective relationships.

The grading of values in a definitive scale leads on to the final distinguishing mark of later childhood: namely, the emergence of will, and subsequently of the personality. The growth of the will, in Piaget's view, is a function of the relatively late development of autonomous moral values; its exercise represents a purposeful choice, i.e. the putting of a higher objective, chosen by the self, before a more immediately seductive, but lower, desire. Will, in this sense, pre-supposes a grading of values; in order for it to be exercised effectively, the child has to *know* which values stand higher than others, which objectives are, in the long run, worth pursuing. And this knowledge, in turn, is a function of the growth of the personality, defined by Piaget as 'a unique system which integrates the self (*le moi*) in a manner that is wholly *sui generis* (to that person)'; it is, that is to say, a 'personal' system, in the double sense that it is specific to one particular individual and that it implies a co-ordination by that individual of all his, or her, own qualities. With the development of the personality in this sense, between the age of eight or nine and the end of adolescence, the ego-centredness of the child is finally overcome, the individual stands on his own feet morally (is *autonomous*, in Piaget's terms), and is ready to assume his place in adult society.

Such, then, are Piaget's main findings on the development of children in our own culture. The crucial point to be noted is the break that takes place around the age of six to seven years; before that, children are not yet ready for social life, they are too absorbed in discovering things for themselves and bending them to their own desires; after it, they embrace social life eagerly. One *caveat* must be entered, however. Throughout his work Piaget stresses that the ages he gives are *relative*, not absolute: that is to say, while all children go through the same main stages, and while the stages succeed one another in the same order, individual children reach the successive stages at different ages. The age of 6 to 7 marks, in the majority of children, the onset of fully social behaviour; some children, however, reach that stage at the age of 5, and others (a few) not until 8 or $8\frac{1}{2}$. But somewhere between the ages of 5 and $8\frac{1}{2}$, all children who are capable of socialisation may be expected to reach it.

One further point may be noted here, before we proceed to transpose

Piaget's findings from our own to cultures of the kind we have been considering in this study. Piaget stresses the rôle of collective games in the socialising process; he sees them, indeed, as forming—between the ages of six years and eleven—the prime expression of that process. Physical work undertaken in common by children of that age-group, he mentions as another expression of it, but as a subsidiary one. In societies living nearer to the bread line than our own, the ratio is reversed. From the age of seven or eight, children have important economic rôles to fill: e.g. among the Hopi, bird-scaring and, latterly, herding sheep and goats by the boys, grinding and fetching water by the girls. Consequently, in such societies, physical work undertaken in common takes the place filled by collective games in our own.

I cannot do more than indicate here the relevance of Piaget's findings to the upbringing of children in kin-based societies.[1] The gist of what I have to say, however, is contained in Mauss's observation, quoted earlier, on the teaching of swimming:

> On commence tout l'apprentissage en habituant l'enfant à se tenir dans l'eau les yeux ouverts . . . *on sélectionne des arrêts et des mouvements* . . . vous voyez qu'il s'agit *d'un enseignement technique* et qu'il y a, comme pour toute technique, *un apprentissage de la nage.*

Socialisation in all its aspects, e.g. learning to walk, to eat, to take care of the body, to talk, requires *an apprenticeship*: not simply to the act, but *to the act as performed by the society into which the child is born*. As example, let us consider briefly the Navajo.

### NAVAJO MOVEMENT, SPEECH, AND CATEGORIES

> One of the most striking differences first noted between Navaho movement and that of the white American, [writes Dr. Bailey, at the outset of her study of Navajo motor habits[2]], is the smoothness and flowing quality of the action. Briefly, the Navaho gestures and moves with sustained, circular motions rather than with the angular, staccato movements characteristic of white culture.

This rhythmic quality characterises Navajo *walking*. Both men and women walk with a long stride in a relaxed, loose-limbed fashion, feet toeing ahead, legs swinging freely from the hips, shoulders drooping slightly forward, arms hanging loosely; the head, however, is held erect, and the general effect is one of ease, relaxation, and control in the walk. *Sitting* postures are defined according to sex. Men commonly squat on their heels, the back resting against a wall or other support about twelve inches from the ground and the arms resting

---

[1] For one, simple reason: that I do not know enough about it. For twenty years now such studies, under the title of *Culture and Personality* studies, have proved a fruitful field in American anthropology; but they have been singularly neglected in this country. Almost the only book that comes to mind, in this context, is Margaret Read's *Children of their Fathers: Growing up among the Ngoni of Nyasaland* (London, 1959).

[2] Bailey (1942), p. 210.

on the knees; women often sit on one hip, both legs turned back towards the opposite side and feet tucked under the body, the arm extended down at the side and the weight of the body supported on the heel of the hand. Younger children adopt their own characteristic posture; older children imitate that of adults, male or female.[1]

Dr. Bailey then runs through the whole gamut of personal, social and work habits (1942, pp. 211–32): from eating, sleeping, combing the hair, washing, nose-blowing, urinating, through shaking hands, embracing, pointing, dancing, child nursing, fondling and cradling the infant, to grinding corn, kneading dough, stirring the pot, spinning wool, weaving, shearing sheep, chopping wood, ball throwing, and shaking the rattle in ceremonial dances; showing how each is done in a specific, and traditionally Navajo, manner.

Regarding the transmission of motor habits, the more basic such as walking and sitting are learned by unconscious imitation, and enforced, where necessary, by public opinion. Thus W. W. Hill, in his field notes (quoted by Bailey, p. 214, n. 10), says that people would talk about a woman who adopted the sitting posture of a man, and would say: 'I wonder what she is doing that for? That doesn't look like a woman.' Other motor habits, such as modes of eating, are acquired partly by imitation and partly by precept, while specific skills such as grinding corn or shooting with bow-and-arrow are taught to children, usually by their parents.

Of body movements requiring training, the most complex are those of the muscles of the tongue and lips, pre-requisite to speech: what we may call, in contrast to *manual* skills, *buccal* and *glossal* skills. Of the many hundreds of sounds that can be produced by different positions of the tongue and lips in combination with the vocal chords, each language has made its own selection, which the child has to master. Consider, in this context, the speech of the Navajo:

> White people despair at learning Navaho, [writes Kluckhorn[2]], not only because of its unfamiliar and difficult sounds, but also because Navahos are accustomed to respond to small variations which in English are either ignored or merely used for expressive emphasis. For example, a small clutch of the breath ('glottal closure'), which the speaker of European languages scarcely notices, often differentiates Navaho words. *Tsin* means 'log', 'stick' or 'tree', whereas *ts'in* (the ' representing glottal closure) means 'bone'. Similarly, *bita* means 'between', but *bita'a'* means 'its wing'.
>
> The Navahos also distinguish quite separate meanings on the basis of pronouncing their vowels in long, intermediate, or short fashion. For example, the words *bito'* (his water) and *bitoo'* (its juice) are absolutely identical except for the fact that the second vowel of the latter is lingered over. Finally, the Navahos, like the Chinese, pay very careful attention to the tones of vowels. . . .

---

[1] These postures, in turn, have a precedent in those assumed by two of the legendary deities, thus making them traditional: Bailey (1942), p. 214, n. 9, quoting W. W. Hill.

[2] Kluckhorn and Leighton (1962), pp. 256–9.

After listing a number of cases of slight variations in vowel length and tone signifying differences in meaning, Kluckhorn goes on:

> A few white persons (children of traders or missionaries) who have learned Navaho as small children, speak 'without an accent'. A very few other whites have learned as adults to speak fluent and correct Navaho, but have failed to acquire certain nuances in the sheer style of speaking. Learners may take comfort against their mistakes from the realization that the only recipe for pronouncing Navaho perfectly is to take the precaution of being born of or among Navahos. The talk of those who have learned Navaho as adults always has a flabby quality to the Navaho ear. They neglect a slight hesitation a fraction of a second before uttering the stem of the word. They move their lips and mouths too vigorously. Native Navaho has a nonchalant, mechanical flavor in ordinary discourse. . . .

At the level of *speech*, pure and simple, i.e. of discrete sounds each of which carries a particular meaning (as the small child might say 'bread', or 'milk', and get what it wants), the spoken tongue may be compared to a code of manual signs (such as that used by the deaf and dumb). But a language is more than an instrument for the conveying of information; it is also, as I have endeavoured to show for the Mota language, a means of categorising experience:

> Every people, [writes Kluckhorn[1]], has its own characteristic classes in which individuals pigeon-hole their experiences. These classes are established primarily by the language through the types of objects, processes, or qualities which receive special emphasis in the vocabulary, and equally, though more subtly, through the types of differentiation or activity which are distinguished in grammatical forms. The language says, as it were, 'Notice this', 'Always consider this separate from that', 'Such and such things belong together'.

As one example of the difficulty younger children have in grasping the principles on which these categories are based, I have cited the case of Piaget's daughter at the age of $6\frac{1}{2}$, regarding the houses in the village, etc. Here is an example of the relevance of such categories, kinship in this case, to daily behaviour:[2]

> In the old days, Navahos meeting each other for the first time established their respective positions in the social world by way of a stereotyped exchange of information; a Navaho is a member of his mother's clan, but is 'born for' his father's clan. The exchange followed these lines:
>
> 'The two of us are of one clan.'
>
> 'He is the one for whom I am born' (i.e. he belongs to my father's clan).
>
> 'He is born for my clan . . . I belong to his father's clan.'
>
> 'We two are born for each other' (i.e. our fathers and mothers are clan brothers and sisters).
>
> 'We started out together in birth' (i.e. our fathers are of the same clan).
>
> 'He is not my relative.'

[1] Kluckhorn and Leighton (1962), pp. 271–2.
[2] Kluckhorn (1960), p. 88.

From the position reached, there emerge at once certain specified modes of behaviour: kinship terms (and behaviour), the kind of joking that can properly be carried on, mutual obligations.

The whole range of categories recognised by any particular people represents, as I have endeavoured to show for the Hopi, their distinctive world-view: a world-view which, in the case of the Hopi at least, is intimately related to the grouping of clans.

### THE IDEA OF THE PERSON

Piaget argues that the comprehension of categories of this kind, being dependent not only on the command of language but also on the prior elaboration of certain logical operations (the 'part' and the 'whole', for example), is not *possible* to the child before the age of five, and is not usually attained until the age of 6 or 7—and sometimes not until 8 or 8½. A break of this kind at the age of 6 or 7 is recognised by some pre-literate peoples. Thus the Yurok, salmon fishers of north-western California,

> make the distinction between a non-sense age and a sense age, which latter marks, in its meaning, if not in its timing, our 'school age'—a differentiation . . . which rests not only on the child's language and locomotor development but also on the development of conscience. Whether a Yurok child belongs in one or the other stage is ascertained by the question repeatedly put to him, 'Can you tell me what I told you yesterday?' If the child can remember with some regularity what he has been told, he is said to have sense, which means that the child can now be held liable for his mistakes . . . Verbal education can begin.[1]

The question arises: how far do kin-based societies formally mark the age of six to seven, or more generally the age of five to eight, as a limit or turning-point in the child's life? And this question itself turns on the idea of the personality held in societies of this kind. At what age do such societies recognise the child as a person? Now the idea of the person is intimately bound up with that of the name, and that of the name with the idea of the soul or spirit:

> Chaque clan, [wrote Mauss[2] on the basis of Boas' Kwakiutl ethnography], a une certaine quantité de noms, rangs, titres. Ce fait donne bien la sensation du fait général: que, dans un clan déterminé, il y a un nombre déterminé d'âmes en voie de perpétuelle réincarnation ou de possession qui, définissant la position de l'individu dans son clan, dans sa famille, dans la société, dans l'ensemble de la vie, définissent sa personalité.

---

[1] Erikson (1943), p. 286: for an account of the ensuing educational process, see ibid pp. 286–90.

[2] Mauss (1929), p. 126. These remarks, made at a meeting of the *Société française de Philosophie* in Paris in answer to a paper by Lévy-Bruhl, were later elaborated by Mauss in his Huxley Memorial Lecture (1938), on 'Une Catégorie de l'Esprit humain: la Notion de Personne, celle de "Moi" ', reprinted in Mauss (1968), pp. 331–62.

Much the same relation between the name and the spirit is to be found among the Eskimo[1]. After quoting analogous material from West Africa, China and Melanesia, Mauss concludes (1929, p. 126: my italics):

Je pense, moi, pouvoir trouver la raison du mythe du prénom identique à l'âme à travers les faits que je viens de vous indiquer. *La personalité, l'âme viennent, avec le nom, de la société.*

We may therefore expect to find that the point when, in any given society, a child is deemed to become a 'person', will be recognised by that society either overtly, in the bestowing on him of a new name or in an initiation of some kind, or covertly; and since ideas regarding the spirit are commonly reflected in modes of burial, such covert recognition is likely to take the form of a change in the mode of burial, in the event of his subsequent death.[2]

### ON BECOMING A PERSON AMONG THE PUEBLOS

In the origin myth of the Rio Grande Tewa,[3] the people were originally living underground beneath a lake far to the north of where they now live, in company with the Supernaturals and animals. A man was sent up on to the earth's surface, to find a way out for the people; but the world above was still *ochu*, 'green' or 'unripe', so he returned to the underworld. Later, six pairs of brothers were sent out, one pair in each of the six cardinal directions. The first five pairs were unable to walk very far because the earth was still soft, but the last pair, when they emerged, found that the ground had hardened somewhat. When the people below heard this, they prepared to leave the underworld. The Summer chief[4] led the way, but as he stepped out on the earth it was still soft, and he sank to his ankles in the mud. Then the Winter chief came out, and as he stepped on the ground there was hoar frost; the ground became hard, and the rest of the people followed. So the Tewa set forth on their wanderings.

The origin myth compares the *ochu* world before emergence, to the *seh t'a* world after emergence. This *ochu/seh t'a* polarity has a number of important references in Tewa thinking. Literally, *ochu* means moist, green or unripe;

---

[1] Mauss (1968), p. 404, and nn. 5 and 6, pp. 446–7, 452–3.

[2] A point that has been noted independently by van Gennep. The conferring of a name, van Gennep points out (1909, pp. 88–90, 218–19, 229–30), both individualises the child, and aggregates him to the community of which he now becomes a member; infants who have not been named, *or not yet initiated*, and so not yet categorised and integrated into their own society, cannot be categorised and integrated into the world of the dead; their bodies, therefore, are commonly buried without the customary rites, 'particularly if the people in question hold that the small child does not yet have a spirit (*âme*)'. On each of these points, van Gennep anticipates the argument of the present chapter – though I was not aware of this, at the time of writing it.

[3] Ortiz (1969), pp. 13–16. In this brief account of Tewa notions, I follow closely the path marked by Ortiz in *The Tewa World: Space, Time, Being, and Becoming in a Pueblo society*, a study of rare insight. Ortiz, himself a Tewa, carried out field work at the pueblo of San Juan on the Rio Grande, between 1963 and 1965.

[4] i.e. the head of the Summer moiety. The Rio Grande Tewa are divided for ceremonial purposes into two moities, Summer people and Winter people, the Summer people having charge of the agriculture-and-warm-weather ceremonies, the Winter people of the hunting-and-cold-weather ceremonies.

*seh t'a* means 'dry food', from *seh,* a cooked dish of any kind, and *t'a,* hardened or dry. Thus, in their simplest, everyday sense, the terms express a moist/dry, unripe/ripe, raw/cooked opposition. In the origin myth, the soft, unhardened earth-surface before emergence is contrasted with the dry, hardened surface after emergence; and the process of becoming *seh t'a* is presented, both here and in other oral traditions of the Tewa, as a gradual one, requiring some time for its completion. Since what occurred before emergence belongs to the spiritual realm, while what occurred after emergence is mundane, the *ochu/seh t'a* polarity is extended to cover this contrast. Finally, and of great interest from our point of view, the terms are applied to the social order and to the life-cycle of the individual.

The Tewa word for 'people' is *towa.*[1] But not all people are 'people'. To understand how this is so, we must describe, very briefly, the life-cycle of the individual. Four days after birth, the infant is named, the purpose of the naming rite being, in the words of Tewa themselves, 'to bring the child in out of the darkness', where it has no identity. Every fourth year, the 'water-pouring' rite is held, in the fall by the Winter moiety and in the following spring by the Summer moiety; at this rite all children between the age of six to seven and ten years, who have not yet undergone the rite, undergo 'water pouring'. Later in life some men undergo a further initiation, entitling them to become office-bearers in one of the eight ritual fraternities which have charge of the ceremonial cycle. Finally, after death, the soul of an initiated person is believed to wander round in the vicinity of the village for four days, before setting off to the underworld.

Now the *ochu/seh t'a* polarity is used to distinguish older children from those up to the age of six or seven who have not yet attained the age of reason:

> Thus, to be not yet *seh t'a* is to be innocent or unknowing . . .: to be innocent is to be not yet Tewa; to be not yet Tewa is to be not yet human; and to be not yet human is to be, in this use of the term, not entirely out of the realm of spiritual existence.[2]

Children below the age of six or seven are still *ochu,* 'unripe'; the water-pouring rite marks the transition from the 'innocent' or 'unknowing' state of early childhood to the state of being *seh t'a*. All Tewa who have undergone water-pouring become *seh t'a towa,* '*seh t'a* (ripe, cooked, browned-off) people', no longer *ochu*; those who have undergone further initiation into one of the fraternities are known as *pa' towa,* 'people (*towa*) who have become (*pa*)'.

We may thus represent the life-cycle of the Tewa individual under the following form, referring to his spiritual status at each stage:

---

[1] The word *towà,* 'human being', is used in two senses in Tewa: to distinguish man from other animals, and to distinguish the Tewa themselves from other men. Human beings, as such, are not considered by the Tewa to be essentially different from other animals: Henderson and Harrington (1914), pp. 9, 12.

[2] Ortiz (1969), p. 16: cf. pp. 37–41.

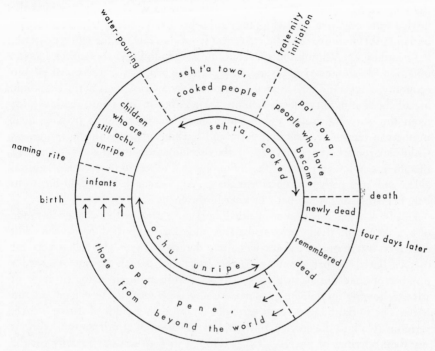

Fig. 54. Tewa life cycle

Six or seven years is the age at which the child is held to be a person of reason, capable of making up his own mind (Ortiz, 1969, pp. 86, 123); the water-pouring rite is the outward sign that his 'ripening' is complete. The change in spiritual status effected by the rite is marked by this: that in the event of a *seh t'a* person dying in the course of a ceremony, all ritual must be postponed for the four days during which the spirit is believed to wander about the village (Ortiz, 1969, p. 100), but not for a child who has not yet undergone water-pouring (ibid. p. 168, n. 12).

Turning now to the Hopi: the Hopi naming rite takes place, as we have seen, on the twentieth day after birth. At the age of six to nine years, both boys and girls undergo katçina initiation. This age coincided, in the old days, with the donning of clothes by Hopi children, with the assuming by them of economic responsibilities, and with a change in mode of burial. Taking these three points in order: in the old days, according to Bourke,[1] children of both sexes went about naked 'until seven, eight, or even nine years' of age; that is to say, in effect, until their katçina initiation. Considerable emphasis is laid, in the various accounts of katçina initiation (e.g. Dozier, 1954, pp. 326–7), on the nakedness of the children when they are whipped by the initiators; and one of

[1] Bourke (1884), p. 113: confirmed by James (1903), p. 53.

the chief duties of a lad's ceremonial 'father' is to weave the kilt which the novice puts on after the whipping. It seems likely, therefore, that katçina initiation formerly marked the transition from the 'raw' to the clothed state.[1]

Regarding the assumption of economic responsibilities, the age of katçina initiation (six to nine years) is the very period when, in the traditional pueblo economy, boys—and girls as well—began to take a serious part in the economic life of the community:[2] boys helping their father in the fields, scaring birds from the growing crops, and herding sheep and goats, girls helping their mothers in the house, grinding corn, and fetching water from the spring. As Goldfrank remarks (1945, pp. 527–8), the first initiation both at Zuñi and among the Hopi is an integral part of the ceremony that ushers in the new agricultural cycle, and 'it is perhaps no accident that . . . [it] occurs when a boy begins to help his father or his mother's brother in the fields . . .'.

Finally, katçina initiation co-incided, in the old days, with a change in mode of burial. A child dying prior to katçina initiation was buried, not in the adult cemetery, but in one of the crevices along the mesa edge.[3] The fullest account of such burials is that given by Barrett (1937, pp. 562–4). Barrett observed a number of child burials in a rock cleft near Mishongnovi, in the summer of 1911, following an epidemic of measles and dysentery in the villages on 2nd Mesa. The burial bundles, each carefully wrapped in a cloth of native weave, were thrown into the crevice, but without any attempt at orientation, without any food offerings or prayer-sticks, without a stick to serve as a ladder for the spirit, and without any covering of earth; in size, the bundles varied considerably, indicating that there was a variation in age from earliest infancy *up to at least several years.*

> This observation . . . would seem to indicate, [Barrett concludes (1937, p. 564)], that, at that particular time at least, younger children as well as infants were accorded this crevice burial, that no attempt was made to fill the crevice with earth, and that the same crevice was used over a considerable period; that apparently no spirit ladder was used, and that apparently offerings were not placed with these child burials.

On 3rd Mesa, however, a 'road' was put down to show the spirit the way to go. For Voth reports (1912*b*, p. 103) that whereas for an adult, on the third day after death, prayer-feathers and a bowl of food were placed beside the grave, and a *püh'tabi* laid on the ground pointing to the west, with a prayer-meal 'road' leading on from it, in the case of a small child the 'road' is made

---

[1] This would be in line with Great Basin Shoshoni practice: both the western Shoshoni and the Northern Paiute distinguish between a small boy (*davici* in one, *na:tsi* in the other) and a lad (*tuivitci*, in both), and the basis of the distinction appears to be that the *tuivitci* wears a breach clout, whereas the small boy does not (Steward, 1938, pp. 315–16).

[2] See, on this point, Aberle (1951), pp. 23–6, Simmons (1942), especially pp. 51, 68–9, 73, 87, and Dozier (1954), pp. 327–8.

[3] Voth (1912*b*), pp. 101–3: Plates xxxiv and xxxv show two such child burials. For the age up to which such crevice burials took place, cf. Titiev (1944), p. 129, and E. and P. Beaglehole (1935), p. 13.

from the grave towards the home of the child, 'because it is believed that the soul [*hikvsi*, breath] of that child returns to the house of its parents and is re-incarnated in the next child that is born in that family'.

In Hopi theory, the souls of the living come from the underworld, to which the dead, in due course, return; but only the dead who have been initiated into full membership of the community:

> Katcina initiation, [writes Eggan (1950, pp. 49–50)], marks the introduction of the child to status in the tribe as a whole. He is here introduced to the ancestors, or 'Cloud People', who return in the form of Katcinas ... The change in ritual status is marked by a new name and the privilege of returning to the underworld at death...

The difference in mode of burial between older and younger children signifies, I suggest, that the soul or 'breath' only becomes definitively attached to the person at the time that the child receives his katçina initiation, that is to say, when he is socially recognised as a 'person', such recognition being expressed by the bestowal on him of a new name. As Mauss held: '*la personalité, l'âme viennent, avec le nom, de la société.*'

As this notion of the child not becoming a 'person' until some years after birth—until, indeed, well after the acquisition of speech—is alien to our own way of thinking and, consequently, hard for us to grasp fully, I propose, since it is central to the theme of this book, to delineate the bed of ideas in which the notion is set and of which it forms an integral part. And as I cannot expect the reader to take on trust my assertion that such-and-such is the case, I shall do so with specific reference to the Omaha.

Among the Omaha,[1] when a child was born, it was regarded not as a member of the tribe (and so, human), but simply as a living being coming forth into the world, hardly to be distinguished from all other, already existing, living forms.

The Omaha believe that all nature, *and all phases of man's conscious life*, are permeated by a force called *wakon'da*; in nature, *wakon'da* is the creative power responsible for the form which any given aspect takes, or for the development which it undergoes, e.g. the shape of a mountain, the growth of a tree, the character of an animal; in man, it is the directive force of which he is conscious within himself. Now there is a term in Omaha, *wakonda-gi*, 'possessed by (or manifesting the action of) *wakon'da*', and this term is applied, in particular, to the early signs of directed action on the part of the child. When the child is first able to sit up, to walk, or to speak, each of these actions is spoken of as *wakonda-gi*; thus, when the child walks for the first time, the act is called *monthin* [to walk] *wakonda-gi*; when he utters his first word, that is *I-e* [to speak] *wakonda-gi*. The ability to walk and to speak, acts denominated as *wakonda-gi*, are thus taken to show that the child is developing into something more than simply 'a new life', is becoming capable of recognition as an individual to whom may be given a name and a place within the tribe.

At this stage in the old days, commonly when the child reached the age of three or four

---

[1] For these notes on the Omaha, see Fletcher and La Flesche (1911), pp. 115–22, 597–601, and Fletcher (1912), pp. 106–8; Alice Fletcher worked for many years among the Omaha, La Flesche was himself an Omaha.

years, the ceremony of 'Turning the Child' took place. By way of this ceremony, under-gone by all Omaha children, the child passed out of that phase in its life wherein it was hardly distinguished from all other living forms into its place *as distinctively a human being*, a member of the kin group into which it had been born, and through this to a recognised place in the tribe. As mark of this change in the child's status, its baby name was thrown away, its feet were clad in new moccasins (to prepare the child for the journey through life), and its *ni'kie* name (i.e. its clan name) was proclaimed to the community at large.

The Tewa, as we have seen, regard the passage from the natural (and non-human) phase of life to the social (and human) phase as one of 'hardening' or 'cooking', i.e. of passing from the 'unripe' (*ochu*) state of infancy to the 'cooked' (*seh t'a*) state of later childhood, the process—which is a gradual one—being completed by the 'water-pouring' rite when the child reaches the age of six or seven. How far is this 'raw'/'cooked' dichotomy common to pueblo culture in general?

Long ago, in Zuñi mythology,[1] there was a time 'when the earth was soft'. At that time animals could become human, and humans could change into animals. During this period, also, the katçinas came in person to the villages. It was at this time that customs originated and took form. Then the earth hardened; things assumed their permanent form, and have remained unchanged ever since.

The Zuñi recognise a class of spiritual beings called *a'wona·wi'lona*, 'the ones who hold our roads'; these include e.g. the Sun, earth, corn, the prey animals and war deities, whose aid may be invoked by the appropriate ritual. These beings, which have consciousness but do not possess human faculties, are grouped together as *käpin ho'i*, 'raw persons'; man, by contrast, is a 'cooked' person. Included among 'the ones who hold our roads', are the *Uwanami*, or 'Cloud people'. Discussing the relation between the dead and the Cloud people, Parsons emphasises (1939, p. 171) that, although the Uwanami are not to be identified with *all* the dead, yet these Cloud people are described as 'our ancestors, the ones who have died'. According to one Zuñi text,

> The Clouds are people, just as we are people. They are our ancestors, the ones who have died. These are the rain. *These become Uwanami, raw people.* When they put on their garments, they are just like the clouds. Therefore they just impersonate clouds with their breath, but they are people.

And it is in keeping with this notion that, just before going out to dance, the Zuñi who is to impersonate the katçina takes from his belt his packet of seeds, spits on it, and says (Parsons, 1939, pp. 423-4):

> Now you shall be my heart. You shall make me into a raw person (spirit). You will bring good fortune for me and for all my people, so that our corn may grow.

So far, then, we may draw the following inferences. First, the Zuñi divide sentient beings into two great classes: 'raw' persons, which includes all super-naturals including the Cloud people and the long dead, and 'cooked' persons, i.e. people or humans (or, more specifically, the Zuñi themselves). Second, humans can become 'raw' again, *either* by putting on the katçina mask, *or*

[1] See, in particular, Bunzel (1932), pp. 480-8.

some of them, by dying and in due course becoming *Uwanami*, 'Cloud people'.[1] The question arises: how do people pass from the 'raw' to the 'cooked' state in the first place?

> At Zuñi, [writes Parsons (1939, pp. 45–6)], the infant is delivered on a heated sand bed, in Zuñi phrase, 'it is cooked'. The unborn beings of Zuñi, the supernaturals, are always referred to as the raw people.

And again (ibid. p. 198):

> The greatest distinction Zuñi can make between a spirit and a man is to call the one a 'raw person' and the other a 'cooked person', referring to the heated sand bed a human infant is placed on at birth.

In the same sense, Lévi-Strauss writes (1964, p. 341):

> En Amérique, les mères pueblo accouchaient au-dessus d'un tas de sable chaud dont l'office était peut-être de transformer l'enfant en 'personne cuite' (par opposition aux êtres naturels et aux objets, naturels ou manufacturés, qui sont des 'personnes crues' . . .).

This use of the hot sand bed at child-birth is confirmed by Mrs. Stevenson (1904, pp. 299–302), but without reference to any distinction between 'raw' and 'cooked'. Further, the hot sand bed has other female uses at Zuñi. According to Eggan (1950, p. 193), the Zuñi girl at puberty used to grind corn all day for her father's mother or sister, 'kneeling on heated sand and observing certain restrictions';[2] and Mrs. Stevenson states (1904, pp. 304–3) that Zuñi women, during menstruation,

> employ themselves with indoor work, usually weaving or grinding, and sit or kneel over heated sand that is spread thickly on the floor. Their robes are caught up around their waists and blankets are fastened around their shoulders, falling loosely to the floor, covering all the sand. Extreme delicacy is observed by the women at this period.

This evidence suggests that the use of heated sand at child-birth does not effect an absolute change of status (i.e. from 'raw' to 'cooked') as Parsons implies, but is, rather, one instance of a series of intermediaries, in Lévi-Strauss's terms (1964, pp. 342–3), between nature and the social order, by means of which the child passes gradually out of the one state into the other.[3] That this is so, receives confirmation from the practice at Acoma and Laguna; for the

---

[1] Whether *all* the dead eventually become Uwanami, is not clear; nor is it clear whether, if they do not, those who do not are classed as 'raw' persons—or whether they fall into some intermediary category.

[2] Among the Yuma Indians, girls were 'roasted' over a bed of hot sand in the course of the puberty rite: Forde (1932), pp. 152–4.

[3] On the rôle of such intermediaries, see below, pp. 486–8. van Gennep is referring to the same thing as Lévi-Strauss, when he speaks (1909, pp. 13–14, 26–7) of *les rites liminaires*; thus for van Gennep, the use of heated sand would be a *liminary* rite, separating the child from *le monde antérieur*.

Keres, not having the Zuñi custom of lying in at child-birth on a heated sand bed (Parsons, 1918, p. 174), nevertheless use the terms 'cooked' and 'raw', but apply them differently (Parsons, 1939, p. 198, n. 2), the 'cooked' being the initiated and the 'raw' the uninitiated.

Turning briefly to the Hopi: the Hopi, as we have seen (above, pp. 26–7), use a bed of sand at child-birth, but not, so far as I know, a heated bed; nor do they refer to the infant as undergoing any process of 'cooking'. In the old days, however, a bed of heated sand was used in infant care;[1] in the evening the mother warmed a pile of sand by the fire, then laid the baby on the sand and covered it over with a rabbit-skin rug; the sand held the warmth, and if the baby wetted in the night, the hot sand absorbed the moisture.

We find, then, a number of elements which we may set out in the following Table:

|  | use of heated sand in infancy | *raw/cooked dichotomy* | | form of initiation |
|  |  | related to use of heated sand | related to initiation |  |
|---|---|---|---|---|
| Tewa | – | – | + | water-pouring rite, age 6 to 9 |
| Keres | – | – | + | katçina initiation, age 8[2] |
| Zuñi | + | + | – | katçina initiation, age 5 to 7[3] |
| Hopi | + | – | – | katçina initiation, age 6 to 9 |

This body of evidence does, I think, indicate a general pueblo cultural pattern of regarding the first six to seven years of life as a period of 'ripening' or 'maturing', before the child is definitively introduced into the community at his (or her) initiation. And it is within this context of belief that Hopi child burial takes its place. For the 'breath' (*hi'ksvi*) of a child that dies prior to its katçina initiation does not proceed on to the underworld; rather, it goes back to the roof of its mother's house, where it hovers among the rafters waiting to be re-born in her next child;[4] only if the mother fails to bear another child, does the un-embodied 'breath' eventually accompany her spirit to the home of the dead.

[1] This information comes from Mae Poling'yowma's grandmother, Mary, who died at Old Oraibi in the spring of 1969, aged about 100 years.

[2] White (1932), p. 135.

[3] Bunzel (1932), p. 541.

[4] Voth (1912b), p. 103: confirmed by Parsons (1939), p. 71, Simmons (1942), p. 30, and Eggan (1950), p. 47.

Now if the first six to seven years of life represent a transition process during which the small child is 'brought in from the cold' through the agency of certain mediatory substances such as heated sand, ashes, and the adoption of clothing, we may expect to find an analogous process by way of which the socialised (i.e. in Zuñi terms, 'cooked') person relinquishes human status. Traces of that process we can detect in certain aspects of pueblo burial ritual. The washing of the dead body and the rubbing of it with corn meal, prior to burial, are clearly the analogue to the washing of the infant's body and the rubbing of *it* with ashes after delivery, both ashes and corn meal being mediatory substances; while the use of *raw* cotton for the mask placed over the face of the dead man[1] mirrors the use of *woven* cotton for the kilt put on by a boy after his katçina whipping. More significant still, is the place of burial. At Oraibi, the greater part of the trash produced in the village is thrown over the mesa lip to the west of the village; on the talus slopes below the mesa lip, the scatter of early pottery and occasional bones exposed by wind and rain suggest that, for some hundreds of years, these slopes have constituted the main burial ground for the pueblo. Excavation of trash piles outside the cliff dwellings (twelfth to thirteenth century) at Tsegi Cañon and at Mesa Verde commonly reveals pueblo burials *in* the trash, such interments being usually ascribed to ease of digging in the soft deposits furnished by the trash. A far more cogent reason, surely, is that implied by Lévi-Strauss (1958, p. 249): namely, that just as clothes are intermediate between 'nature' and 'culture', so ashes—or soot[2]—are intermediary between the hearth and the roof (or between earth and sky), and '*les ordures* (i.e. trash) *entre le village habité et la brousse*', that is, between what is domestic and social, on the one hand, and what is wild on the other.

Regarding the period of transition *out of* social life: for four days, the spirit of the dead person is believed to remain in the vicinity of the village, before starting on its journey to the underworld. But for four *years* after death, according to Parsons (1939, p. 271), Hopi continue to make prayer-sticks for the deceased at Soya'l. Nor is this relation one-way only; for, as Fewkes remarks,[3] 'clan relationship not being severed by death, the deceased members of the clan are regarded as still members of the clan, with the same obligation to the clan as when alive on earth'.

---

[1] Also practised by the Keres: Parsons (1918), p. 180. In van Gennep's terms (1909, pp. 240–1), the use of the mask itself is *un rite liminaire*; thus, Socrates, covering his face with a veil after having drunk the hemlock, 'se séparait ainsi du monde des vivants pour s'agréger au monde des morts et des dieus'. Cf. on this point, Eliade (1968), p. 144.

[2] On soot (*la suie*) as intermediary between *le monde profane* and *le monde sacré*, cf. Eliade (1968), p. 143.

[3] Fewkes (1917), p. 152. Cf. in the Trobriands, the use of the kinship term *tabu* to refer to the ancestral dead as well as e.g. to the living elders of the speaker's natal hamlet: Leach (1958), pp. 130–1, 135, and p. 130, Fig. 1.

Much additional material, along the lines indicated in the latter part of this section, has been collected by Hertz in his study on 'the collective representation of death' (Hertz, 1960, pp. 27–86). Hertz, however, was working in a different conceptual frame to the one adopted here; while he emphasised (pp. 34–52) that the period between dying and the

ON BECOMING A PERSON IN SOUTH INDIA, AND AMONG THE NUER

The pueblo material, set against the context of ideas held by the Omaha, indicates (I suggest) that in the Southwest at least, and probably far more widely in North America, the child is not regarded as in any real sense a member of the community, and so a person, until he (or she) is capable of grasping the fundamental categories upon which the thought-world of that community is based: a point marked, among the pueblos in general, by passage from the 'raw' to the 'cooked' state, and among the Hopi in particular, by katçina initiation. By this event the child's transition out of the 'natural' state of infancy and early childhood to full membership of the community is formally recognised by the bestowing on him of a new name, by the assuming on his part of economic responsibilities, and by his acquiring of the right to be buried in the adult manner—sign of his definitive status as a 'person'.

To show that this event is not restricted to North America, but is, rather, one instance of a *class* of similar events wide spread over other parts of the world and probably, therefore, characteristic of kin-based societies, I append here further instances taken respectively from South India, the Aegean, the Andaman islands, northern Australia, and Africa.

Among the Dravidians of South India, a change in mode of burial analogous to that practised by the Hopi is accompanied, not by any overt form of initiation, but by a major change in grammatical categorisation. To take the latter point first:[1]

> The main division among nouns in Tamil grammar (and Malayalam does not differ significantly) is between what are traditionally known as 'higher class' and 'lower class'—the higher class being further divided into masculine and feminine in the singular. These so-called 'gender' distinctions show in the personal terminations of verbs in Tamil and in the third person pronouns that will be used to replace given nouns. The 'higher' class includes nouns referring to human beings (and to gods and demons)—but only human beings *after they have in some sense the capacity of thought*. That is to say that babies and very small children (along with all other, non-thinking, living beings) belong to the 'lower' class. The pronoun for the latter is *adu*, 'it'.

The age at which the child graduates from being 'it', to being 'he' or 'she', is commonly four to five years. This is the age at which the child first has its hair cut short by the barber,[2] who, as Dumont points out, is also 'le prêtre

---

accomplishment of the final funerary rites marks a prolonged passage *out of* social life, and while he recognised (pp. 80–1) the complementarity between the act of dying and the act of being born, he did not proceed on to the conclusion that the period between being born and full recognition as a 'person' marks an analogous passage *into* social life—even though he quotes (p. 84) the fact that in Indonesia, from which most of his evidence is drawn, the final funerary rites are dispensed with in the case of children who die before reaching the age of seven.

[1] I am indebted to Dr. R. E. Asher, of the Department of Phonetics and Linguistics, University of Edinburgh, for the following paragraph; also, for information as to when the change from being 'it', to being 'he' or 'she', takes place.

[2] Dumont (1957), p. 37.

funéraire' in South Indian society; it is also the age at which the child graduates to the village cemetery. Thus, referring to burial customs among the Pramalai Kallar of Madura district, Dumont writes:[1]

> Les enfants sont enterrés différement suivant leur âge. Jusqu'à quatre ou cinq ans, un enfant est enterré sur le bas-côté de la route près du village . . .; au delà de cinq ans, on enterre au cimetière. . . .

A more radical difference in the mode of disposal of the bodies of small children appears to have been practised in the Aegean, in the archaic period. One of the rooms in the museum at Rhodes exhibits a selection of pots and small objects (*kterismata*) found in graves in the fields around Ialysia, together with two urns standing 2 feet 9 inches high, with mouth-opening 9 inches across:

> Les inhumations commencent du 9 ème jusqu'au début du 6 ème siècle avant J.C. Durant cette période on brûlait les morts avec leur dons et l'on enterrait leur cendres, exception faite pour les enfants qu'on déposait, *sans les brûler*, avec leur dons dans les urnes. . . .

In the Great Andaman, the bodies of infants and small children were disposed of in quite a different manner to that employed for adults,[2] and this difference appears to have corresponded to a difference in the fate of their souls and/or their spirits (the Andamanese distinguish between the two). After death, the spirits of both adults and children go to *cha·ita·n*, the jungle under the earth; but whereas the souls of older children and adults subsequently proceed on to *jere·g*, the land of the dead, where they pursue a life similar to that on earth, the spirits of all children who die before they cease to be entirely dependent on their parents (i.e. those under about six years of age) remain at *cha·ita·n*, where they subsist on the fruit of the *rau*-tree (*Ficus laccifera*).[3]

Among the Murngin of northern Australia, boys undergo circumcision between the ages of six and nine. In the course of the rite a boy is introduced to his clan totems, while the rite itself marks his change in status from that of 'child', *dji-mer-ku-li* (male or female), to that of *yaoerin*, 'young man', and his

---

[1] Dumont (1957), p. 250. In those parts of South India where the bodies of the dead (other than those of small children) are burned, not buried, only that of the *sannyasi*, the holy man who has renounced the world and so, in effect, quitted it before his (physical) death, is interred: 'son décès', as Dumont observes (1958, p. 334, no. 18), 'ne crée pas d'impureté pour les siens, il est interré de façon spéciale, et non brûlé, et devient en somme directement un ancêtre . . .'. Should he subsequently resume social life, he is treated as an untouchable. A similar process of *de-socialisation* occurs when a person is expelled from his caste, the act of expulsion—like the renouncement of the *sannyasi*—being accompanied by the appropriate death ceremonies to cut him off from it (Miller, 1952, p. 160); thus both holy man and outcaste, in his own way, 'dies' socially before he dies physically.

[2] Man (1883), pp. 141–6: cf. Radcliffe-Brown (1922), pp. 106–9.

[3] Man (1883), pp. 161–2. For a careful weighing of Man's evidence, see Radcliffe-Brown (1922), pp. 170–5; Radcliffe-Brown is of the opinion that Man has run together the accounts of several informants into a more coherent and 'logical' version than any single Andaman islander would ever have held.

entry into the male community of the tribe; besides adopting the pubic covering, he becomes subject now to the avoidance rules that govern conduct
between certain relatives, and should he subsequently die, his death—unlike
that of small children and of women—will be attended by the full mortuary
ritual. Since the primary purpose of the mortuary ritual is to ensure the return
of the soul (*warro*) to the totemic water-hole,[1] and since infants are buried
with no rites at all, it seems probable that Murngin regard the acquisition of
the soul as a gradual process which is completed by the time the child is old
enough to be circumcised.

Among the Mbembe (see Vol. 1, pp. 65–6), while all 'normal individuals' are
buried in the village in or by their houses with full rites, small children who die
are buried in the bush without such rites. 'The death of infants', writes Dr.
Harris (1965, p. 61), 'is not regarded as natural; it always raises the suspicion
that the child was not a real human being but a spirit child . . .', adding (p. 61,
n. 1) that no rites are held because 'the child had no social personality'.

Turning now to the link between recognition as a 'person', admission to
membership of the community and the assuming of economic responsibilities,
such a link is explicitly affirmed, e.g. by the Ngoni of Nyasaland:

> Among the Ngoni a child's acquiring of his second teeth, between the ages of
> six-and-a-half and seven-and-a-half, marks a new stage in his development. And it
> was at this stage that the ear-piercing ceremony took place. In contrast to the neigh-
> bouring peoples, the Ngoni had no facial or body markings, and it was the pierced
> ears which showed that they were true Ngoni. In the days of warfare, captives,
> especially boys and men, were forcibly made to have their ears pierced. Sometimes,
> children went to their parents and said, '*We want to be made Ngoni now*'.
>
> At this age, the boys left their own (family) compounds, and took to sleeping in
> the (village) dormitory; they stopped playing childish games, and began instead to
> develop the skills and perform the tasks they would require in adult life—making
> axes and knobkerries, hunting, herding sheep and goats, fighting. At the same time,
> as boys in the dormitory and girls in the girls' circle, they became increasingly
> sensitive to the opinion of their peers—subject, that is, to the social sanctions of
> rebuke and ridicule.[2]

Discussing the age of circumcision in Morocco and Algeria, van Gennep
points out (1909, pp. 101–6) that it is only among orthodox Moslems that the
operation is performed on the seventh day after birth; among the Berber
tribes of the interior, it takes place between the ages of five and ten, and most
commonly at the age of seven or eight—though, in cases of adoption, it may be
done at twenty or later. Regarding its significance, van Gennep specifically
puts circumcision, with the first cutting of the hair and rites associated with
the first dentition, in the category of practices which, by cutting or mutilation

---

[1] See, on this point, Warner (1964), pp. 433–8, and on the general significance of the
circumcision ritual in Murngin life, ibid. pp. 5–6, 120–6, 251–2, 402–3.
[2] Read (1959), pp. 88–91. Cf. Piaget's remarks (above, pp. 314–16), on the growth of
mutual respect between children of this age-group.

of some part of the body, 'modifient d'une façon visible pour tous la person-nalité d'un individu'.[1] Such mutilations, like the wearing of a special costume or the decoration of the body with paint (especially with earth colours), serve as a means of differentiation, the individual so mutilated being thereby admitted to a pre-determined social group:

> Chaque sorte de mutilation étant un procédé de différentiation collective, ... peut servir à différencier un groupement donné de ses voisins.

Finally among the Nuer, as we have seen, a child who dies before his lower teeth have come is buried without mourning and without sacrifice, the link between recognition as a 'person', admission to membership of the com-munity and the assuming of economic responsibilities being implicitly affirmed by Nuer themselves when they say:

> A small child is not a person, *ran*. When he tethers the cattle and herds the goats, he is a person; when he cleans the byres, and spreads the dung out to dry and collects and carries it to the fire, then he is a person.

### THE CATEGORY 'PEOPLE'

The recognition of the child as a 'person' only at the point where he (or she) becomes a member of the community, i.e. accepts the obligations which it imposes, implies a category 'people' made up of all those who have taken a similar step. Such a category is indeed recognised by many peoples in different parts of the world, for whom the term 'people' is synonymous with 'member(s) of (one's own) community'. Thus, in Nuer, the plural of *ran*, 'person', is *Nuer*, 'people'; in the Bantu languages, Shona for example, the word *bantu* itself is the plural of *muntu*, 'a person';[2] the Kwa-speaking groups along the Guinea Coast were so named after their own word for 'people'; in the Southwest, both the Navajo and the Tewa refer to themselves as 'people', while the Daflas of northern Assam apply to themselves a term that means simply 'human being'.[3]

The recognition of a category 'people', comprising the members of one's own community (however, precisely, that is defined), implies a further category embracing all those who are not quite people, that is, strangers, the line between the two being drawn by the differential treatment meted out to the latter. Widely, strangers are regarded with suspicion, often with outright hostility. The ambivalent attitude adopted towards them is brought out by Codrington's remarks on the Banks Islanders. Throughout the islands, writes Codrington (1891, p. 345), a stranger, as such, was generally an enemy to be killed:

> But, he goes on (p. 346), it was often a question whether a castaway was a stranger. Not uncommonly canoes were blown, or drifted, from their own islands to distant islands; the men on board them were not wholly strangers, though personally

[1] Van Gennep (1909), p. 102. Subsequently (p. 104), van Gennep compares the human body to a piece of wood 'que chacun a taillé et arrangé à son idée'.

[2] One assumes that when the first European seamen arrived and asked, probably by means of signs, 'who are you?', they got the answer: 'we are *bantu*, i.e. "people"; who are you?'

[3] C. von Fürer-Haimendorf, *The Apa Tanis and their Neighbours* (London, 1962), p. 7.

unknown; they were men and from known lands, not strange beings like white men from without the world. They were therefore received as guests, sometimes establishing themselves after a while by marriage, sometimes waiting an opportunity to return. Many single canoes from time to time have been blown away, from distant islands, and have drifted to the Banks Islands; in many cases the castaways have been kindly treated, and have added a strain to the native race. Within the last forty years, men from Tikopia have twice been most kindly received at Mota.

Among the Kariera of western Australia, and in the Andamans, strangers were treated with undisguised hostility. Among the Kariera,[1] when a stranger came to a camp, he did not enter it straightway, but sat down at a distance; the old men came out to question him, and only when his exact relationship to each of the people living there had been established, could he be admitted to the camp, since only then did they know how, precisely, to behave towards him. For either a man is my relative, in which case I know how to behave towards him, or he is a stranger; and in that case he must be my enemy and I shall take the first opportunity to kill him, for fear lest he forestall me. Much the same attitude prevailed among the Andamanese, who, until about 1850, attacked all mariners who landed or were wrecked upon their shores.[2]

I have chosen these three examples from isolated communities, in order to demonstrate the attitude adopted towards strangers in its extreme form. But in communities living cheek by jowl with one another, equally damaging, if more subtle, attitudes may prevail. Most communities in Melanesia, according to Hogbin and Wedgwood,[3] have two forms of sorcery, one to cause minor illnesses only, the other to cause death. The first of these is used primarily against one's own kindred, the second against strangers and outsiders, *strangers* in this context being defined as people from nearby settlements to whom one is related neither by blood nor marriage, and *outsiders*, as people from distant settlements. In the old days, however (i.e. before the imposition of European administrations), outsiders ran the risk of being killed on sight, while 'a man with a grievance against strangers had no compunction about trying to encompass their death, either by performing the more lethal kind of sorcery against them himself or by employing someone else to do so on his behalf'. The effective range of sorcery was thus the group of neighbouring villages between which marriage exchanges commonly took place.

This attitude towards outsiders, i.e. to those 'beyond the pale' of one's own community, is correlate to the categorisation referred to above: one treats strangers in such a way because, to a greater or lesser degree, they are not

---

[1] Radcliffe-Brown (1913), p. 151.

[2] Radcliffe-Brown (1922), p. 7. The fact that Radcliffe-Brown's fieldwork was done among two such 'simple' and static communities as those of the Andamanese and the Australian aborigines, has had a lasting effect on English anthropological theory: notably, in its inability to cope with the problem of social change.

[3] Hogbin and Wedgwood (1953), p. 245: confirmed, for Dobu, by Fortune (see above, Vol. 1, p. 241, n. 1).

regarded as 'people' at all, and so the normal canons of 'kyndeness' and humanity do not apply. As Lévi-Strauss remarks (1962*b*, p. 220):

> On a dit, non sans raison, que les sociétés primitives fixent les frontières de l'humanité aux limites du groupe tribal, en dehors duquel elles ne perçoivent plus que des étrangers, c'est-à-dire des sous-hommes sales et grossiers, sinon même des non-hommes: bêtes dangereuses ou fantômes.

Thus the Dinka, while regarding the Nuer as similar to themselves, 'seem scarcely to regard the Azande and other Sudanic-speaking peoples as "people" '.[1]

Taken to its logical conclusion, such an attitude may express itself in *eating* outsiders. This is nicely brought out by the case of the Ibo, who expanded into the savannah country to the north of the middle Cross River in the course of the nineteenth century (see Vol. 1, Fig. 5). The Ibo are divided into a number of separate tribes, the members of which trace descent from a single founding ancestor and so regard one another as relatives:

> The North-eastern Ibo, [writes Jones (1961, p. 123, n. 1)], made a clear distinction between a relative and an enemy. You made war on, took heads from, and ate enemies. You did not make war on relatives, and if you had to fight with them, you used only sticks and stones. If, however, a relative broke the rules and made war on you consistently, he ceased to be a relative. Thus ... by the end of the nineteenth century, some Izi sub-tribes[2] were making war on other Izi sub-tribes, though not to the extent of taking their heads or eating them. Sub-tribes of the other tribes continued to fight each other only with sticks and stones.

Now Lorenz has made the acute observation (1966, p. 70) that there is no such thing, strictly speaking, as cannibalism; one never eats people one recognises as 'people', only people one does not recognise as such.[3] Among the Nuer, as we saw earlier (Vol. 1, p. 13), those who are kith are also kin:

> *kin* derives, through ME *kin*, from OE *cynn*, kindred, (one's own) kind, people or race: cf. OE *cennan*, to beget.
> *kind*: OE *cynde*, whence ME *cunde*, later *kinde*, whence the E. noun *kind*, nature, originally human.
>
> Partridge, *Origins*, p. 329.

> *kith*: OE *cunnan*, to know, OE *cūth*, known, had derivative *cyth*, native land (one's known land)—whence E. *kith*, knowledge, hence (obs) familiar land or district, hence neighbours, friends: whence E. *uncouth*, unknown, therefore strange.
>
> Partridge, *Origins*, p. 73.

---

[1] Lienhardt (1958), p. 108.

[2] The Izi, one of the original tribes of the North-eastern Ibo, numbered about 138,000, subsequently divided into twelve sub-tribes: Jones (1961), pp. 123–4. The internecine warfare between the Izi sub-tribes was probably to some extent 'pathological', induced by European gun-running on the coast.

[3] Thus, in parts of the western Pacific where cannibalism was endemic, human meat was referred to as 'long pig': that is to say, one categorised it as animal, before eating it. The converse of this relation is that one does not eat *pets*, that is, animals that have been, to some extent at least, 'humanised'.

So we may complete the equation: those who are *kith* are also *kind*, and *you do not eat your own kind*.[1]

## THE *COMMUNE* AS A MORAL ENTITY

In our preliminary discussion of the commune (above, Chapter 5), we found that the *commune* has various attributes by which it may be defined. It consists, on the ground, of a number of villages, or other settlements occupying a definite territory. Socially, these villages comprise a marrying circle. Juridically, they form the basic unit within which effective means for settling disputes operate. They commonly form the unit for certain economic and religious activities (markets, festivals), the unit within which an effective public opinion makes itself felt and within which, also, the writ of sorcery is likely to run. In the intervening chapters I have endeavoured to show how a people's initial categorisation of the world is built into the language they speak, and how this may be further elaborated and given affective force through a ceremonial cycle, expressing—in the case of the Hopi—their whole view of the natural world and of their own place in it.

Certain anthropologists, notably Lévi-Strauss, have treated classificatory systems of this kind as though they were, first and foremost, logical constructs: as though, that is to say, they were primarily conceptual tools (*des moyens de penser*), means of grasping the complexity of phenomena by reducing them to simpler terms (pairs of opposites, in Lévi-Strauss's scheme).

> Le principe logique, [writes Lévi-Strauss (1962*b*, pp. 100–1): italics in original], est de toujours *pouvoir opposer* des termes qu'un appauvrissement préalable de la totalité empirique permet de concevoir comme distincts. *Comment opposer* est, par rapport à cette exigence première, une question importante, mais dont la considération vient après. Autrement dit, les systèmes de dénomination et de classement, communément appelés totémiques, tirent leur valeur opératoire de leur caractère formel: ce sont des codes, aptes à vehiculer des messages transposables dans les termes d'autres codes, et à exprimer dans leur système propre les messages reçus par le canal de codes différents.

And later (ibid. pp. 287–8: my italics):

> Comme l'ont montré nos exemples, dans tous les cas, un axe (qu'il est commode d'imaginer vertical) supporte la structure. Il unit le général au spécial, l'abstrait au concret: mais, que ce soit dans un sens ou dans l'autre, l'intention classificatrice peut toujours aller jusqu'à son terme. Celui-ci se définit en fonction d'une axiomatique

---

[1] The idea of humanity or of the unity of mankind, the idea, that is, that all men—by virtue of the reason that is in them—are equal and belong to one community, is perhaps the greatest single contribution brought by our own culture to the thought of the world; its corollary is that certain minimal standards of conduct obtain between them.

The idea itself originated in the Greek city-states in the fourth century B.C. (Glotz, 1915, pp. 12–17). Its later development is bound up with the Stoic/Christian doctrine of Natural Law, a doctrine which, in Troeltsch's words (Barker, 1934, I, p. 206), 'held sway for a thousand years, and dominated the theology, the jurisprudence, the political theory, the politics, and the history of the Middle Ages'.

implicite pour qui tout classement procède par paires de contrastes: *on s'arrête seulement de classer quand vient le moment où il n'est plus possible d'opposer.*

Quand l'intention classificatrice remonte, si l'on peur dire, vers le haut ..., aucune diversité ne l'empêchera d'appliquer un schème sous l'action duquel le réel subira une série d'épurations progressives, dont le terme sera fourni, en conformité avec l'intention de la démarche, sous l'aspect d'une simple opposition binaire (haut et bas, droite et gauche, paix et guerre, etc.). ... La même opération pourra être répétée sur d'autres plans: que ce soit celui de l'organisation interne du groupe social ..., ou le plan spatio-temporel, grâce à une géographie mythique qui, comme le montre un mythe aranda, permet d'organiser l'inépuisible variété d'un paysage par réductions successives aboutissant de nouveau à une opposition binaire (ici, entre directions et éléments, puisque le contraste est placé entre terre et eau).

This approach, while it accounts for the logical processes involved in such classifications, does scant justice (it seems to me) to the emotive force with which they are held: thus, it explains how strangers are differentiated from the members of one's own group (as, let us say, 'them' and 'us'), it does not explain why 'they' should be regarded with such hostility. To understand how ideas are endowed with emotive value, we have to go back to a period in our own history when they were still so:

The sorts of meanings men die for, [writes Danby[1], discussing different views of nature presented in *King Lear*], are at least as real as the fires in which the same men burn, and the meanings of 'Nature' in which Shakespeare is interested are meanings of this sort. They are the structural frames by which men live and work and think. A meaning is not a dictionary sense. It can be a programme of action. The human being who chooses such and such a meaning is deciding for such and such a course of behaviour among his fellows.

The liberal tradition in the last century could not grasp the necessity for either inquisition or martyrdom over the question of a man's ideas. We nowadays are better placed. We see that an idea sometimes represents the life-interest of a group. *It stands for a claim on society and a stake in reality.*[2] One's ideas represent one's rôle as an agent among other agents ... in the field of meaning ideas can be principles of action, too. Conversely, bits of behaviour can have the force of ideas, implying a view of what man really is, and what kind of world surrounds him. A goal towards which he must strive can be proposed. And such goals tend to exclusiveness. All man's goods are jealous goods.

Different views on Nature, therefore, are not differences of opinion only. They are felt as so many stubborn holds that reality has on us and we on it. They are such

[1] J. F. Danby, *Shakespeare's Doctrine of Nature: a Study of King Lear* (London, 1961), p. 16: my italics. Danby argues, in the course of his book, that the principal protagonists in *King Lear*, namely the King himself, Edmund, the Fool, Cordelia, stand for, i.e. represent in their persons, different and conflicting views of Nature current in Elizabethan England.

[2] This comes out, movingly, in a letter written by one of the conspirators a few days before the attempt on Hitler's life on 20 July 1944 (quoted by A. Bullock, *Hitler: a Study in Tyranny*, London, 1962, p. 739):

The assassination, [he wrote], must be attempted at any cost. Even should it fail, the attempt to seize power in the capital must be undertaken. We must prove to the world and to future generations that the men of the German Resistance dared to take the decisive step *and to hazard their lives upon it.* Compared with this object, nothing else matters.

meanings as can become concrete people. *People, in fact, feel themselves to be what they are only so long as these particular meanings hold good.* They cling to them rather than to their lives. Such ideas, Coleridge would say, are not merely regulative but constitutive of our being.

We are accustomed, in our culture, to the idea of economic exchange: to the exchange, in particular, of services and goods, either against each other or for money (*coin*). Mauss, in his *Essai sur le Don: Raison de l'Échange dans les sociétés archaïques* (1924), showed how such commercial transactions are but one type of a far wider and more inclusive network of exchange which forms the ground for social life itself:

> Toutes ces institutions, [he wrote (1968, pp. 163–4: my italics), at the end of his survey of the diverse kinds of gift and prestation to be found in kin-based societies], n'expriment qu'un fait, un régime social, une mentalité définie: *c'est que tout, nourriture, femmes, enfants, biens, talismans, sol, travail, services, offices sacerdotaux et rangs, est matière à transmission et reddition.* Tout va et vient comme s'il y avait échange constant d'une matière spirituelle comprenant choses et hommes, entre les clans et les individus, répartis entre les rangs, les sexes et les générations.

This exchange on the physical plane is mirrored, on the mental plane, by an intellectual exchange: not only is the language of any given community a *koinê* for the handing to and fro of ideas and information, to be a member of that community is to *koinônein*, to share in its common values. To such membership the child is introduced at the age of five or six (or soon after), when, having acquired the techniques of speech, he begins to grasp the common values embodied in the language and behaviour of his community, and to take part in its common life.

These shared values may be reflected outwardly in many, apparently trivial, forms, such as turns of speech, common jokes, special dishes, ways of doing the hair[1] or of dressing,[2] all of which vary from one district to another, e.g. in peasant Europe. Beneath these superficial conformities lies a community of ideas, of ways of looking at the world and at man's place in it, from which the really powerful sanctions on human conduct,[3] namely gossip, ridicule, shaming,

---

[1] Lévi-Strauss remarks on the difference in hair styles from one region to another in peasant Europe, and the rôle these differences played in formulating marriage rules—'on n'épouse que dans la coiffe', he writes (1926*b*, p. 119). Gerald Brenan, in his autobiography *A Life of One's Own* (London, 1962, p. 102), speaks of the Breton peasant women as wearing the starched *coiffe* of their *pays* as late as the summer of 1911.

[2] Benedict (1951), p. 237. Sébillot, discussing the Breton fishermen (1901, pp. v–vi), says that, although they wore almost the same clothes (except on Sundays) as the neighbouring peasants, the two communities hardly mixed at all, and virtually no inter-marriage took place between them: 'les pêcheurs bretons', he writes (ibid. p. 49), 'n'épousent en général que des pêcheuses . . .'.

[3] To the erosion of which, over the last few centuries, the growth of penal systems may be traced: one makes laws, at the point where custom and the traditional sanctions no longer effectively control behaviour. The sixteenth- to seventeenth-century stocks, still to be seen on the green in many English villages, stand midway between the old system and the new.

insult,[1] cursing, fear of sorcery (or directed malice of any kind), and threat of expulsion, draw their strength. For all these depend for their efficacy on values held in common; and it is within the limits of the *commune*, as we have defined that body, that they exercise their power. Thus the *commune*, as well as being a geographical, social and juridical entity, is also, and more significantly, a *moral* one.

★     ★     ★     ★     ★

> That man, [said Aristotle], who, by nature and not merely by temporary ill-fortune, is without a *polis*, is either a poor sort of person or a being higher than man, like the one whom Homer reviled, as being 'without kinsmen, without *themis*, and without hearth . . .'.

Homeric society (or, more accurately, the society of the Archaic period) was made up of a number of *genê* (sing. *genos*). The *genos*, as delineated by Glotz,[2] has all the characteristics of the unilineal descent group of three to four generations' depth, as delineated by Forde and by Fortes (see Vol. I, pp. 155–7): that is to say, all its members trace descent from a common male ancestor; the *genos* owns its own farm land and herds in common; it recognises a head man or chief, who exercises authority over its members, and who has charge of the (ancestral) rites pertaining to the *genos*. The *genos* has its own code of conduct, namely the reciprocal obligations which obtain between members of the same *genos* and enhance its solidarity; knowledge of these duties constitutes *aidôs*, shame. The *genos* is the vengeance group, standing together to require satisfaction for an injury done to any one of its members; conversely, it is the group which accepts responsibility for an injury done by any one of its members. Finally the *genos* has its own justice, *themis*: *themis* only applies to offences committed within the *genos*, namely sacrilege, homicide, incest, and neglect of kinship duties; its ultimate sanction is expulsion from the *genos*:

---

[1] The effectiveness of insult as an agent of social control may be gauged from the following observation by Gann (1918, p. 16: my italics), regarding the Mayas of eastern Yucatan:

> When quarreling among themselves both women and girls use the most obscene language, improvising as they go along, with remarkable quick-wittedness, not binding themselves down to any conventional oaths or forms of invective, but pouring out a stream of vituperation and obscenity to meet each case, *which strikes with unerring fidelity the weak points in the habits, morals, ancestry, and personal appearance of their opponents.*

Within a certain range ridicule and insult may be neutralised by special 'joking relationships' between particular descent groups, whereby the members of the one are permitted to address the members of the other by approbrious epithets, or to jeer at them, without offence being taken (for an example from the Banks Islands, see Vol. I, p. 399, n. 3). Such joking relationships, as Radcliffe-Brown points out (1952, pp. 102–4, 109–11), represent a halfway house between the relations of solidarity and mutual obligation which exist within a given descent group, and the state of active or latent hostility which frequently characterises relations between descent groups allied neither by marriage nor by exchange of services.

[2] See Glotz (1925), pp. 119–22.

Retranché du *génos*, sans foyer, un homme n'est plus protégé par la thémis et n'a plus valeur d'homme: il est *atimos*. L'atimie, dans sa rigueur première, entraîne la proscription: le misérable est traité en ennemi par les siens et doit s'attendre à l'être aussi par les autres.                                          Glotz (1925), p. 122.

Beyond the *genos*, begins *le monde extérieur*. Several *genê* together form a phratry, and several phratries a tribe or *phylê*.[1] The *phylê*, like the *genos*, has its own moral code, *dikê*. Say a murder has been committed. *Dikê* recognises that the injured *genos* has the right to the blood of the murderer, and may seek vengeance on any member of his *genos*. There is only one way, in the short run, to stop hostilities: the flight of the murderer. By his presence, he compromises his kinsfolk, associates them with his crime, defies the gods and men; by his departure, he puts his own people out of reach of reprisals, calms both the divine 'nemesis' and the anger of public opinion. In the long run, however, and when tempers have had time to cool, *dikê* prescribes other ways of restoring amity between the two kin groups set at odds. The murderer may take the place of the deceased man in his *genos*, either by being adopted or by marrying into it;[2] in this way one extends its *aidôs* to yesterday's enemy, one is reconciled by *aidêsis*. Or he may compound his guilt, by offering so many head of cattle or of slaves as blood-price; the indemnity paid and accepted, a treaty of 'friendship', a *philotês*, is concluded between the two kin groups and witnessed by their respective deities.

Thus, in Archaic Greek society, we find three concentric rings surrounding the individual: the *genos* or descent group, the *phylê* or commune, and outsiders. To the first corresponds *themis*, to the second *dikê*. What, then, of the third? Now we saw earlier (Vol. 1, p. 164) that the word for 'stranger' in Welsh is *alltud*, 'man of another *tud* (or commune)'. The equivalent word in Greek is *xenos*, 'stranger', but especially 'a stranger as being entitled to the rights of hospitality', so 'a friend': clearly, to my mind, 'man of another *commune* to one's own', over whom extends one's protection (and that of one's *genos*)— and he reciprocally, like *kula* partners in the Trobriands—since *dikê* no longer protects a man beyond the borders of his own *commune*.

---

[1] The social order itself, whether of *phylê* or of incipient city-state, being referred to, e.g. in Crete in the eighth to seventh century B.C., as the *kosmos*, and the men who directed its affairs as *kosmoi* (Willetts, 1965, pp. 59–62); the cognate verb, *kosmeo*, was used earlier by Homer of dividing into communities or bodies, e.g. the Rhodians were 'divided into three bodies or communities', of settling tribes in occupied territory, or of ordering by tribes and phratries for war. It was the Ionian philosophers of the sixth century B.C., who extended the idea from the demographic and social plane to that of the 'ordering' of the universe, the *kosmos*: Cornford (1930), pp. 538–49.

[2] In which case, presumably, any children he begets will be adopted into the *genos*, to the dead man's 'name': cf. among the Nuer (above, Vol. 1, p. 32), the custom of raising seed to the dead man's name.

# PART FOUR

# ENVIRONMENT
# AND ADAPTATION

# 18

## *The social morphology of kin-based societies: I. the Great Basin Shoshoni*

The term *social morphology* is taken from Mauss's early paper,[1] *Essai sur les variations saisonnières des sociétés Eskimos: étude de morphologie sociale*. In that essay Mauss sets out to study what he calls the *material substrate* of Eskimo societies, that is, 'the form which they take in establishing themselves on the ground, the volume and density of the population, the manner in which the population is distributed, as well as the whole body of *things* (i.e. material objects) which serve as basis for the collective life of the people'. He shows that Eskimo societies have—or at least *had*, at the time when European explorers first traversed the region—a double morphology, corresponding to their seasonal pattern of exploitation of the resources offered by the environment. In winter, walrus, and still more seals, gather at certain points on the coast. The seal, in particular, has need of sheltered places to raise its young, and also of places where the water remains free of ice as long as possible, to enable the animal to come to the surface easily to breathe. The number of such places, whether beaches, islands or promontories, is limited, even on the great lengths of coast ranged by the Eskimo; it is only at these points that it is possible to hunt seal, at least by the methods which the Eskimo dispose of, and consequently, since they are primarily dependent on seal meat for their winter food supply, their winter settlements have to be sited within reach of such beaches or other sheltered places. Directly spring comes, and *leads* appear in the ice, the seals move out either into the open sea, or along the coast to the foot of precipitous cliffs; to reach them, the Eskimo have to disperse as well. In early summer sweet-water fishing, especially for salmon, and hunting of reindeer and other kinds of deer on the high pasturages of the interior, invite the Eskimo to a fully nomadic life and to spread out over vast areas in the wake of the game—until the approach of cold weather warns them to make their way back to their winter settlements.

> En résumé, [writes Mauss[2]], tandis que l'été étend d'une manière presque illimitée le champ ouvert à la chasse et à la pêche, l'hiver, au contraire, le restreint de la

---

[1] First published in *L'Année Sociologique*, vol. ix (1904–5): reprinted in Mauss (1968), pp. 389–477. Mauss's thesis is largely based on Boas' fieldwork among the Central Eskimo.
[2] Mauss (1968), p. 442.

manière la plus étroite. Et c'est cette alternance qui exprime le rythme de concentration et de dispersion par lequel passe cette organisation morphologique. La population se condense ou se dissémine comme le gibier. Le mouvement dont est animée la société est synchronique à ceux de la vie ambiante.

The alternate systole and diastole of Eskimo life is reflected, in Mauss's view, in every aspect of their life: and, in particular, in their social units, in their religious life, and in their attitude to nature. The typical habitat of summer is the tent, and its occupants a single family; sometimes two or three related families will hunt together, more often each hunts on its own. But as winter approaches, all the families dispersed over a particular territory converge on their winter settlement. *There*, the typical habitat is the house, built either of stones, of a wooden frame thatched with turf, or of blocks of snow: its occupants, three or four related families, living under the same roof but each having its own clearly demarcated compartment (*cloison*) of the interior. Several such houses form a settlement, and the mark of *its* unity is the *kashim* or communal house. Apart from rites of birth and of death which may take place at any time of year, the religious life of the Eskimo community is virtually restricted to the winter months, when all its members are concentrated together in their winter settlement; this is the time when myths and folk-tales are handed down from one generation to another, and when the great festivals that ensure the survival both of the animals on which the Eskimo depend (*la fête des vessies*), and of the Eskimo themselves (*la fête des morts*), are performed. And this division between *la vie d'été* and *la vie d'hiver* is further reflected in their whole outlook on the world.[1] Throughout the Central Eskimo groups, people wear all their life, but more especially at the time of the principal ceremonies, an amulet made from the skin either of an animal, or of a bird, which is the one that presides over their month of birth. It seems clear, writes Mauss, that this is one effect of the tendency to class people in different groups according to the season when they are born, i.e. into a 'winter' people and a 'summer' people; and this division of the people into two great categories appears to be attached to a division, still wider and more general, which comprehends the whole of nature.[2] In this way, the very manner in which men and things are classed carries the imprint of the cardinal, ecological opposition between the two seasons.

The social life of the Eskimo thus assumes two clearly contrasted forms, each corresponding to one aspect of their double morphology. Of course, there are transitions between the two; but, in general, it is true to say that the people have two ways of grouping themselves, and to these two forms of grouping correspond two juridical systems, two scales of values (*deux morales*), two kinds

[1] See, in particular, on this most interesting subject, Mauss (1968), pp. 447–50.

[2] Reflected, (*a*) in a number of myths in which the whole body of animal species, and of the cardinal events of nature, is divided into two groups, one of summer and the other of winter; (*b*) in a multitude of ritual interdictions, forbidding e.g. the working of reindeer skin (summer animal) in the winter or of walrus skin in the summer, the eating of salmon meat (summer animal) in the winter or of seal meat in the summer.

of domestic economy, and two kinds of religious life. The groupings themselves are dependent, as we have seen, on the food resources offered by the environment; as these change from one season to another, so the groupings change; and as the form of the groupings changes, 'on voit la religion, le droit, la morale se transformer du même coup'. From this demonstration Mauss draws the far-reaching conclusion:[1] *que la vie sociale, sous toutes ses formes, morale, religieuse, juridique, etc., est fonction de son substrat matériel, qu'elle varie avec ce substrat, c'est à dire avec la masse, la densité, la forme et la composition des groupements humains.*

In this chapter and the next I propose to test Mauss's hypothesis, by applying it, first, to certain Shoshonean societies of the Great Basin, and then, to Hopi society. As one outcome of the enquiry, we may hope to isolate the part played by fraternities in relation to other organs, e.g. kin groups, of pueblo society; and on that basis to proceed, in the final chapter, to a general theory of the rôle of associations in kin-based societies.

### THE SHOSHONEAN-SPEAKING PEOPLES OF THE GREAT BASIN

The task that faces us in this chapter is to show how, in the Great Basin, the aboriginal social groupings—the groupings, that is to say, which the first Europeans found when they penetrated the country 150 years ago and which persisted, in some degree, until the early decades of this century—were dependent, in form, on population density; and how population density was in turn dependent on the food, or more precisely on the protein, resources offered by the environment. Mathematically, this dependence might be expressed thus:

$$s.f. \propto p,$$

where $s.f.$ = social forms, and $p$ = population density; and where $p$ itself varies with the protein resources offered by the environment. To put the relationship in this form is not wayward, its object being to convey that terms are being used, and must be so used if the demonstration is to have any value, exactly. We hypothesise that the kinds of social grouping found in the Great Basin were the outcome of two factors: of the food resources offered by the environment, and of the techniques available to the Shoshoneans for exploiting them. By way of demonstration, we shall be concerned with such practical matters as: lists of seed grasses, distribution of roots, bulbs and tubers, seasonal fluctuation in yield of berries and piñon nuts, vagaries of certain orthopterous and hymenopterous insects, reproductive rate of small rodents and jack rabbits, habits of deer and antelope, and design of such simple tools as digging sticks, wicker baskets, dead-fall traps, nets and brush fences.

The Great Basin itself, the habitat of the Plateau Shoshonean-speaking peoples,[2] extends for some 400 miles from the Sierra Nevada mountains in the

---

[1] Mauss (1968), pp. 474–5.

[2] The Plateau Shoshonean group of languages, also known as 'Numic' (see below, p. 410), comprises three main branches: Northern Paiute, Ute and Southern Paiute, and western

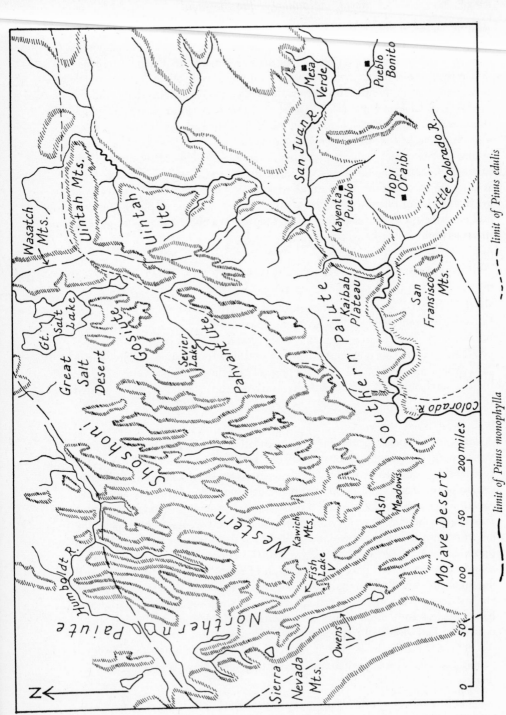

Fig. 55. Basin-Plateau area (south of the Humboldt River). Redrawn from Stewart (1938), figs. 1 and 4.

——— limit of *Pinus monophylla*

- - - - - limit of *Pinus edulis*

west to the piedmont of the Wasatch range in the east (see fig. 55). The country is one of arid valleys, from 5 to 20 miles wide and up to 80 miles long, divided from one another by mountain ranges running from north to south; many of the valleys merge into salt deserts at their lower end. The valley floors lie at around 4,500 feet above sea level, and the ranges that flank them rise a further 4,500 feet, with isolated peaks and ridges reaching to well over 10,000 feet above sea level. The mean annual rainfall over the valley floors averages 8 to 10 inches; on the mountain ranges, however, precipitation is greater and reaches 20, or even 30, inches a year in favoured localities. As more than half of the annual precipitation occurs during the winter months, it is retained as snow until well into summer on the higher ranges, whence it is released gradually in springs and streams.

Passing from the valley floor to the higher slopes of the mountain ranges, one traverses four main vegetational zones.[1] Over vast areas of the valley floor, more especially in the vicinity of salt lakes and around the periphery of salt deserts, the greasewood-shadscale community is dominant: comprising, besides greasewood itself (*Sarcobatus vermiculatus*) and shadscale (*Atriplex confertifolia*), salt-grass, alkali sacaton (*Sporobolus airoides*) and rabbit-brush (*Chrysothamnus graveolens*). This vegetation has very limited value as a food source; in places, it is true, seed-bearing grasses are to be found there after rainfall, but in general the valley floors were only of importance to the inhabitants of the region as the habitat of jack rabbits and of antelope. Where the valley floor gives way to the foothills (5,000 to 6,000 feet), the greasewood-shadscale community is supplanted by the sagebrush community, comprising, apart from sagebrush itself (*Artemisia tridentata*) and small sagebrush (*A. nova*), winterfat (*Eurotia lanata*), hop-sage (*Grayia spinosa*), gray molly (*Kochia vestita*), and other xerophytic shrubs. Edible seeds and roots, e.g. *Oryzopsis, Mentzelia, Stipa, Agropyron, Salvia*, occur in some abundance within this zone, particularly along the banks and in the vicinity of streams emerging from the mountain ranges; also, certain plants the fresh shoots of which could be eaten as 'greens' in the spring. As cottontail rabbits also have their habitat here, this zone afforded a major source of vegetable and animal foods to the Indians. Between 6,000 and 8,000 feet the mountain sides, except in the most precipitous places, carry a mixed growth of piñon and juniper, and it is in the lower reaches of this belt, in the neighbourhood of springs and streams, that the winter encampments of the Shoshoneans were commonly located. Apart from the piñon, the nuts of which

---

Shoshoni (to which is linked Comanche). Plateau Shoshonean and Hopi separated some 3,000 years ago; besides exhibiting structural features characteristic of the Uto-Aztecan family as a whole, they share a stock of nouns derived from the ancestral speech common to both.

[1] The basic similarity between the soils and vegetation of the Great Basin, and that of the Hopi region to the southeast, may be gauged by comparing Kearney's investigation of the soils and vegetation of Tooele Valley (Kearney *et al.*, 1914), and Shantz's survey of plant communities in the Great Basin (Shantz, 1925), with my own findings for the Oraibi valley (Bradfield, 1968 and 1969).

furnished the chief source of winter food, other edible plants—including some of the most important seed-bearing grasses—were to be found at favourable locations within this zone; these grasses, with herbaceous plants, also furnished grazing for fair numbers of deer. Above 8,000 feet, piñon and juniper give way to pine, fir, spruce and aspen, which continue up to the timber line (*c.* 11,000 feet). This zone, or at least the lower reaches of it, is particularly rich in herbaceous plants, including some seed-bearing grasses, in plants bearing edible roots and tubers, and in berry-bearing shrubs such as currant, elderberry, rose and service-berry; all these furnished food, especially in the late summer, when the berries ripened and the roots and tubers were ready for digging. Deer, and in the higher ranges mountain sheep, were also abundant.

At this point, and before proceeding to a detailed account of their ecology, one preliminary fact may be noted; the Shoshonean-speaking peoples of the Great Basin were primarily gatherers of vegetable foods and lower forms of animal life (i.e. fly larvae, ants, grasshoppers, locusts, mice, rats, lizards, snakes), rather than hunters. They utilised nearly 100 species of wild plants (Steward, 1955, p. 105), and this dependence on vegetable foods determined their pattern of settlement; for, since the great majority of the food-bearing plants and shrubs grew on the flanks of the mountains, it was these areas that acted as foci for their encampments. Certain phases of the gathering cycle might take single families or groups of families down to the valley floor for a few days, or even for several weeks, at a time; but it was always to the mountain flanks and to their encampments there that they returned, usually carrying with them at least a part of the harvest they had gathered and storing it there for winter use.

Roughly speaking, there were four main periods in the Shoshonean gathering year: spring, early summer, late summer, and fall. In the spring, stored food was running low. But spring in the Great Basin sees the first growth of new plants as the snows melt, particularly along streams and watercourses in the foothills of the main ranges; a number of these plants provided food, the stems and leaves being either cooked or eaten raw as 'greens'; and as the days lengthened, individual families sallied out from their winter quarters in search of these plants to eke out their dwindling reserve of pine nuts and stored seeds. In early summer (May–June), the seeds of herbaceous plants and grasses begin to ripen, some on the valley floor but most, again, in the moister foothills. At this point, throughout the greater part of the region, families leave their winter encampment and go on trek, often up to 30 or 40 miles from their home base, in search of seeds; some of what they harvest, they consume at once, the remainder they carry back to the vicinity of their winter camps and cache there in grass-lined pits, then go out again in search of more: the harvest period in any one locality being of relatively short duration, since the seeds of most species fall to the ground within a few days or weeks of ripening. In late summer (July–August), edible roots and tubers mature; many of these are to be found on the higher slopes of the mountain ranges, where, with late-ripening seeds and berries, they formed the main standby of many families through until the pine-nut harvest.

Early in the fall (late September–October), the pine nuts begin to ripen. To begin with, the cones are closed tight and have to be roasted for several hours over a smouldering fire before the nuts can be extracted (Dutcher, 1893, pp. 379–80); the first frosts open the cones, but while this makes the nuts easy to harvest, it also sets a limit to the harvesting period since, within a few days, the nuts begin to drop from the cones. The period during which the nuts can be harvested in this state is thus limited to two to three weeks, rarely longer, and it may only be ten days (Steward, 1938, pp. 27–8). During this time families have to gather sufficient nuts to last them, with the seeds and dried roots and berries which they have already cached, through the four winter months from late November to the end of March. Some of the nuts they store in the mountains; the rest they carry down to their winter encampment, usually located either at a spring within the piñon-juniper belt or near a stream in the foothills below, but always within reach of where their seeds and pine nuts have been cached.

Their ultimate dependence on vegetable foods, in conjunction with the limited technical skills available for harvesting and storing them, entailed certain consequences in the social life of the Great Basin Shoshoneans: in short, it put a premium, at least for many months of the year, upon family separatism rather than upon co-operation.[1] Three specific points may be noted here, with regard to seed-bearing plants: in the first place, they usually grow scattered, seldom in dense patches; in the second, since the yield is directly related to rainfall and since rainfall, throughout the Great Basin, is highly erratic, the exact location of crops within any given territory varies widely from year to year; and in the third, as noted earlier, the seeds of most seed-bearing plants fall to the ground within a few days, or at most two or three weeks, of ripening. As a result of the first of these three factors, all seed-gathering activities were carried out by individual families working either on their own or, at most, in conjunction with one or two other families; by far the greater part of the gathering was done by women, and a woman gathered as much, or perhaps a little more, *alone* as she could in company with others—as anyone who has picked wild berries in a party will be aware. As a result of the other two factors, the movements of the Indians were both erratic within any one season, and varied from year to year; single families wandered over their territory from spring to fall, moving from one crop-yielding area to another, as the chance of local rainfall dictated, and staying in each just so long as the resources there lasted. The only partial exception to this rule was furnished by the pine-nut crop. In the late summer, when a family heard reports that the pine nuts seemed promising in a certain area of the mountain range, it arranged its travels so as to arrive there in late October, when the first frosts would have opened the cones and made the nuts ready to

[1] Steward (1955), p. 107: cf. (1938), pp. 20–1. The generalisations made in this paragraph apply, in particular, to the western Shoshoni area of the Great Basin; in certain respects, as we shall see later, conditions were different in Owens Valley, perhaps also on the piedmont of the Wasatch Mountains.

harvest; other families, who had also been foraging for food within a radius of perhaps 20 or 30 miles, converged on the same locality. Once assembled there, however, the individual families camped from a few hundred yards to a mile apart, each family (or group of two or three families) restricting itself by common agreement to a limited tract of trees, from which its members gathered nuts as rapidly as they were able, storing them in earth caches either on the spot or at their winter encampment lower down on the mountain flank. If the harvest were a good one, a winter encampment of this kind might consist of as many as twenty or thirty families (Steward, 1955, pp. 105–7), camped e.g. along the course of a stream within easy visiting distance of one another; in another year, it might number no more than half a dozen.

The three factors noted above had a further important consequence: on population. In a good year the crop of seeds, and especially of pine nuts, was probably sufficient, as Steward remarks (1938, p. 20), to have supported many times the number of inhabitants actually to be found living in the region; but its availability was limited, first by the fact that the seed-bearing plants—though not the piñon trees—were widely scattered, and second, by the fact that the seeds themselves—including pine nuts—ripened and fell before many could be gathered. Further, due to the vagaries of rainfall, the crop itself varied enormously in any one region from one year to the next. One year might provide enough food, especially pine nuts, to support *thousands*, but the next three have few seeds and *no* pine nuts; in such years, crops were only to be found in small quantities in restricted areas, and scarcely sufficed to support the sparse population that had to subsist on them.

Turning now to the sources of animal protein:[1] in certain areas, and at some times of year, insects—notably ants, grasshoppers, crickets and locusts—and their larvae filled an important place in the Shoshonean dietary. Most snakes, with the occasional exception of the rattlesnake, were eaten; also lizards, when they were large enough to warrant the trouble of catching and preparing them. Quail, duck, and mud-hen were taken, and fish, wherever there were lakes or a river which held them.[2] But probably the major source of animal protein, at least among all western Shoshoni groups, was provided by rodents and other small mammals. As a food source, these had great advantages, particularly over larger game. In the first place, several species of small burrowing rodents occur in extensive colonies, usually in comparatively fertile places where they feed on seeds and roots; in such localities they can be taken in worthwhile numbers, without the hunter having to move any great distance from his camp. Secondly, all of them reproduce quickly, so that killing them does not diminish their numbers for any length of time. Considerable effort was expended in taking them; they were either dug out with a digging stick, pulled from their holes

---

[1] See, in particular, Steward (1938), pp. 32–40.

[2] Stansbury, who travelled in the region in the 1840s, describes the construction of willow weirs in the vicinity of the Great Salt Lake, perhaps by the Gosiute, for the purpose of trapping fish: quoted by Lowie (1924), p. 200.

by means of a rodent skewer, smoked out, flooded out, or killed with dead-fall traps. Two of these methods, dead-fall traps and flooding,[1] have been described by Egan (quoted by Steward, 1938, pp. 138–9), who travelled in the Great Basin in the 1850s and 1860s. Both accounts refer to the Gosiute, to the south of the Great Salt Lake. In one instance, Egan met an Indian whose 'plan was to go up one side of the canyon, setting the traps wherever he saw the sign of rats, and the same down the other side. The next day, taking the same route, gathering the catch, and re-setting the traps. The rats . . . were 6 to 8 inches long . . .' On another occasion Egan saw eight or ten women in Creek Hollow, diverting water by means of little ditches into gopher holes; in part of a day some of them acquired *up to half a bushel*, with several days' work ahead, and one woman got twenty-five to thirty within half an hour; the rodents were skinned, eviscerated, and dried without removing the bones.

Among the rodents taken in this way were various species of pocket gophers (*Geomydae*), ground squirrels (*Citellus*), and prairie dogs (*Cynomys*). Other rodents, living among the rocks in the foothills and on the mountain flanks, were taken when the opportunity offered, usually by running down and killing with sticks and stones; among these were chipmunks and pack-rats.[2] Only two disadvantages weighed against these small burrowing rodents as a food source: first, since each of them weighed less than a pound, large numbers had to be taken to make a meal; second, most species hibernated during the winter and so were not available at the time when food shortage was most acute, i.e. in late winter and early spring.

Halfway between the small rodents described above, and the relatively scarce large game (antelope, deer, and mountain sheep), come rabbits; and here a distinction has to be drawn between cottontails and jack rabbit. Cottontails were smaller, and more limited in number, than jack rabbits, and were to be found mainly in scrub, in the foothills bordering the valleys, where they were most readily taken either in snares or with bow and arrow; consequently, they were never the object of communal drives, but were taken by individual hunters supplementing the food supply of their families either at the winter encampments or when collecting seeds in the foothills. Jack rabbits, by contrast, lived on the open, sage-dotted valley floor; and while their speed and ability to hide made them difficult for single hunters to take with bow and arrow, their large and rapidly multiplying herds rewarded communal drives (Steward, 1938, pp. 38–9), the rabbits from a large area being driven—between wings of sage-brush—into a line of nets, where they were dispatched with sticks and stones. Rabbit drives of this kind were held by all Shosohnean groups in the fall, commonly in association with the fall festival, and were a major communal activity. Not only were jack rabbits more numerous than cottontails, they were also considerably heavier, weighing (on average) $5\frac{1}{2}$ lbs. against the cottontail's

---

[1] Both these methods were also practised by the Hopi: Hough (1918), pp. 285–6.

[2] Simpson, in the 1870s, met a Woodruff Valley Paiute with twenty-seven rats for food: quoted by Steward (1933), p. 255, n. 57.

2 to 2½ lbs., and so providing more meat; they also furnished skins, used for making rabbit-skin blankets and mantles.

Finally, there were the large game: antelope, found—like jack rabbits—on the valley flats, and hunted communally, usually with the aid of V-shaped sagebrush corrals into which the animals were driven; deer and mountain sheep, found in the mountains and hunted either by lone hunters or by small parties of experienced men, often with the help of dogs.

Despite the importance of animal protein as a supplement to the mainly vegetarian diet of the Shoshoneans, it remained only a supplement, and the annual migration in search of food was directed with reference to plant rather than animal species. The reasons for this are clear. Of the two groups of animals, i.e. insects and small rodents, on which the Shoshoneans chiefly depended for animal protein during the spring and summer months, insects—notably grasshoppers, crickets and locusts—were to be found principally on the valley floor, occurring there in some summers in such abundance as to furnish a major source of food; when this happened, perhaps once in every three or four years, families finding themselves in the proximity of swarms of locusts or crickets joined together to hunt them (see below, p. 358), but the occurrence of such swarms was too unpredictable to determine the course of the migratory cycle. The small burrowing rodents, since they lived on the same roots and seeds as the Shoshoneans themselves, were to be found chiefly in those localities which individual families were in the habit of visiting *in any case*; the hunting of these small animals, consequently, dovetailed in with the gathering of the seeds and roots on which both relied for their subsistence.[1] Of larger game, the two most important, jack rabbits and antelope, were both the object of communal hunts, enterprised at that time of year (October–November) when groups of families were already assembled for the pine-nut harvest.

Throughout the Great Basin area, the individual family was, for the greater part of the year, the independent economic unit, fending for itself and supplying its own needs. Within the family, men's work and women's work were complementary (Steward, 1938, pp. 44–6). *Women* did virtually all seed gathering, though men helped to some extent in collecting pine nuts; they prepared food, including the grinding of the seeds on metates, did all the cooking, made baskets and most of the clothing. *Men* did all large-game hunting, including that of jack rabbits, made digging sticks and other tools (including, in the old days, chipped-flint tools), wove their own rabbit nets either from twine or fibres of wild flax, and sewed together rabbit-skin blankets; they built the winter encampments, and assisted women in such tasks as hunting rodents, carrying firewood and water, transporting seeds, and gathering some of the material for making baskets. The sexual division of labour thus covered all essential pursuits of Shoshonean life. From an early age children were taught the tasks appropriate to their sex (Steward, 1933, p. 291). When boys were about 10 years of age,

---

[1] At a number of points in his account, Steward refers to the robbing of rodent stores by the Shoshoneans as one source of seeds.

their fathers taught them hunting, making bows and arrows for them, the boys practising on rabbits and other small game; at 14, they accompanied their fathers deer-hunting. Girls, correspondingly, at the age of 12 or 14 were taught seed gathering and women's work.

I remarked earlier that certain characters of seed-bearing plants, in particular the fact that they seldom grow in dense patches and that their yield varies directly with rainfall, had a direct relation to population; this relation we must now examine briefly (Steward, 1938, pp. 46–9). Over the whole of the Basin-Plateau area the mean population density was probably, at the time the first Europeans entered the area, one person to about 16 sq. miles. But within the area, density varied widely according to the fertility of the different regions, itself dependent on rainfall. Extremely arid regions had the lowest density; thus the Gosiute of Skull Valley and the Deep Creek Mountains, who numbered 256 persons in the 1860s, ranged over an area of about 120 × 50 miles, or 6,000 sq. miles (excluding the Great Salt Desert), giving a population density of one person to *c.* 24 sq. miles; while the western Shoshoni of the Kawich Mountains, with 120 persons ranging over 2,000 sq. miles, fell near the mean of one person to 16 sq. miles. But where high elevation attracted increased rainfall, or the presence of mountain ranges produced perennial springs and streams, the population was much denser: for example, the piedmont of the Wasatch Mountains, with one person to *c.* 4 sq. miles, and Owens Valley, in the far west, with one person to 2 sq. miles. To the significance of these figures, particularly in their bearing on social structure, I shall return later; in the meantime, they may be summarised as follows:

| location | population[1] (c. 1861–70) | area in sq. miles[2] | sq. miles per person |
|---|---|---|---|
| all of Nevada .. .. .. .. | *c.* 7,000 | 110,700 | 16 |
| Gosiute (Skull Valley, Deep Creek Mts.) | 256 | 6,000 | 24 |
| Western Shoshoni (Kawich Mountains) | 120 | 2,000 | 16 |
| Northern Paiute (Fish Lake Valley) .. | *c.* 100 | 800 | 8 |
| Pahvant Ute (Sevier Lake region) .. | *c.* 1,000 | 4,000 | 4 |
| Northern Paiute (Owens Valley) .. | *c.* 1,000 | 2,000 | 2 |

[1] Figures taken from Steward (1938), pp. 48–9: except that for Northern Paiute (Owens Valley), taken from Steward (1933), p. 237.

[2] The figure for Nevada includes deserts, the other figures have been pared down to exclude (uninhabitable) desert. If areas of uninhabitable desert accounted for 25 per cent of

This concludes our introduction to the Great Basin and its aboriginal in-habitants. I proceed now to a detailed account of the economy, and social structure, of four representative Shoshonean-speaking groups: namely, the Gosiute of Skull Valley and the Deep Creek Mountains, Northern Paiute of Fish Lake Valley, Northern Paiute of the northern section of Owens Valley, and Southern Paiute of the Ash Meadows region.

### THE GOSIUTE OF SKULL VALLEY AND THE DEEP CREEK MOUNTAINS

The Gosiute habitat[1] is one of the least favourable in the entire Shoshoni region. Lying between the fertile piedmont of the Wasatch mountains to the east and the relatively high terrain of central Nevada to the west, it is an area of true desert and pre-desert. Most of the valleys in the region are relatively low, rarely above 4,500 feet, and consequently arid; few of the mountain ranges have sufficient altitude to intercept moisture in any quantity. The only fertile areas are Deep Creek Valley and Trout Creek, which lie on either side of the lofty Deep Creek range, to the southwest of the Great Salt Desert, and scattered localities with perennial springs and streams in the Oquirrh and Cedar moun-tains, bounding Tooele and Skull Valleys, immediately south of Great Salt

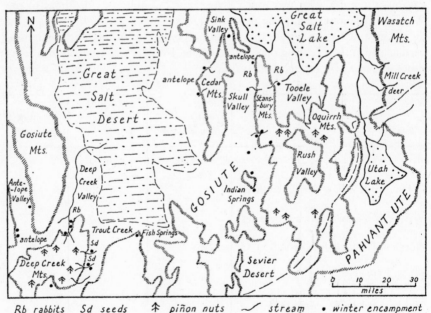

Rb rabbits    Sd seeds    ⚹ piñon nuts    ⁓ stream    • winter encampment

Fig. 56. Territory of the Gosiute Indians.

the land surface in the Basin-Plateau region, then the mean population density will have been one person to *c*. 12 sq. miles, overall.

[1] The outline of this account of the Gosiute is based on Steward (1938), pp. 132–41. Most of the ethno-botanical detail comes from Chamberlin's article (1911) on 'The Ethno-botany

Lake. The rest of the Gosiute area had only a few, widely separated, sources of water.

The population was as sparse as anywhere in the Great Basin. When Powell and Ingalls visited the region in 1872 (Steward, 1938, pp. 132–3), the Gosiute were 'scattered in very small bands, cultivating the soil about little springs here and there . . .'. They fell unto two main groups:

(*a*) a northeastern group, around Skull Valley, with winter encampments in the Cedar and Oquirrh Mountains; this group numbered 149.

(*b*) a southwestern group, chiefly in Deep Creek and Trout Creek Valleys, with winter encampments in the Deep Creek range, numbering 107.

Like other western Shoshoni groups, the Gosiute placed their chief dependence for food[1] on vegetal products, notably on 'greens', seeds, bulbs and tubers, berries, and pine nuts.

*Greens, and seeds:*

In the spring, the Gosiute left their winter encampments and went in search of certain kinds of plants, the leaves and stems of which they boiled and ate as 'greens'. Amongst these were leaves of arrow-root, of *Cymopterus longipes*, of native watercress, of cancer-root, of a plumed thistle, of mountain mint; the lower, tender stems of bulrush; also, the first shoots of *Ferula multifida*.

As among all western Shoshoni groups, seeds provided the staple diet during the summer months. While many kinds of plants were a source of seeds, the bulk of the seeds eaten came from the *grasses*, from a species of nettle (*Urtica*), and from members of the *Chenopodiaceae*. Most of the common grasses furnished seeds, e.g. the following ten species:[2] *Agropyron repens*, blue-joint grass, *Cinna arundinacea*, rood reed grass, *Deschampsia caespitosa*, hair grass, *Elymus canadensis*, wild rye, *Festuca tenella*, fescue grass, *Glyceria distans*, manna grass, *Glyceria aquatica*, reed meadow grass, *Oryzopsis cuspidata*, mountain rice, *Poa californica*, meadow grass, and *Poa tenuifolia*, bunch grass. Among seed-bearing plants were *Triglochin maritimum*, arrow grass, and an unidentified species of *Urtica*.[3] Of these grasses and plants, the two most important as food source were moun-

---

of the Gosiute Indians', of particular value since Chamberlin saw Gosiute culture before its final disintegration; further details have been taken from Chamberlin (1908), Lowie (1924), and Reagan (1934).

[1] On Gosiute subsistence, see Steward (1938), pp. 137–9, and, especially, Chamberlin (1911), pp. 336–44.

[2] Chamberlin (1911), p. 360 *et seq.* One species of wild amaranth was also used, by some of the western Shoshoni, as a seed source (Steward, 1938, p. 306: cf. Kelly, 1964, p. 42). This is of interest, in that, far to the south in Mexico and Guatemala, various species of amaranth were cultivated as grain crops in pre-Spanish times (Sauer, 1950a, pp. 567–73), and one species, perhaps with a cultivated chenopod, formed one of the three staple crops of that area—the other two being maize and beans. A number of Mexican pueblos, usually those in rather out-of-the-way places, still plant fields of grain amaranth to-day (ibid. p. 577).

[3] The only two species of *Urtica* (nettle) native to Utah and Nevada are *Urtica breweri* and *Urtica gracilis*. In habitat, both range from the valleys and canyons of the artemisia belt, upward through the pinyon, to the aspen belt: I. Tidestrom, *Flora of Utah and Nevada* (Contrib. U.S. National Herbarium, vol. 25: Washington, 1925), p. 141.

tain rice, called *wai*, and the unidentified species of nettle, known as *tui*; the first of these occurs widely throughout the region and was formerly a major food-source, while wild seeds of *tui* were collected in one season and sown the following spring, on land where brush had been burned off in the fall, and harvested later in the summer.[1]

The seeds of these grasses, and of other seed-bearing plants, were all gathered in much the same way. The seeds were first collected in conical woven baskets, about 30 inches wide by 3 feet deep, into which they were brushed straight from the plant with the aid of basketry fans;[2] they were then carried to some convenient place near the camp, and subsequently threshed and winnowed; after roasting over live coals in shallow baskets, the greater part of the seeds was stored in grass-lined pits in the ground, covered over with brush, for winter use. When required for eating, the grain was ground into meal on the metate; the meal thus produced was eaten chiefly in the form of a porridge or gruel, or was baked into crude scones.

In addition to grasses, various chenopods, growing abundantly over the valley floor and the flats, afforded a great quantity of nutritious seeds; in some localities, indeed, certain species of *Atriplex* and *Chenopodium* are found growing so thickly over wide areas that they would seem to have furnished, as Chamberlin remarks, a food supply 'limited only by the capacity of the Indians to harvest it'. Of these, *Atriplex confertifolia*, known as *suñ*, is abundant on alkaline flats throughout the region and occurs in enormous profusion in the more favoured places; in such localities this plant was much depended on, the seeds being gathered like those of the grasses.[3] Other chenopodiaceous plants that contributed large quantities of seeds were *Salicornia herbacea*, samphire, common around brackish water and over damp alkaline areas, and *Chenopodium capitatum*, goosefoot.

Of *Crucifera* furnishing edible seeds, the most important seems to have been the hedge mustard, *Sisymbrium canescens*, known as *poi'ya*; and of the borage family, a species of *Lithospermum*, called *tso'ni-baip*. Especially nutritious were the seeds beaten from the heads of a number of the *Compositae*; among these may be mentioned the sunflower,

---

[1] Steward (1938), p. 138. This must, I think, be the cultivation to which Powell and Ingalls referred in 1872 (see above, p. 355); Steward states specifically (p. 138) that there was no horticulture, by the Gosiute, of *domesticated* plants.

[2] It may be remarked, in passing, that the Shoshonean-speaking peoples of the Great Basin represented, in the literal sense, a *basket-maker culture*: as well as seed-gathering equipment, all containers needed for domestic use were made of basketry; also, cradles. For a full description of Great Basin (Northern Paiute) basketwork and cradles, see Kelly (1932), pp. 120–35, and Plates 23–31; for the extensive use of basketry in traditional Hopi culture, cf. Hough (1918), pp. 263–70; and for Hopi cradles, Hough (1918), p. 241 and Plate 25, and W. and M. G. Dennis (1940), pp. 108–10.

Archaeological findings at Danger Cave near Wendover, on the western edge of the Great Salt Desert, indicate that a Gosiute-type economy has persisted in the region since the end of the Ice Age. After listing the similarities between the economy of the prehistoric inhabitants, as evidenced by the archaeological remains, and that of the Gosiute, Dr. J. D. Jennings concludes (1957, p. 3):

> The parallel between the historically observed Shoshoni cultures and the inferences warranted about the archaeologically derived cultures, is so close that we assume no significant shifts in economy, in general balance with the environment, or in cultural orientation to have occurred since man first invaded the Basin. Further, a socio-political organization and a cultural orientation very like that of the historic tribes are postulated for all of the cultures of the Great Basin for the past 10,000 years.

[3] The Hopi, incidentally, use the leaves of this plant as 'greens'.

*Helianthus annuus,* known as *i'üm-pi,* the seeds of which were a much valued source of food and oil among the Gosiute (Chamberlin, 1911, p. 371).

### Roots, tubers, and bulbs:

These mostly came into season between June and September, and were an alternative food-source to seeds.

Bulbs of the lily, *Calochortus nuttallii,* known as *si'go,* were dug up, roasted in pits lined with hot stones, and eaten; when not required for immediate consumption, the bulbs were stored for winter use, being dried and placed in grass-lined pits whence they were taken as needed and then, most commonly, cooked with meat in the form of stews. Another member of the lily family furnishing an edible bulb, though less important as a food-source than *si'go,* was *Fritillaria pudica,* a yellow-flowered species blooming in the mountains in early spring. The Camassia, *pa' sigo,* was used extensively where available, being similarly cooked by roasting with hot stones; the bulbs of the wild onion, *küñ'ga,* and of the common spring beauty (*Claytonia caroliniana*), *dzi'na,* were also eaten in season.

One of the most highly sought after of all plant foods among the Gosiute[1] was the wild carrot (*Carum gardneri*), *yam'pa,* found in abundance in favourable locations on the higher mountains. It grows to a height of four feet, and has swollen, tuberous roots; it is these that were eaten. The usual method of cooking the roots was to roast them in pits lined with hot stones, in which they were covered and left overnight; being filled with starchy material, the roots were not only sweet and pleasant to the taste, but highly nutritious. Like *si'go* bulbs, the roots of the wild carrot were dried in quantity and stored for winter use.

### Berries, currants, fruit:

Berries formed an important element in Gosiute diet, being both eaten in late summer when they ripen and preserved in large quantities for winter use. For preserving, the berries were mashed, spread out on the rocks in the sun, and allowed to dry thoroughly; the dried fruit was then put in pits lined with grass, covered over with leaves of sage, then cedar bark and finally with earth. For use in winter, the dried fruit was ground on the metate, mixed with seed meals and sometimes with meat, and then boiled.

Of fruits of this kind, the service-berry (*Amelanchier alnifolia*), *ti'üm-pi,* was the principal source. The native currants, general term *po'go-nüp,* were gathered and preserved in the same way; these included the black currant (*Ribes aureum*), various other species of Ribes, wild cherry (*Prunus demissa*), wild rose, and lemon berry (*Rhus trilobata*). The prickly pear (*Opuntia rutila*), also, was formerly used as a food, the spines being removed and the joints roasted over hot coals.

### Pine nuts:

As among other western Shoshoni groups, the nuts of *Pinus monophylla* were a major food-source of the Gosiute; as late as *c.* 1910, the invariable journey into the mountains each fall for the pine-nut harvest was still looked upon as a great fixed event of the year (Chamberlin, 1911, p. 377). As with wild-seed areas, there was no ownership of pine-nut tracts; groups of families assembled in localities where the crop happened to be good that

[1] Chamberlin (1911), pp. 339–40, 365: cf. Reagan (1935b), pp. 21–2.

year, and agreed among themselves that each family would pick from one particular tract. Skull Valley people commonly procured pine nuts from the Oquirrh mountains, south of Tooele Valley, and Deep Creek people from the Deep Creek range; the latter range furnished the more reliable supply, and if the Oquirrh crop failed, families from that region made their way down to the Deep Creek mountains where they sometimes remained all winter, returning to their own territory in the spring.

After gathering, the cones were roasted over a slow fire, and the nuts then knocked out with a stone. Further roasting, if found necessary, was done in ovens. The nuts were then either carried down to the winter encampment, or cached in pits on the mountain side. For eating, they were commonly ground into meal on a metate.

Turning now to the sources of animal protein: all the early travellers in the region stress the importance of insects, lizards and small rodents, in the diet of the Gosiute. They are described, in various accounts (see Steward, 1938, pp. 134–5, 138–9), as eating ants, grasshoppers, black crickets, lizards, snakes, gophers, field rats, and rabbits.

### Ants (a'ni):

Reagan (1934, p. 54) describes how, in the Deep Creek country, there is a large red ant that makes a large bushy mound for a home. 'In the old times the Goshutes [Gosiute] used to go to these ant hills and collect the ants and the ant eggs in a basket, take them home and boil them into a soup. . . .' They also, according to the same authority, made a soup out of fly larvae.

### Crickets, grasshoppers, locusts, and cicadas:

An abundance of food[1] was furnished at times by the black cricket (*Anabrus simplex*), *ma'so*, by the cicada (*Cicada septendecim*), *gi'a*, and by certain species of locust, *a'tuñ*. In some summers, crickets occur in this region in vast swarms, or 'armies'; on these occasions they afforded an easily obtainable, abundant, and highly relished food-supply to the Gosiute. For immediate eating, the crickets were placed in pits lined with hot stones, covered over and left until thoroughly roasted; alternately, they were dried and preserved for winter use in baskets or other receptacles covered over in pits. The cicada and its larvae, and locusts, afforded a similar source of food; they, too, were either roasted for immediate consumption or dried and stored for winter use.[2]

Regarding grasshoppers, Lowie quotes (1924, p. 195) an interesting account written by one of the Franciscan fathers, probably about 1850, describing a grasshopper 'drive' among one of the western Shoshoni groups in Utah (the Gosiute, in all probability). The principal portion of the Shoshoni territory, runs the account, is covered with wormwood and various species of artemisia [the writer is clearly referring here to the valley floors], in which 'the grasshoppers swarm by myriads'; these parts are consequently most frequented by the inhabitants, and when the grasshoppers are sufficiently numerous, the people hunt them together:

> They begin by digging a hole, ten or twelve feet in diameter by four or five deep; then, armed with long branches of artemisia, they surround a field of four or five

---

[1] See, particularly, Chamberlin (1908), pp. 82–3, and (1911), pp. 336–7.
[2] The Hopi also, in the old days, used to go out and collect locusts (*ma'hü*) when these appeared in large numbers in the summer; they roasted them with salt, as they do popcorn today, and ate them: information from Mae Poling'yowma's grandmother, Mary.

acres, more or less, according to the number of persons who are engaged in it [the hunt]. They stand about twenty feet apart, and their whole work is to beat the ground, so as to frighten up the grasshoppers and make them bound forward. They chase them towards the centre by degrees—that is, into the hole prepared for their reception. Their number is so considerable that frequently three or four acres furnish grasshoppers sufficient to fill the reservoir or hole.

The grasshoppers caught in this way were treated in one of three ways. For immediate eating, they were either boiled in a soup, or transfixed along the length of pointed sticks and roasted (by setting the sticks in the ground around the fire); alternately, they were crushed into a kind of paste, which was then dried and kept for future use.

Various kinds of shrimp were treated in the same manner as crickets and grasshoppers; indeed, the Gosiute likened the one to the other, calling shrimps *ma'so pañ'witc*, 'fish cricket'. All these arthropods, however, had one feature in common, namely, that their occurrence was too unpredictable for them to form a reliable, annual item in Gosiute diet; in years when they were abundant, they afforded a major source of food, then for several years they were of no importance.

### Lizards, snakes, and small rodents:

Certain of the larger desert lizards, as well as snakes, were formerly eaten by the Gosiute: Chamberlin (1911), p. 336. But their principal standby, throughout the spring and summer months, were the small rodents which lived on the same roots and seeds as the Gosiute themselves. I have already quoted accounts (above, p. 351) of the hunting of rats, and of gophers, by means of deadfall traps in the one case, and of flooding in the other. Ground squirrels (*kim'ba*), everywhere present, were also hunted in spring and early summer, being either trapped or shot with bow and arrow; chipmunks (*ho'i*), mountain rats (*ka'*), and cottontail (*ta'bo*), were taken in the foothills and higher up on the mountain flanks.

### Jack rabbits:

The major source of animal protein throughout the fall and winter months was, undoubtedly, the jack rabbit.[1] Exceedingly common throughout the region, particularly on the valley floors where it bred in large numbers, this animal was highly important to the Gosiute, both as a source of meat and of fur for clothing and blankets. Every fall, especially in November after the pine-nut harvest, it was the custom to hold great rabbit drives, in which all the families in a particular valley co-operated. The common procedure was either to set up a line of nets with wings of sagebrush, or to construct a V-shaped funnel of greasewood or sage, some hundreds of yards long, with a hole at the apex leading into an underground trench; in either case, the hares from a wide area were driven into the enclosure by the combined efforts of men, women and children, whence they ran either into the line of nets or into the trench, and were killed there with sticks and stones.

Drives of this kind commonly lasted for several days, the hunters moving to a different part of the valley floor each day. Great numbers of hares were killed. After the hunt, the meat was dried and preserved for winter use, while the skins were dressed and cut into

---

[1] See, particularly, Chamberlin (1908), pp. 95–6, and (1911), p. 336: cf. Steward (1938), pp. 38–9.

strips; later, these fur strips were sewn together into blankets,[1] or made into clothes which were warm and very serviceable.

*Antelope, deer, and mountain sheep:*

Of large game, the most important were antelope and deer, mountain sheep being relatively scarce in Gosiute territory. Deer were commonly taken either by lone hunters or by small parties of men working together, though in the Deep Creek range small surrounds were held under the direction of the valley chief. Antelope were fairly numerous on the valley floor and were the object of communal hunts, usually undertaken in the fall before the first snow fell, in the course of which the animals were driven between walls of sagebrush, often extending for many miles across the bench lands. These walls were semi-permanent constructions,[2] put into repair each time a hunt was held, with openings along their course; although the antelope can jump, he did not usually do so, but ran the length of the wall until he came to an opening, through which he would pass to the outside, to be killed there by Indians hiding behind the brush. Alternately, the animals were driven the whole length of the corridor into a sagebrush corral, and despatched there. Egan gives a graphic account (quoted by Steward, 1938, pp. 34–5) of one such hunt, held at the northern end of Antelope Valley about twenty miles northwest of Deep Creek, in the course of which between twenty and thirty antelope were caught in this manner. But he observes that such hunts could be held only once every ten or twelve years in any one locality, since it takes that length of time for the animals to increase in sufficient number to make a drive of this kind worthwhile.

The ecological conditions under which the Gosiute lived, in conjunction with the techniques at their disposal for exploiting such resources as the environment offered, determined in certain respects the pattern of their social life. For six to seven months, from the break-up of the winter camps late in March until the onset of the pine-nut harvest in October, individual families—or, at most, groups of two or three families—foraged on their own, *of necessity*, given the distribution of seed plants and Gosiute techniques of seed gathering; only on rare occasions, during these months, did larger groups of families co-operate, e.g. in a grasshopper 'drive'. In October, they converged on selected localities in the mountain ranges where the pine-nut crop was known to be promising, and for the next few weeks groups of families, numbering from half a dozen to a dozen, were engaged in each locality gathering the pine-nut harvest. November saw the largest social gatherings known to the Gosiute. Early in that month, after the first frosts had opened the pine cones and eventually rendered further picking uneconomical, and before the first snows made travelling difficult, the fall festival was celebrated. Such evidence as we have for the Gosiute (Steward, 1938, pp. 139–40) indicates that, in the normal course, all the families whose winter encampments lay on the flanks of the mountains

[1] Each blanket requiring the fur of from fifty to seventy-five jack rabbits: Steward (1933), p. 269. Cf. among the Hopi, Hough (1918), p. 262.

[2] Reagan observes (1934, p. 54) that remains of these sagebrush walls were still to be seen, at a number of places on the bench lands around the Deep Creek range, in the early years of this century; cf. Chamberlin (1911), pp. 335–6, for remains of such fences in the Cedar Mountain range.

bordering a particular valley co-operated together under a valley chief, who directed both the festival itself and the rabbit drives which everywhere accompanied it. In practice this meant that, provided the pine-nut crop was adequate in each region, Skull Valley people and Deep Creek people held their own independent festivals under the direction of their own valley chief. Communal antelope drives were also held at this time, but these were directed by an antelope shaman.

Late in November, when the first snows heralded the onset of winter, the families which had assembled to take part in the fall festival and the accompanying rabbit drives made their way back to their winter encampments on the mountain flanks, and to the stores of seeds, roots, berries and pine-nuts, which they had cached nearby.

All western Shoshoni groups, including the Gosiute, held the fall festival; among most groups it was the major, and among some the *only*, such communal gathering held in the course of the year. The Gosiute also held a spring festival (Steward, 1938, pp. 45, 139), in the course of which they performed the circle dance, *to bring rain and to make seeds grow*. This dance Steward believes to be[1] a borrowed form of the Bear dance of the Utes; Reagan, also, says (1934, p. 52) that the Gosiute had their own version of the Bear dance, while farther to the south, the Southern Paiute of Kaibab Plateau had songs for both Bear dance and circle dance (Sapir, 1911, p. 455, n. 2). In the spring, as we have seen, the Gosiute sowed wild seeds on land they had burned off in the fall. Regarding the Hopi *powa'mu*, Stephen says (1936, p. 238) that one of its purposes was to exorcise the cold, and Simmons (1942, p. 20) that it was held 'in order to melt the snows, banish cold weather, and prepare the fields and gardens for planting'. We thus get the series:

| Ute *bear dance* | / | Gosiute *circle dance* | / | Hopi *powa'mu* |
| (to mark the | | (to bring rain and | | (to banish the cold |
| melting of the snow) | | make seeds grow) | | and prepare the fields) |

NORTHERN PAIUTE OF FISH LAKE VALLEY

Fish Lake Valley[2] lies some 20 miles to the northeast of Bishop Creek, which is in Owens Valley. It is 40 miles long from north to south, and 8 to 10 miles wide. The valley floor lies about 5,000 feet above sea level, and is generally arid. High mountains rise on either side of the valley, the White Mountains to the west and the Silver Peak to the east, but only the White Mountains give rise to a few small streams reaching the valley floor from the west. The vegetation it supports is, consequently, mainly xerophytic, and of limited value for food.

Originally, i.e. around 1870, the valley supported a population of about 100 persons, distributed among eight more or less permanent encampments. When

---

[1] Steward (1938), p. 184: (1955), pp. 113-14.
[2] For a brief account of the Northern Paiute of Fish Lake Valley, see Steward (1938), pp. 61-6.

Steward worked in the area in the early 1930s, there were six encampments, with a total population of sixty to seventy persons. The encampments were all located on the west side of the valley, on the streams which issue from the White Mountains; they were occupied all the year round, except for a few weeks during the summer and fall when trips were made for seeds and pine nuts. Of the six encampments the largest was Sohodühatü, near the southern end of the valley, with four families in residence; the other encampments had either one, or two, families each.

)))  *irrigated land*  ⎯ᴸᴸᴸ⎯ *marsh*  /// *wild seed area*

Fig. 57. Fish Lake Valley.

A vivid picture of subsistence activities in Fish Lake Valley is given by one of Steward's informants, MH. She described the seasonal activities of her family as follows:

Their usual winter home was at Tu:na'va, on a creek on the west side of the valley. In early spring they procured Joshua tree buds from the foothills of the Silver Peak range, and sand-grass and *Mentzelia* seeds from the vicinity of Pan'üva, 10 miles to the north. Then they went 5 miles northeast to Yo:gamatü, taking the seeds with them. The principal crop at Yo:gamatü was *nahavita*, a species of *Eleocharis*, which grew on irrigated ground there; this was the only irrigated plot in the valley. In moist places near Yo:gamatü, they also dug *tupu'si* roots, a species of *Brodiaea*. In late June they made their way back to Sühühoi, at the foot of the White

Mountains; there, and at other nearby places where the crops were good, they gathered seeds of *mono*, love grass (*Eragrostis secundiflora*), of *pasi'da* (probably *Salvia columbaria*), of porcupine grass (*Stipa speciosa*), and sunflower, carrying them back to Tu:na'va to store for winter use. In the late summer, they gathered berries of *Ribes* and *Lycium* on the mountain sides, dried them, and carried them back to Tu:na'va. In the fall they ordinarily went for pine nuts to the Silver Peak range to a place called Tohoyavi, some 10 miles directly east of Tu:na'va. All the families in a single encampment usually went to the same place for pine nuts, travelling in a body, but once arrived there, each family picked on its own tract; families carried as many nuts as possible down to the winter encampment, the remainder they cached in brush-lined pits in the mountains, bringing them down when needed (usually in the spring).

As among the western Shoshoni, animal foods were of secondary importance. Cater-pillars, fish, lizards, and small rodents, were eaten whenever available. Jack rabbits were to be found within a few miles of the various streams in the valley; in the fall, people from all over the valley assembled for rabbit drives, directed by the valley chief or his deputy, or by some experienced hunter. Deer and mountain sheep were taken in the White Mountains, usually by small parties of skilled men; large game, even when taken by a lone hunter, was divided among all the members of the encampment, the hunter keeping only the hind quarter for himself and his family. Antelope occurred chiefly in the plains at the foot of the Silver Peak range, where they were the object of communal hunts.

Compared with the Gosiute, the Northern Paiute of Fish Lake Valley show advances in three particular respects. Due to the poverty of their environment the Gosiute, as we have seen, had to range great distances, often as much as 30 or 40 miles, in search of vegetable foods. As a consequence of this *ecological* fact, even their winter encampments lacked stability; families who lived cheek by jowl one winter might find themselves camped in different mountain ranges the next. And as a consequence of this *social* fact, all Gosiute social groupings larger than the family—or, at the widest, a group of two or three closely related families—lacked cohesion; families who intended wintering around a particular valley came together, in November, to take part in the fall festival and its con-comitant rabbit drives, but not all the families who co-operated in one year would necessarily be there the next. In each of these respects, the Fish Lake Valley people differed. The valley itself, and the mountain ranges which bordered it, afforded all essential food supplies within carrying distance of the winter encampments; these encampments, in consequence, were more or less permanent settlements, occupied all the year round, and though the families who lived in them might still go off on trek for a few days, or even for a few weeks, at a time, they always returned to them bringing with them the seeds or pine-nuts which they had gathered on their expedition.

This stability of settlement was reflected, in turn, in the cohesiveness of their larger social groupings. As with the Gosiute, the principal social gathering was the fall festival, commonly held at Sohodühatü near the southern end of the valley, and directed by the valley chief.[1] Some weeks beforehand, the valley

[1] Who was also, sometimes at least, chief of Deep Springs Valley to the southwest: Steward (1938), p. 61.

chief sent messages to the various settlements to announce when, and where, it was to be held; then, after the pine-nut harvest and before returning to their winter encampments, the people assembled for the festival, *nüga süwüduwa'du* (dance gathering), and for the rabbit drives which accompanied it. Both, commonly, lasted for six days, the people driving rabbits during the day, and feasting and dancing at night; each morning the hunters went out to a different part of the valley, but returned in the evening to the settlement where the festival was being held. Since the *same* families came together each fall for the festival, and co-operated in the rabbit drives, this gave them a cohesiveness that was lacking to the analogous group among the Gosiute. Among both, however, chiefship remained a nebulous affair, limited (in the main) to the direction of the fall festival and of the rabbit drives which accompanied it.

### NORTHERN PAIUTE OF OWENS VALLEY

Owens Valley is a deep trough,[1] more than 100 miles long and some 15 to 20 miles wide. On the west it is dominated by the Sierra Nevada range, with crests rising to over 12,000 feet; heavy snowfall on these summits is preserved in lakes, snowfields, and even glaciers, from which streams flow out into the otherwise arid valley and finally seep into swamps in the lowlands, whence they are drained off by Owens River. On the damp lands of the valley floor, various plants bearing edible roots and tubers grow in abundance, while the foothills carry a rich cover of seed-bearing grasses. Owens River itself carries fish, and the flats beyond it, antelope and jack rabbit, while the arid Inyo and White Mountains to the east support extensive tracts of piñon.

The comparative fertility of the region they inhabited profoundly affected the territorial and social organisation of the Owens Valley Paiute. Their encampments were clustered along the streams emerging from the Sierra Nevada range (see Fig. 58), which afforded an excellent source of fresh water. Since all essential food resources were to be found within a day's walk—12 to 15 miles—of these sites, the families occupying any one such cluster tended to form permanent associations or villages, exploiting their own, defined territory. Each village had its name, taken from some prominent feature in the locality, the northern section of the valley (i.e. from Panatü to a few miles north of Bishop's Creek) being divided into four districts of this kind:

*Pitanapatü*, 'south place', the area to the south of the big bend in Owens River, on either side of Bishop's Creek: 18 camps.

*Utütü' üwitü*, 'hot place' (from the warm springs located there), extending down the valley to 3 miles north of Big Pine Creek: 6 camps.

*Tu'va-wohamatü*, 'natural mound place', embracing the land on either side of Big Pine Creek: 12 camps.

---

[1] For a brief account of the Owens Valley Paiute, see Steward (1938), pp. 50–7, and for a detailed account, Steward (1933), pp. 235–335. The latter, upon which I draw heavily in the following account, represents Steward's major contribution to Great Basin ethnography.

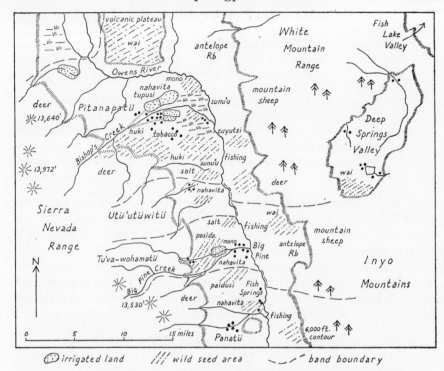

(⊙) irrigated land     /// wild seed area     ‿⌣‿ band boundary

Fig. 58. Owens Valley, northern section. Redrawn from Stewart (1933), map 2, and
(1938), Fig. 7.

*Panatü*, the area to the south of Big Pine Creek, including Fish Springs: 6
camps.

Each territory was roughly a long, narrow rectangle, stretching across Owens
Valley from the upper slopes of the Sierra Nevada range in the west, to the
upper slopes of the White and Inyo Mountains in the east. Since each territory
embraced the various life zones, all the local varieties of essential foods were
to be found within it.

The three principal plant zones were: the damp lands of the valley floor,
irrigated in a number of places by means of the streams emerging from the
Sierra Nevada range; the foothills on either side of the valley, including the
volcanic plateau to the north of the big bend in Owens River; and the mountain
slopes, up as far as the timber-line (*c.* 11,000 feet). Each of these zones furnished
essential foods.[1] The damp lands of the valley floor were the principal source
of roots and tubers, of rushes, and of some seed-bearing grasses:

---

[1] For plant foods, see Steward (1933), pp. 242–6. Steward's account of the ecology of the
Northern Paiute of Owens Valley may be compared with that given by Kelly (1932,
pp. 75–104) of the ecology of the Northern Paiute of Surprise Valley, 300 miles to the
north-north-west.

*tupu'si*, probably *Brodiaea capitata*. This plant yielded a kind of ground nut, which formed a major item in O.V. Paiute diet. It requires damp ground, and was grown, with *na'havita*, on the irrigated land at Pitanapatü. Harvested in the fall, the plants being dug with a digging stick of mountain mahogany; the greater part of the crop was dried and stored, being subsequently roasted and ground into flour.

*na'havita*, a species of *Eleocharis*, spike rush, bearing a number of bulbs. Grown, with *tupu'si*, on irrigated land at Pitanapatü, and also at Tu'va-wohamatü. Harvested, and prepared, in the same way as *tupu'si*: the two crops formed the principal root crops used by O.V. Paiute.

*paidusi*, wild onion: harvested from wet places in the spring, and eaten green with salt.

Salt, *öña'vi*, was scraped up with the hand from certain alkali flats, e.g. north of Big Pine Creek, where a characteristic species of brush, *tona'vi*, grew; it was mixed with water in a basket, and the paste moulded into flat cakes about 8 inches in diameter, for storage and trade (Steward, 1933, p. 250).

Two kinds of rush, *Phragmites communis* and *Juncus balticus*, both fairly common in the immediate vicinity of Owens River, were used as a source of sugar;[1] in both cases the sugar, formed on the leaves of the plant, was shaken into baskets, moulded into balls, then warmed and eaten.

Among seed-bearing grasses growing on moist ground were the following:

*mono*, *Eragrostis secundiflora*, love grass. Very important: grows on moist ground near Owens River, and on irrigated land, e.g. at Tu'va-wohamatü.

*pau'poniva*, unidentified seed plant. Very important: grows below the irrigated land at Bishop's Creek, and over a wide area to the south of this.

*sunu'u*, a species of *Agropyron*, wheat grass. Common near Owens River, especially on the swampy ground to the south of Bishop's Creek.

*wai'ya*, *Elymus condensatus*, giant rye grass. Very important: grows below the irrigated land around the mouth of Bishop's Creek. Muir, who watched the harvesting of the crop in 1870, said that the grain grew about 6 feet high, bearing heads from 6 to 12 inches long, with seeds about ⅜ inch long; the Indian women were 'gathering it in baskets, bending down large handfuls, beating it out, and fanning it in the wind'.

*pa'kii*, sunflower, was widely distributed over damp ground, and irrigated in some localities. It was harvested in August, the flowers being dried in the sun, then threshed and winnowed. Another plant harvested in similar manner was *ku'ha*, (unidentified) bearing a large yellow flower.

The foothills bordering the valley were the source of a further group of seed-bearing grasses, of certain 'greens', of sage and tobacco, and of various species of cactus:

---

[1] *Phragmites communis* is the reed, *pa'kab*, of the Hopi clan name (Whiting, 1939, p. 66); Professor Eggan tells me (1968) that Hopi children still chew the stem of this reed, or rush, for its sweetness.

*hu'ki*, *Stipa speciosa*, porcupine grass. Grows on the foothills, near where Bishop's Creek emerges from the mountains; harvested in late spring, the seeds being much favoured for making into a gruel.

*pasi'da*, probably *Salvia columbaria*. Occurs on sunny slopes in the vicinity of Bishop's Creek. The whole plant was gathered when dry, and the seeds threshed out: used for gruels and mushes.

*wai*: two species were *Oryzopsis hymenoides*, sand bunch grass, and *Oryzopsis miliacea*, rice grass. Widely distributed over foothills, and on the volcanic tableland at the north end of the valley. Very important as a food source: harvested in early summer, the seeds being beaten from the plant, then roasted and ground into flour.

*cuyutsi*, a species of *Parosela*, pea family, perhaps iron root: grows on foothills south of Bishop's Creek.

*posi'da*, *Trifolium tridentatum*, tomcat clover. Grows on foothills, e.g. north of Big Pine Creek; entire plant used, without cooking, as 'greens' in the spring.

*sawa'va*, *Artemisia tridentata*, common sage. The seeds were collected, roasted and ground into flour, generally mixed with other seeds, in times of food shortage.

*pa'müpi*, *Nicotiana attenuata*, tobacco. None was actually planted in Owens Valley, but semi-cultivation occurred at a number of places, e.g. along the foothills south of Bishop's Creek. Land was burned off in the spring, the ground cleared, and partly grown plants were pruned to increase leaf size; men cleared the ground, women did the remainder of the work (Steward, 1933, p. 319). The leaves were gathered in late summer, dried, ground, moistened, and made into balls 5 or 6 inches in diameter for keeping.

The mountain slopes were the principal source of berries, of certain plants used for making 'tea', and of pine nuts. The two principal berries collected were elderberry, *Sambucus mexicana*, gathered in the Sierra Nevada range, and golden currant, *Ribes aureum*; the berries were either eaten fresh, or boiled in water, or spread on rocks to dry in the sun, then stored in buck-skin bags for winter use. A mint tea was made by boiling the leaves of the tule mint, *Mentha arvensis*, in water; and 'mountain tea' by boiling the needles of *Ephedra viridis*, Mormon tea, found in moist places on mountain sides.

Pine-nut areas lay principally in the Inyo and White Mountains, to the east of Owens Valley. Each village owned its own pine-nut territory; within this territory the area was sub-divided into family plots, each bounded by natural landmarks. The plots were owned by men and inherited by their sons; a woman picked on her husband's plot.[1] The trip for pine nuts was made in the fall; the

---

[1] Steward (1933), p. 241: this was also the case among the Southern Paiute (Ash Meadows), cf. Steward (1938), p. 183. At George's Creek, however, farther south in Owens Valley, pine-nut tracts *were owned by women* and inherited matrilineally. This is in line with an analogous difference in the ownership of irrigated land (Steward, 1938, pp. 52–4): in the northern part of Owens Valley, the irrigated land belonged to all the families in the village, and each family gathered where it liked on irrigated land; in the southern part, each woman owned a sub-division of the irrigated land. Throughout Owens Valley, *wild-seed areas* belonged to the village in the territory of which they lay; but in some cases particular wild-seed areas appear to have belonged to particular families, as was the case with pine-nut tracts—and with irrigated plots in the south.

village headman, having noted the ripening of the nuts, announced the trip a few days in advance. On arriving in the mountains, each family went to its own plot. The greater part of the gathering was done by women, using long sticks— up to 12 feet long—to beat the cones from the trees. When the harvest was complete, a part of the nuts gathered were carried down to the village straight-away; the rest were cached, and brought down later. If the harvest were very abundant, people sometimes remained in the mountains for a part of the winter.

Pine nuts were the major food of the O.V. Paiute, as of other Shoshoni groups; so we need to know what kind of quantity a family might expect to gather in any one season.[1] It is clear, first, that the crop itself varied greatly from year to year; this, in turn, affected the quantity of nuts that could be gathered. Estimates vary from 7 or 8 lbs. of nuts per person per day (Dutcher's estimate), up to 30 or 40 lbs. a day. Four persons, quoted by Steward (1938, p. 27), once picked 300 lbs. in a week, a rate of 10 to 12 lbs. per person per day; at this rate, a single gatherer would pick one bushel (56 lbs.) in four to five days, or about six bushels in the four weeks or so that gathering lasted. In fact, this latter figure probably represents a mean: i.e. in a good year an active picker might pick as much as ten or twelve bushels of nuts, and in a poor year as little as one or two bushels. Steward reckons, further, that a family of five or six might eat about a bushel of nuts a week, if this were its staple fare; so that a harvest of, say, eighteen bushels (three gatherers) would barely last through the four winter months (late November to the end of March)—'consequently', as he remarks (1938, p. 27), 'it is not difficult to see why starvation by early spring was very common'. Perhaps here, however, Steward is referring more to the western Shoshoni than to the O.V. Paiute; for the latter, when the pine nuts failed, were able to fall back on *wai'ya* (giant rye grass), *mo'no* (love grass), *tupus'i* ('ground nut'), *na'havita* (bulbs of the spike rush), and other seeds and roots gathered during the summer.[2]

Regarding the actual gathering and preparation of seeds and roots (Steward, 1933, pp. 239–42): women, often working in groups, gathered seeds by beating them from the plants, with seed beaters, into conical baskets. The heads of some plants, e.g. sunflowers, were picked, carried home, threshed and winnowed. Tubers and roots were dug with sharp, pointed digging-sticks of mountain mahogany, or robbed from rodent stores.[3] Both seeds and roots were stored in grass-lined pits, for winter use. For cooking, seeds were first roasted, then ground on a metate, *mat^a*, a slab of rock about 12 inches by 18 inches and 2 to 5 inches thick, with another, oval-shaped stone, into a fine flour; this was either

---

[1] Steward's early estimate (1933, p. 241) of 30 to 40 bushels per person seems much too high in the light of his own later, more conservative, discussion (1938, pp. 27–8). The estimates I have reached are based on Steward's later figures, taken in conjunction with Dutcher's observations (1893, pp. 379–80); Dutcher observed a party of women gathering pine-nuts in the mountains above Death Valley, in the fall of 1891.

[2] Steward (1934), pp. 432–3.

[3] Gophers were regarded as women, because they gathered *tüpüs'i* nuts and other seeds: Steward (1936a), p. 389, n. 57.

baked into scones, or mixed with water and boiled into a mush or gruel. For the latter, several different kinds of seeds were generally used, pine-nut being the base; meat was often added, to make a stew. The whole was cooked in a clay pot and stirred with a looped stick; for eating, people sat round in a circle and dipped their middle and index fingers into the bowl, and sucked.

Turning now to meat (Steward, 1933, pp. 255–6): grasshoppers and crickets were almost certainly eaten in the past, also the larvae of ants, wasps, bees, and other insects; *piüga*, the fleshy caterpillar of *Coloradia pandora* occurring on *Pinus jeffreyi*, was collected in July when about to pupate, roasted, spread out in the sun to dry, then stored for winter use. Lizards were eaten, and snakes sometimes. Some fishing was done in Owens River, but fish was relatively unimportant in O.V. Paiute dietary (Steward, 1938, p. 54). Quail, caught in noose traps, were broiled on coals; waterfowl, taken in the early morning by hunters concealed in blinds (Steward, 1933, p. 255), included geese, spoonbill, mallard, pintail, teal and other ducks generically called *pü'yü*; sage hens (*ka'hu*), grouse (*hü'ja*), and bluejays (*tcai*), were also eaten. Small burrowing rodents were dug out of their holes; others such as ground squirrels were taken in baited, dead-fall traps, i.e. tilted rocks, supported by sticks, which dropped when the bait underneath was gnawed. Mice (*puña'ji*), gophers (*mü'iyu*), ground squirrels (*a'ñwa*), wood rats (*ka'wa*), chipmunks (*tava'y$^a$*), porcupines (*mü'ha*), and badgers (*hu'na*), were all eaten, being roasted buried in hot ashes. Cottontail rabbits (*ta'vots*) were taken in snares attached to birch rods, set across their runs. Jack rabbits (*ka'mu*) were the object of communal drives, undertaken chiefly in the fall, under the direction of the village headman, in connection with the fall festival; the drives took place on the valley floor to the east of the river, the rabbits being driven out of the scrub, which was sometimes set alight, into a line of nets where they were killed with sticks and stones. Antelope, likewise found on the valley floor to the east of the river, were also the object of communal hunts. Deer and mountain sheep were usually hunted by small parties of experienced men in the Sierra Nevada mountains, sometimes with the help of dogs; occasionally, heavy snows drove the animals down from the high mountains into the pine-nut belt. As with jack rabbits, the meat of larger game was cut into strips, dried, smoked, and left hanging for winter use.

While the general ecology of Owens Valley resembles that of the western Shoshoni area, its comparative fertility, as I remarked earlier, profoundly affected the territorial and social organisation of the people who lived there. We are now in a position to see wherein this difference lay. The presence of perennial streams, emerging at intervals of 2 to 15 miles from the Sierra Nevada mountains, afforded both a supply of fresh water to support a cluster of camps, and food resources of sufficient abundance and reliability for the families who resided in each cluster to be sure of finding enough to eat within a day's journey[1] of their home-base. The availability of fresh water led to the establishment of permanent villages at the more favoured sites, while the habitual use by the same group of families, of the resources that lay within walking distance of their encampment, led to the concept that each such village had exclusive rights

---

[1] The farthest they had to go was to the pine-nut tracts in the Inyo and White Mountains: perhaps an eight-hour journey—about twelve miles across the river, and a climb of 2,000 to 3,000 feet.

(Steward, 1955, p. 108) to the seed, root and pine-nut tracts within its territory. The independence of each group, *vis-à-vis* other groups of the same kind, was expressed in a common name (e.g. *pitanapatü*), in the ownership of its own village site and of the seed and root tracts, including irrigated areas, that lay within its territory,[1] and in the co-operation of its members in the upkeep of the irrigated areas, in pine-nut gathering and in communal hunts. It was further expressed, as we have now to see, in a common chiefship, in the holding of its own fall festival and mourning ceremony, and in the possession of a communal sweat house.

Districts, e.g. *pitanapatü*, were political units, each with a head man to direct such communal activities as its constituent families engaged in. Head men were called *pogina'vi*. Formerly, head men were, in Steward's words (1933, p. 304), 'intelligent, persuasive leaders, though not always skilled hunters, who organised and perhaps led pine-nut trips, rabbit drives, communal hunting and fishing, war parties, and fall dances and festivals'. At *pitanapatü*, the headman chose the irrigator, subject to popular approval; he was also responsible for the erection and upkeep of the communal sweat house. There is some conflict in the evidence (Steward, 1933, p. 305: 1938, p. 56), regarding the part played by the headman in settling disputes between members of his own district. It seems likely that serious disputes, e.g. disputes involving homicide or wife stealing, could only be settled by the disputants themselves and their kin. Less serious disputes, e.g. conflicts over pine-nut tracts, were usually adjudicated by the headman; the latter conflicts were brief, and never involved weapons more serious than slings, which did little damage;[2] also, fear of witchcraft appears to have aided pacific settlement (Steward, 1933, p. 305).

Six-day festivals, involving dances, gambling and rabbit drives, were held by each independent village in the fall, following the pine-nut harvest. These were planned in advance and directed by the headman. Neighbouring districts arranged their festivals in series, so that people from one village could attend the festival in another after completing their own. In the fall, also, each district celebrated its own annual mourning ceremony, the primary purpose of which was to terminate the period of mourning during which relatives of a deceased person were required to abstain from meat and fat, to refrain from washing, and to avoid any festivities. This ceremony requires a brief excursus on Northern Paiute mortuary customs.[3] At death, the body was wrapped in an animal-skin blanket and taken to the burial ground, the relatives sprinkling pine nuts and seeds on the ground for the ghost. In the evening friends and relatives carried

---

[1] The title to the territory, and to the food resources contained within it, lay in *all* the people of the district: Steward (1933), p. 305.

[2] Cf. the quarrels between Sarakatsan shepherds, in northern Greece, over grazing for their sheep and goats: as Campbell points out (1964, pp. 97, 264), the shepherds were careful only to fight with weapons, e.g. shepherds' crooks, which, while capable of causing ugly wounds, rarely killed.

[3] On burial rites, see, in particular, Steward (1933), pp. 296–9: and on the annual mourning ceremony, Steward (1938), p. 55.

some of the dead man's property, e.g. bow and arrow, and other things of daily use, to burn at the grave, and scattered more seeds; at midnight the property was burned, and the deceased's most cherished articles—beads, clothing, etc.— buried with him; sometimes, also, the house in which he had lived was burned. Mourning, which lasted until the following fall, entailed the avoidance of meat and fat,[1] remaining at home and not seeing many people, and not bathing; the face was streaked with tears and dirt, to show that a person was in mourning. Mourning was terminated at the annual mourning ceremony, in the course of which the relatives of those who had died during the preceding year were ceremonially washed, and were exhorted to forget the dead and to start on a new life; in this way their grief was symbolically washed away, and at the same time all the dead of the past year were commemorated by burning certain articles which had been saved from their funerals.[2] The ceremony concluded with a feast at which those who had been in mourning ate meat for the first time. Each ceremony of this kind was led by the headman of the district, and was attended by visitors from neighbouring villages.

Finally, each independent village in Owens Valley had its own sweat house,[3] *mu:sa*. The headman directed its construction, and it was owned in common by all the families resident there. In practice, the sweat house was used by men alone, and served several purposes. It was, in the first place, the *men's house*, a place for sleeping in for old men and for young men not yet married; here the men of the village gathered in the evenings, particularly in winter, to smoke, sing, play games, relate myths,[4] and discuss communal affairs. But the sweat house also had a religious function. About once a month, in winter, it was used for sweating; at these sessions, which usually took place after hunting or other strenuous work, the men of the village gathered in the sweat house, praying individually while they sweated, then plunged into a pool of ice-cold water always located nearby. To what extent smoking also had a religious function, is not clear. Only men smoked, women never, and they smoked sparingly, generally in the sweat house, in the evenings; there was no set ritual, however, the pipe being passed from one man to another in any convenient manner (Steward, 1933, pp. 319–20). But the fact that it was chiefly older men who smoked, that 'doctors', i.e. shamans, smoked while curing, and that others 'blew out smoke to blow away disease', suggests that smoking, among the Shoshonean-speaking peoples of the Great Basin as among the Hopi, had to do

---

[1] Meat was also *tabu* to a woman during her menstrual periods (Steward, 1936a, p. 386, n. 50); and both meat and fat, for a month after child-birth (Steward, 1933, p. 290).

[2] Cf. among the Hopi, the making of prayer-sticks and *nakwa'kwosi*(s) for the recently dead, at the Soya'l: see above, pp. 119–21.

[3] On the construction and uses of the communal sweat house among the O.V. Paiute, see Steward (1933), pp. 265–6, and (1938), pp. 54–5; for a drawing of the communal sweat house at Big Pine Creek, see Steward (1933), Fig. 4.

[4] Myths could not be related in the summer; in the fall, 'after the snakes had disappeared', was the proper time to tell them (Steward, 1936a, p. 357, n. 3). Songs, dances, myths, and games were, in the main, communally owned (Steward, 1933, p. 305); their repetition and re-enactment, in the sweat house, must have been a potent source of village solidarity.

with the 'thought' of the smoker, i.e. was a form of prayer—perhaps, specifically, a prayer for rain. Among the Owens Valley Paiute a lad smoked for the first time, and commenced to sleep at the sweat house (Steward, 1933, p. 294), after killing his first deer, usually at the age of 16 or 17.

The ownership and use of a communal sweat house is particularly significant, in Steward's view (1938, p. 55), as indicating the degree of stability and concentratedness attained by the settlements of the Owens Valley Paiute. The western Shoshoni were on the whole too scattered, and the individual families too unsettled during much of the year, to make the building of a communal sweat house worthwhile; instead, individual men constructed small sweat houses near their winter camps, for sweating alone. Among the Owens Valley Paiute, sweating was still a major function of the sweat house. But grafted on to this original function were the other communal uses we have enumerated, the sweat house serving in turn as dormitory, work centre, recital hall and village parliament.

### SOUTHERN PAIUTE OF ASH MEADOWS AND THE PAHRUMP VALLEY

Much of the territory occupied by the Southern Paiute resembles that of the western Shoshoni to the north: a succession, that is to say, of arid mountain ranges and sage-covered valleys. In the region of Ash Meadows and the Pahrump Valley, it becomes still more arid and takes on some of the features of the Mojave Desert which borders it to the southwest. But while certain of the plant species found there differ from those found in the western Shoshoni habitat, the basic ecology of the two groups was similar, with one exception: that all Southern Paiute groups appear to have practised some horticulture. Even this feature, however, did not alter their way of life in any very fundamental manner, serving rather as an adjunct to wild-seed gathering than as a substitute for it.

When Powell and Ingalls travelled through the Ash Meadows and Pahrump Valley region around 1870, the population appears to have been divided into four groups, as follows (Steward, 1938, pp. 181–2):

Ash Meadows: 31 (mixed Shoshoni and Southern Paiute)
Amargosa Desert area: 68 (mixed Shoshoni and Southern Paiute)
Indian Springs Valley, over towards Cane Spring: 18 (Southern Paiute)
Pahrump Valley: 56 (Southern Paiute).

This gives 173 persons, ranging over a total area of some 2,600 sq. miles: or, one person to roughly 16 sq. miles.

The Ash Meadows Southern Paiute, with whom this account is chiefly concerned,[1] lived in camps located beside streams in the foothills to the south

---

[1] And about whom, of the western group of Southern Paiute, we are most fully informed: see Steward (1938), pp. 180–5. On the southern Paiute of Kaibab Plateau, to the east, Sapir's lexical work (1930, 1931) forms a rich vein, little worked as yet: though Isabel Kelly in her descriptive account of their ethnography (1964, pp. 5–142), based on field work done in 1932, makes some use of it, as also of Sapir's manuscript notes.

of the Amargosa Desert (see Fig. 59); these camps were occupied on and off all the year round, but foraging expeditions in search of seeds and game took individual families up to 30 or 40 miles from home, often for several weeks at a time. The natural environment of the region is similar to, perhaps rather harsher than, that of Beatty and the Kawich Mountains to the north; its greatest asset is the Spring Mountains which, rising to a height of nearly 12,000 feet, afford abundant pine nuts and wild seeds, and some game. In the fall, families made their way there for the pine-nut harvest, either on their own or in small parties; the valley chief announced when the nuts were ripe, but had no

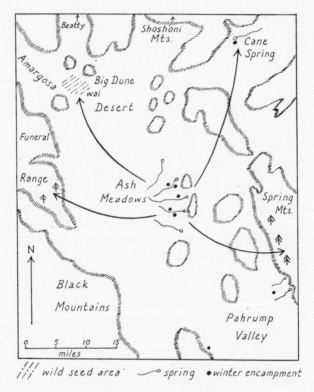

Fig. 59. Territory of the Ash Meadows Paiute.

authority in managing the trip or the gathering. Arrived in the mountains, each family picked on its own tract, until snow made further picking impossible. The gathering process was like that of the western Shoshoni. Women did the greater part of the work, pulling the cones from the trees by means of long poles, each having a fire-bent hook at the end; the cones were gathered into conical baskets, *a'hus*, and carried to a pile, where they were roasted to extract the nuts (cf. Dutcher, 1893, pp. 379–80). All the nuts extracted in this way, together with loose nuts gathered off the ground, were carried down to the winter encampment; other nuts were left in the cones and stored in the mountains, in grass- or brush-lined pits covered over with grass, brush and earth. Pine-nut tracts were owned by men, and inherited by their sons; women gathered on their husband's plot. Permission to gather on a tract was readily extended to families owning tracts in areas where the crop had failed; thus, Shoshoni from the Amargosa Desert area were often invited to pick on the Spring Mountains, and when the crop there failed, Ash Meadows Southern Paiute were invited to pick in the Shoshoni Mountains, to the north.

Mesquite, which ripens in August, was fairly abundant at Ash Meadows, where families owned groves; screw beans, also ripening in August, were a further important food source, both kinds of beans being gathered in considerable quantities and stored for winter use. Other wild-seed plants grew more sparsely over wide areas, and the tracts of these were not family-owned. Of these, the two most important were *ko'*, and *wai*. The former, a species of *Mentzelia* ripening in the spring, grows in the hills; Ash Meadows people gathered the seeds either in the Funeral Range to the west, or in the vicinity of Cane Spring some 40 miles to the northeast, both of which localities were also visited by western Shoshoni. *Wai*, sand bunch grass (*Oryzopsis hymenoides*), grows in the Amargosa Desert area, particularly at Big Dune some 30 miles to the northwest; it ripens in early summer, and as this grass is often found many miles from water, it was necessary for Ash Meadows people, when they went to gather the seeds, to carry water on the journey in a basketry olla.

Ash Meadows marked the northern limit of aboriginal horticulture (Steward, 1938, pp. 183–4). Crops grown were corn, squash, and sunflowers. Cultivation entailed planting plots of moist soil near streams, together with some use of irrigation;[1] according to Steward (p. 183), there was no question of inheritance of such plots, because the crop was destroyed, even if about to bear a harvest, at the death of the owner. Not all families owned plots; those without land exchanged wild-plant foods for cultivated crops. But neither cultivated nor wild vegetable foods were available in sufficient quantity to permit all-the-year-round settlement in the one place; after sowing the plots in the spring, families went off in search of wild seeds; in early summer, as the crop ripened, they returned to harvest and store it; then they set off again, in search of the roots and berries which tided them over until pine nuts were ready for picking late in October.

Hunting played a very minor rôle in Southern Paiute economy, due to the prevailing aridity and the consequent scarcity of game. Ash Meadows people usually went to the Spring Mountains for deer, but sometimes took them in the Shoshoni Mountains; because of the long distances involved, they butchered them on the spot, dried the meat and skins, and carried these home in nets.

---

[1] Probably by digging ditches to convey water to the plots, as was done to bring water to the irrigated land at Bishop's Creek, in Owen's Valley (Steward, 1930, pp. 149–56); the course of the ditches there is shown on the map (Fig. 58), the two ditches leaving the stream just below the *k* of *Bishop's Creek*.

Mountain sheep, formerly fairly numerous, were mostly taken in the Funeral range; like deer, they were hunted either by individuals or by small groups of skilled hunters. Antelope were few and far between, and communal antelope drives, which played so prominent a part in western Shoshoni communal enterprise, were evidently not practised. Jack rabbits were taken with traps or surrounded by fire, neither method involving more than a handful of men.

In the absence of communal antelope hunts or rabbit drives, the only important communal activity serving to unite the members of nearby camps was the annual fall festival, which commonly lasted three or four days and terminated with mourning rites. Each district, e.g. Ash Meadows, Pahrump Valley, held its own festival, under the direction of its own chief; indeed, the primary function of the chief was to arrange and direct the annual festival for his group of camps. He announced the festival some months in advance, and from time to time, in the course of the dances[1] and other rites, made speeches. On the last night buck-skins and other property, which had been accumulated for the purpose, were burned in the name of persons who had died within the year.

Regarding the political organisation of the Southern Paiute of Ash Meadows and the Pahrump Valley, Steward remarks (1938, p. 181) on the absence among them of 'well-defined, named political bands'. Certainly, when Powell and Ingalls visited the region a hundred years ago, they found the people to be roughly divided into groups, the several families of which wintered at favourable sites in fairly close proximity to one another, foraged the same general terrain in search of seeds and roots during the spring and summer, owned groves of screw beans and mesquite in the same valley, and gathered pine nuts in the same mountain range in the fall. But the only truly communal activity in which they all took part was the annual fall festival and the mourning rites which followed it, directed by the head man of the group on behalf of all its members. Apart from this, there was little cohesion between the several families that made up the group, beyond that furnished by kinship and marriage alliance.

### THE STRUCTURE OF SHOSHONEAN SOCIETY

This completes the ethnography of the four Shoshonean-speaking groups, i.e. the Gosiute, Northern Paiute of Fish Lake Valley, Northern Paiute of Owens Valley, and the Ash Meadows Southern Paiute, whose socio-political structure we have now to consider.[2] Mauss, it will be recalled, argued that social life, under all its forms, is a function of its 'material substrate' and that it varies with that substrate, 'that is to say, with the mass, the density, the form and the composition of the human groupings' of which it is made up. We have now to see

---

[1] One of these dances, according to Steward (1938, p. 184), was the circle dance, 'a borrowed form of the Ute bear dance'; if this is the case, then it must have changed its nature on the way, since the Ute bear dance was, essentially, a spring dance (see Steward, 1932).

[2] See, for the whole of this section, Steward (1938), pp. 230–62.

how far Mauss's rule applies to the Shoshonean-speaking peoples of the Great Basin, under the following rubric:

ecological data → human groupings → socio-political forms.
          (a)                              (b)

### (a) Effect of ecological data in shaping human groupings

Among the western Shoshoni (Steward, 1938, pp. 232–3), of whom we have taken the Gosiute as representative, *plant harvesting* was the main subsistence activity. For the greater part of the year, as we have seen, families necessarily travelled alone or in very small groups, gathering seeds, roots and berries over a wide area; they ordinarily ranged 20 miles or more in each direction from their winter encampment. Their itinerary, also, was not fixed; seasonal variations in rainfall, and consequently in crop growth, often required that they alter their routine from one year to the next. The most permanent association of families was at winter encampments. These were sites where certain families habitually remained during the months when vegetable foods could not be had and when, consequently, they depended on the stores laid up during the summer and fall; necessary conditions for such sites were accessibility to stored seeds, especially pine nuts, water, wood for house building and firewood, and absence of extremely low winter temperatures. These conditions were most often fulfilled either at springs within the piñon-juniper belt or, lower down, near streams emerging from the mountain flanks; encampments tended, therefore, to cluster with regard to the mountain ranges rather than valleys. But whether they were sited at springs in the mountains, scattered along the course of streams, or clustered in colonies, depended upon the quantity of foods which could be gathered and stored within convenient distance of each camp; in some places families had to camp alone, in more favoured localities several families were in the habit of spending the winter together in semi-permanent encampments. All such arrangements were dependent, however, on the annual seed harvest, particularly of pine nuts; for just as, in the spring and summer, people had often to modify their itinerary from year to year as local rainfall or other factors affected plant growth, so the erratic occurrence of the pine-nut crop required that a family, or group of families, might have to winter in different mountain ranges in successive years.

The small game, i.e. insects, lizards, burrowing rodents, and cottontail, with which the western Shoshoni supplemented their mainly vegetarian diet, hardly modified the régime imposed upon them by their search for plant foods. The individual family was necessarily the independent economic unit; from spring to fall it foraged the foothills and valley floor within range of its winter encampment, usually on its own, sometimes in company with one or two other families, its movements dictated by the successive occurrence of 'greens', seeds, roots, and berries. In each locality the members took such game, e.g. cottontail in the foothills, gophers and rats in the canyon walls, lizards on the valley floor, as the environment offered; only rarely, and then usually in the case of large hatches of insects such as crickets, grasshoppers, and locusts, did several families go out of their way to exploit a non-vegetarian food source. The only major exception to the economic independence of the single family was furnished by the communal deer, antelope, and jack-rabbit drives, which commonly took place in the fall when the pine-nut harvest had already brought together a number of families; their primary purpose, as we have seen, was to provide meat for winter, and skins for clothing and blankets. But even the rabbit drives which everywhere accompanied the fall festival rarely lasted for more than a week, and those taking part rarely numbered, at least among the western Shoshoni (Steward, 1938, p. 231), more than two dozen families. Moreover, since different species of game occurred in different localities, e.g. deer in the mountains, antelope and jack rabbit often in different parts of a valley, it was by no means always the *same* group of families who came together for communal hunts. Families, as Steward observes (1938, p. 233), travelled from their encampment, or from wherever they happened to be gathering seeds or pine nuts, to the most convenient location, and often co-operated with very different people in successive hunts:

> They might join families from across their valley for a rabbit drive, go to a neighbouring valley to hunt with its residents in an antelope drive, travel in another direction to a marsh to join in a waterfowl drive, and associate with immediate neighbours to hunt deer in their own mountains. If their own pine-nut crop failed the next year, they might be thrown into association with still other people for these hunts.

The techniques available to the western Shoshoni for exploiting the resources of their environment were, as we have seen, extremely simple; and this fact, taken in conjunction with the variability from one year to another in the resources themselves, was reflected in many aspects of their life, particularly in their property concepts (Steward, 1938, pp. 253–4). Objects belonged to persons who expended work on them and used them. All natural resources, with the sole exception of eagle nests, were free to anyone. This was not communal ownership; as Steward remarks, it was not ownership *at all*, because no group whatever claimed natural resources. Water, seed-gathering and hunting areas, salt deposits, were freely utilised by anyone. But once work had been done on the products of natural resources, they became the property of the person or family doing the work. Willow groves could be used by anyone, but baskets made of willow belonged to their makers. Wild seeds could be gathered by anyone, but once harvested, they belonged strictly to the family doing the task, though they might be shared with other families; when wild seeds were sown, as sometimes by the Gosiute, the crop belonged to whoever sowed the seeds (1938, p. 253). Women owned their baskets and other objects (e.g. stones for grinding seeds) used by them, while men owned hunting equipment, especially rabbit nets, and other things peculiar to their sex. The family as a whole appears, among the western Shoshoni, to have owned the house itself. The principal exception to the rule that property was owned within the household, was large game. A hunter who killed e.g. a deer, was entitled to keep the skin and one of the hind quarters for his own family, but was obliged to share the remainder with the other families in the encampment; rabbits killed in rabbit drives belonged to the man in whose net they were caught.

Apart from eagle nests, the western Shoshoni lacked any form of ownership of land or resources on it. No group habitually and exclusively utilised any clearly defined territory for hunting, fishing, or seed gathering. This fact Steward ascribes (1938, p. 254) to their ecology. The people were primarily gatherers of seeds, including pine nuts. The sparse and erratic occurrence of vegetable foods required that territories exploited by different groups of families not only should vary from year to year, but should often overlap. There was no competition for vegetable foods, because good crops, especially of seeds, ripened and fell to the ground so quickly that people could not possibly gather all of them. When the crop in one locality failed, people went elsewhere; if crops were poor everywhere, everyone went hungry. And this applied as much to piñon areas as to wild-seed tracts; for when a particular tract yielded well, it afforded more nuts than could possibly be harvested. Families consequently travelled to the locality of a good supply, were welcomed by the local residents, and often cached their nuts and remained there for the winter; the following year might find the same groups encamped in quite different mountain ranges.

Under such conditions, ownership of vegetable foods resources would, as Steward points out (1938, p. 254), have been a disadvantage to everyone. Had hunting been the main subsistence activity, this might not have been the case. In the western Shoshoni area, however, seed gathering rather than hunting determined the economic routine; men accompanied their families to seed tracts, and hunted where they had an opportunity. Consequently hunting areas, like seed areas, overlapped and could not advantageously have been owned.

In contrast to the western Shoshoni, may be set the Northern Paiute of the northern section of Owens Valley. In Owens Valley, as we have seen, the population was comparatively dense, stable, and settled in more or less permanent villages sited along the streams emerging from the Sierra Nevada mountains. The country was fertile, and all essential foods and materials, i.e. seeds, roots and tubers, piñon nuts, game, salt, firewood, were to be found within a range of 10 to 15 miles of each village. Consequently, instead of travelling during much of the spring and summer in search of seeds and roots and often (due to the vagaries of the pine-nut crop) having to spend the fall and winter in distant ranges, the Owens Valley Paiute were able to harvest the main foods offered by the environment by keeping within a day's walk of their home-village. Further, the presence of perennial streams, and the consequent use of patches of irrigated land, ensured comparatively reliable seed- and tuber-crops within the valley; the harvest from these patches was shared out between the families living in that district and served as a store which offset, to some extent, the erratic yield of wild seeds and, particularly, of pine nuts. Game, also, was to be found in relative abundance, antelope and jack rabbit on the valley floor, deer and mountain sheep in the mountains flanking the valley, enabling the same group of families readily to co-operate each year in communal hunts and rabbit drives.

All these factors, i.e. the comparative density of the population, the presence of streams and the availability of wild seeds and game within a limited range of them, the use of irrigated patches on the valley floor and of pine-nut tracts on the mountain sides, contributed, in Steward's view (1938, pp. 233–4, 255–6), to the emergence among the Owens Valley Paiute of clearly defined territories, with band ownership of the seed and game resources found within each territory. Specifically, these resources comprised: wild-seed tracts on the valley floor and on the adjoining foothills, irrigated plots on the alluvial fans of streams, fishing rights in Owens River, salt pans near the river, piñon tracts on the mountain slopes, and hunting territory. And just as the availability of these resources within a certain range of the village sites conduced to the linking of a number of families into corporate bands, so habitual co-operation in exploiting the resources of their territory contributed to the cohesion of the families within each band.

Within the framework of communal band ownership of resources in Owens Valley, there was some ownership, particularly of pine-nut tracts, by individual families; certain families, at least, habitually picked from the same areas, which they regarded as their own and defended against trespassers. In the northern section of the valley, these tracts were owned by men, and handed down to their sons; in the south, at least around George's Creek, they were owned by women and handed down matrilineally, as were, also, rights to plots of irrigated land.

The Fish Lake Valley people fall, ecologically, somewhere between the western Shoshoni and the Owens Valley Paiute. As with the latter, all essential food resources were to be found either within the valley or on the mountains flanking it. But the habitat was far less fertile than Owens Valley; consequently, the population was sparser, and individual families had to forage far more widely in search of seeds and roots. In the sense, however, that individual families always returned to the same winter encampments, and that the same families habitually co-operated in pine-nut gathering, rabbit drives and communal hunts, the inhabitants of the valley may be regarded as forming a single corporate band: with this difference, that whereas, in Owens Valley, the encampment of each such band formed a single cluster and its total territory ran to not more than *c.* 150 sq. miles, in Fish Lake Valley the camps were dotted about the valley at a number of localities, and the total area exploited ran to about 800 sq. miles.

The Southern Paiute of Ash Meadows and the Pahrump Valley resembled the western Shoshoni in the harshness of their environment, and in the consequent absence among them of band ownership of wild-seed and hunting territories. As with the Gosiute, individual families often had to travel 40 miles or more from their home base, in search of seeds and sometimes, also, of pine nuts, and over much of this area they interleaved with western Shoshoni from the north. But they differed from the western Shoshoni in practising some horticulture, i.e. of corn, squash, and sunflowers; and while this was not sufficient to modify their relationship to the environment in any radical way, it had two principal effects on their subsistence pattern. In the first place, the growing of crops, like the use of irrigated plots by the Owens Valley Paiute, reduced to some extent their dependence on wild seeds, while the need of individual families to return to harvest, and store for winter use, the crops they had planted, increased the stability of their home camps. In the second place, the practise of horticulture may have introduced (Steward, 1938, pp. 234-5, 256) the concept of land ownership. Among the Ash Meadows Southern Paiute, particular families were said to have owned the land they cultivated,[1] as well as groves of mesquite and screw beans, and pine-nut tracts; and it may well be, as Steward argues (p. 235), that 'ownership of pine-nut, mesquite, and screw-bean groves was an extension of the concept applied first to cultivated lands and was made more practicable by the comparatively fixed subsistence routine'.

## (b) Relation between human groupings and socio-political forms

Four elements in Shoshonean life contributed to social cohesion in large groups.[2] These were: kinship, marriage alliance, economic co-operation between families exploiting the same terrain (e.g. communal pine-nut gathering, rabbit drives, antelope and deer hunts), and social co-operation, e.g. communal festival and mourning ceremonies, use of a common sweat house.

Taking kinship and marriage alliance first:[3] among the western Shoshoni, as we have seen, the household was the independent economic unit during the greater part of the year; it foraged either on its own, or in company with one or two other families, and the household head was its leader. Nevertheless, though the exigencies of the food quest often forced related families apart, they sought one another's proximity, and especially wintered together, wherever possible. Very small encampments frequently consisted exclusively of related families, and larger encampments usually had many that were related. Several marriage practices contributed to this condition—post-marital residence was usually either matrilocal or patrilocal, rarely independent; if there were unrelated families in an encampment, their children often married one another

---

[1] This appears to contradict the statement (above, p. 374) that the plots were not inherited. In fact, the Ash Meadows Paiute practice seems to represent a very fine point where the plots were owned but not inherited; presumably, on the death of the owner, they became common land again.

[2] Four, that is, before the introduction of horses. The introduction of horses enabled certain of the Shoshonean-speaking peoples, particularly the northern Shoshoni, Utes, and perhaps also some of the Southern Paiute, to group themselves into large, war-making bands; but this was a late, and eccentric, development. It also enabled the Comanche to break out of the Great Basin altogether, into the Plains.

[3] See Steward (1938), pp. 237-9, 244-6.

and remained there; when brothers and sisters married sisters and brothers, they tended to re-assemble at the same winter site. This high degree of relationship between the families in an encampment enhanced its solidarity, even when common economic and social activities failed to do so. A practical aspect of this solidarity was the willingness to share food with relatives; and whenever it was economically possible, related families travelled together in the food quest. They also tended to participate in the same communal activities. The headman, therefore, especially of the smaller encampments, was usually the most vigorous and competent member of the related families which made up the majority of its population. The importance of kinship in village control decreased, however, in proportion to the size of the encampment; in larger encampments, made up of several kin groups nearly equal in size, no single one of these groups was able to dominate the village.

To a very large extent, at least among the western Shoshoni, a group of related families constituted the socio-political unit. Part cause and part consequence of this, was the tendency to ally families through multiple marriages. Several preferred usages permitted multiple inter-family unions; it was preferred that brothers from one family should marry sisters from another, or that a brother and a sister from one family should marry a sister and a brother of another, a practice reflected in kinship terms and which also appears in several genealogies (Steward, 1938, p. 245). The levirate and sororate were widespread, and cross-cousin marriage was also practised in some localities. Multiple interfamily marriages of the latter kind were, in Steward's words (p. 245), 'a simple device for strengthening, and the sororate and levirate for continuing, an alliance between two families'; though there is no obvious reason, as he goes on to remark, why cross-cousin marriage should have been developed in some localities but not in others.

Nevertheless, practices of the kind outlined above for allying kin groups were often nullified, in the event, by harsh economic necessity. Despite the preference for multiple inter-family unions, the frequency of separation often undid what these marriages had accomplished, and allied kin groups were forced by food shortage in the different regions to live widely apart and beyond effective contact with each other. It was this element of economic uncertainty, and consequent population fluidity, that prevented, in Steward's view (1938, p. 246), the crystallisation of a fixed set of duties and obligations between affines.

Turning now to the means of integrating larger groups:[1] political organisation and control, as Steward observes (1938, p. 246), are commensurate with the activities requiring co-operation and management; they must be understood in terms of specific activities. Throughout the Basin-Plateau area, the people of different localities exhibited a wide variation in political organisation, ranging from (among the western Shoshoni) the small group of related families wintering together in the mountains under the direction of the senior man of the

[1] See Steward (1938), pp. 246-53.

group, to the corporate bands of the Owens Valley Paiute, living in permanent villages and made up of several unrelated kin groups under the lead of a recognised headman. Throughout the region, however, the latter's authority was restricted to certain definite activities, principally either of an economic nature, e.g. arranging pine-nut gathering, communal rabbit drives, etc., or socio-religious in character, e.g. organising the fall festival and the mourning rites which in some places accompanied it; consequently, just as the position of chief was a function of the kind of co-operating groups to be found in different localities, so his authority was a function of the kind of activities in which those groups habitually co-operated. Basin-Plateau political groups as such, and consequently their chiefs, had virtually no interest in disputes between individuals; these were settled by relatives, usually close kin, of the parties involved.

Among all western Shoshoni, from the Snake River in the north to the Panamint Valley in the south, and also among the Southern Paiute at least of the Death Valley and Ash Meadows region, the largest permanent organisation was the winter encampment, which, in those places where it reached a certain size and stability, may be termed a village. There were no defined groups larger than the village. Names were sometimes applied to the inhabitants of wider areas, e.g. '*Mentzelia* seed-eaters' to the inhabitants of the Reese River area, *wai-diika* ('*wai*-eaters') to those of the next valley to the west; but the boundaries of such areas were never clearly defined, and the people so designated had no organisation as a group (Steward, 1938, pp. 247–8).

Each encampment, or village, was named after some salient feature of its locality; as proximity to water was essential to its siting, it was often named after a nearby spring or creek. Some encampments, as we have seen, comprised a small number of related families, who, after ranging widely in search of seeds and tubers during the spring and summer, came together again in the fall for the pine-nut harvest and spent the winter together in the vicinity of their cached stores; since such groups were liable to vary in composition from year to year, they had no formal headman, their communal activities being in the charge of the senior man of the several families comprising the group at any given time. Many larger villages, particularly those occupying more or less permanent sites, had a single headman over a number of years, often referred to (by modern Shoshoni informants) as the 'village chief'. So far as 'chief' implies permanent authority over an identifiable group, the term, as Steward points out (1955, pp. 114–15), is a misnomer; for this man had virtually no authority, and he served only one function (expressed in his title, *degwani*, 'talker'), namely, to collect and retail information about where food could be found.

> Since the Shoshoneans were constantly on the verge of starvation, especially at the end of the winter, knowledge of where greens, seeds, rabbits, insects, and other foods were to be had, made the repository of such information the most important person in the village. (Steward, 1955, p. 115).

In other words, the principal task of the *degwani* was to keep himself informed about the ripening of plant foods in the different localities foraged by his people, to impart this information to them, and, if all the families travelled to the same pine-nut tract, to organise the trip and arrange where each family was to pick. Even in this field, his authority was strictly limited; he gave directions only to families who chose to co-operate, and any family was free at any time to pursue its own, independent course.

Spring, then, was a time of great scarcity among the Shoshoneans; the winter supply of pine nuts and other cached foods was running low, and people waited expectantly for the appearance of the first 'greens' to supplement their meagre diet. The fall, by contrast, was a season of relative affluence, and it was in the fall, in connection with the pine-nut harvest, that the only big yearly festival of the western Shoshoni was celebrated. It was held soon after the pine-nut harvest, generally lasted five or six days, and was accompanied by daily rabbit drives; indeed, it is not too much to say that the fall festival, over by far the greater part of the western Shoshoni area, was *made possible* by the temporarily increased food supply produced by the pine-nut crop and by rabbit drives. Its essential motivation, however, was non-economic; for people *desired* social intercourse with friends and relatives rarely seen during the rest of the year; they *wished* to dance and gamble, and, in some localities, to hold religious observances (Steward, 1938, p. 237). Each locality celebrated its own fall festival, and the size of groups united by festivals depended on the locality. In some localities, festivals were held either at the main village, or at a place within the district where there happened to be an abundance of food; in such cases the village headman, i.e. the *degwani*, commonly took charge, the function of directing the annual festival fell in with his other duties, and the size of the group united by the festival roughly coincided with that produced by economic activities, such as pine-nut gathering and communal hunts. In other localities, among the Deep Creek Gosiute for example, the fall festival served to bring together many scattered groups of families, otherwise independent of one another in their day-to-day life, into a temporary assemblage wider than any that they formed a part of during the remainder of the year; commonly, then, as in the Deep Creek region, the fall festival—and the rabbit drives accompanying it—was directed by a valley chief, whose special rôle was restricted to the communal activity and fell into abeyance at its conclusion.

The religious observances that accompanied the fall festival were, primarily, the rites attendant on the annual mourning ceremony, celebrated by the Owens Valley Northern Paiute, by the Ash Meadows Southern Paiute, and perhaps, also, by some western Shoshoni groups, at the conclusion of that festival. Burial rites, as we have seen, were performed immediately after death, and as they were attended only by close relatives and fellow villagers of the deceased, brought together only those who were already in the habit of co-operating in daily affairs. But the annual mourning ceremony, carried out at the end of the fall festival, in the course of which the last pieces of property of those who had died during the preceding year were burned and their kinsmen were released from mourning, must surely have fostered, among those attending the festival, both their solidarity and their sense of forming a group—if only by its emphasis on those who had *left* the group. But, as Steward observes (1938, p. 237), too little is known either about the rites themselves, or of who participated in them, to be able to say more than this.

In sum then we may say, regarding the western Shoshoni, that the largest socio-political groups known to them in their traditional economy, i.e. before the introduction (among some peripheral groups) of the horse, were groups of families which exploited a vaguely defined, common territory and which were in the habit, when conditions allowed, of harvesting pine nuts and wintering together in the same locality. Commonly, most of the families making up such a group were related to one another by kinship ties, or linked by marriage alliance; they took part in a number of economic activities, e.g. pine-nut gathering, rabbit drives, deer and antelope hunts, which benefitted from co-operation; these activities mostly occurred in the fall, and were directed by a headman, to whom it also fell to organise the fall festival, the annual event marking the high point of group solidarity. Certain features, however, were lacking to these western Shoshoni groups, to prevent their becoming corporate, land-holding bands. In the first place, the territories they exploited were not clearly defined; often, indeed, the areas foraged by neighbouring groups overlapped. Nor was there any ownership, in any strict sense of the term, of the resources offered by the environment; families gathered where they chose, and wherever rainfall and local conditions offered the best crop. In the second, and corollary to the first, the groups were not stable in their composition; individual families might detach themselves, and either join other groups or winter on their own, from one year to the next, depending on the vagaries of the available food supply and, particularly, of the pine-nut crop. And this, in turn, affected the strength of the social ties uniting each group: for just as (above p. 381) the frequency of separation brought about by food shortage prevented the emergence of a fixed set of duties and obligations between affines, so the solidarity engendered by co-operation in such communal activities as rabbit drives, and by the fall festival itself, was dependent on the *same* families co-operating in them from year to year.

By contrast to the very loose social organisation of the western Shoshoni, the Northern Paiute of Owens Valley were traditionally grouped into corporate, land-holding bands; and this difference is to be ascribed, primarily, to their ecology. At root, the resources offered by Owens Valley are comparable to those offered by the western Shoshoni environment; a similar range of food plants grows there, and the same insects, grubs, wildfowl, rodents and game, are to be found in the one region as in the other. But, due to the proximity of the Sierra Nevada mountains and to the perennial streams which emerge from them, Owens Valley is unusually fertile compared with other parts of the Great Basin. The valley was able, consequently, to support a relatively dense population clustered in camps along the streams, and as all essential food sources lay within a day's walk of the several village sites, each cluster of camps became the nucleus of a corporate band. Two essential features thus distinguish the corporate band of the Owens Valley Paiute, from the looser groupings of the western Shoshoni: first, it comprised the *same* group of families from one year to the next: second, it *owned* a clearly defined territory, the resources of which its members had sole right to exploit.

Just as the resources offered by Owens Valley were basically similar to those offered by the western Shoshoni habitat but enriched by the proximity of a high mountain range, so the social ties linking the families within the corporate band were similar to those at work among the western Shoshoni—but strengthened by day-to-day contact and co-operation between them. Everywhere in the Great Basin the individual family remained the economic unit, dependent on its own efforts for its subsistence. In Owens Valley, as elsewhere in the region, the basic ties between families were those of kinship on the one hand, and of marriage alliance on the other. But, in Owens Valley, the habitual co-operation of the *same* group of families in exploiting the resources of their *own* territory, including the harvesting of wild-seed and pine-nut tracts, the sharing of irrigated land, and participation in communal rabbit and antelope hunts, gave a content and meaning to these ties which was not to be found—at least, not as a matter of course—among the western Shoshoni.

The solidarity thus engendered within the corporate band was reflected in three related institutions, each of which is to be found among the western Shoshoni, but in a far more developed form among the Owens Valley Paiute: namely, the fall festival, chiefship, and the sweat house. Among the Owens Valley Paiute, each main village or cluster of camps held its own fall festival, under the direction of its own headman; people from other villages might be, and frequently were, invited to attend, but essentially the fall festival was a village affair and terminated with the annual mourning ceremony for those of its members who had died since the previous festival. The position and functions of the village headman, in Owens Valley, were commensurate with the extended scope of communal affairs there (Steward, 1938, p. 250): he looked after —or appointed someone to look after, on his behalf—the plots of irrigated land, directed individual families in their wild-seed and pine-nut gathering cycle, organised rabbit drives and communal hunts (though specialist hunters, or, in the case of antelope hunts, shamans, usually directed these), and presided over the fall festival and its concomitant rites. He was also responsible for the building and upkeep of the communal sweat house, itself—among the Owens Valley Paiute—an important mark of village solidarity; for whereas the western Shoshoni were in general too unsettled, and their encampments too small, to make the construction of a communal sweat house worthwhile, each cluster of camps in Owens Valley had a communal sweat house of its own, which served both as meeting-house and dormitory for the men of the village, where they discussed communal affairs and practised crafts during the day time, and where they smoked and recounted the myths of their people on the long winter evenings.

Earlier (above, p. 361) I argued that the circle dance of the western Shoshoni, performed in the spring to bring rain and to make seeds grow, was the analogue to the Hopi *powa'mu*. Of the content of their fall festival, of its purpose even, virtually nothing is recorded; but from its seasonal character and its co-incidence with rabbit hunting, from the relation of the annual mourning rites to it, and from the fact that a lad smoked for the first time after killing his first deer, I take it to be the analogue to the Hopi *wü'wütçim* ceremony and to *wü'wütçim* initiation of young men.[1] To the question of the mourning rites themselves, and to what event in the Hopi cycle they correspond, I shall return in the next chapter.

[1] On the place of rabbit hunting and of tobacco smoking in the Hopi *wü'wütcim* ceremony, see above, pp. 284–8.

# 19

# *The social morphology of kin-based societies: II. The Hopi*

'Remembering', wrote Bartlett,[1] at the outset of his enquiry into the nature of that act, 'is a function of daily life, and must have developed so as to meet the demands of daily life.'

The gist of the argument being advanced in this Part should by now, I think, be clear to the reader. It is, briefly, that—like remembering—the forms of social life are 'a function of daily life, and must have developed so as to meet the demands of daily life'. Following closely in Steward's footsteps, I have endeavoured to show how, against a broadly similar ecological ground stretching from the Sierra Nevada to the Wasatch Mountains, the Shoshonean-speaking peoples developed certain forms of social life in response to the demands of their daily life there; and further, how a modification of the environment in one particular region, Owens Valley, led to the development of more complex forms of social organisation in that region. I propose now to extend the survey to the Hopi, treating the Hopi—as we have already the Owens Valley Paiute—as a local variant on a basic Shoshonean theme.

## THE HOPI, AS A LOCAL VARIANT OF SHOSHONEAN SOCIETY

The root ecological difference between the Hopi region and that of the western Shoshoni to the north lies, not in the vegetation and soils of the two regions (which, as I have shown elsewhere, are broadly similar), nor in volume of rainfall, but in the fact that, due to local hydrographic conditions, certain alluvial fans in the vicinity of the Hopi mesas receive sufficient surface run-off to permit regular annual cultivation. These fans are of a limited acreage: in the case of Oraibi, some 1,600 to 1,800 acres of cultivable land within a radius of 4 miles of the village. Nor did the Hopi ever, until very recent times, give up the seed and root gathering techniques of their Shoshonean congeners; at least until the later decades of the nineteenth century, 'greens', wild seeds, roots, berries and piñon nuts, still filled a considerable place in their dietary,[2] particularly as a standby in years when the yield from cultivated crops was unduly

---

[1] F. C. Bartlett, *Remembering: a Study in Experimental and Social Psychology* (Cambridge, 1967: first published, 1932), p. 16.

[2] Cf. on this point, Fewkes (1896), and Hough (1898).

low.[1] Nevertheless, the regular use of the alluvial fans lying within a circum-scribed range of their home-base, for the growing of corn, beans and squash, enabled the Hopi to achieve a density of population, and *a resultant complexity of social organisation*, unknown either to the western Shoshoni or to the Owens Valley Paiute. This complexity we have now to examine.

Taking the Kawich Mountain region as representative—in regard to popula-tion density—of the western Shoshoni, the district of *pitanapatü* (Bishop's Creek) as representative of the Owens Valley Paiute, and the pueblo of Oraibi as representative of the Hopi, we get the following figures for the number of people exploiting a given area:

| people and location | number of inhabitants[2] | area exploited | population density |
|---|---|---|---|
| Western Shoshoni, Kawich Mountain region | about 120 | gathering area lay within a radius of 25 miles of winter encampments: *c.* 2,000 sq. miles | one person to 16 sq. miles |
| Northern Paiute, district of *pitanapatü* | about 150 | area of territory, roughly 16 × 20 miles: *c.* 320 sq. miles | one person to 2 sq. miles |
| Hopi, pueblo of Oraibi | about 660 | agricultural area lay within radius of 4 miles of village: gathering area, roughly 16 × 10 miles: *c.* 160 sq. miles | four persons to 1 sq. mile |

Very roughly we may say that the Owens Valley Paiute, at one person to 2 sq. miles, were eight times ($2^3$) more concentrated than the western Shoshoni; and that the Hopi, at four persons to one square mile, were eight times ($2^3$) more concentrated than the Owens Valley Paiute. A significant difference,

[1] It has to be borne in mind, also, that the corn cobs found on early pueblo sites are much smaller than those grown in historic times, and that it required many centuries of selection to produce the latter; consequently, the yield from such fields as were cultivated must, at first, have been considerably less than it later became. The change from a primarily wild-seed gathering, to a primarily agricultural, economy is not an all-or-nothing affair; it may be expected to have taken place gradually, over some hundreds of years.

[2] The figures are those for the decade 1861–70; for the first, see Steward (1938), pp. 110–12, and for the second, Steward (1933), p. 237. For the Hopi figure, and the reports upon which it is based, see Appendix 4 to my paper (1971), 'The changing pattern of Hopi agriculture'. Regarding the Oraibi gathering area, I suppose that this extended for about eight miles up and down the valley from the village, and for about five miles to the east and west.

however, may be noted between the two equations, as regards the *kind* of concentration: that between the western Shoshoni and the O.V. Paiute being primarily ($2^3$) due to a reduction in the territory ranged; that between the O.V. Paiute and the Hopi primarily ($2^2$) to an increase in the number of inhabitants carried (due to the use of agricultural techniques), and only secondarily ($2^1$) to a reduction in the area of the territory exploited.[1]

Turning now to notions of property: the western Shoshoni, as we have seen (above, p. 378), lacked any form of ownership of land or of the resources on it. No established group of families habitually made use of any clearly defined territory for gathering seeds, roots and pine nuts; individual families foraged where they liked, and where the vagaries of rainfall led them. All natural resources were free to anyone, on the principle 'first come, first served'; only when work had been expended, e.g. in gathering seeds, did things become the property of those who had worked on them. The only exception to this rule were eagle-nesting cliffs, which seem to have belonged to individual families.[2] Among the Owens Valley Paiute, we find a marked development in the practise of ownership. Throughout the valley, each village owned the territory within foraging distance, in the sense that the families living there exercised exclusive rights over the resources to be found on it. Further, within the territory belonging to the village, certain resources were the property of individual families; thus, in the northern section of the valley, pine-nut tracts (perhaps, also, some wild-seed tracts) belonged to men and were inherited by their sons, while in the southern section (George's Creek) pine-nut tracts, and also plots of irrigated land, belonged to women and were inherited matrilineally. Among the Southern Paiute of Ash Meadows, though wild-seed tracts were open to all, mesquite and screw-bean groves belonged to individual families who had exclusive gathering rights over them.

Among the Hopi, property rights centred on agricultural land,[3] that is to say, on the alluvial fans which furnished the greater part of it. These were originally allotted, according to Hopi tradition, to the clans that first settled in the pueblo, but have been held, for as far back as we have knowledge, by the matrilineages of which the clans are made up. To bring out the significance of

[1] This point would be brought out more clearly still if comparison were made, not with Oraibi, but with the three villages on 1st Mesa where the population, before the smallpox outbreak of 1852–3, was roughly double that of Oraibi.

[2] This is confirmed, for the Southern Paiute of Kaibab Plateau, by Kelly (1964, pp. 92–3), who states that ownership of eyries usually passed from father to son. Among the Luiseño Indians of Southern California, it may be noted, eagle-nesting cliffs were owned by the (patrilineal) descent groups: Sparkman (1908), pp. 226–7.

[3] There is no trace, so far as I know, of any form of clan ownership of wild-seed tracts among the Hopi—unless some form of proprietary right is to be read into Simpson's observation (1953, p. 54) that 'berry patches scattered over many miles of open country are still visited regularly by Hopi women'.

Eagle-nesting cliffs, however, were traditionally owned by clans; and Professor Eggan tells me (1968) that certain trapping areas, to the south of Oraibi, were also formerly owned by clans. Springs were village-owned, and rock-cut cisterns on the mesa top were owned by matrilineages.

this fact, we have first to describe the kinship system of the Great Basin Shoshoneans, then to compare it, briefly, with that of the Hopi.[1]

As a start, let us compare our own kinship system with that of the western Shoshoni, taking the Deep Creek Gosiute as example (p. 391).

Both systems are *bilateral*: that is to say, in neither system is there any bias towards tracing descent either through the patriline or through the matriline. This is illustrated by the terms used for parallel cousins:[2] there is no tendency, in either system, to link parallel cousins, *either* on the father's side *or* on the mother's side, with siblings. The English system is, further, completely symmetrical: i.e. terms for grandparent, uncle/aunt, cousin, nephew/niece, grandchild, are precisely the same on either side. Gosiute, like English, distinguishes between the father and the father's brother, between the mother and the mother's sister, between brother/sister and cousin, and between own child and nephew/niece. And it is symmetrical as regards terms for cousin.[3] But it distinguishes, as English does not, between the father's close kin (i.e. *his* mother and father, brother and sister) on the one hand, and the mother's close kin (i.e. *her* mother and father, brother and sister) on the other; and, in the descending generation, between the brother's son/daughter and the sister's son/daughter.

Two principles underlie the interpretation of *any* kinship system: first, like other forms of social life, a given kinship system is 'a function of daily life, and must have developed so as to meet the demands of daily life'; second, its terminology embodies a classification, by means of which certain relatives are grouped together *as the same sort of people*, in relation to the speaker: e.g. in English, but in relatively few other systems, the mother's sister and the father's sister (and also, incidentally, the mother's brother's wife and the father's brother's wife) are regarded as 'the same sort of person', namely *aunt*. The question we have to answer, is: what *kind* of classification is embodied in the Gosiute system, and to what needs of daily life does the classification respond?

English and western Shoshoni society, while differing in almost every other respect, have one thing in common: both lay an extreme emphasis on the nuclear family as the unit of social life. So far as the western Shoshoni are concerned, this emphasis was forced on them by the exigencies of seed gathering in that harsh environment. Only the single family—or, at the most, a group of two or three families—was sufficiently mobile, and its over-all requirements

[1] In the discussion that follows, I have relied chiefly, for the Shoshonean material, on Steward (1933), pp. 299–301, and (1938), Appendix C, pp. 284–306: for the Hopi material, on Lowie (1929), pp. 367–83, and Eggan (1949), pp. 122–43: and for theoretical bias, on White (1939), pp. 566–73.

[2] *Parallel* cousins are the children (a) of father's brother and (b) of mother's sister; *cross* cousins, the children (a) of father's sister and (b) of mother's brother.

[3] The Skull Valley Gosiute, however, who practised preferential marriage with the father's sister's daughter (and prohibited marriage with the mother's brother's daughter), used special terms to distinguish father's sister's son and daughter from other cousins: Steward (1938), pp. 140–1.

ENGLISH KINSHIP SYSTEM

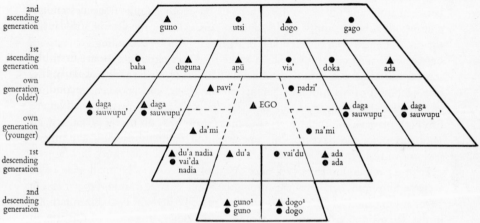

KINSHIP SYSTEM OF DEEP CREEK GOSIUTE

[1] As with the mother's brother–sister's child relation, the grandfather–grandchild and grandmother–grandchild terms are reciprocal: i.e. a woman calls her son's child *utsi*, and her daughter's child *gago*. This use of reciprocal terms is a characteristic feature of kinship systems of North America west of the Rocky Mountains: Lowie (1929), pp. 366–7.

sufficiently modest, to be able to gather enough seeds to survive there in lean years; in the fall and winter, it is true, a number of such families commonly camped near one another in the vicinity of the pine-nut crop, but each family camped on its own and the same families did not necessarily camp together in successive years. So far as our own society is concerned, we do not have to enter here into the historical reasons for the emphasis; all we need say is that, for the last six hundred years, the nuclear family has in point of fact been the primary social unit throughout the developed part of western Europe, including England.[1]

Now if, as westerners, we look at our own kinship system from the inside (and this, after all, is the only system we can ever know *at first hand*), we see—or at least in my own case I see—a number of nuclear families, i.e. in the generation above my own, those of an aunt and uncle and *their* children, and in my own generation, those of a cousin and his (or her) spouse and *their* children, each on complete equality of footing one with another. This fundamental aspect of our kinship system is reflected in the terminology: no distinction is made between aunts and uncles on the father's or the mother's side, nor any between cousins; all alike are aunts, uncles, and cousins. Among the Gosiute, this is not the case. There, a clear distinction is drawn, at least in the ascending generations, between the nuclear families which make up Ego's close kin: between, in the second ascending generation, the nuclear families of his father's parents on the one hand and of his mother's parents on the other, and between, in the first ascending generation, those of his *baha* (father's sister), his *duguna* (father's brother), his *doka* (mother's sisiter), and his *ada* (mother's brother). To understand why this is so, we have to shift our attention from subsistence activities to patterns of residence.

First, let us remind ourselves once again of the extremely small scale of all western Shoshoni social groups: among the Skull Valley Gosiute, 149 persons in 1870, among the Deep Creek Gosiute 107 persons, perhaps two dozen families in the one group and eighteen to twenty in the other. In groups of this size, in which choice of marriage partner was limited by the distance people could travel on foot, everybody *must* have been related to everybody else, within (at the most) second or third cousinship. Common to all Shoshonean-speaking peoples of the Basin-Plateau area was the very simple form of exchange, whereby a brother and sister of one family marry a sister and brother of another family: a custom that is reflected in the extension of the term for the mother's brother to the father's sister's husband, and of the term for father's sister to the mother's brother's wife.[2] Widespread throughout the region was the practice,

---

[1] That is to say, roughly, from Chaucer's day. For the stages by which, between the twelfth and the fourteenth centuries, the nuclear family detached itself from earlier, and wider, kin groups, see Marc Bloch (1968), pp. 200–6: a process marked by the gradual emergence of hereditary patronyms. Patronyms appear to have emerged first at the upper end of the social scale, e.g. Plantagenet, after the sprig of broom (*genesta*, *genet*) which Geoffrey of Anjou plucked on his way to the Second Crusade.

[2] Steward (1938), pp. 285, 287–8.

in some cases preferential, of cross-cousin marriage,[1] reflected in the further extension of those terms to the father-in-law and to the mother-in-law respectively, and representing a rather more complex kind of exchange: i.e. the taking of a father's sister's daughter representing a return for the girl *given* in the preceding generation, and the taking of a mother's brother's daughter implying a marriage circle in which *we* take girls from one family and *they* take theirs from another (who perhaps, in turn, take theirs from *our* family). Common, also, was the practice whereby two or three brothers from one family marry two or three sisters from another.

Regarding post-marital residence: among the Gosiute (Skull Valley and Deep Creek), post-marital residence 'was said to be matrilocal for about a year *as a kind of bride service*, and thereafter depended upon circumstance'.[2] A survey of nine other western Shoshoni groups, stretching from the Inyo Mountains in the west to the Great Salt Desert, shows a definite tendency towards eventual *patrilocal* residence:

*Little Lake:* matrilocal until birth of first child, then independent, though preferably patrilocal: Steward (1938), p. 84.

*Panamint Valley:* matrilocal until birth of first child, then independent: p. 85.

*Death Valley:* matrilocal for about a year, then independent: p. 91.

*Beatty:* no rule of post-marital residence: p. 99.

*Kawich Mountains:* of six marriages recorded, four were patrilocal, two matrilocal: p. 112.

*Reese River:* temporary matrilocal residence, during which the boy hunted for his parents-in-law in a kind of bride service: permanent residence usually patrilocal: p. 109.

*Little Smoky River:* strong preference for permanent patrilocal residence: p. 131.

*Spring Valley:* residence determined by the various factors of food supply and individual preference: in two villages, all the families were those of several brothers: p. 131.

*Ruby Valley:* some couples went at once to the boy's home to live, but most stayed with the wife's family for a year, in a kind of bride service, or until the first child was born. Permanent residence ... depended upon circumstances of food supply and preference: at least in the case of headmen, it was commonly patrilocal: pp. 150–1.

In Fish Lake Valley, one informant asserted 'that residence after marriage was matrilocal until the birth of a child, when the couple set up an independent household' (Steward, 1938, pp. 67–8); the latter, in practice, appears to have been virilocal or uxorilocal according to circumstance, and in some cases couples simply moved to more sparsely settled areas. Among the Ash Meadows Southern Paiute (1938, p. 185), there was no rule of post-marital residence.

Among the Owens Valley Paiute, there appears to have been some difference between the northern and southern halves of the valley. In the northern villages (Steward, 1933, p. 295), residence was generally matrilocal for the first year after marriage, the husband contributing food to the support of his wife's parents; a year of patrilocal, then independent residence followed, 'the place being chosen by the girl, the house built by the boy's

---

[1] Steward (1938), pp. 285, 288–90. As regards the Gosiute, Skull Valley Gosiute preferred that a man marry his father's sister's daughter, and prohibited his marrying his mother's brother's daughter; Deep Creek Gosiute permitted marriage with either cross-cousin. Both groups prohibited marriage between parallel cousins.

[2] Steward (1938), p. 140: my italics.

family'. In the southern half of the valley, there was a strong preference for matrilocal residence, perhaps connected—in Steward's view (1938, p. 57)—with female ownership of valley seed plots there.

Reviewing this evidence: the pattern appears to have been, among all groups, for the newly married couple to spend the first year of married life at the bride's home, the husband performing services for the wife's parents.[1] About the time of the birth of their first child,[2] they *either*, among the western Shoshoni, moved back to the boy's home, *or* set up camp on their own. A similar rule applied among the Northern Paiute of Fish Lake Valley, and *probably*, also, in the northern half of Owens Valley. In the southern half of Owens Valley, however, while the couple might (as in the north) return for a few years to the boy's home, they tended to settle eventually in the village where the girl's parents lived and where she might expect, in due course, to inherit valley seed plots.

Now the essential feature to be noted regarding post-marital residence in *all* Shoshonean groups is that, whether the newly-married couple eventually settled in the vicinity of the boy's home, in the vicinity of the bride's home, or on their own, they established an independent household: i.e. they did *not* merge into an already existing residential unit. Assuming, as I believe to have been the case, that among the western Shoshoni residence tended (after an initial phase of matrilocality) to be patrilocal, then the combined effect of the rules for the choice of marriage partner with the rule of post-marital residence will have been to 'place' the families in any particular group, in relation to two co-ordinates: first, whether they were a potential source of marriage partners to Ego and his siblings, and second, where they commonly resided. Thus, to take the Deep Creek Gosiute as example, all the eighteen or twenty families that made up the group will have fallen, from the point of view of the growing child, into one or four defined classes:[3] i.e. families of our *duguna*, living near

---

[1] During which time, evidently (Steward, 1938, p. 243), 'his general acceptibility and hunting prowess were ascertained'. The four qualities looked for in a young man, according to a Uintah Ute myth (Mason, 1910, p. 329), were that he should be a good worker and a good hunter: equable in temper: that he should 'know everything', i.e. all the things needed for survival: and that he should have a full complement of relatives, i.e. to come to his aid in time of need.

[2] Sometimes not until several children had been born, 'because the aid of the maternal grandmother was sought, in childbirth and infant care': Steward (1938), p. 243.

[3] The Kariera of Western Australia (see, in particular, Radcliffe-Brown, 1913, p. 147 *et seq*) have gone one stage farther than this and put all local residential groups into one of two categories, *ngaju maru*, 'we people', and *bahu maru*, 'they people', the first referring to those local groups into which Ego may not marry (including his own), the second to those local groups into which he may marry. Like the western Shoshoni, the Kariera practise marriage of a brother and sister with a sister and brother, and cross-cousin marriage with either cross cousin. They further divide the whole tribe into four sections, Ba, Bu, Pa and Ka, which regulate marriage; since a man of Ba may only marry a woman of Bu and *her* children belong to Pa, and a man of Bu may only marry a woman of Ba and *her* children belong to Ka, and since post-marital residence is patrilocal, each local group is *either* Ba-Pa *or* Bu-Ka (the one taking its wives from the other). The local groups, when plotted on a map of the tribal area (Romney and Epling, 1958, Fig. 1, p. 61), form a chequerboard;

us in the encampment of our *guno* (father's father), whose children we don't marry: families of our *baha*, living *way over there* (pointing, e.g. in the direction of Trout Creek), whose children we may marry: families of our *ada*, living in the encampment of our mother's father (*dogo*), whose children, also, we may marry: and families of our *doka*, living over *there* (e.g. Antelope Valley), whose children we may not marry.[1]

A kinship system, as I said earlier, is 'a function of daily life, and must have developed so as to meet the needs of daily life'. To do its job, it has to embody a classification: 'kinship terms', as Leach remarks (1958, p. 143), 'are category words, by means of which the individual is taught to recognise the significant groupings in the social structure into which he is born'. The significant groupings in the social structure of the Gosiute are the nuclear families; consequently, it is these that the kinship system differentiates.

Like the Gosiute kinship system, that of the Owens Valley Paiute (p. 397) is *bilateral*, i.e. there is no bias towards tracing descent either through the patri-line or through the matriline; like Gosiute, also, it distinguishes between the father's brother and the mother's brother, between the father's sister and the mother's sister, and between brother's son/daughter and sister's son/daughter. The principal difference between the two systems is that O.V. Paiute not only, like Gosiute, distinguishes older brother/sister from younger brother/sister, but extends these terms to cousins,[2] cross as well as parallel. This difference it would be nice to correlate, (*a*) with the O.V. Paiute prohibition on marriage with cousins of either kind (Steward, 1933, p. 294, n. 125), and (*b*) with the existence in the valley of settled villages and the resultant proximity of closely related families (and so, of both kinds of cousin living cheek by jowl with own brothers and sisters): were it not for the fact that the kinship systems of some western Shoshoni groups exhibit the same feature.[3]

---

and this chequerboard distribution is clearest in precisely those regions, i.e. along rivers and in the vicinity of the sea coast, *where ecological conditions favor relatively more stable residence* (p. 63). Regarding the relation between the section system and the kinship system as a whole, Romney and Epling point out (ibid. p. 64) that while the kinship terms are in great part *relative* (i.e. to any two persons using them), the section terms are *absolute* in the sense that they impose a formal pattern on the whole society.

[1] Due to the uncertainties of Gosiute seed-gathering, one should add the rider *tending to reside in such-and-such locality* after each family or group of families.

[2] It may be that, as on occasions among the Tewa of Hano, the older brother/sister, younger brother/sister, terms refer, when extended to cousins, to the age of the father's brother or of the mother's sister in relation to Ego's own father or mother: i.e. that I call 'older brother', *any* son of my father's 'older brother'.

[3] The Skull Valley Gosiute, for example, who practise preferential marriage with the father's sister's daughter and who do *not* have settled villages, yet—on occasions—extend *pavi'/da'mi* and *padzi'/na'mi* terms to cousins, parallel and cross: Steward (1938), pp. 297–9.

Steward himself holds (1938, p. 289) that the smallness of their encampments, 'wherein one was unlikely to live in the proximity of many cousins', may have contributed to the frequent failure by western Shoshoni to distinguish cousins from brothers and sisters. My own view is that such conditions *favoured* the differentiation of cousins from brothers and sisters, and that it was the relative *largeness* of O.V. Paiute villages, wherein one *was* likely to live in the proximity of many cousins, that favoured their merging into a single class (particularly where this was joined to a rule against marrying any of them).

Turning now to Hopi kinship terminology: the fundamental difference between the Shoshonean, and the Hopi, systems lies in the following features of the latter:

in the ascending generation, Hopi classes the father's brother—and other males whom the father calls 'brother'—with the father (*ina'a*), and the mother's sister—and other females whom the mother calls 'sister'—with the mother (*iñü'ü*).

in Ego's own generation, Hopi classes the father's sister's son with the father (*ina'a*), and the father's sister's daughter with the father's sister (*ikya'a*). Further, a man classes his mother's brother's child with his own child (*iti'i, iti'i-ma'na*), and a woman classes her mother's brother's child with her own brother's child (*imü'yi*).

in the descending generation, a man classes his brother's child—and the child of any male whom he calls 'brother'—with his own child (*iti'i, iti'i-ma'na*), while a woman classes her sister's child—and the child of any female whom she calls 'sister'—with her own child (*iti'i, iti'i-ma'na*). A man applies a separate term (*iti'waiya*) to his sister's child, while a woman classes her brother's child with the child of her own son or daughter (*imü'yi*).

To understand the *meaning* of these features of the Hopi system, we must make a brief excursus into kinship theory. A kinship terminology, as I remarked earlier, embodies a classification, by means of which certain relatives are grouped together *as the same sort of person*, in relation to the speaker. The question that faces us, is: what principle of similarity lies behind the Hopi use of the terms *ikya'a, ina'a, iñü'ü, iti'i* (woman speaking), *iti'waiya* (man speaking), and *imü'yi* (woman speaking)? For answer, we have to cast our minds back to the primary distinction between the Hopi social order and that of their Shoshonean congeners: namely, that where the Shoshoneans were (in the main) seed gatherers, owning the resources of their territory in common (except, in special areas, where certain seed and root tracts were family-owned), the Hopi were (primarily) agriculturalists and the principal resource of their territory, i.e. agricultural land, was owned by particular (matri-)lineages. In both, the household or family was the primary economic unit; but whereas, among the western Shoshoni (and still, to some degree, among the Owens Valley Paiute), the family was also the primary social unit, among the Hopi its place—e.g. in the upbringing of children, discharge of obligations, succession to ceremonial knowledge and office—was either shared with, or taken by, the body of closely related families that made up the (matri-)lineage.[1]

A kinship nomenclature, says White,[2] is a mechanism whose function is the classification of relatives. In communities (like that of the western Shoshoni)

---

[1] The continued place held by the nuclear family *within* a lineage system has been nicely put by Miss B. Freire-Marreco (1914, p. 283). Discussing the rôle of the men of other clans married to women of our clan, she says (speaking in the voice of a Tewa girl):

> One among them—*nabi tada*, my father—stands in a close and tender relation to myself and my sisters and brothers. He and my mother and my brothers and sisters and I form a little camp of our own, as it were, in the midst of the crowded household life; we sit together to eat and talk, and sleep together on my mother's own sheepskins and blankets.

[2] In this excursus, I follow closely in White's footsteps: see White (1939), an article of admirable incisiveness and lucidity.

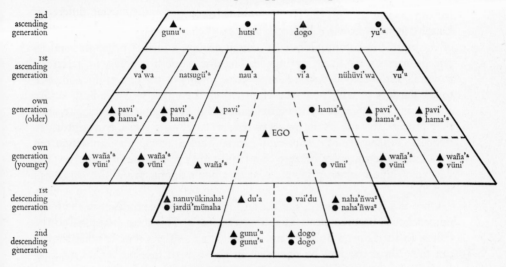

KINSHIP SYSTEM OF OWENS VALLEY PAIUTE

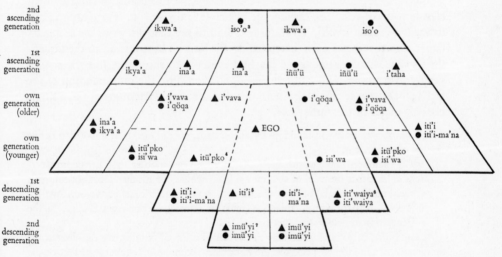

HOPI KINSHIP SYSTEM

[1] or *duivi'tci*, the common Shoshonean stem for 'lad'.

[2] *naha'ñwa*, sister's son or daughter (man speaking): sex is designated by adding 'boy', or 'girl': Steward (1933), p. 300, n. 148. A woman calls her sister's son and daughter *du'ya* and *vatu'*, and her brother's child *yara'*.

[3] *iso'o*, father's mother, also applied to father's eldest sister.

[4] A woman speaker applies the term *itü'pko* to her younger sister, as well as to her younger brother.

[5] *iti'i/iti'i-ma'na* is the generic word for 'child'. A man uses it for his own child, for the child of his brother, and for his mother's brother's child; a woman uses it for her own child, and for the child of her sister.

[6] *iti'waiya* is the word used, by a male speaker only, for his sister's child.

[7] A woman speaker applies the term *imü'yi* to her brother's child, and to her mother's brother's child, as well as to her own grandchild: i.e. in general, to those who address her as *iso'o* or *ikya'a*.

lacking descent groups, the classification is based on a single principle: that of kinship, in what Lowie calls (1929, pp. 382-3) the 'ordinary genealogical sense of the word'; in communities *with* descent groups, a further principle is introduced—namely, the lineage principle. The first classifies people with reference to families, the second with reference to segments of the community, that is, to the lineages of which e.g. the Hopi village is composed. Since both family and lineage are engaged in doing the same thing, classifying relatives, and since they proceed from different points of reference, they are rivals, competitors, so to speak, *in the game of relative-classification.* Thus a person may be designated by a kinship term, *either* because of a family link, *or* because of a lineage link, depending upon which principle is at that point dominant (White, 1939, pp. 567-8).

Once this idea is grasped, the reason for the *apparent* anomalies in the Hopi nomenclature become clear. Take the term *ina'a.* This term is applied to the father, to the father's brother, and to the father's sister's son. In what respect can these three relatives be regarded, in the eyes of the speaker, as *the same kind of person?* well, quite simply, as 'members (male) of the lineage (or clan) from which our mother took her consort'. Marriage, as we have seen earlier, among the Hopi is an alliance between lineages; at this point, therefore, in the classification of relatives, the lineage principle is dominant. *We,* with our bias towards a *familial* kinship terminology, tend to say that the word *ina'a* 'means' father, and that it has been 'extended' to the father's brother and to the father's sister's son. But this, unless we can find evidence to show that it is the case, is simply to read our own cultural pre-suppositions into the interpretation of the facts; all that the terminology tells us is that the Hopi system groups in a single class all males of the father's lineage.[1]

At a number of points in the Hopi kinship system, we can discern the working of the lineage principle: e.g.

    *ina'a,* 'member (male) of the lineage from which our mother took her consort':
    *ikya'a,* 'member (female) of the lineage from which our mother took her consort':
    *i'taha,* 'member (male) of our own lineage, in the generation(s) above our own':
    *iti'waiya* (man speaking), 'member (male or female) of our own lineage, in the generation(s) below our own':

At one point, in particular, namely in the classification of cousins, we can discern the dominance of the familial principle. As in certain Shoshonean systems (e.g. that of the Owens Valley Paiute), Hopi classes parallel cousins on *both* sides with brothers and sisters: whereas, if the lineage principle were dominant, we should expect (in a matrilineal

---

[1] A further danger in translating e.g. *ina'a* as 'father', is that we tend to carry over, in considering the class of relatives designated by the term, our own mode of behaviour towards the particular relative: i.e. bearing subconsciously in mind our own pattern of respect for the father, we conclude that, since the father's sister's son is addressed as 'my father' by Hopi, he must be held in respect by them. But the classification of kin, in itself, is neutral; the fact that a society puts a number of relatives, including the father, into a single class, does not necessarily mean that that *kind* of relative is looked up to; he may be, but whether he is or not, is a matter of empirical observation—it cannot be deduced from the terminology.

system) only the mother's sister's children to be classed with Ego's own siblings, and the father's brother's children to be classed separately.

The term *iti'i/iti'i-ma'na* shows the lineage principle at work, but in a different sense according to the sex of the speaker. For a woman speaker, whose child belongs to her own lineage, *iti'i/iti'i-ma'na* refers to any child of her own lineage, including her own child, of the generation below her own; for a male speaker, *iti'i/iti'i-ma'na* is the obverse of *ina'a*, and refers to the child of any man of his own lineage, including his own child. The term *imü'yi*, as used by a woman speaker, is rather similar; since her daughter's child belongs to her own lineage, a woman applies the term to any child of her own lineage of the 2nd descending generation (i.e. to whom she herself stands as *iso'o*, 'grandmother'); as the obverse of *ikya'a*, she applies it to the child of any man of her own lineage (i.e. to whom she herself stands as 'father's sister' or, in modern Hopi parlance, as 'aunt'), including her own brother's child and her son's child.

### ECOLOGY, RESIDENCE AND SOCIAL STRUCTURE

At this point, let us resume the argument. The reader will have observed by now that the writer is endeavouring to keep three balls in the air at the same time: one to do with the ownership of resources, one to do with kinds of post-marital residence, and one to do with the emergence (among the Hopi) of (matri-)lineages. Among the western Shoshoni, virtually *all* resources were held in common; post-marital residence was either independent, or patrilocal; and the individual family was the unit of social, as well as of economic, life. Among the Owens Valley Paiute, while many resources (e.g. game, wild-seed tracts) were still held in common, certain resources (*some* seed and root tracts, and pine-nut tracts) were owned by individual families, including—in the southern half of the valley (George's Creek)—plots of irrigated land handed down in the female line; post-marital residence was either patrilocal or matrilocal, with a strong preference for matrilocal residence in the southern half of the valley; and while the individual family was still the unit of economic life, the group of families that made up each separate community had become, in certain definite respects (e.g. organisation of festivals, ownership of a communal sweat house, holding of mourning ceremonies), the unit of *social* life. Among the Hopi, while certain limited resources (e.g. wild-seed tracts) remained the property of the community as a whole, the principal resource, namely agricultural land, was vested in (matri-)lineages; post-marital residence was firmly matrilocal; and the individual family or household, while it remained the *primary* economic unit, was no longer wholly autonomous—in the traditional Hopi economy it relied to a considerable degree, e.g. in communal sowing and harvesting parties, bird-scaring, spreading of flood waters, on the co-operation at least of other families in the same lineage.

The question that faces us now is to resolve the structural relationship between these three aspects of Basin-Plateau social life, namely ownership of resources, post-marital residence, and the transition from family to lineage; and I propose to do so by way of a consideration of marriage with the father's sister's daughter. Among the Hopi, post-marital residence was, and still to a large extent is to-day, matrilocal; among the Owens Valley Paiute, it *tended* to be matrilocal, but was often patrilocal, especially in the northern half of the valley, where pine-nut tracts were owned by men and handed down patrilineally; among the western Shoshoni, it was either patrilocal or independent. Now, Titiev has emphasised[1] that, whether patrilocal or matrilocal, there are two fundamentally different types of post-marital residence: one, where the bridal pair take up *independent* quarters in the village of either the boy's or the girl's parents, the other, where they are expected to move into a habitation *already occupied* by the parents and other relatives of one or other of them. The second type Titiev defines as 'the principle of *unilocal* residence', to distinguish it from *simple* matrilocal or patrilocal residence, which implies only that they settle down in the general vicinity either of the bride's home, or of the boy's. Among the Shoshonean-speaking peoples of the Great Basin, post-marital residence, whether matrilocal,[2] patrilocal, or independent, was definitely of the first type. Among the Hopi, it was of the second type: the young man and his bride traditionally shared the actual house occupied by the girl's mother; only after the birth of two or three children did they move into a house of their own, and commonly, then, into one in close proximity to that of her parents. The immediate effect of the practice of *unilocal* residence is, as Titiev points out (1943c, pp. 518–19), to merge the newly married pair with the occupants of a single, recognisable, already existent residential unit, controlled and dominated by the kinsfolk of either the bride or the groom; its long-term effect, when consistently followed over many generations, is to lead to the formation of *permanent residential nuclei*, the core of which is composed—in a matrilocal society —of a woman, her daughters and grand-daughters, with their respective husbands and children, each such nucleus occupying the same residence—at least so far as its female members are concerned—from birth to death.

Let us now turn to marriage with the father's sister's daughter. The Skull Valley Gosiute, as we have seen (above, p. 390, n. 3), practised preferential marriage with the father's sister's daughter: that is, a man chose as his wife the daughter of his *baha*. Now marriage entailed, among the western Shoshoni, a minimum of obligations between the two families engaged in the alliance. This, for two reasons: first, because, as Steward has pointed out, you cannot have elaborate obligations between two families whose movements are as erratic as those of the western Shoshoni commonly were; second, because, due to the poverty of the environment and the limited technology available for exploiting such resources as it offered, there was very little storable surplus, e.g. of food, for discharging such obligations. In short, the only secure lien was on the immediate product of the labour of a person living in close proximity to you. And this, as we have seen, is the form the marriage obligation took: among the Gosiute, post-marital residence was 'matrilocal for about a year as a kind of

---

[1] Titiev (1943c), especially pp. 516–19.

[2] I shall return in a minute to discuss the question of the initial year's residence in the bride's home.

bride service, and thereafter depended upon circumstances' (Steward, 1938, p. 140); in other groups (e.g. Little Lake and Panamint Valley, ibid. pp. 84–5), it was matrilocal until the birth of the first child; farther north, in the Reese River area, a period of 'temporary matrilocal residence, during which the boy hunted for his parents-in-law in a kind of bride service', was followed by (usually) patrilocal permanent residence (ibid. p. 109); in Ruby Valley, to the west of the Great Salt Desert, some couples went at once to the boy's home to live, but most 'stayed with the wife's family for a year, in a kind of bride service or until the first child was born'.[1] In other words, in groups (like that of the Skull Valley Gosiute) practising preferential marriage with the father's sister's daughter, the boy went to the encampment of his father's sister, lived there for about a twelve-month working for his parents-in-law (and incidentally proving his ability to keep his wife[2]), then either took her back to his own home to live, or set up camp with her in a new locality altogether.

Among the Hopi, there are strong indications of a former practice of preferential marriage with the father's sister's daughter,[3] or rather, with one of that class of relatives, of his own generation, whom Ego calls *ikya'a*. This distinction is crucial. For, among the Hopi, the rule of post-marital residence not *near*, but *in*, the household of the girl's parents (i.e. Titiev's 'principle of *unilocal* residence') led to the formation of *permanent residential nuclei*, extending from generation to generation in the female line. The term *ikya'a* (as applied to a girl of a man's own generation), while it may originally have referred to the father's sister's daughter (i.e. in a strict kinship sense), thus early came to mean 'girl of my father's natal unit', *natal unit* being defined here (cf. Titiev, 1956, pp. 855, 861–2) as the group of closely related families that formed the core of one of these residential nuclei. This was the group into which a man moved on marrying: a group the men of which stood to him as *ina'a* and the women as *ikya'a*,[4] and to whom he, in turn, stood as *iti'i* and *imü'yi*, respectively.

The marriage of a lad to his father's sister's daughter represents, as I have remarked earlier, a simple form of exchange: in return for a girl given in one generation, her daughter is taken in the next.[5] A link between two families is

[1] Steward (1938), p. 150. This pattern, i.e. of an initial period of matrilocal residence as a kind of bride-service, is confirmed, in general, by Lowie (1924), pp. 275–8.

[2] The analogue to this period of service by the young man to the bride's family among the western Shoshoni is the month's service, spent chiefly in grinding corn and cooking, rendered by the bride to the young man's family among the Hopi.

[3] Titiev (1938), pp. 105–11: cf. for the Tewa of Hano, Freire-Marreco (1914), p. 286. Since we are using the practice simply to illustrate the working of the lineage principle, we do not have to determine here how common it may have been at any particular stage in Hopi history. Eggan's view (1950, p. 121) is that 'cross-cousin marriage is a useful device for integrating small, relatively stable groups such as were characteristic of early Hopi history': in effect, that it represents a stage of development through which Hopi society has passed and come out the other side, leaving a residue in present-day Hopi attitudes between the relatives involved. Certainly, such attitudes still persist.

[4] The husbands of his father's sisters he addressed as *ikwa'a*, the same term he applied to his own father's father.

[5] Or, alternatively, in return for the sexual and economic services rendered by a man in one generation, his son reciprocates the services in the next.

thus established over two generations; and the existence of this link is affirmed, in the interim between the two marriages, by the tie which binds a lad to his father's sister (whose daughter he is expected, in due course, to marry). The strength of this tie may be taken as a measure of the strength of the alliance. Among the western Shoshoni, due to the conditions outlined above (the uncertainties of a gathering economy, and the lack of a storable food surplus), this tie can never, I think, have been a strong one; indeed, the only reference I have come across, expressing a young man's duty to his father's sister, is that he was obliged to 'keep his *baha*'s mouth plugged with fat', i.e. to keep her supplied with game (Steward, 1938, p. 171)—and it is by no means clear, from the context, whether this refers to the time *before*, or *after*, his marriage to her daughter. Among the Hopi, on the other hand, the tie binding a lad to his father's sister was an extremely close one; it was she, as we have seen (above, p. 27 *et seq.*), who bathed him soon after birth and bestowed one of her clan names on him twenty days later, and who made frequent gifts to him as he grew up; and it was she, in particular, for whom he hunted rabbits as a lad, and for whom, as a young man, he went on salt expeditions.[1]

The strength of the tie binding a lad to his father's sister is one *term* of the strength of marriage alliance in Hopi society: not of the strength of individual marriages (these, in point of fact, quite frequently break down), but of the strength of the ties created by alliance between two kin groups. Among the western Shoshoni (e.g. Skull Valley Gosiute), the marriage of a man and a girl in one generation (even of a brother and a sister with a sister and a brother), and of their son and the man's sister's daughter in the next, created—in the conditions of Great Basin life—only a relatively weak link between two nuclear families; the marriage itself was followed by a year's residence in the vicinity of the bride's parents, during which the young man worked or hunted for them; after that, the couple settled, commonly, where the exigencies of the food quest led them. Among the Hopi, the matter was quite other. Marriage itself was an alliance between two matrilineal, residential nuclei, sealed by elaborate exchanges of food and other gifts, and setting in train a whole series of reciprocal obligations between the kin groups so allied; the closeness of the ties between a lad and his father's sister(s) was one expression of these reciprocal obligations; and his eventual marriage, where this took place, with a girl of his father's *natal unit* (i.e. with a girl of his own generation whom he called *ikya'a*), reaffirmed—in the reverse direction—the alliance already established between the two kin groups by his father's marriage to his own mother.

The fundamental difference between the effects of (in western Shoshoni society) marriage with the father's sister's daughter, and (in Hopi society)

---

[1] In the Great Basin, also, salt was virtually the only object for which people might travel long distances: much of it came from Saline Valley, to the east of the Inyo Mountains, whence it was bartered to the Owens Valley Paiute, and thence, in return for sea-shells, across the Sierra Nevada Mountains: Steward (1938), pp. 45, 78. Formerly the Hopi, too, made occasional journeys across the desert country to the Pacific coast to fetch sea-shells: Mearns (1896), p. 392.

marriage with a girl of one's father's natal unit called *ikya'a*, is due to the presence, among the Hopi, of permanent residential nuclei of unilineal kin, reflected in the kinship terminology.[1] The *proximate* cause of this grouping of unilineal kin in permanent residential nuclei, we have attributed to the practice of post-marital residence whereby the newly married couple settle not *near*, but *in*, the household of the parents of either one of them (in the case of the Hopi, in the household of the bride's parents); its *ultimate* cause is traceable to a different system of work, and to different concepts of the ownership of resources.

Among the western Shoshoni, as we have seen, there was virtually no individual or family ownership of resources; wild-seed tracts were free to anyone to harvest, and, at least in one locality (Egan Cañon), even land that had been sowed with wild seeds in the spring might be reaped by anyone. Among the Ash Meadows Southern Paiute, while there was no ownership of wild-seed tracts, cultivated plots, groves of mesquite and screw beans, and pine-nut tracts belonged to individual families and, in the case of pine-nut tracts, were handed down by a man to his sons; cultivated plots were not inherited, however, since the crop was destroyed at the death of the owner. Among the Northern Paiute of Owens Valley, all wild-seed, root and pine-nut tracts were owned by the corporate bands in whose territory they lay; within this general ownership, pine-nut tracts, and perhaps, also, some seed tracts, belonged to individual families. In the northern section of the valley, pine-nut tracts were handed down by a man to his sons, and in the south, by a woman to her daughters; in the south, too, valley seed plots were owned by women, and were handed down matrilineally. Among the western Shoshoni, *post-marital residence* was either patrilocal or independent; among the Ash Meadows Southern Paiute, there was no rule of post-marital residence; in the northern section of Owens Valley, it was either patrilocal or matrilocal, but the boy's family were responsible for building the house; in the southern section of Owens Valley, there was a strong preference for matrilocal residence, 'perhaps connected', in Steward's view (1938, p. 57), 'with female ownership of valley seed plots. This tended to convert small villages into female lineages, which approximated [to] but failed actually to be exogamous matrilineal bands.'

In other words, where the principal resources were held in common, post-marital residence tended to be either patrilocal or independent; where owned by men and handed down to their sons, it tended to be patrilocal; and where owned by women and handed down to their daughters, it tended to be matrilocal. Nevertheless, throughout the Great Basin area (including Owens Valley), the bridal pair settled *in the vicinity of*, rather than *with*, the parents of either one of them; and to this fact may be attributed the failure of permanent residential nuclei of unilineal kin to emerge there. Why was this the case? Because, I think, neither the practice of a small amount of agriculture (as among the Ash

---

[1] The link between kinship terminology and residence was noted many years ago by Lowie (1929, p. 380: my italics at end):

> What possible reason *can* be given for calling all the female descendants through females of the paternal aunt by the same term as the paternal aunt herself, unless it be the fact that all these females are members of the same clan *or, to put it more cautiously, unless they are aligned together by some cause, such as common residence, that is correlated with the clan idea?*

Meadows Southern Paiute), nor the ownership and handing-down of pine-nut tracts or valley seed plots (as among the Owens Valley Northern Paiute), was sufficient *in itself* to compel a rule of *unilocal* post-marital residence. Only where agriculture came to assume an important (rather than a subsidiary) rôle in the total economy, and where, in consequence, agricultural land became the primary resource of the community, and where, further, its exploitation required the co-operation of several families (rather than of a single family planting on its own), were the conditions fulfilled for such a rule to become general: i.e. for the newly-married couple, *as a rule*, not to set up house on their own, but to merge into a larger group owning and exploiting its own share of the principal resource of the community, namely agricultural land.

The only Shoshonean-speaking people amongst whom this development, i.e. the establishment of a rule of *unilocal* post-marital residence, has taken place, at least to the east of the Sierra Nevada Mountains, is the Hopi; and the archaeological record in the plateau region to the south-east of the Colorado River gives a fair indication of the stages by which the transformation was effected—though it does not, of course, tell us whether the people living in the sites were Hopi-speaking or not. The crucial changes appear to have occurred, in the San Juan basin, in the late Basketmaker to early Pueblo periods,[1] that is, from *c.* A.D. 600 to 900. At the beginning of that period, the inhabitants of the region, though already practising *some* horticulture, were primarily dependent—like the Great Basin Shoshoneans of the nineteenth century—on seed gathering and hunting for their subsistence; they lived in caves or on open camp sites, and moved seasonally in search of food. As among the Shoshoneans, such an economy precluded the emergence of settled villages. By the end of the period,[2] the inhabitants were grouped in small clusters of houses, commonly referred to as 'pit lodges'; at least in the San Juan drainage area, the small house clusters of this period are generally located at no great distance from one another in the regions of arable land (Steward, 1955, p. 162). A typical settlement of this kind is the village of Shabik'eshche, in the Chaco, dated by tree-ring dating to

---

[1] For a summary of the archaeological evidence to the 1940's, see Reed (1946), Eggan (1950), pp. 123–30, and Steward (1955), p. 161 *et seq.* Since then much additional work has been done, notably in the Glen Canyon area to do with the flooding of Lake Powell, and in the upper basin of the Little Colorado; some of this later work is referred to in the text and in footnotes.

The distinctive branch of Basketmaker and early Pueblo culture that developed in the San Juan basin is known as the Anasazi culture. It lasted for rather more than a thousand years, coming to an end around A.D. 1300; at that time the entire San Juan drainage was abandoned, probably on account of arroyo-cutting caused by prolonged rain-lack (Reed, 1946, p. 303).

[2] The development appears to have been set off initially by the introduction into the Southwest, around A.D. 700, of a fresh strain of eight-rowed corn which crossed with the strains already being grown there to produce new hybrids, adaptable to higher altitudes and more drought-resistant than the old, yielding a heavier crop and one easier to mill; the new hybrids were capable of supporting a larger population than the old, and facilitated expansion out onto lands previously unsuited to corn-growing (Gallinat, 1965, pp. 353–5).

around A.D. 750. It consisted of early and late settlements, each having a cluster of about nine houses; to the south of Chaco Cañon, for some 30 to 40 miles, sites of the same period (Basketmaker III–Pueblo I) are numerous—'they may be found on ridges and low mesas along almost every former watercourse there'.[1]

Small house clusters of this kind, located near one another in the vicinity of watercourses, *must* have involved—so far as land-ownership is concerned—small farm plots, not extensive hunting-and-gathering tracts; that the clusters housed unilineal descent groups, living on or near their farm land, is consistent with their size (Steward, 1955, pp. 161–2), for if each house sheltered a family of five to six persons, a cluster of six to eight houses would have numbered some thirty to forty-five persons (about the size of a lineage); and from their distribution it seems likely that, as population increased, small lineages budded off, each setting up a new cluster at no great distance from its neighbours and formerly close kin.

If we accept that the small house clusters of the early Pueblo period housed unilineal descent groups living in close proximity to their farm land, the question still remains: what particular factors led to the establishing of a rule of *unilocal* post-marital residence, the establishing of such a rule (we have postulated earlier) being precursor to the emergence of descent groups of that kind? And the answer is to be looked for, I suggest, in two further features of the archaeological record: namely, (*a*) field systems, and (*b*) stone-lined storage chambers, both found in association with settlements of the period.

The study of field systems has been much neglected in the Southwest. The pioneer study of such systems, fundamental to an understanding of pueblo ecology, has been that undertaken by Dr. R. B. Woodbury and his colleagues at Point of Pines, in the San Carlos region, 175 miles south-south-east of the Hopi villages; and it is to that study[2] that I now turn.

The Point of Pines prehistoric settlements are sited at the northern foot of the Nantack Ridge (average elevation, *c.* 6,000 feet), about 65 miles east of Globe, Arizona. 'The northern foot of Nantack Ridge', writes Dr. Woodbury (1961, p. 1), 'breaks up into small, low, subsidiary ridges fingering out towards the prairie, separated from each other by small, flat valleys drained by intermittent streams. These low ridges and small open

---

[1] Vivian and Mathews (1964), p. 29. Similar house clusters, rather later in date (*c.* A.D. 950 to 1150), are found fairly densely over the Rainbow Plateau region to the east of Navajo Mountain, 75 miles north of the Hopi villages; many of these settlements are located near seeps or springs, nearly all have areas of arable land nearby, and some also show traces of terracing and linear borders: Lindsay *et al* (1968), pp. 20–1, 121–36, 364–5.

[2] Woodbury (1961), especially pp. 8–38. Since then, a further study of prehistoric field systems has been carried out by A. J. Lindsay (1961), on the delta of Beaver Creek near the mouth of the San Juan River, 75 miles to the north of the Hopi villages. Besides terrace walls, and linear and grid borders (as at Point of Pines), the Beaver Creek people constructed stone-lined ditches to carry water to areas which could not be farmed without irrigation. The associated small house clusters date from A.D. 1050 to about 1250, occupancy of the site being terminated by dissection of the alluvial floor of the valley consequent on the rain-lack which hit the San Juan drainage in the later thirteenth century.

valleys provided the prehistoric population with village locations that were above the level of the prairie, close to the higher, forested slopes of the main ridge but also close to the lands used for farming.' The earliest occupation of the region goes back to about 2000 B.C.; at that time it was occupied by small groups of people who lived by hunting and gathering, and it seems probable, from the available evidence, that the economy of these groups changed little for the next 1,500 to 2,000 years. The subsequent development of the area is outlined by Dr. Woodbury in the following words (1961, p. 6):

> By the first century of the Christian era, agriculture had certainly begun in the Point of Pines area; small-scale cultivation would have been a supplement to wild plants and game. The scarcity of occupational remains for the first millenium of the Christian period suggests that the population must have still been small, and it may be that farming had not yet assumed the dominant role it later had. The first extensive evidence of settled life in the Point of Pines area comes from Crooked Ridge Village, occupied from about the fourth to the seventh centuries. By A.D. 1000, masonry architecture begins to appear and slightly larger villages developed. This was probably accompanied by a slow growth of population and a gradual increase in the importance of farming. The population peak was reached in the fourteenth century, when several large towns were occupied simultaneously, the largest of them covering 4 acres and containing about 800 ground floor rooms. Thereafter, population declined, the larger towns being partly in ruins, and during the fifteenth century the entire area was quite rapidly abandoned by the farming peoples who had occupied it with such apparent success for the preceding centuries.[1]

Closely associated with the prehistoric settlements in the Point of Pines area are elaborate remains of early field systems. These remains are of three main kinds: first, *terrace walls*, consisting of rough walls of unshaped boulders built in series across the bottom of small, rocky stream beds that carry storm water from a wide area of hill-side or ridge top; second, *linear borders*, i.e. long lines of boulders or smaller stones, often stretching for some hundreds of yards and arranged in roughly parallel or concentric lines down the steeper hill-sides; thirdly, *grid borders*, or lines of stones arranged at right angles to each other to form a grid pattern, usually found either on gentler slopes or on the valley floor, sometimes in association with boundary markers and/or field shelters. The purpose of all three principal works is, in general terms, similar: namely, to conserve the soil, and to spread the run-off from summer storms so that it sinks into the ground instead of running away with its silt load.

Field works of this kind are virtually impossible to date *on their own*. In some cases, however, they are closely associated with nearby settlements which can be dated. I append opposite a list (based on Woodbury, 1961, pp. 16–34), of five representative field areas of the early period.

Dr. Woodbury makes clear (p. 30) that his estimates of field area are *minimal*, since they include only the area actually delineated by surviving field works. Since many stream bottoms and hill sides were probably farmed without *any* field works, the total area under cultivation was undoubtedly much greater than the figures given: a multiple as high as × 6 may even be reasonable.[2]

---

[1] This abandonment may have co-incided with the arrival of the White Mountain Apache in the area.

[2] Within an area of about 100 sq. miles, there are scores of similar farm sites which have not been mapped and measured. Woodbury estimates (1961, pp. 37–8) that as many as

| name of site | associated settlement | date | kind of field works | area of farm land |
|---|---|---|---|---|
| Clover Park site (Arizona W:9:30) | village ruin, comprising six rooms | A.D. 900–1150 | linear borders + terrace walls | 2 acres |
| Arizona W:10:8 | small village, consisting of about six pit houses | A.D. 1000–1150 | linear borders + grid borders | 2½ acres |
| Arizona W:10:114 | — | (?) A.D. 1000–1150 | linear borders + terrace walls | 3½ acres |
| Arizona W:10:115 | (?) Turkey Creek site | (?) A.D. 1000–1150 | linear borders | 12 acres |
| Arizona W:10:116 | — | (?) A.D. 1000–1150 | linear borders | 2½ acres |

Two points may be made here, with regard to these field works and to the agricultural system to which they were concomitant. In the first place, their construction entailed a very considerable outlay of time and energy on the part of their builders. General to the Great Basin Shoshoneans, as we have seen, was the notion that an object belonged to the person or persons who had expended work on it; in the Great Basin, however, there was no real concept of *land* ownership, the nearest approach to such a notion being found in Owens Valley, where exclusive rights to the crop of certain wild-seed, root and pine-nut tracts were vested in particular families. It was, I suggest, the interaction of a *general* notion of ownership of the kind current among the Great Basin Shoshoneans, with the *particular* labour of clearing and terracing fields entailed in prehistoric agriculture, that gave rise to the idea of land as an heritable asset.

The second point is that farming, on the scale implied by the field works at Point of Pines, profited from, even if it did not necessarily involve, co-operation. In seed gathering, as we have seen, co-operation is at a discount; individual families, at least in the conditions of the Basin-Plateau region, could do better working on their own than they could in association with other families. In

---

1,000 acres may originally have been terraced or bordered by stone alignments, and that the total area under cultivation may, at its peak, have risen to over 6,000 acres. These figures are commensurate with my own from the Oraibi valley, i.e. some 2,500 acres of farm land out of a total area of about 50 sq. miles; and I have estimated *there* that each matrilineage held from 40 to 60 acres of farm land.

the kind of farming practised at Point of Pines, this is no longer the case: a system of terrace walls, designed to break the force of a flash flood, is *more* efficient when carried the whole length of a gully than when limited to one section of it;[1] the labour of e.g. scaring birds from the growing crops may be halved, or even further reduced, by siting the fields of two, or several, families in close proximity to one another, while traditional Hopi practice attests the advantage of communal parties for sowing and harvesting. Moreover, the development of agriculture itself underwent profound changes between *c.* A.D. 600 and 900. Besides improved strains of maize due to selection, beans were now added to the previous corn-squash complex.[2] Improved seed, in conjunction with new crops, produced surpluses for reserve storage: a fact that is reflected in the presence of slab-lined storage chambers, in association with the house clusters of this period.[3] Complementary to increased yield went improvements in metates and manos for grinding the corn and beans harvested;[4] and this leads on to the final point I wish to mention here, namely, the rôle of grinding in pueblo life. For the rise of agriculture to a dominant place in their economy had far-reaching effects on the division of labour in those groups where it occurred.

Among all the groups of Great Basin Shoshoneans, as we have seen (above, p. 352), there was a rough-and-ready division of labour between the sexes; men did all the hunting of large game, took most smaller game, built houses and camps, collected materials for basketry, and sometimes lent a hand with seed and pine-nut gathering; women did all the preparing and cooking of food and most of the seed gathering, made baskets, took some of the smaller game, and were mainly responsible for the upbringing of small children. But this division of labour remained *within* the family; even though a man and a woman, by and large, undertook different tasks, they co-operated closely in those tasks. In traditional pueblo e.g. Hopi life, this was no longer the case: a man's work lay essentially in the fields (and, to some extent, in the kiva), in the company of other men, a woman's work essentially in the house, in the company of other

---

[1] In one site at Point of Pines (Woodbury, 1961, pp. 24–6), nearly 200 terrace walls, with an average length of 20 metres and an estimated height of 50 cm., were built in three adjoining gullies; this system, which conserved about 5 acres of garden land, extended over more than 1,000 yards of drainage. As Woodbury points out, this is as much masonry as might be used in a fifty- or seventy-five-room pueblo, although (as he says) less difficult to lay up.

[2] Eggan (1950), p. 123. At Point of Pines, the following cultivated plants have been identified: maize (*Zea mays*), kidney beans (*Phaseolus vulgaris*), tepary beans (*P. acutifolius*), and squash (*Cucurbita mixta*); at the Tularosa cave site, 75 miles to the north, these were supplemented by sunflowers (*helianthus*) and, from around A.D. 700 on, by cotton (Cutler, 1952).

[3] Eggan (1950), p. 123: slab-lined, I suppose, in order to inhibit the depredations of rats and mice. The size of such stored reserves is indicated by one room at Point of Pines, which contained approximately 25 bushels of charred corn: Woodbury (1961), p. 35.

[4] For these improvements in design, see Eddy (1964), pp. 8–9 and Fig. 1. The new techniques for grinding corn were accompanied by grinding bins, for storing the ground flour (Eggan, 1950, p. 129), and by improved methods of cooking (Hough, 1928, p. 69).

women. And this differentiation took place, we may suppose, over many centuries, coeval with the rise of agriculture to a dominant place in pueblo economy.

Of women's work, grinding was the epitome: it has been estimated, by Owens (1892, p. 164), that in the traditional pueblo economy a woman spent on average three hours a day, every day of her working life, grinding corn. Thus, in place of a man and a woman co-operating in the food quest (as among the western Shoshoni), one finds *a group of men* co-operating in work in the fields, and *a group of women* co-operating in work at home;[1] and it was this fact, I suggest, that led to the establishing of a rule of *unilocal* post-marital residence.[2] For, at marriage, a choice had to be made: *either* the bride remained with her grinding unit, i.e. the group of women of her natal household who habitually ground corn together, in which case the man came to live with her and joined the group of men who worked that household's fields; *or* the young man remained with his field-working unit, i.e. the group of men of his natal household who habitually worked together in the fields, in which case the girl came to live with him and joined the group of women who ground that household's corn. In western Pueblo society, the former choice was taken: mainly, I suggest, because of the precedent tendency, among the seed-gathering peoples of the Basin-Plateau area, for seed-gathering to be women's work and for valley seed plots to belong to women.[3]

[1] This aspect of traditional pueblo economy has been expressed by Miss B. Freire-Marreco (1914, p. 282), speaking—again in the voice of a Tewa girl—of the men of other clans who are married to our clanswomen:

> These are the men who support, or should support, the household, bringing their yearly crops to their wives to be stored and administered by *saja* [mother's mother, in Tewa: the senior woman of a clan or household], killing sheep (if they have any), and bringing firewood at frequent intervals.

[2] The germ of the idea put forward here is to be found in Eggan (1950, pp. 129, 131). Eggan believes that improved techniques for grinding corn, and the greater efficiency obtained by women grinding together in small groups, was an important factor in maintaining the matrilineal-matrilocal character of western Pueblo society. My own view is more radical: that it was the formation of corn-grinding groups (of women) on the one hand, and of field-working groups (of men) on the other, coeval with the development of *field*-agriculture (as distinct from casual sowing of valley bottoms), that gave western Pueblo society that character.

[3] Precedent, that is, to the actual working of *fields* by men. I see no need to postulate, as Steward does (1955, p. 169), that women originally tilled the soil (particularly as, among the Owens Valley Paiute, it was men who cleared the ground for tobacco plants and who were in charge of the irrigation ditches); it is enough, surely, that women were the original seed-gatherers, and that valley seed plots tended to belong to them.

Had the alternative precedent, of patrilocal residence and male ownership of pine-nut tracts, been followed, then, doubtless, the fields would have belonged to men and patrilocal-patrilineal descent groups would have emerged—as has, in fact, taken place among the Luiseño Indians of Southern California (Kroeber, 1925, pp. 686–7). To this extent, I am in agreement with Kroeber (1938, p. 308), who regarded such elements of social structure as *unilineal descent groups* 'as secondary and often unstable embroideries on the primary patterns of group residence and subsistence patterns'. Whether the descent groups that emerge trace descent in the male or the female line, seems, indeed, almost a matter of chance. But I disagree with Kroeber when he characterises such groups as *unstable*; they are, surely, as stable as the economic conditions to which they are the response.

o

While, therefore, the emergence of localised matrilineal descent groups among the western Pueblos may be attributed in the long run to the adoption of agriculture (Steward, 1955, p. 172), the chain linking the two events is an indirect one. With the adoption of field-agriculture, farm land became the principal resource of the community, in place of seed and root tracts; the working of the fields required co-operation; the labour expended gave rise to the notion that the fields themselves belonged to the families who had done the work on them, while the co-operation required led to the merging of several closely related families either under the same roof or in a cluster of contiguous houses (Titiev's rule of *unilocal* residence); the owning of farm land in common served to bind together the several families in the (matri-)lineage, and its handing-down—together with that of stone-built houses—to preserve the continuity of that body from one generation to another.

Reflected in the whole process is the increased density of population, consequent upon a more ample and assured food-supply brought about by the change from a dominantly seed-gathering, to a dominantly agricultural, economy.[1] And at this point, before proceeding further, we may take our leave of Mauss. Mauss, it will be remembered, argued *que la vie sociale, sous toutes ses formes . . . est fonction de son substrat matériel, qu'elle varie avec ce substrat, c'est à dire avec la masse, la densité, la forme et la composition des groupements humains*; and I said earlier (above, p. 345) that we were to test that hypothesis, first with regard to certain Shoshonean-speaking peoples of the Great Basin, and then with regard to the Hopi. That task I consider now to be discharged: a comparison of western Shoshoni, Owens Valley Paiute, and western Pueblo social organisation reveals profound differences in, e.g. classification of kin, reciprocal obligations, concepts of ownership, between peoples of the same linguistic stock; these differences may be traced directly back to variations in the density, the form and the composition of their respective groupings, variations which are themselves related (as we have seen) to the means at the disposal of each group for exploiting the resources of its environment.

### DIFFERENTIATION OF THE NUMIC LANGUAGES

Hopi, as I remarked earlier (above, p. 262), is the southeasterly outrider of the northern or Shoshonean branch of the Uto-Aztecan language family. This branch is itself divided into four groups, namely Luiseñic, spoken in the coastal region of Southern California: Tübatulabal, spoken in the Kern River region immediately to the west of the Sierra Nevada watershed above the lower half

---

[1] This point has been noted independently by Goldschmidt, in his enquiry (1948, pp. 444–56) into why a mature lineage system *failed to develop* among the tribes of Central California. 'I would postulate', he writes (ibid. p. 452), 'that the need for clan organization and its particular value to the community appears when the population reaches a certain density and size. Usually such density is the product of technological developments, particularly the adoption or invention of horticultural techniques. But it is not horticulture in itself which appears to be crucial.'

of Owens Valley: Hopi, spoken only in the Hopi villages: and Plateau Shoshonean, spoken over an area of not less than 200,000 sq. miles, extending for about 500 miles N.N.W. from the Colorado River at Grand Canyon and for 400 miles E.N.E. from the Sierra Nevada Mountains. The Plateau Shoshonean languages are also known as 'Numic', after the stem *nyum-* or *nyam-*, common to all the members of the group and signifying, in Shoshoni, 'people' or 'tribe' (and in Hopi, 'clan').

The languages of the Numic group, besides exhibiting structural features common to all the Uto-Aztecan tongues, also have a common stock of nouns derived from the ancestral speech ('proto-Numic') before its differentiation; many of these they share with Hopi. To give an idea of the range of objects covered and of the degree to which the nouns have preserved their original form, I append here a list of name-words for twenty-one objects in the environment, taken respectively from Northern Paiute, western Shoshoni (Kawich Mountains/Gosiute), Pahvant Ute, Southern Paiute (Kaibab Plateau), and Hopi:[1]

| *English* | *Northern Paiute* | *Western Shoshoni* | *Pahvant Ute* | *Southern Paiute* | *Hopi* |
|---|---|---|---|---|---|
| badger | *hu'na* | *huna'ᵃ* | *u:na'mpüts* | *üna'mpüts* | *hona'ni* |
| bow/arrow | *hu/a'dü* | *hu/edu* | *u/ats* | *hu/a'tcü* | *(ho')hü/a'out* |
| cottontail | *tavo* | *tavu'tsi* | *tavü'ts* | *tavu'ts* | *ta'vo* |
| coyote | *iça'ᵃ* | *ija'pü* | *yoho'vuts* | *süna'v* | *isau'û* |
| basketry cradle | *hu'pa* | *gohnu* | *kan* | *qö'nu* | *ta'pi* |
| gopher | *mü'yu* | *yuavits* | *mu:iyu'mpüts* | *müyü'mpüts* | *mü'yi* |
| hand | *mai* | *ma'ᵃ* | *ma'avi* | *ma* | *ma'a* |
| house | *no'bi* | *gahni* | *kahni* | *qa'ni* | *ki'hu* |
| grinding stone | *ma'ta* | *bo:to* | *ma:dᵃ* | *ma'ra* | *ma'ta* |
| moon, month | *miia* | *miia'ᵃ* | *mü''togots* | *müa* | *mü'iyawû* |
| mountain | *toya'vi* | *toyavi* | *kaiv* | *qaivᵃ* | *tükya'ovi* |
| north | *kwi'wi* | *kwina'hipu* | *kwiyü'm* | *?* | *kwini'wi* |
| pinyon | *tu'ba* | *tuba'ᵃ* | *tuvᵃ* | *tü'va* | *tuve'e* |
| rattlesnake | *togo'a* | *togoa* | *toxo'avi* | *togo'avi* | *tçü'a* |
| rock | *tu'pi* | *tümbi* | *tump:ⁱ* | *tü'mpi* | *tü'bka* (cañon) |
| salt | *öña'vi* | *üñavi* | *oa'vi* | *oa-vi* | *ö'ñga* |
| smoke | *kwi:p* | *kukwi'p* | *kwii'p* | *qwi:* | *kwi'kwici* (is smoking) |
| snow | *nuva'vi* | *taha'vi* | *nuva'vi* | *nüva-vi* | *nü'va* |
| sun | *ta'va* | *tave''nⁱ* | *tav:ᵃ* | *ta:va* | *ta'wa* |
| sunflower | *akü* or *pakü* | *akü:* | *akü'mp* | *a'qü-mpü* | *akau'wosi* |
| water | *pa'ya* | *pa* | *pa* | *pa* | *pa'* |

---

[1] The first three of these are taken from Steward (1938), Appendix B, pp. 272–84, the fourth from Sapir (1931), and the fifth from my own information and from the Glossary to Stephen's *Hopi Journal* (1936).

Lexico-statistic analysis of the languages of the Shoshonean branch of Uto-Aztecan, taken in conjunction with the present geographical distribution of the languages, indicates the following sequence:[1]

the original 'home land' of the undifferentiated language, i.e. Luiseñic/Tübatulabal/Hopi/Plateau Shoshonean or 'proto-Numic', lay in the southwestern corner of the Great Basin, in the Spring Mountain/Panamint Mountain/Owens Valley region. Between 3,500 and 3,000 years ago, Luiseñic broke away from the common stem, as the forbears of the present-day Shoshonean-speaking peoples of southern California pushed westward towards the sea.

Between 3,200 and 2,900 years ago, Hopi separated from the Tübatulabal-Numic group: i.e. by around 1000 B.C. (taking the lower date), Hopi had either already become, or was well on the way to becoming, a separate language no longer mutually intelligible with Numic and Tübatulabal, though still retaining—as it does to-day—many words in common with them.

Between 2,700 and 2,400 years ago, the same process happened to Tübatulabal: i.e. by around 600 B.C., Tübatulabal had separated from Numic, leaving the speakers of the (as yet undifferentiated) Numic in sole possession of the original 'home land'.

During the next 600 to 700 years Numic itself split into three groups, so that, by around A.D. 100, three separate languages occupied the old 'home land': i.e. a northwestern group in the Owens Valley/Lake Mono region, a central group in the Panamint Mountain region, and a southeastern group in the Spring Mountain/Vegas Valley region.

About a thousand years ago, there began a great movement northward and eastward which carried Numic far beyond the borders of its original home land. This spread appears to have been undertaken by each of the three groups independently, the northwestern group penetrating north towards the Humboldt River, the central group northeast towards Great Salt Lake, and the southeastern group east towards the Kaibab Plateau and beyond. During the next 500 years each of these groups itself split into two, to give the present geographical distribution of the Numic or Plateau Shoshonean languages: the northwestern group into *Mono*, concentrated in the Owens Valley/Lake Mono region, and Northern Paiute (or *Paviotso*), spread over a vast area to the north; the central group into Panamint Shoshoni, concentrated around the Panamint mountain range, and western Shoshoni, spread over the whole area from there to Great Salt Lake and the Wasatch piedmont; and the southeastern group into Chemehuevi, concentrated in the Vegas Valley region, and Southern Paiute/Ute, extending in a 150-mile wide corridor along the north bank of the Colorado River to the Uintah Mountains.

The lexical evidence indicates that the original Hopi speakers were in linguistic touch with their Numic congeners until about 1000 B.C., after which time the two groups drew apart; and that the three main groups of Numic speakers remained in close geographical touch with one other until about A.D. 1000, after which time they too diverged from each other as a consequence of their centrifugal spread from the old home land into the Great Basin.

[1] I present here a brief summary of the main conclusions reached by Lamb (1958, pp. 96–9), by Hale (1958, p. 107), by Hopkins (1965, pp. 49–51, 57–8), and by Goss (1966, pp. 10–13, 29–30). The technique of lexico-statistic analysis is still young, and Lamb, in particular, stresses the tentativeness of conclusions based upon it.

Turning to the ceremonies of the Numic speakers: we have seen that there is a *general* similarity between the ritual observances of the three groups (represented, in our analysis, by the Northern Paiute of Owens Valley, the Gosiute, and the Southern Paiute of Ash Meadows). Common to all, in one form or another, are: a fall festival associated with rabbit hunting, an annual mourning ceremony (for those who have died in the course of the year) following the fall festival,[1] *probably* some kind of smoking rite (associated with hunting) for young men, and a spring festival, taking the form either of a Bear dance or a circle dance, directed to the melting of the snows, the emergence of animals from hibernation, rain and the growth of plants.

Now I have suggested above that the analogue to the fall festival of the Great Basin Shoshoni is the Hopi Wü'wütçim ceremony; the analogue to the smoking rite for young men, Wü'wütcim initiation; and the analogue to the Bear dance or circle dance, the Hopi Powa'mu ceremony. What, then, is the analogue to the annual mourning rites of the Great Basin Shoshoni? And the answer, I suggest, is the Hopi Soya'l. That ceremony, it will be recalled, has a strong 'mourning' element; the great majority of the prayer-sticks and *nakwa'kwosi(s)* made in the course of it (see above, pp. 119–21) are *for* the dead, either the long-dead, the ancestors, or the recent and remembered dead. And this element, I believe, constitutes the original core of the Soya'l, to which all its other aspects—for increase of animals, fertility of corn, turning the Sun in his path—are accessory. If this is the case, we may ask, how has the mourning ceremony become detached from Wü'wütçim? And the answer, I suggest, is to be looked for in the part played by the stars in its timing. The fall festival itself is tied to the pine-nut harvest; while its timing may oscillate from year to year around a given date, it can never move very far from it. But if the timing of the annual mourning rites were originally fixed by observation, say, of the rising time of Orion and the Pleiades, or of their crossing of the meridian, as the emphasis on the observing of those constellations by Hopi in the course of Soya'l suggests that it may well have been, then we can see how, as a result of the precession of the equinoxes, the rites themselves may have become detached from the fall festival to which they were adjunct:

> The effect of precession, [writes Dr. M. F. Ingham, of the Department of Astrophysics, Oxford, to whom I referred the matter], is to cause the vernal equinox to occur each year some $20\frac{1}{2}$ minutes before the Earth has made a complete orbital revolution about the Sun. Thus, relative to the time at which a given star is due south at midnight, which relates to a particular point in the Earth's orbit, the equinoxes, i.e. the seasons, occur $20\frac{1}{2}$ minutes earlier each year. Thus a ceremony fixed by the culmination of a particular star takes place at a steadily increasing interval after the vernal equinox. In the past, therefore, the ceremony took place earlier than now, the displacement amounting to fourteen days per thousand years. Hence, a ceremony which was celebrated on 15 February two thousand years ago would fall due to-day on 15 March.

[1] Steward (1938), p. 184.

What I am suggesting is that, at the time (1200 to 1000 B.C.) when the original Hopi speakers became separated from their Numic congeners, i.e. at the time they 'came out of' the Great Basin, the fall festival and the annual mourning rites were still linked, and were fixed by the date of the pine-nut harvest, which also co-incided with a particular position of Orion and the Pleiades in the night sky; that the Hopi, on leaving the Great Basin, took the position of Orion and the Pleiades for the timing of their annual mourning rites, while retaining the date of the pine-nut harvest for that of the fall festival; and that after 2,000 years, i.e. by around A.D. 800, the mourning ceremony had fallen some twenty-eight days behind the fall festival, so that it coincided now with the winter solstice. At this point, due to the growing importance of agriculture in pueblo economy, the rites became tied to solar observation, acquiring in the process the various solstitial and agricultural attributes with which, as the Soya'l,[1] they were still invested a thousand years later.[2]

In support of this thesis, it may be noted that the Luiseño Indians of southern California, whose forbears broke away from the Numic-Tübatulabal stem at about the same time as the forbears of the Hopi (Goss, 1966, pp. 29–30), hold an annual mourning ceremony, in the course of which eagles are ceremoniously killed and buried: that Orion and the Pleiades figure prominently in Luiseñic songs and ritual: and that the spirits of the dead are themselves *identified with the stars of the Milky Way*.[3]

### THE ORIGIN OF HOPI CEREMONIALISM

I come now to the most obscure aspect of pueblo culture we have to face: namely, whence came Hopi ceremonialism? And before proposing an answer,[4] I shall define the question itself more precisely.

The archaeological record for the plateau region of northeastern Arizona shows the emergence there, from the 1st to 4th centuries A.D., of small-scale farming communities, dependent for their subsistence in part on the corn and squash which they grew on the valley bottoms but in large measure, still, on

---

[1] The word appears to be derived either from *so'ya*, the planting stick thrust into the grave (Stephen, 1936, p. 825), or from *so'ʾa*, '(they) are dead', plural of *mo'ki*, '(he) is dead'. In the old days the Hopi were known to their neighbours, e.g. to the Southern Paiute (Sapir 1931), as the *Mo'ki* or *Moqui*, no one quite knows why. Perhaps it was due to the part played by the annual mourning rites in their ceremonial cycle, as compared with their Shoshoni congeners.

[2] Parsons, also, queries (1936, pp. 508–9) whether the Soya'l at Oraibi was primarily a solstice celebration.

Steward, observing (in 1931) that the Unitah Ute Bear dance was then held in March, not in February as it had once been, ascribed this to a change to agrarian pursuits on the part of the Utes; but perhaps this retardment, too, was due to the precession of the equinoxes.

[3] Kroeber (1925), pp. 675–82. The Milky Way (*soñwuka*, in Hopi) crosses the meridian about an hour behind Orion, and is the only constellation (galaxy), apart from Orion and the Pleiades, named by the Hopi.

[4] This section was written during May and June, 1972, a year after the completion of the remainder of the book; it was only then, for the first time, that I felt able to answer the question posed in it.

the products of gathering and hunting. The linguistic evidence indicates that the forbears of the Hopi separated from their Numic congeners, and 'came out' of the Great Basin, around 1,000 B.C.; the evidence of physical anthropology,[1] that there has been no significant change of physical type in the agriculturalists of the region over the last 1,750 to 2,000 years. On these grounds it seems a reasonable inference that the forbears of the present-day Hopi formed a part of the original farming population of the plateau.

In earlier chapters (notably 12 to 14) I have described the ceremonial cycle of the Hopi as this existed when first recorded by outside observers at the end of the 19th century, together with the individual ceremonies of which the cycle was composed and the elements out of which the ceremonies themselves are built up; and I argued that it is these elements, notably the use of corn meal and feathers, of *nakwa'kwosi*(s) and *pa'ho*(s), of pigments and of smoking, that are likely to furnish the key to the meaning of Hopi religion. Subsequently, as the outcome of a study of Great Basin Shoshoni culture, I have suggested that the principal winter ceremonies of the Hopi have analogues in the winter ceremonies of their Shoshoni congeners, Wü'wütçim in the fall festival of the Shoshoni, Soya'l in the annual mourning rites, and Powa'mu—the fragment of it having to do with the banishing of cold and the return of warm weather—in the circle or bear dance; that one at least of the principal Hopi deities, Masau'u, is of northern origin; and that one element in the Hopi complex, namely tobacco smoking, is pre-figured in Shoshoni religious practice. These features of the cycle, I concluded, the Hopi owe to their Shoshoni inheritance.

But this legacy falls far short of the complete cycle; and it falls short in two principal respects. In the first place, a whole segment of the cycle running from Powa'mu—the other fragment of it—through the Uñkwa'ti ceremony to the Flute[2] and the Marau', and having to do with the germination and growth of corn, is missing from it: as are the deities, Mü'iyiñwa and Sun, chiefly associated with that segment, together with the majority of the key elements in the complex as a whole, notably corn meal, feathers, cotton thread and pigments. In the second place, and perhaps more significantly, the *principle* of the cycle itself, of a system even, is in large measure absent. All accounts of Shoshoni life agree on the relative casualness of their social groupings, and consequently of

---

[1] Seltzer (1944), pp. 32–3. Seltzer's conclusions are based on a comparison between the physical type represented by the inhabitants of the modern pueblos, Zuñi in particular, and that represented by the physical remains associated with Basketmaker and Pueblo sites in the same area.

[2] I shall not discuss further here the question of the katçinas. No signs of a katçina cult have been found at Kiet Seel and Betatakin ( *fl.* A.D. 1250–85), and I follow Eggan in regarding it as a 14th century introduction into the region.

A pointer to that origin may be furnished by the amaranth plant. Grain amaranths, as we have seen (above, p. 355, n. 2), formed one of the three staple crops grown in Mexico and Guatemala prior to A.D. 1500; amaranth seeds are included in the most sacred bundles at Zuñi (Parsons, 1939, p. 22); and the Hopi plant *ko'mo* (a variant of *A. cruentus*), formerly cultivated in the gardens as a source of the red dye used in *piki* bread distributed at katçina dances, is a northern outrider, modified by careful selection for pigment, of the cultivated grain amaranths of Mexico and Guatemala (Sauer, 1950a, pp. 601–2: 1950b, pp. 412–15).

the ceremonies they performed: those families that gathered in a mountain range for the pine-nut harvest performed the fall festival and the mourning rites that accompanied it; perhaps if the same families were still together in the spring, they did the circle or bear dance; the following fall they might be scattered to the four winds. But the essential feature of the Hopi cycle, before it began to disintegrate seventy years ago, was its interlockedness; each phratry grouping was responsible for one principal ceremony in the cycle, individual clans were responsible for specific items (e.g. offering corn meal, smoke, water) in all the ceremonies, and the efficacy of any one ceremony depended on the carrying-out of those preceding and following it. Thus there would be no point in doing Powa'mu, to exorcise the cold and prepare the ground for planting, unless Wü'wütçim and Soya'l had previously been done to ensure that cold and snow had actually occurred.

If, then, we are to seek the origin of that part of the ceremonial cycle that came to the Hopi from outside their Shoshoni inheritance, we have to look for two related pieces: the *actual items*, namely the ritual elements, deities and ceremonies which are missing from the cycle, or the analogues from which these may have derived; and the *principle* capable of combining these items, with items drawn from other sources, into a comprehensive system. If, further, we can point to an *external correlate* having nothing directly to do with the other two, but serving as a marker to the process of their transfer, we may take this as confirmatory evidence that the search has not been in vain.

The place where I propose to look for these two pieces, and for the external correlate that accompanied them, is in the Yucatan peninsula.[1] The particular items within the Hopi cycle upon which I shall concentrate are, as to ceremonies, the germination and corn-growth fragments of the Powa'mu and Uñkwa'ti,[2] and the Flute; as to deities, Mü'iyiñwa, Sun and the Cloud deities; as to ritual complexes, the four- (or six-) directions system, and the ceremonial day count; as to ritual elements, corn meal, feathers, cotton thread and ceremonial colours. If it can be shown that each of these items can be parallelled *in detail* in the classic Maya culture of the 4th to 7th centuries A.D., and that that culture contains within itself the principle by which these items may be synthesised into a system; and if, further, an external correlate can be pointed to, which is common to ancient Maya culture and to the pueblo culture contemporaneous with it; then I think we may conclude that that culture was the ultimate source upon which the Hopi drew for the elaboration of their ceremonial cycle.[3]

[1] Following, in this, certain hints thrown out by Fewkes seventy-five years ago (1894 *c*, and *d*). In all the literature on the Pueblos, these two papers by Fewkes—and the one by Ferdon referred to below—are the only ones known to me to tackle the question posed in this section; Fewkes wrote them after studying the *Codex Tro-Cortesianus* in Madrid during the winter of 1892–3.

[2] The plumed serpent fragment of the Uñkwa'ti, following Ferdon (1955, pp. 11–12, 21–2), I hold to be a 12th century introduction from Mexico.

[3] That the elements in question came from the south, i.e. from Meso-America, can hardly be doubted: the question is, from where, and when? The test of a Maya origin hangs on the degree of closeness of parallellism between them in the two cultures.

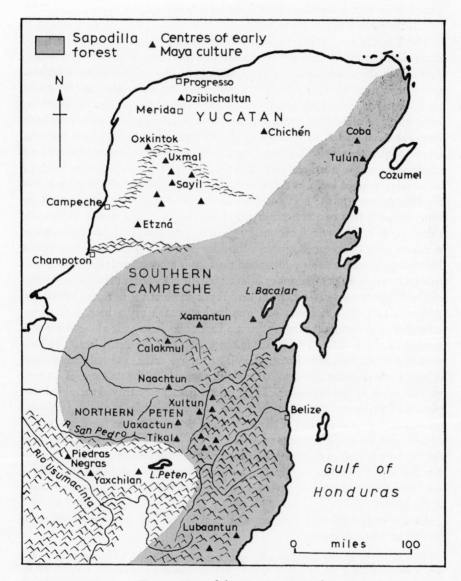

Fig. 60. Map of the Yucatan Peninsula.

The task that faces us is one of great delicacy, however; for what I am endeavouring to demonstrate is how an ideational complex may be shown to have passed from one culture to another, without being able to show the steps by which the passage was accomplished.

The Yucatan peninsula (Fig. 60), as Coe remarks,[1] is a single, great limestone shelf jutting up into the blue waters of the Gulf of Mexico. Travelling south from the northern tip of the peninsula (in the neighbourhood of Progreso), one traverses four principal zones: a flat limestone plain hardly raised above sea level, stretching for about 75 miles inland to the foot of the Puuc hills; a belt of increasingly hilly country, also about 75 miles wide, stretching from the Puuc hills to a few miles south of Etzná; a belt about 300 miles wide of more hilly country still, embracing the southern two-thirds of the state of Campeche and the northern part of Petén; and, finally, the southern lowland area embracing the basin of the Usumacinta River and its tributaries draining the hilly country to the north and the mountain chain to the south. Of these four belts, the first two are covered by low, thorny jungle, rarely more than thirty feet in height, which eventually gives way to xerophytic scrub along the northern coast of the peninsula; the third by high monsoon forest, dominated by mahogany trees and sapodillas; and the fourth by grassland savannah, interspersed by swampy depressions or *bajos* which fill with water in the rainy season.

The vegetational gradient, from xerophytic scrub at the northern tip of the peninsula to monsoon forest and grassland savannah at its base, is a direct reflection of the rainfall: ranging from a bare 20 inches a year along the north coast, to a mean of 60 to 70 inches in the region of Lake Petén Itzá. The two northern zones, also, are virtually bereft of surface water, the only sources of drinking water being the *cenotes*, or *chens*, formed by the collapse of underground caves in the limestone. These *cenotes* have necessarily determined the pattern of settlement in the northern half of the peninsula, as the dependence on an uncertain rainfall has of the agriculture practised there; for while Maya culture, and the *milpa* farming on which it was based, evidently originated in the southern region in the neighbourhood of the great centres at Tikal, Uaxactun and Lake Petén Itzá, it spread at an early date (i.e. around the 4th century A.D.) into the more arid country to the north, undergoing certain modifications in the process.

All the early authorities[2] agree on the extraordinary importance of corn (maize) in Maya culture:

---

[1] Coe (1971), p. 27. On the geography and phyto-geography of the Yucatan peninsula, see, besides Coe (1971, pp. 23–33), Bequaert (1933, pp. 513–22), Lundell (1934, pp. 258–64), and Morley (1946, pp. 6–13).

[2] Of the early sources, by far and away the most important is de Landa's *Relación de las Cosas de Yucatán*, written in 1566 and re-discovered in 1863. Arriving in the country as a Franciscan friar soon after the Conquest, de Landa stayed on for many years as bishop of Mérida; what he writes applies, therefore, primarily to the northern half of the peninsula. Quotations from the *Relación* are taken either from Morley (1946), from Thompson (1954), or from Tozzer's edition (1941); Spanish-speaking readers may prefer to consult the Spanish edition by Garibay, K. (1966).

If one looks closely, [writes an early Spanish chronicler[1]], one will find that everything they did and talked about had to do with maize; in truth, they fell little short of making a god of it. And so great is the delight and gratification they got and still get out of their *milpas* [corn fields], that because of them they forget wife and children and every other pleasure, as if their *milpas* were their final goal in life and the ultimate source of their felicity.

The clearing, burning, planting, weeding and harvesting of his corn field occupied the greater part of the time of the Maya peasant of the Classic period, and the growth of corn of his thoughts (so far as these can be inferred from the monuments), as they do of his successor today.[2] These farming activities furnished the frame for the Maya year.

The crucial event in the Maya farming year is the burning of the bush at the end of the dry season. The timing of this event was set, in the ancient culture, by observation of the sun's rising or setting behind fixed points on the horizon.[3] Today, it is often set by the chirping of cicadas:

Cicadas, [writes Morley (1946, p. 35)], are honoured weather prophets among the Maya. If one variety called *choch* chirps for a long time, it will rain; if another called *chipit-tin* chirps continually, it will be dry. Often the time for the important agricultural activity of burning the cornfield is determined by the chirping of these little insects.

The planting of the cornfield is described by de Landa in the following words (Tozzer, 1941, pp. 96–7):

The Indians have the good habit of helping each other in all their labours. At the time of sowing ... [they] join together in groups of twenty, more or less, and all together they do the work of all of them (each doing) his assigned share, and they do not leave it until everyone's is done.[4]

They plant in many places, so that if one fails the others will suffice. In cultivating the land they do nothing more than clear the brush, and burn it in order to sow it afterwards. From the middle of January to April they work it and then when the rains come they plant it, which they do by carrying a small sack on their shoulder, and with a pointed stick, they make a hole in the ground, dropping in five or six grains, covering them with the same stick. And when it rains, it is marvelous how it grows.

[1] *Chronica de la Santa Provincia del Santissimo Nombre de Jesus de Guattemala*, cap. vii (16th century MS.), quoted by Morley (1946), p. 21, and by Thompson (1954), p. 234. Morley himself (ibid. pp. 441–2) speaks of corn as the alpha and oméga of Maya life; virtually every aspect of Maya culture, he says, can be traced directly back to the complex of ideas that grew up around corn.

[2] See, on this point, Gann (1918), p. 20: Thompson (1930), pp. 41–2: and Morley (1946), pp. 141–50. The milpa itself is regarded as *zuhuy*, as is the maize growing within it, and to be treated with respect; literally 'virgin', unsullied, the word *zuhuy* refers especially to what is appropriate to or associated with the gods: Redfield (1941), pp. 120–1.

[3] At Copan, in western Honduras, stelae appear to have been set up for this purpose: Morley (1946), pp. 144–6, 308.

[4] That is to say, they worked on each man's *milpa* in turn until all were sown. This sharing of work extended to many aspects of Maya life, e.g. the building and thatching of houses, and weaving (by women): Tozzer (1941), p. 96, n. 428.

| our months | weather | farming | ceremonial cycle[1] | patron deities | Maya months |
|---|---|---|---|---|---|
| January | | | making new idols of the gods | Itzamna, Bacabs, Chacs, all deities | chen |
| | | clearing the fields | oc na, renovating the temples of the Chacs | Chacs | yax |
| February | dry season | | | | zac |
| | | | to appease the hunting deities for having shed blood in the chase | hunting deities | ceh |
| March | | | | | mac |
| | | burning the brush | to ensure rain for the corn, and a good year | Itzamna, Chacs | kankin |
| April | | | | | muan |
| | | planting the corn | to ensure rain for other crops (cacao) | Chacs, and bee deities | pax |
| May | | | | | kayab |
| June | | | summer dances | | cumhol / uayeb |
| | | growing season | New Year's rites, and renewal of tools and utensils | Itzamna, Bacabs, Chacs, all deities | pop |
| July | rainy season | | | | uo |
| | | weeding | for curing of disease / for successful hunting[3] / for successful fishing[3] | Ixchel, Itzamna / hunting deities / fishing deities | zip |
| August | | | | | zotz |
| | | bending the cornstalks | for abundance of honey[4] | Bacabs, especially the bee deities (Muzencabs) | tzec |
| September | | | | | xul |
| | | harvesting the corn | for flowers for the bees / anointing all utensils with sacred blue pigment / making new idols of the gods | Muzencabs, the bee deities / Itzamna, Bacabs, Chacs, all deities / Itzamna, Bacabs, Chacs, all deities | yaxkin |
| October | | | | | mol |
| November | dry season begins[2] | | | | |
| December | | | | | |

Before each of the main stages in the agricultural cycle, namely cutting the forest, burning the brush and sowing the corn, during the ripening of the corn (for rain), and at the harvest, periods of fasting and continence were—and still, in the more remote areas, are[1]—observed, and prayers and oblations offered to the appropriate deities. Describing these observances today, Thompson writes (1954, p. 248):

> In many parts of the Maya area, particularly in the western highlands of Guatemala, offerings of turkeys, various preparations of maize, beans and squash seeds, as well as flowers, are still made to pagan deities. In Yucatan, offerings are still made to the Chacs, and in the remoter villages of the peninsula no Maya will start to clear his land or plant his crop without an oblation, usually of copal and *posole*, to the gods of the soil (the black smoke of the copal represents the rain clouds; *posole* is a popular maize gruel).

These agricultural observances form but one aspect of the elaborate complex of Maya ceremonialism, to which we may now turn.

A number of major ceremonies filled the Maya calendar (see the *Farming and ceremonial calendar*, opposite); other, lesser rites responded to particular needs. All alike followed a similar pattern, and this pattern, common to all Maya rites and ceremonies, was made up of seven elements.[2]

(i) *A preliminary period of fasting and abstinence:*

> The abstinences which they generally subjected themselves to, [wrote de Landa (Tozzer, 1941, p. 107)], were of salt in their stews, and pepper, which was a very hard thing for them. They kept apart from their wives for celebration of all their feasts.
>
> They always entered on the offices of their feasts with fastings . . . And in some of the fastings of their festivals they neither ate flesh nor had intercourse with their wives.

---

[1] On present-day *milpa* farming in the rain-forest area, see Cook (1919), and Thompson (1930), pp. 41–55: on the religious rites that accompany the farming cycle there, Gann (1917), and (1918), pp. 42–8, and Thompson (1930), pp. 61–2, 106–14: and on *milpa* farming in the scrub-forest area of northern Yucatan, Steggerda (1941), pp. 89–139. The best general introduction to conditions of life in northern Yucatan, is still J. L. Stephens' *Incidents of Travel in Yucatan* (1843).

[2] Morley (1946), pp. 216–20, 236.

---

*Footnotes to Calendar opposite.*

[1] Morley (1946), pp. 254–5. This is the Maya calendar as given by de Landa (Tozzer, 1941, pp. 151–66); for the correlation of the Maya months as given by de Landa, with the equivalent dates in the Gregorian calendar, see Thompson (1925), p. 122.

[2] This is the date of onset in the northern part of the peninsula, e.g. around Chichén Itzá; farther south, in Petén, the rainy season may not finish until late in December.

[3] The lakes, in the southern half of the peninsula, being now filled with water; the previous month is called *uo* in Maya, after the frogs which croak at the height of the rainy season.

[4] Bee-keeping figured prominently in ancient Maya economy, the bees being kept in hollow log-hives. Honey and wax were collected both from domestic bees, and from wild bees in the woods: de Landa (Tozzer, 1941), pp. 193–4. October, November and December are the months when flowers are most abundant in northern Yucatan: Bequaert (1933), p. 514.

In addition to these restrictions on meat, salt and sexual intercourse, they also painted their bodies black, the black pigment being made (Tozzer, 1941, p. 89, n. 378: p. 125, n. 577) either from the soot of burning copal, collected on the inside of a special vessel, or from corn smut.

(ii) *Selection, in advance, of an auspicious day to celebrate the rite.*

(iii) *Expulsion of the evil spirit from the midst of those taking part:*

> In any festival or solemnity that this people celebrated in honour of their gods, they always began by chasing away from themselves the evil spirit, in order to perform the ceremony the better. And the driving him off was done sometimes by prayers and benedictions, which they had for this purpose; at other times by worship, offerings and sacrifices, which they offered for this purpose.
>
> de Landa: Tozzer (1941), p. 138.

(iv) *Incensing of the images, and aspersing:*

Incense was constantly burned in the course of the ceremonies, evidently (Thompson, 1954, pp. 253–4) to the deities of the four cardinal directions. Copal gum was used to produce the smoke for the incensing; the copal was ignited from 'virgin fire', *zuhuy kak*, fire made with a fire drill for the purpose (Tozzer, 1941, p. 153, n. 759). The aspersing, also, had to be done with water that was *zuhuy*, 'virgin': that is to say, water 'which they brought from the hollows of the trees or of the rocks in the forests' (de Landa: Tozzer, 1941, p. 105), where it had not been contaminated by contact with the soil.

(v) *Prayer, and sacrifice:*

> Then they drove away the evil spirit, as usual, [writes de Landa (Tozzer, 1941, p. 165), in an account of a typical ceremony], with much solemnity. This ended, the praying and offering gifts and incensing went on.

Offerings made to the gods included flowers, simple offerings of food, *tortillas*, beans, honey, incense, the first fruits of the fields, cooked meat in sauces, jade, shell beads, pendants and feathers (Morley, 1946, p. 217: Thompson, 1954, p. 248); also, on occasions, the blood of fish, fowl, dog, deer, and child,[1] the victim being killed with a flint or obsidian knife plunged into the ribs just below the left breast, the still-beating heart plucked out and the blood smeared on the face of the idol in whose honour the ceremony was being held.

(vi) *Dancing:*

Dances formed an essential part of every ceremony, and dances are represented on stelae and murals from the earliest period. Thus one of the murals from Bonampak (see Thompson, 1954, Pl. 17b), dated to *c.* 800 A.D., shows masked dancers on the left, probably impersonating the gods, a single seated figure at a drum, musicians beating turtle shells in the centre, and others shaking gourd rattles on the right.

(vii) *A purificatory rite, and concluding feast:*

Most Maya ceremonies, according to Thompson (1954, p. 254), included a purificatory

---

[1] On the ground that children, too, were *zuhuy*, 'virgin'. The general practice of human sacrifice was a late, and eccentric, development in Maya culture due to Mexican influence: Gann (1918), p. 57, cf. Tozzer (1941), p. 115, n. 533.

rite; and all concluded with a feast at which *balche*, fermented honey, was drunk in order
to drive evil from the bodies of those taking part.

The ritual core of this sequence I take to be: prayer, sacrifice, and dancing.
Of the first, de Landa writes (Morley, 1946, p. 204):

> . . . all the services, which they made to their gods, were for no other purpose than
> that they [the gods] should give them life, health and sustenance.

Of the offerings that accompanied the services, he says (Thompson, 1954,
p. 248):

> And other things which they had, they used to offer. They removed and offered
> the hearts of some animals; others they offered whole. Some were alive, some dead;
> some raw, some cooked. They also made offerings of bread and wine, maize prepa-
> rations and *balché* [fermented honey], and of every kind of food and drink which
> they used.

Finally, of dances of Spanish origin which he witnessed, Thomas Gage, an
English Dominican friar, wrote in 1648 (Thompson, 1954, p. 258):

> When I lived amongst them, it was an ordinary thing for him who in the dance
> was to act St. Peter or John the Baptist, to come first to confession, saying that they
> must be holy and pure like that saint whom they [were to] represent, and must
> prepare themselves to die. So likewise he that acted Herod or Herodias, and some of
> the soldiers that in the dance were to speak and accuse the Saints, would afterwards
> come to confess of that sin, and desire absolution as from blood guiltiness.

This quotation, as Thompson remarks, illustrates how completely the dancer
identified himself with the part he took, such being a natural attitude 'in a
society which had always held dancing to be essentially a religious ritual'.

The relation between man and god which thus emerges is one in which man
approaches the deity in whose power it lies to bestow the benefit he desires,
with an offering of food, incense or other goods, in return for which the deity,
if so minded, bestows the benefit desired: a relation that may be further
mediated, in the course of the greater ceremonies of which they are the object,
by the impersonation of the deities themselves by masked dancers. And at this
point, before enquiring into the nature of the deities whose aid was thus
invoked, we may break our narrative to see how far these aspects of Maya
culture are reflected in aspects of Hopi culture which we considered earlier.
This I shall do briefly, for it is not my purpose to prove a case; indeed I doubt
whether the case is susceptible of proof, since it is a movement of ideas not of
things that I am endeavouring to demonstrate. What I shall do, rather, is to
indicate the main parallels which, to my mind, exist between ancient Maya and
Hopi culture.

The first and most obvious of these parallels concerns the *form* of Maya and
Hopi ceremonies. In each a period of sexual continence, and of abstinence from
salt and meat, plays a major part; each is preceded by a preliminary rite,
'prayer-stick making' in the Hopi case, setting the time for the ceremony itself;

in each, prayer, offerings to the deity and dancing, form the core of the ritual; and in each, the ceremony itself is terminated by a purificatory rite, followed by a public feast. But a significant difference between the two may also be noted: whereas, in the Maya case, the ceremony opens with the expulsion of the evil spirit—conceived as an external entity—from the midst of those taking part, and the offerings to the deity at a later stage include not only seeds and agricultural produce but also the hearts (and blood) of sacrificial animals, among the Hopi the expulsion of the evil spirit has been replaced by the expelling of evil and rancour *from the hearts of the participants themselves*, while the offerings to the deity are restricted to corn meal, pollen, honey and feathers. In other words, the Hopi have taken the cruder, external elements of the Maya system and internalised, or *spiritualised*, them.

Regarding the *purpose* as distinct from the form of the ceremonies, de Landa's words that 'all the services, which they made to their gods, were for no other end, nor for any other purpose than that they [the gods] should give them life, health and sustenance', need no emphasis. And with de Landa's words in mind, we may return to the deities from whom these benefits were to be obtained.

Apart from Hunab Ku, the creator, who appears to have withdrawn early from the world he created and to have had little further to do with it, three principal deities dominated the Maya imagination, namely Itzamna, Chac (or the four *chacs*), and the Young Corn-god:[1]

*Itzamna*, the leading deity, was lord of the heavens, and also of Day and Night; as lord of the Day, he was intimately associated with the Sun deity, Kinich Ahau. One of the characteristic features of Maya deities is their ability to appear under different aspects. In Maya belief, the Sun crossed over the earth by day and spent the night in the underworld, returning to the upper world the next morning; it seems likely on this ground that Kinich Ahau, the Sun deity, is simply a special manifestation of Itzamna in the latter's capacity as lord of the Day, i.e. as the Sun.[2]

But Itzamna also has a link with rain, and with growing crops.[3] In company with the Chacs, he was invoked in the rain-making ceremony that took place at the time of the burning of the brush, in April. Further, he was addressed as *Itzamna t'ul*, Itzamna 'of the dripping water', and one source attributes to him the remark: 'I am the *itz* (dew) of heaven, I am the *itz* of the clouds'. According to the Motul dictionary, *itz* is 'milk, tear, sweat, semen, resin or gum that coagulates from trees, bushes and some grasses'. The word as Thompson remarks (1939, pp. 152–3), clearly refers to liquids that exude drop by drop; and this piece of evidence, along with the designation *t'ul*, leads Thompson to conclude (ibid. p. 160) that, in addition to his aspect as Sun deity,

---

[1] In the three surviving Maya codices, Chac is represented 218 times, Itzamna 103 times, and the Young Corn-god 98 times; Ah Puch, the deity in control of death, is represented 88 times, and the next three deities 134 times (between three). Ixchel, the patroness of childbirth and weaving, also appears in the codices, but Morley does not say (1946, pp. 230–1) how many times she is represented.

[2] Both Joyce (1914, pp. 227–8), and Morley (1946, pp. 222–3), reach this conclusion tentatively; Tozzer (1941, pp. 145–6, n. 707) equates Itzamna unequivocally with the Sun.

[3] Thompson (1939), pp. 152–61: confirmed by Tozzer (1941), pp. 145–6, n. 707. In his most recent work (1972, pp. 53–4), Thompson associates Itzamna with vegetation in general, and with the soil, on the basis of the glyphs by which the deity is represented.

Itzamna is closely connected with rain falling from the skies, and so, indirectly with the growing crops. He was almost certainly looked on as four-fold, each of his aspects being associated with one of the world colours and world directions.

*Chac, the god of rain*, was a rain-god primarily, and by association, god of lightning and thunder: hence by extension, god of fertility and agriculture in a broad sense, that is of the idea of growth and germination, and so by still further extension, even of the corn-fields.[1] He was a benevolent deity like Itzamna, with whom he is linked in certain important ceremonies, always the friend of man, *associated with creation and life*.

The rain-god, however, was regarded not only as a single deity but also as four deities, a different Chac for each of the four cardinal directions, each direction having its own special colour: red Chac of the east, white Chac of the north, black Chac of the west, yellow Chac of the south. And here we enter the realm of Maya cosmology,[2] for Maya believed that the sky was sustained by four gods, the Bacabs, who stood at the four sides of the world; each of these directions, or sides of the world, was associated with one of the four cardinal colours, 'almost every element in Maya religion and not a few parts of the Maya calendar being connected with one world direction and its corresponding colour' (Thompson, 1954, p. 225). Thus at each of the four sides of the world stood a sacred *ceiba* or wild cotton tree, the tree of abundance from which the food of mankind first came, of the colour belonging to that direction; in its branches perched a bird, and associated with it were a stone, vines, turkey, corn, all of the requisite colour. And there is reason to believe that a fifth tree, whose colour was blue-green,[3] was set in the centre.

The Chacs were intimately associated with, and in popular imagination probably merged into, the four sky-bearers or Bacabs. The Chacs, too, sat at the four corners of the world; in their hands they held calabashes and from these they sprinkled rain on the earth, hence they were sometimes known as 'the sprinklers'.[4] The little frogs, called *uo*, whose croaking announces rain, are their attendants and musicians; and they were also referred to, on occasions, as *mensabak*, 'maker(s) of the black soot or smut', representative of the dark rain clouds which they were believed to send.[5]

The four Bacabs, or Chacs, were also closely linked with the four Muzencabs, the patron deities of bee-keeping, and especially with the senior of these, Hobnil, whose name evidently refers to the hollow log-hives in which the Maya kept their bees. Their particular ceremony, to ensure a bountiful supply of honey, was held in October towards the end of the rainy season; like the Chac/Bacabs, they were associated with the four cardinal directions, as the following extract from a post-Conquest ritual makes clear:

[1] Morley (1946), p. 224: de Landa, describing (Tozzer, 1941, p. 161) the *oc na* festival, says that it was held in honour of the Chacs, 'whom they regarded as the gods of the corn-fields'.

[2] On Maya cosmology, see Thompson (1954), pp. 224–6: and, more recently, Coe (1971), pp. 175–6.

[3] The colour, that is to say, of jade and/or of blue corn; the other four world colours, namely black, red, white and yellow, are the colours of the other four kinds of corn grown in Meso-America and in the Southwest (Simpson, 1953, p. 52).

[4] According to de Landa (Tozzer, 1941, pp. 162–3, and n. 848), the rain-making ceremony in April was preceded by a short rite known as *tup kak*, 'putting out the fire', in the course of which a pile of faggots was lighted and subsequently extinguished by the four Chacs with pitchers of water: their action evidently symbolising (Long, 1923, p. 174) the putting out of the fires on the burning *milpas* prior to the sowing of the corn.

[5] Tozzer (1941), p. 125, n. 577.

The red flint is the stone of the red Muzencab, the red ceiba . . . his arbor which is set in the east. The red bullet tree is their tree, the red sapodilla, the red vine . . ' reddish are their turkeys, red toasted corn is their maize, etc.

Whether, therefore, the Chacs and the Muzencabs were in origin separate deities from the sky bearers, or whether they simply represent different aspects of the Bacabs, is of little import beside the fact that, in Maya popular opinion, the sky bearers were identified as patron deities both of rain and of the bees.[1]

*The Young Corn-god*, third deity in frequency of representation in the codices, was 'a deity of vegetation in general and of maize in particular' (Thompson, 1954, p. 230). He is always represented as a youth, often with an ear of corn as his head-dress or with flowing hair to represent the 'beard' on the corn. A stela from Piedras Negras,[2] Petén, dated A.D. 746, shows him kneeling on the ground dropping grains of corn into a hole; he wears a maize head-dress, and carries a seed bag in his left hand; the lower half of the panel shows the Earth mother reclining under the earth's surface.

In the Codices, the Young Corn-god (whose Maya name is unknown) is shown engaged in a variety of agricultural pursuits. He would thus seem to have been the patron deity of husbandry, as well as 'essentially . . . a corn-god, representing the spirit, not only of the growing corn, but also of the mature cereal' (Morley, 1946, p. 226). Like Itzamna and the Chacs, he was a benevolent deity, a god of life, prosperity, abundance and fruitfulness, and is never shown associated with the symbols of death.

Regarding these three deities, several points may be made. There is no doubt, first, that all three are aboriginal Maya.[3] Their relative standing, however, did not remain constant either in time or place. From the very earliest period, if we are to judge by the surviving monuments, veneration of the Chacs was predominant in the more arid country of northern Yucatan.[4] In course of time, also, the Young Corn-god, even in the central region where early representations of him are most frequent, appears to have declined in importance *vis-à-vis* the Chacs and some of his fertility attributes to have passed to the latter; so it has come about that, today, it is the Chacs whose aid is sought by the Maya peasants not only of Yucatan but also of the more rainy regions to the south.[5]

---

[1] See, on this point, Thompson (1954), pp. 215–16: cf. Tozzer (1941), p. 157, nn. 795 and 796.

[2] Morley (1946), Pl. 54c, shows the whole stela; Thompson (1954), Pl. 10b, the upper half only. See further, on this stela, the *additional note* on p. 441.

[3] See, on this point, Morley (1946), p. 223, and Thompson (1954), pp. 114, 228–9, for Itzamna and the Chacs; and the depicting of the Young Corn-god on stelae of the Classic period, for that deity.

[4] The region of scrub forest, that is to say, from Etzná northward, embracing the area of the Chenes and Puuc cultures of the Classic period. Joyce pointed out many years ago (1914, pp. 346–50), as Morley (1946, pp. 222–3) and Alberto Ruz (1970, pp. 88–90, 96) have done more recently, that the buildings in this region, e.g. at Kichmool, Uxmal, Kabah, Labná, Sayil, Chichén *viejo*, are distinguished from those in the Central (Petén) region by the riot of Chac masks with which they are decorated: a point which the reader may confirm by brief reference to the *Guide Bleu* (Boulanger, 1968, pp. 859–67, 892–4). It is not too much to say, indeed, that the ceremonial centres in northern Yucatan represent a *Chac* culture.

[5] Thompson (1954), p. 230: cf. for specific areas, Gann (1918), p. 48, and Thompson (1930), pp. 61–2, 106–9, 114.

The predominance of the Chacs in northern Yucatan from earliest times, and their usurpation of the place once held by other deities in the Central (Petén) region, both stem, I suggest, from the conditions of *milpa* farming. Thompson, who carried out field work in the upper basin of the Belize River (about 50 miles southeast of the early Maya centres at Tibal and Uaxactun), characterises the sapodilla forest area in these words (1930, pp. 227–9):

> Mountain Cow Water Hole [the base from which he worked] is situated in rolling limestone country thickly covered with tropical rain forest. The rainfall during most of the season is heavy, and only during the months of February, March, April, and May can one count with any certainty on a spell of dry weather. The soil is rich, although somewhat shallow, but in the valleys is to be found deep soil as good as any in the whole peninsula.
>
> Practically every hillside between Benque Viezo [15 miles away] in the north, and the Mountain Cow area in the south, is terraced. The terraces are faced with rough blocks of limestone, and vary in width according to the slope of the hill on which they are situated.

L. H. Owers, in *The Geology of British Honduras* (1928), speaks of virtually the whole of the limestone plateau being covered with abandoned agricultural terraces; and Lundell states (1933, pp. 72–3) that linear borders are to be found in many areas in southern Campeche, i.e. to the south of Etzná.

In limestone country, hill soils are more fertile than their lowland equivalent; so it is natural that the Mayas should have chosen them for their *milpas*. The terraced slopes are relatively gentle, however, and would be quite usable for *milpa* crops without terracing and with no attendant risk of erosion (Wright *et al*, 1959, p. 112). They must, therefore, have conferred some other advantage. Now the tropical rain forest presents two principal obstacles to the *milpero*.[1] In the first place, on account of the size of the trees growing there, the initial labour of clearing the land for the cornfield is very much greater than in the more arid country to the north; in the second, the increased moisture causes secondary growth to appear before the felled trees have dried sufficiently for burning.

The effect of terracing is to create a series of silt-traps across the slope, often extending right round the head of a valley; in places, indeed, some 6 to 8 feet of soil, additional to the two feet already present, has accumulated during the centuries and the original retaining walls are now buried under 2 to 3 feet of soil. Two principal advantages follow: in the first place, the fertility of the soil is renewed through the annual wash-down of new material, especially of organic phosphates, from the steeper slopes above; in the second, the deeper soil

---

[1] Redfield, in particular, stresses (1941, pp. 6–7, 10–11) the difficulties attached to *milpa* farming within the rain-forest belt; it is clear from his account that an assured dry spell in March–April, to ensure good burning of the brush, is nearly as important for the *milpero* as an assured wet spell in May–June, to ensure germination of the seed. The wide gap between the group of early settlements in the southeast of the peninsula (Tikal-Uaxactún), and the group in the northwest (Uxmal-Kabáh), is probably due to the hazards of *milpa* farming in the intervening rain forest.

serves to hold the available moisture longer. On these grounds, Wright _et al_ conclude (1959, pp. 113–14) that the terracing of limestone slopes in the rain-forest region, allied with hand weeding, permitted far more regular cropping of the land than would have been possible without terracing—or than is practised in the same area today, now that the terraces have fallen out of use.

The essential features of _milpa_ farming as practised in the rain-forest region of the pensinsula in the Classic period are, then: an assured rain supply, relatively deep soil and agricultural terracing, permitting the repeated use of the more desirable patches of land. None of these three conditions are present in the northern scrub forest. The soil, apart from local pockets in the limestone, is extremely thin, often no more than a few centimetres in depth:

> Yucatan, [wrote de Landa,[1] referring to the northern half of the peninsula], is the country with least earth that I have seen, since all of it is one living rock and has wonderfully little earth ... and it is marvelous that the fertility of this land is so great on top of and between the stones, so that everything that grows in it grows better and more abundantly amongst the rocks than in the earth: because on the earth which happens to be in some parts, neither do any trees grow, nor do the Indians sow their seeds in it, nor is there anything except grass. And among the stones and on top of them they sow, and all their seeds spring up, and all the trees grow and some so large that they are marvelous to see. The cause of this is, I believe, that there is more moisture and it is preserved more in the rocks than in the earth.

The rainfall, while apparently fairly abundant (e.g. around 36″ a year at Campeche, and 48″ at Chichen Itzá), is in fact very unreliable. As Redfield observes:[2]

> While the seasonal alternation [between summer and winter] is marked and regular, the total amount of annual rainfall is subject to great fluctuation. During some years three or four times as much rain falls as in other years. Thus, although the agriculturalist may count upon the coming of the rains, he may not count upon the coming of enough rain.

Finally the lie of the land, and in particular, as one moves north from Etzná, the increasing flatness of the country, renders it unsuited to terracing.

Thus, in moving out of the southern rain forest into the more arid, scrub forest to the north, the early Maya had to modify very considerably the _milpa_-farming techniques suited to the former, substituting a true shifting cultivation[3]

---

[1] Tozzer (1941), p. 186: cf. on the thinness of the soil in northern Yucatan, Lundell (1934), pp. 263–4, Steggerda (1941), pp. 89–92, and Morley (1946), p. 11. Bequaert also comments (1933, p. 514) on the porosity of such soil as there is.

[2] Redfield (1941), p. 5: cf. on the climate around Chichén Itza, Steggerda (1941), pp. 130–6.

[3] One, that is to say, in which fields are in use for only two years before being allowed to revert to bush: Steggerda (1941), p. 114.

My own observations, made on a brief visit to northern Yucatan early in July, 1972, indicate that in moving into the scrub-forest area the Maya hit upon a modified form of flood-water farming. Flood-water farming, as Kirk Bryan observed (1929, pp. 444 _et seq._), involves the use of a volume of rain falling over a larger area on a smaller area, the water for the more regular use of fields permitted by agricultural terracing; and it was as corollary to this change in technique, and to the increasing dependence on an uncertain rainfall as they moved farther north, that the Chacs or rain-gods came to the fore as the principal objects of veneration among the northern Maya.[1]

Returning now to the deities in general, one further point may be noted: namely, the strongly dualistic nature of Maya religion. The principal deities were seen as being engaged in a constant struggle, the benevolent deities bringing thunder, lightning and rain to fructify the corn and ensure plenty, the malevolent ones causing hurricanes or drought, which spoil the corn and bring famine in their train. This contest is graphically depicted in the Codices, where Chac the rain-god is shown (Morley, 1946, Fig. 10) tending a young fruit-tree, while behind him follows Ah Puch, the death-god, who breaks the tree in two.

The dualistic bias in Maya religion is expressed very clearly in the character of Ixchel, the patron deity of conception and child-birth, and of weaving:[2]

*Ixchel*, who may or may not be associated with the moon, has four undeniable attributes in Maya belief:

*as deity in control of conception, pregnancy and child-birth*, i.e. of human procreation in general, being referred to as 'the goddess of making children': de Landa (Tozzer, 1941, p. 129, and n. 599).

*as inventor and patroness of weaving*, being depicted in the Codices either spinning thread or weaving at a loom, and referred to in the texts as 'she of the 13 skeins of coloured thread'.

*as grandmother*, being depicted in the Codices as an old woman, referred to in texts as 'our grandmother', and held to be, *inter alia*, grandmother to the Bacabs: Thompson (1939), p. 137, and p. 148, n. 39.

*as spider*: a Maya text, given in full by Thompson (1939, p. 148), specifically links spider, whose colour appears to have been blue-green, with its grandmother Ixchel, 'she of the thirteen skeins of dyed thread'. Subsequently, Ixchel herself appears to have become identified with spider (ibid. p. 168), and the spider's web to have been the symbol of one of the four Bacabs or sky-bearers.

---

being led from the one to the other either by a watercourse or by direct run-off from an adjoining talus slope. In either case, the water comes from *outside* the field. Quite commonly, in northern Yucatan, a *milpa* field embraces a local pocket of soil, an acre or two in extent *together with the limestone slopes forming the edges of the pocket*; the whole area is sown with corn but the floor of the pocket more regularly than the walls, where planting is necessarily restricted to crannies in the rock. In this way the rain falling over one area, i.e. over the limestone slopes, is utilised on another, i.e. on the floor, though both lie within the confines of the *milpa* (one part of which serves as catchment area for the other).

[1] In keeping with their predominance there is the fact that the *cenotes* are regarded as the especial abode of the Chacs, that the plants growing around the *cenote* are used in their ceremonies, and that the frogs, toads and tortoises living near the *cenotes* are their 'pets': Redfield (1941), p. 117.

[2] On the ambivalent character of Ixchel, see Thompson (1939), pp. 132–7, 147–8, 166–8, and (1954), pp. 227–8: cf. Morley (1946), pp. 181, 230–1, and for an illustration of her weaving at a loom taken from the *Codex Tro-Cortesianus*, ibid., fig. 45. Ixchel, like her consort Itzamna, is an aboriginal Maya deity (Thompson, 1954, p. 114); her link with the moon may well be a later, Mexican import.

Ixchel also has some link, probably through the spider's web/cloud association, with rain, and it is this link that furnishes the other side to her character: for while, as patroness of pregnancy and childbirth, inventor of weaving and 'grandmother', she was a friendly deity and generally well disposed towards mankind, she is also depicted on occasions in the Codices as 'an old and hostile water-goddess', sender of floods and cloudbursts on the unsuspecting people.

This concludes our account of the principal Maya deities,[1] and again I shall allude only briefly to what I hold to be the significant Hopi analogues. Clearly, first, virtually the whole of the Hopi colour-directional system and the ascription of plants, birds, cultigens, etc., to the colour-directions (see above, pp. 92–3), is pre-figured in Maya cosmology; that the five principal colours have got out of order at some point on their journey is of less weight than the fact that the same five colours are made use of, that these are the colours of the five main kinds of corn, and that they serve as the basis for ascribing other natural phenomena to their appropriate classes or 'directions'.

Regarding the deities themselves, the Chacs or Bacabs are evidently the Cloud deities of the Hopi, the chiefs of the Directions, who sit at the four cardinal points and send rain to fall on the Hopi land. The Young Corn-god of the Maya, whose name is for ever unknown, is none other than Mü'iyiñwa:[2]

> And here (at the Below, *at'kyami*) sits the deity regarded as the maker of all life germs. He sits upon a flowery mound on which grows all vegetation. He wears a mask[3] of clouds of all these five colours, and before it flutter all the butterflies. Speckled corn and sweet corn grow there, and melons, cotton, beans, squash ...

*Ta'wa*, Sun, who as he journeys over the earth sees the prayer-offerings of the Hopi and comes to them, and inhales their essence, and places them in his girdle and takes them with him as he goes in at the west, represents the Maya Itzamna in his aspect as Sun deity.[4] And here a further parallel may be noted. For the ancient Maya fixed the timing of their agricultural cycle, as did the Hopi until recent times, by observation of the sun's rising and setting behind fixed points on the horizon, while their present-day descendants use the chirping of cicadas for the same purpose.

[1] I have not dealt with the gods of death and destruction, or, for that matter, with many other aspects of Maya culture, because I am concerned here only with that fragment of the culture that proved acceptable to the early Pueblos: namely, its *positive* aspects.

[2] His Hopi name being derived, perhaps, from that of the Muzencab(s), the Maya bee deities: bees, it will be remembered (above, p. 110), are the 'pets' of Mü'iyiñwa.

[3] In the second of the two papers cited above (1894d, pp. 266–7), Fewkes pointed out that, in the Maya codices and on bas-reliefs of the archaic period, the Maya deities are depicted holding their masks in their *left* hand; he compares this specifically (ibid. p. 267, n. †) with the Hopi use of the left hand for putting on and taking off the mask, as well as for sprinkling sacred corn meal.

[4] The glyph for Itzamna in his vegetational aspect shows the head of the deity with the symbol for vegetal growth (*bil*), a sprouting maize seed, emerging from a cavity in the forehead, while that for the Sun is commonly post-fixed by a sign representing the Sun's rays: Thompson (1972), pp. 53–4, 64–5. This combination of signs is perhaps reflected in the Hopi clan name, *Sun's forehead*, said to represent the Sun's 'brow' as it rises above the horizon.

And finally Ixchel, the Hopi 'Spider woman', patroness of conception, pregnancy and childbirth, grandmother, old hag, inventor of weaving . . . :

> She has a good breath, bad breath, and a breath. She can cause good or evil to happen, or she can remain passive. She knows everybody in the world. . . .

To understand *her* significance, we have to understand the place of weaving in Maya culture:[1]

> Weaving to the Maya woman was a sacred undertaking, just as the working of his land was to her husband. Indeed, women of the Guatemalan highlands still offer a prayer before starting to weave a new textile. It was not chance that the moon goddess [i.e. Ixchel], the special patroness of women, was credited with the invention of weaving. . . .

Now I have suggested earlier that the Hopi (or their forbears), in taking over the main structure of Maya ceremonialism, internalised or *spiritualised* certain of its cruder elements, namely the expulsion of the evil spirit—conceived as an external entity—and the offering of the heart of a sacrificial victim, substituting for these elements the expelling of evil from their own hearts and their coming to the office of the deity themselves with pure hearts. That process of *spiritualisation*, they took a stage further. Early accounts of the Maya stress the multitude of their images,[2] and the heterogeneity of the offerings that were made to them. In both respects, Hopi culture is marked by an extreme austerity; only in the most solemn ceremonies do wooden figures appear at all,[3] and even then the offerings that are made to them are of the simplest: corn meal, pollen and honey.

And the reason for this is to be looked for, I suggest, in the place ascribed to cotton and feathers in Hopi religion. Taking over the sacred nature of cotton, and probably of feathers too, the Hopi transmuted it to their own ends; spinning and weaving cotton became men's work, to be done in the kiva,[4] and the principal objects for which cotton was woven were ritual objects, namely the wedding *o'va* needed by the bride on her journey to the after-world, the breech clout worn by men in the course of all major ceremonies, and the cotton mask laid over a dead person's face prior to burial, while cotton thread itself was required chiefly for making prayer 'roads', *pa'ho*(s) and *nakwa'kwosi*(s). Now the whole object of the prayer-offering is that it 'stands for' whatever it is that is desired:

---

[1] Thompson (1954), p. 181: for the actual technique of Maya weaving, see Morley (1946), pp. 405–9. Two kinds of cotton were grown by the Maya: de Landa (Tozzer, 1941), p. 200, and n. 1099.

[2] See, on this point, de Landa (Tozzer, 1941, p. 108 *et seq.*); the wooden images were carved out of the wood of *ku che*, 'divine tree', the Spanish cedar. Whether Hopi *kya*, 'sacred', comes from the same stem as Maya *ku*, I must leave for etymologists to determine.

[3] This does not refer to katçina figures which, besides being late in origin, were primarily educational in purpose and were restricted, by and large, to children.

[4] The sacred character of which, so far as it has one apart from the ceremonies that take place in it, may derive from this source.

A man makes a prayer-stick because he wants something good, some benefit.

Feathers are used in prayer-sticks and breath-feathers, because they are *ka-püʼtü*, 'not heavy', light; and Cloud, and all the other chiefs, desire them to make the fringe of feathers with which to decorate their foreheads.

The Hopi barters his prayer-offerings with those chiefs for the benefits he desires to receive from them. He exchanges prayer-sticks and breath-feathers for material benefits.

As Sun journeys over the earth, he sees the prayer-sticks and breath-feathers, and comes to them and inhales their essence and takes them. He places them in his girdle and when he goes in at the west to the Below, he gives them, all that he has collected through the day's journey, to Müʼiyiñwa. Müʼiyiñwa knows all prayer-sticks and breath-feathers, and as he takes them up one by one, he looks at each . . . [and] those that are ill made, *or made by men of evil hearts*, he casts away, saying: 'this one is from a bad man, *ka-hoʼpi*, a foolish one'.

Thus what, in Maya religion, is still in large measure a corporeal relation between man and the image of the deity, mediated by way of carnal offerings and dependent for its efficacy on their size,[1] has become among the Hopi a predominantly spiritual relation between man and deity, mediated by way of prayer-sticks and breath-feathers and dependent for its efficacy on the purity of heart of whoever makes and offers them. Benefits are still sought, but prayer and thought-power, not material offerings, are the means by which they are to be obtained.[2]

I said earlier that, apart from specific ritual elements that might be common to Maya and Hopi ceremonialism, we were to look for the *principle* capable of combining these elements into a system, and for an *external correlate* marking the passage of the whole complex, i.e. of elements and principle together, from the one culture to the other. To these two concluding matters, and to the ceremonial day count, I now turn.

All Maya religious festivals, as well as important stages in the agricultural cycle such as cutting the forest, burning the brush and sowing the fields, were preceded by a period of abstinence and fasting; this period of continence lasted for 13 days, as it still commonly does today in the remote parts of Guatemala and Honduras.[3] The period of 13 days represents a 'week' in the Maya sacred

[1] As is shown by the graded scale of the offerings made, ranging from (say) a fowl or fish to, on great occasions or in dire stress, a human child.

[2] I am inclined to think that, in the most general sense, the Maya idols, the more important of which were made of wood (de Landa: Tozzer, 1941, pp. 110–11, 159–61) and which were painted with either a black or a blue-green pigment (Tozzer, 1941, p. 117, n. 537: p. 160, n. 826), were transmuted into the twin sticks—one faceted—of the Hopi *paʼho*, typically painted (above, pp. 52–3) blue-green and black. Thus what, among the Maya, had been an image to which offerings were brought, became among the Hopi the *vehicle* by which prayers were conveyed; and the ceremony at which great numbers of these were made, celebrated by the Maya in late December, the Hopi merged with the mourning rites of their Shoshoni forbears to produce the Soyaʼl.

[3] Thompson (1954), p. 135: and for the 13-day period of abstinence in old Maya culture, de Landa (Tozzer, 1941), p. 152.

year, the *tzolkin* or 'count of days'. To understand the nature of this 'week', requires an excursus on Maya time-reckoning.

The Maya system of counting was vigesimal: that is to say, they had separate names for numbers up to 20, as the 3rd Mesa Hopi still have,[1] while for larger numbers they counted in multiples of 20, e.g. in Hopi *lö'p sunat* (two 20s), *pa'yip sunat* (three 20s), *na'löp sunat* (four 20s). The *tzolkin* or 'count of days' was arrived at[2] by taking the numerals from 1 to 13 and prefixing them, one by one, to the twenty Maya day-names, as it might be (if *we* had twenty day-names, not seven) *one Monday, two Tuesday, three Wednesday* . . .; when the 14th day-name was reached, the numeral *one* was applied to it again, and so on, thus making a single *tzolkin* or 'sacred year' of 260 days (20 'weeks' of 13 days each) before *one Monday* occurred again. This time-period was, in Morley's words,[3] 'the most fundamental fact of their religion [i.e. of the religion of the common people], since it determined for everybody the very pattern of his or her ceremonial life'. This it did because each of the thirteen days of the 'week' was dedicated to one of the thirteen deities who presided over the upper world, and the god of the particular day upon which a person was born became his guardian deity.

Quite separate from the 'count of days' or *tzolkin*, was the *haab* or calendar year of 365 days, made up of 18 months of 20 days each (the 20 named days), known as *uinal*, plus a closing 'month' of 5 days and 6 hours.[4] These 19 months were each named (see above, p. 420), and important ceremonies were associated with many of them: thus the ceremony to the bee deities, for abundance of honey, was held in *tzec*, the 5th month (mid October) after the celebration of the New Year's rites, that for the Making of new Idols in *mol*, the 8th month (late December), that for the Renovation of the temples of Chac in *yax*, the 10th month (early February), and that to ensure rain for the corn in *mac*, the 13th month (early April), the latter two ceremonies being the Maya analogues to the moisture-and-corn-growth fragment of the Hopi Powa'mu and to the Uñkwa'ti.[5] In this way the Maya calendar furnished a frame both for the ceremonial cycle and for the agricultural labours to which the cycle referred.[6] Each year, further, was associated with one of the four cardinal directions and with the Bacab associated with that direction;[7] there were thus four kinds of year, i.e. red, white, black and yellow, each having certain ceremonies peculiar to it and to no other.

The Maya conceived the world as having thirteen heavens, arranged in layers, the lowest being the earth itself; over each presided one of the thirteen gods of the upper world, who also presided over one of the days of the sacred 'week'. And there were nine underworlds, also arranged in layers, over each of which presided one of the nine gods of the lower world, the ninth and lowest underworld being Mitnal, ruled by Ah Puch, the lord of Death; and corresponding to these nine gods was a cycle of nine nights, over

---

[1] Or had, until recently: Colton (1941), pp. 35–6.

[2] See Morley (1946), pp. 265–9.

[3] Morley (1946), p. 267. The *tzolkin* or 'sacred year' of 260 days, roughly equal to nine moons, was still in use in the highlands of Guatemala forty years ago: Lothrop (1928), pp. 653–4. For its Hopi analogue, see the *additional note* on p. 441.

[4] Giving, in practice, a sixth day every four years: Tozzer (1941), pp. 133–4.

[5] Fewkes, also, compares (1894c, p. 33, n. †) the Hopi *powa'mu*, in the course of which the kivas are renovated and re-plastered, to the Maya *oc na* ceremony for the renovation of the temples of the Chacs.

[6] The link between calendar, ceremonial cycle, and agricultural labours, is stressed by Alberto Ruz (1970), pp. 22, 65–7.

[7] Morley (1946), pp. 243–4: cf. Thompson (1934), pp. 211–15.

each of which one of these gods ruled.[1] Thirteen and nine were thus, in Morley's words (1946, p. 204), 'the two most sacred numbers among the Maya, the former corresponding to the number of gods of the Upper World and the latter to the number of gods of the Lower World'. Together with the number of the cardinal directions, they recur in present-day Maya practice. Thus, when a boy reaches the age of four months, he is carried for the first time on his mother's hip, not in her arms:

> The number of months is placed at four, [writes Thompson (1930), p. 110], because the corners of the *milpa* are four in number, and his future life will be bound up with the *milpa*. His god father carries him nine times round the table set in the centre of the hut; at each circuit he places a small tortilla in his mouth.

A Maya woman generally resumes her household duties *nine* days after the birth of her child; there are nine days of prayer for thanksgiving, and nine nights of prayer after the death of a relative. When the *milpa* is to be burned, *thirteen* bowls of *zaca* (food) are offered to the gods of the bush.[2]

The numbers 4, 9, 13 and 20 furnish the key to the Hopi ceremonial day count. That count, it will be remembered (above, p. 61), begins with *yü'ñya*, 'going in'; this is followed by a first sequence of four days, one for each of the four cardinal directions, and then by a second sequence of four days, making nine days in all. On the ninth day the dance (*ti'kive*) is held, and this initiates the third sequence of four days, during which the leaders of the ceremony (*wi'mi*) fast in the kiva and continue to observe ritual tabus; making a total of thirteen days. The 13-day 'week' thus survives among the Hopi in the thirteen days of ritual abstinence observed over all major ceremonies, and the 20-day 'month' in the twenty days' seclusion to which the new-born child is subject (see above, p. 27): both periods starting, as among the Maya, with day 0.

To sum up the evidence adduced so far: what I believe happened was that a nexus of ideas, having to do with moisture, with the germination and growth of corn, and with the return of warm weather, was carried from northern Yucatan into the pueblo region[3] at the formative point, i.e. around A.D. 700, in the development of Pueblo culture. This nexus of ideas was represented, as to ceremonies, by the moisture-and-corn-growing fragment of the Hopi Powa'mu and Uñkwa'ti, and probably, in view of the part played by the Flutes in sun-watching (and by *ma'hü*, cicada, in Flute symbolism), by the nucleus of the Flute; as to deities, by the Young Corn-god (represented by Mü'iyiñwa), by the Chacs (the Hopi Cloud deities), and by Itzamna in his aspect as Sun god; as to structural complexes, by the colour-directional system and by the ceremonial day count; as to ritual elements, by corn meal, feathers, pigments and cotton thread. These elements the Pueblos elaborated, in conjunction with

[1] On the nine Maya gods of the night, see Thompson (1932), Appendix III, pp. 414–18.

[2] These examples are cited from Steggerda (1941), pp. 64–5; others may be found in the index to Thompson (1930), pp. 208–13.

[3] Probably by sea to the mouth of the Rio Grande, and then up the Rio Grande valley; the turquoise deposits southwest of Santa Fé may have been the original lure: Ball (1941), pp. 22–7, and Pl. 4. Knowledge of stone terracing may have passed to the Pueblo region by the same route. On Maya boat-building, see Gann (1918), pp. 28–9.

elements derived from other sources (their Shoshoni inheritance, in the Hopi case), into ceremonial cycles of their own.

Since each such cycle is tied to the particular environment in which it was first elaborated, and since these cycles with their attendant groupings of clans are themselves ways of classifying nature and of acting upon it, we may say that what was transferred was not primarily a set of cultural traits but, rather, *a means of organising experience*; and that only among the Hopi, the most westerly and the most isolated of the Pueblos, has the cycle that was elaborated, together with the vigesimal system of counting that probably went with it, survived in anything like its original form.[1]

The *principle* for elaborating such cycles was furnished by the Maya calendar itself, while the driving force for their elaboration came from the need for assurance of rain and corn-growth, consequent upon the change-over from a predominantly gathering to a predominantly agricultural economy: life itself being now dependent upon moisture and germination.

The *external correlate* marking the passage of this nexus of ideas from one culture to the other is cranial deformation, which appears in the Southwest for the first time around A.D. 700 and spreads rapidly through the Pueblo region.[2] Regarding the Maya practice, de Landa wrote (Tozzer, 1941, p. 125):

> The women brought up their little children with all the roughness and nakedness in the world, since four or five days after the infant was born, they placed it stretched out upon a little bed, made of osiers and reeds; and there with its face upwards, they put its head between two small boards one on the back of the head and the other on the forehead, between which they compressed it tightly; and there they kept it suffering until at the end of several days, the head remained flat and moulded,[3] as was the custom of all of them.

This custom, which serves e.g. in the 11th century representations at Chichén Itzá to distinguish Mayas from Mexicans, occurs very early in Maya culture. On many of the carved jades and bas-reliefs of the Classic period, the artificial flattening of the head may be noted (Tozzer, 1941, p. 88, n. 372), while of all the deities represented in the Codices the Young Corn-god shows the greatest degree of head deformation.[4]

---

[1] Rather as remnants of Elizabethan English still survive in the mountain valleys of eastern Kentucky and Tennessee: H. L. Mencken, *The American Language* (New York, 1936), pp. 124–9.

[2] See Kidder (1917), pp. 110–11, and Reed (1946), pp. 296–9; two kinds of cranial deformation were practised in the Pueblo region, lambdoid and vertical occipital.

[3] Causing a flattening that is especially marked above the brow, and rather less so over the occiput. The original purpose of the frontal flattening may have been to make a ledge for the carrying-strap with which all heavy loads were, and sometimes still are, supported; according to Gann (1918, pp. 15–16), Maya men are capable of carrying loads of 150 lbs. for up to 20 miles in this way. If this was indeed its purpose, it was forgotten when the practice of cranial deformation passed to the Pueblo region.

[4] Morley (1946), p. 225. The Hopi maidens' butterfly whorls may well have come from the same source: 'they dress the hair of the little girls, until they reach a certain age', wrote de Landa (Tozzer, 1941, p. 126), 'in four or two horns, which are very becoming to them'.

If the Maya culture of northern Yucatan be accepted as the source of Pueblo ceremonialism,[1] then this in turn throws light on one final aspect of Southwestern ethnography. Many years ago Ruth Benedict drew attention to the extraordinary isolation of the pueblos of the Southwest, as a single Apollonian group surrounded by peoples of predominantly Dionysian bent.[2] We can now see whence that character came: for classic Maya culture was deeply Apollonian, as much in the desire for moderation and the emphasis which it laid on the group rather than the individual, as in the serenity and impersonality of its art.[3] This character the Pueblos inherited, at the same time as they took over the complex of ideas centred around rain and corn-growing from which they elaborated their ceremonial cycles. The two, I believe, went together: to work this sort of cycle, you must be this kind of person. Perhaps they could only accept the ideas, because they already had an affinity for the character. However that may be, over the last twelve hundred years character and way of life have become indissolubly linked, so indissolubly that Ruth Benedict was able to say, with truth, of the Pueblo resistance to mescal and other stimulant drugs embraced by their neighbours: 'It is not that it is a religious tabu; it is deeper than that, *it is uncongenial*'.

## INTEGRATION OF THE PUEBLO COMMUNITY

The emergence of unilineal descent groups in western Pueblo society—and, subsequently, of multi-lineage villages, as indicated by the archaeological remains (Steward, 1955, pp. 166–8)—carried with it certain dangers for the community. Chief amongst these was the danger of fission; for the stronger a man's loyalty to his own kin, the weaker, proportionately, the ties binding him to other

[1] Even if this is not accepted, the argument of the present chapter is not materially affected, since all that *that* requires is that the nexus of ideas delineated above should have reached the Pueblo area from the south around A.D. 700. While I feel myself that the parallels between the *Chac* culture of northern Yucatan and that of the Pueblo region are too close to be accounted for other than by a direct link, it is the case that certain elements in the nexus, notably the colour-directional system, the ceremonial day count and the prominence of a rain-god, are common to both Mexican and Mayan cultures of the classic period (300–850 A.D.). That being so, others—and particularly those more familiar with the Mexican evidence—may well reach a different conclusion to the one presented here.

[2] Benedict (1928), pp. 572–81: the idea of cultures being basically either Apollonian or Dionysian, Benedict drew from Nietzche's *The Birth of Tragedy*. A subsequent study of Navajos and Mayas, carried out by Steggerda and Macomber (1939), showed that the most marked difference between these two groups lay in the Navajos' extreme fear of death and disease, and the Mayas' small regard for it; it would be interesting to know how far the two attitudes are characteristic of Dionysian and Apollonian cultures generally.

[3] This judgement is based on Thompson's characterisation of Maya culture (1954, pp. 262–5), itself based on a lifetime's study of the monuments and texts in relation to the present-day Maya: cf. in the same sense, Steggerda (1941), pp. 25, 37–43, 85–6, Redfield (1941), pp. 127–30, and Morley (1946), pp. 28–32. Nearly all students of the Maya comment on their co-operativeness, sociability, sense of humour, lack of aggression, and lack of ambition or sense of competition; even the drunkenness to which they are prone is, in large measure, ritual in origin (Gann, 1918, p. 34).

members of the community.[1] This fact has been put very clearly by Miss B. Freire-Marreco, at the conclusion of her discussion (1914, pp. 281-5) of the usage of kinship terms among the Tewa of Hano:

> Here, [she writes, speaking in the voice of a Tewa girl and having enumerated the terms in common use], the circle of familiarity, marked by the use of kinship terms, ends so far as our own village is concerned. The rest are merely 'the people', *towa*, of doubtful friendliness, always capable of hostility, jealousy, and ingratitude towards us as a clan. Not that our *tada'i* [members of the father's clan] and *t'ete'i* [members of the mother's father's clan] are always exempt from these failings—they often offend us or leave us in the lurch. But their defection is a definite grievance— 'they ought to help us, because they are our *tada'i*' (or *t'ete'i*, as the case may be), whereas the rest of the people are almost normally disagreeable! *towa to'a we di mudi!*—'the people are not good'—is as common a saying with the Tewa as *Ho'pi ka Ho'pi* is with their Hopi neighbors.
>
> Outside our own village we claim and recognise relationship with members of clans corresponding to our own. *Maemae'i*—men of the clan—from all the Hopi villages visit us: they come to our house to eat and sleep; our women offer to wash and comb their hair, our men let them into good bargains. Our grievances against our fellow-villagers are discussed with them quite freely, and *it is taken for granted that they will take our side of the question.*'
>
> (1914, pp. 284-5: my italics in last sentence).

Against this fissiparous tendency may be set the strengthened ties engendered by marriage alliance. Among the Great Basin Shoshoneans, a marriage link between two families entailed few obligations between them: chiefly, as we have seen, because the movements of individual families were too erratic, and because there was little surplus of storable food for expressing such obligations. In western Pueblo society, the same sequence of events which led to the emergence of unilineal descent groups created the conditions for firm alliances between them: namely, that the groups themselves formed stable residential nuclei, with large reserves of storable food at their disposal. *Pari passu*, consequently, with the emergence of such groups, and offsetting to some extent the effects of their crescent solidarity, went the development of a network of marriage alliances between them, expressed in the whole series of reciprocal obligations, both of food and services, with which we are familiar from the Hopi example.[2]

---

[1] Campbell, in his study of kinship among the Sarakatsans of northern Greece (1964, especially pp. 213-15, 256-7), has come to much the same conclusion. 'A man's work, affections, and moral obligations', he writes (p. 257), 'are almost exclusively contained within the one small group [his close kin]. The commitment of energy, physical resources, or deep affection to an unrelated person is a kind of betrayal.'

Yet both Goldschmidt (1948, pp. 453-4), and Eggan (1950, pp. 116-17), regard lineages and, particularly, clans as having important integrative functions for the community; Goldschmidt, indeed, holds this to be the primary *function* of clans. This I cannot see; except where, as among the Nuer, there is a fiction of kinship embracing the whole community, it seems to me that unilineal descent groups are potentially—and often in practice—divisive, not integrative.

[2] The same point has been made by Dumont, in quite a different context. 'Tout se passe', he writes, referring to the Pramalai Kallar (1957, p. 162: my italics), 'comme si, *plus le*

Regarding the wider integration of the community: among the western Shoshoni, as we have seen, this was effected almost solely by the holding of a fall festival, by the communal game drives and mourning ceremonies which generally accompanied it, by the recognition—for specific purposes—of a headman or valley chief, and, among the Owens Valley Paiute, by the ownership and use of a common sweat house. The development of agriculture among the western pueblos, with their consequent dependence upon agriculture for the survival of the increased population which agriculture had made possible, led to an enormous proliferation of ceremonialism among them: to the elaboration, in short, of that liturgy, or ceremonial cycle, the principal elements of which we have recorded in the earlier chapters, and the primary purpose of which was to ensure the rain and fertility needed for the continued well-being of the community. This ceremonialism in itself, became a powerful integrative force in Pueblo society, in two senses: one practical, the other spiritual. In the first sense, the correct performance of any *one* ceremony in the cycle depended on the co-operation of men from several different clans, while the correct performance of the whole cycle depended on the co-operation of men from *all* the different clans represented in the village. In the second sense, the co-operation required had to be both willing and spontaneous, a quarrel of any kind invalidating the ceremonial (Parsons, 1939, p. 153). This point, namely, the tremendous emphasis on *conformity* and the need felt for *unanimity* in the ritual, has been stressed by Barbara Aitken in her account of Hopi religion:[1]

> The co-operation on which the Hopi lay most stress, [writes Mrs. Aitken (1930, p. 376)], is a spiritual co-operation. The clans and the societies 'take care of each other', the chiefs 'take care of all their children', by contributing their special rain-making ceremonies and their 'thought'. What is required by Hopi public opinion is unanimous confidence—a constant, hopeful enthusiasm for the general prosperity.

This creates, as I have suggested earlier (above, p. 193, n. 3), a spiritual community. And Mrs. Aitken goes on to point out, using Oraibi as example, how schism in a pueblo commonly takes a religious form, and how its normal effect is to break up the pueblo bodily and lead to the formation of one or two (or more) new villages—'winners as well as losers desert the place where the common life has come to grief' (p. 384).

---

*principe unilinéaire tend à s'affirmer, et plus en même temps il est contraint de souligner l'alliance comme un principe corrélatif de sa propre distinction.* Ce qu'on sait comparativement permet ici de hasarder l'idée que ce développement est le fait des Pramalai Kallar.'

[1] Aitken (1930), pp. 372–84. Mrs. Aitken died last year (1968), and I would like to place on record here the debt which all students of the western Pueblos owe to her all-too-scanty writings on the Hopi-Tewa of 1st Mesa. As Miss B. Freire-Marreco, she resided at Hano for several months in the spring of 1913, and subsequently made valuable contributions to Pueblo ethnography in the fields of kinship (1914), of ethnobotany (1916), and of religion (1930). In a letter written shortly before her death, Mrs. Aitken told me that she was still in correspondence with the Tewa lady of the Corn clan who had looked after her in that village more than fifty years earlier.

The development of a spiritual community, based on shared values, is reflected in the means of settling disputes within the pueblo. Among the western Shoshoni, disputes and hostilities arising from e.g. wife-stealing, theft or homicide, were settled between the families concerned; none of these was a 'crime' against the community, for the community did not exist in any corporate or legal sense (Steward, 1955, pp. 114–15). Violations of custom threatened families, not larger socially integrated groups; the very concept of crime, as Steward points out, pre-supposes some kind of supra-family level of integration, some collectivity, which has a common purpose that must be protected against anti-social behaviour by its members. Nor, among the western Shoshoni, was there any person, or group of persons, specifically charged with the settling of disputes; each valley commonly recognised its own headman or 'talker', but his duties were restricted, in the main, to the organising of the fall festival and the communal rabbit drives which accompanied it. The Owens Valley Paiute present a definite advance, in the matter of public order. Each district, as we have seen (above, p. 370), was a political unit, under the direction of its own headman; and while his powers of imposing a settlement were limited, he was expected to intervene in less serious disputes, both within his own village and between members of different villages. Moreover, the use of a communal sweat house, and the discussion of affairs which took place in it, implies the development of a public opinion the weight of which could be brought to bear against those who transgressed its *mores*. Among the western Pueblos, also, the organs for settling disputes were rather rudimentary.[1] Each pueblo had its own *ki'k moñwi*, but his duties were primarily ritual, and while disputes over land were sometimes referred to him, his rôle in settling them was conciliatory rather than judicial; in some of the villages, the War chief disposed of certain powers for maintaining order within the pueblo, and in others, again, the Kwan and Al fraternities appear to have exercised similar functions. But none of these were very effective means of restoring peace, once it had been broken; and in any case, as Eggan has pointed out (1950, p. 119), the use of force is antithetical to Hopi ideology.

This weakness in the authority structure of the Hopi village was compensated for by—may, indeed, be attributed to—the strength of the shared values to which I have referred above, inculcated by the Hopi methods of child upbringing (epitomised as following the Hopi 'path') and constantly re-affirmed by participation in the ceremonial cycle.[2] Breaches of the code, defined as not

[1] Titiev (1944), pp. 64–8: cf. Eggan (1950), pp. 106–9.

[2] For a sensitive handling of the interaction between these two aspects of Hopi life, see D. Eggan (1956), especially pp. 350–66.

Laura Thompson, in *The Hopi Way* (Thompson and Joseph, 1944, pp. 132–3), argues that much of this social code was *internalised* by the Hopi in the form of an individual conscience. While agreeing with this part of her thesis, I think it is the weakness of Dr. Thompson's account of Hopi integration (Thompson, 1945, especially pp. 542–6), that, were things precisely as she says they are, one would be at a loss to explain why quarrels *ever* broke out in the Hopi village (so well integrated were its inhabitants).

following the Hopi 'path', were regarded as offences against the whole community, in that they threatened the harmony on which its well-being depended. In spite of this all the villages have been beset with factions, and where these factions become strong enough, they have led to village splitting;[1] but the very fact that pueblo splitting has not occurred *more* frequently than it has, may be ascribed, ultimately, to the strength of the common values which all Hopi share.

A ceremonial cycle, however elaborate, does not require fraternities to conduct it, as the case of the hill Talis (see above, Chapter 3) demonstrates; nor can we ascribe to the Hopi fraternities political functions either within the village, of the kind exercised by the associations of the Yakö and the Mbembe (above, Chapter 2), or between villages, of the kind exercised by *tamate liwoa* in the Banks Islands. To what cause, then, are we to attribute the emergence of fraternities in western Pueblo society? The answer, I think, is that they are primarily *structural*, in the same sense that marriage alliance is structural; and that, just as alliance developed *pari passu* with the crystallisation of unilineal descent groups (as a balance to the inward-lookingness of the latter), so also—perhaps at a rather later date—did the fraternities.[2] By furnishing another set of cross links between the members of different clans, they put a further check on the fissiparous tendencies of the latter. That this development, none the less, took place early in the history of western Pueblo society,[3] is indicated by one piece of linguistic usage; for, embedded in current speech, are the two parameters by which, in that society, a person is 'placed'—by, that is to say, his clan membership on the one hand, and his fraternity membership on the other:

*nü Pa'tki wüñwa*, 'I am water-house clan-member', and
*nü Tcü'b wimkya*, I am antelope fraternity-member';

and it would be as erroneous, as Voth points out (1912*b*, p. 134, n. 1), to use *wiwimkya* to designate the members of a clan or a phratry, as it would be to use *nyamü* for those of a fraternity. The term *nyamü* comes down, as we have seen, from the common Numic stem for 'people', its shift in meaning signifying

[1] Eggan (1950), p. 119, cf. (1964), pp. 182–3. Parsons makes the point (1939, p. 108) that even where the pueblo is divided, it is a question of group against group, not of individual rebellion.

[2] If, following Kroeber (1938, p. 308), we describe unilineal descent groups as *secondary*, then fraternities are *tertiary*: in the sense that they come into existence to solve certain problems posed by the prior emergence of unilineal descent groups—using *prior* in a logical, rather than a strictly temporal, sense.

Professor Eggan suggests (1968) that the *strength* of fraternity ties may, in fact, be due to the relative weakness of the ties of alliance in Hopi society; the nub of the whole system, as he points out, lies in the choice of ceremonial 'father', who often is, but need not be, a man of the father's clan.

[3] As to the *order* in which the fraternities developed, I think we must assume—as the interpretation of the myth recorded on pp. 294–5 indicates—that the four Tribal Initiation fraternities, i.e. Wü'wütçim, Singers, Ahl and Kwan, and possibly the Marau', were the first to crystallise, and that these set the pattern subsequently followed by the Blue and Gray Flute, Lako'n, Antelope, Snake.

a shift from semi-nomadic to settled village life; *wimkya* is derived from *wi'mi*, the ceremony around which each fraternity is organised and the growth of which, we may suppose, coincided with the change-over from a gathering to a predominantly agricultural economy.[1]

[1] Dozier, also, relates (1960, pp. 149–50) the growth of Hopi ceremonialism to the dependence on agriculture, combined with the uncertainty of the rainfall and the lack of any technological means (e.g. irrigation ditches) for ensuring an adequate water supply to the fields: 'Confronted with this problem', he writes (p. 150), 'the Hopi have understandably resorted to a complex ceremonialism which emphasizes the magical control of the weather.'

I think myself that the word 'magical' inadequately describes the richness and subtlety of Hopi religious belief; but I am in agreement with Dozier's main thesis.

***

*Additional note to p. 426.*

The bringing together of Young Corn-god and Earth mother, on the stela from Piedras Negras, is strikingly paralleled by the link between Mü'iyiñwa and Tü'wa-poñya-tümsi in Hopi thinking. The corn-growing attributes of the former deity are attested in the Emergence myth, in one version of which (Voth, 1905c, p. 39) the Hopi were accompanied by Mü'iyiñwa, '. . . his body consisted *entirely of corn*, his feet being ears of corn, so that he could not move very fast'. Mü'iyiñwa stands as brother to Tü'wa-poñya-tümsi, whose generative powers are characterised in the passage quoted earlier (above, p. 110):

> She is the mother of all living things, . . . and all vegetation; plants suck from her breast a nourishing liquid, it passes up from their roots to their flowers and fruit, and animals and man eat of this vegetation, hence Tü'wa-poñya-tümsi is mother of all life.

The Hopi configuration of ideas could hardly be closer to that represented on the stela from Piedras Negras.

*Additional note to p. 433.*

The former observance by Hopi of a ceremonial 'year' of 8 to 9 moons' duration, three such 'years' covering 24 months, is attested by a single surviving piece of evidence. Writing around 1888, Stephen noted (1940b, p. 23):

> The seasons are reckoned by periods called 'lesser-years', each consisting of eight moons, beginning with the new moon of November, at the full of which the New Year festival called *keli* [*ke'le*, 'novice', i.e. the Wü'wütçim ceremony] is celebrated. The first lesser-year ends in the following June; the second begins with the July moon and ends with February; the third begins with March and ends with October, and this third period is called the Year of the Great Moon.

As a solar year comprises approximately $12\frac{3}{8}$ lunations (19 years = 235 lunations), the 'lesser year' of the Hopi spanned $8\frac{1}{4}$ moons, in contrast to $8\frac{3}{4}$ of the Maya *tzolkin*.

P

# 20

# *The nature of associations*

A theory that claims to account for associations, of the kind treated here, must be capable of answering three questions about them: first, why such associations are virtually restricted to men; second, why, though they occur in widely separated parts of the world between which there can hardly have been at the relevant time any physical contact or exchange, they yet exhibit marked similarities of form; third, why they are found in some societies but not in others. For answer to the first of these three questions, I draw on certain earlier theories, notably on those put forward by Schurtz (1902) and by van Gennep (1908), read in the light of recent studies by ethologists on primate societies. The answer to the second is implicit in the material presented in the earlier chapters of this book and will already, I think, have occurred to the perceptive reader; the answer to the third, as I hope to show, follows from that given to the second. Let us begin, therefore, with an outline of Schurtz's theory of associations.[1]

Schurtz sets off by drawing a distinction between *natural* and *artificial* groupings: blood-relation groupings, i.e. groups of kinsmen, he calls natural or primary; voluntary associations, i.e. those developing between people unrelated by blood, he calls artificial or secondary.[2] The prevalent drive in women, he argues, is towards the natural or primary grouping, that of the family; this grouping, in effect, satisfies the associational needs of a woman, and no further groupings are formed with other women. In males, by contrast, there is an inborn drive to group with other males and, arising from this, to develop the groups so formed into tightly-knit organisations. These groups are the *artificial* or secondary ones, referred to above. They may crystallise, in any given society, e.g. around the need to find food or to band together for defence, but the source of their cohesion lies in the associational needs of males, needs which are not satisfied by the groupings of family and kin; for men, in contrast to women, such associations are necessary and mean enhanced living and opportunity for competition, while for the societies in which they occur they introduce an element of diversity, requisite for development over and beyond the narrow limits set by the *natural* groupings of family and kin.

Regarding their actual form, Schurtz traces the origin of all such male

[1] I am indebted to Mrs. M. Michaelis for providing me with a *résumé*, in English, of the gist of Schurtz's *Altersklassen und Männerbünde* (Berlin, 1902).

[2] The two kinds of bond corresponding to *les liens de nécessité*, and *les liens de volonté*, of French sociologists.

groupings to the initiation of boys, whereby they are taken from their families at or around puberty, subjected commonly to certain ordeals, and 're-born' as men, that is, as members of the adult male community, fitted to undertake the duties and responsibilities required of them. There are, in Schurtz's view, three principal forms which such groupings may assume. Where the initiatory groups retain their original form, all those who pass through initiation at the same time constituting a single grouping, a system of age-groups results. Where, however, initiation simply admits the lad to a group which includes virtually all the male members of the community, you have what Schurtz defines as a 'club', such as *suqe* in the Banks Islands, which may in turn have its own internal grading— regarded by Schurtz merely as age-grades transformed; clubs of this kind are purely social in purpose, and their activities are normally held in public. The crucial step from the 'club' to the third kind of grouping, the secret society or fraternity, occurs—in Schurtz's view—when two conditions are fulfilled:

> when there is an element of *exclusiveness* in the membership, i.e. when not *all* the adult males of the community are admitted but only some, by what- ever criterion—status, wealth, 'pure' descent, or whatever—these may be chosen;
>
> when the members recognise each other, are marked, by the use of e.g. a *secret* language, *secret* signs, and/or by sharing in a restricted cult.

The secret society or fraternity is thus distinguished from the 'club' by the fact that it has a limited membership, that its members recognise one another by certain signs, that its activities commonly have a religious nexus, and that some at least of these activities are pursued in secret.[1]

To sum up: in Schurtz's view, age-groups, 'clubs' and secret societies form a graded series in a chain of social forms developed by males. The driving force in their development lies in the male need to associate, which is not satisfied by family and descent groupings. They have a common origin in boys' initia- tion, whereby young males are withdrawn from family life and segregated as a preparation for taking part in such all-male groupings, while, from the point of view of the societies in which they occur, they provide the diversity requisite for development over and beyond the limits set by the primary groupings of family and kin.

This theory of Schurtz's is taken a stage further by a remark of van Gennep's (1908, p. 330):

> En principe, [writes van Gennep, referring to the status of women in primitive societies], elle n'appartient pas à la société générale, laquelle n'est constituée que par les hommes ayant passé par les rites d'agrégation à la communauté. Elle rentre ainsi dans la même catégorie que l'étranger.

---

[1] de Jonghe observes (1923, p. 388) that secret societies are, strictly speaking, 'closed' societies rather than 'des sociétés vraiment secrètes'; everyone knows who the members are, where they meet and when; what they do *not* know is, what goes on at the meetings.

And subsequently (p. 331), referring to children:

> Dans les sociétés demi-civilisés, les enfants rentrent dans la même catégorie que les femmes. . . .

What van Gennep is saying here, in effect, is that society itself, as conceived among primitive peoples, is formed by the body of its adult and sub-adult male members who have been aggregated to that body by rites of initiation, while women and juveniles remain, strictly speaking, outside it (not having been so initiated); in other words, that the artificial or secondary associations of which Schurtz speaks are, simply, rather more clearly defined variations on a theme inherent in the structure of society itself.[1] This structure must also, then, be derived from the innate drive to associate, postulated by Schurtz as characterising the human male.

Now to say that the male drive to associate is inborn, is to say that it is genetically determined; to say that it is genetically determined, that it is the end-result of a process of selection; and to say that it is the end-result of a process of selection, that it reflects environmental or ecological pressures acting, *at some time in the past*, on the evolving species. The problem that faces us, therefore, is to isolate the environmental and ecological factors, in response to the pressure of which the proto-hominids developed the male drive to associate (which, in turn, gave to primitive human society its characteristic form). To do this effectively, requires a long excursus on the structure of primate societies.

## COMPARATIVE STRUCTURE OF PRIMATE SOCIETIES

Man is a primate, the nearest relatives to man among the primates are the great apes (orangs, gorillas and chimpanzees), and the ape whose social organisation most nearly approximates to that of the early proto-hominids is, probably, the chimpanzee—a ground-living biped of the forest floor and, like man, a tool-user and bed-maker. First, therefore, let us consider chimpanzees in their natural habitat, to see how far their social organisation has been moulded by their ecology.

### (a) Habitat, and social organisation, of wild chimpanzees[2]

Primarily, chimpanzees are animals of the forest, their geographical range corresponding roughly with the extent of the African equatorial rain forest. This fact is related to their feeding habits. Chimpanzees live mainly on fruit, supplementing this with leaves, seeds, pith and bark, and, at certain seasons, with insects; being large primates, they have to spend six or seven hours a day in active feeding, and much of the rest of the time in moving from one feeding

---

[1] One might almost say that they are *distilled* versions of its essence.

[2] This section is based chiefly on the Reynolds' account (1963, 1965) of chimpanzees in the Budongo Forest, Uganda, supplemented by Kortlandt's observations (1962) of chimpanzees living around a plantation in the eastern Congo, and—especially for their diet —by Jane Goodall's (1963) of chimpanzees on the eastern littoral of Lake Tanganyika.

area to another, in order to subsist on a predominantly fruit diet. Thus, of sixty-one kinds of vegetable food collected by Jane Goodall, thirty-three were fruits, seventeen leaves or leaf buds, four seeds, and the remaining seven blossoms, stems or bark. Of the food actually eaten, 90 per cent is found growing in trees; the animals commonly spend from one half to three quarters of the daylight hours in trees, and in the great majority of cases they make their sleeping nests in them. To conclude from these figures, however, that chimpanzees are primarily tree-dwelling animals who sometimes come down to earth, would be a great over-simplification.

In the first place, chimpanzees are not entirely restricted to the rain forest. Within its borders, they are found around the edge of, and venture into, land that has been cleared for cultivation; outside it they occur, not only in the gallery forests that fringe the watercourses traversing the savannah, but also in areas adjacent to the forest where the forest itself thins out to woodland-savannah. In the second place, many of their essential activities are carried out on the ground. Thus, to travel over distances of more than 50 yards, chimpanzees nearly always come down to the ground; while there, they often stop to eat the leaves of small plants, to pick the pith from stalks, to gather ripe fruits which have fallen to earth, and to collect the larvae of gall flies or termites from their nests.[1] Forest-dwelling chimpanzees, also, have a network of tracks at ground level, which they use for moving from one feeding area to another; and, when disturbed by humans, they invariably descend to the ground to make good their escape.

These terrestrial adaptations account for further aspects of chimpanzee life. Where the animals are protected, or at least not molested by man, their principal feeding patterns may become ground-oriented. Thus, in the group studied by Kortlandt in the eastern Congo, the pawpaws grown on the plantation adjoining the forest became a major item in the diet of the chimpanzees living there, particularly of the females with young offspring. Throughout his account, and especially in the photographs illustrating it, Kortlandt stresses the terrestrial habits of his chimpanzees:

> In the wild, [he writes (1962, pp. 133–4)], they behave like such basically terrestrial animals as baboons. The chimpanzees I watched had created an elaborate road system in the forest . . ., [and] on the plantation hill, where they were apparently safe from leopards, some of them even slept in nests on the ground. Moving around on the plantation and, as far as I could judge, in the forest, they walked on the ground from tree to tree, avoiding any climbing that was not absolutely necessary. When they did climb, they moved very cautiously, as if afraid they might fall. When a chimpanzee in a tree suspected the presence of a human being, it immediately fled back to the ground.

In the open, Kortlandt continues (p. 134), chimpanzees spend a good part

[1] Observed by Goodall in the Gombe Stream Reserve (1963, pp. 42–4). The method employed is by 'fishing': the animal breaks off a grass stalk, pokes it into the termite mound, leaves it a minute or two, then withdraws the stalk and sucks off the insects adhering to it.

of the time *on two legs*, walking and running in a nearly erect and almost human posture; this mode of travel, which accounted for between 10 and 15 per cent of the distance covered by the animals when they were fully at ease, is evidently adopted either to free their hands, e.g. for eating or carrying fruit, or to gain a better view of their surroundings. In this way, in more open habitats such as the Gombe Stream Reserve, a group of chimpanzees may cover 6 or 7 miles in a day, feeding in a clump of trees here, moving on across an open patch and feeding lightly on the way, settling for an hour or so in a second clump, then moving on to another farther on.

Before discussing the significance of these findings, we must take a brief look at the social organisation of forest-dwelling chimpanzees. Our chief source here is the Reynolds' study of the chimpanzees of the southwest corner of the Budongo Forest in Uganda.[1] Broadly speaking, forest-dwelling chimpanzees are divided into small bands, a number of which form the population of a particular area of the forest. The bands themselves are of three kinds. First, there are 'mothers' bands', usually consisting of two to five mothers, each with a dependent infant, and sometimes one or two other females as well. Then there are 'bands of males', consisting of four or five fully mature, adult males, one of which usually acts as leader of the group; these bands of males are closely-knit units, the members of which stay together for several months and are often seen grooming one another. Finally, there are 'adult bands', containing adults of both sexes and sometimes a few juveniles, but never any mothers with dependent young. Now while these bands may retain their structure for periods ranging from a few weeks to several months, they are not permanent or stable associations. Individual animals readily move from one band to another, or even, on occasions, go off to forage on their own. Two bands may join together temporarily; often, for example, an all-male band will join up with a mothers' band when one of the females comes into oestrus, staying with it until her oestrus is finished. Again, during the three principal fruit seasons of the year, namely the fig season in March–April, *Pseudospondias* in late May and June, and *Maesopsis* in August–September, large mixed groups of chimpanzees are to be found feeding—and vociferating loudly—in neighbouring clumps of trees; as the supply of fruit declines, the several bands leave the trees and disperse into the forest, to come together again at the next harvest.

Now it will be realised that, as the membership of bands is itself unstable, as bands vary in the distances they travel—all-male bands being, in this respect, the most adventurous and mothers' bands the least so—and as chimpanzees are shy animals, it is very difficult to work out the precise number of chimpanzees living in even a restricted area of the forest. However, after following band movements for several months and plotting their routes on large-scale maps, Dr. and Mrs. Reynolds found that they were able to divide the study area (see Fig 61) into three regions, each of about 6 to 8 sq. miles, with a population of

[1] See, especially, V. Reynolds (1963), pp. 96–8, and V. and F. Reynolds (1965), pp. 396–403; their findings are borne out by Kortlandt's, in the eastern Congo (1962, pp. 132–3).

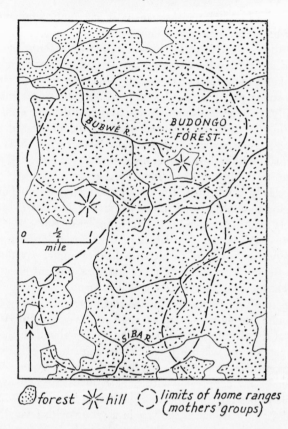

Fig. 61. Home ranges of chimpanzees in the southwest corner of Budongo Forest, Uganda. Re-drawn from V. Reynolds (1965), fig. 12a, p. 402.

about seventy animals to each region. Within each region are located certain feeding areas, sleeping trees and ground routes, which are habitually used by the bands of that region; the bands within a region interact more frequently, and more intimately, with other bands within it than with bands outside its borders; and while adult bands, especially all-male bands, may explore adjoining areas and even join up temporarily with neighbouring bands, the mothers' bands with their attendant young commonly keep to the habitual areas within their own region, only venturing outside it as part of a general movement in response to seasonal food distribution, such as the *Maesopsis* fruit harvest.

Thus, [writes Dr. Reynolds (1963, p. 100)], while one cannot speak of 'territories' in regard to chimpanzees, there are what can be termed as 'habitual ranges'. Animals in a region, although often dispersed in small groups [i.e. bands], are bound together from infancy by ties of familiarity with a particular stretch of forest, and the knowledge of its key feeding areas, and the habitual routes from one place to another.

From this account of their social organisation, certain preliminary conclusions may be drawn. In the first place, chimpanzee groups are not closed social groups; the bands into which a local population will be found at any one time to be divided are constantly changing membership, splitting apart, meeting others and joining them, congregating and dispersing. Much of this alternate dispersal and congregating of bands occurs in response to seasonal changes in the food supply, and this leads on to a second point: that the different kinds of bands play different rôles in the food quest of the population as a whole. Mothers' bands, as we have seen, are far more 'conservative' than adult bands, tending to remain within their own regions most of the time, and even restricting themselves to familiar places within those regions. Adult bands, by contrast, and especially bands of males, are far more adventurous, often moving from one region to another; their range is thus considerably greater than that of the mothers, and may extend up to 10 sq. miles or more.[1]

Now chimpanzees in the wild lack any strict male dominance hierarchies based on aggression, such as characterise (for example) savannah baboons. Doubtless, as Reynolds remarks (1963, pp. 100–1), dominant males are present; but the two channels through which male dominance is commonly expressed, namely competition for prized food items and preferential access to females in oestrus, are quite simply not points of conflict between them. When food is abundant, as at the ripening of various fruits, it is *so* abundant that there is no need to compete for it; when it is scarce, the animals disperse in small bands which forage on their own. Again, the Reynolds found no evidence of competition by males for copulating with females in oestrus; on most occasions when a female in oestrus was observed, she was in the company of one attentive male only, and even when she was in a group with several adult males, and one of these was known on other grounds to be a leader, he showed no special interest in her.

Within a chimpanzee population, leadership appears to be expressed primarily within, and through, the bands of males. These bands commonly comprise some four or five mature, adult males, one of whom usually acts as leader and whom the others tend to follow. These male bands, as we have seen, are the adventurers of the population; it is they who forage farthest, often passing out of their own 'home' region into an adjoining one. Consequently, they are commonly the first to discover trees newly in fruit or other food sources, whereupon they call and drum loudly in excitement,[2] so attracting other bands— particularly the bands of mothers—to the area. The formation of the male bands themselves, and the development of drumming as a means of signalling over long distances (up to 3 or 4 miles, in fact), appear therefore to be special adaptations to the forest environment: the one as a means of locating the food sources upon which the population is dependent for its survival, the other of

[1] V. and F. Reynolds (1965), pp. 402–3.
[2] V. and F Reynolds (1965), pp. 413–15, 423–4: cf. V. Reynolds (1966), p. 445.

communicating the information to the biologically significant fraction of that population, namely to the bands of mothers.

Turning now to the relation between habitat and social organisation, the following inferences may be drawn:

First, the forest environment is a relatively 'easy' one, food is plentiful at most times of the year, *either* scattered through the forest *or*, at the fruit seasons, concentrated on particular trees or groves of trees. The loosely organised, unstable bands of a local chimpanzee population appear to be, then, an efficient—and flexible—adaptation to these conditions.

Second, predation pressure in the forest is not sufficient, in itself, to have modified the social organisation. Defence against predators, chiefly leopards (and humans), is achieved by a combination of concealment, running away, and climbing into trees; these means of escape are compatible with the 'dispersed' band organisation described above.

Thirdly, the failure of chimpanzees to move out of the forest and exploit, to any significant degree, the woodland savannah, cannot be due to their arboreal habits; given suitable conditions, they are quite at home on the ground. It must be ascribed, therefore, to some other cause: tentatively, we may suggest at this stage, to their failure to develop—since the conditions of the forest do not require it—a form of social organisation capable of providing defence on the ground, in the open, against grassland predators.

The object of the next two sections will be to determine:

(i) by comparison with forest-dwelling baboons, how far the 'loose' kind of social organisation characteristic of wild chimpanzees is, indeed, an adaptation to their forest environment;

(ii) by comparison with savannah baboons, what kind of social organisation is needed in order to effect a move out of the forest into the savannah.

### (b) Social organisation of forest-dwelling baboons

The forest-living baboons we may choose for comparison are those studied by Dr. T. E. Rowell,[1] living along the Ishasha River on the Congo-Uganda border. The river itself is permanent, fast-flowing and cold; it flows northward in a shallow trough, some 400 to 600 yards wide, through the surrounding grassland (see Fig 62). On either side of the river there is a strip of gallery forest, on average about a quarter of a mile wide; in some places the forest fills the trough, in others there is a strip of coarse wet grass or patchy bush between the forest edge and the border of the trough. The river meanders through the forest, undermining old trees (which then fall, often making bridges across it) and leaving new areas to be recolonised, so that the vegetation there is very varied. Outside the trough the savannah grassland extends to east and west,

---

[1] Rowell (1966). Dr. Rowell observed the baboon troops living along the Ishasha River over a period of two years, from the spring of 1963 to the spring of 1965.

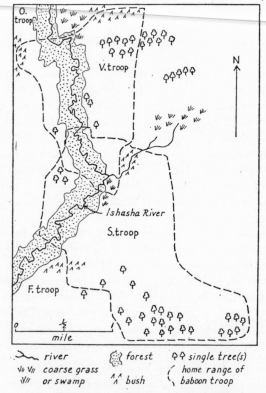

Fig. 62. Home ranges of forest-living baboons along the Ishasha River, Uganda.
Re-drawn from Rowell (1966), Fig. 4, p. 355.

broken here and there by patches of scrub, by single acacia trees or by groves of fig and acacia.

Apart from the 'olive' baboons (*Papio anubis*) which are the object of our study, colobus monkeys, chimpanzees and *C. ascanius* live in the gallery forest, and *C. aethiops* in the savannah grassland. The coarse wet grass of the trough is grazed by hippos; elephants are also common, and their—and hippos'—grazing and browsing have made wide tracks through the forest which are used by all other species. Potential predators include lions, leopards, and possibly, serval cats.

The food supply afforded by this habitat is both rich and varied. It includes many different kinds of fruit, seeds, leaves and berries; indeed, as Dr. Rowell remarks (1966, p. 358), 'a complete list of plants eaten [i.e. by baboons] would probably be approximate to the botanical species list for the area'. Broadly speaking, however, the vegetable foods eaten by these baboons fall into two main classes: those of forest origin, and those found in the grassland savannah. Among the former are the fruits of *Pseudospondias* and fig, seeds from the pods of *Cynometra*, and the flowers and seeds of *Parkia filicoidea*. The latter are much more varied, and include: the flowers and seeds of *Acacia sieberiana* (both are a valuable source of protein), figs, the buds and fruit of *Maerua edulis* (a common shrub in the grassland), the fruit of *Capparis tomentosa* and berries of *Securinega virosa* (both are common shrubs of low bush and grassland), mushrooms, and the new shoots, storage leaf bases and seed heads of many grasses (another valuable source of protein). The mainly vegetarian diet of these baboons is supplemented by animal protein, and this, again, is found chiefly in the savannah grassland: insects, mainly grasshoppers and butterflies, are grabbed as opportunity offers, birds' nests investigated, and occasional lizards caught and eaten. Also, on six occasions observed by Rowell (1966, pp. 359–60), African hares (*Lepus capensis*) were coursed by baboons after being flushed in open grass, and on four of these they were successfully caught and eaten; as this works out at one hare taken for every thirty hours spent by baboons in the appropriate vegetation, it represents over the year, as Dr. Rowell points out, a considerable protein input into the baboon population, as well as predation pressure on the hares.

Now this division of their food supply into two main categories, according to source, corresponds to a distinction between the behaviour of the baboons in the forest, where they sleep, rest, and do the greater part of their feeding (spending 60 to 70 per cent of their waking hours there), and in the grassland where they are, essentially, foragers. When foraging, says Dr. Rowell (1966, p. 360), 'the animals give the impression of looking for something—insects and hares were always caught during this activity'. When scared, they make a bee-line for the forest:

> In respect of flight distance, [she writes (p. 361)], the baboons behaved like animals that 'felt at home' in the forest, but made potentially dangerous sorties into the open, rather like grassland animals.

On the basis of this distinction between their behaviour in the forest and in grassland, Dr. Rowell concludes (p. 364) that:

> the baboon might be considered *not* as a primate adapted to life in the grassland but as an unusually versatile forest dweller which managed to survive where forest cover was (recently) lost, but which still uses patches of trees where they are available, and which, given the opportunity for choice, is more at home in forest.

This conclusion is of particular interest in relation to the social organisation of these forest-living primates, to which we may now turn.

The area studied by Dr. Rowell extends for some four miles along the river itself and about a mile on either side, giving a total area of around 8 sq. miles. Within this area lived four baboon troops, F, S, V and O, each of between thirty and fifty animals.[1] The troops were strung along the river, each having

---

[1] V troop had, in fact, increased from forty-five to fifty-eight animals by the end of Dr. Rowell's stay, but appeared then to be on the point of splitting.

a home range of 1½ to 2 sq. miles, with some overlap of ranges particularly in the forest belt fringeing the river. Each troop tended to move as a whole, especially when it ventured out into the savannah grassland to forage or to the isolated groves of acacia and fig trees to feed in them. However, the larger troops sometimes divided into two (or more) smaller parties which might follow different routes during part of the day, while neighbouring troops, particularly (in this case) S and F troops, were in fairly frequent contact with each other and sometimes joined together on joint foraging expeditions. Nor are the troops themselves 'closed' units; adult males, and possibly juveniles as well, were seen to move from one troop to another and to establish themselves, at least temporarily, there. In spite of such movements, no doubt was felt in the field as to the identity of the different troops, probably because each had a stable nucleus of known individuals; in particular, no female, and certainly no adult female, was ever seen to exchange troops, and in the short term, as Dr. Rowell observes (p. 354), 'it is probably the conservatism of the females that is the basis of troop identity'.

Regarding their actual composition, the smallest of the four troops (S) numbered thirty-two individuals, and contained five adult and sub-adult males, five adult females, sixteen juveniles and six infants (up to 1 year). The males in the troop are not, however, graded in any kind of dominance hierarchy, nor do they play any very prominent part in troop defence. Whereas, among savannah baboons, the males form a ring around the troop and interpose themselves between its more vulnerable members and any predator that may threaten them, among these forest-dwelling baboons—when they venture out into the grassland—the males, while keeping a general look-out and 'co-operating together in policing the environment', do not regard it as their duty to protect the females and young; indeed, in the face of any serious threat, a general *sauve qui peut* ensues, the whole troop rushing helter-skelter to the safety of the forest, 'with the big males well to the front and the last animals usually the females carrying heavier babies'.[1]

The absence of any effective troop defence by the males Dr. Rowell ascribes (p. 363), in part to the relatively short distances usually travelled between feeding stations, and in part to the protection afforded against predators by thick cover and forest. The absence of a dominance hierarchy among the adult males she ascribes to the plentiful food supply to be found in the forest, together again with its thick cover:

> The abundance of food and its scattered distribution means, [she writes[2]], that there is rarely competition for it; disputes are seen over some isolated prized items—

[1] Rowell (1966), p. 362. Dr. Rowell stresses, however, that great concern is shown for stragglers; the whole troop will wait for up to half an hour for a mother to finish grooming her infant and catch up, and no animal is ever left behind on foraging expeditions.

[2] Rowell (1966), p. 363: cf. (1967), pp. 229–30, where Dr. Rowell argues that dominance hierarchies are the outcome of agonistic behaviour, and that agonistic behaviour is, in large measure, the consequence of competition at a restricted food source—natural or artificial.

seedlings growing in elephant dung, and mushrooms. In an environment where the food competition situation occurs more frequently, it may be that tensions can be sustained until a hierarchical social structure develops. Another factor to be considered is the density of cover. In thick brush disputes are often ended when visual contact is lost—perhaps in an open environment they continue longer and have a more lasting effect.

The social organisation of these forest-dwelling baboons falls, then, somewhere between that of the forest-living chimpanzees described in the last section and that of the savannah baboons we shall consider in the next, having certain features in common with each. They have the troop organisation characteristic of savannah baboons; but their troops are not as 'closed' as those of savannah baboons, the males within them are not graded in any kind of dominance hierarchy nor do they co-operate together to any marked degree in group defence. Conversely, they have a rather 'tighter' organisation than that of forest-living chimpanzees, but share with them the lack of a dominance hierarchy and the relative absence of agonistic behaviour between males. To the significance of these findings in terms of their ecology, we may return when we have described the adaptations achieved by their cousins in the savannah.

### (c) Savannah baboons, ecology and social structure

Savannah baboons are the most widespread of the baboons of Africa, occurring in grassland, woodland and forest edge, from Tibesti to the Cape and across the continent from Dakar to Mombasa. They are, in fact, the 'common' baboons of the game reserves of Kenya and Tanzania, Zambia, Rhodesia and South Africa.[1] Slight differences in morphology and habitat have led to their being classified as three separate species, namely: *P. ursinus*, the chacma baboon, occurring chiefly in the arid and semi-arid steppe region of Southwest Africa and Angola, and over the grasslands and wooded steppe of South Africa; *P. cyanocephalus*, a lankier, longer-tailed form, found in woodland and woodland savannah over much of Rhodesia, Zambia, Tanzania, Malawi and Mozambique; and *P. anubis*, the 'olive' baboon, widespread over the whole savannah belt north of the equator, and down into Kenya and Uganda to the edges of the Congo forest. Each of these species, however, merges into the next without a break, and it seems simpler[2] to regard them as a single species of savannah baboon, which has developed relatively minor differences of morphology, diet and social organisation in response to local conditions, than as three separate species. This, at least, is the view taken here; and where, in the preceding section, we described their response to forest-living, we have now to consider the range of adaptations elicited from the same species by a woodland savannah and arid savannah environment, respectively.

---

[1] On the distribution of savannah baboons, see in particular Hall (1966), pp. 52–62. The only other species of *Papio* at all widely distributed are the drill and mandrill, in the Cameroons and the forest region of the lower Congo basin, and the desert baboon (*P. hamadryas*) in eastern Ethiopia and Somalia.

[2] DeVore and Hall (1965), pp. 20–1.

Throughout the region,[1] baboons are both primarily vegetarian, and eclectic, in their feeding; fruit plays a much smaller part in their total diet, however, than it does among forest-living baboons. In the Cape region they are recorded as eating ninety-four different species of vegetable food,[2] made up of bulbs, roots and tubers which they dig from the ground, flowers of shrubs and plants, small plants pulled up whole and eaten, buds and leaves, seeds, berries, cones, and cultivated crops such as mealies. Considerable quantities of cockroaches and termites are eaten, as shown e.g. in S.W. Africa by faecal analysis, also termite larvae, locusts, grasshoppers, spiders and crickets, birds' eggs and young (chiefly of ground-nesting species), and lizards. On the Atlantic coast of S.W. Africa, mussels, limpets and other shell fish are collected from the rocks at low tide and furnish a major source of protein to the local baboon population; inland in South Africa, lambs, and in Kenya-Tanzania young antelopes, are taken at the appropriate season. Viewed in ecological perspective, say DeVore and Hall (1965, p. 43), the most significant aspect of this diet is the ability shown by baboons to adapt to different habitats and to exploit whatever staple food items the local environment has to offer; a catholic diet, they go on (p. 52), together with a social organisation which permits the group to move into open areas in relative safety, explain why a single species has been able to spread over most of sub-Saharan Africa.

Savannah baboons are organised in troops; indeed troop organisation, for reasons we shall consider presently, is pre-requisite to their life on the ground in the savannah. Our first task, therefore, is to determine the size, composition and range of these troops. As model, let us take savannah baboon troops in Kenya and Tanzania.[3] Nine baboon troops in Nairobi National Park, numbering 374 animals in all, ranged from 12 to 87 animals each, giving a mean of 42 ($\pm$ 14); ten troops in the Amboseli Reserve numbered 562 animals, giving a mean of 56 ($\pm$ 14). In the Amboseli Reserve, five larger troops numbered 88, 94, 103, 171 and 185 animals, respectively. All these large troops, however, were liable to split into two troops, each going off to forage on its own for the day and usually, though not always, joining up with the other fragment at nightfall; thus the troop of 103 often split into two troops of 66 and 37, each troop having a centre, a periphery, and all the characteristics of an independent troop. It seems likely, say DeVore and Washburn (1963, pp. 339–41), that this kind of splitting represents the first stage in the formation of a new troop:

[1] The region, that is, from Kenya in the north, down through Tanzania and Rhodesia to South Africa, within which recent studies of savannah baboons have been carried out. The studies drawn upon in this account are those of Hall (1962a, 1962b, 1963) on baboons in S.W. Africa, the Cape and Rhodesia (Zambezi valley), and of DeVore and Washburn (1963) on baboons in Kenya and Tanzania; the results of these studies are correlated by DeVore and Hall (1965), and by Hall and DeVore (1965).

[2] This compares with eighty-five different species of edible food plants utilised by the Kung Bushmen of the Kalahari Desert. Vegetable foods comprise 60–80 per cent (by weight) of the total diet of these Bushmen, and of this the mongongo nut, the staple food, accounts for roughly one half: R. B. Lee (1968), p. 33.

[3] See, in particular, DeVore and Washburn (1963), pp. 338–46.

It appears that large troops may become unstable, and that divisions occur in troops larger than 70 individuals which are not seen in the small troops. If this division persists, and if the division contains a normal age-sex distribution, a new troop may result.

On this ground we may put typical troop-size, in the woodland-savannah region of Kenya and Tanzania, at from 40 to 70 animals, troops tending to become unstable above the latter number.

Hall, who carried out baboon counts in the Zambezi valley, in South Africa (Drakensberg Mountains, and the Cape) and Southwest Africa, got the following figures (1963, pp. 3–7):

| area | number of troops counted | numerical range | mean size |
|---|---|---|---|
| Zambezi valley .. .. .. | 18 | from 12 to 109 | 46 |
| South Africa .. .. .. | 15 | from 15 to 80 | 34 |
| Southwest Africa .. .. .. | 20 | from 8 to 65 | 27 |

He found, further, in four counts taken on the slopes of the Drakensberg Mountains, that the number of baboons per troop fell progressively, the higher one ascends the mountain: i.e. from 48 baboons per troop in the lower valleys (4,000 to 5,000 feet), to 18 per troop in the higher valleys and on the face of the escarpment (c. 6,000 feet). This difference in size of troops Hall correlated with the available food supply; in the lower reaches of the valleys, fruit, seed and leaf-bearing trees and shrubs are relatively abundant, whereas, higher up, they scarcely occur at all so that bulbs, tubers and grasses must provide the staple diet.

Turning now to the distances covered by savannah baboons and the extent of their home ranges: in Nairobi National Park, the daily range covered by a baboon troop varies from 2 to 3, up to 6 or 7, miles. In the Cape Reserve, day ranges average 3 to 4 miles; in S.W. Africa, the largest baboon troop observed, numbering 65 animals, covered 12 miles on one occasion, the route being a long loop in shape which took the troop a straight-line distance of 5 miles from its sleeping-place. These, and other, observations of troop movements indicate that a baboon troop moves in the course of the year over an area which averages, in open savannah country, between 8 and 16 sq. miles.[1] This area constitutes its

[1] See, in particular, Hall (1962a), pp. 192–6, DeVore and Washburn (1963), pp. 348–63, and DeVore and Hall (1965), pp. 31–8. Population density of baboons in Nairobi National Park is about ten per square mile, compared with twenty-eight per square mile in Rowell's study of forest-living baboons; in the arid environment of S.W. Africa, it may be as low as three or four per square mile.

'home range'; for the home range of SR troop, Nairobi National Park, which measures roughly $3\frac{1}{2} \times 4\frac{1}{2}$ miles (an area of 15·75 sq. miles), see Fig. 63. Within a given habitat, the figure itself is independent of troop size; it is likely, however, to fall near the upper limit in an arid environment where vegetation is scarce and day-ranging consequently longer, and near the lower limit where vegetation is richer, e.g. on the forest fringes, or where other sources of food, such as cultivated crops or visitors' titbits, are available to the animals. The fact that there is a relative constancy in home-range size, based on the distance that baboons can comfortably travel in the course of the day and forage at the same

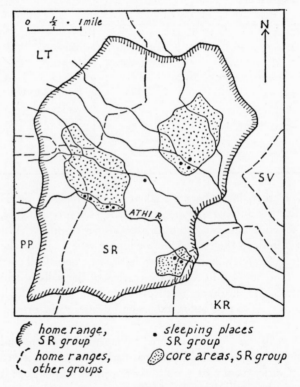

Fig. 63. Home ranges of savannah baboons, Nairobi National Park, Kenya. Re-drawn from DeVore and Hall (1965), Fig. 6*b*, p. 35.

time, indicates the *kind* of link we may expect to find between troop size and environment: namely (Hall, 1963, pp. 6, 11–14), that the baboon troop grows to a certain size, the limit of which is set by the food supply available to it within a home range of 8 to 16 sq. miles *in that particular habitat*. Hence, the smaller troops in S.W. Africa, the Cape Reserve and the upper valleys of the Drakensberg Mountains, and the larger troops in the Zambezi valley, Kenya and Tanzania.

The 'home range' of any particular baboon troop is structured around its principal sleeping-places—clumps of trees, commonly, in woodland savannah, granite kopjes in the high veldt, and vertical cliffs in S.W. Africa—and noon-day resting-places, the distribution of food plants and water-holes, and the existence of well-worn tracks. This is the tract of country familiar to the animals, beyond which it is virtually impossible to drive them. Within the home range, certain areas are used far more frequently than others; these constitute its 'core areas'. Although on the periphery the home range of one troop often overlaps with the home ranges of its neighbours, overt aggression between troops is extremely rare; this is partly because only the 'core areas' of a troop are used at all frequently and these rarely overlap, and partly, also, because their daily routines tend to keep troops apart. Another reason, however, appears to be that agonistic behaviour is worked out within the troop rather than outside it; thus, even when neighbouring troops meet at the same water-hole, they nearly always do so amicably.

All the evidence indicates that savannah-baboon troops in the wild are discrete social units, with little or no interchange between units, and that each troop is organised around a dominance hierarchy of adult males.[1] A typical troop of savannah baboons has from three to ten adult males, from six to twenty adult females,[2] and juveniles and infants roughly equal to the number of adults. When the troop is moving through open country, the females with offspring and the young juveniles cluster in the group's centre, around the most dominant and protective adult males; other males surround this central group, moving ahead, behind, and on either side. This arrangement of the troop places the females and young in the safest position, at its centre, and any predator approaching the troop will first encounter adult males. Should he press an attack, the females and juveniles hurry ahead, while the adult males continue walking slowly forward; within a few seconds, the adult males are interposed between the predator and the rest of the troop, acting as a screen to cover its withdrawal. Clearly, in an environment such as that of the Kenya game reserves where there are many large predators including lions, leopards, cheetahs, wild dogs, hyenas and jackals, such an adaptation is of extreme importance for the survival of the troop. Before discussing its evolutionary significance, however, we may first consider the behavioural patterns upon which it is based: namely, those of male dominance.

Male dominance, within a troop of savannah baboons, is expressed by five principal criteria:[3] priority of access to females in full oestrus; frequency of

[1] On the social organisation of savannah baboons, see Hall (1962b), pp. 323–7, DeVore and Washburn (1963), pp. 342–7, DeVore (1964), pp. 28–31, and Hall and DeVore (1965), pp. 54–71.

[2] The apparent discrepancy in sex ratio between adult males and adult females is probably due to the fact that females mature in roughly half the time that males do: DeVore and Hall (1965), p. 41. Partly, however, it may be due to the greater exposure of young males to predators.

[3] Hall (1962b), pp. 326–7: 'presenting', in the text, is the standard gesture of submission among savannah baboons.

aggressive episodes by the dominant male against other individuals, male and
female, within the troop; frequency with which other animals in the troop
present to, and groom, him; success in causing another male to relinquish a
prized food item or feeding spot; and priority of aggressive-defensive action
against intruders. The simplest form of male dominance is when one animal
fills the dominant rôle, *tout court*, as in S troop in the Cape Reserve, studied by
Hall; there one adult male, the largest of the three in the troop, mated exclusively with the mature females at peak of oestrus, walked at the centre of the
group of mothers with recently-born infants when the troop was on the move,
took the leading part in maintaining order within the troop, and went ahead
of it and threatened when an eland cow charged the troop. A more complex
pattern, giving rise to a true dominance hierarchy, is that found in the SR troop,
in Nairobi National Park, numbering twenty-eight animals. In this troop there
were six large adult males, approximately equal in size; of these, two, nicknamed Dano and Kula, were considerably more dominant—in terms of the
five criteria listed above—than the other four, and on several occasions when
these two met away from the other males, Kula was the more dominant of the
two. However, whenever Kula challenged Dano *within* the confines of the troop,
the latter was always supported by two of the other four males, while Kula
was unable to muster any such support; this meant that, within the troop, Dano
was always in control, since he stood at the head of a 'central hierarchy' of three
adult males, against which the others were unable to combine effectively. Thus,
a male's position in the dominance hierarchy is a combination of his abilities
*as an individual*, i.e. his fighting qualities, and of his *co-operative* abilities, that is,
of his success in combining with other males against a potential challenger. So,
further, the stability of the dominance hierarchy itself in a complex troop like
the SR troop, and its effectiveness in operating against outside enemies, derive
from its being based on the combined strength of a cluster of males who
commonly act together, rather than on the individual fighting ability of any
one of them.

We have seen that there is an *upper* limit, of about seventy to eighty animals,
to the size of a stable baboon troop, set by the extent of day-ranging that baboons can easily accomplish in relation to the available food supply: in the sense
that too large a troop will have to spend too much time on the move to be able
to forage efficiently. We now see that there is a *lower* limit, of around twenty-
four to twenty-eight animals, to a stable baboon troop in open country where
large predators abound.[1] When the troop is away from trees, foraging in open
country, it relies for protection on the defensive rôle of its adult males. This
rôle, in turn, is dependent on the powerful muscles and large canines of the
adult males, whose weight is roughly twice that of the adult females; and on
the dominance hierarchy, which enables them to act together in group defence.

---

[1] Crook and Gartlan, in particular, make the point (1966, p. 1201) that, below a certain
group size, the rôle of the adult males in defence becomes rapidly less efficient.

But in order for this defence to be effective, there need to be not less than four to six adult males to co-operate in it: which implies a troop of not less than twenty-four animals.

We are now in a position to assess the evolutionary significance of the troop organisation characteristic of savannah baboons. Very briefly we may say that their grouping in stable troops of twenty-eight to seventy animals, the organisation of those troops around a dominance hierarchy of adult males, and the marked sexual dimorphism shown by males in those features which best equip them for defence, are the condition of their survival on the ground, in the open, in the presence of large predators such as lions, leopards and cheetahs; and further, that these elements probably developed some ten to twelve million years ago, in the late Miocene and early Pliocene, as the African rain forest retreated in the face of increasing aridity and those species that were ready to adapt to the change, as chimpanzees were evidently not, took to life in the woodland-savannah and eventually in the arid savannah. Now we noted, at the end of the previous section, the relatively low frequency of agonistic behaviour shown by forest-dwelling baboons and the absence among them of dominance hierarchies; and we ascribed this, following Dr. Rowell, in part to the abundance of food in the forest, so that there is little competition for it, and in part to the density of cover, so that disputes—even when they occur—peter out as soon as visual contact is lost.[1] In the savannah, conditions are different. There, while the troop itself, when it is foraging, may be spread out over a distance of a quarter of a mile or more measured along and across its line of march, each of its members is keenly aware of what his companions are up to; this, in turn, gives rise to increased social interaction between them, and this, among adult males, to competition for prized food items and for differential access to females in oestrus. The increased size and marked aggressiveness of adult male savannah baboons are thus, in Crook and Gartlan's view,[2] the *outcome* of the transition from forest to savannah life, being pre-adaptive to their organisation in dominance hierarchies and co-operative activities in group defence: both of which developed in direct response to predatory pressures in the new environment, and have evidently been lost again in their forest-living congeners.

We have postulated that the size and organisation of savannah baboon troops are a response to the interplay of two factors, food resources and predation pressure; and we have found that, in relatively rich savannah habitats with high

---

[1] On the relation between visual awareness and a dominance hierarchy, cf. Chance (1967), p. 510.

[2] Crook and Gartlan (1966), p. 1201. This line of reasoning is powerfully supported by studies of captive primates. Both Rowell (1967, pp. 229–30), and Gartlan (1968, pp. 99–102), point out that levels of aggression are far higher in captivity than are normally found in wild populations. Dr. Rowell specifically links a high frequency of agonistic behaviour with competition at a restricted food source; Gartlan suggests that high levels of aggression, and consequent marked dominance hierarchies (also found among captive baboons), are the result of increased social interaction following the move from forest to savannah—and still more so in captivity, which 'is essentially an impoverished habitat' (1968, p. 89).

predator pressure, these factors result in troops near (or above) the upper limit[1] of a 28–70 range. In harsher environments where food is in very short supply, a troop of even thirty to fifty animals may no longer be an effective foraging unit,[2] in that the troop will be unable to cover a sufficient feeding area in a day without exhausting its members. In such environments, and especially in areas where predators are rare and the need for a group of adult males to protect its weaker members is minimal, we may expect to find both smaller troops and a tendency for troops to divide into foraging parties: each such party tending to range more or less independently during the day and perhaps, though not necessarily, joining up with other parties at communal sleeping cliffs or escarpments by night. This, in fact, is the pattern assumed by the baboon population in the more arid parts of S.W. Africa, where troop size averages between twenty-three and twenty-seven,[3] and where foraging parties of a single adult male, with several breeding females and their young, are not uncommon. This, however, is only an extreme variation, in response to local conditions, on a general pattern of social organisation common to savannah baboons from the borders of the Sahara to the Cape.

For an adaptation to an arid environment which is now genetically determined in a single species, we have to go to the social organisation of the desert or hamadryas baboon of eastern Ethiopia.

### (d) Desert baboons, ecology and social structure

Savannah baboons, as we have seen, are spread over a vast area of Africa extending from the borders of the Sahara to the Cape, in habitats varying from arid savannah to gallery forest, and at altitudes ranging from sea level up to 6,500 feet. In the extreme north-east of this area, they are eventually replaced by the desert baboon, *P. hamadryas*, which lives in the arid brush-land of the eastern Sudan, the eastern lowlands of Ethiopia, Somalia and S.W. Arabia. The first comprehensive study of hamadryas baboons was carried out by two Swiss ethologists, Kummer and Kurt, in the Erer Gota region of eastern Ethiopia in 1960–1; and it is on their work[4] that I draw in the account that follows.

The village of Erer Gota (see Fig. 64) is sited at about 4,000 feet above sea level, in the eastern foothills of the Ethiopian *massif*. Six to seven miles to the south rise the Ahmar Mountains, while about the same distance to the north the Danakhil Plain begins, extending northward into the distance. A strip of foothills about 15 miles wide, stretching in an east-west direction and cut by

---

[1] DeVore and Washburn suggest (1963, pp. 341–2) that, within a given habitat, size in itself may confer certain benefits, in that a small troop commonly yields to a large troop when they meet at water-holes or at desirable food sources within the home-ranges of both; this gives a large troop an advantage over a smaller one, at seasons when supplies are limited.

[2] DeVore and Hall (1965), p. 43. The point is that, if there are only a few food items per acre, a large troop has to move on from one feeding area to another more frequently than a small troop, and so expend more energy on the food quest.

[3] Hall (1963), pp. 3–7, (1965), pp. 81–4, and (1966), pp. 67–70.

[4] See Kummer and Kurt (1963), and, in far richer detail, Kummer (1968).

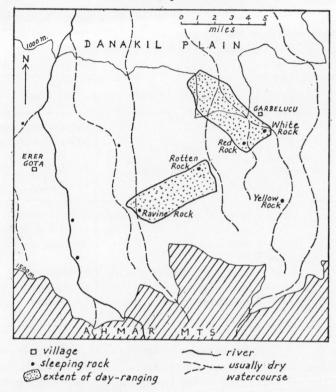

Fig. 64. Day-ranging of hamadryas baboons in Erer Gota area, Ethiopia.
Re-drawn from Kummer (1968), Fig. 11, p. 24, and Fig. 66, p. 166.

many, usually dry watercourses carrying the drainage from the mountains and
petering out in the desert to the north, lies between the two, and it was in this
region that Kummer and Kurt carried out their survey. The hillsides are thickly
wooded with acacias, the beans and dry leaves of which form the staple diet
of the hamadryas population throughout the dry season (October to March);
the cliffs that line the watercourses furnish safe sleeping-places, while their sandy
beds are a source of water to the animals, who, in the dry season, dig drinking
holes in the floor by scooping out the damp sand with their hands.[1] Counts of
all the animals on the six sleeping-rocks between Erer Gota and the village of
Garbelucu, 14 miles to the east, numbered 450 animals in an area measuring
roughly 14 by 8 miles; this gives a population density of about four per sq.
mile. Potential predators in the region include a few lions and cheetahs,
hyenas, and jackals; in the twelve months of Kummer and Kurt's survey,
however, no contacts between predators and baboons were observed, nor was
any evidence of such contacts found.

[1] Kummer (1968), pp. 163–4. Kummer suggests (p. 156) that the survival of hamadryas
in pre-desert areas may depend, in part, on their habit of digging for water, 'a behaviour
which has not been reported in the savanna baboons'.

The diet of hamadryas baboons, like that of savannah baboons, is overwhelmingly vegetarian. The principal food sources exploited in the Erer Gota region are listed in the following table (cf. Kummer, 1968, p. 161):

| season | months | principal food | where found | % |
|---|---|---|---|---|
| rainy season | April to early September | grass seeds<br>other food | picked from ground<br>picked from ground | 44<br>8 |
| | | | | ........ |
| | | acacia shoots and flowers<br>fruits of *Dobera glabra* | by climbing<br>by climbing | 45<br>3 |
| dry season | late September to March | beans and dry leaves of acacia<br>sisal leaves<br>roots and tubers | fallen to ground<br>pulled from ground<br>dug from ground | 6<br>5<br>4 |
| | | | | ........ |
| | | beans and dry leaves of acacia<br>leaves of *Dobera glabra*<br>green leaves of deciduous trees | by climbing<br>by climbing<br>by climbing | 78<br>4<br>3 |

Acacia flowers, and grass seeds, are preferred to any other type of food; both are abundant during the rainy season, especially in the northerly part of the habitat. The soft, bitter base of sisal leaves, and the thick waxy leaves of the evergreen *Dobera glabra*, though available throughout the year, are only eaten in the dry season, when they supplement the dry leaves and beans of acacia. Locusts are eaten, in large quantities when procurable, at the onset of the rains. Only one instance of possible predation on small mammals was observed, a young antelope, which may or may not have been killed by the baboons.

The daily routine of the animals remains essentially unchanged through the year. All hamadryas baboons sleep on vertical cliffs from 50 to 80 feet high; there are a number of such sleeping rocks in the region, and on any given night between 30 and 150 animals will be found congregated at each of them. The size of these sleeping parties[1] depends solely on the availability of sleeping rocks, in conjunction with the local food supply: where cliffs are few and food supply rich, as in the vicinity of agriculture (the animals feeding on grain and field produce when they have the chance), sleeping parties are large; where cliffs are plentiful and food supply sparse, sleeping parties are small—they may be as

[1] Rather unfortunately, Kummer (1968) refers to these unstable sleeping parties as 'troops', and to the smaller, stable groups of which they are composed, as 'bands'. However, he makes quite clear in his concluding analysis (pp. 153–6) that it is the 'bands' that are the homologue to the savannah baboon troop. In the present account I retain the term 'band' for the smaller, stable group; use the term 'sleeping party' when referring to the animals that congregate at a particular sleeping rock for the night; and refer to the daytime foraging body as a troop.

low as fifteen to twenty animals. An hour or so after sunrise the whole body sets off, commonly in the same direction, moving rapidly along open ridges or river beds without pausing to feed or drink; after about an hour the speed decreases, the column becomes looser, and individual 'one-male units' break away from the main body and begin to feed. By noon the main body comes to a halt, with the animals spread out over an area as much as half a mile in extent. Individual parties may lose contact with the main body, and may proceed on to another sleeping rock to spend the night; most of them, however, begin to make their way back to the rock they left that morning, feeding in a leisurely manner as they move.

The basic integer of hamadryas social organisation is the 'one-male unit',[1] consisting, at its peak, of a single adult male plus two to five females, most of whom are adult, with their offspring up to one to one-and-a-half years of age. About one in three 'one-male units' are accompanied by one or more sub-adult males as 'followers'; the latter are groomed now and then by the adult females of the unit, but rarely copulate with them. Some males of all age-classes (other than juveniles still living in their natal units) live outside such units, though still within the troop; observation shows that about 20 per cent of the adult males in a troop live outside 'one-male units'.

The integrity of the 'one-male units' within the troop is expressed in the following ways:

(*a*) *increased social intercourse between members*, expressed particularly in physical contact, e.g. mutual grooming, sleeping in one another's arms. Of all social activity, mutual grooming takes up the largest amount of an adult baboon's time; at the sleeping rock(s), 15 to 25 per cent of all the time that animals were under observation was taken up with grooming (Kummer, 1968, p. 44). Grooming commonly takes place between the unit leader and his several females, but sometimes one of the sub-adult males attached to the unit will groom with one of the females.

(*b*) *spatial coherence:* the members of the 'one-male unit' always stick together within the troop, both at the sleeping rock and when foraging in the open; on the rare occasions when it leaves the troop, it does so as a unit. The leader disciplines his female(s), either by staring hard at an erring one to 'bring her to heel', or by biting her on the back of the neck; correspondingly, females close in on their leader if another male approaches too closely, or in the face of any outside threat. Units rarely intermingle within the troop, each unit being held together by potential threat from its leader.

(*c*) *sexual activity:* without exception, adult males copulate only with females of their own unit (Kummer, 1968, p. 41). Oestrus females, on the other hand, may copulate not only with their own unit leader, but also with sub-adult or

---

[1] On the structure of the one-male unit, see in particular Kummer (1968), pp. 29–83: cf. Kummer and Kurt (1963), pp. 8–16.

juvenile males from outside the unit; if the unit leader observes this, however, he will chase off the young male, neck-bite the female, and probably mount her himself. But females never leave the unit to form temporary consort-pairs with other males outside it; the 'one-male unit' is the social frame for the sexual activity of adult hamadryas baboons, and within it infants are conceived, born and brought up.[1]

(*d*) *persistence in time:* two of the 'one-male units' observed by Kummer and Kurt (1963, p. 14) were observed for 103 and 124 days respectively, no change in composition being noted during that time.

The hamadryas population is found, then, to be fragmented into units consisting of one adult male plus several females with their offspring. These units associate with each other and with single males in larger bodies, namely bands and sleeping parties. No females are found to live outside such one-male units; about one in five adult males, by contrast, have no unit to lead. The peak of a unit's size is reached when the leader is in his early prime. In later prime and old age, the male's restrictive behaviour becomes less intensive; his activity gradually shifts, as we shall see, from leading the unit to directing the travel of the band or the troop.

At this point we may break our account of the structure of the hamadryas troop, to trace the behavioural roots of the grouping tendencies found in young males. 'Nearest neighbour' and 'social interaction' studies of young hamadryas baboons[2] show that male infants of six months to one year tend to leave their mothers far more often than female infants of the same age, and that play-groups of that age include more male infants than females. During the second year of life, the juvenile males' tendency to join predominantly male play-groups is still more pronounced; towards the end of this period some of them no longer sleep with their maternal units, but spend the night in a group of their male peers, sleeping on a separate ledge of the cliff in a cluster of juvenile and sub-adult males. The peak of this attraction between juvenile males is reached at around two years and shortly after. At this age the juvenile males still join the maternal unit during travel and foraging, but when the troop settles to rest, they assemble near its periphery and start to wrestle and chase one another. A single sub-adult or adult male often forms the centre of a play-group of this kind, keeping an eye on the wrestling and playing. Juvenile females of two years or older tend to join such play-groups only if they are built up in this way around an older male; if such a potential protector is not present, only a very few young females—the 'tomboys' of the hamadryas world—are likely to join in, and the boys will greatly outnumber the girls.

During their third year, young males still join the group of juvenile males, but play-fighting becomes progressively less frequent and more inhibited. Instead, towards the end of their third year, they tend to form pair bonds with other

[1] Kummer and Kurt (1963), p. 15.
[2] See, in particular, Kummer (1968), pp. 89–92.

males of their own age, often sitting alone, or in pairs grooming one another, near the troop's periphery. This tendency to separate reaches its peak at sub-adulthood (fourth year of life). Then, fairly suddenly, females begin to appear with increasing frequency among a young male's neighbours; the male himself begins to separate from the members of his own age-sex class, as he either joins a 'one-male unit' as follower, or becomes leader of one himself.[1] As Kummer remarks (1968, p. 92): 'the long growing period in a predominantly male company has come to an end'.

Resuming our account of troop structure: actual counts of hamadryas sleeping parties show that, while the numbers of animals congregating at particular cliff-faces vary from night to night, groups of identifiable animals are commonly to be found sleeping at the same rock. This suggests that the larger bodies of animals consist of separable components which usually, but not always, associate together. It is these components that constitute bands, *the largest stable groups in hamadryas social organisation*.[2] These entities are not apparent under normal circumstances, i.e. within the larger sleeping parties or foraging bodies. Their existence is inferred on the following grounds:

(*a*) *sleeping counts:* if counts of sleeping parties are repeated often enough, the same figures tend to recur. Thus, in fifty counts made at Ravine Rock and the nearby Rotten Rock, the figures 62 or 63 were found four times, 68 twice, and 81 or 82 five times. Further, on several occasions Kummer and Kurt encountered a single old male, nicknamed Rosso, travelling in the same area and leading a column of 43 animals apart from the main sleeping party.

(*b*) *foraging parties:* en route Kummer and Kurt often encountered large, isolated parties which would arrive at the sleeping rock independently of each other and, once there, tended to use different areas of the cliff face for sleeping; twelve out of nineteen counts of such parties in the Erer Gota area numbered between thirty and sixty animals.

(*c*) *fighting within a larger body:* one spontaneous battle was observed, as well as four others which were induced by emptying corn in a pile near the sleeping rock. The battle begins with skirmishes between individual one-male units; gradually, however, the larger body breaks into two (or more) smaller bodies, which round off, cease fighting among themselves, *and re-direct their aggression against the other bands*: e.g. one such band may withdraw, *en masse*, to an adjoining hillside and proceed to threaten the band still at the feeding site, periodically running against it and trying to drive it away. In all the cases observed by Kummer and Kurt, these smaller bodies or bands numbered between twenty and ninety animals; and this number, as Kummer remarks (1968, pp. 106,

---

[1] Starting, commonly, with a single young female as consort. Females of eighteen months to two years may already become the first consort of a young leader: Kummer (1968), p. 60.

[2] On the structure of hamadryas bands, see Kummer (1968), pp. 99–106, 148–9.

148–9), corresponds roughly to the size of the foraging parties which split off from one another *en route*. Further, as we shall see, at the departure of the larger bodies from the sleeping rock in the morning, it is parties of this size which, acting independently of each other, determine the direction of march of the whole body:

> It seems more probable, [concludes Kummer (1968, p. 106)], that the bands appearing on route, during battle, and during the break of camp are identical and remain constant over long periods of time, than that they are formed *ad hoc* by different animals on each occasion. However, we have as yet no evidence for this assumption.

Now while the basic integers of hamadrayas society are the one-male units described earlier, when the animals are actually foraging in the open the one-male units are frequently to be found associated in 'two-male teams', co-ordinated in their activities by their leaders. These 'two-male teams' are, as Kummer observes,[1] among the most fascinating phenomena in the social organisation of the hamadryas, and the way in which they work furnishes the key to understanding the co-ordination of movement in larger bodies. Each team consists of a younger and an older unit leader. When travelling, the two leaders frequently interact with each other, while their females restrict their interactions to their own units. The essential features of the two-male team are: (*a*) that the two males assume different rôles; (*b*) that they concur in making decisions.

The common order of march is for the younger of the two males to lead the way, followed by his females, then by the females of the older male, and finally by the older male himself. Changes of direction are commonly initiated by the younger of the two males; he also presses the combined party to break camp in the morning, by leaving the sleeping rock in a given direction. His advances, however, are only taken as 'proposals'. The older male watches these advances from the back, but only follows when the proposal concurs with his own intended direction; if he disagrees with the route proposed, he remains seated, his own females then remain seated also, and probably also the females of the younger male, leaving the latter out on a limb (metaphorically). Should the younger male fail, after several tries, to initiate the march in *any* direction approved by the older, then the older may come to the front and take the lead himself for a time, until the younger is prepared to continue in the direction indicated.

Thus in the two-male team, as Kummer points out, initiative and decision are divided functions: the younger and less influential leader takes the *initiative* or I-rôle, while the *decision* making or D-rôle is taken by the older. The two-male team goes through several stages, however. In stage 1, the older male assumes both I- and D-rôles, i.e. he leads the whole team, the junior male

---

[1] On the working of the two-male team and the I-D system, see Kummer (1968), pp. 124–37.

bringing up the rear and complying, in the majority of cases, with his 'proposals'; in stage 2, as described above, the junior male leads the way and makes 'proposals', while the senior brings up the rear, accepting or rejecting the proposals made, and sometimes substituting proposals of his own; finally, in stage 3, although by now the aged male has released his last female, he still displays the traits of a D-male, bringing up the rear and exercising control over the team's movements. The essential feature of the two-male team is that, in all cases observed, a younger male accompanies an older, and that it is the older animal who plays the decisive rôle in determining the direction of travel taken by the team as a whole; this is so even when he leads fewer females than his younger partner, and even, as in the case of an old animal, *when he leads no females at all*. The significance of this fact surely is, as Kummer emphasises (p. 137), that, by directing the younger leader towards favourable feeding spots, the older partner is able to pass on his own acquired knowledge—which may be of high survival value in an area of scarce resources—to the younger.

Passing on now to the sources of cohesion within the hamadryas band:[1] Kummer concludes, from the way in which sleeping parties move off in the morning, i.e. by a series of 'pseudopods' led by I-males, one of which is eventually accepted by the D-males near the centre, that the same mechanism operates for larger bodies of animals as for two-male teams. Co-operative behaviour between males, notably the facing and shifting of posture that takes place between adult males within a troop or sleeping party, he calls 'notifying behaviour'. And the largest group between the adult males of which direct relations, as evidenced by 'notifying behaviour', exist, is the band: the group, that is to say, of six or eight one-male units comprising the 'pseudopods' into which the sleeping party shapes itself before setting off in the morning, and the foraging bodies into which it often breaks up later in the day. Thus dyadic relations between adult males, expressed through 'notifying behaviour' and through the extended I-D system of the pseudopods, effectively integrate the movements of up to about fifty animals (Kummer, 1968, p. 141).

One question remains to be answered: namely, how one-male units, and two-male teams, are able to form stable bands at all—seeing that their leaders keep carefully out of one another's reach and indulge in none of the kinds of behaviour, such as mutual grooming and play, that appear generally to reinforce associations among primates. Preliminary observations, made on five sub-adult males of one troop over nearly a month, showed that each of the five males interacted with a stable set of partners throughout the period; that the number of partners interacted with by each individual ranged from three to six; and that the majority of these appeared in every session in which that animal was observed. These observations suggest, in Dr. Kummer's view (1968, pp. 106–8), that young males before the unit-leading stage interact with a relatively stable, and restricted, set of peers; that this set of peers may form the nucleus of a later

[1] On the internal cohesion of the hamadryas band, see Kummer (1968), pp. 138–41, 148–50.

band; and that there are, consequently, within the larger sleeping and foraging bodies, sets of unit-leaders[1] who know one another sufficiently well to stick together and fight as a band even when the unity of the larger body has broken down.

The significance of these findings can perhaps best be assessed in terms of hamadryas day-ranging. In the 15-mile wide strip of foothills surveyed by Kummer and Kurt (see Fig. 64), nine cliff faces were utilised as permanent or temporary sleeping-places, the average distance between them being about 4 miles, with $1\frac{1}{4}$ and 5 miles at the extremes. Apart from one exceptionally short route of $2\frac{1}{4}$ miles, the other eight day-routes mapped ranged from 6 to 12 miles, with an average of $8\frac{1}{2}$; in six out of the eight cases, the animals set out from, and returned to, the same rock, the return route commonly running parallel to the outward journey. Also, the direction in which they set out from a given rock nearly always followed the same course, probably reflecting the distribution of the main food plants, the acacias. On the basis of these eight day-ranges, it appears that the areas exploited by the hamadrayas troops based on two sets of adjacent sleeping rocks covered roughly $6 \times 2\frac{1}{2}$ miles, or 15 sq. miles each. It has to be remembered, however, that these are not 'home-ranges' in the sense of the home-ranges characteristic of savannah baboons: in the first place, the animals congregating at a particular cliff face for the night may comprise the members of two or three bands; in the second, a given band may go off and spend the night, or several nights, on the cliff face of a neighbouring troop, before returning to its own more habitual ledges. The pattern of land use among desert baboons is thus altogether more fluid than among savannah baboons; and this fluidity may itself be a response to life in a very harsh habitat, enabling the local hamadryas population of a region to respond flexibly to relatively minor fluctuations in climate or rainfall. In this case, while the fragmentation of the population into one-male units and two-male teams is probably necessary to enable the members to survive on their own home ground through periods of seasonal scarcity, the grouping of these smaller units into bands may be necessary to ensure their survival within the region as a whole over a period of decades or centuries.

There are, in conclusion, two aspects of hamadryas organisation which I wish to examine, in relation to the general argument of this chapter: first, the nature of the internal bonds which hold the society together, and second, the degree to which its structure may be regarded as an adaptation to a marginal environment.

> Essentially, [writes Kummer (1968, p. 150)], the hamadryas society is an exclusive society of males, the females being distributed among its members as controlled dependents who have no active part in the life of the higher units. Consequently, the hamadryas organisation is based on two types of social bonds: the bond between the adult male and his female, and the bond among the adult males.

[1] A set of four to six peers of this kind might well form the nucleus for a band of thirty to sixty animals, particularly if two or three of them were also either I- or D-males of two-male teams.

The male-female bond is, so far as the female is concerned, an exclusive bond between two animals, which depends for its existence on active enforcement by the male:

> The hamadryas female, [says Kummer (1968, pp. 120–1)], is merely a social appendage of her male whose constant watch virtually prevents her from contacting other troop members. As a stranger, she is retrieved by a male with as little preliminaries as if she were a young juvenile.
>
> The dependent hamadryas females, like juveniles, *are precluded from full troop membership.* . . .

And subsequently (p. 132):

> In a hamadryas troop, the conspicuous adult males alone form the connecting knots in the network of animals. Above the unit level, individuals without grey mantles [characteristic of adult males] do not have to be taken into account by others.[1]

While, then, it is the male-female bond, based on mutual grooming and sexual reciprocity, and backed—on the part of the male—by threats, which lies at the root of the one-male units, it is the multiple bonds established between males which holds a band together. Such male-male bonds are not enforced by threats; nor do they rely for their strength on any overtly sexual content.[2] They seem, rather, to develop from the interaction that takes place between males and from the mutual attraction to which this gives rise.[3] Thus at all stages before—and even for some time after—they have females, sub-adult and newly adult males preferentially sit close to each other and groom. At the unit-leading stage, the male-male attraction is less obvious; at close quarters, it is counteracted by the males' tendency to keep their units from mixing, the leaders avoiding each other's immediate proximity and never grooming one another. But while unit leaders are now spatially isolated from each other at the centres of their social territories and only communicate at a distance, the *rapport* between them—expressed by way of 'notifying behaviour'—is sufficiently strong to give cohesion to the band as a sleeping, foraging and, on ocasions, fighting body.

Savannah baboons have adapted to the relatively impoverished habitat (compared, that is, with the forest) of the savannah, and to the heavy predation pressure to which they are exposed there, by grouping themselves into 'closed' troops and by evolving powerful, aggressive males, capable of jointly driving

---

[1] Elsewhere (1968, p. 152), Kummer refers to 'the extreme degree to which the hamadryas society is patterned by males', in contrast to savannah baboons where females are relatively free to interact with all adults, male or female, of their troop.

[2] Clearly, the wrestling and playing that take place between juvenile and sub-adult males are 'homosexual' in a sense, i.e. in the sense that they take place between individuals of the same sex; but the specifically sexual element in such activities receives no emphasis in Kummer's account of them (1968, pp. 60, 67, 89–92). It is rather like asking, in our own society, whether football is a homosexual game.

[3] On the nature of the male-male bond among hamadryas, see Kummer (1968), pp. 151–3. Chance also stresses (1962, pp. 20–1) the spontaneous nature of the attraction between males, and its persistence in time, e.g. among Japanese macaques.

even fairly large predators away from the group. This, we argued, was the condition of their exploitation of the new environment created by the retreat of the rain forest. In the hamadryas habitat, food resources, at least in the dry season, are even sparser than in the arid parts of the savannah: predation pressure, however, is considerably less severe. Already, among savannah baboons living in the extremer regions, there is a tendency for troops to break down into smaller foraging parties, often consisting of a single adult male with a group of females and their offspring. In hamadryas populations, in a still harsher environment, the same process has been carried a stage further; under conditions of great seasonal food scarcity, the population has become fragmented into one-male units with the females permanently allocated to individual adult males, and this pattern, in place of being a temporary response to local conditions, has become genetically fixed in the species. Thus, as Kummer observes (1968, p. 155):

> the social re-organisation of the hamadryas has partly abandoned the advantage which the closed group of the savanna type provided in the defence against predators. It has created small family groups with only one fighter [or two, in the case of the foraging two-male teams], but it has thereby increased the species' ability to disperse and to exploit the sparse and scattered food resources of its habitat.

That the fragmentation of the hamadryas population into one-male units is a direct response to the harshness of their pre-desert environment, is powerfully supported by Crook's study (1966b) of the social organisation of gelada baboons, *Theropithecus gelada*, in the mountain region of Ethiopia. At harvest time, in conditions of food plenty, geladas congregate in herds of 300 to 400 animals in the vicinity of the fields and threshing floors; but at other times of year, particularly towards the end of the dry season, and in areas where agriculture is not practised, they are found widely dispersed in 'one-male units' and 'all-male groups', which forage independently of one another—though they may share the same line of sleeping cliffs. Crook argues[1] that the fragmentation of the population into 'one-male units', characteristic of both hamadrayas and geladas, is an adaptation to sparse feeding resources, seasonally more limiting even than those exploited by savannah baboons, e.g. in S.W. Africa.

The troop itself has not, however, disappeared from hamadryas organisation, though it has undergone a sea change. Among savannah baboons, as we have seen, the troop is built around a dominance hierarchy of adult males, based on the fighting abilities of the individual males within it and on their capacity for co-operation.[2] Both these factors are necessary to its cohesion. In the hamadryas band the first plays little or no part, while the second has assumed the main rôle. Among hamadryas males, as Kummer remarks (1968, p. 153), dominance in the usual restricted sense, i.e. as the ability of one animal to displace another from a desired object, may be assumed to be present; but its effects on troop

---

[1] Crook (1966b), pp. 252–8: cf. Crook and Gartlan (1966), pp. 1201–2.
[2] On the latter point, cf. Crook (1966a), pp. 64–7.

life are minimal. The functional order between them derives, as he points out, not from the ability to displace, but from the amount of attention and compliance received from other males in choice of travel routes, feeding spots, etc.: from, that is to say, their capacity to co-operate effectively and to elicit co-operation from their peers. And it is on this capacity, and the bonds to which it gives rise, that the hamadryas band relies for its cohesion.

### SOCIAL ORGANISATION OF THE PROTO-HOMINIDS

The crucial event in the evolution of the proto-hominids appears to have been the forest recession which set in, over the whole of central Africa, in the late Miocene and continued through the Pliocene. It was this event which forced them to take the first *step* along the path leading to the development of man. To understand in what sense this was so, requires some knowledge of human anatomy, since the step in question turned on the move from brachiating to walking. We may begin, therefore, with a definition of the former.

All primates are potential brachiators,[1] a *brachiator* being an animal that uses the fore-limb to suspend and propel the body from above. *Semi-brachiators* use the fore-limb sometimes for suspending the body from above, and sometimes for supporting it from below (i.e. for walking on all fours). *Quadrupeds*, which may be arboreal or ground-living, use the fore-limb chiefly for the purpose of supporting the body from below, although occasionally the arms may be used to suspend the body for brief periods. Regarding the hind-limb, brachiators use the hind-limb sometimes to suspend the body from above and sometimes to support it from below; semi-brachiators use the hind-limb to support the body from below, and to propel it forwards in leaping from branch to branch; quadrupeds use the hind-limb largely to support the body from below, but also to propel it forwards in locomotion and in jumping, short of leaping. Brachiators are the only group who use their hind-limbs principally for the purpose of suspending the body; the distinction, in terms of hind-limb activity, between semi-brachiators and arboreal quadrupeds is largely a behavioural one, in that semi-brachiators employ the hind-limb for *leaping* when moving through the forest canopy, arboreal quadrupeds for jumping from one branch to another. Thus semi-brachiation, among Old World primates, involves a specialised activity of both fore-limbs and hind-limbs, reflected in their morphology; conversely, the morphology of these organs furnishes a key to the habitats of their owners.

Now there appears to be a link between brachiating and the development of habitual bipedalism. Most primates can stand, and walk bipedally, *if they require to* (Napier, 1964, p. 683). However, specialised brachiators, i.e. the common run of Old World monkeys, have developed an extreme prehensility of the feet which makes this difficult for them, while specialised quadrupeds

---

[1] On brachiation, and the relation between brachiation and bipedalism, see Napier (1964), pp. 678–85.

which have taken to ground-living, such as savannah baboons and macaques, have become so accustomed to using the fore-limb for supporting the body from below that they find an upright posture hard to maintain for long.

> It seems, therefore, that one must look for the antecedent stage of hominid bipedalism not among the fully specialised brachiators nor among specialised quadrupeds adapted to ground-living life, but among agile forms that employed their fore-limbs in suspending the body, and their hind-limbs in supporting and propelling it in such a manner as to promote mobility of the hips without incurring the specialisations associated with extreme prehensility of the feet (Napier, 1964, p. 685):

that is to say, among the semi-brachiators.

The two organs likely to tell us most about the transition from brachiating to the adoption of an upright posture and of bipedal walking, are the foot and the hand, since both undergo fundamental modifications of function in the process. The modifications undergone by the foot centre around the transmission of weight.[1] Among arboreal monkeys which have retained a quadrupedal mode of progression, weight is transmitted chiefly through the middle digit of the foot which is also the longest; the fact that baboons have retained the primitive weight line through the middle digit, even in their terrestrial habitat, strongly suggests their development from quadrupedal monkeys. In brachiators and semi-brachiators, by contrast, especially as body weight increased and the grasping functions of the foot took precedence over the propulsive function, the *hallux* (big toe) became increasingly opposable to the other four digits. In the feet of apes, we find that weight is transmitted to the branch not through the third digit, but through the webbing between digits 1 and 2. Thus, in both chimpanzees and lowland gorillas (which are largely arboreal), the big toe is widely separated from digit 2, for grasping branches; in the mountain gorilla (which is largely terrestrial) and in man, by contrast, the opposability of the big toe has been almost or completely lost, and weight is transmitted chiefly by way of the big toe. The fact of this shift of load line, together with the increase in length of the big toe (relative to digits 2 and 3), strongly suggests that the hominids evolved from a primate which had already increased somewhat in weight *and* had developed semi-brachiation, but that they subsequently lost the opposability of their big toe when, on taking to the ground, the foot changed from being a tactile grasping organ to a locomotor prop (Campbell, 1967, pp. 131, 136).

Turning now to the upper limb, brachiators, on the whole, have long arms. Thus in gibbons and orangs, both of which are arboreal, the arms are much longer than the legs; in chimpanzees and gorillas, they are a little longer; but in man, who is wholly terrestrial (apart from small boys), the legs are considerably longer than the arms, i.e. the legs have lengthened in response to bipedalism. It is in the changing morphology of the primate hand, however,

[1] On the evolution of the foot in primates, see Campbell (1967), pp. 128–36.

that changes in function may be traced most clearly.[1] Among brachiators the hand is, first and foremost, a grasping organ. Now there are two ways of achieving a hold on a branch with the hand: one, typical of the prosimians (tree shrews, lemurs, etc.), by opposing the *pollex* (thumb) to the other digits, so that the branch can be encircled between thumb and digits; the other, typical of brachiators, by lengthening the phalanges of digits 2, 3, 4 and 5, so as to hook around the branch with all four acting together.

The latter course has been followed by the African apes, i.e. chimpanzees and gorillas; the ligaments have tightened up, so that the hand retains a curved, hook-like shape, and when these animals walk on all fours, their weight is taken on the knuckles which cannot be flattened (unlike baboons, which walk on their palms). In the Old World monkeys, however, and in man, the opposability of the thumb has not been lost; rather, it has been retained and put to other purposes, e.g. for procuring food, cleaning the body, caring for the infant, picking up and throwing sticks and stones.

Monkeys, apes and man, as Campbell emphasises (1967, pp. 161–2), are almost the only animals that fiddle about with things, i.e. extract them from their surroundings, turn them over, examine their form and texture, and carry them about. This ability is dependent in man, in whom it reaches its fullest development, on two pre-adaptations:

(*a*) on the evolution of the opposable thumb, and the consequent development of a precision grip. This anatomical feature man shares with the Old World monkeys; a baboon, for example, as Campbell points out (1967, p. 159), has a grip between thumb and fingers sufficiently precise to extract the sting from a scorpion. In man, this has been carried a stage further with the development of a saddle joint at the base of the thumb, permitting a 45° rotation as well as movement in two planes, plus a lengthening of the phalanges to carry a heavier musculature (Campbell, 1967, pp. 163–4).

(*b*) on the move to the ground and the adoption of an habitual upright posture, so freeing the hand from any residual weight-bearing or grasping function and allowing the further perfecting of the precision grip. This factor is shared to some degree by the African apes, especially chimpanzees, amongst whom food carrying, simple tool using, and the throwing of sticks and stones in agonistic display, have all been reported; their ability to handle objects is limited, however, by the lack of an opposable thumb, and they can move neither fast nor far when carrying things in their hands.

As I said earlier, it was the forest recession which set in during the later Miocene (around 12,000,000 years ago), and the conditions of relative aridity which persisted through most of the Pliocene,[2] that forced the proto-hominids out of

---

[1] On the evolution of the hands of primates, see Campbell (1967), pp. 157–65.

[2] Our knowledge of the climatic sequence in sub-Saharan Africa is based chiefly on studies by botanists and entomologists of the Kalahari sands: Robinson (1964), pp. 409–10.

Q

their easy-going niche in the tropical rain-forests of central Africa into the woodland savannah—and eventually into the grassland savannah—to which the rain forest gave way, so setting them on the path that led to the development of man. We are now in a position to assess what this change involved.

To take advantage of any major environmental change and exploit a new habitat, a population must be to some degree *pre-adapted*,[1] i.e. have the potentiality for developing the characteristics required for success in it. To take a single example: man, in company with (other) brachiating and semi-brachiating primates, has a relatively stiff spine; this in itself was of advantage to him in developing an upright posture, such a posture being in turn a necessary pre-adaptation for his subsequent move from the forest floor to the plains. Anatomical evidence of this kind[2] suggests that the proto-hominids were, in origin (i.e. in the later Miocene), a population of 'ape-men' living either in the forest or on the borderland where forest gives way to woodland savannah, equally at home in the trees upon which they relied for fruit, edible leaves, seeds and honey, and on the ground which they exploited for roots and tubers, berries, grubs and insects; able to walk on two legs, and so with hands free for foraging and carrying things over short distances, though not as yet fully erect in posture; and with a social organisation, initially, not unlike that of forest living and forest-fringe chimpanzees. In short, bipedal, omnivorous, manually acquisitive and mentally inquisitive, non-territorial and loosely organised in 'open' groups.[3]

Two features in this way of life especially pre-adapted the proto-hominids for their move out of the forest into a woodland-savannah habitat: first, an omnivorous diet (with the dentition and digestive processes that go with it), and second, the adoption of an habitual upright posture. The two features are related. A woodland-savannah habitat has enough trees to provide some of the forest fruits, such as figs, to which forest-dwelling species are accustomed; on the other hand, it places a greater premium on ground foods such as berries, roots, grass seeds, plant stalks, nuts and mushrooms. Further, it has enough trees to offer ready escape from predators. Now this is precisely the environment in which an habitual upright posture would be an advantage: in the first place, for spotting predators; and in the second, to release the hands for foraging and carrying food.[4]

And it is here that the inquisitiveness which appears to be characteristic of the great apes, and particularly of their young, comes into its own; for it seems

[1] Campbell (1967), pp. 84–5, 96–7.

[2] Together with the fossil remains of *Proconsul*, from Miocene lake beds in East Africa: Campbell (1967), pp. 79–83.

[3] Reynolds (1966) emphasises this aspect of their organisation: on other aspects, cf. Kortlandt and Kooij (1963), especially pp. 65–8, Crook (1966a), pp. 67–9, Crook and Gartlan (1966), p. 1202, and Campbell (1967), pp. 170–4, 200–4.

[4] Napier (1967), pp. 64–5: cf. Kortlandt (1962), p. 134. Kortlandt, in particular, suggests that walking on two legs may have evolved primarily *as a result of manual dexterity*, rather than (as has usually been supposed) manual dexterity having evolved as a result of upright posture.

likely that it was their flexibility in diet and behaviour which enabled the proto-hominids to exploit the food resources offered by their new environment. Chimpanzees, as we have seen, use simple tools for procuring food, and are capable, under the conditions of 'impoverished habitat' afforded by captivity, of developing many manipulative skills. But in the wild chimpanzees have remained, broadly speaking, within the forest zone with its abundant food supply, and their learning proficiency has not been fully utilised. The recession of the rain forest, and the lengthening dry season which accompanied (and caused) it, would however have been precisely the conditions for eliciting this response from a species prepared to show it; and we may suppose that it was under these conditions that the proto-hominids developed their tool-using propensities, probably in the first instance digging sticks—to supplement hands —in getting at deep-rooting bulbs and tubers in the drier areas, and took to eating reptiles, small animals, eggs and nestlings of birds, etc., to supplement their mainly vegetarian diet.[1] The use of tools for collecting vegetable foods, an increase in meat-eating, and the move to ground-living which these imply, conduced to the adoption of an habitual upright posture such as we find in the *Australopithecines*: the fossil remains of which (in their archaeological setting), dating from the early phase of the Pleistocene (*c.* 1,800,000 years ago), under climatic conditions rather similar to those of the present day, and found through the savannah belt of Africa east of 29° E., show them to have been bipedal, simple tool users, supplementing their vegetarian diet[2] with birds, lizards and rodents.

So long as the proto-hominids stayed in the woodland savannah and retained some of their brachiating propensities, they were relatively safe from predators; consequently, their social organisation need have been no 'tighter' than that of present-day chimpanzees. But once they ventured outside this habitat into the grassland savannah, with its scattered clumps of trees perhaps two to three miles apart, *or*—as we should probably put it—once the woodland savannah in which they had been living gave way to grassland savannah as a result of the increasing aridity of the late Pliocene, they were no longer safe from their enemies. Now savannah baboons, as we have seen, are able to survive in open country only as a result of their highly evolved social structure,[3] and this condition probably applies to primates in general:

[1] Robinson (1964), pp. 410–12. Kortlandt and Kooij also suggest (1963, p. 83) that, whereas a constant rain-forest habitat discourages predatory habits, a savannah habitat with fluctuating climate is likely to promote predation on other species.

[2] The fossilised jaw and dentition of *Australopithecus africanus* indicate that, while this hominid was still largely vegetarian, he was eating less tough food than his forbear *A. robustus*, perhaps as a result of the use of simple tools for pounding roots and seeds: Campbell (1967), pp. 181–2, 200–2.

[3] Even this, however, has not enabled them to live in areas totally bereft of either trees, cliffs or kopjes, where large predators abound; the absence of such refuge sites, as DeVore and Hall point out (1965, pp. 50–1), may deny baboons access to areas otherwise rich in food resources.

At any rate it seems, [writes Campbell (1967, p. 335)], that plains life for such a defenseless creature as a primate necessitates the rapid evolution of a means of co-operative defense and a binding social structure.

In savannah baboons, this structure takes the form of relatively tightly-knit 'closed' troops, of an average size of thirty to seventy animals, centred around a dominance hierarchy of adult males. This form of social organisation we may regard as one of the two primary adaptations enabling savannah baboons to exploit the savannah habitat, the other being their omnivorous diet.

Now it seems reasonable to suppose that the proto-hominids, in moving out into the grassland savannah, evolved some similar form of troop structure in response to the predation pressure they met there.[1] But the 'closed' troop structure characteristic of savannah baboons is only one form of such social organisation. In desert baboons, as we have seen, for whom predation pressure is much less severe but seasonal food scarcity much more so, the local population tends to fragment into separately foraging 'one-male units' and 'two-male teams'; these are the functional units of hamadryas society and, at least during the dry season, the larger stable groups—the bands—take form only transiently at sleeping rocks or at locally abundant food sources. It seems rather likely that a process analogous to the fragmentation of the hamadryas population in its extreme habitat may have taken place among the proto-hominids, both there in response to similar ecological conditions, and in the grassland savannah as a consequence of the development of defensive weapons: chiefly, of the spear.[2] Two or three proto-men armed with wooden spears would have been a match for all but the largest predators; and it was probably the use of defensive weapons, together with the increasing accuracy with which stones could now be thrown,[3] that permitted, even in a savannah habitat, the fragmentation of the troop into smaller foraging parties and the exploitation by the latter of areas previously closed to them, as to present-day savannah baboons, by lack of refuge sites. I am inclined, on these grounds and by analogy with recent gatherer societies living in arid environments, to see the social organisation of the Australopithecines as one of small foraging parties and 'one-male units', spread in a loose web over a given area, no more territorial than are hamadryas baboons in *their* habitat, and retaining, like them, a 'shadow' band structure capable of assuming definite form for purposes of exploiting locally abundant food sources, of inbreeding, and perhaps, on occasions, of co-operative defence

---

[1] Recent evidence from the Swartkrans cave site in the Transvaal indicates that, in open grassland conditions, the predators in question are likely to have been leopards: Brain (1970), pp. 115-18, and especially Fig. 6.

[2] Cf. Kortlandt (1962), pp. 136-8. Crook and Gartlan remark (1966, p. 1202) that the possession of even simple weapons would compensate for the gross sexual dimorphism in size and musculature found e.g. in savannah baboons, but not in man.

[3] Largely restricted, if present-day performance is any guide, to males. Kortlandt and Kooij argue (1963, p. 65) that the move to predominant ground-living (with consequent decline in brachiating), preferably in a semi-open habitat, is pre-requisite for the evolution of the genetic basis for the ability to throw and aim proficiently.

against large predators.[1] If this is accepted, then we may hypothesise, by analogy with hamadryas, the kinds of social bonds which are likely to have held the Australopithecine community together.

Essentially, as we have seen, the cohesion of the hamadryas band is dependent on the *rapport* established between its adult male unit-leaders, expressed in 'notifying behaviour'. This *rapport* is patterned on, derives from, precedent male-male bonding within the hamadryas local community: notably, on the 'best friend' relation, established between two juveniles soon after leaving their natal units, and expressed in sitting together, mutual grooming, etc.; on the 'age-group' relation, established between the sub-adult males of the local community and expressed in playing together, wrestling, etc., and also in mutual grooming between chosen friends; and on the 'sponsor-novice' relation, established between an older (adult) and a younger (adult or sub-adult) male within the framework of the 'two-male team', and expressed in co-operation in daily foraging activities and in joint protection of their respective 'families'. If the Australopithecines, in response to environmental pressures common to both, evolved a social organisation of hamadryas type, and if their local communities were held together by social bonds similar to those that ensure the cohesion of the hamadryas band, then we can deduce the kind of genetically determined behaviour patterns, e.g. of personal friendship between co-equals, mutual esteem between age-mates, and respect/patronage between a younger and an older male, which they are likely to have bequeathed to their successors and which furnished raw material for the next step in hominid evolution: namely, the development of co-operative hunting.

### THE ADVENT, AND EFFECTS, OF CO-OPERATIVE HUNTING

The evolution of *Homo erectus* from *Australopithecus africanus* spanned the period, roughly speaking, from 1,200,000 to 200,000 years ago. The first step in the process was the development of a striding gait. The immense power of the human stride comes in part from the length of the human leg, and in part from the action of three muscles acting in turn: *biceps femoris* (hamstring muscle) brings the body forward over the knee, *gluteus maximus* (buttock muscle) completes extension at the hip, *gastrocnemius* (calf muscle) gives a final lift and levers the body forward, using the forefoot as a fulcrum.[2] The pelvis of *Australopithecus* indicates that this little hominid, though erect or nearly erect in posture, could scarcely have been a strider:

[1] Thus among gelada baboons, which, like hamadryas, are organised in one-male units—and all-male groups—but lack any definite troop or band structure, several males may co-operate together in keeping off an attack by dogs while the females and young run for safety down the cliff face: Crook (1966a), pp. 64–5. This is an advance on the *sauve qui peut* observed by Dr. Rowell among her forest-dwelling *P. anubis* baboons.

[2] On the action of these three muscles, see *Gray's Anatomy* (30th ed., 1949), pp. 646–7, 653, 660–1, and especially pp. 674–5. It is clear, from the account given there, that the main propulsive force in human walking is provided by the *Gastrocnemius* muscle. In running, the action of *Gastrocnemius* is reinforced by that of the Quadriceps group on the front of the thigh, which, by powerfully extending the knee, increases the thrust of the forefoot against the ground.

For *Australopithecus*, [writes Napier (1967, p. 65)], walking was something of a jog trot. These hominids must have covered the ground with quick, rather short steps, with their knees and hips slightly bent; the prolonged stance phase of the fully human gait must surely have been absent.

Fossil bones, from Olduvai in particular, indicate[1] that 'in East Africa, more than a million years ago, there existed a creature whose mode of locomotion was essentially human': i.e. who walked with a striding gait.

Now human walking is primarily, as Napier states (1967, p. 62), an adaptation for covering long distances with economy of effort. The Australopithecines already supplemented their mainly vegetarian diet with birds and rodents; savannah baboons, as we have seen, course and catch hares which they accidentally put up in the grassland, besides exerting quite heavy predation pressure on young gazelles in areas where the habitats of the two species overlap. It seems reasonable to suppose, on these grounds, that the primary purpose served by a striding anatomy was to enable the successors of *Australopithecus africanus*, probably working together in two-man pairs, to track and run down deer and gazelle over long distances, *in much the same way as the Hopi until recently did in their equally arid environment.*[2] The increased musculature required for human walking may be seen, therefore, as a response to the directed running-down of game of the size of deer and antelope—individuals of which, as the Hopi case shows, can readily be killed (when exhausted) by a single man with his bare hands. The development of such musculature must in turn have increased the extent of hominid day-ranging, say from the four to six miles (out, and back, from a home base) typical of savannah and desert baboons, to eight to ten miles out and back; and this extension of range, by bringing a wider variety of vegetable food sources within day-walking distance of the foraging unit,[3] would have permitted the hominids access to areas of sparse resources, especially arid areas, previously denied to them.

Not all game animals, however, are amenable to running down by a single hunter or by a pair of hunters working together: some because of their strength, and some because they only occur in herds from which individuals cannot be separated. Such animals, in the Southwest and the Great Basin, are the elk and the mountain sheep; and these are best hunted, at particular seasons, by parties of hunters acting according to an agreed plan. What the equivalent species were

---

[1] Napier (1967), p. 66: cf. on the fossil bones of *Homo erectus* from Olduvai, Napier (1964), pp. 698–700.

[2] It is hard for us to realise, I think, the *kind* of distances that can be covered by humans on foot. I was told at Oraibi of a Hopi who, charged with a message for the Agent at Keam's Cañon, left Moenkopi at sunrise, ran to Oraibi (where he ate breakfast) and on to Keam's Cañon, passed through Oraibi on his way back and re-entered Moenkopi as the sun was setting: a distance of between 130 and 140 miles, in about seventeen hours. For the running-down of deer and antelope by Hopi, see above, p. 275.

[3] An increase in day-ranging from, say, four to eight miles out and back from a home-base, quadruples the exploitable area, i.e. from around 50 to 200 sq. miles. If several home-bases are available to the foraging unit(s), then we approach the extent of western Shoshoni foraging areas.

in the Old World I am not sure, perhaps the powerfully horned ungulates like (?) wildebeeste and oryx. But whatever they were, it was in relation to them that the second great step in the evolution of *Homo erectus* was taken: namely, the development of co-operative hunting.[1]

We have postulated that the social organisation of the Australopithecines consisted of small foraging parties, analogous to those of hamadryas, spread in a loose web over the countryside, the knots of the web being tied to refuge sites and water holes, with 'shadow' local communities—analogous to the hamadryas band—ready to be activated under suitable conditions, e.g. of food abundance, for in-breeding, or for defence. The extension in day-ranging, consequent upon the adoption of a fully striding gait, would have brought more of these foraging parties into close social contact with one another; and we have already delineated the kind of co-operative behavioural patterns which, by analogy with hamadryas, are likely to have been present in the genetic make-up of the Australopithecines, assuming that they developed a similar type of social organisation. We may suppose, therefore, that it was the co-operative behavioural patterns inherited from the Australopithecines which enabled their successors to respond to the opportunity offered by their newly-acquired striding gait, to develop co-operative hunting as a means of exploiting the last major food source hitherto denied them: namely, that of the large game animals too well protected, too swift or living in too inaccessible a habitat, to be killable by a single man on his own or by two men working together.[2]

This brings us to the final point I wish to discuss here: the increase in brain size, and particularly in the size of the forebrain, that accompanied these changes. From our knowledge of fossil remains and their cranial capacity, two points stand out clearly[3]: first, the great spurt in brain size occurred between the lower and middle Pleistocene, between (that is to say) *Australopithecus africanus* on the one hand and *Homo erectus pekinensis* on the other, i.e. between *c.* 1,200,000 and 200,000 years ago; second, the increase in brain size coincided roughly with the development of co-operative hunting by the early hominids. Now co-operative hunting, since it depends for its success on foresight and planning, requires a communication system far more elaborate and subtle than any available to baboons and chimpanzees; no other primate but man, so far as we know, is able to communicate even so simple a message as: 'I will meet you by that tree over there at noon.' But this is of the essence of effective co-operative hunting; and it was in response to needs of this kind, we may suppose,

---

[1] Campbell (1967), pp. 339–40: cf. DeVore (1964), p. 34, Crook and Gartlan (1966), p. 1202.

[2] As to the size of the social units required, these probably numbered—at the appropriate hunting seasons—thirty to fifty individuals, depending on local resources, yielding a hunting party of six to ten adult males; the inbreeding group, dialect tribe or *deme*, is likely to have comprised eight or ten local bands of this kind. For these figures, see Birdsell (1968), pp. 231–6, and the ensuing discussion, especially pp. 245–8.

[3] Campbell (1967), pp. 230–4.

that speech itself developed.[1] And, co-eval with speech, the use of fire for cooking, and an increasing reliance on tools and weapons, all three character-istic of the middle Pleistocene (*c*. 200,000 years ago); and later, as man pushed north into colder latitudes during the late Pleistocene (*c*. 80,000 years ago), the adoption of simple skin clothing.[2]

Now a process which begins as an option may end by becoming an essential, as we have seen with Hopi farming. Much the same seems to have happened in the case of co-operative hunting; what probably began—and may have re-mained—in the African savannah, and perhaps even in the more arid areas adjoining it, as a useful but non-essential supplement to a diet furnished sub-stantially by vegetable foraging and small-game chasing, became in more northerly latitudes where vegetable resources were less abundant,[3] and especially in response to climatic fluctuation (the later glaciations), a condition of survival there. To say this is to imply that middle and late Palaeolithic communities, at least in the Old World outside Africa, depended for their life on the strength of the co-operative bond between their adult males: in other words, what in the Australopithecines (by analogy with hamadryas) had been relatively loose attachments, based on mutual attraction in the case of age-mates and on recipro-cal duties in the case of the leaders of two-male teams, had become, in later Ice Age man, bonds *necessary* for the continued existence of the social group.

It is not far-fetched therefore to hold, as Emlen holds (1966, pp. 416–17), that initiation itself, and the tests of fortitude which often accompany initiation, may have their roots in primitive hunting-party organisation, where the degree to which one hunter could rely on and work closely with another 'might

[1] The enlargement of the fore-brain being, in a general sense, a response to the needs of social life in a word-using community: i.e. it furnished the physical basis for the infinitely subtle give-and-take of *human* relations. Just as the mid- and hind-brain and their associated tracts are responsible for maintaining the body in actual space (lesions there giving rise to various forms of ataxia), so the frontal lobes evidently are for maintaining the *person* in social space—a lesion there commonly first manifesting itself in disorders of behaviour: F. A. Elliott, Brodie Hughes and J. W. Aldren Turner, *Clinical Neurology* (London, 1952), pp. 60–2, 556–9.

[2] See Clark and Piggott (1970), p. 30 (on speech), pp. 36–8 (on the use of fire), pp. 38–42 (on tools and weapons), pp. 48–50 (on the adoption of clothing).

The spread of the early hominids into more northerly latitudes in the late Pleistocene brought them, for the first time, into contact with bears. Bears, like the higher primates (chimpanzees, gorillas and man), are chiefly vegetarian but may also eat meat, are pre-dominantly ground-living but can climb trees to pick fruit or get honey, are able to walk upright, have lost their tails, urinate standing up, and make beds to sleep in: hence, on all these counts, their place in the mythology of virtually all peoples north of 36° N. On the evo-lution in the middle Pleistocene of the brown, cave and black bear from the ancestral species, *Ursus etruscus*, see B. Kurten (1957), pp. 70–6.

[3] This point is stressed by R. B. Lee (1968), pp. 42–8. Lee shows, by comparison of recent hunter-gatherer communities, that as one moves farther from the tropics the amount of food contributed by gathering progressively declines, and that contributed by hunting and/or fishing progressively increases: e.g.

Hadza (East Africa), gathering 80 per cent, hunting 20 per cent;
Andamanese, gathering 50 per cent, hunting/fishing 50 per cent;
Ainu (Japan), gathering 30 per cent, hunting/fishing 70 per cent;
Yukaghir (Siberia), gathering 10 per cent, hunting/fishing 90 per cent.

be a matter of life and death not only to the hunter but to his entire group': particularly when we remember that the social relationships formalised at initiation, namely the relationship between sub-adult males of the same age-group, and that between an older and a younger male (sponsor and novice), are precisely those which the early co-operative hunters are likely to have inherited from their Australopithecine forbears.

I conclude, on these grounds, that Schurtz was right in postulating an innate, i.e. genetically determined, tendency to associate on the part of human adult and sub-adult males. I agree, further, with van Gennep that 'la société générale', among primitive peoples, 'n'est constituée que par les hommes ayant passé par les rites d'agrégation à la communauté';[1] and with Schurtz, that age-sets and male associations are, simply, secondary elaborations on this basic theme. I disagree radically, however, with van Gennep's analysis of the nature of these *rites d'agrégation*; and it is to that subject, since it forms an integral part of the theory of associations which I propose to offer, that we may now turn.

### LES RITES DE PASSAGE

van Gennep starts from the premise[2] that for the individual, whatever his society, life consists in a succession of stages through which he passes:

> C'est le fait même de vivre qui nécessite les passages successifs d'une société spéciale à une autre et d'une situation sociale à une autre: en sorte que la vie individuelle consiste en une succession d'étapes dont les fins et commencements forment des ensembles de même ordre — naissance, puberté sociale, mariage, . . . mort. Et à chacun de ces ensembles se rapportent des cérémonies dont l'objet est identique: faire passer l'individu d'une situation déterminée à une autre situation toute aussi déterminée.  p. 4.

The ceremonies, whereby the passage from one stage or from one social situation to another is effected, fall into ceremonial sequences; since they have the same object, the sequences, though not identical in detail, follow the same general pattern; it is this general pattern which van Gennep has in mind when he refers to all such sequences as comprising a single class, that of *les rites de passage*:

> Les rites de passage se retrouve donc, à la base, des ensembles cérémoniels qui accompagnent, facilitent ou conditionnent le passage de l'un de ces stades de la vie à un autre, ou d'une situation sociale à une autre. . . .  p. 267.

---

[1] Cf. Kummer's characterisation of hamadryas society (above, p. 469): 'Above the unit level, individuals without grey mantles do not have to be taken into account.'

How far this male-oriented view of society is determined by the greater *visio-spatial* ability of the primate male (as against the female), I must leave for others to judge; the gene for the ability itself is evidently carried on the X-chromosome, that is to say, it is sex-linked: see 'The biology of sex differences', by Dr. J. Gray, in *The Times Saturday Review* for 11 December 1971, p. 6.

[2] For the general account of his theory that follows, see van Gennep (1909), pp. 3-4, 13-14, 271-6.

The pattern common to all the sequences is that of separation from one group (or stage), followed by an interim or waiting period, and then by integration into another group (or stage). On the basis of this common pattern, van Gennep sub-divides each ceremonial sequence into three: namely, *rites préliminaires* (i.e. *de séparation*), *rites liminaires* (i.e. *de marge*), and *rites post-liminaires* (i.e. *d'agrégation*). In theory, every full *rite de passage* should be divisible into these three categories; conversely, any single ceremonial element should be apportionable to one or other of them.

The greater part of van Gennep's book[1] is taken up with a detailed study of the rites that accompany pregnancy and child-birth, infancy, initiation, betrothal and marriage, death and burial. In these chapters van Gennep shows, convincingly to my mind, how the ritual that accompanies each of these events is divisible into the three stages he has delineated, first separating the individual concerned from *le monde antérieur*, then subjecting him (or her) to a period o suspense, and finally integrating him into the new group which the rites—and the co-incident physiological changes—have qualified him to join. One point only I wish to draw attention to here: namely that, in his treatment of each of the principal steps in the life-cycle of the individual, van Gennep specifically compares the status of the person concerned to that of an outsider or stranger. Thus, referring to pregnancy, he writes (1909, p. 58) that, from the moment that the woman is *enceinte*,

> elle se trouve dans un état physiologique et social temporairement anormal: rien de plus naturel alors qu'elle soit traitée comme l'est le malade, *l'étranger*. . . .

Referring to the rites surrounding birth and infancy (1909, p. 72):

> il y a, là, une attitude de défense de même ordre que celle que prend la collectivité à l'égard de *l'étranger*. Or, de même que l'étranger, l'enfant doit d'abord être séparer de son milieu antérieur.

Of marriage, van Gennep writes (1909, p. 201):

> Que les cérémonies du mariage présentent des analogies, souvent même des identités de détail avec *l'adoption*, c'est là un fait qui semblera normal à qui se rappelle qu'en définitive, dans le mariage, il s'agit de l'agrégation d'*un étranger* à un groupement.

And of death (1909, pp. 235–6):

> Quant aux rites d'agrégation à l'autre monde, ils sont l'equivalent de ceux de *l'hospitalité*, de *l'adoption*. . . .

Finally, discussing the licence which commonly prevails during the period of initiation, and again during the period between burial and the last rites for the dead, van Gennep writes (1909, pp. 161–3):

---

[1] i.e. Chapters iv to viii, pp. 57–236 or 180 pages out of 280.

Pendant toute la durée du noviciat, les liens ordinaires, tant économiques que juridiques, sont modifiés, parfois même nettement rompus. *Les novices sont hors de la société*, et la société ne peut rien sur eux et d'autant moins qu'ils sont proprement sacrés et saints, par suite intangibles, dangereux. . . . En sorte que si d'une part, les tabous, en tant que rites négatifs, élèvent une barrière entre les novices et la société générale, de l'autre, celle-ci est sans défense contre les entreprises des novices. Ainsi s'explique un fait qui a été relevé chez de très nombreuses populations: c'est que pendant le noviciat, les jeunes gens peuvent voler et piller tout à leur aise, on se nourrir et s'orner aux dépens de la communauté.

La presque généralité du fait dont il s'agit est d'ailleurs assez connue, mais pour en comprendre le mécanisme dans le cas que j'indique, il convient de rappeler qu'une licence générale, une suspension de la vie sociale, marquent également les interrègnes et la période entre les funérailles provisoires et les funérailles définitives. C'est ainsi peut-être que s'expliquerait aussi, au moins en partie, la licence sexuelle qui prend place, chez un certain nombre de peuples, entre le début des fiançailles (*betrothal*) et la termination du mariage par appropriation de la femme à un homme déterminé. Si la suspension des règles ordinaires de vie ne conduit pas toujours à de tels excès, elle n'en constitue pas moins un élément essentiel des périodes de marge.

van Gennep, then, divides every *rite de passage* into three parts: *rites prélimi-naires*, *rites liminaires* (ou *de marge*), and *rites post-liminaires*. The notion of the *marge*, or *limes*, van Gennep draws directly from the no-man's land lying between the territories of two neighbouring peoples. Each body of people, he points out (1909, pp. 19–21), has its own territory over which its inhabitants exercise their own rights and prerogatives; such a territory is commonly marked e.g. by upright stones or posts, or by prominent landmarks; around it stretches a neutral band, the marches, to cross which, and so to pass from the territory of one people to that of another, involves certain formalities. Such rites, i.e. of passage, obtain not only between two territories, but also when proceeding from one village to another, even from one house to another: 'la porte', as van Gennep remarks (pp. 26–7), 'est la limite entre le monde étranger et le monde domestique . . ., ainsi "passer le seuil" signifie s'agréger à un monde nouveau.'

This notion of the *marge* or *limes* is allied, in van Gennep's theory, to another: that of the division between the sacred and the profane. For the territory of a particular people is not only theirs, it is also sacred:

Un espace déterminé du sol est approprié par un groupement déterminé de telle manière que pénétrer, étant étranger, dans cet espace réservé, c'est commetre un sacrilège au même titre que pénétrer, étant profane, dans un bois sacré. . . .

pp. 20–1.

In van Gennep's *schema*, the sacred/profane dichotomy has no absolute value; rather, it characterises aspects of certain situations. Thus a man, resident in his own house, lives in the profane: 'il vit dans le sacré dès qu'il part en voyage et se trouve, en qualité d'étranger, à proximité d'un camp d'inconnus'. Similarly, a girl who is pregnant becomes *sacrée* with regard to the other women of the social group, who then constitute, *vis-à-vis* the pregnant girl, *un monde profane.* In this way the individual, at the point when he makes the physical crossing from one territory to another or the social crossing from one group to another, finds the sacred/profane dichotomy hingeing upon himself (*pivoter sur lui-même*).

The three 'legs' upon which van Gennep's formulation rests, namely the physical crossing of a frontier or *limes*, the alternation of the sacred and the profane, and the transference of both aspects to the social plane, stand out clearly in his own summary (1909, pp. 23–4) of the object of his book:

> Ces zones, [he writes, speaking of the marches between two neighbouring territories], sont ordinairement un désert, un marécage et surtout la forêt vierge, où chacun peut voyager et chasser de plein droit. Étant donnée le pivotement de la notion du sacré, les deux territoires appropriés sont sacrés pour qui se trouve dans la zone, mais la zone est sacrée pour les habitants des deux territoires. Quiconque passe de l'un à l'autre se trouve ainsi matériellement et magico-religieusement, pendant un temps plus ou moins long, dans une situation spéciale: il flotte entre deux mondes. C'est cette situation que je désigne du nom de *marge*, et l'un des objets du présent livre est de démontrer que cette marge idéale et matérielle à la fois se retrouve, plus ou moins prononcée, dans toutes les cérémonies qui accompagnent le passage d'une situation magico-religieuse ou sociale à une autre.

Before criticising this theory, let us look at the *detail* of van Gennep's work. And for this purpose I take his treatment (1909, pp. 107–25) of the rites that accompany initiation into, respectively, totemic groups (Australia), secret societies or fraternities (Guinea Coast, Congo, Melanesia), and age-sets (east Africa): a central part, it will I think be granted, of the whole theory. In spite of manifold differences in detail, these all follow, as van Gennep is able convincingly to demonstrate, a common pattern:

> separation from *le monde antérieur*, 'death' of the novice—physical tests (of endurance), special food, special language, learning of the customary code, *peintures corporelles (en blanc, en rouge)*, *mutilations corporelles*, learning the steps of dances—'re-birth' of the novices, *les initiés agissent comme des nouveaux nés, ils re-apprennent tous les gestes … de la vie commune*, sharing a meal, wearing of special clothes, re-integration into the community.

Not all these features are likely to figure in any one initiatory sequence, but they form a repertory of elements out of which such sequences are commonly built. Let us take three of these elements in more detail:

(*a*) *hair:* different modes of dressing the hair, as van Gennep points out (1909, pp. 238–40), mark different stages in the social life of the individual—'c'est que les cheveux sont, par leur forme, leur couleur, leur longeur et le mode d'arrangement, un caractère distinctif aisément reconnaissable, tant individuel que collectif'.

(*b*) *special (or secret) languages:* in the course of many initiatory ceremonies, especially during the period of *marge*, a special language is employed, consisting sometimes in a vocabulary totally different to that in common use and sometimes merely in the avoidance of certain words in ordinary speech. van Gennep sees this (1909, p. 241) as a phenomenon of the same kind as the changing of clothes, physical mutilations, *l'alimentation spéciale* (*tabous alimentaires*), i.e. as a process of differentiation.

(*c*) *carrying* (*le portage*): this practice is found very widely in the ceremonies whereby the individual passes through life, e.g. at birth, initiation, marriage (crossing the threshold), enthroning, funerary rites; 'le sujet de la cérémonie ne doit pas, pendant un temps plus ou moins long, toucher la terre'. van Gennep sees this (1909, pp. 265–6) as a typical *rite de marge*:

> pour montrer qu'à ce moment l'individu n'appartient ni au monde sacré ni au monde profane, ou encore qu'appartenant à l'un des deux, on ne veut pas qu'il se ré-agrège mal à propos à l'autre, on l'isole, *on le maintient dans une position intermédiaire, on le soutient entre ciel et terre....*

Now every single element in the sequence of initiatory rites is pre-figured in the development of the child during the first five to six years of life: from washing and carrying the infant, through feeding, the acquisition of motor skills, learning to speak and to walk, and sharing in a common meal, to dressing the hair and the assumption of clothing. The interpretation I am proposing is that these initiatory rites, and by extension all the other ceremonial sequences— e.g. of betrothal and marriage, and especially of death and burial—which van Gennep groups with them as *rites de passage*, have nothing whatever to do, except by remote analogy, with the rites that sometimes accompany passage from one territory to another, and *everything to do with the physiological and social transition from birth to social maturing* (at the age of six to seven): in short, that it is the development of the child during the first five to six years of life, culminating in his (or her) recognition as a 'person', not any physical journeying from one country to another, which furnishes the model for the rites that accompany passage from one social grade to another.

In support of this interpretation, consider first the part played by birth, or re-birth, in *rites de passage*. Again and again in his account of such rites, van Gennep stresses the importance of birth, yet at no point does he satisfactorily explain, *in terms of his own theory of crossing a frontier*, why this element should play so central a part in the various sequences. The nearest he comes to offering such an explanation is when he writes (1909, p. 262), lamely to my mind:

> 'L'idée logique' de ces parallélismes [i.e. de la mort, et de la naissance] ... c'est que passer d'un état à un autre, c'est 'dépouiller le vieil homme', c'est 'faire peau neuve' littéralement.

But if the sequences themselves are based on the process of 'cooking' the child preparatory to his (or her) admission to the community, it is obvious why the representation of birth should form an essential element in them.

Consider, further, the significance of *la première fois*. van Gennep points out (1909, pp. 249–54), rightly I am sure, the importance of 'the first time'. Anything done for the first time, e.g. the *first* cutting of the hair,[1] the *first* dentition, the *first* period (for a girl), the *first* intercourse, the birth of the *first* child, looking for the *first* time on a sacred object, any one of these events may, and usually does, mark the passage from one social grade to another. There is no particular reason, in terms of crossing a *limes* or frontier, why this should be so: but every reason in terms of child development, where everything is done for the first time.

Consider, finally, the case of strangers. In 'primitive' societies, as van Gennep points out (1909, pp. 36–50), there are really only two things you can do to strangers, either kill them or accept them. And if you decide to accept them, then you must first submit them to the whole series of *rites de marge*, namely salutations, shaking hands, exchange of presents, eating and drinking together, sometimes even loan of women for the night, by way of which they are, if only temporarily, integrated into one's own group:

> Ici encore on se donne la main ou on se frotte le nez, on se sépare du monde extérieur en ôtant ses souliers, son manteau, sa coiffure, on s'agrège en mangeant ou en buvant ensemble. . . . Bref, on s'identifie d'une manière ou d'une autre à ceux qu'on rencontre, fût-ce pour un moment.     p. 46.

The same sequence characterises adoption:

> Les rites de détail de l'adoption sont identiques à ceux qui ont été déjà signalisés: échanges (de sang, de cadeaux, etc.); lien, voile, siège communs; allaitement (*suckling*) réel ou simulé; naissance simulée, etc.     pp. 53–4.

For van Gennep, the treatment of strangers and, *a fortiori*, of those who are adopted into a social group, furnishes the model for the *rites de passage* whereby the individual passes from one category or stage to another within his own society; hence the emphasis he lays, to which I have drawn attention (above, p. 482), on the similarity in status between the individual undergoing such rites and a stranger. In the interpretation of these rites offered here, the treatment of strangers is peripheral to the main problem, while adoption—with its *allaitement*, and its *naissance simulée*—is a straight 'take' of the physiological and social processes of birth, suckling, and upbringing: i.e. an alternative form of admission to the community, copied from the real one.

The second 'leg', upon which van Gennep's theory rests, is that of the alternation between the sacred and the profane. My criticism here is not so much that the sacred/profane dichotomy is mistaken as that it lacks bite, is too vague to serve any useful purpose.[2] In place of it, let us try Lévi-Strauss's nature/culture

---

[1] Among the Hopi, as we have seen (above, p. 35), it was only when a girl obtained her *naso'me* hair dressing that she could properly be buried in the adult cemetery; each subsequent change in her status was marked by a further change in hair style (Hough, 1918, pp. 248–51).

[2] That this is indeed so, is *almost* admitted by van Gennep himself when he writes (1908, p. 330), in another context, that

> chez les demi-civilisés le domain du sacré est beaucoup plus vaste que chez nous, au point qu'il n'est guère d'activité sociale qui ne participe à un moment ou à un autre du rite magico-religieux.

dichotomy. After describing how Pueblo mothers lay the new-born infant on a bed of hot sand to 'cook' it, Lévi-Strauss continues (1964, pp. 341–2):

> Chez plusieurs peuplades de la Californie, on installait les jeunes accouchées et les filles pubères dans des fours (*ovens*) creusés dans le sol; après les avoir recouvertes de nattes, puis de pierres chaudes, on les faisait consciencieusement 'cuire'. Cette pratique s'accompagnait d'autres, dont la diffusion est encore plus grande: ainsi l'emploi obligatoire, surtout pour les filles pubères, de peignes (*combs*) et de gratte-tête (*head-scratcher*) leur évitant de porter la main à leurs cheveux ou à leur visage, et aussi de tubes à boire, et de pinces pour saisir les aliments.
>
> Cette rapide évocation d'usages ... permet au moins d'en offrir une définition provisoire: on fait 'cuire' des individus intensément engagés dans un processus physiologique:[1] nouveau-né, accouchée, fille pubère. La conjonction d'un membre du groupe social avec la nature doit être médiatisée par l'intervention du feu de cuisine, à qui revient normalement la charge de médiatiser la conjonction du produit cru et du consommateur humain, et donc par l'opération duquel un être naturel est, tout à la fois, *cuit et socialisé*. ...
>
> A la fonction médiatrice de la cuisine symbolique, s'ajoute celle des ustensiles: le gratte-tête, le tube à boire, la fourchette, sont intermédiaires entre le sujet et son corps, présentement 'naturalisé', ou entre le sujet et le monde physique.

To the head-scratcher, comb, drinking-tube and fork, as intermediaries between the person and the natural world (including his own body), Lévi-Strauss subsequently adds (1964, p. 344) saddle, stockings, and clothes.[2]

Lévi-Strauss's theory of mediatory substances and/or acts easing the passage from the 'raw' or natural state to the 'cooked' and socialised offers, to my mind, a much better 'fit' to the available evidence than van Gennep's theory of *rites liminaires*, standing between the sacred and the profane. Moreover, the idea of such intermediaries is already implicit in van Gennep's handling of some of his material; thus, discussing rites of pregnancy and child-birth, he says (1909, p. 67):

> On notera le rôle des *intermédiaires*, qui, ici comme pour les autres cérémonies, n'ont pas seulement pour objet de neutraliser l'impureté ..., mais bien *de servir réellement de pont, de chaîne, de lien*, bref de faciliter les changements d'état, sans secousses sociales violentes, ni arrêts brusques de la vie individuelle et collective.

To conclude: I agree with van Gennep that the ceremonial sequences whereby the passage of the individual from one social stage to another is effected, follow

---

[1] A piece of usage which Lévi-Strauss appears to have missed, and which powerfully supports his general argument, is the (crude) English expression: to 'have a bun in the oven', to refer to a pregnant, and especially an unmarried, girl. The expression occurs, e.g. in the script to the film *A Taste of Honey*.

[2] Nakedness itself being a part of the natural (raw, *cru*) world: cf. the English expression, quoted by Lévi-Strauss, to 'sleep in the raw'. This, I think, is probably the reason for the tabu on sexual intercourse laid on those taking part in (Hopi) ceremonies: cf. the divorce formula spoken by the Swahili husband (quoted by van Gennep, 1909, p. 205, n, 1), 'Je ne veux plus avoir affaire à ta nudité ...': every act of sexual union involving, to some extent, a return to nature.

a common pattern; against van Gennep, I hold that the model upon which they are based is the process whereby the child passes from being a puling infant, and so barely human, to being a 'person'. Following Lévi-Strauss, I see the latter process essentially as a passage from nature to culture, 'mediated' by such objects as spoons, forks, combs, head-scratchers, clothing, shoes, and by such acts as being laid on hot sand, having the head washed with yucca suds and the body rubbed with ashes, being carried, walking, sleeping on a bed, dressing the hair, and speech. And I suggest that the re-employment of such inter-mediaries in the ceremonial sequences whereby the individual passes from one social stage to another later in life is due to the fact that, at each such passage, the person concerned to a greater or lesser extent *returns to a natural state*—as van Gennep himself recognised when, referring to the licence which commonly prevails during periods of initiation, he spoke of the novices as being '*hors de la société*', and so, in his terms, '*proprement sacrés et saints, par suite intangibles, dangereux . . .*'.[1]

In support of this thesis, consider briefly the elements employed in the Hopi *wü'wütçim* initiation (above, pp. 101-4, 111-12). The novices enter the kiva naked except for a white kilt, without shoes, and with their hair loose; they are *carried* down the ladder and across the floor of the kiva,[2] and placed on a blanket where they sit with their knees drawn up to their chins—in imitation, perhaps, of the position taken up by the foetus in the womb. Their bodies are rubbed over with a yellow pigment, and for three days they sit huddled in a corner of the kiva, naked except for their breech clouts, with a blanket stretched over the kiva hatch to keep the sun's rays from falling on them. During this time they are treated *as infants*; they are fed by their ceremonial 'fathers', a special food (*tumoyi*) is prepared for them, they are provided each with a pottery spoon (*akua*), presumably for taking some kind of broth, and with a wooden scratcher, so that they will not have to use their nails for scratching their head or body.[3] Finally, early on the fifth morning, their heads are washed in yucca suds, each novice has his new name bestowed on him, and either now or later, we may suppose, they don the special costume (*kel napna*) which marks their 'emergence' as fully fledged members of the tribe.

---

[1] Above, p. 483. The contrast between the sacred/profane, and the natural/cultural, dichotomies is here seen at its sharpest: i.e. are the novices 'dangerous' because they are *saint*(s), or because they are *cru*(s)? Either answer accounts for their being treated as 'strangers'.

[2] Among the Murngin, when the women go out to the lily swamps or oyster beds to gather food, babies and small children are carried astride their mothers' necks and put their hands around her forehead. An identical method is adopted by the men, when they carry boys to the circumcision ritual: Warner (1964), pp. 115, 257, 275-6.

[3] Both spoons and scratchers being 'intermediaries', in Lévi Strauss's terms: cf. the use of the head-scratcher in the puberty rite for Hopi girls, above, p. 34. It may be, too, that the emphasis laid on rabbit hunting in *wü'wütçim* initiation owes less to rabbits as a source of meat (above, p. 288) than to rabbits as a source of the skins which, throughout the Great Basin and among the Hopi, were cut up and sewn into blankets: blankets also being inter-mediary between the raw and the cooked.

The Tewa, as we have seen (above, p. 322), make a distinction between children below the age of six or thereabouts, who are *ochu*, 'green' or 'unripe', and those of riper years who are *seh t'a*, 'cooked':

> ... to be not yet *seh t'a* is to be innocent or unknowing; to be innocent is to be not yet Tewa; to be not yet Tewa is to be not yet human. ...

The process of becoming human involves the adoption of all those habits which distinguish humans from animals, e.g. being carried as an infant, being weaned and fed on cooked food, learning to walk on two legs, using spoons for eating and cups for drinking, dressing the hair, wearing clothes, learning to speak, to sing and to dance. Now all these items were evolved during the middle and late Pleistocene;[1] and if, as Emlen holds, initiatory rites have their origin in primitive hunting-party organisation, then it seems reasonable to suppose that they should have taken as model the passage from nature to culture,[2] the first appearance of which coincides with the development of co-operative hunting among the early hominids.

### THE FORM, AND OCCURRENCE, OF ASSOCIATIONS

At this stage, before proceding to our concluding analysis of associations, let us remind ourselves of the salient features which distinguish them on the ground. For this purpose, I take the secret societies of the lower Congo Basin, delineated by de Jonghe sixty years ago:[3]

> The word generally used in the lower Congo region to designate the ceremonies that take place at puberty is *nkimba*; they may also, however, be referred to as *kimpasi*, from *fua kimpasi*, '(he) passes through the ceremony of re-birth'. All boys pass through the *nkimba* ceremony, between the ages of 10 and 14 years.
>
> Parallel to the *nkimba* ceremonies, and in large measure based on them, are the *ndembo* rites; these take place either at puberty or later, and give access to specific cults. The distinction between *nkimba* and *ndembo* is, therefore, that where *nkimba* admits the novice to adult male membership of the community, *ndembo* admits him to membership of a subsection of that community. Since the rites in both cases are based on the pattern of re-birth, either may be referred to as *kimpasi*. In the account of them that follows, I describe the *nkimba* rites primarily, noting any deviation in the *ndembo* rites as it occurs.

[1] On the use of tools and of fire for cooking, on the development of speech and the adoption of clothing, see above, p. 480, n. 2. Washburn and DeVore point out (1961, p. 96) that the mother-child relationship characteristic of humans is dependent on bipedal locomotion; mothers who cannot carry things, as they justly remark, cannot carry babies.

[2] It has to be borne in mind that at this stage of human development—as in any rapidly evolving species—a certain proportion of infants, lacking the necessary gene complex, would have failed to make the transition and been weeded out by a process of natural selection, so emphasising the status of those who completed it successfully. A trace of this is perhaps still to be seen in the anxiety with which mothers watch for the 'stages' in a child's development—smiling, sitting up, cutting the first tooth, walking on two legs, saying the first word, and so on.

[3] de Jonghe (1907), especially pp. 17–57. The element of re-birth, which plays so prominent a part in the rites described by de Jonghe, has been stressed by many writers on secret societies: e.g. for Melanesia, by Rivers (1922), pp. 25–31, and (1924), pp. 122–4, and for North America, by Loeb (1929), p. 257 *et seq.*

Plusieurs villages, [according to de Jonghe (1907, pp. 24–5)], se groupent autour d'un village chef-lieu, d'un *banza*, pour former un *nkimba* [i.e. a bush school]: les chefs décident de l'opportunité de convoquer les jeunes gens; chaque village est représenté par une demi-douzaine de néophytes. Si nous prenons en moyenne soixante-dix néophytes, nous nous trouvons en présence d'un groupement d'une douzaine de villages, où les croyances et les coutumes seront uniformes du fait de l'éducation commune des enfants.

The bush school for both *nkimba* and *ndembo* takes place in the forest or the bush, well outside the village; for *nkimba*, it lasts about six months. On arrival at the 'school', the novices are stripped of all their clothes; their bodies are rubbed all over with white clay,[1] and for six months they go about naked in the bush—'c'est qu'*étant morts*, ils ne doivent pas sortir de leur retraite et se montrer aux hommes'. At some time during this period, perhaps immediately on their arrival, a new name is bestowed on each novice; they undergo certain ordeals, notably whipping and the administration of a narcotic; they learn a secret language,[2] are instructed in certain arts and crafts, e.g. how to build huts and to fish, and in the medicinal properties of plants, learn songs and how to dance, and above all, the code of local customs known as *kiziles*.

During all this time, the novices 'ne vivent pas sous le régime du droit commun. Ils jouissent de certains privilèges; ils sont soumis aussi à certaines défenses' (de Jonghe, 1907, p. 50). They must not, for example, sleep inside a hut, but only on the naked earth. They are forbidden to wear a woven loincloth, or to wash themselves. They must not use plates of any kind, but must eat off the ground—according to one account they have to throw the food to the ground before conveying it to the mouth. They may drink only water, not wine, and are restricted to a vegetarian diet, even palm oil and ground nuts being forbidden them. Above all, they must abstain from sexual relations throughout the period of the bush school, and are allowed no contact whatever with their own family or village.

Finally, at the conclusion of the initiatory period, the novices wash the white clay from their bodies, assume a new woven loincloth, and adorn their arms and legs with metal rings. Then they are hoisted on the backs of the older *nkimba*, and carried in triumph to the village:

Les *néo-zinkimba*, [writes de Jonghe (1907, pp. 54–5)], font semblant de revenir d'un autre monde et en sont pour ainsi dire persuadés. Ils ne veulent d'abord reconnaître que les anciens *zinkimba*. Ils semblent ignorer leur propre mère. Ils font semblant *de ne pouvoir marcher, de ne pas connaître les manières de cette vie. Ils mangent par terre, font des grimaces, mordent,* etc. Et tous d'en avoir pitié, de les excuser, puisqu'ils viennent d'un autre monde. Enfin, on se reconnaît: on présente le fils à sa mère, le frère à sa soeur, le fiancé à sa fiancée.

They drink wine, eat meat. But henceforth the novice may only be addressed by his new name, and anyone who inadvertently uses his old one, has to pay a forfeit: '*il était mort et il renaît à la vie*'.

Within the detail of these rites, the crucial point—in the sense that it furnishes the clue to the real nature of associations—is, I suggest, the learning of a secret

---

[1] Red, in the case of the *ndembo*: de Jonghe (1907), p. 45.

[2] *Ndembo* also have a secret language, quite different from that of the *nkimba*: de Jonghe (1907), p. 50.

language.[1] Initiatory rites, I have argued above (p. 485), are modelled on the passage from nature to culture; the hinge on which this passage turns is furnished by mastery of one's natal tongue. But consider what such mastery implies:

> Chaque dialecte, [writes van Gennep,[2] referring to those of the Australian aborigines], n'assumerait-il pas la fonction d'une langue spéciale vis-à-vis de tous les autres, malgré l'absence d'une langue générale proprement dite, langue spéciale consciemment voulue, *telle en tant que facteur vital du maintien et de l'autonomie du groupement parlant ce dialecte?*

And these special languages, he concludes (1908, p. 337):

> ne sont que l'un des innombrables moyens par lesquels les collectivités de tout ordre maintiennent leur existence et résistent aux pressions de l'extérieur. Elles sont à la fois un moyen de cohésion pour ceux qui les emploient, et un moyen de défence contre l'étranger . . ., la notion d'étranger se marquant autant dans le domaine de la parenté, de la religion, du droit, que dans le domaine politique. L'un de ces caractères par quoi se différencie l'étranger sera, en outre de la couleur de peau, du facies, du costume: la langue.
>
> Ainsi la langue spéciale joue, à l'intérieur de la société générale, le rôle que chaque langue générale joue vis-à-vis des autres langues générales. *C'est l'une des formes de différentiation, formes voulues, et nécessaires à la vie même en société.*

Morphologically, it seems to me, associations or secret societies are characterised by three diacritical features:[3]

(*a*) they are entered *by a process of initiation*, the novice being sponsored, commonly, by someone who is already a member;

(*b*) at some stage in the process of initiation, novices are introduced to *something known only to members*, e.g. a riddle, a song, a fetish, a mask, a dance, a ritual, or esoteric learning of any kind. Whatever this something is, it is always cultural, and knowledge of it confers membership of the fraternity; consequently,

(*c*) whoever stumbles on that knowledge, whether by accident or design, *must either be put to death or be himself initiated to membership of the fraternity*:

> If any outsider came across their path, [wrote d'Almada in *Rios de Guiné*[4]], he was either killed or made a member.

---

[1] Mauss, also, draws attention to this (1947, p. 123) as one of the distinguishing marks of a secret society or fraternity: cf. on this point, Lévi-Bruhl (1910), p. 210.

[2] van Gennep (1908), p. 336. van Gennep adds a footnote (p. 336, n. 3) that, at Zuñi, 'each fraternity employs a dialect different from that of the others'; for the possible use of a special language within Hopi fraternities, cf. Bourke (1884), p. 190, n. 2.

[3] These are rather, though not radically, different from the three enumerated by Morton-Williams (1960), p. 362.

[4] Quoted by Rodney (1967), pp. 243–4: cf. the attitude to strangers adopted by the Kariera, the Andamanese and the Banks Islanders, above, pp. 333–4.

I have argued, above (p. 488), that initiatory rites are themselves modelled on the transition from the natural state to the cultural, and that the crucial element in that transition is the acquisition of a given language. We have seen, further, that one of the prime functions of a language is to maintain the integrity of the group speaking it as their natal tongue; in this sense every such group constitutes a secret society, to membership of which the child is admitted, with his parents as sponsor, by the process of learning its language and absorbing the categories implicit in it. And this, I suggest, is the reason why fraternities in different parts of the worlds exhibit marked similarities of form: _because they are based on the same model, namely that of the societies in which they occur_.[1] Hence the attitude they take to outsiders who stumble on their secret by accident.

Functionally, associations come into existence in response to certain pressures, to fulfil certain requirements: they are there, as Robin Fox says of kinship systems,[2] 'because they answer certain needs—do certain jobs'. The particular job associations do, I hold, is to counter the fissiparous tendencies inherent in the emergence of unilineal descent groups as the principal asset-holding bodies in settled _communes_, tendencies which, unchecked, might lead to the disintegration of the marrying-in group. Since these assets are, commonly, either livestock or farm land, the development of associations is secondary to that of either herding or agriculture.[3] To do their job, they make use of initiatory elements pre-figured in the culture of hunter and gatherer bands.[4]

The question arises, finally, why associations are found in some parts of the world and not in others. And the answer is to be looked for, I suggest, in the kind of societies where they occur. In the analysis given above (Chapter 5, last section but one) of the secret societies of the African forest belt, I drew a fundamental distinction between, on the one hand, the cultures of the rain forest, characterised by compact village settlement, a multiplicity of local dialects and the presence of secret societies, and those of the savannah, on the other, characterised by a dispersed type of settlement, wide distribution of a few major languages, and the development of age-sets; and I suggested that this dis-

[1] Cf. Larock (1932), p. 86: 'une société secrète est un petit groupe formé à l'image du grand . . .'.

[2] Fox (1967), p. 25. A similar approach, refreshingly realistic in the context of kinship studies, is adopted by Powell in his recent paper (1969a) on Trobriand kinship; Powell argues (pp. 178–80, 198–200) that the distinctive features of a kinship system must be derived, not from what all kinship systems have in common, i.e. from the biological 'raw material' of reproduction, but from what each culture has that is unique to it, i.e. as an ecological adaptation to a given environment.

[3] The thesis is not contradicted by the fact that certain Plains Indian tribes, who neither owned stock nor practised agriculture, had military associations, age-graded in some cases: since, as Lowie showed many years ago (1916, pp. 946–54), these are likely to have originated with the farming Indians along the Missouri River, and to have been transmitted by them to the Indians of the Plains. Apart from their overt functions in settling disputes and punishing wrongdoers, the Plains Indian military associations furnished, in Lowie's view (1960, pp. 254–9), 'a potential instrumentality for territorial integration'.

[4] Cf. smoking as a form of hunting initiation among the western Shoshoni, pre-figuring _wü'wütçim_ initiation among the Hopi.

tinction was rooted in a radically different mode of exploiting the resources offered by the two habitats. Subsequently, in the analysis (concluding section of Chapter 17) of the *commune* as a moral entity, I showed that to belong to a community means to share in its common values, to accept a certain view of the world and of man's place in it, and that a child born into the community is admitted to membership of it when, at the age of five or six, having mastered the technique of speech, he begins to grasp the common values embodied in its language and behaviour. Finally, in the present section, I have argued that secret societies or fraternities are modelled on, are a microcosm of, the societies in which they are found; and that they arise in response to definite needs, namely to check the fissiparous tendencies inherent in the crystallisation of uni-lineal descent groups.

Associations are likely to occur, therefore, only in societies where the model upon which they are based is comparatively clear-cut, in societies, that is to say, where—due to local patterns of settlement and physiography—the follow-ing equation is, or is nearly, satisfied:

$$commune = \text{ethno-linguistic unit} = \text{'people'}:$$

as where one *commune* is clearly demarcated from its neighbours by tracts of forest, as in West Africa and the Congo Basin, by sea as in Melanesia, or by desert as in the Southwest. Where, due to different patterns of settlement and physiography, one *commune* merges into the next with no clear geographical or linguistic limit between them, as in the savannah belt of Africa, the conditions for their emergence are not fulfilled and other bodies, such as age-sets, take their place. Many societies have developed neither associations nor age-sets; but whether a given society develops the one or the other is primarily due, I hold, to the relationship in which that society stands to the environment which it exploits.

As to the process whereby new social forms and institutions emerge, no one to my knowledge has given a better account than van Gennep himself, referring to the origin of secret languages—though even he, I think, over-emphasises the *conscious* element in their emergence:

> Pour une théorie des langues spéciales, [writes van Gennep (1908, p. 327: my italics)], il faut se rappeler qu'il existe dans la vie sociale des conditions spéciales, plus exactement des besoins collectifs spéciaux auxquels répondent des institutions déterminées. Ces besoins peuvent demeurer latents quelque temps, et jusqu'au moment où ils émergent dans les consciences individuelles leur satisfaction demeure potentielle. Mais du jour où l'émergence se produit souvent, à plus de reprises, et chez des individus plus nombreux, et de plus en plus rapprochés par de mêmes besoins, la tendance se manifeste, d'abord sporadiquement et timidement, puis avec une puissance peu à peu accrue, à l'unification des efforts *en vue de la création d'institutions nouvelles nécessaires*.

# Appendix to Part 4

## On the regulation of numbers in kin-based societies, with special reference to North American Indians[1]

The general impression of early travellers through both the eastern and western parts of North America, and only excepting the Great Plains area (where the acquisition of the horse and of firearms had wrought great changes in aboriginal habits), appears to have been[2] that the Indian tribes were predominantly sedentary, i.e. organised in more or less clearly defined territories, and that their population was well below the level which the supply of game, fish, nutritious roots, seeds and berries would *apparently* have allowed.

> Even the practice of agriculture, [wrote Powell (1891: 1966, p. 114)], with its result of providing a more certain and bountiful food supply, seems not to have had the effect of materially augmenting the Indian population. At all events, it is in California and Oregon, a region where agriculture was scarcely practised at all, that the most dense aboriginal population lived. There is no reason to believe that there ever existed within the limits of the region included in the map [the linguistic map which accompanies Powell's paper], with the possible exception of certain areas in California, a population equal to the natural food supply. On the contrary, there is every reason for believing that the population at the time of the discovery might have been many times more than it actually was, had a wise economy been practised.

With Powell's concluding sentence we may, perhaps, take issue. Were the upper limit to the population of any given area set, as we have seen to be the case with the Great Basin Shoshoni (above, p. 350), by the yield of its natural resources in a bad year—or a bad run of years—rather than in a good year, then the relation between food supply and numbers may have been much closer than he admits. But the general drift of his remarks is clear: that, *in the days before— and in the early days of—European contact, the Indian population of North America was relatively low in numbers, and stable.*

Why, given the potential rate of increase of human—as of other mammalian—populations,[3] was this so?

---

[1] This Appendix was written in July–August, 1971, after the completion of the main book. The theory outlined in it had been forming in my mind, under the weight of the Shoshoni and Hopi evidence, over the previous two years.

[2] See J. W. Powell (1891: 1966), pp. 106–16.

[3] The Hutterite communities in the United States and Canada have probably come nearest to realising the *potential* fecundity of the species. Descended from 400 pioneers who

An explanation commonly advanced[1] is: disease, of one kind or another. First, therefore, we may examine the evidence for disease in the aboriginal population of North America, under five principal heads: namely, nutritional lack, parasites, chronic infection, acute epidemic infection, and infant mortality.

(*a*) *Nutrition.* The general impression conveyed again by early travellers and ethnographers through western North America is that, apart from high infant mortality (to which I shall return presently), the Indians were long-lived and rather healthy.[2]

This impression is confirmed both by archaeological evidence, and by more recent studies among hunter-gatherer populations in other parts of the world. Thus Hough, who spent some thirty years excavating prehistoric sites in the Southwest, noted (1928, p. 67) that the skeletal material from that area was singularly free from signs of disease or malnutrition in adults. And Dunn, summarising more recent work among hunter-gatherer communities, writes:[3]

> *Patent, and perhaps even borderline, malnutrition is rare.* Dietary resources, even in arid environments, are diverse: typical sampling of these resources by modern hunter-gatherers in ecosystems relatively undisturbed by outsiders seems to provide at least the minimum protein, carbohydrate, fat, mineral, and vitamin requirements. Many workers have commented on the relatively good nutritional status of hunter-gatherers in comparison with neighbouring agriculturalists or urban dwellers.

(*b*) *Parasites.* Parasites, notably intestinal parasites, by impairing their host's general health tend to lower his resistance to other, more serious infections. In hunting and gathering groups, the most common infection is helminthic (Alland, in Dunn, 1968, p. 244). It is significant, therefore, that in a study of more than fifty coprolites from Lovelock Cave, Nevada, Dunn himself (1968, p. 222) found no eggs or larvae of parasitic helminths:

> Because of the extraordinary state of preservation of certain pseudo parasites— mites and nematodes—we were able to conclude, with a fair degree of certainty, that the ancient people represented by these specimens were in fact free of a whole series of intestinal helminths, including flukes, tapeworms, and important nematodes such as hookworm and *Ascaris*.

---

emigrated from eastern Europe in the 1870s, condemning all forms of birth control and placing a high value on child-bearing, they now number some 15,000 persons; this represents an increase of between 3½ and 4 per cent a year (roughly twice that of the Navajo over the same period), or a doubling of the population every eighteen to twenty years. See 'Hutterites thrive on Bible dogma', in *The Times Science Report* for 9 January 1969, summarising an article in *Population Bulletin*, vol. 24 (1968), no. 2.

[1] Actually, this explanation is usually put forward in the inverse form: that the *increase* of population which followed European intervention, e.g. among the Navajo after 1870, was due to improved sanitation and medical care.

[2] Much of the evidence, by travellers such as Catlin, Bancroft and Schoolcraft, is collected by Carr-Saunders (1922), pp. 158–9, 171–2.

[3] Dunn (1968), p. 223: italics in original. In the discussion (ibid. pp. 243–5) following Dunn's paper, both Woodburn and Alland confirmed his view: Woodburn quoting paediatricians from Makerere College Medical School, to the effect that Hadza children were 'one of the best-nourished groups they had seen in East Africa'.

(*c*) *Chronic (bacterial) infection.* Under this heading, diseases like tuberculosis—and leprosy—at once come to mind. Now there is no doubt that negroes, North American Indians and Eskimos, amongst others, are more susceptible to tuberculosis than are most Europeans. The reason for this difference appears to be[1] that, European communities having been parasitised by *Myco. tuberculosis* for the past 3,000 years, the more susceptible individuals in each generation have been eliminated and only those with some degree of inherited immunity—or the capacity to develop such immunity—have survived. The particular example points a general lesson: that populations living in relative isolation in a particular habitat over some thousands of years, as the Indians in North America have evidently lived, are likely to reach a state of biological equilibrium with their local bacteria, the humans in course of time becoming more resistant to the parasites (and their toxins) and the parasites becoming less noxious to the humans.[2]

On this ground it appears unlikely that chronic infections such as tuberculosis, due to indigenous bacterial mutants, can ever have played more than a marginal rôle in controlling numbers in hunter-gatherer groups. When they first evolve, or when they are introduced from outside to populations enjoying no inherited immunity, they are *too* lethal, while communities that survive their first onslaught develop some degree of immunity to them.

(*d*) *Acute epidemic infection.* Regarding acute infections, the decimating epidemics of the eighteenth and nineteenth centuries, notably smallpox, measles, scarlet fever and influenza, were all introduced from outside to populations enjoying no inherited immunity against them.

There appear, further, to be sound theoretical reasons why dispersed communities of hunter-gatherers should *not* develop acute epidemic-causing organisms of their own. Consider measles. The measles virus has no reservoir other than its human host and, since life-long immunity follows infection, persistence of the virus is dependent on a continuous supply of susceptible recruits to the population. Black has recently shown (1966, pp. 207–11), on the basis of measles case reports from a number of island communities over a period of fifteen years, that breaks in the continuity of measles transmission—and so extinction of the virus in the absence of reintroduction from outside—occur in all such communities of less than 70,000 to 100,000 persons. He postulates that populations sufficient to support continued propagation of the virus did not exist in primitive societies[3], and consequently that the measles virus must have evolved since the development of the early riverain civilisations.

[1] R. Hare, *An Outline of Bacteriology and Immunity* (London, 1956), p. 106. Morse, after a careful survey (1961, pp. 495–502) of fourteen possible cases of spinal tuberculosis in pre-Columbian skeletal material, says that in only three of these is tubercular infection a likely diagnosis, and that, even in these three, other disease could have caused the same picture. In the absence of evidence to the contrary, he concludes (p. 503) that the pre-contact American Indians did *not* suffer from tuberculosis.

[2] This process has been noted by Lack (1954), pp. 168–9, 177; also by Alland (Dunn, 1968, p. 244), who refers to it as a kind of 'genetic sieve'.

[3] The critical community size for *varicella* (chicken-pox), by contrast, appears to have been less than 1,000 persons, due to the ability of this virus to remain latent for long periods

*(e) Infant mortality.* Evidence furnished by the early travellers and ethno-graphers[1] indicates that infant mortality among the North American Indians was very high; and that it was chiefly due to exposure, to lack of proper care and to lack of proper feeding.

Infant mortality, in this context, may be divided into mortality during the milk period, and post-weaning mortality—up to, say, three to four years of age. The commonest cause of such mortality today, in both periods, is epidemic gastro-enteritis spread by flies. This cause is unlikely to have been operative in dispersed, pre-contact hunter-gatherer communities: for the general reason out-lined in the previous section, and for the particular reason that breast-fed infants rarely suffer from epidemic gastro-enteritis,[2] the mother's milk evidently containing antibodies to the local strains of gut bacilli responsible for it.

The evidence set out above points to two preliminary conclusions: first, that, among the dispersed gathering-and-hunting communities of North America, neither parasites nor infectious disease played any significant part in keeping numbers down; second, that high infant mortality, particularly in the post-weaning period, due in part to lack of proper feeding (? protein imbalance) and in part to exposure (lack of clothing is specifically mentioned in some of the early reports), undoubtedly did play such a part.

And at this point, before proceeding further, we need to clarify the concepts we are to use.

If the population of the aboriginal communities of North America was indeed stable, or—which is much the same thing—if numbers fluctuated within rela-tively narrow limits, the chances of this being due to a fortuitous balance between losses and replacement are very small indeed. If the balance is not fortuitous, then it must be due to a homeostatic mechanism of some kind whereby, as numbers rise in a given community, factors come into operation to reduce them again—and conversely, as numbers fall, the same (or other) factors operate to raise them. Such a mechanism requires both an input of information, to register changes in the system (in this case, rise or fall in numbers), and con-trolling factors capable of counter-acting the changes registered. Since a rise or fall in numbers affects the density of the population, such controlling factors are said to be *density*-dependent. Their mode of operation has been delineated by Nicholson in these words (1933, p. 135: italics in original), referring to animal populations:

> For the production of balance, it is essential that a controlling factor should act more severely against an average individual when the density of animals is high, and less severely when the density is low. In other words, *the action of the controlling factor must be governed by the density of the population controlled.*

---

in man—and to break out periodically as shingles (*herpes zoster*): Black (1966), p. 210, cf. Bartlett (1968), pp. 11-12.

[1] Summarised by Carr-Saunders (1922), pp. 159-61, 172.

[2] See Patterson and Lightwood, *Sick Children* (London, 1956), p. 135.

It is evident, says Nicholson (ibid. p. 136), that physical factors such as climate cannot furnish a homeostatic mechanism of the kind postulated, *even though climate destroys large numbers of individuals in a given community.* Suppose, he says, that the animals in a certain population would increase one hundredfold in each generation if unchecked, and also that, on the average, climate destroys 98 per cent of the animals. Clearly, the number of animals would be doubled in each successive generation if no other factors intervened. Climate would never check this progressive increase, for it would continue to destroy only 98 per cent, its action being uninfluenced by the density of the animals. If, however, there were some other factor, such as a natural enemy, the action of which were influenced by their density, the destruction of the remaining 1 per cent needed to check increase would soon be accomplished. One is tempted to conclude that, because climate destroys 98 per cent of the animals and the natural enemy only 1 per cent, the limitation of numbers is predominantly due to climate. But, argues Nicholson, it is the natural enemy which is *wholly* responsible for control, since climate, by itself, would permit the density to go on increasing indefinitely.

Clearly, infectious disease, the effect of which is progressively augmented by over-crowding, may be both a powerful agent of natural selection *and* a density-dependent factor of the kind postulated by Nicholson. But there appears good ground for thinking that infectious disease only became a major selective agent,[1] and presumably *pari passu* a population-controlling factor, with the development of agriculture and the enlarged population-units—villages and, later, towns —which agriculture made possible. The high infant mortality due to exposure and lack of proper care characteristic of the gatherer-hunter communities of North America, while also no doubt serving as a powerful selective agent, was— I suggest—insufficiently density-dependent to act as a population-controlling factor.[2] We are therefore led to ask what factor, or combination of factors, was both sufficiently sensitive to density and capable of exerting sufficient leverage on numbers, to keep their populations well *within* the limits set by the available food supply. This seems to me to be the crux of the problem. And for answer I propose to go in the first instance to other mammal communities, and in particular to those resident on the Kaibab Plateau, Arizona, to see what kind of factors operate there.

The Kaibab Plateau[3] lies directly to the north of the Grand Canyon of the Colorado River. It measures about 32 miles across, and 40 to 45 miles from north to south: a total

---

[1] See, on this point, Haldane (1957), pp. 328–9; Haldane refers there to an earlier paper of his own, in *Ricerca Scientifica* (Roma), vol. 19 (Suppl.), which I have not been able to consult.

[2] To argue that it did act as such a factor, one would have to show that the degree of exposure and lack of care was markedly greater at high than at low densities, either in the community as a whole or in individual families. This seems doubtful, as the older children probably helped look after the younger and so a child in a large family may actually get *more* attention than one in a small family: as often happens among the Hopi.

[3] The account that follows is based on that given by Rasmussen (1941), especially pp. 231–6: cf. for the biotic communities of the southern third of the plateau, Hoffmeister (1971), pp. 13–27.

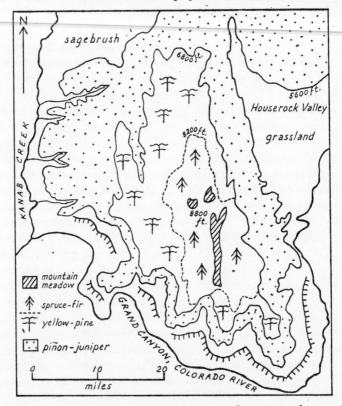

Fig. 65. Kaibab Plateau, Arizona, showing the principal vegetational zones. Redrawn from Rasmussen (1941), p. 233.

area of between 1,300 and 1,400 square miles (see Figure 65). Of this area a central core, rather less than half the total area in extent and rising above the 6,800 feet contour, is covered by coniferous forest—yellow pine from 6,800 to 8,200 feet, spruce and Douglas fir from 8,200 to 8,800 feet, with montane grassland on the highest ridges (up to 9,200 feet); around this central core, from 6,800 feet down to 5,600, lies a belt of piñon-juniper woodland with characteristic shrub undergrowth (cliff rose, sagebrush, Mormon tea, Apache plume), varying in width from two to twelve miles. To the south and west the plateau is bounded by rugged escarpments falling to Grand Canyon and Kanab Creek respectively, to the northwest by a fault line, and to the east by a monoclinal fold where the strata dip down between 2,000 and 3,000 feet to the floor of Houserock Valley. The edges of the plateau are seamed by steep-walled canyons, the effect of which, particularly to the east, south and west, is to form a barrier to the movement of most animals—either into or out of the area.

The two animals, with whose ecology we shall be chiefly concerned in this account, are mule deer and mountain lion. The mule deer passes the summer and rears its young in the coniferous forest, i.e. above the 6,800 feet contour, descending in the fall to the piñon-juniper woodland to winter there; the mountain lion, being largely dependent on the mule deer for food, follows it. Apart from minor losses of fawns to coyote, the only other deer predators operating on the Kaibab Plateau prior to the arrival of ranchers in the 1880s were wolves, and the Paiute: wolves were evidently too few in number[1] to have seriously affected the deer population; the Paiute are reckoned (Rasmussen, 1941, p. 235) to have accounted for about 800 deer a year, out of a total herd of around 4,000.

In 1906 the Kaibab Plateau was declared a game reserve, and the hunting of deer was prohibited. At the same time there was a marked decrease in the number of domestic sheep grazed in the area,[2] and government hunters were employed in killing the main predators. During the first ten years of this régime some 600 mountain lions were killed, and during the next six years 74, together with about 3,000 coyote and 120 bobcats. The effects of this policy on the deer herd are best described in Rasmussen's words (1941, pp. 236–7):

> The decrease in competition for forage, the check on natural enemies and the prevention of killing by man caused an increase in the deer herd in this ideal deer range. The deers' habits and the topography of the country prevented a scattering of deer to adjacent ranges. The increase was allowed to go on without check for sixteen years, until the estimated 4,000 of 1906 had become an enormous herd of near 100,000 in 1924. The peak was reached, the range depleted, and the deer population started downhill. There were deaths by thousands from malnutrition and related causes.

Between 50,000 and 60,000 animals are estimated to have died in the winters of 1924–5 and 1925–6. In 1924, hunting was again permitted on the Plateau; during the next seven years some 15,000 deer were removed by hunting, and by the end of 1930 the herd was down to an estimated 20,000. Even this number, however, was excessive in view of the damage that had been done to the range; during the 1930s, the herd continued to decrease slowly, and by the end of the decade was estimated to number 10,000 animals.

From this account of the deer 'irruption' on Kaibab Plateau between 1906 and 1924, two points may engage our attention. The first concerns the relation between deer and vegetation.[3] So long as deer keep well within the limits set by the available food supply, a heavy growth of palatable shrubs may develop in favourable locations within the range; in the mountains of the Great Basin, notably the Wasatch range and the Kaibab Plateau, such 'storage' of food shrubs—particularly of *Cowania* (cliff rose) and *Cercocarpus*—appears to have taken place on a large scale prior to 1900. When the brake on deer numbers on the Kaibab Plateau was relaxed in the years following the declaration of the game reserve in 1906, this 'stored' food stood ready to support the rapid growth of population which in fact took place. As deer pressure increases, however, these palatable shrubs are progressively crippled by over-browsing; their reproduction is inhibited, and as a result their place tends to be taken by unpalatable species. Deer pressure thus gives worthless foods a competitive advantage, and in the long run, as Leopold points out (p. 172), 'the whole flora tends to shift its composition in a direction unfavourable for deer'. Since, in cold climates, the critical season for deer in terms of food supply is winter, it is the winter range that bears the brunt of over-browsing. A run of mild winters may mask the over-browsed state of the winter range, by allowing the deer to use the lower slopes of the summer range in winter, but this can only put off the evil day. Sooner or

---

[1] Between 1906 and 1931, thirty wolves were killed on Kaibab Plateau, exterminating the species there.

[2] Sheep had been introduced on to the Plateau in the 1880s; from 1906 to 1924, the number grazed there varied between 9,000 and 15,000.

[3] See, in particular, Leopold *et al.* (1947), pp. 172–5.

later the reduced forage on the winter range will cut back the deer population to that number which it is capable of supporting—as happened, on the Kaibab Plateau, in the winters of 1924-5 and 1925-6.

The second point concerns the relation between deer and their predators. All the recorded irruptions of deer in western North America have followed, and none preceded, measures of predator control:

> Since irruptions co-incide both in time and space with greatly reduced predation by wolves or cougars, [writes Leopold (1947, p. 176)], and since they are not known to have occurred in the presence of these predators, there is a strong presumption that over-control of these predators is a pre-disposing cause.

Wolves having been too few in number to have seriously affected the issue, mountain lions must have played the primary rôle in controlling the deer population on the Kaibab Plateau. Recent studies of mountain lions in central Idaho,[1] and in Utah and Nevada,[2] show that individual animals occupy their own distinct winter territories, ranging in size from 15 to 25 sq. miles, the male ranges in a given area forming one mosaic and the female ranges another mosaic superimposed on the first; that mule deer constitute by far their major food, making up nearly 80 per cent of that taken in winter and 65 per cent in summer; and that a single lion kills, on average, one deer a week during the cold winter months (November to April), and perhaps more often during the summer. Transposing these findings to the Kaibab Plateau: if the winter range of the deer there covered some 700 to 800 sq. miles, this area would have supported a resident population of about sixty mountain lions, and a resident population of this size would have culled the deer herd at a rate of around 3,200 head a year.

The changes that took place in the inter-relationship between deer and mountain lion, following the declaration of the game reserve in 1906, are probably too complex to be fully reconstructible now. Something on the following lines may have occurred: the initial killing of lions, together with the prohibition on hunting by the Paiute, would have released the 'brake' on deer numbers. As the numbers of deer rose, the reproductive rate of the lion population would have increased in response to the increased food supply.[3] The increase in their reproductive rate must, however, have been more than balanced by the campaign against them on the part of government hunters; by 1917 the mountain lion population was clearly on the wane,[4] and deer numbers were free to rise unchecked.

The Kaibab Plateau example shows that there are two possible mechanisms whereby balance may be maintained in animal populations in a wild state: one *extrinsic*, the other *intrinsic*. The deer population on the plateau was held in check primarily by extrinsic means, namely by predation: any increase in deer numbers was checked by the action of the mountain lions, and it was only after the latter had been drastically reduced by human intervention that the deer

---

[1] Hornocker (1969), Fig. 1, p. 460.

[2] Robinette *et al.* (1959), p. 272.

[3] The ability of populations of carnivores such as foxes, cats and lions, to respond to changes in the numbers of their prey by changes in their own reproductive rate, is well established: see Lack (1954, pp. 46, 210-11), for foxes and lynxes, and Wynne-Edwards (1962, pp. 490-1, 513), for cats and lions.

[4] Before 1917 the killing of mountain lions had run at a rate of fifty to sixty a year; after 1917 (and up to 1931), though the campaign continued, the rate fell to an average of twelve a year.

population was free to rise to the ceiling set by the food resources of the environment.[1]

The mechanism of control of the mountain lion population is more complex. To elucidate it, I propose to outline the theory of regulation of numbers by *intrinsic* means, recently put forward by Wynne-Edwards (1962). This theory is woven out of three strands: namely, territory, competition, and group selection. A given stock of animals, argues Wynne-Edwards (1962, pp. 141–2), tends to persist generation after generation in the same locality. This 'group' is not a haphazard assembly of individuals thrown together into a particular habitat; rather, it is a population largely of common descent, 'self-perpetuating and potentially immortal'. As such, it will have its own distinctive complement of genes distributed among its members, and can be expected to differ somewhat in its gene-complement from neighbouring local groups of the same species.

Now it is clearly to the advantage of the local group to limit its population to that number which does not press unduly hard on the resources available to it, whether those resources be the seeds or berries of plants, or a species of prey animal: since a local group which failed to do this would end by exhausting those resources and so, in effect, signing its own death warrant. This danger is averted, in Wynne-Edwards' view (1962, pp. 449–65), by competition between the members of the local group: competition, not for the food supply itself, but for certain objects which *stand for* the food supply. Each local group, being confined—apart from emigration of surplus members and pioneers—to its own locality, has certain traditions applying specifically to that locality. These local traditions, referring in birds to knowledge of nesting sites, feeding places, food-storage and singing points, and in mammals to use of customary dunging places, rubbing and marking posts, dens, warrens, trails and territories, tend to be extremely stable; they may survive for hundreds, even thousands of years. Since the number of such objects in each locality is finite, and since knowledge of them is invested in self-perpetuating local groups, they set a limit to the population of such groups; and it is compettiton for these objects, carried on according to rules accepted by all the members of the group, that determines which of its members shall stay to breed there, and which shall either fail to breed or be forced out into more marginal habitats.[2]

The acceptance of these conventional goals as objects of competition, and the elaboration of rules governing competition for them, are both—in Wynne-Edwards' view (pp. 18–21, 141–2, 450–1)—group-characters, *evolved through selection at group level*. What is inherited, in the case of such group-characters, is the capacity to respond correctly in the interests of the community as a whole, rather than in the purely selfish interests of the individual. Consider, he says,

[1] Such *extrinsic* means of control are also found to operate in populations of White-tailed Deer, American Elk, Moose, Mountain Sheep and Pronghorn Antelope: see Lack (1954), pp. 121–2, 170–3, 176.

[2] In animals living in bands or herds, much the same function is performed by dominance hierarchies, except that, there, competition is for a place in the hierarchy: see Wynne-Edwards (1962), pp. 134–40.

reproductive rate. If selection acted all in favour of the individual (as it does in the case of physiological or anatomical characters), there would be an over-whelming premium on higher and ever higher individual fecundity provided it resulted in leaving more progeny than one's fellows. Manifestly, this does not happen, since in many species annual reproductive rate is varied according to the current needs of the population as a whole; in such cases it is no longer a question of this individual or that leaving progeny to posterity, but of the group itself producing that number of young consistent with the resources available to it. Selection thus promotes the interests of the social group as an evolutionary unit in its own right; and if, in any particular group, this mechanism fails and individuals take to putting their own interest before that of the community of which they are members, the stock itself will suffer and, in the long run, its territory will be taken over by neighbouring stocks with more successful systems.

Each of the three strands in Wynne-Edwards' theory has a respectable pedi-gree in biological thinking. Thus W. H. Burt, in his study of chipmunks, ground squirrels and mice,[1] stressed the link between territoriality and the regulation of numbers; only those females, he pointed out, that can find suitable nesting sites will be successful in raising young, the remainder being forced out of the home range to seek their fortunes in new and unknown habitats. Nicholson, in the article cited earlier,[2] argued that competition furnishes the primary means of limiting animal numbers in populations where extrinsic factors are not operative. Darwin himself, in *The Origin of Species*, recognised the importance of group-selection:

> Natural selection, [he wrote[3]], will modify the structure of the young in relation to the parent, and of the parent in relation to the young. In social animals it will adapt the structure of each individual for the benefit of the whole community: if the community profits by the selected change.

And Allee (1940, pp. 154–60) linked the idea of competition *within* the com-munity with that of competition *between* communities: with 'the resulting survival of the more fit systems'.

It remained, however, for Wynne-Edwards to take these three strands and weave them into a single model, showing the *process* whereby numbers may be

---

[1] Burt (1940), especially pp. 52–6: in a subsequent paper on lemming voles (1949, pp. 25–7), Burt refers to territoriality as 'a kind of governor in preventing over-population'.
[2] Nicholson (1933), pp. 168–74. Errington, also, postulated (1946, pp. 227–8) a link between the strong territoriality characteristic of birds and many mammals, increased intraspecific competition (especially just before the breeding season), and population density.
[3] Darwin (1872: 1951), p. 87. Subsequently in the same work, as examples of the selection of characters in the interest of the community rather than of the individual, Darwin cites the bee's sting (p. 213), and the evolution of castes of worker ants (pp. 297–302).
Another case is furnished by the alarm calls of many flocking birds: these, as Tinbergen remarks (1965, p. 55: cf. pp. 73–4), are a clear example of an activity which serves the group but endangers the individual. If selection acted purely at an individual level, one would expect the individuals that gave alarm calls to have been eliminated.

effectively regulated in animal communities. The two essential components in such a system are, first, a means of registering actual changes in population density within the community, and, second, a means of bringing about whatever changes are needed to restore the balance when it is disturbed. The first of these two functions is performed, in Wynne-Edwards' model, by competition:[1] as population density rises, the intensity of competition for those *things* which are the object of conventional competition in that particular group rises also; the intensity of competition itself furnishes the gauge of population density, and when this rises sufficiently, it will evoke a response to bring the pressure down. If the mechanism is working properly, this response ought to occur before the safe limit of numbers is reached, before—that is to say—permanent damage has been done to the resources of the habitat.

The second function, the relief of pressure, is performed—in Wynne-Edwards' model—either by emigration of surplus members out of the locality or by a lowered reproductive rate, or by a combination of the two. The first of these two 'valves' is straightforward, and needs no particular elucidation.[2] The second is more complex. The essential point here is not so much birth rate *per se* (though this, of course, enters into the equation), as recruitment to the adult population: recruitment being defined, in this context, as 'admission to full membership of a population normally capable of sustaining itself by reproduction'. The gist of Wynne-Edwards' argument (1962, pp. 487–92, 502–15) is that potential fecundity, in all animal species, being considerably greater than is normally required simply to maintain the population at its current level, is only fully utilised when a state of under-population exists and numbers need to be rapidly raised;[3] under normal stable conditions, while the 'annual reproductive enterprise' of any particular community is commonly on the generous side (to take care of emergencies), there are a number of stages in the process of raising recruits to the adult population *at which homeostatic adjustments can, and do, take place*. Such means of adjustment include, in mammals, resorption of embryos (known to occur in rodents and foxes), variation in litter-size (in rabbits, domestic sheep, lions), variation in frequency of pregnancy (in rats, musk-rats, cats), and variation in rates of litter-mortality—due chiefly to inadequate lactation, neglect of the young and/or cannibalism. These homeostatic adjustments

[1] Wynne-Edwards (1962), pp. 14–16, 132–3: a large part of his book (Chapters 11 to 16, pp. 193–388) is taken up with a description of the various modes of competition found in animal communities. He argues that *epideictic* displays of one kind or another, i.e. displays in which all the males of a local population 'show off' to one another, frequently furnish the stage for such competition.

[2] Cf. Wynne-Edwards (1962), pp. 480–2. A classic case of the emigration, and subsequent death, of surplus members of the population is furnished by the Red Grouse on the moors of Scotland and northern England: see Watson *et al.* (1970), pp. 14–19, 30–1.

[3] The capacity for rapid increase is well illustrated in the case of many rodents. Thus populations of brown rats in the city of Baltimore, having been reduced between 50 per cent and 90 per cent by intensive trapping and poisoning, were found to recover at a rather constant rate of about 4 per cent of their original levels each month, due primarily to greater frequency of pregnancy in the surviving females: see Emlen *et al.* (1948), and Davis (1951), pp. 459–61.

R

are called into play *ultimately* by imbalance between a given population and the environmental resources upon which it is dependent, and *proximately* by increased competition for the conventional goals which 'stand for' those resources, the physiological changes that actually bring about the regulation of reproductive output being mediated by the mammals' endocrine system.[1]

Such, in outline, is the model proposed by Wynne-Edwards for the governing of numbers in animal communities where outside factors are not operative; and it was, I suppose, by *intrinsic* means of this kind that the mountain lion population of the Kaibab Plateau was controlled prior to the advent of European hunters.

This model Wynne-Edwards extends to primitive human communities. Such communities, he argues (1962, pp. 187–91), quoting the Australian aborigines, the Eskimos and the North American Indians, are also—like animal communities—territorial; and, like animal communities, they keep their numbers well within the limits set by the resources available to them. But in humans, as in animal species, potential fecundity is well in excess of that needed to replace current numbers, even allowing for a high rate of infant mortality; so their populations, also, must be under homeostatic control 'like those of other wild animals', except that, in human communities, control is exercised by means of abstention from intercourse, induced abortion and infanticide, sanctioned by tribal custom (pp. 491–2). In animal communities, as we have seen, communal displays of one sort or another provide an opportunity for assessing population density, alternative to that furnished by direct competition for territories or status. In human communities this function is discharged by tribal gatherings. Citing the initiation ceremonies of the Australian aborigines and the midsummer festivals of some North American Indian tribes, Wynne-Edwards concludes (pp. 219–20):

> Gatherings like these appear to be the only possible source of what knowledge exists regarding changes in numbers in the population, and to be the basis, therefore, on which tribal customs relating to sexual abstinence, infanticide and other forms of birth-control are built up, reinforced or relaxed.

The weakness of Wynne-Edwards' theory, *as applied to primitive human communities,* lies—to my mind—not in the idea of balance between a local population and the exploitable resources upon which it is dependent; this idea I believe to be right. It lies, rather, in the proposed mechanism whereby balance is achieved. According to the theory, population, at least in a gatherer-hunter economy, should be stabilised at that number which is able to survive in the worst year likely to be encountered, in a generation say, in that particular environment. The question is: how are numbers kept *down*, in a run of good years, to that level which can survive—in the absence of any stored surplus—in a bad year: i.e. how is the population kept *within*, rather than on the verge of,

---

[1] Wynne-Edwards (1962), pp. 505–6. The latter aspect, which receives relatively scant attention from Wynne-Edwards, has been treated in detail by Christian and Davis (1964), and by Christian, Lloyd and Davis (1965): see below, pp. 511–12.

the carrying capacity of the habitat? This question Wynne-Edwards nowhere faces squarely. He implies, however, that the result is achieved by some kind of conscious foresight:[1] i.e. that the local population comes together for a festival or religious ceremony, is made aware then—through the increased excitement and interaction that takes place (equivalent to the *epideictic* displays of birds and mammals)—that its numbers are rising to a level beyond that which the resources of its territory can support, and proceeds to take one or more of the measures needed to restore them to their former level.

This model appears to me to be defective, on three counts. I find it hard to see, first, what factor is really equivalent to the competition for territory, breeding sites or other desired objects, which, in animal communities, acts as a gauge of increasing pressure on resources. Communal gatherings, such as those of the Great Basin Shoshoni, appear on the whole to be much more co-operative than competitive; nor does it help to shift the emphasis to status, since, in the complex value systems characteristic of human societies, there is no simple correlation between status and permission-to-breed.[2] Second, the means for controlling numbers requires of the community as a group a degree of foresight and directed action which gatherer-hunters rarely show *in their other activities*. This is not to say that abstention from intercourse, abortion and infanticide do not occur in such societies; it is simply to query whether they are practised there consistently enough and with sufficient purpose to act in the way the model requires. Finally, and more radically, there is, to my mind, a fault line running between the afferent and the efferent sides of the model: so far as Wynne-Edwards postulates a gauge of increasing pressure on resources, he postulates one that is—by and large—subconscious, namely a communal state of awareness borne in on people at a ceremony or festival, whereas the response he postulates is, by and large, conscious and dependent on voluntary action. I find it hard to see precisely how the one is converted into the other.[3]

---

[1] The most explicit statement to this effect is to be found on p. 542 of his book: the chief difference, he says there, between the means of control in animal communities and in primitive human communities is that whereas, in the former, control is exercised through physiological adaptations, in the latter it is exercised chiefly through traditional tribal customs; these, he argues, besides being more flexible than the physiological adaptations found in animals, 'are also open to insight modification by the tribal authorities'.

[2] This point has been made by Mary Douglas (1966, p. 272), in her *critique* of Wynne-Edwards' theory. Dr. Douglas goes on to suggest that we should, therefore, shift our attention away from subsistence to prestige and to 'the relation between the prestige structure and the economic basis of prosperity'.

[3] I can understand either an overt system, such as that reported by Laughlin (1968, p. 242) of some Eskimo groups, where people get together and say, in effect, 'look, we've got too many children, we must do something about it'; *or* a covert one, such as that postulated by Wynne-Edwards for animal communities, where information is fed in and the response is mediated on, so to speak, a physiological level—in much the same way as, in the body, a rise in blood $CO_2$ elicits deeper breathing. What I find hard to accept is a covert/overt system, whereby information is fed in on the physiological level and the response is mediated on the level of conscious action. It may be that Wynne-Edwards would argue, in the latter case, that the response is in a sense involuntary since it is dependent on tribal custom: but in *that* case, who decides whose baby is to be left outside for the night?

While, therefore, I think that Wynne-Edwards is right in postulating a balance between population and resources in gatherer-hunter communities, the model he proposes appears to me inadequate to explain how that balance is achieved. Before presenting an alternative, let me summarise the criteria that such a model should satisfy. It has to show, first, how rising pressure on resources is registered in the system: and second, how numbers may be effectively regulated, without invoking the foresight and directed action which gatherer-hunter communities, rarely evincing in their other activities, are unlikely to evince in this one. It has, thirdly, to demonstrate a link between input of information and effector response: in other words, to show how an imbalance registered in the system elicits the response needed to correct it. Finally, it should, ideally, be able to show how the limits themselves may vary in response to long-term, e.g. climatic, changes in the habitat and in the resources which it offers. This last requirement we shall find to be the hardest to satisfy: the model which I propose now to offer failing, I think, on this count.

This model concerns *names* and *naming*. Briefly, it holds that each community has, or originally had, a finite stock of personal names, and that this finite stock of names, being directly related—in number—to the resources available to the community, furnished a gauge of increasing pressure on those resources. First, therefore, let us consider the function of names in 'primitive' communities. There is a fair amount of evidence that, in many such communities, personal names have little or nothing to do with designating the person named.[1] In such communities he may be addressed, or referred to, by a kinship term, or by a nickname referring to some personal idiosyncrasy or form of behaviour or place of origin.[2] Alternatively, he may have a 'real' name, bestowed ceremonially, and a secondary name for common use: in which case the 'real' name is often kept secret, sometimes even from the person himself.[3] What, then, if it is not to designate a person, is the true function of the name? And for answer, I refer the reader back to the facts presented in Chapter 17 of this book, and in particular to that link which Mauss divined (above, p. 321) between the personality, the soul, and the name. The primary purpose of the name, on this reckoning, is to admit the child—or other outsider, in case of adoption—to full membership of the community, and to recognise him *as a person*.[4]

---

[1] See, on this point, Reichard (1938), pp. 450–1.

[2] Cf. the stock of nicknames in common use in the army—'Dusty' (Miller), 'Nobby' (Clark), 'Lofty', 'Shorty', 'Chips' (a carpenter), 'Sparks' (an electrician), 'Ginger' (red-head), 'Geordie' (a Tynesider), 'Taffie' (a Welshman), 'Jock' (a Scotsman), etc.

[3] Larock (1932), p. 53, 79–86.

[4] Thus, among the Murngin, there is a distinction between a man's personal—or camp—name, which he receives from his mother's kinsfolk, and his totemic or sacred name which he receives from his own, i.e. his father's, clan. The sacred name is taken from some part of the totemic complex of the clan to which he belongs, and refers directly or indirectly to the totem (Warner, 1964, pp. 26, 62, 152, 380–1); and it is introduction to the totemic complex, at circumcision, that separates the boy from the uninitiated children and women.

This theme has been taken up and developed in detail by Larock, in his *Essai sur la valeur sacrée et la valeur sociale des noms de personnes dans les sociétés inférieures.*[1] From Larock's analysis, three points emerge clearly:

first, *the child's real existence (l'existence véritable de l'enfant) only begins from the moment he receives a name:*

> Jusqu'à ce moment c'est un être sans personnalité, sans contact avec les membres du clan, vivant ou mort, privé de toute virtualité religieuse ou sociale, une chair sans âme. Pourvu d'un nom, *de son nom,* l'enfant n'est plus cette chair sans 'âme' qu'il etait auparavant[2].

Second, *the name bestowed on the child is, very commonly, that of an ancestor either in the paternal or maternal line.*

A part of *la valeur sacrée*, which attaches to the name, Larock traces to the belief in the re-living (*réviviscence*) of the ancestor through the intermediary of the name:

> Qu'est-ce qui se passe dans l'enfant, [he asks[3]], au moment où il reçoit son nom? Il est investi d'une force sacrée . . ., *l'âme d'un ancêtre descend soudain en lui,* le groupe le reconnaît pour un des siens, il n'est plus seulement un être quelconque de chair vivante: il a une personnalité. . . .

And later (p. 65) he suggests that, rather than the custom of naming-after-an-ancestor being derived from a belief in re-incarnation, the belief in re-incarnation may be derived from the naming custom.

Third, *in many societies the number of names from which the child's parents—or other name-giver(s)—must choose, is rigorously fixed:*

> Souvent, aussi, l'ordre dans lequel le même nom passera des ascendants aux descendants est specifié par l'usage. Les dénominations même, du moins celles que l'enfant reçoit en premier lieu [i.e. *son nom véritable*], sont distribués d'une façon qui ne varie pas[4].

And, subsequently, discussing the limited stock of personal names possessed by the community, he writes (p. 85):

> Comme les noms constituent les réserves les plus précieuses [*de la collectivité*], il importe de les préserver, d'en fixer scrupuleusement le nombre — de là les listes de noms, de les imposer solonellement aux nouveaux-nés — de là les rites collectifs, de les sauvegarder enfin contre toute atteinte. . . .

---

[1] Larock (1932), especially pp. 27–95, 170–4.

[2] Larock (1932), p. 29, and 58. The use of the *personal* name to mark the child's entry into the community has been carried to its logical conclusion by the Yuma Indians, amongst whom women do not have personal names at all while boys receive theirs at the time of the nose-piercing rite at the age of 7 or 8: Forde (1932), pp. 149–50.

[3] Larock (1932), pp. 37–8: cf. pp. 32–4, 61–4.

[4] Larock (1932), pp. 51–2: Larock quotes, at this point, the naming practices of the Sioux and other Plains groups.

This last quotation brings out an aspect of naming upon which Larock lays great emphasis: that is, the emotional 'charge' with which names are invested.[1] This emotional 'charge' constitutes, in his view, the original, primordial significance of names and naming; and it is only as this 'charge' weakens that the social element (*la valeur sociale*) in naming, of names (that is) as designations, comes to the fore and gradually replaces the religious element (*la valeur sacrée*), of names (that is) as bearers of soul and personality, as their primary function.

Let us now consider what happens when a body of hunter-gatherers moves, or originally moved, into a new territory for the first time. To begin with, we may suppose, the move is followed by a period of trial and error, i.e. oscillation of numbers, until eventually the population becomes stabilised within those limits which the resources of the territory permit, *by whatever mechanism numbers are stabilised in comparable primate groups*. At this point the numbers are converted into a finite stock of personal names, the number of names corresponding—give or take a few—to the carrying capacity of the territory and being related directly to that particular habitat. As members of the community die, their names are taken, after a decent interval, by their descendants, commonly their grandchildren or great-grandchildren. Should the population begin to rise and to press upon the available resources, the pressure will be reflected in a growing dearth of personal names. To begin with, this dearth will no doubt be accommodated by shortening the interval between a man's dying and the re-use of his name; as it becomes more acute, it will give rise to increasing anxiety within the families that are short of names to bestow on their children.

In mammal species such as rats, mice, voles, rabbits, woodchucks and dogs, in laboratory populations of which homeostatic controls have been found to operate, these controls operate in part through increased mortality of adults, i.e. in response to over-crowding, and in part through reduced recruitment into the population. Both responses are mediated through the endocrine system, the former by way of the pituitary-adrenocortical axis, the latter by way of the pituitary-gonadal axis; both are ultimately under central nervous control, by way of the hypothalamus. Responses serving to reduce recruitment into the population have been found to operate at each main stage in the reproductive process. They may include any one or more of the following:[2] delayed sexual maturation (of females), prolonged oestrus cycles, diminished ovulation and implantation, increased intra-uterine mortality (and/or resorption) of foetuses, reduced litter-size, inadequate lactation and/or neglect of the young. The sum of the actions of these two broad categories, i.e. of increased mortality and reduced recruitment, is, in the words of Christian *et al.* (1965, p. 568):

> to slow the growth of a population and eventually to maintain the population at a level below that which would exhaust the environmental resources. These

[1] Larock (1932), pp. 9, 170–4: cf. in the case of the Banks Islands, Vol. 1, pp. 370–1.
[2] See, in particular, Thiessen and Rodgers (1961), pp. 447–8, Christian and Davis (1964), pp. 1551–2, and Christian *et al.* (1965), pp. 502–3, 568.

endocrine functions therefore have survival value for the species, even though the effects on many individuals may be deleterious.

Two points may be noted regarding the means of homeostatic control found in sub-primate mammal populations. First, they require an actual state of over-crowding to exist before they come into operation. Given such a state, the increased population density leads to increased competition and social strife, due, primarily, *to increased number of interactions between individuals*;[1] social strife, and the aggression which accompanies it, in turn act—by way of the hypo-thalamic-pituitary axis—to elicit the changes in endocrine balance needed to increase mortality and decrease natality. Competition within an already crowded community is thus the gauge in response to which the control mechan-ism is brought into play. Second, the pivot of the whole system is the point of entry into the sub-adult and adult breeding community: it is the increasing pressure within the latter body, in relation to limited resources, that sets off the control mechanism.

Now this mechanism is relatively crude, in that numbers have *first* to rise considerably, to increase competition to that point at which the controls needed to bring them down again are called into operation.[2] A finer mechanism would be one in which the gauge registered current recruitment against current loss *directly*, and in which control was exercised wholly on recruitment, i.e. with *no* loss among those already admitted to the community. A gauge of this kind would be set, ideally, at the point of entry into the sub-adult and adult breeding community, so as to regulate the flow into it. Such a gauge is furnished, I suggest, in undisturbed gatherer-hunter communities, by *naming*: ideally, as among the Owens Valley Paiute,[3] by naming at or after the age of walking (by which time the hazards of infancy and early childhood have been surmounted), with the name of a deceased grandparent or other lineal forbear.

In animal communities, control is exercised in part, as we have seen, by way of increased mortality among existing members of the community, and in part by way of decreased natality among prospective members. The stimulus for both means of control is the increasing competition and social strife to which increasing population density gives rise: competition, and aggression, acting by way of the pituitary-adrenocortical axis to increase mortality, and by way of the pituitary-gonadal axis to decrease natality. Now in humans, the primary agent acting on the pituitary-gonadal axis—and so affecting the various stages of the reproductive process including menstruation, ovulation, implantation, the *in utero* health of the foetus, and lactation—is *anxiety*, mediated from the

---

[1] Christian and Davis (1964), pp. 1552–3.

[2] This is probably one reason for the enormous oscillations found in some mammal populations, e.g. those of lemmings and voles, in the wild; another reason is the relatively short breeding periods of these mammals.

[3] Steward (1933), p. 292. Among the Owens Valley Paiute, the name was bestowed on the child by the father's family; among the Hopi, the right of conferring the name has passed to the father's clan.

higher centres of the brain to the anterior lobe of the pituitary via the hypothalamus.[1] We might therefore expect that a means of controlling population which worked *wholly* on the recruitment side of the recruitment-loss equation (such as we have postulated above) would, in humans, be activated by anxiety rather than, as in other mammals, by competition; and this, I suggest, is the function of the emotional 'charge' attached to names in primitive communities, i.e. to generate the anxiety needed to set these controls in operation.

In this model the *ultimate* factor limiting population is, as in the model proposed by Wynne-Edwards, the food resources offered by the environment; the *proximate* factor is furnished by the finite stock of personal names 'owned' by the community.[2] Control is exercised through anovulatory cycles, reduced implantation, spontaneous abortion, etc., caused by changes in hormonal balance; such changes, mediated via the hypothalamic-pituitary axis, are set in train by anxiety in response to a dearth of available names, anxiety—of sufficient strength to initiate the sequence—being generated by the emotional 'charge' attached to names in primitive hunting-and-gathering communities. An involuntary, cultural means of control is thus put in place of the natural regulation found in other mammalian species,[3] and of the voluntary means of control postulated by Wynne-Edwards.

As corollary to this model, we may infer that the practice of naming, a feature shared by all human communities of which we have knowledge, evolved originally as a means of regulating numbers, at that point in man's development where:

(*a*) the reproductive processes of females were coming increasingly under the control of the developing cerebral cortex;[4] and

(*b*) a means of controlling population that involved the mortality—or forced emigration—of existing members of the breeding community, such as is found in other mammals, was becoming increasingly incompatible with the growing respect accorded to the individual *as a person*.[5]

---

[1] For clinical evidence of the effects of mental strain and fear on human reproductive processes, see an early paper by Theobald (1936), pp. 1038–41; for further evidence, and for the channel by which anxiety exerts its effect on reproductive processes, see Harris (1955), especially pp. 62–4, 70–1, 93–5, 118–27, 153–8.

[2] For the distinction between *ultimate* and *proximate* factors in population control, see Lack (1954), pp. 5–6, 36–7, 61–6.

[3] Using the terms *nature* and *culture* in the sense that Lévi-Strauss uses them. Calhoun, however, discussing (1952, pp. 143–7) the population dynamics of brown rats, points out that animal communities too may enjoy a culture. As soon, he says, as a group of animals begins to condition its environment by building trails, nests, burrows and the like, this affects the social behaviour of the animals themselves; 'this alteration of the habits and social behavior of one generation by the activities of generations which precede it represents a cultural process', a process which, in turn, exercises a controlling influence upon population dynamics through its effect on reproductive capacity, growth rate, mortality rate, incidence of disease, etc.

[4] See, on this point, Beach (1947), especially pp. 307–10, and Harris (1955), pp. 281–3.

[5] As evidenced by the burial customs of Middle Palaeolithic hunters: Clark and Piggott (1970), pp. 50–2.

Set in a wider perspective, human communities appear to have passed through three stages in population control. In the earliest stage, that of the proto-hominids, when man was still—by and large—a prey species, the means of control was probably in part *extrinsic*, by way of predation (Brain, 1970), and in part *intrinsic*, on the lines proposed by Wynne-Edwards for other mammal communities. With the development of weapons and group hunting, and the change in status from prey to predator, the means of control became, we may suppose, primarily intrinsic; in place, however, of the *natural* regulation of numbers found in other mammal communities, a *cultural* mechanism—that of naming—was evolved. The change from hunting-and-gathering to agriculture, and the increased reproduction that agriculture facilitated,[1] in conjunction with the greater weight that lineage systems accord to child-bearing,[2] evidently put this mechanism under increasing strain; and at this point, I suggest, it began to be supplemented by *voluntary* measures such as abstention from intercourse, induced abortion and the deliberate exposure of unwanted children.

[1] As happens, also, in populations of mice and voles that have taken to an 'agricultural' life: see Linduska (1942), pp. 359–62.

The change from hunting-and-gathering to agriculture and/or herding is not necessarily, however, accompanied by any marked increase in population: thus, in the two centuries (A.D. 1600 to 1800) during which the Navajo made this transition, their numbers—in a virtually empty habitat—only increased from a little under 4,000 to a little over 6,000 (Johnston, 1966, pp. 135–6). During the next sixty-five years, however, their numbers nearly doubled.

[2] See, on this point, B. Benedict (1970). It would be interesting to know to what extent, if at all, matrilineages and patrilineages differ in this respect: whether, for instance, a greater weight on child-bearing is correlated with the greater value attached to pre-marital virginity in patrilineal societies.

# References

GENERAL WORKS, AND WORKS RELATING TO SOUTH INDIA, THE
MEDITERRANEAN AND WESTERN EUROPE

Barker, E. (1934): *Natural Law and the Theory of Society*, by Otto Gierke: with a lecture on *The Ideas of Natural Law and Humanity*, by Ernst Troeltsch, translated with an introduction by Ernest Barker (2 vols., Cambridge).

—(1948): *The Politics of Aristotle*, translated with notes by Ernest Barker (Oxford).

Binchy, D. A. (1943): 'The linguistic and historical value of the Irish Law Tracts', *Proc. Brit. Acad.*, vol. xxix, pp. 195–227.

—(1970): *Celtic and Anglo-Saxon Kingship*. O'Donnell Lectures for 1967–8 (Oxford).

Black, M. (1962): 'Linguistic relativity: the views of Benjamin Lee Whorf', *Models and Metaphors: Studies in Language and Philosophy* (New York), ch. xiv, pp. 244–57.

—(1968): *The Labyrinth of Language* (London).

Bloch, M. (1924): *Les Rois Thaumaturges: étude sur le caractère surnaturel attribué à la puissance royale particulièrement en France et en Angleterre* (Strasburg).

—(1964): *Les Caractères originaux de l'histoire rurale française* (Paris): 1st ed. Oslo, 1931.

—(1968): *La Société féodale* (Paris): 1st ed. Paris, 1939–40.

Boyce, A. J., Küchemann, C. F. and Harrison, G. A. (1967a), 'Neighbourhood knowledge and the distribution of marriage distances', *Ann. Human Genet.*, vol. 30, pp. 335–8.

—(1967b): 'A demographic and genetic study of a group of Oxfordshire villages', *Human Biology*, vol. 39, pp. 251–76.

Brown, P. (1971): 'The rise and function of the holy man in Late Antiquity', *J. Roman Studies*, vol. lxi, pp. 80–101.

Campbell, J. K. (1964): *Honour, Family and Patronage: a Study of Institutions and Moral Values in a Greek Mountain Community* (Oxford).

Cornford, F. M. (1930): 'Mystery religions and pre-Socratic thought', in *Cambridge Ancient History*, vol. iv (1930), ch. xv, pp. 522–78.

Dodds, E. R. (1951): *The Greeks and the Irrational* (Berkeley, Calif.).

Dumont, L. (1953): 'The Dravidian kinship terminology as an expression of marriage', *Man*, vol. 53, no. 54, pp. 34–9.

—(1957a): 'Hierarchy and marriage alliance in South Indian kinship', *Occasional Papers*, *R. Anthrop. Inst.*, no. 12, pp. 1–45.

—(1957b): *Une Sous-caste de l'Inde du sud: organisation sociale et religion des Pramalai Kallar* (Paris).

—(1958): 'Le renoncement dans les religions de l'Inde', Frazer Lecture for 1958: reprinted in *Homo hierarchicus* (1966), Appendix B, pp. 324–50.

—(1966): *Homo hierarchicus: essai sur le système des castes* (Paris).

Eliade, M. (1968): *Le Chamanisme et les techniques archaïques de l'extase* (Paris).

Emmet, D. M. (1958): *Function, Purpose and Powers* (London).

Entwistle, W. J. (1953): *Aspects of Language* (London).

Fox, R. (1965): 'Prolegomena to the study of British kinship', in *Penguin Survey of the Social Sciences 1965* (ed. Gould, J.), pp. 128–43.

—(1967a): *Kinship and Marriage: an Anthropological Perspective* (London).

—(1967b): 'In the beginning: aspects of hominid behavioural evolution', *Man, J. Royal Anthrop. Inst.*, vol. 2 (new series), no. 3, pp. 415–33.

Frankfort, H. and H. A. (1946): 'Myth and reality', Introduction to *The Intellectual Adventure of Ancient Man: an Essay on Speculative Thought in the Ancient Near East* (Chicago), pp. 3–27.

Frankfort, H. (1951): *The Birth of Civilization in the Near East* (London).

Gardiner, A. H. (1932): *The Theory of Speech and Language* (Oxford).

Gellner, E. (1958): 'Time and theory in social anthropology', *Mind*, vol. lxvii, pp. 182–202.

—(1962): 'Concepts and society', reprinted from *Transact. 5th World Congress of Sociology* (Washington), pp. 1–23.

—(1963): 'Nature and society in social anthropology', *Philosophy of Science*, vol. xxx, pp. 236–51.

Glotz, G. (1915): 'Le droit des gens dans l'antiquité grecque', *extrait des Mémoires présentés à l'Acadamie des Inscriptions et Belle-Lettres* (Paris), tome xiii, pp. 1–17.

—(1925): *Histoire grecque: 1. Des origines aux guerres médiques* (Paris).

Goodchild, R. G. and Ward Perkins, J. B. (1949): 'The *Limes Tripolitanus* in the light of recent discoveries', *J. Roman Studies*, vol. xxxix, pp. 81–95.

Graven, J. (1927): *Essai sur l'évolution du droit pénal valaisan* (Lausanne).

Halliday, W. R. (1933): *Indo-European Folk-Tales and Greek Legend* (Cambridge).

Hertz, R. (1960): 'Contribution à une étude sur la représentation collective de la mort', *L'Année sociologique*, vol. x (1907), pp. 48–137: English translation by Needham, R. and C., in *Death* and *The Right Hand* (London, 1960), pp. 27–86, 117–54, 163–71.

Isaacs, S. (1930): *Intellectual Growth in Young Children* (London).

—(1933): *Social Development in Young Children* (London).

Kardiner, A. (1939): *The Individual and his Society* (New York).

—(1945): *The Psychological Frontiers of Society* (New York).

Kluckhorn, C. (1936): 'Some reflections on the method and theory of the *Kulturkreislehre*', *Amer. Anthrop.*, vol. 38, pp. 157–96.

Larock, V. (1932): *Essai sur la valeur sacrée et la valeur sociale des noms de personnes dans les sociétés inférieures* (Paris).

Leach, E. R. (1945): 'Jinghpaw kinship terminology: an experiment in ethnographic algebra', *J. Royal Anthrop. Inst.*, vol. 75, pp. 59–72.

—(1951): 'The structural implications of matrilateral cross-cousin marriage', *J. Royal Anthrop. Inst.*, vol. 81, pp. 23–55.

—(1954): *Political Systems of Highland Burma* (London).

—(1957): 'Aspects of bridewealth and marriage stability among the Kachin and Lakher', *Man*, vol. lvii, no. 59, pp. 50–5.

—(1962): 'On certain unconsidered aspects of double descent systems', *Man*, vol. lxii, no. 214, pp. 130–4.

Lévi-Strauss, C. (1949): *Les Structures élémentaires de la parenté* (Paris).

—(1958): *Anthropologie structurale* (Paris).

—(1962a): *Le Totémisme aujourd'hui* (Paris).

—(1962b): *La Pensée sauvage* (Paris).

—(1964): *Le Cru et le cuit* (Paris).

Lewis, C. S. (1936): *The Allegory of Love. A Study in Medieval Tradition* (Oxford).

—(1964): *The Discarded Image. An Introduction to Medieval and Renaissance Literature* (Cambridge).

McIlwain, C. H. (1932): *The Growth of Political Thought in the West: from the Greeks to the End of the Middle Ages* (New York).

MacNeill, J. (1911): 'Early Irish population-groups: their nomenclature, classification, and chronology', *Proc. R. Irish Acad.*, vol. xxix, section C, no. 4, pp. 59–114.

Mauss, M. (1929): 'L'âme et le prénom', *Bull. de la Societé Française de Philosophie*, vol. xxix, pp. 124–7.

—(1947): *Manuel d'ethnographie* (Paris).

—(1968): *Sociologie et anthropologie*, with introduction by C. Lévi-Strauss: 4th ed. Paris, 1968 (1st ed. 1950).

Miller, E. J. (1952): 'Village structure in north Kerala', *Econ. Weekly* (Bombay), vol. 4, pp. 159–64.

—(1954): 'Caste and territory in Malabar', *Amer. Anthrop.*, vol. 56, pp. 410–20.

Myres, J. L. (1943): *Mediterranean Culture*. Frazer Lecture for 1943 (Cambridge), pp. 1–52.

Onians, R. B. (1951): *The Origins of European Thought about the Body, the Mind, the Soul, the World, Time, and Fate* (Cambridge).

Opie, I. and P. (1967): *The Lore and Language of Schoolchildren* (Oxford), 1st ed. 1959.

Palmer, L. R. (1950): 'The Indo-European origins of Greek justice', *Transact. Philolog. Soc.* (London), pp. 149–68.

—(1956): 'The concept of social obligation in Indo-European: a study in structural semantics', *Collection Latomus* (Brussels), vol. xxiii, pp. 258–69.

—(1963): *The Interpretation of Mycenaean Greek Texts* (Oxford).

Piaget, J. (1923): *Le Langage et la pensée chez l'enfant* (Neuchâtel), 5th ed. 1962.

—(1924): *Le Jugement et le raisonnement chez l'enfant* (Neuchâtel), 5th ed. 1963.

—(1936): *La Naissance de l'intelligence chez l'enfant* (Neuchâtel), 5th ed. 1966.

—(1937): *La Construction du réel chez l'enfant* (Neuchâtel), 3rd ed. 1963.

—(1945): *La Formation du symbole chez l'enfant* (Neuchâtel), 3rd ed. 1964.

—(1946): *La Développement de la notion de temps chez l'enfant* (Paris).

—(1964): 'Le développement mental de l'enfant', in *Six Études de psychologie* (Geneva), pp. 7–86.

Pirenne, H. (1929): *Histoire de Belgique. I. Des origines au commencement du xiv<sup>e</sup> Siècle* (Brussels).

—(1970): *Mahomet et Charlemagne* (Paris): 1st ed. Brussels, 1936.

Radcliffe-Brown, A. R. (1950): Introduction to *African Systems of Kinship and Marriage*, ed. Radcliffe-Brown and Daryll Forde (Oxford), pp. 1–85.

—(1952): *Structure and Function in Primitive Society* (London).

Ritter, H. (1948): 'Irrational solidarity groups. A socio-psychological study in connection with Ibn Khaldûn', *Oriens* (Leiden), vol. 1, pp. 1–44.

Rosenthal, E. I. J. (1962): *Political Thought in Medieval Islam* (Cambridge).

Rosenthal, F. (1958): *The Muqaddimah: an Introduction to History, by Ibn Khaldûn*, translated from the Arabic by Franz Rosenthal, with introduction (3 vols., New York).

Rostovsteff, M. (1957): *The Social and Economic History of the Roman Empire*, 2nd ed. revised by P. M. Frazer (Oxford): 1st ed. 1926.

Schurtz, H. (1902): *Altersklassen und Männerbünde* (Berlin).

Sébillot, P. (1901): *Le Folk-lore des pêcheurs* (Paris).

Southern, R.W. (1965): 'Medieval humanism—II: scientific humanism', *The Listener*, vol. lxxiv, pp. 377–8.

—(1967): *The Making of the Middle Ages* (London), 1st ed. 1953.

Stenton, D. M. (1965): *English Society in the Early Middle Ages* (4th ed. London, 1965), 1st ed. 1951.

Stenton, F. M. (1924): *Introduction to the Survey of English Place-Names*, ed. Mawer, A. and Stenton, F. M. (Cambridge), vol. I, part 1, chs. iii and ix.

Stephenson, C. (1941): 'The origin and significance of feudalism', *Amer. Hist. Rev.*, vol. 46, pp. 788–812.

Strayer, J. R. (1965): 'Feudalism in Western Europe', in *Feudalism in History*, ed. Coulborn, R. (Hamden, Conn.), pp. 15–25.

van Gennep, A. (1908): 'Essai d'une théorie des langues spéciales', *Revue des études ethnographiques et sociologiques* (Paris), pp. 327–37.

—(1909): *Les Rites de passage* (Paris).

Watkins, C. (1966): 'Italo-Celtic revisited', in *Ancient Indo-European Dialects*, ed. Birnbaum and Puhvel (Berkeley and Los Angeles), pp. 29–50.

White, L. (1962): *Medieval Technology and Social Change* (Oxford).

Willetts, R. F. (1965): *Ancient Crete: a Social History* (London).

Winch, P. (1963): *The Idea of a Social Science and its Relation to Philosophy* (London).

---

## WORKS ON THE ETHNOGRAPHY OF THE SOUTHERN SUDAN, WEST AFRICA, AND RELATED AREAS

Bascom, W. R. (1942): 'The principle of seniority in the social structure of the Yoruba', *Amer. Anthrop.*, vol. 44, pp. 37–46.

Baumann, H. (1928): 'The division of work according to sex in African hoe-culture', *Mem. Internat. Inst. African Languages and Cultures*, no. 5, pp. 289–319.

—(1957): *Les Peuples et les civilisations de l'Afrique*, by Baumann, H. and Westermann, D. (French translation by Homburger, L., Paris, 1957), part I, pp. 13–438.

Beattie, J. H. M. (1964a): 'Bunyoro: an African feudality?', *J. African History*, vol. v, pp. 25–36.

—(1964b): *Other Cultures* (London).

Brown, P. (1951): 'Patterns of authority in West Africa', *Africa*, vol. xxi, pp. 261–78.

Chowdhury, K. A. and Buth, G. M. (1970): '4500-year-old seeds suggest that true cotton is indigenous to Nubia', *Nature*, vol. 227, pp. 85–6.

de Jonghe, E. (1907): 'Les sociétés secrètes au Bas-Congo', extrait de la *Revue des Questions scientifiques* (Brussels), pp. 1–74.

—(1923): 'Les sociétés secrètes en Afrique', *Congo*, 4ᵉ année, no. 2, pp. 388–403.

de Schlippe, P. (1956): *Shifting Cultivation in Africa: the Zande System of Agriculture* (London).

Dieterlen, G. (1955): 'Mythe et organisation sociale au Soudan français', *J. de la Société des Africanistes*, tome xxv, pp. 39–76.

—(1959): 'Mythe et organisation sociale en Afrique occidentale', *J. de la Société des Africanistes*, tome xxix, pp. 119–38.

Drachoussoff, V. (1947): 'Essai sur l'agriculture indigène au Bas-Congo', *Bull. Agricole du Congo Belge*, vol. 38, no. 3, pp. 471–582.

Evans-Pritchard, E. E. (1931): 'Mani, a Zande secret society', *Sudan Notes and Records*, vol. xiv, pp. 105–48.

—(1933): 'The Nuer, tribe and clan: i–iv', *Sudan Notes and Records*, vol. xvi, pp. 1–53.

—(1934): 'The Nuer, tribe and clan: v–vii', *Sudan Notes and Records*, vol. xvii, pp. 1–57.

—(1935): 'The Nuer, tribe and clan: vii–ix', *Sudan Notes and Records*, vol. xviii, pp. 37–87.

—(1936a): 'The Nuer, age-sets: x–xi', *Sudan Notes and Records*, vol. xix, pp. 233–69.

—(1936b): 'Daily life of the Nuer in dry season camps', in *Custom is King: Essays Presented to R. R. Marett* (London), pp. 291–9.

—(1937): 'Economic Life of the Nuer: I', *Sudan Notes and Records*, vol. xx, pp. 209–45.

—(1938): 'Economic Life of the Nuer: II', *Sudan Notes and Records*, vol. xxi, pp. 31–77.

—(1939): 'Nuer time-reckoning', *Africa*, vol. xii, pp. 189–216.

—(1940a): *The Nuer. A Description of the Modes of Livelihood and Political Institutions of a Nilotic People* (Oxford).

—(1940b): 'The Nuer of the Southern Sudan', in *African Political Systems*, ed. Fortes and Evans-Pritchard (Oxford), pp. 272–96.

—(1940c): *The Political System of the Anuak* (London).

—(1940d): 'The political structure of the Nandi-speaking peoples of Kenya', *Africa*, vol. xiii, pp. 250–67.

—(1944a): 'Cyrenaican tribes: Habitat and way of life', *Handbook on Cyrenaica* (Benghazi), part vii, pp. 1–12.

—(1944b): 'Tribes and their divisions', *Handbook on Cyrenaica* (Benghazi), part viii, pp. 1–17.

—(1945): 'Some aspects of marriage and the family among the Nuer', *Rhodes-Livingstone Papers*, no. 11.

—(1946): 'Nuer bridewealth', *Africa*, vol. xvi, pp. 247–57.

—(1947a): 'A note on courtship among the Nuer', *Sudan Notes and Records*, vol. xxviii, pp. 115–26.

—(1947b): 'Further observations on the political system of the Anuak', *Sudan Notes and Records*, vol. xxviii, pp. 62–97.

—(1948a): 'Nuer marriage ceremonies', *Africa*, vol. xviii, pp. 29–40.

—(1948b): 'Nuer modes of address', *Uganda Journal*, vol. 12, pp. 166–71.

—(1949a): 'Burial and mortuary rites of the Nuer', *African Affairs*, vol. 48, pp. 56–63.

—(1949b): 'Nuer curses and ghostly vengeance', *Africa*, vol. xix, pp. 288–92.

—(1949c): 'Nuer rules of exogamy and incest', in *Social Structure: Studies Presented to A. R. Radcliffe-Brown* (Oxford), pp. 85–103.

—(1950): 'Kinship and the local community among the Nuer', in *African Systems of Kinship and Marriage*, ed. Radcliffe-Brown and Daryll Forde (Oxford), pp. 360–91.

—(1951): *Kinship and Marriage among the Nuer* (Oxford).

—(1953): 'The Nuer concept of spirit in its relation to the social order', *Amer. Anthrop.*, vol. 55, pp. 201–14.

—(1956): *Nuer Religion* (Oxford).

—(1960): 'The Organization of a Zande kingdom', *Cahiers d'études africaines*, vol. i, no. 4, pp. 5–37.

Firth, R. (1951): Review of *The Web of Kinship among the Tallensi* (by Fortes, M.), *Africa*, vol. xxi, pp. 155–9.

Forde, C. Daryll (1934): *Habitat, Economy and Society: a Geographical Introduction to Ethnology* (London).

—(1937): 'Land and labour in a Cross River village, southern Nigeria', *Geographical Journal*, vol. xc, pp. 24–47.

—(1938): 'Fission and accretion in the patrilineal clans of a semi-Bantu community in southern Nigeria', *J. Royal Anthrop. Inst.*, vol. lxviii, pp. 311–38.

—(1939a): 'Government in Umor', *Africa*, vol. xii, pp. 129–61.

—(1939b): 'Kinship in Umor', *Amer. Anthrop.*, vol. 41, pp. 523–53.

—(1941): *Marriage and the Family among the Yakö* (London).

—(1946): 'A village economy in the eastern palm belt', in *The Native Economies of Nigeria*, ed. Daryll Forde and Scott (London), pp. 44–64.

—(1947): 'The anthropological approach in social science', *Advancement of Science*, vol. iv, no. 15, pp. 213–24.

—(1948): 'The integration of anthropological studies', *J. Royal Anthrop. Inst.*, vol. lxxviii, pp. 1–10.

—(1949): 'Integrative aspects of Yakö first fruit rituals', *J. Royal Anthrop. Inst.*, vol. lxxix, pp. 1–10.

—(1950a): 'Ward organisation among the Yakö', *Africa*, vol. xx, pp. 267–89.

—(1950b): 'Double descent among the Yakö', in *African Systems of Kinship and Marriage*, ed. Radcliffe-Brown and Daryll Forde (Oxford), pp. 285–332.

—(1953): 'The cultural map of West Africa: successive adaptations to tropical forests and grasslands', *Transact. New York Acad. Sciences*, series ii, vol. 15, pp. 206–19.

—(1958a): *The Context of Belief* (Liverpool).

—(1958b): 'Spirits, witches and sorcerers in the supernatural economy of the Yakö', *J. Royal Anthrop. Inst.*, vol. lxxxviii, pp. 165–78.

—(1961): 'The governmental rôles of associations among the Yakö', *Africa*, vol. xxxi, pp. 309–22.

—(1962): 'Death and succession: an analysis of Yakö mortuary ritual', in *Essays on the Ritual of Social Relations*, ed. Gluckman, M. (Manchester), pp. 89–123.

—(1963a): 'Rôle des sociétés dans le cérémonial funéraire des Yakö', *Cahiers d'études africaines*, vol. iii, no. 11, pp. 307–17.

—(1963b): 'Une analyse sociologique des formalités matrimoniales chez les Yakö', *Cahiers d'études africaines*, vol. iii, no. 12, pp. 447–57.

—(1964): *Yakö Studies* (Oxford).

Forde, C., Daryll and Jones, G. I. (1950): *The Ibo and Ibibio-speaking Peoples of South-eastern Nigeria*. Ethnographic Survey of Africa, ed. Daryll Forde (London).

—(1956): *Efik Traders of Old Calabar* (Oxford).

Fortes, M. and S. L. (1936a): 'Food in the domestic economy of the Tallensi', *Africa*, vol. ix, pp. 237–76.

Fortes, M. (1936b): 'Ritual festivals and social cohesion in the hinterland of the Gold Coast', *Amer. Anthrop.*, vol. 38, pp. 590–604.

—(1936c): 'Kinship, incest and exogamy of the northern territories of the Gold Coast', in *Custom is King: Essays Presented to R. R. Marett* (London), pp. 239–56.

—(1937a): 'Communal fishing and fishing magic in the northern territories of the Gold Coast', *J. Royal Anthrop. Inst.*, vol. lxvii, pp. 131–42.

—(1937b): 'Marriage Law among the Tallensi', Government Printing Dept., Accra, pp. 1–23.

—(1938): 'Social and psychological aspects of education in Taleland', Supplement to *Africa*, vol. xi, pp. 1–64.

—(1940): 'Political system of the Tallensi', in *African Political Systems*, ed. Fortes and Evans-Pritchard (Oxford), pp. 237–71.

—(1944): 'The significance of descent in Tale social structure', *Africa*, vol. xv, pp. 362–85.

—(1945): *The Dynamics of Clanship among the Tallensi* (Oxford).

—(1949): *The Web of Kinship among the Tallensi* (Oxford).

—(1953a): 'The structure of unilineal descent groups', *Amer. Anthrop.*, vol. 55, pp. 17–41.

—(1953b): 'Analysis and description in social anthropology', *Advancement of Science*, vol. x, no. 38, pp. 190–201.

—(1959a): *Oedipus and Job in West African Religion* (Cambridge).

—(1959b): 'Descent, filiation, and affinity', *Man*, vol. lix, no. 309, pp. 193–7: no. 331, pp. 206–12.

—(1961): 'Pietas in ancestor worship', *J. Royal Anthrop. Inst.*, vol. 91, pp. 166–91.

—(1963): 'Ritual and office in tribal society', in *Essays on the Ritual of Social Relations*, ed. Gluckman, M. (Manchester), pp. 53–88.

Fortes, M. and Mayer, D. Y. (1966): 'Psychosis and social change among the Tallensi of northern Ghana', *Cahiers d'études africaines*, vol. vi, no. 21, pp. 5–40.

Goody, J. (1963): 'Feudalism in Africa', *J. African History*, vol. iv, pp. 1–17.

Hair, P. E. H. (1967a): 'Ethnolinguistic continuity on the Guinea Coast', *J. African History*, vol. viii, pp. 247–68.

—(1967b): 'An Ethnolinguistic inventory of the Upper Guinea Coast before 1700', *African Language Review*, vol. 6, pp. 32–70.

—(1968): 'An ethnolinguistic inventory of the Lower Guinea Coast before 1700: Part I', *African Language Review*, vol. 7, pp. 47–73.

—(1970): Personal communication.

Harley, G. W. (1941a): 'Notes on the Poro in Liberia', *Papers of Peabody Museum* (Cambridge, Mass.), vol. xix, no. 2, pp. 1–39, with plates.

—(1941b): *Native African Medicine* (Cambridge, Mass.).

—(1950): 'Masks as agents of social control in north-east Liberia', *Papers of Peabody Museum* (Cambridge, Mass.), vol. xxxii, no. 2, pp. 1–45, with plates.

Harris, R. (1962a): 'The influence of ecological factors and external relations on the Mbembe tribes of south-east Nigeria', *Africa*, vol. xxxii, pp. 38–52.

—(1962b): 'The political significance of double unilineal descent', *J. Royal Anthrop. Inst.*, vol. 92, pp. 86–101.

—(1965): *The Political Organization of the Mbembe, Nigeria* (London).

Harris, W. T. (1950): 'The idea of God among the Mende', in *African Ideas of God*, ed. Edwin Smith (London), pp. 277–97.

Harris, W. T. and Sawyerr, H. (1968): *The Springs of Mende Belief and Conduct* (Oxford).

Hofstra, S. (1937a): 'Personality and differentiation in the political life of the Mende', *Africa*, vol. x, pp. 436–57.

—(1937b): 'The social significance of the oil palm in the life of the Mendi', *Internat. Archiv. für Ethnographie* (Leiden), band xxxiv, pp. 105–18.

—(1941): 'The ancestral spirits of the Mendi', ibid., band xxxix, pp. 177–96.

—(1942): 'The belief among the Mendi in non-ancestral spirits', ibid., band xl, pp. 175–82.

—(1963): Personal communication.

Jackson, H. C. (1923): 'Nuer of the Upper Nile Province', *Sudan Notes and Records*, vol. vi, pp. 59–106, 123–89.

Jones, G. I. (1961): 'Ecology and social structure among the north-eastern Ibo', *Africa*, vol. xxxi, pp. 117–34.

—(1961): 'Ibo age organisation with special reference to the Cross River and north-eastern Ibo', *J. Royal Anthrop. Inst.*, vol. 92, pp. 191–211.

Kup, A. P. (1961): *A History of Sierra Leone, 1400–1787* (Cambridge).

Leuzinger, E. (1963): *African Sculpture: A Descriptive Catalogue* (Rietberg Museum, Zurich).

Lewis, I. M. (1965): 'Problems in the comparative study of unilineal descent', in *The Relevance of Models for Social Anthropology* (A.S.A. Monographs 1, London), pp. 87–112.

Lienhardt, G. (1957): 'Anuak village headmen', *Africa*, vol. xxvii, pp. 341–54.

—(1958a): 'Anuak village headmen', *Africa*, vol. xxviii, pp. 23–35.

—(1958b): 'The Western Dinka', in *Tribes without Rulers: Studies in African Segmentary Systems*, ed. Middleton, J. and Tait, D. (London), pp. 97–135.

—(1961): *Divinity and Experience: the Religion of the Dinka* (Oxford).

Little, K. L. (1947): 'Mende political institutions in transition', *Africa*, vol. xvii, pp. 8–23.

—(1948a): 'Land and labour among the Mende', *African Affairs*, vol. 47, pp. 23–31.

—(1948b): 'The Mende farming household', *Sociological Review*, vol. xl, pp. 37–56.

—(1948c): 'The Poro society as an arbiter of culture', *African Studies*, vol. 7, pp. 1–15.

—(1948d): 'The function of "Medicine" in Mende society', *Man*, vol. xlviii, no. 142, pp. 127–30.

—(1949): 'The rôle of the secret society in cultural specialisation', *Amer. Anthrop.*, vol. 51, pp. 199–212.

—(1951a): *The Mende of Sierra Leone* (London).

—(1951b): 'The Mende rice farm and its cost', *Zaïre* (Brussels), vol. v, pp. 227–73, 371–89.

—(1953): 'The study of "social change" in British West Africa', *Africa*, vol. xxiii, pp. 274–83.

—(1954): 'The Mende in Sierra Leone', in *African Worlds*, ed. Daryll Forde (Oxford), pp. 111–37.

—(1965): 'The political function of the Poro: Part I', *Africa*, vol. xxxv, pp. 349–65.

—(1966): 'The political function of the Poro: Part II', *Africa*, vol. xxxvi, pp. 62–72.

Malcolm, J. M. (1939): 'Mende warfare', *Sierra Leone Studies*, vol. xxi, pp. 47–52.

Maquet, J. J. (1961): 'Une hypothèse pour l'étude des féodalités africaines', *Cahiers d'études africaines*, vol. ii, no. 6, pp. 292–314.

Migeod, F. W. H. (1916a): 'The Poro society: the building of the Poro house', *Man*, vol. xvi, no. 61, pp. 102–8.

—(1916b): 'Mende songs', *Man*, vol. xvi, no. 112, pp. 184–91.

Middleton, J. (1958): 'The political system of the Lugbara of the Nile-Congo Divide', in *Tribes without Rulers: Studies in African Political Systems*, ed. Middleton, J. and Tait, D. (London), pp. 203–29.

Morton-Williams, P. (1960): 'The Yoruba Ogboni cult in Oyo', *Africa*, vol. xxx, pp. 362–74.

Paulme, D. (1956): 'Structures sociales en pays Baga', *Bull. de l'Inst. franç. d'Afrique noire,* tome 18, sér. B, pp. 98–116.

Peristiany, J. G. (1951): 'The age-set system of the pastoral Pokot', *Africa,* vol. xxi, pp. 188–206, 279–302.

—(1954): 'Pokot sanctions and structure', *Africa,* vol. xxiv, pp. 17–25.

Rattray, R. S. (1932): *The Tribes of the Ashanti Hinterland* (2 vols., Oxford).

—(1936): 'Totemism and blood groups in West Africa', in *Custom is King: Essays presented to R. R. Marett* (London), pp. 19–32.

Read, M. (1959): *Children of their Fathers: Growing up among the Ngoni of Nyasaland* (London).

Roberts, D. F. (1956): 'Demography of a Dinka village', *Human Biology,* vol. 28, pp. 323–49.

Rodney, W. (1967): 'A reconsideration of the Mane invasions of Sierra Leone', *J. African History,* vol. viii, pp. 219–46.

Samuel, P. (1950): 'Agriculture équatoriale bantou et agriculture européenne', *Bull. Agricole du Congo Belge,* vol. 41, no. 3, pp. 579–660.

Schwab, G. and Harley, G. W. (1947): *Tribes of the Liberian Hinterland.* Papers of the Peabody Museum (Cambridge, Mass.), vol. xxxi, pp. 1–526, with plates.

Seligman, C. G. (1934): *Egypt and Negro Africa: a Study in Divine Kingship.* Frazer Lecture for 1933 (London).

Seligman, C. G. and B. Z. (1932): *Pagan Tribes of the Nilotic Sudan* (London).

Smith, E. W. (1934): 'Indigenous education in Africa', in *Essays Presented to C. G. Seligman* (London), pp. 319–34.

Thomas, N. W. (1920): 'Secret societies (African)', in Hastings' *Encyclopedia of Religion and Ethics,* vol. xi, pp. 287–303.

Udo Ema, A. J. (1938): 'The Ekpe Society', *Nigeria,* no. 16, pp. 314–16.

Wallis, C. B. (1905): 'The Poro of the Mendi', *J. African Society,* vol. 4, pp. 183–9.

Worsley, P. M. (1956): 'The kinship system of the Tallensi: a revaluation', *J. Royal Anthrop. Inst.,* vol. 86, pp. 37–74.

Wylie, K. C. (1969): 'Innovation and change in Mende chieftaincy, 1880–1896', *J. African History,* vol. x, pp. 295–308.

---

## WORKS ON THE ETHNOGRAPHY OF NORTH-WESTERN MELANESIA, THE NEW HEBRIDES AND BANKS ISLANDS, AND RELATED AREAS

Allen, M. (1964): 'Kinship terminology and marriage in Vanua Lava and East Aoba', *J. Polynesian Soc.,* vol. 73, pp. 315–23.

Austen, L. (1938): 'Seasonal gardening calendar of Kiriwina, Trobriand Islands', *Oceania,* vol. xi, pp. 237–53.

—(1946): 'Cultural changes in Kiriwina', *Oceania,* vol. xvi, pp. 15–60.

Baker, J. R. (1928): 'Notes on New Hebrides customs, with special reference to the intersex pig', *Man*, vol. 28, no. 81, pp. 113–18.

—(1929): 'The northern New Hebrides', *Geographical J.*, vol. 73, pp. 305–25.

Baker, J. R. and Harrisson, T. H. (1936): 'The seasons in a tropical rain-forest (New Hebrides)', *J. Linnaean Soc. London (Zoology)*, vol. 39, pp. 443–63.

Barrau, J. (1958): 'Subsistence agriculture in Melanesia', *Bull. Bernice P. Bishop Museum* (Honolulu), no. 219, pp. 1–111.

Bartlett, H. H. (1929): 'Color nomenclature in Batak and Malay', *Papers Michigan Acad. Science, Arts and Letters*, vol. 10, pp. 1–52.

Bateson, G. (1932): 'Social structure of the Iatmül people of the Sepik river', *Oceania*, vol. ii, pp. 245–91, 401–53.

Burkill, I. H. (1951): 'The rise and decline of the greater yam in the service of man', *Advancement of Science*, vol. vii, no. 28, pp. 443–8.

—(1953): 'Habits of man and the origins of the cultivated plants of the Old World', *Proc. Linnaean Soc. London*, Session 164, part 1, pp. 12–42.

Burkill, I. H. *et al.* (1935): *A Dictionary of the Economic Products of the Malay Peninsula* (2 vols., London).

Capell, A. (1938): 'The stratification of after-world beliefs in the New Hebrides', *Folk-Lore*, vol. 49, pp. 51–85.

—(1939): 'The word *Mana*: a linguistic study', *Oceania*, vol. ix, pp. 89–96.

—(1949): 'The concept of ownership in the languages of Australia and the Pacific', *Southwestern J. Anthrop.*, vol. 5, pp. 169–89.

—(1960): 'Language and world view in the Northern Kimberley, Western Australia', *Southwestern J. Anthrop.*, vol. 16, pp. 1–14.

Codrington, R. H. (1881): 'Religious beliefs and practices in Melanesia' *J. Anthrop. Inst.*, vol. x, pp. 261–316.

—(1885): *The Melanesian Languages* (Oxford).

—(1891): *The Melanesians: Studies in their Anthropology and Folk-Lore* (Oxford).

Codrington, R. H. and Palmer, J. (1896): *A Dictionary of the Language of Mota* (London).

Conklin, H. C. (1955): 'Hanunóo color categories', *Southwestern J. Anthrop.*, vol. 11, pp. 339–44.

Coote, W. (1883): *The Western Pacific, being a Description of the Groups of Islands to the North and East of the Australian Continent* (London).

Elkin, A. P. (1932): 'The *Kopara*: the settlement of grievances', *Oceania*, vol. ii, pp. 191–8.

—(1938): 'The nature of Australian languages', *Oceania*, vol. viii, pp. 127–69.

—(1964): *The Australian Aborigines*: 3rd ed. (New York: American Museum of Natural History).

Firth, R. (1936): *We, the Tikopia* (London).

—(1940): 'The analysis of Mana: an empirical approach', *J. Polynesian Soc.*, vol. 49, pp. 483–510.

—(1949): 'Authority and public opinion in Tikopia', in *Social Structure: Studies Presented to A. R. Radcliffe-Brown*, ed. Fortes, M. (Oxford), pp. 168–88.

Firth, R. and Davidson, J. W. (1944): *Pacific Islands*, vol. III: *Western Pacific*. Geographical Handbook Series, Naval Intelligence Division (London), chs. xii-xiv (New Hebrides and Banks Islands), pp. 511–606.

Fortune, R. F. (1932): *Sorcerers of Dobu* (London).

—(1934): 'A note on some forms of kinship structure', *Oceania*, vol. iv, pp. 1–9.

Fox, C. E. (1947): 'Phonetic laws in Melanesian languages', *J. Polynesian Soc.*, vol. 56, pp. 58–118.

—(1948a): 'Passives in Oceanic languages', *J. Polynesian Soc.*, vol. 57, pp. 2–29.

—(1948b): 'Prefixes and their functions in Oceanic languages', *J. Polynesian Soc.*, vol. 57, pp. 227–55.

Giddens, A. (1964): 'Suicide, attempted suicide, and the suicidal threat', *Man*, vol. 64, no. 136, pp. 115–16.

Gluckman, M. (1963): 'Gossip and scandal', *Current Anthropology*, vol. 4, pp. 307–16.

Guiart, J. (1963): *Structure de la Chefferie en Mélanésie du Sud*. Travaux et Mémoires de l'Institut d'Ethnologie (Paris), no. lxvi, pp. 1–688.

Hogbin, H. I. (1936): 'Mana', *Oceania*, vol. vi, pp. 241–74.

Hornell, J. (1943): 'Outrigger devices: distribution and origin', *J. Polynesian Soc.*, vol. 52, pp. 91–100.

Ivens, W. G. (1927): *Melanesians of the South-East Solomon Islands* (London).

—(1930): 'A note on "A-mbat"', *Man*, vol. 30, no. 36, pp. 49–51.

—(1931): 'The place of *vui* and *tamate* in the religion of Mota', *J. Royal Anthrop. Inst.*, vol. 61, pp. 157–66.

—(1934): 'The diversity of culture in Melanesia', *J. Royal Anthrop. Inst.*, vol. 64, pp. 45–56.

Keesing, R. M. (1964): 'Mota kinship terminology and marriage: a re-examination', *J. Polynesian Soc.*, vol. 73, pp. 294–301.

Lane, R. B. (1961): 'A reconsideration of Malayo-Polynesian social organisation', *Amer. Anthrop.*, vol. 63, pp. 711–20.

Layard, J. W. (1930): 'Malekula: flying tricksters, ghosts, gods, and epileptics', *J. Royal Anthrop. Inst.*, vol. 60, pp. 501–24.

—(1934): 'The Journey of the Dead from the small islands of north-eastern Malekula', in *Essays Presented to C. G. Seligman* (London), pp. 113–42.

—(1942): *Stone Men of Malekula* (London).

Leach, E. R. (1950): 'Primitive calendars', *Oceania*, vol. xx, pp. 245–62.

—(1958): 'Concerning Trobriand clans and the kinship category *tabu*', in *The Developmental Cycle in Domestic Groups* (ed. Goody, J., Cambridge), pp. 120–45.

—(1961): 'Two essays concerning the symbolic representation of time', in *Re-thinking Anthropology* (London), pp. 124–36.

—(1964): 'Anthropological aspects of language: animal categories and verbal abuse', in *New Directions in the Study of Language* (ed. Lenneberg, E. H., Boston), pp. 23–63.

Lee, D. D. (1940): 'A primitive system of values', *Philosophy of Science*, vol. 7, pp. 355–78.

Lévy-Bruhl, L. (1910): 'La mentalité des primitifs dans ses rapports avec les langues qu'ils parlent', in *Les Fonctions mentales dans les sociétés inférieures* (Paris, 9th ed. 1951), ch. iv, pp. 151–203.

—(1935): 'Le temps et l'espace du monde mythique', *Scientia* (Bologna), vol. lvii, pp. 139–49.

Lounsbury, F. G. (1965): 'Another view of the Trobriand kinship categories', *Amer. Anthrop.*, vol. 67, pp. 142–85.

Malinowski, B. (1916): 'Baloma: the spirits of the dead in the Trobriand Islands', *J. Royal Anthrop. Inst.*, vol. 46, pp. 353–430.

—(1918): 'Fishing in the Trobriand Islands', *Man*, vol. 18, no. 53, pp. 87–92.

—(1920a): 'War and weapons among the natives of the Trobriand Islands', *Man*, vol. 20, no. 5, pp. 10–12.

—(1920b): 'Kula: the circulatory exchange of valuables in the archipelagoes of eastern New Guinea', *Man*, vol. 20, no. 51, pp. 97–105.

—(1920c): 'Classificatory particles in the language of Kiriwina', *Bull. School Oriental Studies* (London), vol. I, part iv, pp. 33–78.

—(1922): *Argonauts of the Western Pacific* (London).

—(1923): 'The problem of meaning in primitive languages', Supplement I to *The Meaning of Meaning* (by Ogden, C. K. and Richards, I. A., London), pp. 450–510.

—(1926a): 'Myth in primitive psychology'. Frazer Lecture for 1925.

—(1926b): *Crime and Custom in Savage Society* (London).

—(1927a): *Sex and Repression in Savage Society* (London).

—(1927b): 'Lunar and seasonal calendar in the Trobriands', *J. Royal Anthrop. Inst.*, vol. 57, pp. 203–15.

—(1932): *Sexual Life of Savages in North-Western Melanesia*, 3rd ed. (London).

—(1935): *Coral Gardens and their Magic* (2 vols., London).

Man, E. H. (1882): 'On Andamanese and Nicobarese objects', *J. Anthrop. Inst.*, vol. xi, pp. 268–94.

—(1883): 'On the aboriginal inhabitants of the Andaman Islands', *J. Anthrop. Inst.*, vol. xii, pp. 69–175, 327–434.

Mauss, M. (1924): *Essai sur le don: forme et raison de l'échange dans les sociétés archaïques. L'Année sociologique*, tome i (nouvelle série), pp. 30–186: reprinted in Mauss (1968) pp. 143–279.

Meillet, A. (1906): 'Comment les mots changent de sens', *L'Année sociologique*, tome ix, pp. 1–38.

Needham, R. (1958): 'The formal analysis of prescriptive patrilateral cross-cousin marriage', *Southwestern J. Anthrop.*, vol. 14, pp. 199–219.

—(1960): 'Lineal equations in a two-section system: a problem in the social structure of Mota (Banks Island)', *J. Polynesian Soc.*, vol. 69, pp. 23–30.

—(1964): 'The Mota problem and its lessons', *J. Polynesian Soc.*, vol. 73, pp. 302–14.

Powell, H. A. (1952): 'Cricket in Kiriwina', *The Listener*, vol. xlviii, pp. 384–5.

—(1957): 'An analysis of present-day social structure in the Trobriand Islands', Ph.D. thesis (unpublished), London University.

—(1960): 'Competitive leadership in Trobriand political organisation', *J. Royal Anthrop. Inst.*, vol. 90, pp. 118–45.

—(1968): Personal communication.

—(1969a): 'Genealogy, residence and kinship in Kiriwina', *Man, J. Royal Anthrop. Inst.*, new series, vol. 4, no. 2, pp. 177–202.

—(1969b): 'Territory, hierarchy and kinship in Kiriwina', *Man J. Royal Anthrop. Inst.*, new series, vol. 4, no. 4, pp. 580–604.

Radcliffe-Brown, A. R. (1913): 'Three tribes of Western Australia', *J. Royal Anthrop. Inst.*, vol. 16, pp. 143–94.

—(1918): 'Notes on the social organisation of Australian tribes', *J. Royal Anthrop. Inst.*, vol. 21, pp. 222–53.

—(1922): *The Andaman Islanders* (Cambridge).

—(1931): 'The social organisation of Australian tribes', *Oceania*, vol. i, pp. 34–63, 206–46, 322–41, 426–56.

Rawcliffe, D. A. (1967): Personal communication.

Rivers, W. H. R. (1914): *The History of Melanesian Society* (2 vols., Cambridge).

—(1918): 'Dreams and primitive culture', reprinted from *Bull. John Rylands Library* (Manchester), vol. 4, pp. 1–28.

—(1920): 'The concept of "soul-substance" in New Guinea and Melanesia', *Folk-Lore*, vol. 31, pp. 48–61.

—(1922): 'The symbolism of rebirth', *Folk-Lore*, vol. 33, pp. 14–33.

—(1924): *Social Organization* (London).

—(1926): 'Irrigation and the cultivation of taro', in *Psychology and Ethnology* (London), pp. 262–81.

Romney, A. K. and Epling, P. J. (1958): 'A simplified model of Kariera kinship', *Amer. Anthrop.*, vol. 60, pp. 59–74.

Sauer, C. O. (1952): *Agricultural Origins and Dispersals*. Amer. Geograph. Soc., Bowman Memorial Lectures, series 2, pp. 1–110.

Seligman, C. G. (1910): *The Melanesians of British New Guinea* (Cambridge).

Sommerfelt, A. (1938): *La Langue et la société: caractères sociaux d'une langue de type archaïque* (Oslo).

—(1944): 'Is there a fundamental mental difference between primitive man and the civilised European?', 26th Earl Grey Memorial Lecture, Newcastle-upon-Tyne.

Spencer, J. E. and Hale, G. A. (1961): 'The origin, nature and distribution of agricultural terracing', *Pacific Viewpoint* (Wellington, N.Z.), vol. 2, pp. 1–40.

Tambiah, S. J. (1968): 'The magical power of words', *Man, J. Royal Anthrop. Inst.*, vol. 3, no. 2, pp. 175–208.

Warner, W. Lloyd (1964): *A Black Civilization: a Study of an Australian Tribe*, 1st ed. New York, 1937: revised ed. 1964.

Webb, A. S. (1937): 'The people of Aoba, New Hebrides', *Mankind*, vol. 2, no. 4, pp. 73–80.

Wedgwood, C. H. (1927): 'Death and social status in Melanesia', *J. Royal Anthrop. Inst.*, vol. 57, pp. 377–97.

—(1930*a*): 'Some aspects of warfare in Melanesia', *Oceania*, vol. i, pp. 5–33.

—(1930*b*): 'The nature and functions of secret societies', *Oceania*, vol. i, pp. 129–45.

Wedgwood, C. H. and Hogbin, H. I. (1953): 'Local grouping in Melanesia', *Oceania*, vol. xxiii, pp. 241–76.

—(1954): 'Local grouping in Melanesia', *Oceania*, vol. xxiv, pp. 58–76.

N.B. there is also an extensive literature in French, on the northern New Hebrides, by *Pères* Suas, J. B. *et* Tattevin, E., in *Anthropos*, vols. vii, ix, xvi, xvii, xxiii, xxiv, xxvi; and by the latter, in *La Revue des Missions* (3e et 4e année, 1926–7). This I have not had the time to consult.

WORKS ON THE ETHNOGRAPHY OF THE SOUTHWEST, THE GREAT
BASIN, AND RELATED AREAS

Aberle, D. F. (1951): 'The Psychosocial analysis of a Hopi life-history', *Comparative Psychology Monographs* (University of California), vol. 21, no. 1, pp. 1–133.

Aitken, B. (*née* Freire-Marreco, B.) (1930): 'Temperament in native American religion', *J. Royal Anthrop. Inst.*, vol. 60, pp. 363–87.

Anderson, A. (1961): 'Mammals of Mesa Verde National Park, Colorado', *Univ. Kansas Publ., Mus. Nat. Hist.*, vol. 14, no. 3, pp. 29–67.

Bailey, F. L. (1940): 'Navaho foods and cooking methods', *Amer. Anthrop.*, vol. 42, pp. 270–90.

—(1942): 'Navaho motor habits', *Amer. Anthrop.*, vol. 44, pp. 210–34.

Ball S. H. (1941): 'The mining of gems and ornamental stones by American Indians', *Smithsonian Inst., Bureau of Amer. Ethnology*, Bulletin 128, pp. 1–78.

Bannister, B. (1964): 'Tree-ring dating of the archaeological sites in the Chaco Canyon region, New Mexico', *Southwestern Monuments Assoc., Technical Series*, vol. 6, no. 2, pp. 116–214.

Barrett, S. A. (1937): 'An observation of Hopi child burial', *Amer. Anthrop.*, vol. 39, pp. 562–4.

Bartlett, K. (1931): 'Prehistoric pueblo foods', *Museum of Northern Arizona, Museum Notes*, vol. 4, no. 4, pp. 1–4.

—(1964): 'Edible wild plants of Northern Arizona', *Plateau*, vol. 16, pp. 11–17.

Beaglehole, E. and P. (1935): 'Hopi of the Second Mesa', *Memoirs Amer. Anthrop. Assoc.*, no. 44, pp. 1–65.

Beaglehole, E. (1936): 'Hopi hunting and hunting ritual', *Yale Univ. Publications in Anthropology*, no. 4, pp. 1–26.

—(1937): 'Notes on Hopi economic life', *Yale Univ. Publications in Anthropology*, no. 15, pp. 1–88.

Beaglehole, P. (1935): 'Census data from two Hopi villages', *Amer. Anthrop.*, vol. 37, pp. 41–54.

—(1937): 'Foods and their preparation', *Yale Univ. Publications in Anthropology*, no. 15, pp. 60–71.

Benedict, R. (1928): 'Psychological types in the cultures of the Southwest', *Proceedings 23rd Internat. Congress Americanists* (New York), pp. 572–81.

—(1935): *Patterns of Culture* (London).

—(1951): 'Dress', in *Encyclopedia of the Social Sciences*, ed. Seligman, E. R. A. and Johnson, A. (New York), vol. 5, pp. 235–8.

Benson, S. B. (1935): 'A biological reconnaissance of Navajo Mountain, Utah', *Univ. Calif. Publ. Zoology*, vol. 40, no. 14, pp. 439–55.

Bourke, J. G. (1884): *The Snake-Dance of the Moquis of Arizona, being a Narrative of a Journey from Santa Fé, New Mexico, to the Moqui Indians of Arizona* (New York): facsimile edition, Chicago, 1962.

Bradfield, R. M. (1968): 'Hopi names for certain common shrubs, and their ecology', *Plateau*, vol. 41, no. 2, pp. 61–71.

—(1969): 'Soils of the Oraibi valley, Arizona, in relation to plant cover', *Plateau*, vol. 41, no. 3, pp. 133–40.

—(1970): 'Birds of the Hopi region, their Hopi names, and notes on their ecology', unpublished MS.

—(1971): 'The changing pattern of Hopi agriculture', *R. Anthrop. Inst., Occas. Paper,* no. 30, pp. 1–66.

Bunzel, R. L. (1932): 'Introduction to Zuñi ceremonialism', *47th Annual Report, Bureau of American Ethnology* (Washington), pp. 467–544.

Bryan, K. (1929): 'Flood-water farming', *Geographical Review,* vol. xix, pp. 444–56.

Carter, G. F. (1945): 'Plant geography and culture history in the American southwest', *Viking Fund Publications in Anthropology,* no. 5, pp. 1–140.

Chamberlin, R. V. (1908): 'Animal names and anatomical terms of the Goshute Indians', *Proc. Acad. Nat. Sciences of Philadelphia,* vol. lx, pp. 74–103.

—(1911): 'The ethno-botany of the Gosiute Indians of Utah', *Memoirs Amer. Anthrop. Assoc.,* vol. 2, pp. 329–405.

Colton, H. S. (1941), 'Hopi number systems', *Plateau,* vol. 14, no. 2, pp. 33–36.

—(1947a): 'What is a kachina?', *Plateau,* vol. 19, no. 3, pp. 40–7.

—(1947b): 'Hopi deities', *Plateau,* vol. 20, no. 1, pp. 10–16.

Coville, F. V. (1892): 'The Panamint Indians of California', *Amer. Anthrop.,* vol. v (old series), pp. 351–61.

Curtis, E. S. (1922): *The North American Indian:* vol. xii. *The Hopi.*

Cushing, F. H. (1892): 'Manual concepts: a study of the influence of hand-usage on culture-growth', *Amer. Anthrop.,* vol. v (old series), pp. 289–317.

—(1896): 'Outlines of Zuñi creation myths', *13th Annual Report, Bureau of American Ethnology* (Washington), pp. 321–447.

—(1923): 'Origin myth from Oraibi', *J. Amer. Folk-Lore,* vol. 36, pp. 163–70.

Cutler, C. (1952), 'A preliminary survey of plant remains of Tularosa cave', in *Mogollon cultural continuity and change,* Fieldiana (Chicago), vol. 40, ch. x, pp. 461–79.

Dean, J. S. (1967): 'Chronological analysis of Tsegi Phase sites in northeastern Arizona', Ph.D. thesis in Dept. of Anthropology, University of Arizona, Tucson, pp. 1–705.

Dennis, W. (1940): *The Hopi Child.* University of Virginia Institute for Research in the Social Sciences, Monograph no. 26, pp. 1–204

—(1941): 'The socialization of the Hopi child', in *Language, Culture, and Personality: Essays in memory of Edward Sapir* (ed. Spier, L., *et al.,* Menasha, Wis.), pp. 259–71.

Dennis, W. and M. G. (1940): 'Cradles and cradling practices of the Pueblo Indians', *Amer. Anthrop.,* vol. 42, pp. 107–15.

Dennis, W. and Russell, R. W. (1940): 'Piaget's questions applied to Zuñi children', *Child Development* (Baltimore), vol. 11, pp. 181–7.

Dorsey, G. A. and Voth, H. R. (1901): 'The Oraibi Soyal ceremony', *Field Columbian Museum, Anthrop. Series,* vol. 3, pp. 1–59.

Douglas, C. L. (1966): 'Amphibians and reptiles of Mesa Verde National Park, Colorado', *Univ. Kansas Publ., Mus. Nat. Hist.,* vol. 15, no. 15, pp. 711–44.

Douglass, A. E. (1935): 'Dating Pueblo Bonito and other ruins of the southwest', *Nat. Geograph. Soc. Tech. Papers,* Pueblo Bonito Series no. 1.

Dozier, E. P. (1954): 'The Hopi-Tewa of Arizona', *Univ. Calif. Publ. Amer. Arahaeology and Ethnology,* vol. 44, no. 3, pp. 259–376.

—(1960): 'The Pueblos of the southwestern United States', *J. R. Anthrop. Inst.,* vol. 90, pp. 146–60.

—(1965): 'Southwestern social units and archaeology', *Amer. Antiquity,* vol. 31, no. 1, pp. 38–47.

Dutcher, B. H. (1893): 'Piñon gathering among the Panamint Indians', *Amer. Anthrop.*, vol. vi (old series), pp. 377–80.

Earle, E. and Kennard, E. A. (1938): *Hopi Kachinas* (New York), pp. 1–40, pl. xxviii.

Eddy, F. W. (1964): 'Metates and manos: the basic grinding tools of the Southwest', Museum of New Mexico (Santa Fé), *Popular Series Pamphlets*, no. 1, pp. 1–10.

Eggan, D. (1943): 'The general problem of Hopi adjustment', *Amer. Anthrop.*, vol. 45, pp. 357–73.

—(1949): 'The significance of dreams for anthropological research', *Amer. Anthrop.*, vol. 51, pp. 177–98.

—(1952): 'The manifest content of dreams: a challenge to social science', *Amer. Anthrop.*, vol. 54, pp. 469–85.

—(1956): 'Instruction and affect in Hopi cultural continuity', *Southwestern J. Anthrop.*, vol. 12, pp. 347–70.

—(1957): 'Hopi dreams, and a life history sketch', *Microcard Publications of Primary Records in Culture and Personality*, ed. Kaplan, B. (Madison, Wis.), vol. 2, no. 16, pp. 1–147.

—(1961): 'Hopi dreams: second series', ibid., vol. 3, no. 9, pp. 1–77.

—(1966): 'Hopi dreams in cultural perspective', in *The Dream and Human Societies*, ed. von Grunebaum, G. E. and Callois R. (Berkeley), pp. 237–65.

Eggan, F. (1949): 'The Hopi and the lineage principle', in *Social Structure: Studies presented to A. R. Radcliffe-Brown*, ed. Fortes, M. (Oxford), pp. 121–44.

—(1950): *Social Organisation of the Western Pueblos* (Chicago).

—(1954): 'Social anthropology and the method of controlled comparison', *Amer. Anthrop.*, vol. 56, pp. 743–63.

—(1964): 'Alliance and descent in Western Pueblo Society', in *Process and Pattern in Culture*, ed. Manners, R. A. (Chicago), pp. 175–84.

—(1966): *The American Indian: Perspectives for the Study of Social Change* (New York).

—(1968): Personal communication.

Erikson, E. H. (1943): 'Observation on the Yurok: childhood and world image', *Univ. Calif. Publ. Amer. Archaeology and Ethnology*, vol. 35, no. 10, pp. 257–302.

Ferdon, E. N. (1955): 'A trial survey of Mexican–Southwestern architectural parallels', *Monogr. School Amer. Research* (Santa Fé), no. 21, pp. 1–39.

Fewkes, J. W. (1891): 'The meaning of the Moki snake dance,' *J. Amer. Folk-Lore*, vol. iv, pp. 129–38.

—(1892a): 'A few summer ceremonials at the Tusayan pueblos', *J. Amer. Ethnology and Archaeology*, vol. ii, pp. 1–160.

—(1892b): 'The ceremonial circuit among the village Indians of northeastern Arizona', *J. Amer. Folk-Lore*, vol. v, pp. 33–42.

—(1894a): 'The snake ceremonials at Walpi', *J. Amer. Ethnology and Archaeology*, vol. iv, pp. 1–126.

—(1894b): 'The Walpi flute observance', *J. Amer. Folk-Lore*, vol. vii, pp. 265–87.

—(1894c): 'On certain personages who appear in a Tusayan ceremony', *Amer. Anthrop.*, vol. vii (old series), pp. 32–52.

—(1894d): 'A study of certain figures in a Maya Codex', *Amer. Anthrop.*, vol. vii (old series), pp. 260–74.

—(1896): 'A contribution to ethnobotany', *Amer. Anthrop.*, vol. ix (old series), pp. 14–21.

—(1897a): 'Tusayan katcinas', *Smithsonian Inst., Bureau of Amer. Ethnology, 15th Annual Report*, pp. 247–313.

—(1897b): 'Tusayan snake ceremonies', *Smithsonian Inst., Bureau of Amer. Ethnology, 16th Annual Report*, pp. 267–312.

—(1898a): 'The growth of the Hopi ritual', *J. Amer. Folk-Lore*, vol. xi, pp. 173–94.

—(1898b): 'The winter solstice ceremony at Walpi', *Amer. Anthrop.*, vol. xi (old series), pp. 65–87, 101–15.

—(1900a): 'The new-fire ceremony at Walpi', *Amer. Anthrop.*, vol. 2, pp. 80–138.

—(1900b): 'Tusayan migration traditions', *Smithsonian Inst., Bureau of Amer. Ethnology, 19th Annual Report*, part 2, pp. 573–634.

—(1900c): 'Property-right in eagles among the Hopi,' *Amer. Anthrop.*, vol. 2, pp. 690–707.

—(1902): 'Minor Hopi festivals', *Amer. Anthrop.*, vol. 4, pp. 482–511.

—(1903): 'Hopi katcinas', *Smithsonian Inst., Bureau of Amer. Ethnology, 21st Annual Report*, pp. 3–126.

—(1910): 'The butterfly in Hopi myth and ritual', *Amer. Anthrop.*, vol. 12, pp. 576–94.

—(1917): 'An initiation at Hano in Hopiland, Arizona', *J. Washington Acad. Sciences*, vol. vii, pp. 149–58.

—(1922): 'Oraibi in 1890', *Amer. Anthrop.*, vol. 24, pp. 268–83.

Fewkes, J. W. and Owens, J. G. (1892): 'The La'lakon-ta: a Tusayan dance', *Amer. Anthrop.*, vol. v (old series), pp. 105–29.

Fewkes, J. W. and Stephen, A. M. (1892a): 'The Na-ac-naiya: a Tusayan initiation ceremony', *J. Amer. Folk-Lore*, vol. v, pp. 189–221.

—(1892b): 'The Mamzrau'ti: a Tusayan ceremony', *Amer. Anthrop.*, vol v (old series), pp. 217–45.

—(1893): 'The Pa'lü-lü-koñ-ti: a Tusayan ceremony', *J. Amer. Folk-Lore*, vol. vi, pp. 269–84.

Fisher, A. K. (1896): 'A partial list of Moki animal names', *Amer. Anthrop.*, vol. ix (old series), p. 174.

—(1903): 'A partial list of the birds of Keam Canyon, Arizona', *The Condor*, vol. 5, pp. 33–6.

Fletcher, A. C. (1912): 'Wakonda-gi', *Amer. Anthrop.*, vol. 14, pp. 106–8.

Fletcher, A. C. and La Flesche, F. (1911): 'The Omaha tribe', *27th Annual Report, Bureau of American Ethnology* (Washington), pp. 15–672.

Forde, C. Daryll (1931): 'Hopi agriculture and land ownership', *J. Royal Anthrop. Inst.*, vol. 61, pp. 357–405.

—(1932): 'Ethnography of the Yuma Indians', *Univ. Calif. Publ. Amer. Arch. and Ethn.*, vol. 28, no. 4, pp. 83–278.

—(1934): 'The Hopi and Yuma: flood farmers in the North American desert', in *Habitat, Economy and Society* (London), ch. xii, pp. 220–59.

Freire-Marreco, B. (1914): 'Tewa kinship terms from the Pueblo of Hano, Arizona', *Amer. Anthrop.*, vol. 16, pp. 269–87.

Galinat, W. C. (1965): 'The evolution of corn and culture in North America', *Econ. Botany*, vol. 19, no. 4, pp. 350–7.

Goldenweiser, A. A. (1910): 'Totemism, an analytical study', *J. Amer. Folk-Lore*, vol. xxiii, pp. 179–293.

Goldfrank, E. S. (1945): 'Socialization, personality, and the structure of Pueblo society (with particular reference to Hopi and Zuni)', *Amer. Anthrop.*, vol. 47, pp. 516–39.

—(1948): 'The impact of situation and personality on four Hopi Emergence myths', *Southwestern J. Anthrop.*, vol. 4, pp. 241–62.

Goldschmidt, W. (1948): 'Social organization in native California and the origin of clans', *Amer. Anthrop.*, vol. 50, pp. 444–56.

Goss, J. A. (1966): 'Culture-historical inference from Utaztecan linguistic evidence', paper presented at symposium on Utaztecan Pre-history held at Reno, Nevada, in May 1966, pp. 1–68.

Gregory, H. E. (1916): *The Navajo Country*. U.S. Geological Survey, Water Supply Paper 380 (Washington).

Haeberlin, H. K. (1916): 'The idea of fertilization in the culture of the Pueblo Indians', *Memoirs Amer. Anthrop. Assoc.*, no. 3, pp. 1–56.

Hale, K. (1958): 'Internal diversity in Uto-Aztecan', *Internat. J. Amer. Linguistics*, vol. 24, pp. 101–7.

Hallowell, A. I. (1926): 'Bear ceremonialism in the northern hemisphere', *Amer. Anthrop.*, vol. 28, pp. 1–175.

Hargrave, L. L. (1939): 'Bird bones from abandoned Indian dwellings in Arizona and Utah', *The Condor*, vol. xli, pp. 206–10.

Henderson, J. and Harrington, J. P. (1914): 'Ethnozoology of the Tewa Indians', *Smithson. Inst., Bureau Amer. Anthrop.*, Bulletin no. 56, pp. 1–76.

Hill, W. W. (1936): 'Navajo warfare', *Yale Univ. Publications in Anthropology*, no. 5, pp. 1–19.

—(1938): 'The agricultural and hunting methods of the Navajo Indians', *Yale Univ. Publications in Anthropology*, no. 18, pp. 1–194.

Hoffmeister, D. F. (1971): *Mammals of Grand Canyon* (Urbana, Ill.)

Hopkins, N. A. (1965): 'Great Basin pre-history and Uto-Aztecan', *Amer. Antiquity*, vol. 31, pp. 48–60.

Hough, W. (1898): 'Environmental interrelations in Arizona', *Amer. Anthrop.*, vol. xi (old series), pp. 133–55.

—(1915): *The Hopi Indians* (Cedar Falls, Iowa).

—(1918): 'The Hopi Indian Collection in the United States National Museum', *Proceedings of the U.S. National Museum*, vol. 54, pp. 235–96, and Pls. 19–53.

—(1928): 'Ancient pueblo subsistence', *Proceedings 23rd Internat. Congress Americanists* (New York), pp. 67–9.

Humphrey, N. D. (1941): 'A characterisation of certain Plains associations', *Amer. Anthrop.*, vol. 43, pp. 428–36.

James. G. W. (1903): *The Indians of the Painted Desert Region* (London).

Jennings, J. D. (1953): 'Danger Cave: a progress summary', *El Palacio* (Santa Fé, N.M.), vol. 60, no. 5, pp. 179–213.

—(1957): 'Danger Cave', *Univ. Utah Anthrop. Papers*, no. 27, pp. 1–328.

Jennings, J. D. and Norbeck, E. (1955): 'Great Basin pre-history: a review', *Amer. Antiquity*, vol. 21, pp. 1–11.

Johnston, D. F. (1966): 'An analysis of sources of information on the population of the Navajo', *Smithsonian Inst., Bureau of American Ethnology*, Bulletin 197, pp. 1–220.

Kearney, T. H. *et al.* (1914): 'Indicator significance of vegetation in Tooele Valley, Utah', *J. Agric. Research*, vol. 1, pp. 365–417.

Kelly, I. T. (1932): 'Ethnography of the Surprise Valley Paiute', *Univ. Calif. Publ. Amer. Archaeology and Ethnology*, vol. 31, no. 3, pp. 67–210, and Pls. 17–32.

—(1934): 'Southern Paiute bands', *Amer. Anthrop.*, vol. 36, pp. 548–60.

—(1936): 'Chemehuevi shamanism', in *Essays in Anthropology presented to A. L. Kroeber* (Berkeley, Calif.), pp. 129–42.

—(1964): 'Southern Paiute Ethnography', *Univ. Utah Anthrop. Papers*, no. 69, pp. 1–194.

Kennard, E. A. (1937): 'Hopi reactions to death', *Amer. Anthrop.*, vol. 39, pp. 491–7.

Kennard, E. A. and Yava, A. (1944): 'Field Mouse goes to war: *Tusa'n homi'chi tu'wvöta'*, U.S. Department of the Interior, Bureau of Indian Affairs, Phoenix (Ariz.), pp. 1–76.

Kidder, A. V. (1917): 'Prehistoric cultures of the San Juan drainage', *Proc. 19th Internat. Congress Americanists* (1915), pp. 108–13.

Kluckhorn, C. (1945): 'The personal document in anthropological science', in *The Use of Personal Documents in History, Anthropology, and Sociology*: Social Science Research Council, Bulletin 53, pp. 77–173.

—(1960): 'Navaho categories', in *Culture in History: Essays in honor of Paul Radin*, ed. Diamond, S. (New York), pp. 65–98.

Kluckhorn, C. and Leighton, D. (1962): *The Navajo*. 1st ed. 1946 (revised ed. New York, 1962).

Kluckhorn, C. and Macleish, K. (1955): 'Moencopi variations from Whorf's Second Mesa Hopi', *Internat. J. Amer. Linguistics*, vol. 21, pp. 150–6.

Kroeber, A. L. (1917): 'Zuni kin and clan', *American Museum of Natural History, Anthrop. Papers*, vol. 18, part 2, pp. 39–204.

—(1925): *Handbook of the Indians of California*. Smithsonian Inst., Bureau of Amer. Ethnology, Bulletin 78, chs. 39–42, pp. 574–610, and chs. 46–7, pp. 648–88.

—(1938): 'Basic and secondary patterns of social structure', *J. Royal Anthrop. Inst.*, vol. 68, pp. 299–309.

Lamb, S. M. (1958): 'Linguistic prehistory in the Great Basin', *Internat. J. Amer. Linguistics*, vol. 24, pp. 95–100.

Lee, D. D. (1938): 'Conceptual implications of an Indian language', *Philosophy of Science*, vol. 5, pp. 89–102.

—(1944): 'Linguistic reflection of Wintu thought', *International J. Amer. Linguistics*, vol. 10, pp. 181–7.

—(1959): 'The conception of the self among the Wintu Indians', in *Freedom and Culture* (New York), pp. 131–40.

Leighton, D. and Kluckhorn, C. (1948): *Children of the People: the Navaho Individual and his Development* (Cambridge, Mass.).

Lewton, F. L. (1912): 'The cotton of the Hopi Indians: a new species of *Gossypium*', *Smithsonian Misc. Coll.*, vol. 60, no. 6, pp. 1–10, and Pls. 1–5.

Lincoln, E. P. (1961): 'A comparative study of present and past mammalian fauna of the Sunset Crater and Wupatki areas of Northern Arizona', M.Sc. thesis, University of Arizona, Tucson, pp. 1–62

Lindsay, A. J. (1961): 'The Beaver Creek agricultural community on the San Juan River, Utah', *American Antiquity*, vol. 27, pp. 174–87.

Lindsay, A. J. *et al.* (1968): 'Survey and excavations north and east of Navajo Mountain, Utah, 1959–62', *Mus. Northern Arizona Bull.*, no. 45, pp. 1–400.

Linton, R. (1940): 'Crops, soils and culture in America', in *The Maya and their Neighbors* (New York), pp. 32–40.

Lipe, W. D. (1970): 'Anasazi communities in the Red Rock Plateau, Southeastern Utah', in *Reconstructing prehistoric Pueblo societies* (ed. W. A. Longacre, Albuquerque, N.M.), pp. 84–139.

Loeb, E. M. (1929): 'Tribal initiations and secret societies', *Univ. Calif. Publ. Amer. Archaeology and Ethnology*, vol. 25, no. 3, pp. 249–88.

Lowie, R. H. (1916): 'Plains Indian age-societies: historical and comparative summary', *American Museum of Natural History, Anthrop. Papers,* vol. xi, pp. 877–984.

—(1924): 'Notes on Shoshonean Ethnography', *American Museum of Natural History, Anthrop. Papers,* vol. 20, part 3, pp. 185–314.

—(1925): 'A women's ceremony among the Hopi', *Natural History* ( American Museum of Natural History), vol. 25, pp. 178–83.

—(1929): 'Notes on Hopi clans', and 'Hopi kinship', *American Museum of Natural History, Anthrop. Papers,* vol. 30, parts 6 and 7, pp. 303–88.

—(1960): 'Property rights and cöercive powers of Plains Indian military societies', reprinted in *Lowie's Selected Papers in Anthropology,* ed. Du Bois, C. (Berkeley, Calif.), pp. 247–61.

Mason, J. A. (1910): 'Myths of the Uintah Utes', *J. Amer. Folk-Lore,* vol. xxiii, pp. 299–363.

Means, F. C. (1960): 'The Hopi religion and dry farming', in *Sunlight on the Hopi Mesas* (Philadelphia), ch. 14, pp. 119–28.

Mearns, E. A. (1896): 'Ornithological vocabulary of the Moki Indians', *Amer. Anthrop.,* vol. ix (old series), pp. 391–403.

Mindeleff, C. (1891): 'A study of Pueblo architecture, Tusayan and Cibola', *Smithsonian Inst., Bureau of Amer. Ethnology, 8th Annual Report,* pp. 1–228.

Morgan, W. (1932): 'Navaho dreams', *Amer. Anthrop.,* vol. 34, pp. 390–405.

Nequatewa, E. (1931): 'Hopi *Hopi-wi'me*: the Hopi ceremonial calendar', *Museum of Northern Arizona, Museum Notes,* vol. 3, no. 9, pp. 1–4.

—(1933): 'Hopi courtship and marriage: 2nd Mesa', *Museum of Northern Arizona, Museum Notes,* vol. 5, no. 9, pp. 41–54.

—(1936): 'Truth of a Hopi, and other clan stories from Shungo'povi', *Museum of Northern Arizona Bulletin,* no. 8, pp. 1–112.

—(1943): 'Some Hopi recipes for the preparation of wild plant foods', *Plateau,* vol. 16, pp. 18–20.

—(1946): 'The place of corn and feathers in Hopi ceremonies', *Plateau,* vol. 19, no. 1, pp. 15–16.

Olin, G. (1954): *Animals of the Southwest Deserts.* Southwestern Monuments Association (Globe, Ariz.), Popular Series no. 8.

Ortiz, A. (1969): *The Tewa World: Space, Time, Being, and Becoming in a Pueblo Society* (Chicago).

Owens, J. G. (1892): 'Natal ceremonies of the Hopi Indians', *J. Amer. Ethnology and Archaeology,* vol. ii, pp. 161–75.

Page, G. B. (1940): 'Hopi agricultural notes', issued by U.S. Department of Agriculture, Soil Conservation Service, May 1940.

Parsons, E. C. (1917): 'Zuni conception and pregnancy beliefs', *Proceedings 19th Internat. Congress Americanists* (1915), pp. 379–83.

—(1918): 'Notes on Acoma and Laguna', *Amer. Anthrop.,* vol. 20, pp. 162–86.

—(1921a): 'Hopi mothers and children', *Man,* vol. 21, no. 58, pp. 98–104.

—(1921b): 'Getting married on 1st Mesa', *Scientific Monthly,* vol. 13, pp. 259–65.

—(1922a): 'Oraibi in 1920', *Amer. Anthrop.,* vol. 24, pp. 283–94.

—(1922b): 'Shungo'povi in 1920', *Amer. Anthrop.,* vol. 24, pp. 294–8.

—(1923): 'The Hopi Wöwöchim ceremony in 1920', *Amer. Anthrop.,* vol. 25, pp. 156–87.

—(1924): 'Tewa kin, clan, and moiety', *Amer. Anthrop.,* vol. 26, pp. 333–9.

—(1925): *A Pueblo Indian Journal 1920–21*, ed. Parsons, E. C.: *Memoirs Amer. Anthrop. Assoc.*, no. 32, pp. 1–123.

—(1926): 'The ceremonial calendar of the Tewa of Arizona', *Amer. Anthrop.*, vol. 28, pp. 209–29.

—(1927): 'Witchcraft among the Pueblos: Indian or Spanish?', *Man*, vol. 27, no. 70, pp. 106–12: no. 80, pp. 125–8.

—(1932): 'The kinship nomenclature of the Pueblo Indians', *Amer. Anthrop.*, vol. 34, pp. 377–89.

—(1933): 'Hopi and Zuni ceremonialism', *Memoirs Amer. Anthrop. Assoc.*, no. 39, pp. 1–108.

—(1936): Introduction and notes, appendices and glossary, to *Hopi Journal of Alexander M. Stephen. Columbia Univ. Contributions to Anthropology*, vol. xxiii, parts 1 and 2.

—(1939): *Pueblo Indian Religion* (2 vols., Chicago).

Phillips, A., Marshall, J., and Monson, G. (1964): *The Birds of Arizona* (Tucson, Ariz.).

Pinkley, J. M. (1965): 'The Pueblos and the turkey: who domesticated whom?', *Amer. Antiquity*, vol. 31, pp. 70–2.

Powell, J. W. (1891): 'Indian linguistic families of America north of Mexico', *7th Annual Report, Bureau of American Ethnology* (Washington), pp. 1–42: reprinted by Univ. Nebraska Press, Lincoln (1966), pp. 82–218.

Reagan, A. B. (1934): 'The Gosiute (Goshute), or Shoshoni-Goship Indians of the Deep Creek region, in Western Utah', *Proc. Utah Acad. Science, Arts and Letters*, vol. xi, pp. 43–54.

—(1935a): 'Some names of the Ute Indians of Utah, followed by a selected list of words used by the Indians of the State', ibid. vol. xii, pp. 1–39.

—(1935b): 'Ute myths', ibid., vol. xii, pp. 46–9.

Reed, E. K. (1946): 'The distinctive features and distribution of the San Juan Anasazi Culture', *Southwestern J. Anthrop.*, vol. 2, pp. 295–305.

Reed, V. Z. (1896): 'The Ute bear dance', *Amer. Anthrop.*, vol. ix (old series), pp. 237–44.

Reichard, G. A. (1938): 'Social life', in *General Anthropology* (ed. Boas, F., New York), ch. ix, pp. 409–86.

—(1948): 'Navajo classification of natural objects', *Plateau*, vol. 21, no. 1, pp. 7–12.

Robbins, C. S., Bruun, B., and Zim, H. S. (1966): *Birds of North America, a Guide to Field Identification* (New York).

Robbins, W. W., Harrington, J. P., and Freire-Marreco, B. (1916): 'Ethno-botany of the Tewa Indians', *Smithsonian Inst., Bureau of Amer. Ethnology*, Bulletin 55, pp. 1–124.

Sapir, E. (1911): 'Song recitative in Paiute mythology', *J. Amer. Folk-Lore*, vol. 23, pp. 455–72.

—(1916): 'Time perspective in aboriginal American culture: a study in method', *Canada Dept. Mines Geolog. Survey, Anthrop. Series*, Memoir 90, pp. 1–87.

—(1930): 'Southern Paiute, a Shoshonean language', *Proc. Amer. Acad. Arts and Science*, vol. 65, no. 1, pp. 1–296.

—(1931a): 'Southern Paiute Dictionary', ibid., vol. 65, no. 3, pp. 536–730.

—(1931b): 'Conceptual categories in primitive languages', *Science*, vol. 74, p. 578.

—(1949): *Selected Writings in Language, Culture and Personality* (Berkeley, Calif.).

Sauer, J. D. (1950a): 'The Grain Amaranths: a survey of their history and classification', *Ann. Missouri Botan. Garden*, vol. 37, pp. 561–632.

—(1950b): 'Amaranths as dye plants among the Pueblo peoples', *Southwestern J. Anthrop.*, vol. 6, pp. 412–15.

Seltzer, C. C. (1944): 'Racial prehistory in the Southwest and the Hawikah Zuñis', *Papers Peabody Museum Amer. Arch. and Ethn.*, vol. xxiii, no. 1, pp. 1–37.

Shantz, H. L. (1925): 'Plant communities in Utah and Nevada', in *Flora of Utah and Nevada* by Tidestrom, I. (*Contrib. U.S. National Herbarium*, Washington, vol. 25), pp. 15–23.

Simmons, L. W. (1942): *Sun Chief: the Autobiography of a Hopi Indian*, ed. Simmons, L. W. (New Haven, Conn.).

Simpson, R. D. (1953): 'The Hopi Indians', *Southwest Museum Leaflets* (Los Angeles), no. 25, pp. 1–91.

Sparkman, P. S. (1908): 'The culture of the Luiseño Indians', *Univ. Calif. Publ. Amer. Arch. and Ethn.*, vol. 8, no. 4, pp. 187–234.

Stephen, A. M. (1889): 'Tribal boundary marks', *Amer. Anthrop.*, vol. ii (old series), p. 214.

—(1893): 'The Navajo', *Amer. Anthrop.*, vol. vi (old series), pp. 345–62.

—(1898): 'Pigments in ceremonials of the Hopi', *Arch. Internat. Folk-Lore Assoc.*, vol. i, pp. 260–5.

—(1929): 'Hopi tales', ed. Parsons, E. C.: *J. Amer. Folk-Lore*, vol. 42, pp. 1–72.

—(1936): *Hopi Journal of Alexander M. Stephen*, ed. Parsons, E. C.: *Columbia Univ. Contributions to Anthropology*, vol. xxiii, parts 1 and 2, pp. 1–1417

—(1940a): 'Hopi Indians of Arizona', *The Masterkey* (Southwest Museum, Los Angeles), vol. 13, no. 6, pp. 197–204: vol. 14, no. 1, pp. 20–27, no. 3, pp. 102–9. no. 4, pp. 143–9, no. 5, pp. 170–9, no. 6, pp. 207–15. Reprinted as:

—(1940b): 'Hopi Indians of Arizona', *Southwest Museum Leaflets*, no. 14, pp. 1–47.

Stevenson, M. C. (1904): 'The Zuñi Indians', *23rd Annual Report, Bureau of American Ethnology* (Washington), pp. 1–634.

Steward, J. H. (1930): 'Irrigation without agriculture', *Papers Michigan Acad. Science, Arts and Letters*, vol. 12, pp. 149–56, and Pl. xxxvii.

—(1931): 'Notes on Hopi ceremonies in their initiatory form', *Amer. Anthrop.*, vol. 33, pp. 56–79.

—(1932): 'A Uintah Ute Bear dance, March, 1931', *Amer. Anthrop.*, vol. 34, pp. 263–73.

—(1933): 'Ethnography of the Owens Valley Paiute', *Univ. Calif. Publ. Amer. Archaeology and Ethnology*, vol. 33, no. 3, pp. 233–350, and Pls. 1–10.

—(1934): 'Two Paiute autobiographies', ibid., vol. 33, no. 5, pp. 423–38.

—(1936a): 'Myths of the Owens Valley Paiute', ibid., vol. 34, no. 5, pp. 355–440.

—(1936b): 'The economic and social basis of primitive bands', in *Essays in Anthropology Presented to A. L. Kroeber* (Berkeley, Calif.), pp. 331–50.

—(1937a): 'Ecological aspects of southwestern society', *Anthropos*, vol. 32, pp. 87–104.

—(1937b): 'Linguistic distributions and political groups of the Great Basin Shoshoneans', *Amer. Anthrop.*, vol. 39, pp. 625–34.

—(1938): 'Basin-Plateau aboriginal socio-political groups', *Smithsonian Inst., Bureau of Amer. Ethnology*, Bulletin 120, pp. 1–346.

—(1940): 'Native cultures of the Intermontane (Great Basin) Area', *Smithsonian Miscellaneous Collections*, vol. 100, pp. 445–502.

—(1951): 'Levels of socio-cultural integration: an operational concept', *Southwestern J. Anthrop.*, vol. 7, pp. 374–90.

—(1955): *Theory of Culture Change* (Urbana, Ill).

—(1968): 'Causal factors and processes in the evolution of pre-farming societies', in *Man the Hunter,* ed. Lee, R. B. and DeVore, I. (Chicago), ch. 34, pp. 321–34.

Stewart, G. R. (1940): 'Conservation in Pueblo agriculture: I. Primitive practices; II. Present-day flood water irrigation', *Scientific Monthly*, vol. 51, pp. 201–20, 329–40.

Thompson, L. (1945): 'Logico-aesthetic integration in Hopi culture', *Amer. Anthrop.* vol. 47, pp. 540–53.

—(1950): *Culture in Crisis: a Study of the Hopi Indians* (New York).

Thompson, L. and Joseph, A. (1944): *The Hopi Way* (Chicago).

Titiev, M. (1937a): 'A Hopi salt expedition', *Amer. Anthrop.*, vol. 39, pp. 244–58.

—(1937b): 'The use of kinship terms in Hopi ritual', *Museum of Northern Arizona, Museum Notes*, vol. 10, no. 3, pp. 9–11.

—(1938): 'The problem of cross-cousin marriage among the Hopi', *Amer. Anthrop.*, vol. 40, pp. 105–11.

—(1939): 'Dates of planting at the Hopi Indian pueblo of Oraibi', *Museum of Northern Arizona, Museum Notes*, vol. 11, no. 5, pp. 39–42.

—(1940): 'A Hopi visit to the Afterworld', *Papers Michigan Acad. Science, Arts and Letters*, vol. 26, pp. 495–504.

—(1942): 'Notes on Hopi witchcraft', ibid., vol. 28, pp. 549–57.

—(1943a): 'Hopi snake handling', *Scientific Monthly*, vol. 57, pp. 44–51.

—(1943b): 'Two Hopi tales from Oraibi', *Papers Michigan Acad. Science, Arts and Letters*, vol. 29, pp. 425–37.

—(1943c): 'The influence of common residence on the unilateral classification of kindred', *Amer. Anthrop.*, vol. 45, pp. 511–30.

—(1944): *Old Oraibi: a study of the Hopi Indians of Third Mesa*. Papers of the Peabody Museum, Cambridge (Mass.), vol. xxii, no. 1, pp. 1–277.

—(1950): 'The religion of the Hopi Indians', in *Forgotten Religions* (New York), pp. 363–78.

—(1956): 'The importance of space in primitive kinship', *Amer. Anthrop.*, vol. 58, pp. 854–65.

Vivian, G. and Mathews, J. W. (1964): 'Kin Kletso: a Pueblo III community in Chaco Canyon, New Mexico', *Southwestern Monuments Assoc., Technical Series*, vol. 6, no. 1, pp. 1–115.

Voegelin, C. F. and F. M. (1957): *Hopi Domains: A Lexical Approach to the Problem of Selection. Indiana Univ. Publications in Anthropology and Linguistics*, Memoir 14 (Baltimore), pp. 1–82.

Voth, H. R. (1900): 'Oraibi marriage customs', *Amer. Anthrop.*, vol. 2, pp. 238–46.

—(1901): 'The Oraibi Powamu ceremony', *Field Columbian Museum, Anthrop. Series*, vol. 3, pp. 60–158.

—(1903a): 'The Oraibi summer snake ceremony', ibid., vol. 3, pp. 262–358.

—(1903b): 'The Oraibi Oaqöl ceremony', ibid., vol. 6, pp. 1–46.

—(1905a): 'Oraibi natal customs and ceremonies', ibid., vol. 6, pp. 47–61.

—(1905b): 'Hopi proper names', ibid., vol. 6, pp. 63–113.

—(1905c): 'The traditions of the Hopi', ibid., vol. 8.

—(1912a): 'The Oraibi Marau ceremony', ibid., vol. 11, pp. 1–88.

—(1912b): 'Brief miscellaneous Hopi papers', ibid., vol. 11, pp. 90–149.

—(1912c): Catalogue to *The Henry R. Voth Hopi Indian Collection at Grand Canyon, Arizona*: first published 1912, republished, ed. Byron Harvey (Phoenix, Ariz.), 1967, pp. 1–40.

S

Wallis, W. D. (1936): 'Folk tales from Shumopovi, Second Mesa', ed. Parsons, E. C.: *J. Amer. Folk-Lore*, vol. 49, pp. 1–68.

Wallis, W. D. and Titiev, M. (1944): 'Hopi notes from Chimopovy', *Papers Michigan Acad. Science, Arts and Letters*, vol. 30, pp. 523–55, and Pls. i–xx.

Watson, J. B. (1943): 'How the Hopi classify their foods', *Plateau*, vol. 15, no. 4, pp. 49–52.

White, L. A. (1932): 'The Acoma Indians', *47th Annual Report, Bureau of American Ethnology* (Washington), pp. 17–192.

—(1939): 'A problem in kinship terminology', *Amer. Anthrop.*, vol. 41, pp. 566–73.

—(1942): 'Keresan Indian color terms', *Papers Michigan Acad. Science, Arts and Letters*, vol. 28, pp. 559–63.

—(1943): ' "Rohona" in Pueblo culture', ibid., vol. 29, pp. 439–43.

—(1944): 'Notes on the ethnobotany of the Keres', ibid., vol. 30, pp. 557–68.

—(1945): 'Notes on the ethnozoology of the Keresan Pueblo Indians', ibid., vol. 31, pp. 223–43.

—(1946): 'Miscellaneous notes on the Keresan Pueblos', ibid. vol., 32, pp. 365–73.

Whorf, B. L. (1935): 'The comparative linguistics of Uto-Aztecan', *Amer. Anthrop.*, vol. 37, pp. 600–8.

—(1936): Notes on the glossary to *Hopi Journal of Alexander M. Stephen*, ed. Parsons, E. C.: *Columbia Univ. Contributions to Anthropology*, vol. xxiii, part 2, pp. 1198–1326.

—(1946): 'The Hopi language, Toreva dialect', in *Linguistic Structures of Native America*, Viking Fund Publications in Anthropology, no. 6, pp. 158–83.

—(1956): *Language, Thought, and Reality: Selected Writings of Benjamin Lee Whorf*, ed. Carroll, J. B. (Cambridge, Mass.).

Wittfogel, K. and Goldfrank, E. S. (1943): 'Some aspects of Pueblo mythology and society', *J. Amer. Folk-lore*, vol., 56, pp. 17–30.

Woodbury, A. M. and Russell, H. N. (1945): 'Birds of the Navajo Country', *Bull. Univ. Utah*, vol. 35, no. 14 (*Biological Series*, vol. ix, no. 1), pp. 1–160, map.

Woodbury, R. B. (1956): 'The antecedents of Zuñi culture', *Transact. New York Acad. Science*, series II, vol. 18, no. 6, pp. 557–63.

—(1961): 'Prehistoric agriculture at Point of Pines, Arizona', *Memoirs of the Society for American Archaeology*, no. 17, pp. 1–48.

Wright, B. and Roat, E. (1965): 'This is a Hopi kachina', Museum of Northern Arizona (Flagstaff, Ariz.), pp. 1–29.

---

## WORKS ON THE ETHNOGRAPHY OF THE YUCATAN PENINSULA

Bequaert, J. C. (1933): 'Botanical notes from Yucatan', in *The Peninsula of Yucatan* (ed. G. C. Shattuck), Carnegie Inst. Wash., Publ. no. 431, ch. xxvii, pp. 505–24.

Boulanger, R. (1968): *Mexico* (Hachette World Guides, Paris): ch. 41–7, pp. 830–903.

Coe, M. D. (1971): *The Maya* (London).

Cook, O. F. (1919): 'Milpa agriculture, a primitive tropical system', *Smithson. Inst. Ann. Report* (1919), pp. 307–16 and Pl. 1–15.

Gann, T. W. F. (1917): 'The *chachac*, or rain ceremony, as practised by the Maya of southern and northern British Honduras', *Proc. 19th Internat. Congress Americanists* (1915), pp. 409–18.

—(1918): 'The Maya Indians of southern Yucatan and northern British Honduras', *Smithson. Inst. Bur. Amer. Ethn.*, Bulletin no. 64, pp. 5–142.

Garibay, K., A. M. (1966): *Relación de las Cosas de Yucatán* by Fray Diego de Landa, with introduction by A. M. Garibay (Mexico).

Joyce, T. A. (1914): *Mexican Archaeology: an Introduction to the archaeology of the Mexican and Mayan civilizations of pre-Spanish America* (London).

Long, R. C. E. (1923): 'The burner period of the Mayas', *Man*, vol. 23, no. 108, pp. 173–6.

Lothrop, S. K. (1928): 'A modern survival of the ancient Maya calendar', *Proc. 23rd Internat. Congress Americanists* (New York), pp. 652–5.

Lundell, C. L. (1933*a*): 'The agriculture of the Maya', *Southwest Rev.*, vol. xix, pp. 65–77.

—(1933*b*): '*Chicle* exploitation in the sapodilla forest of the Yucatan peninsula', *Field and Lab.*, vol. ii, no. 1, pp. 15–21.

—(1934): 'Preliminary sketch of the phyto-geography of the Yucatan peninsula', *Carnegie Inst. Contrib. Amer. Arch.*, vol. ii, no. 12, pp. 255–321.

Morley, S. G. (1946): *The Ancient Maya* (Stanford, Calif.).

Page, J. L. (1933): 'The climate of the Yucatan peninsula', in *The Peninsula of Yucatan* (ed. G. C. Shattuck), Carnegie Inst. Wash., Publ. no. 431, ch. xx, pp. 409–22.

Redfield, R. (1941): *The Folk Culture of Yucatan* (Chicago).

Ruz, L., A. (1970): *The Civilization of the Ancient Maya* (Inst. Nac. de Anth. e Hist., Mexico).

Steggerda, M. (1941): 'Maya Indians of Yucatan', *Carnegie Inst. Wash.*, Publ. no. 531, pp. 1–280 and Pl. 1–32.

— and Macomber, E. (1939): 'Mental and social characteristics of Maya and Navajo Indians, as evidenced by a psychological rating scale', *J. Social Psychol.*, vol. 10, pp. 51–9.

Stephens, J. L. (1843): *Incidents of Travel in Yucatan* (1st ed. 1843: paperback ed., 2 vols., New York, 1963).

Thompson, J. E. S. (1925): 'The meaning of the Mayan months', *Man*, vol. 25, no. 71, pp. 121–3.

—(1930): 'Ethnology of the Mayas of southern and central British Honduras', *Field Mus. Nat. Hist., Anthrop. Series*, vol. xvii, no. 2, pp. 23–213 and Pl. i–xxiv.

—(1931): 'Archaeological investigations in the southern Cayo District, British Honduras', ibid. vol. xvii, no. 3, pp. 214–362 and Pl. xxv–lii.

—(1932): 'The solar year of the Mayas at Quirigua, Guatemala', ibid. vol. xvii, no. 4, pp. 363–421.

—(1934): 'Sky bearers, colors and directions in Maya and Mexican religion', *Carnegie Inst. Contrib. Amer. Arch.*, vol. ii, no. 10, pp. 209–42.

—(1935): 'Maya chronology: the correlation question', ibid. vol. iii, no. 14, pp. 51–104.

—(1939): 'The moon goddess in Middle America, with notes on related deities', *Carnegie Inst. Contrib. Amer. Anthrop. and Hist.*, vol. v, no. 29, pp. 120–73.

—(1954): *The Rise and Fall of Maya Civilisation* (Norman, Oklahoma).

—(1972): *Maya hieroglyphs without tears* (British Museum, London).

Tozzer, A. M. (1941): 'Landa's *Relación de las Cosas de Yucatán*: a translation', *Papers Peabody Mus. Amer. Arch. and Ethn.*, vol. xviii, pp. 1–394.

Willey, G. R. *et al* (1965): 'Prehistoric Maya settlements in the Belize valley', *Papers Peabody Mus. Amer. Arch. and Ethn.*, vol. liv, pp. 1–589.

Wright, A. C. S. *et al.* (1959): 'Land use in British Honduras: Report of the British Honduras Land Survey team', *Colonial Research Publ.* (H.M.S.O., London), no. 24, pp. 1–327.

WORKS ON PRIMATE ETHOLOGY, AND ON THE REGULATION OF
NUMBERS IN ANIMAL AND HUMAN COMMUNITIES

Allee, W. C. (1940): 'Concerning the origin of sociality in animals', *Scientia*, vol. lxvii, pp. 154–60.

—(1949): 'Animal aggregations', in *Principles of Animal Ecology* (by Allee, W. C. *et al.*, Philadelphia), ch. 23, pp. 393–419.

Bartlett, M. S. (1968): 'Biomathematics', an Inaugural Lecture (Oxford).

Beach, F. A. (1947): 'Evolutionary changes in the physiological control of mating behavior in mammals', *Psychol. Review*, vol. 54, no. 6, pp. 297–315.

Benedict, B. (1970): 'Population regulation in primitive societies', in *Population Control*, ed. Allison, A. (London), pp. 165–80.

Black, F. L. (1966): 'Measles endemicity in insular populations: critical community size and its evolutionary implication', *J. Theoret. Biol.*, vol. 11, pp. 207–11.

Birdsell, J. B. (1968): 'Some predictions for the Pleistocene, based on equilibrium systems among recent hunter-gatherers', in *Man the Hunter*, ed. Lee, R. B. and DeVore, I. (Chicago), pp. 229–40.

Brain, C. K. (1970): 'New finds at the Swartkrans Australopithecine site', *Nature*, vol. 225, pp. 1112–19.

Burt, W. H. (1940): 'Territorial behavior and populations of some small mammals in southern Michigan', *Misc. Publ. Mus. Zool.*, *Univ. Michigan*, no. 45, pp. 1–58.

—(1943): 'Territoriality and home range concepts as applied to mammals', *J. Mammalogy*, vol. 24, pp. 346–52.

—(1949): 'Territoriality', *J. Mammalogy*, vol. 30, pp. 25–7.

Calhoun, J. B. (1952): 'The social aspects of population dynamics', *J. Mammalogy*, vol. 33, pp. 139–59.

Campbell, B. G. (1967): *Human Evolution: an Introduction to Man's Adaptations* (London).

Carr-Saunders, A. M. (1922): *The Population Problem: a Study in Human Evolution* (Oxford).

Chance, M. R. A. (1961): 'The nature and special features of the instinctive social bond of primates', in *Social Life of Early Man* (ed. Washburn, S. L.), Viking Fund Publ. Anthrop., no. 31, pp. 17–33.

—(1967): 'Attention structure as the basis of primate rank orders', *Man, J. R. Anthrop. Inst.*, vol. 2, no. 4, pp. 503–18.

Christian, J. J. (1950): 'The adreno-pituitary system and population cycles in mammals', *J. Mammalogy*, vol. 31, pp. 247–59.

Christian, J. J. and Davis, D. E. (1964): 'Endocrines, behavior, and population', *Science*, vol. 146, pp. 1550–60.

Christian, J. J., Lloyd, J. A. and Davis, D. E. (1965): 'The role of endocrines in the self regulation of mammalian populations', *Recent Progress in Hormone Research*, vol. 21, pp. 501–78.

Clark, G. and Piggott, S. (1970): *Prehistoric Societies*. 1st ed. 1965: 2nd ed. (London), 1970.

Crook, J. H. (1966a): 'Co-operation in primates', *Eugenics Rev.*, vol. 58, pp. 63–70.

—(1966b): 'Gelada baboon herd structure and movement: a comparative report', *Symp. Zool. Soc. Lond.*, no. 18, pp. 237–58.

Crook, J. H. and Gartlan, J. S. (1966): 'Evolution in primate societies', *Nature*, vol. 210, no. 5042, pp. 1200–3.

Darwin, C. (1872): *The Origin of Species*. 6th ed. 1872: The World's Classics, Oxford, 1951.

Davis, D. E. (1951): 'The relation between level of population and pregnancy of Norway rats', *Ecology*, vol. 32, pp. 459–61.

DeVore, I. (1964): 'The evolution of social life', in *Horizons in Anthropology*, ed. Sol Tax (Chicago), pp. 25–36.

DeVore, I. and Washburn, S. L. (1963): 'Baboon ecology and human evolution', in *African Ecology and Human Evolution* (ed. Howell, F. C. and Bourlière, F.), Viking Fund Publ. Anthrop., no. 36, pp. 335–67.

DeVore, I. and Hall, K. R. L. (1965): 'Baboon ecology', in *Primate Behavior: Field Studies of Monkeys and Apes*, ed. DeVore, I. (New York), pp. 20–52.

Douglas, M. (1966): 'Population control in primitive groups', *Brit. J. Sociology*, vol. 3, pp. 263–73.

Dunn, F. L. (1968): 'Epidemiological factors: health and disease in hunters and gatherers', in *Man the Hunter*, ed. Lee, R. B. and DeVore, I. (Chicago), pp. 221–8, and ensuing discussion, pp. 243–5.

Emlen, J. M. (1966): 'Natural selection and human behaviour', *J. Theoret. Biol.*, vol. 12, pp. 410–18.

Emlen, J. T., Stokes, A. W. and Winsor, C. P. (1948): 'The rate of recovery of decimated populations of brown rats in nature', *Ecology*, vol. 29, pp. 133–45.

Errington, P. L. (1946): 'Predation and vertebrate populations', *Quart. Rev. Biol.*, vol. 21, pp. 144–77, 221–45.

Gartlan, J. S. (1968): 'Structure and function in primate society', *Folia Primat.*, vol. 8, pp. 89–120.

Goodall, J. (1963): 'Feeding behaviour of wild chimpanzees: a preliminary report', *Symp. Zool. Soc. Lond.*, no. 10, pp. 39–47.

Haldane, J. B. S. (1957): 'Natural selection in man', *Acta Genetica et Statistica Medica* (Basel), vol. 6, pp. 321–32.

Hall, K. R. L. (1962a): 'Numerical data, maintenance activities and locomotion of the wild chacma baboon, *Papio ursinus*', *Proc. Zool. Soc. Lond.*, vol. 139, pp. 181–220.

—(1962b): 'The sexual, agonistic and derived social patterns of the wild chacma baboon, *Papio ursinus*', *Proc. Zool. Soc. Lond.*, vol. 139, pp. 283–327.

—(1963): 'Variations in the ecology of the chacma baboon, *Papio ursinus*', *Symp. Zool. Soc. Lond.*, no. 10, pp. 1–28.

—(1965): 'Behaviour and ecology of the wild patas monkey, *Erythrocebus patas*, in Uganda', *J. Zool. Lond.*, vol. 148, pp. 15–87.

—(1966): 'Distribution and adaptations of baboons', *Symp. Zool. Soc. Lond.*, no. 17, pp. 49–73.

Hall, K. R. L. and DeVore, I. (1965): 'Baboon social behaviour', in *Primate Behavior: Field Studies of Monkeys and Apes* (ed. DeVore, I., New York), pp. 53–110.

Harris, G. W. (1955): *Neural Control of the Pituitary Gland.* Monographs of the Physiological Society (London), no. 3.

Hornocker, M. G. (1969): 'Winter territoriality in mountain lions', *J. Wildlife Manag.*, vol. 33, pp. 457–64.

Jewell, P. A. (1966): 'The concept of home range in mammals', *Symp. Zool. Soc. Lond.*, no. 18, pp. 85–109.

Kortlandt, A. (1962): 'Chimpanzees in the wild', *Scient. Amer.*, vol. 206 (5), pp. 128–38.

—(1965): 'On the essential morphological basis for human culture', *Current Anthrop.*, vol. 6, pp. 320–6.

Kortlandt, A. and Kooij, M. (1963): 'Proto-hominid behaviour in primates', *Symp. Zool. Soc. Lond.*, no. 10, pp. 61–88 and Pls. 1 to 3.

Kummer, H. (1968): *Social Organization of Hamadryas baboons: a Field Study* (Chicago).

Kummer, H. and Kurt, F. (1963): 'Social units of a free-living population of Hamadryas baboons', *Folia Primat.*, vol. 1, pp. 4–19.

Kurten, B. (1957): 'The bears and hyenas of the interglacials', *Quaternaria*, vol. 4, pp. 69–81.

Lack, D. (1954): *The Natural Regulation of Animal Numbers* (Oxford).

Laughlin, W. S. (1968): 'The demography of hunters: an Eskimo example', in *Man the Hunter*, ed. Lee, R. B. and DeVore, I. (Chicago), pp. 241–3.

Lee, R. B. (1968): 'What hunters do for a living, or, How to make out on scarce resources', in *Man the Hunter*, ed. Lee, R. B. and DeVore, I. (Chicago), pp. 30–48.

Lee, R. B. and DeVore, I. (1968): 'Problems in the study of hunters and gatherers', in *Man the Hunter*, ed. Lee, R. B. and DeVore, I. (Chicago), pp. 3–12.

Leopold, A., Sowls, L. K. and Spencer, D. L. (1947): 'A survey of over-populated deer ranges in the United States', *J. Wildlife Manag.*, vol. 11, pp. 162–77.

Linduska, J. P. (1942): 'Winter rodent populations in field-shocked corn', *J. Wildlife Manag.*, vol. 6, pp. 353–63.

Lorenz, K. (1966): *On Aggression* (London).

Morse, D. (1961): 'Pre-historic tuberculosis in America', *Amer. Rev. Respir. Diseases*, vol. 83, pp. 489–504.

Napier, J. R. (1964): 'The evolution of bipedal walking in hominids', *Arch. Biol.* (Liège), vol. 75, Supplement, pp. 673–708.

—(1967): 'The antiquity of human walking', *Scient. Amer.*, vol. 216(4), pp. 56–66.

Nicholson, A. J. (1933): 'The balance of animal populations', *J. Animal Ecol.*, vol. 2, pp. 132–78.

—(1954): 'An outline of the dynamics of animal populations', *Austr. J. Zoology*, vol. 2, pp. 9–65.

Rasmussen, D. I. (1941): 'Biotic communities of the Kaibab Plateau, Arizona', *Ecol. Monogr.*, vol. 11, no. 3, pp. 229–75.

Reynolds, V. (1963): 'An outline of the behaviour and social organisation of forest-living chimpanzees', *Folia Primat.*, vol. 1, pp. 95–102.

—(1966): 'Open groups in hominid evolution', *Man, J. R. Anthrop. Inst.*, vol. 1, no. 4, pp. 441–52.

—(1968): 'Kinship and the family in monkeys, apes and man', *Man, J. R. Anthrop. Inst.*, vol. 3, no. 2, pp. 209–23.

Reynolds, V. and F. (1965): 'Chimpanzees of the Budongo Forest', in *Primate Behavior: Field Studies of Monkeys and Apes*, ed. DeVore, I. (New York), pp. 368–424.

Robinette, W. L., Gashwiler, J. S. and Morris, O. W. (1959): 'Food habits of the cougar in Utah and Nevada', *J. Wildlife Manag.*, vol. 23, pp. 261–73.

Robinson, J. T. (1964): 'Adaptive radiation in the Australopithecines and the origin of man', in *African Ecology and Human Evolution* (ed. Howell, F. C. and Bourlière, F.), Viking Fund Publ. Anthrop., no. 36, pp. 385–416.

Rowell, T. E. (1966): 'Forest living baboons in Uganda', *J. Zool. Lond.*, vol. 149, pp. 344–64.

—(1967): 'Variability in the social organization of primates', in *Primate Ethology* (ed. Morris, D., London), pp. 219–35.

Theobald, G. W. (1936): 'A centre, or centres, in the hypothalamus controlling menstruation, ovulation, pregnancy and parturition', *Brit. Medical J.*, 1936 (vol. 1), pp. 1038–41.

Thiessen, D. D. and Rodgers, D. A. (1961): 'Population density and endocrine function', *Psychol. Bull.*, vol. 58 (6), pp. 441–51.

Tinbergen, N. (1965): *Social Behaviour in Animals, with Special Reference to Vertebrates* (Oxford), 1st ed. 1953: paperback ed. 1965.

Washburn, S. L. and DeVore, I. (1961): 'Social behavior of baboons and early man', in *Social Life of Early Man* (ed. Washburn, S. L.), Viking Fund Publ. Anthrop., no. 31, pp. 91–105.

Washburn, S. L. and Lancaster, C. S. (1968): 'The evolution of hunting', in *Man the Hunter*, ed. Lee, R. B. and DeVore, I. (Chicago), pp. 293–303.

Watson, A., Jenkins, D. and Miller, G. R. (1970): 'Grouse management', The Game Conservancy (Fordingbridge, Hants.), Booklet no. 12, pp. 1–78.

Wynne-Edwards, V. C. (1962): *Animal Dispersion in Relation to Social Behaviour* (Edinburgh).

---

# Hopi Ceremonial Index

The Index spans pp. 46–305 of the present volume, with scattered references drawn from chapters 10–11 and 17–20; it is restricted to ceremonial material too detailed to go into the General Index. General and comparative items within that span will be found in the General Index.

# General Index

The index covers general and comparative items for the whole book, together with detailed material drawn from volume 1, pp. 1–247, and from volume 2, pp. 1–45, 306–513. Detailed material of a linguistic nature, drawn from pp. 248–418 of volume 1, will be found in the *Mota Index* (at the end of that volume); detailed material of a ceremonial nature, drawn mainly from pp. 46–305 of the present volume but also from chapters 10–11 and 17–20, will be found in the *Hopi ceremonial index* (preceding this one). References to authors quoted in the text are included in this index.

Abacus, use of, in 12th century England, i, 377 n
Abstinence, abstention, as a sign of 'respect' among the Nuer, i, 26: from food, as a sign of mourning in the Banks Islands, 290–1: ritual, among the Hopi, see *ceremonial index*: from meat and fat, by the Northern Paiute, ii, 370–1, 371 n: from salt, meat and sex, by the Maya, 421–2, 432–3
Acreage, of Yakö farms, i, 35: of Tale farms, 74: of Mende farms, 109: in rain-forest cultivation, 184–5, 185 nn: of Trobriand gardens, 201–2, 202 n: of village territory, in the Banks Islands, 274: of farm land, sets a limit to the population of the Hopi village, ii, 6–8: cultivated by the Hopi, 387–8, 406 n: of farm land, at Point of Pines, 406 n, 407, 408 n: of the *milpa* (Maya), 428 n
Adoption, of Dinka into a Nuer lineage, i, 23, 24: into the Yakö patriclan, 48 and n: of strangers into the community, ii, 482, 486
Adultery, Tale definition of, i, 96: consequences of, in the Trobriands, 236, 240: payment for, in the Banks Islands, 299: as cause of disputes, 336: as mark of bad character, 345: punished by *tamate*, 346 n
Affection(s), seat of (Banks Islands), i, 341–3, 348: how conceived, 356–7: new ideas of, in 12th century Europe, 357 n

Age-mates, among the Yakö, i, 43: their rôle in marriage preliminaries, 47–8: among the Mende, 137: their aid invoked by pastoral Pokot, 170–1: growth of mutual respect among, ii, 314–15, 332
Age-sets, rôle of, in Nuer society, i, 27–8, 33: among the Yakö, 43–4: among the Mbembe, 63: of the north-eastern Ibo, 68: typical of the savannah, 181–2: associated with millet-growing culture, 183: and with dispersed pattern of settlement, 187
Aggression, lack of, among the Maya, ii, 436 n: rôle of, among savannah baboons, 459 and n: among hamadryas baboons, 465
Agriculture, different kinds of, determine patterns of settlement, i, 184–7: adoption of, in the Southwest, ii, 404–8: effects of this, on social structure, 408–10: on reproduction, 513 and n
Aitken B. (*née* Freire-Marreco), quoted, on the place of the nuclear family within the lineage, ii, 396 n: on the rôle of men married into the clan, 409 n: on clan unity, 437: on co-operation within the pueblo, 438: her fieldwork at Hano, and tribute to, 438 n
Alkaloid(s), use of, for stunning fish, i, 176: as fish poisons, 263
Alliance, marriage, between minimal lineages among the Nuer, i, 20: binds

T

Eagle(s), ownership of nesting cliffs, by the Hopi, ii, 9, 389 n: and in the Great Basin, 377–8, 389: taking of, by the Hopi, 239–40: and by the Luiseño Indians, 414

Earth, the 'sacred one of', among the Nuer, i, 30–3: the Mbembe *okpobam* a cult of, 66–7: Talense cult of, 96–8, 102–3: the 'wife' of Ngewo (Mende), 130: inauguration of a new *rí*, a symbolic mating with, 163: cult of, as a sanction, 173: typical of the forest belt, 179: e. mother of the Maya, and her Hopi analogue, ii, 426, 441 n

Economic activities, age of assuming, among the Nuer, i, 21: ii, 333: among the Yakö, i, 37, 43: among the Talense, 77: among the Mende, 117: in the Trobriands, 228: among the Hopi, ii, 25 and n, 224, 324: among the Ngoni, 332: among the Great Basin Shoshoni, 352–3

Egan, 19th century traveller in the Great Basin, quoted on the catching of rodents, ii, 351: on the hunting of deer, 360

Eggan D., on the traumatic effect of katçina initiation (Hopi), ii, 86 n: on the prominence of Masau'u in Hopi dreams, 268 and n: quoted on *wü'wütçim* dream, 270: on rabbit-hunting dream, 285: on dreams where a character changes into an animal, 302–3: on Hopi child upbringing, 439 n

Eggan F., on Hopi matriclans, i, 57 n: on date of introduction of katçinas, ii, 194 n, 415 n: on the phratry groupings as conceptual linkages, 199 n: quoted, on badger as medicine animal, 220: on sparrowhawk as symbol of bravery, 289: on pueblo clan names and nature, 297: on the moisture-corn complex, 298: on the meaning of katçina initiation, 325: on the use of heated sand, at Zuñi, 327: on cross-cousin marriage, 401 n: on the integrative function of lineages, 437 n: on the strength of fraternity ties, 440 n

Elder(s), rôle of, among the Yakö, i, 40–2: Talense, 87: Mende, 112: hill Pokot, 170–1: see, also, under *big men*

Eliade M., on circum-polar shamanism, ii, 288

Elkin A. P., on the nature of social obligation, i, 295 n: on the speech of the Australian aborigines, 372

Emergence, Trobriand myths of, i, 199–200: hole of, 205 n: rank of clans established at, 237: for Hopi myth of, see *ceremonial index*

Emlen J. M., quoted, on the origin of initiatory rites, ii, 480–1, 489

Emmet D. M., on cursing as a sanction, i, 31 n

Entwistle W. J., quoted, on the notion of number, i, 377 n: on the function of particles, 382

Epidemic(s), attributed to malignant spirits, in the Trobriands, i, 235: among hunter-gatherers, ii, 497–8

Erikson E. H., quoted, on non-sense and sense age among the Yurok, ii, 320

Eskimo(s), social morphology of, ii, 343–5: regulation of numbers among, 507 n

Evans-Pritchard E. E., ethnographer of the Nuer, i, 9–33 *passim*: his field work, 9–10: on district and lineage, 18 n: attended mortuary ceremony, 24: quoted, on age among the Nuer, 27–8: on the rôle of age-sets, 28: on the settling of disputes, 29: on the solidarity of village and district, 33: on Azande witchcraft, 169 n

Exchange, of yams against fish, in the Trobriands, i, 207 and n: forms of, in the Banks Islands, 301–2: Hopi word for, ii, 54 n: Mauss quoted on, 338: see, also, under *prestation(s)*

Expulsion, from one's caste in south India, i, 168 n: ii, 331: as a sanction, among the hill Pokot, i, 170–1: of the spirits, at the end of the *milamala* festival (Trobriands), 217: from the village, 240: of ghost, in the Banks Islands, 289–90: of a stranger, 335: threat of, as a sanction, ii, 338–9

Faction(s), within the Hopi village, ii, 440 and n

Faint, fainting, Mende idea of, i, 124: Banks Islands idea of, 287

Fall festival, of the Great Basin Shoshoni, ii, 278–80, 287 n, 287–8, 288 n, 360–1, 363–4, 370–1, 375, 383–4: Hopi analogue to, 386

301.34          v.II          43071
B727n

Bradfield, Richard M.
A natural history of
associations.

301.34          v.II          43071
B727n